T0259922

Lecture Notes in Computer Science   14444

Founding Editors

Gerhard Goos
Juris Hartmanis

Editorial Board Members

The series Lecture Notes in Computer Science (LNCS), including its subseries Lecture Notes in Artificial Intelligence (LNAI) and Lecture Notes in Bioinformatics (LNBI), has established itself as a medium for the publication of new developments in computer science and information technology research, teaching, and education.

LNCS enjoys close cooperation with the computer science R & D community, the series counts many renowned academics among its volume editors and paper authors, and collaborates with prestigious societies. Its mission is to serve this international community by providing an invaluable service, mainly focused on the publication of conference and workshop proceedings and postproceedings. LNCS commenced publication in 1973.

Jian Guo · Ron Steinfeld
Editors

Advances in Cryptology – ASIACRYPT 2023

29th International Conference on the Theory
and Application of Cryptology and Information Security
Guangzhou, China, December 4–8, 2023
Proceedings, Part VII

 Springer

Editors
Jian Guo 🆔
Nanyang Technological University
Singapore, Singapore

Ron Steinfeld 🆔
Monash University
Melbourne, VIC, Australia

ISSN 0302-9743   ISSN 1611-3349 (electronic)
Lecture Notes in Computer Science
ISBN 978-981-99-8738-2   ISBN 978-981-99-8739-9 (eBook)
https://doi.org/10.1007/978-981-99-8739-9

This Springer imprint is published by the registered company Springer Nature Singapore Pte Ltd.
The registered company address is: 152 Beach Road, #21-01/04 Gateway East, Singapore 189721, Singapore

Paper in this product is recyclable.

Preface

The 29th Annual International Conference on the Theory and Application of Cryptology and Information Security (Asiacrypt 2023) was held in Guangzhou, China, on December 4–8, 2023. The conference covered all technical aspects of cryptology, and was sponsored by the International Association for Cryptologic Research (IACR).

We received an Asiacrypt record of 376 paper submissions from all over the world, and the Program Committee (PC) selected 106 papers for publication in the proceedings of the conference. Due to this large number of papers, the Asiacrypt 2023 program had 3 tracks.

The two program chairs were supported by the great help and excellent advice of six area chairs, selected to cover the main topic areas of the conference. The area chairs were Kai-Min Chung for Information-Theoretic and Complexity-Theoretic Cryptography, Tanja Lange for Efficient and Secure Implementations, Shengli Liu for Public-Key Cryptography Algorithms and Protocols, Khoa Nguyen for Multi-Party Computation and Zero-Knowledge, Duong Hieu Phan for Public-Key Primitives with Advanced Functionalities, and Yu Sasaki for Symmetric-Key Cryptology. Each of the area chairs helped to lead discussions together with the PC members assigned as paper discussion lead. Area chairs also helped to decide on the submissions that should be accepted from their respective areas. We are very grateful for the invaluable contribution provided by the area chairs.

To review and evaluate the submissions, while keeping the load per PC member manageable, we selected a record size PC consisting of 105 leading experts from all over the world, in all six topic areas of cryptology. The two program chairs were not allowed to submit a paper, and PC members were limited to submit one single-author paper, or at most two co-authored papers, or at most three co-authored papers all with students. Each non-PC submission was reviewed by at least three reviewers consisting of either PC members or their external sub-reviewers, while each PC member submission received at least four reviews. The strong conflict of interest rules imposed by IACR ensure that papers are not handled by PC members with a close working relationship with the authors. There were approximately 420 external reviewers, whose input was critical to the selection of papers. Submissions were anonymous and their length was limited to 30 pages excluding the bibliography and supplementary materials.

The review process was conducted using double-blind peer review. The conference operated a two-round review system with a rebuttal phase. After the reviews and first round discussions the PC selected 244 submissions to proceed to the second round and the authors were then invited to participate in an interactive rebuttal phase with the reviewers to clarify questions and concerns. The remaining 131 papers were rejected, including one desk reject. The second round involved extensive discussions by the PC members. After several weeks of additional discussions, the committee selected the final 106 papers to appear in these proceedings.

The eight volumes of the conference proceedings contain the revised versions of the 106 papers that were selected. The final revised versions of papers were not reviewed again and the authors are responsible for their contents.

The PC nominated and voted for two papers to receive the Best Paper Awards, and one paper to receive the Best Early Career Paper Award. The Best Paper Awards went to Thomas Espitau, Alexandre Wallet and Yang Yu for their paper "On Gaussian Sampling, Smoothing Parameter and Application to Signatures", and to Kaijie Jiang, Anyu Wang, Hengyi Luo, Guoxiao Liu, Yang Yu, and Xiaoyun Wang for their paper "Exploiting the Symmetry of Z^n: Randomization and the Automorphism Problem". The Best Early Career Paper Award went to Maxime Plancon for the paper "Exploiting Algebraic Structure in Probing Security". The authors of those three papers were invited to submit extended versions of their papers to the Journal of Cryptology. In addition, the program of Asiacrypt 2023 also included two invited plenary talks, also nominated and voted by the PC: one talk was given by Mehdi Tibouchi and the other by Xiaoyun Wang. The conference also featured a rump session chaired by Kang Yang and Yu Yu which contained short presentations on the latest research results of the field.

Numerous people contributed to the success of Asiacrypt 2023. We would like to thank all the authors, including those whose submissions were not accepted, for submitting their research results to the conference. We are very grateful to the area chairs, PC members and external reviewers for contributing their knowledge and expertise, and for the tremendous amount of work that was done with reading papers and contributing to the discussions. We are greatly indebted to Jian Weng and Fangguo Zhang, the General Chairs, for their efforts in organizing the event and to Kevin McCurley and Kay McKelly for their help with the website and review system. We thank the Asiacrypt 2023 advisory committee members Bart Preneel, Huaxiong Wang, Kai-Min Chung, Yu Sasaki, Dongdai Lin, Shweta Agrawal and Michel Abdalla for their valuable suggestions. We are also grateful for the helpful advice and organization material provided to us by the Eurocrypt 2023 PC co-chairs Carmit Hazay and Martijn Stam and Crypto 2023 PC co-chairs Helena Handschuh and Anna Lysyanskaya. We also thank the team at Springer for handling the publication of these conference proceedings.

December 2023   Jian Guo
                                                                    Ron Steinfeld

Organization

General Chairs

Jian Weng   Jinan University, China
Fangguo Zhang   Sun Yat-sen University, China

Program Committee Chairs

Jian Guo   Nanyang Technological University, Singapore
Ron Steinfeld   Monash University, Australia

Program Committee

Behzad Abdolmaleki   University of Sheffield, UK
Masayuki Abe   NTT Social Informatics Laboratories, Japan
Miguel Ambrona   Input Output Global (IOHK), Spain
Daniel Apon   MITRE Labs, USA
Shi Bai   Florida Atlantic University, USA
Gustavo Banegas   Qualcomm, France
Zhenzhen Bao   Tsinghua University, China
Andrea Basso   University of Bristol, UK
Ward Beullens   IBM Research Europe, Switzerland
Katharina Boudgoust   Aarhus University, Denmark
Matteo Campanelli   Protocol Labs, Denmark
Ignacio Cascudo   IMDEA Software Institute, Spain
Wouter Castryck   imec-COSIC, KU Leuven, Belgium
Jie Chen   East China Normal University, China
Yilei Chen   Tsinghua University, China
Jung Hee Cheon   Seoul National University and Cryptolab Inc,
                             South Korea
Sherman S. M. Chow   Chinese University of Hong Kong, China
Kai-Min Chung   Academia Sinica, Taiwan
Michele Ciampi   University of Edinburgh, UK
Bernardo David   IT University of Copenhagen, Denmark
Yi Deng   Institute of Information Engineering, Chinese
                             Academy of Sciences, China

Patrick Derbez   University of Rennes, France
Xiaoyang Dong   Tsinghua University, China
Rafael Dowsley   Monash University, Australia
Nico Döttling   Helmholtz Center for Information Security,
                                Germany
Maria Eichlseder   Graz University of Technology, Austria
Muhammed F. Esgin   Monash University, Australia
Thomas Espitau   PQShield, France
Jun Furukawa   NEC Corporation, Japan
Aron Gohr   Independent Researcher, New Zealand
Junqing Gong   ECNU, China
Lorenzo Grassi   Ruhr University Bochum, Germany
Tim Güneysu   Ruhr University Bochum, Germany
Chun Guo   Shandong University, China
Siyao Guo   NYU Shanghai, China
Fuchun Guo   University of Wollongong, Australia
Mohammad Hajiabadi   University of Waterloo, Canada
Lucjan Hanzlik   CISPA Helmholtz Center for Information
                                Security, Germany
Xiaolu Hou   Slovak University of Technology, Slovakia
Yuncong Hu   Shanghai Jiao Tong University, China
Xinyi Huang   Hong Kong University of Science and
                                Technology (Guangzhou), China
Tibor Jager   University of Wuppertal, Germany
Elena Kirshanova   Technology Innovation Institute, UAE and I. Kant
                                Baltic Federal University, Russia
Eyal Kushilevitz   Technion, Israel
Russell W. F. Lai   Aalto University, Finland
Tanja Lange   Eindhoven University of Technology, Netherlands
Hyung Tae Lee   Chung-Ang University, South Korea
Eik List   Nanyang Technological University, Singapore
Meicheng Liu   Institute of Information Engineering, Chinese
                                Academy of Sciences, China
Guozhen Liu   Nanyang Technological University, Singapore
Fukang Liu   Tokyo Institute of Technology, Japan
Shengli Liu   Shanghai Jiao Tong University, China
Feng-Hao Liu   Florida Atlantic University, USA
Hemanta K. Maji   Purdue University, USA
Takahiro Matsuda   AIST, Japan
Christian Matt   Concordium, Switzerland
Tomoyuki Morimae   Kyoto University, Japan
Pierrick Méaux   University of Luxembourg, Luxembourg

Benjamin Wesolowski	CNRS and ENS Lyon, France
Shuang Wu	Huawei International, Singapore, Singapore
Keita Xagawa	Technology Innovation Institute, UAE
Chaoping Xing	Shanghai Jiao Tong University, China
Jun Xu	Institute of Information Engineering, Chinese Academy of Sciences, China
Takashi Yamakawa	NTT Social Informatics Laboratories, Japan
Kang Yang	State Key Laboratory of Cryptology, China
Yu Yu	Shanghai Jiao Tong University, China
Yang Yu	Tsinghua University, Beijing, China
Yupeng Zhang	University of Illinois Urbana-Champaign and Texas A&M University, USA
Liangfeng Zhang	ShanghaiTech University, China
Raymond K. Zhao	CSIRO's Data61, Australia
Hong-Sheng Zhou	Virginia Commonwealth University, USA

Additional Reviewers

Amit Agarwal
Jooyoung Lee
Léo Ackermann
Akshima
Bar Alon
Ravi Anand
Sarah Arpin
Thomas Attema
Nuttapong Attrapadung
Manuel Barbosa
Razvan Barbulescu
James Bartusek
Carsten Baum
Olivier Bernard
Tyler Besselman
Ritam Bhaumik
Jingguo Bi
Loic Bidoux
Maxime Bombar
Xavier Bonnetain
Joppe Bos
Mariana Botelho da Gama
Christina Boura
Clémence Bouvier
Ross Bowden

Pedro Branco
Lauren Brandt
Alessandro Budroni
Kevin Carrier
André Chailloux
Suvradip Chakraborty
Debasmita Chakraborty
Haokai Chang
Bhuvnesh Chaturvedi
Caicai Chen
Rongmao Chen
Mingjie Chen
Yi Chen
Megan Chen
Yu Long Chen
Xin Chen
Shiyao Chen
Long Chen
Wonhee Cho
Qiaohan Chu
Valerio Cini
James Clements
Ran Cohen
Alexandru Cojocaru
Sandro Coretti-Drayton

Anamaria Costache
Alain Couvreur
Daniele Cozzo
Hongrui Cui
Giuseppe D'Alconzo
Zhaopeng Dai
Quang Dao
Nilanjan Datta
Koen de Boer
Luca De Feo
Paola de Perthuis
Thomas Decru
Rafael del Pino
Julien Devevey
Henri Devillez
Siemen Dhooghe
Yaoling Ding
Jack Doerner
Jelle Don
Mark Douglas Schultz
Benjamin Dowling
Minxin Du
Xiaoqi Duan
Jesko Dujmovic
Moumita Dutta
Avijit Dutta
Ehsan Ebrahimi
Felix Engelmann
Reo Eriguchi
Jonathan Komada Eriksen
Andre Esser
Pouria Fallahpour
Zhiyong Fang
Antonio Faonio
Pooya Farshim
Joël Felderhoff
Jakob Feldtkeller
Weiqi Feng
Xiutao Feng
Shuai Feng
Qi Feng
Hanwen Feng
Antonio Flórez-Gutiérrez
Apostolos Fournaris
Paul Frixons

Ximing Fu
Georg Fuchsbauer
Philippe Gaborit
Rachit Garg
Robin Geelen
Riddhi Ghosal
Koustabh Ghosh
Barbara Gigerl
Niv Gilboa
Valerie Gilchrist
Emanuele Giunta
Xinxin Gong
Huijing Gong
Zheng Gong
Robert Granger
Zichen Gui
Anna Guinet
Qian Guo
Xiaojie Guo
Hosein Hadipour
Mathias Hall-Andersen
Mike Hamburg
Shuai Han
Yonglin Hao
Keisuke Hara
Keitaro Hashimoto
Le He
Brett Hemenway Falk
Minki Hhan
Taiga Hiroka
Akinori Hosoyamada
Chengan Hou
Martha Norberg Hovd
Kai Hu
Tao Huang
Zhenyu Huang
Michael Hutter
Jihun Hwang
Akiko Inoue
Tetsu Iwata
Robin Jadoul
Hansraj Jangir
Dirmanto Jap
Stanislaw Jarecki
Santos Jha

Ashwin Jha

Dingding Jia

Yanxue Jia

Lin Jiao

Daniel Jost

Antoine Joux

Jiayi Kang

Gabriel Kaptchuk

Alexander Karenin

Shuichi Katsumata

Pengzhen Ke

Mustafa Khairallah

Shahram Khazaei

Hamidreza Amini Khorasgani

Hamidreza Khoshakhlagh

Ryo Kikuchi

Jiseung Kim

Minkyu Kim

Suhri Kim

Ravi Kishore

Fuyuki Kitagawa

Susumu Kiyoshima

Michael Klooß

Alexander Koch

Sreehari Kollath

Dimitris Kolonelos

Yashvanth Kondi

Anders Konring

Woong Kook

Dimitri Koshelev

Markus Krausz

Toomas Krips

Daniel Kuijsters

Anunay Kulshrestha

Qiqi Lai

Yi-Fu Lai

Georg Land

Nathalie Lang

Mario Larangeira

Joon-Woo Lee

Keewoo Lee

Hyeonbum Lee

Changmin Lee

Charlotte Lefevre

Julia Len

Antonin Leroux

Andrea Lesavourey

Jannis Leuther

Jie Li

Shuaishuai Li

Huina Li

Yu Li

Yanan Li

Jiangtao Li

Song Song Li

Wenjie Li

Shun Li

Zengpeng Li

Xiao Liang

Wei-Kai Lin

Chengjun Lin

Chao Lin

Cong Ling

Yunhao Ling

Hongqing Liu

Jing Liu

Jiahui Liu

Qipeng Liu

Yamin Liu

Weiran Liu

Tianyi Liu

Siqi Liu

Chen-Da Liu-Zhang

Jinyu Lu

Zhenghao Lu

Stefan Lucks

Yiyuan Luo

Lixia Luo

Jack P. K. Ma

Fermi Ma

Gilles Macario-Rat

Luciano Maino

Christian Majenz

Laurane Marco

Lorenzo Martinico

Loïc Masure

John McVey

Willi Meier

Kelsey Melissaris

Bart Mennink

Charles Meyer-Hilfiger

Victor Miller

Chohong Min

Marine Minier

Arash Mirzaei

Pratyush Mishra

Tarik Moataz

Johannes Mono

Fabrice Mouhartem

Alice Murphy

Erik Mårtensson

Anne Müller

Marcel Nageler

Yusuke Naito

Barak Nehoran

Patrick Neumann

Tran Ngo

Phuong Hoa Nguyen

Ngoc Khanh Nguyen

Thi Thu Quyen Nguyen

Hai H. Nguyen

Semyon Novoselov

Julian Nowakowski

Arne Tobias Malkenes Ødegaard

Kazuma Ohara

Miyako Ohkubo

Charles Olivier-Anclin

Eran Omri

Yi Ouyang

Tapas Pal

Ying-yu Pan

Jiaxin Pan

Eugenio Paracucchi

Roberto Parisella

Jeongeun Park

Guillermo Pascual-Perez

Alain Passelègue

Octavio Perez-Kempner

Thomas Peters

Phuong Pham

Cécile Pierrot

Erik Pohle

David Pointcheval

Giacomo Pope

Christopher Portmann

Romain Poussier

Lucas Prabel

Sihang Pu

Chen Qian

Luowen Qian

Tian Qiu

Anaïs Querol

Håvard Raddum

Shahram Rasoolzadeh

Divya Ravi

Prasanna Ravi

Marc Renard

Jan Richter-Brockmann

Lawrence Roy

Paul Rösler

Sayandeep Saha

Yusuke Sakai

Niels Samwel

Paolo Santini

Maria Corte-Real Santos

Sara Sarfaraz

Santanu Sarkar

Or Sattath

Markus Schofnegger

Peter Scholl

Dominique Schröder

André Schrottenloher

Jacob Schuldt

Binanda Sengupta

Srinath Setty

Yantian Shen

Yixin Shen

Ferdinand Sibleyras

Janno Siim

Mark Simkin

Scott Simon

Animesh Singh

Nitin Singh

Sayani Sinha

Daniel Slamanig

Fang Song

Ling Song

Yongsoo Song

Jana Sotakova

Gabriele Spini

Marianna Spyrakou

Lukas Stennes

Marc Stoettinger

Chuanjie Su

Xiangyu Su

Ling Sun

Akira Takahashi

Isobe Takanori

Atsushi Takayasu

Suprita Talnikar

Benjamin Hong Meng Tan

Ertem Nusret Tas

Tadanori Teruya

Masayuki Tezuka

Sri AravindaKrishnan Thyagarajan

Song Tian

Wenlong Tian

Raphael Toledo

Junichi Tomida

Daniel Tschudi

Hikaru Tsuchida

Aleksei Udovenko

Rei Ueno

Barry Van Leeuwen

Wessel van Woerden

Frederik Vercauteren

Sulani Vidhanalage

Benedikt Wagner

Roman Walch

Hendrik Waldner

Han Wang

Luping Wang

Peng Wang

Yuntao Wang

Geng Wang

Shichang Wang

Liping Wang

Jiafan Wang

Zhedong Wang

Kunpeng Wang

Jianfeng Wang

Guilin Wang

Weiqiang Wen

Chenkai Weng

Thom Wiggers

Stella Wohnig

Harry W. H. Wong

Ivy K. Y. Woo

Yu Xia

Zejun Xiang

Yuting Xiao

Zhiye Xie

Yanhong Xu

Jiayu Xu

Lei Xu

Shota Yamada

Kazuki Yamamura

Di Yan

Qianqian Yang

Shaojun Yang

Yanjiang Yang

Li Yao

Yizhou Yao

Kenji Yasunaga

Yuping Ye

Xiuyu Ye

Zeyuan Yin

Kazuki Yoneyama

Yusuke Yoshida

Albert Yu

Quan Yuan

Chen Yuan

Tsz Hon Yuen

Aaram Yun

Riccardo Zanotto

Arantxa Zapico

Shang Zehua

Mark Zhandry

Tianyu Zhang

Zhongyi Zhang

Fan Zhang

Liu Zhang

Yijian Zhang

Shaoxuan Zhang

Zhongliang Zhang

Kai Zhang

Cong Zhang

Jiaheng Zhang

Lulu Zhang

Zhiyu Zhang

Chang-An Zhao
Yongjun Zhao
Chunhuan Zhao
Xiaotong Zhou
Zhelei Zhou

Zijian Zhou
Timo Zijlstra
Jian Zou
Ferdinando Zullo
Cong Zuo

Sponsoring Institutions

- Gold Level Sponsor: Ant Research
- Silver Level Sponsors: Sansec Technology Co., Ltd., Topsec Technologies Group
- Bronze Level Sponsors: IBM, Meta, Sangfor Technologies Inc.

Contents – Part VII

Post-quantum Cryptography

ANTRAG: Annular NTRU Trapdoor Generation
Making MITAKA as Secure as FALCON

Thomas Espitau[1] , Thi Thu Quyen Nguyen[2] , Chao Sun[3(✉)] ,
Mehdi Tibouchi[4] , and Alexandre Wallet[5]

[1] PQShield SAS, Paris, France
[2] IDEMIA & Normandie Univ., UNICAEN, ENSICAEN, CNRS, GREYC,
Paris, France
thi-thu-quyen.nguyen@inria.fr
[3] Osaka University, Suita, Japan
c-sun@ist.osaka-u.ac.jp
[4] NTT Social Informatics Laboratories, Yokosuka, Japan
mehdi.tibouchi@ntt.com
[5] IRISA, Univ. Rennes 1, Inria, Bretagne-Atlantique Center, Rennes, France
alexandre.wallet@inria.fr

Abstract. In this paper, we introduce a novel trapdoor generation technique for Prest's hybrid sampler over NTRU lattices. Prest's sampler is used in particular in the recently proposed MITAKA signature scheme (Eurocrypt 2022), a variant of the FALCON signature scheme, one of the candidates selected by NIST for standardization. MITAKA was introduced to address FALCON's main drawback, namely the fact that the lattice Gaussian sampler used in its signature generation is highly complex, difficult to implement correctly, to parallelize or protect against side-channels, and to instantiate over rings of dimension not a power of two to reach intermediate security levels. Prest's sampler is considerably simpler and solves these various issues, but when applying the same trapdoor generation approach as FALCON, the resulting signatures have far lower security in equal dimension. The MITAKA paper showed how certain randomness-recycling techniques could be used to mitigate this security loss, but the resulting scheme is still substantially less secure than FALCON (by around 20 to 50 bits of CoreSVP security depending on the parameters), and has much slower key generation.

Our new trapdoor generation techniques solves all of those issues satisfactorily: it gives rise to a much simpler and faster key generation algorithm than MITAKA's (achieving similar speeds to FALCON), and is able to comfortably generate trapdoors reaching the same NIST security levels as FALCON as well. It can also be easily adapted to rings of intermediate dimensions, in order to support the same versatility as MITAKA in terms of parameter selection. All in all, this new technique combines all the advantages of both FALCON and MITAKA (and more) with none of the drawbacks.

J. Guo and R. Steinfeld (Eds.): ASIACRYPT 2023, LNCS 14444, pp. 3–36, 2023.
https://doi.org/10.1007/978-981-99-8739-9_1

Keywords: Post-quantum cryptography · Hash-and-sign lattice-based signatures · NTRU trapdoors · Discrete Gaussian sampling

1   Introduction

1.1   Hash-and-Sign Lattice-Based Signatures

From GGH to FALCON. FALCON [34] is one of the three signature schemes already selected for standardization in the NIST post-quantum competition. It represents the state of the art in *hash-and-sign* lattice-based signatures, one of the two main paradigms for constructing lattice-based signatures alongside Lyubashevsky's Fiat–Shamir with aborts [24,25] (which is also represented among the final selected candidates of the NIST competition in the form of DILITHIUM [26]).

This makes FALCON the culmination of a long line of research in constructing signature schemes from *lattice trapdoors.* The basic idea, which dates back to the late 1990s with the GGH [22] and NTRUSign [23] signature schemes, is to use as the signing key a "good" basis (the *trapdoor*) of a certain lattice allowing to approximate the closest vector problem within a good factor, and as the verification key a "bad" basis which allows to test membership but not decode large errors. The signature algorithm then hashes a given message to a vector in the ambient space of the lattice, and uses the trapdoor to find a relatively close lattice point to that vector. The difference is the signature, which is verified by checking that it is small and that its difference with the hashed vector does indeed belong to the lattice.

The GGH scheme, as well as several successive variants of NTRUSign, were eventually broken by statistical attacks [10,21,29]: it turned out that signatures would leak partial information about the secret trapdoor, that could then be progressively recovered by an attacker. This problem was finally solved in 2008, when Gentry, Peikert and Vaikuntanathan (GPV) [20] showed how to use Gaussian sampling in the lattice in order to guarantee that signatures would reveal no information about the trapdoor.

GPV Signatures over NTRU Lattices. In order to instantiate the GPV framework efficiently in practice, one then needs lattices with compact representation and efficiently computable trapdoors, which has so far been achieved using module lattices over rings—in fact, mostly rank-2 modules over cyclotomic rings, exactly corresponding to NTRU lattices (although higher rank modules, namely ModNTRU lattices, have been shown to be usable as well in certain ranges of parameters [7]). This was first carried out by Ducas, Lyubashevsky and Prest (DLP) [9], who analyzed trapdoor generation for power-of-two cyclotomic ring NTRU lattices and constructed corresponding GPV-style signatures. DLP signatures are compact, but the signing algorithm is rather slow: quadratic in the dimension $2d$ of the lattice. This is because the lattice Gaussian sampling algorithm that forms the core of its signing procedure (namely Klein–GPV sampling, in essence a randomized version of Babai's nearest plane algorithm for approximate CVP) cannot directly take advantage of the algebraic structure of the lattice, and thus operates on the full $(2d) \times (2d)$ matrix of the lattice basis as well as its Gram–Schmidt orthogonalization.

FALCON is a direct descendant of the DLP scheme, that replaces the generic, quadratic complexity Klein–GPV sampler in signature generation by an efficient, quasilinear complexity lattice Gaussian sampler that *does* take advantage of the ring structure. Specifically, that new algorithm is constructed by randomizing the Fast Fourier Orthogonalization (FFO) algorithm of Ducas and Prest [12], and operates in a tree-like fashion traversing the subfields of the power-of-two cyclotomic field over which the NTRU lattice is defined. This makes FALCON particularly attractive in various ways: it offers particularly compact signatures and keys (providing the best bandwidth requirements of all signature schemes in the NIST competition), achieves high security levels in relatively small lattice dimensions, and has both fast signing and very efficient verification speeds.

However, the FFO-based Gaussian sampler is also the source of FALCON's main drawbacks: it is a really contrived algorithm that is difficult to implement correctly, parallelize or protect against side-channels. It is also really difficult to adapt to other rings than power-of-two cyclotomics, which drastically limits FALCON's versatility in terms of parameter selection: in fact, recent versions of FALCON in the NIST competition only target either the lowest NIST security level (using cyclotomic fields of dimension 512) or the highest (using fields of dimension 1024) and nothing in-between.[1]

1.2 The Hybrid Sampler and MITAKA

The Peikert and Hybrid Samplers. After the publication of the DLP paper, Ducas and Prest explored and analyzed other approaches for lattice Gaussian sampling over NTRU lattices, as discussed in depth in Prest's Ph.D. thesis [32], with a view towards overcoming the quadratic complexity of the naive Klein–GPV sampler. While the introduction of the FFO sampler was the final step of that exploration, they also considered two other major approaches along the way, which also achieve quasilinear complexity (see also [11]).

The first approach was not actually novel: it was the ring version of Peikert's lattice Gaussian sampler [30], which is the randomization of the Babai rounding algorithm for approximate CVP, just like Klein–GPV is the randomization of Babai's nearest plane. For NTRU lattices, this algorithm consists of independent one-dimensional Gaussian samplings for each vector component (hence a linear number in total), as well as 2×2 matrix-vector products over the ring, amounting to a constant number of ring multiplications, that are all quasilinear when using FFT-based fast arithmetic. Thus, Peikert's sampler for NTRU lattices is quasilinear as required. However, Ducas and Prest analyzed the *quality* of NTRU

---

[1] The earliest version of the FALCON specification [33] also included an intermediate parameter set of dimension 768, but the corresponding algorithms were so complicated that it was eventually dropped.

trapdoors (generated in the same way as DLP) with respect to Peikert's sampler, and found that it was much worse than for Klein–GPV, both concretely and asymptotically. In other words, for the same choice of parameters, it would reduce security considerably to instantiate DLP with Peikert's sampler instead of Klein–GPV (and to recover the same security, a large increase in the dimension of the underlying ring, and hence the size of keys and signatures, would be required).

As a kind of middle ground between Peikert (fast but less secure) and Klein–GPV (secure but much slower), they introduced as a second approach the *hybrid sampler*, which uses the same structure as Klein–GPV (a randomized nearest plane algorithm) but over the larger ring instead of over $\mathbb{Z}$. In the rank-2 case of NTRU, this reduces to just two "nearest plane" iterations consisting of Gaussian sampling over the ring, which is itself carried out using Peikert's sampler with respect to a short basis of the ring. This algorithm remains quasilinear, but achieves a significantly better quality than Peikert for DLP-style NTRU trapdoors, although not as good as Klein–GPV. Concretely, for those NTRU trapdoors over the cyclotomic ring of dimension 512 (resp. 1024), signatures instantiated with the hybrid sampler achieve a little over 80 bits (resp. 200 bits) of classical CoreSVP security, compared to over 120 bits (resp. 280 bits) for Klein–GPV.

Pros and Cons of Hybrid vs. FFO. This substantial security loss is presumably the main reason that led to the hybrid sampler being abandoned in favor of the FFO sampler (which achieves the same quality as Klein–GPV but with quasilinear complexity) in the FALCON scheme. Indeed, security aside, the hybrid sampler has a number of advantages compared to the FFO sampler of FALCON: it is considerably simpler to implement, somewhat more efficient in equal dimension, easily parallelizable and less difficult to protect against side-channels; it also has an online-offline structure that can be convenient for certain applications, and it is easier to instantiate over non power-of-two cyclotomics, making it easier to reach intermediate security levels.

For these reasons, the use of the hybrid sampler to instantiate signatures over NTRU lattices was recently revisited by Espitau et al. as part of their proposed scheme MITAKA [15]. One of the key contributions of that paper is an optimization of trapdoor generation for the hybrid sampler that mitigates the security loss by making it possible to construct better quality trapdoor in reasonable time. Combined with the various advantages of the hybrid sampler, this allows the authors of MITAKA to achieve a trade-off between simplicity and security that they argue can be more attractive than FALCON. However, despite their efforts, MITAKA remains substantially less secure than FALCON in equal dimension (it loses over 20 bits of classical CoreSVP security over rings of dimension 512, and over 50 bits over rings of dimension 1024), with a much slower and more contrived key generation algorithm as well. In particular, MITAKA falls short of NIST security level I in dimension 512 and of level V in dimension 1024, making it less than ideal from the standpoint of parameter selection.

1.3 Contributions and Technical Overview of This Paper

In this paper, we introduce a novel trapdoor generation technique for Prest's hybrid sampler that solves the issues faced by MITAKA in a natural and elegant fashion. Our technique gives rise to a much simpler and faster key generation algorithm than MITAKA's (achieving similar speeds to FALCON), and it is able to comfortably generate trapdoors reaching the same NIST security levels as FALCON. It can also be easily adapted to rings of intermediate dimensions, in order to support the same versatility as MITAKA in terms of parameter selection (just with better security). All in all, this new technique achieves in some sense the best of both worlds between FALCON and MITAKA.

NTRU Trapdoors and Their Quality. In order to give a overview of the technical ideas involved, we need to recall a few facts about NTRU trapdoors and their quality with respect to the Klein–GPV and hybrid samplers. For simplicity, we concentrate on the special case of power-of-two cyclotomic rings $\mathscr{R} = \mathbb{Z}[x]/(x^d + 1)$. Over such a ring, an NTRU lattice is simply a full-rank submodule lattice of $\mathscr{R}^2$ generated by the columns of a matrix of the form:

$$\mathbf{B}_h = \begin{bmatrix} 1 & 0 \\ h & q \end{bmatrix}$$

for some rational prime number q and some ring element h coprime to q. Note that this can also be described as a lattice of pairs $(u, v) \in \mathscr{R}^2$ such that $uh - v = 0 \bmod q$.

A trapdoor for this lattice is a relatively short basis:

$$\mathbf{B}_{f,g} = \begin{bmatrix} f & F \\ g & G \end{bmatrix}$$

where the basis vectors (f, g) and (F, G) are not much larger than the normalized volume $\sqrt{\det \mathbf{B}_h} = \sqrt{q}$ of the lattice. Since those vectors belong to the lattice, we have in particular that $g/f = G/F = h \bmod q$. Moreover, since the determinants are equal up to a unit of $\mathscr{R}$, we can impose without loss of generality that $fG - gF = q$.

Using the trapdoor $\mathbf{B}_{f,g}$, lattice Gaussian samplers are able to output lattice vectors following a Gaussian distribution on the lattice of standard deviation[2] a small multiple $\alpha\sqrt{q}$ of the normalized volume $\sqrt{q}$. The factor α is the *quality*, and depends both on the trapdoor and on the sampler itself. The lower the quality, the better the trapdoor, and the higher the security level of the resulting signature scheme. For the Klein–GPV sampler, one can show that the quality α is ($1/\sqrt{q}$ times) the maximum norm of a vector in the Gram–Schmidt orthogonalization of the basis $\mathbf{B}_{f,g}$ regarded as a $(2d) \times (2d)$ matrix over $\mathbb{Z}$, whereas for the hybrid sampler, it is similar but with the Gram–Schmidt orthogonalization over $\mathscr{R}$ itself.

---

[2] The actual standard deviation also includes an additional factor (the smoothing parameter of the ring) which we omit in this overview for simplicity's sake.

Those quantities admit a simple expression in terms of the *embeddings* of the ring elements f and g. Recall that the embeddings are the d ring homomorphisms $\varphi_i \colon \mathcal{R} \to \mathbb{C}$; when elements of $\mathcal{R}$ are seen as polynomials, these embeddings are simply the evaluation morphisms $\varphi_i(u) = u(\zeta_i)$ where the ζ_i's are the d primitive $2d$-th roots of unity in $\mathbb{C}$. Then, quality of the basis $\mathbf{B}_{f,g}$ with respect to the Klein–GPV sampler admits the following simple expression:

$$(\alpha_{\mathrm{GPV}})^2 = \max \left(\frac{1}{d} \sum_{i=1}^{d} \frac{|\varphi_i(f)|^2 + |\varphi_i(g)|^2}{q}, \ \frac{1}{d} \sum_{i=1}^{d} \frac{q}{|\varphi_i(f)|^2 + |\varphi_i(g)|^2} \right).$$

Similarly, the quality with respect to the hybrid sampler satisfies:

$$(\alpha_{\mathrm{hybrid}})^2 = \max_{1 \leqslant i \leqslant d} \left(\max \left(\frac{|\varphi_i(f)|^2 + |\varphi_i(g)|^2}{q}, \ \frac{q}{|\varphi_i(f)|^2 + |\varphi_i(g)|^2} \right) \right).$$

Note that $|\varphi_i(f)|^2 + |\varphi_i(g)|^2 = \varphi_i(ff^* + gg^*)$ where the star denotes the complex conjugation automorphism of $\mathcal{R}$ (defined by $x^* = 1/x = -x^{d-1}$). Thus, put differently, one can say that a trapdoor $\mathbf{B}_{f,g}$ achieves quality α or better for the Klein–GPV sampler if and only if the embeddings of $(ff^* + gg^*)/q$ and of its inverse are at most α *on average*, whereas quality α or better is obtained for the hybrid sampler if *all* of the embeddings of these values are at most α. This shows in particular that the quality of a given trapdoor is always at least as good for Klein–GPV as it is for the hybrid sampler, which explains why it may be easier in practice to construct good quality trapdoors for the former than for the latter.

Trapdoor Generation in FALCON *and* MITAKA. Now, the way trapdoors are generated in FALCON is by sampling f and g according to a discrete Gaussian in $\mathcal{R}$ (which can easily be done by sampling the coefficients as discrete Gaussians over $\mathbb{Z}$) so that their expected length is a bit over $\sqrt{q}$, and verifying using the condition above that the quality with respect to the Klein–GPV (or equivalently FALCON's) sampler is $\alpha_{\mathrm{FALCON}} = 1.17$ or better, and restarting otherwise (the value 1.17 here is chosen roughly as small as possible while keeping the number of repetitions relatively small).

The approach to generate trapdoors in MITAKA is similar using the quality formula for the hybrid sampler, and a target quality of $\alpha_{\mathrm{MITAKA}} = 2.04$ in dimension 512 (and slightly increasing as the dimension becomes larger). Doing so directly would take too many repetitions, however; therefore, the candidates for f and g are actually obtained by linear combinations of smaller Gaussian vectors and by applying Galois automorphisms to generate many candidate vectors (f, g) from a limited number of discrete Gaussian samples. Using that approach, MITAKA achieves the stated quality with a comparable number of discrete Gaussian samples as FALCON; its key generation algorithm is much slower, however, as it has to carry out an exhaustive search on a much larger set of possible candidates.

Our ANTRAG *Strategy: Annular NTRU Trapdoor Generation.* In both FALCON and MITAKA, however, the overall strategy is to generate random-looking candidates (f, g) of plausible length, and repeat until the target quality is reached. In this paper, we suggest a completely different strategy that is in some sense much simpler and more natural: just pick the pair (f, g) uniformly at random in the set of vectors that satisfy the desired quality level. We propose and analyze this approach specifically for the hybrid sampler.[3]

Concretely, yet another way of reformulating the quality condition for the hybrid sampler is to say that the quality is α or better if and only if for all the embeddings φ_i, one has:

$$q/\alpha^2 \leqslant |\varphi_i(f)|^2 + |\varphi_i(g)|^2 \leqslant \alpha^2 q.$$

In other words, for each embedding, the pair $\big(|\varphi_i(f)|, |\varphi_i(g)|\big)$ lies in the *annulus* $A\big(\sqrt{q}/\alpha, \alpha\sqrt{q}\big)$ bounded by the circles of radii $\sqrt{q}/\alpha$ and $\alpha\sqrt{q}$—or more precisely, in the *arc* $A_\alpha^+ = A^+\big(\sqrt{q}/\alpha, \alpha\sqrt{q}\big)$ of that annulus located in the upper-right quadrant of the plane since those absolute values are non-negative numbers. Our approach is then to sample f and g by their embeddings (i.e., directly in the Fourier domain), and select those embeddings uniformly and independently at random in the desired space. Namely, we sample $d/2$ pairs (x_i, y_i) in the arc of annulus A_α^+, and set the i-th embedding of f (resp. g) to a uniformly random complex number of absolute value x_i (resp. of absolute value y_i).

An obvious issue is that the elements f and g constructed in this way will generally not lie in the ring itself: after mapping back to the coefficient domain by Fourier inversion, their coefficients are *a priori* arbitrary real numbers instead of integers. But this is easy to address: we simply round coefficient-wise to obtain an actual ring element.

A second issue is that this rounding step will not necessarily preserve the quality property we started from: the embeddings of the rounded values do not necessarily remain in the correct domain. In fact, the probability that *all* embeddings remain in the correct domain after rounding is very low. But there is again a simple workaround: we just carry out our original continuous sampling in the Fourier domain from a slightly smaller annulus than the target one. Instead of picking the pairs (x_i, y_i) in A_α^+ as above, we sample them uniformly in some $A^+(r, R)$ with r slightly larger than $\sqrt{q}/\alpha$ and R slightly smaller than $\alpha\sqrt{q}$. This considerably increases the probability that, after rounding, all of the pairs $\big(|\varphi_i(f)|, |\varphi_i(g)|\big)$ will in fact end up in A_α^+.

And voilá: the description above is essentially a complete trapdoor generation algorithm for the hybrid sampler, that easily reaches the same NIST security

---

[3] One could consider doing so for Klein–GPV as well, but this appears less relevant for two reasons. First, since 1.17 is already quite close to the theoretical optimal quality of 1, and since the number of repetitions in FALCON's key generation is fairly modest, there is not much to gain in the Klein–GPV setting. Second, the space of key candidates has a less elegant geometric description, making it more difficult to sample uniformly in it. Extending the approach to MODFALCON [7], however, could be an interesting, albeit challenging, avenue for future research.

Table 1. Comparison with FALCON and MITAKA for the same dimensions 512 and 1024 and the same modulus $q = 12289$ (excerpt from Table 4).

	FALCON [34]		MITAKA [15]		This paper	
d	512	1024	512	1024	512	1024
Quality α	1.17	1.17	2.04	2.33	1.15	1.23
Classical sec.	123	284	102	233	124	264
Key size (bytes)	896	1792	896	1792	896	1792
Sig. size (bytes)	666	1280	713	1405	646	1260

levels as FALCON. Concretely, we target $\alpha = 1.15$ in dimension 512 (even better than FALCON's 1.17) and $\alpha = 1.23$ in dimension 1024 (which comfortably exceeds the 256 bits of classical CoreSVP security corresponding to NIST level V), and with those numbers, we achieve key generation speeds close to FALCON's, while benefiting of all the advantages of MITAKA in terms of simplicity of implementation, efficiency, parallelizability and so on as far as signing in concerned.

Our Contributions. The main contribution of this paper is to introduce, analyze and implement the ANTRAG trapdoor generation algorithm for the hybrid sampler described above.

The analysis includes a heuristic estimate of the success probability of sampling in the required domain, as well as a discussion of possible attacks on the resulting keys (and even though our security analysis is in a very optimistic model for the attacker, we find no weakness as long as the original sampling domain $A^+(r, R)$ is not chosen to be extremely narrow), and concrete parameters to instantiate a signature scheme.

We also provide a full portable C implementation of the corresponding signature scheme [36] based on those of FALCON and MITAKA. In fact, since the C implementation of MITAKA did not include the key generation algorithm, our implementation is the first complete implementation of the corresponding paradigm. This implementation lets us compare the performance of our key generation with FALCON's, and we find that they are quite close.

Although most of the previous discussion was in the context of power-of-two cyclotomics, our approach also extends with little change to other base rings such as the cyclotomic rings with 3-smooth conductors considered in MITAKA (and we actually provide an analysis in a more general setting still). In particular, it is still possible to map candidate continuous random values generated in the Fourier domain to the ring by coefficient-wise rounding (we could consider other decoding techniques, but this one is sufficient for our purposes; it was in fact already used in the original ternary version of FALCON: see [33, Algorithm 10]). This only changes the distribution of the "rounding error" and hence the success probability slightly, but the analysis carries over easily. It follows that our approach supports the same versatility as MITAKA in terms of parameter selection (Table 1).

2   Preliminaries

For two real numbers $0 \leqslant r \leqslant R$, we denote by $A(r, R)$ the *annulus* limited by radii r and R, i.e. the following subset of the plane $\mathbb{R}^2$: $A(r, R) := \{(x, y) \in \mathbb{R}^2 \mid r^2 \leqslant x^2 + y^2 \leqslant R^2\}$. We also denote by $A^+(r, R)$ the arc of annulus in the upper-right quadrant of the plane, i.e., $A^+(r, R) := \{(x, y) \in A(r, R) \mid x, y \geqslant 0\}$.

When f is a real-valued function over a countable set S, we write $f(S) = \sum_{s \in S} f(s)$ assuming that this sum is absolutely convergent. We note $\lfloor \cdot \rceil$ the rounding of a real number to its closest integer. We extend this notation for the coefficient-wise rounding of polynomials. If $\mathbf{x} = (x_1, \ldots, x_k)$ is a random variable, we let $\mathbb{E}[\mathbf{x}]$ the expected vector and $\mathrm{Cov}(\mathbf{x})$ its covariance matrix. The variance of a scalar random variable x is denoted by $\mathrm{Var}[x]$.

Write $\mathbf{A}^t$ for the transpose of any matrix $\mathbf{A}$. A lattice $\mathscr{L}$ is a discrete additive subgroup in a Euclidean space. When the space is $\mathbb{R}^m$, and if it is generated by (the columns of) $\mathbf{B} \in \mathbb{R}^{m \times d}$, we also write $\mathscr{L}(\mathbf{B}) = \{\mathbf{B}x \mid x \in \mathbb{Z}^d\}$. If $\mathbf{B}$ has full column rank, then we call $\mathbf{B}$ a basis and d the rank of $\mathscr{L}$. When the ambient space is equipped with a norm $||\cdot||$, the volume of $\mathscr{L}$ is $\mathrm{vol}(\mathscr{L}) = \det(\mathbf{B}^t\mathbf{B})^{1/2} = |\det(\mathbf{B})|$ for any basis $\mathbf{B}$.

2.1   Cyclotomic Fields

Let m be a positive integer, and $d = \phi(m)$ be the degree of the m-th cyclotomic polynomial Φ_m (ϕ is the Euler totient function). Let ζ to be a m-th primitive root of 1. Then for a fixed m, $\mathscr{K} := \mathbb{Q}(\zeta)$ is the cyclotomic field associated with Φ_m, and its ring of algebraic integers is $\mathscr{R} := \mathbb{Z}[\zeta]$. The field automorphism induced by $\zeta \mapsto \zeta^{-1} = \bar{\zeta}$ corresponds to the complex conjugation, and we write f^* the image of $f \in \mathscr{K}$ under this automorphism. We have $\mathscr{K} \simeq \mathbb{Q}[x]/(\Phi_m(x))$ and $\mathscr{R} \simeq \mathbb{Z}[x]/(\Phi_m(x))$, and both are contained in $\mathscr{K}_{\mathbb{R}} := \mathscr{K} \otimes \mathbb{R} = \mathbb{R}[x]/(\Phi_m(x))$. Each $f = \sum_{i=0}^{d-1} f_i \zeta^i \in \mathscr{K}_{\mathbb{R}}$ can be identified with its coefficient vector $(f_0, \cdots, f_{d-1}) \in \mathbb{R}^d$. The complex conjugation operation extends naturally to $\mathscr{K}_{\mathbb{R}}$, and $\mathscr{K}_{\mathbb{R}}^+$ is the subspace of elements satisfying $f^* = f$.

The cyclotomic field $\mathscr{K}$ comes with d complex field embeddings $\varphi_i : \mathscr{K} \to \mathbb{C}$ that maps f seen as a polynomial to its evaluations at ζ^k where $\gcd(k, m) = 1$. This defines the so-called canonical embedding $\varphi(f) := (\varphi_1(f), \ldots, \varphi_d(f))$. It extends straightforwardly to $\mathscr{K}_{\mathbb{R}}$ and identifies it to the space $\mathcal{H} = \{v \in \mathbb{C}^d : v_i = \overline{v_{d/2+i}}, 1 \leqslant i \leqslant d/2\}$. Note that $\varphi(fg) = (\varphi_i(f)\varphi_i(g))_{0 < i \leqslant d}$. When needed, this embedding extends entry-wise to vectors or matrices over $\mathscr{K}_{\mathbb{R}}$. We let $\mathscr{K}_{\mathbb{R}}^{++}$ be the subset of $\mathscr{K}_{\mathbb{R}}^+$ which have all positive coordinates in the canonical embedding. We have a partial ordering over $\mathscr{K}_{\mathbb{R}}^+$ by $f \succ g$ if and only if $f - g \in \mathscr{K}_{\mathbb{R}}^{++}$. The algebra $\mathscr{K}_{\mathbb{R}}$ is also equipped with a norm $N_{\mathscr{K}}(x) = \prod_i \varphi(x)$, which extends the standard field norm.

The next technical lemma is useful in our analyses, and is obtained by elementary trigonometric identities.

Lemma 1. *Let* $\zeta = \exp(i\theta)$ *with* $\theta = \frac{2k\pi}{m}$ *and* $\gcd(k, m) = 1$ *be a* m-th *primitive root of the unity, and* $d = \phi(m)$. *Let* $S(\theta) = \sum_{j=0}^{d-1} \zeta^{2j}$. *We have*

$S(\theta) = \frac{\sin(\theta d)}{\sin \theta} e^{i\theta(d-1)}$ and

$$\operatorname{Re} S(\theta) = \frac{1}{2} + \frac{\sin((2d-1)\theta)}{2 \sin \theta} \quad and \quad \operatorname{Im} S(\theta) = \frac{\sin(d\theta) \sin((d-1)\theta)}{\sin \theta}.$$

Remark 1. If m is a power of 2 then $2d = m$ so we always have $S(\theta) = 0$.

2.2 NTRU Lattices

This work deals with free $\mathscr{R}$-modules of rank 2 in $\mathscr{K}^2$, or in other words, groups of the form $\mathscr{M} = \mathscr{R}\mathbf{x} + \mathscr{R}\mathbf{y}$ where $\mathbf{x} = (x_1, x_2), \mathbf{y} = (y_1, y_2)$ span $\mathscr{K}^2$. Given $f, g \in \mathscr{R}$ such that f is invertible modulo some prime $q \in \mathbb{Z}$, we let $h = f^{-1}g$ mod q. The NTRU module determined by h is $\mathscr{L}_{\mathrm{NTRU}} = \{(u, v) \in \mathscr{R}^2 : uh - v = 0 \mod q\}$. Two bases of this free module are of particular interest:

$$\mathbf{B}_h = \begin{bmatrix} 1 & 0 \\ h & q \end{bmatrix} \quad and \quad \mathbf{B}_{f,g} = \begin{bmatrix} f & F \\ g & G \end{bmatrix},$$

where $F, G \in \mathscr{R}$ are such that $fG - gF = q$ and (F, G) should be relatively small. This module is usually seen as a lattice of volume q^d in $\mathbb{R}^{2d}$ in the coefficient embedding.

We equip the ambient space $\mathscr{K}_\mathbb{R}^2$ with the inner product $\langle \mathbf{x}, \mathbf{y} \rangle_\mathscr{K} = x_1^* y_1 + x_2^* y_2$. The well-known Gram-Schmidt orthogonalization procedure for a pair of linearly independent vectors $\mathbf{b}_1, \mathbf{b}_2 \in \mathscr{K}^2$ is defined as

$$\widetilde{\mathbf{b}}_1 := \mathbf{b}_1, \widetilde{\mathbf{b}}_2 := \mathbf{b}_2 - \frac{\langle \mathbf{b}_1, \mathbf{b}_2 \rangle_\mathscr{K}}{\langle \mathbf{b}_1, \mathbf{b}_1 \rangle_\mathscr{K}} \cdot \widetilde{\mathbf{b}}_1.$$

One readily checks that $\langle \widetilde{\mathbf{b}}_1, \widetilde{\mathbf{b}}_2 \rangle = 0$. The Gram-Schmidt matrix with columns $\widetilde{\mathbf{b}}_1, \widetilde{\mathbf{b}}_2$ is denoted by $\widetilde{\mathbf{B}}$ and we have $\det \widetilde{\mathbf{B}} = \det \mathbf{B}$. We also let $|\mathbf{B}|_\mathscr{K} = \max(||\varphi(\langle \widetilde{\mathbf{b}}_1, \widetilde{\mathbf{b}}_1 \rangle)||_\infty, ||\varphi(\langle \widetilde{\mathbf{b}}_2, \widetilde{\mathbf{b}}_2 \rangle)||_\infty)^{1/2}$.

Lemma 2. *Let $\mathbf{B}_{f,g}$ be a basis of an NTRU module and $\mathbf{b}_1 = (f, g)$. We have $\sqrt{q} \leqslant |\mathbf{B}_{f,g}|_\mathscr{K}$ and*

$$|\mathbf{B}_{f,g}|_\mathscr{K}^2 = \max \left(||\varphi(\langle \mathbf{b}_1, \mathbf{b}_1 \rangle_\mathscr{K})||_\infty, \left\| \frac{q^2}{\varphi(\langle \mathbf{b}_1, \mathbf{b}_1 \rangle_\mathscr{K})} \right\|_\infty \right).$$

2.3 Gaussian and Chi-Squared Distributions

For $\mu \in \mathbb{R}$ and $\sigma > 0$ we let $\mathcal{N}(\mu, \sigma^2)$ be the normal distribution of mean μ and standard deviation σ, that is, the continuous distribution over $\mathbb{R}$ with density proportional to $\exp\left(-(x-\mu)^2/(2\sigma^2)\right)$. In higher dimensions, for Σ a positive definite matrix and a vector $\mu \in \mathbb{R}^k$, we let $\mathcal{N}(\mu, \Sigma)$ be the normal distribution of density proportional to $\exp\left(-\frac{1}{2}(x-\mu)^t \Sigma^{-1}(x-\mu)\right)$.

Let $T \sim \mathcal{N}(\mu, \sigma^2 \mathbf{I}_k)$ be a k-dimensional spherical normal random vector. The random variable $\|T\|^2$ follows a *non central chi-squared distribution of degree k, non-centrality $c := \|\mu\|^2$ and scaling σ^2*, denoted by $\chi^2(k, \sigma^2; c)$. Its expectation, variance and cumulative distribution function are described by the following classical result.

Lemma 3. *Let U be a random variable distributed as $\chi^2(k, \sigma^2; c)$. We have $\mathbb{E}[U] = \sigma^2 k + c$ and $\mathrm{Var}[U] = 2\sigma^2(\sigma^2 k + 2c)$. For $0 \leqslant a < b$, we have $\mathbb{P}[a \leqslant U \leqslant b] = Q_{k/2}(\sqrt{c}/\sigma, \sqrt{a}/\sigma) - Q_{k/2}(\sqrt{c}/\sigma, \sqrt{b}/\sigma)$, where $Q_{k/2}$ is the Marcum Q-function of order $k/2$.*

Moreover, the Marcum Q-function Q_m of integer order m satisfies the following inequalities.

Lemma 4 ([3,35]). *For integer m and $u, v \geqslant 0$, the following inequalities hold:*

$$Q_m(u,v) \geqslant 1 - \frac{1}{2}e^{-(u-v)^2/2} \qquad\qquad if\, u \geqslant v;$$

$$Q_m(u,v) \leqslant e^{-(v-u)^2/2} \cdot \left(1 + \frac{(v/u)^{m-1} - 1}{\pi \cdot (1 - u/v)}\right) \qquad\qquad if\, u \leqslant v.$$

We also note that the independent sum of a $\chi^2(k, \sigma^2; c)$ variable and a $\chi^2(k', \sigma^2; c')$ variable, for the same scaling σ^2, follows a $\chi^2(k + k', \sigma^2; c + c')$ distribution.

In the general case where $T \sim \mathcal{N}(\mu, \Sigma)$, let $\lambda_i > 0$ be the eigenvalues of the positive definite symmetric matrix Σ. If P is an orthogonal matrix that diagonalizes Σ, let $\nu = (\nu_1, \ldots, \nu_k) := P\mu$. Then $\|T\|^2 \sim \chi^2(1, \lambda_1; \nu_1^2) + \cdots + \chi^2(1, \lambda_k; \nu_k^2)$. This distribution is called the *weighted sum of k independent non central chi-squared variables*. There is no known closed form for its cumulative distribution function, but there exist tools to evaluate it numerically (e.g., the Python package `chi2comb`).

3   New Trapdoor Algorithms for Hybrid Sampling

3.1   Hash-then-Sign Over Lattices in a Nutshell

The rationale behind this design is that a signature corresponds to a *short* Gaussian vector in a lattice $\mathscr{L}_{\mathrm{NTRU}}$ centered at the hash of a (salted) message. On the one hand, these vectors can only be generated efficiently with the knowledge of a trapdoor $\mathbf{B}_{f,g}$, that is, a basis with good quality for a given sampling method. On the other hand, verifying amounts to checking lattice membership and that the vector is indeed shorter than a threshold. For the sake of completeness, we recap this design in the form of high-level, generic algorithms KeyGen, Sign, Verify corresponding to the current efficient instantiations.

In Algorithm 1, the procedure Sample differs from FALCON to MITAKA. The former relies on the FFO sampler (a Fast-Fourier-like version of the GPV sampler [20], while the latter prefers the simpler hybrid sampler of Ducas-Prest [11]. Lattice membership is implicitly checked at the first step of Algorithm 2. We finish the section with a high-level description of KeyGen in Algorithm 3. Its purpose is to generate a pair $(h, \mathbf{B}_{f,g})$ where $\mathbf{B}_{f,g}$ should have a good quality with respect to the selected instantiation of Sample. For simplicity, we omit in

---

Algorithm 1: Signing

Input: A message $\mathtt{m}$, a trapdoor $\mathbf{B}_{f,g}$, a standard deviation parameter σ
Result: the first component s_0 of $\mathbf{s} = (s_0, s_1) \in \mathscr{R}^2$ such that $\mathbf{c} - \mathbf{s}$ has a distribution close to $D_{\mathscr{L}_{\mathrm{NTRU}}, \mathbf{c}, \sigma}$.

1 $r \xleftarrow{\$} \{0,1\}^{320}$
2 $\mathbf{c} \leftarrow (0, \mathsf{H}(\mathtt{m}||r))$
3 $\mathbf{v} \leftarrow \mathtt{Sample}(\mathbf{B}_{f,g}, \mathbf{c}, \sigma)$
4 $(s_0, s_1) \leftarrow \mathbf{c} - \mathbf{v}$
5 **return** s_0

Algorithm 2: Verification

Input: A message $\mathtt{m}$, a salt r, $s_0 \in \mathscr{R}$, a public key h and a threshold β
Result: Accept or reject

1 $s_1 \leftarrow \mathsf{H}(\mathtt{m}||r) + s_0 h \bmod q$
2 **if** $\|(s_0, s_1)\| > \beta$ **then**
3 | Reject.
4 **end if**
5 Accept.

---

its description the additional secret data related to the sampler. The procedure $\mathtt{GoodPair}$, our focus in this work, outputs $(f, g) \in \mathscr{R}^2$ with the guarantee that the basis $\mathbf{B}_{f,g}$ output by $\mathtt{NTRUSolve}$ will have quality α or better for the choice of $\mathtt{Sample}$.

3.2 NTRU Trapdoors in FALCON and MITAKA

With respect to Prest's hybrid sampler, an NTRU trapdoor $\mathbf{B}_{f,g}$ has a quality α defined as

$$\alpha = |\mathbf{B}_{f,g}|_{\mathscr{K}} / \sqrt{q}, \tag{1}$$

where we recall that $|\mathbf{B}_{f,g}|_{\mathscr{K}}^2 = \max\left(\|\varphi(ff^* + gg^*)\|_\infty, \left\|\frac{q^2}{\varphi(ff^* + gg^*)}\right\|_\infty\right)$. The quality with respect to the Klein–GPV sampler admits a similar expression.

In hash-and-sign signatures, security against forgery attacks is driven by the standard deviation of the sampler, which is essentially $\alpha\sqrt{q}$. As the smaller the value of α, the harder forgery becomes, the goal of $\mathtt{KeyGen}$ in schemes such as DLP [9], FALCON [34] and MITAKA [15] is to construct in reasonable time bases $\mathbf{B}_{f,g}$ with α as small as possible (and in particular, smaller than a given threshold related to the acceptance radius of signature verification). In other words, the goal is to instantiate efficiently the procedure $\mathtt{GoodPair}$.

An important observation regarding NTRU trapdoors is that the knowledge of the first basis vector (f, g) alone is sufficient to determine the quality of the whole basis (see for example Lemma 2 for MITAKA). As a result, to test if a

---

Algorithm 3: Generic NTRU Trapdoor generator

Input: A degree d, a modulus q, a target quality α
Result: a public key $h \in \mathscr{R}$ and the trapdoor $\mathbf{B}_{f,g}$
1 $(f, g) \leftarrow \texttt{GoodPair}(d, q, \alpha)$
2 $\mathbf{B}_{f,g} \leftarrow \texttt{NTRUSolve}(f, g, q)$
3 $h \leftarrow gf^{-1} \bmod q$
4 **return** $(h, \mathbf{B}_{f,g})$.

---

vector (f, g) can be completed into a trapdoor $\mathbf{B}_{f,g}$ reaching the desired quality threshold, it is not necessary to compute the second vector (F, G), which is a notoriously costly operation, even accounting for optimizations such as [31].

In DLP, FALCON and MITAKA, GoodPair is a trial-and-error routine, generating many potential candidate first vectors (f, g) and testing whether they satisfy the required quality threshold. The candidates themselves are generated as discrete Gaussian vectors in $\mathscr{R}^2$ with the correct expected length. In that way, FALCON reaches quality $\alpha = 1.17$ with respect to its FFO-based sampler (that admits the same quality metric as Klein–GPV). Doing this directly for the hybrid sampler, as discussed in [32], only achieves quality $\gtrsim 3$ in dimension 512, and even larger in higher dimensions. As a result, the MITAKA paper has to introduce randomness recycling and other techniques on top of this general approach in order to increase the number of candidates and improve the achievable quality; with those improvements, MITAKA reaches $\alpha = 2.04$ in dimension 512 (which translates to 20 fewer bits of security compared to FALCON, and is thus unfortunately not sufficient to reach NIST security level I).

3.3 ANTRAG: Annular NTRU Trapdoor Generation

The main contribution of this paper is a novel instantiation of GoodPair for the hybrid sampler, resulting in a NTRU trapdoor generation algorithm achieving much better quality than MITAKA, while reaching the same security NIST levels as FALCON.

The intuition behind our new approach stems from the following observation. For a fixed $\alpha \geqslant 1$, requiring a trapdoor $\mathbf{B}_{f,g}$ to satisfy $|\mathbf{B}_{f,g}|_{\mathscr{K}} \leqslant \alpha\sqrt{q}$ is equivalent to enforcing that for all $1 \leqslant i \leqslant d$, we have

$$\frac{q}{\alpha^2} \leqslant |\varphi_i(f)|^2 + |\varphi_i(g)|^2 \leqslant \alpha^2 q, \tag{2}$$

(where we recall that the $\varphi_i(f)$ are the *embeddings* of f in $\mathbb{C}$, and similarly for g). Equivalently, this means that for all i, the pair $(|\varphi_i(f)|, |\varphi_i(g)|)$ belongs to the arc of annulus $A_\alpha^+ := A^+(\sqrt{q}/\alpha, \alpha\sqrt{q})$.

Algorithm 4: Candidate pairs from uniform annulus sampling

Input: $0 < r < R$, the radii of $A^+(r, R)$
Result: $z, z' \in \mathbb{C}$ such that $(|z|, |z'|)$ is uniformly distributed in $A^+(r, R)$
1 $u \hookleftarrow \mathcal{U}\left([r^2, R^2]\right)$
2 $\rho \leftarrow \sqrt{u}$
3 $\theta \hookleftarrow \mathcal{U}\left([0, \pi/2]\right)$
4 $(x, y) \leftarrow (\rho \cos\theta, \rho \sin\theta)$ /* $(x, y) \hookleftarrow \mathcal{U}\left(A^+(r, R)\right)$ */
5 $\omega, \omega' \hookleftarrow \mathcal{U}\left([0, 2\pi]\right)$
6 $(z, z') \leftarrow (x \cdot e^{i\omega}, y \cdot e^{i\omega'})$
7 **return** (z, z')

It is thus natural to try and sample f and g *from their embeddings* (i.e., in the Fourier domain), by picking the pairs $(\varphi_i(f), \varphi_i(g))$ as *uniform* random pairs of complex numbers such that satisfying the condition that the pair of their magnitudes belongs to A_α^+: in other words, pick (x_i, y_i) uniformly at random in A_α^+ and then sample $\varphi_i(f)$ and $\varphi_i(g)$ as uniform complex numbers of magnitudes x_i and y_i respectively. Note that only $d/2$ pairs are needed, as the remaining ones are determined by conjugation.

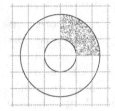

Fig. 1. $(|z|, |w|)$ is sampled uniformly in the annulus $A^+(r, R)$.

Moreover, sampling uniformly in an annulus (or, as in our case, an arc of annulus) in polar coordinates (ρ, θ) is easy: it suffices to sample the angle θ and the *square* ρ^2 of the radial coordinate uniformly in their respective ranges. This is because the area element in polar coordinates is $\rho \, d\rho \, d\theta = \frac{1}{2} d(\rho^2) \, d\theta$. This gives rise to Algorithm 4 for sampling the pairs of embeddings.

However, one soon realizes that the real polynomials $\tilde{f}, \tilde{g}$ corresponding to the embeddings generated by the Algorithm 4 (via the inverse Fourier transform φ^{-1}) do not always have integer coefficients, and hence do not generally correspond to ring elements. In general, they are elements of the $\mathbb{R}$-algebra $\mathscr{K}_\mathbb{R}$.

In order to obtain actual ring elements, a natural solution is to round those real polynomials $\tilde{f}, \tilde{g}$ coefficient-wise. This yields $f = \lfloor \tilde{f} \rceil$ and $g = \lfloor \tilde{g} \rceil$ in $\mathscr{R}$, which are potential candidates for a trapdoor. It turns out, however, that if one starts from $\tilde{f}, \tilde{g}$ uniform with their embeddings of magnitude in A_α^+, the resulting rounded ring elements are very unlikely to also have their embeddings of magnitude in that arc of annulus. Thus, they do not typically give rise to a trapdoor of the desired quality. This is because rounding adds an additive term (essentially uniformly distributed in $[-1/2, 1/2)$) to each coefficient, which translates to an additive "error" on each embedding, making it unlikely that the embeddings all remain in the desired domain.

A straightforward workaround is to compensate this decoding error by sampling the embeddings of $\tilde{f}, \tilde{g}$ from a narrower annulus $A^+(r, R)$ for some radii

---

Algorithm 5: ANTRAG trapdoor generation

Input: The degree d, the modulus q, a target quality α, and starting radii r, R such that $\sqrt{q}/\alpha < r < R < \alpha\sqrt{q}$.

Result: $f, g \in \mathscr{R}^2$ such that $\frac{q}{\alpha^2} \leqslant |\varphi_i(f)|^2 + |\varphi_i(g)|^2 \leqslant \alpha^2 q$ for all i.

1 **repeat**
2   **for** $1 \leqslant i \leqslant d/2$ **do**
3   using Algorithm 4, sample $(z_i, w_i) \in \mathbb{C}^2$ uniformly such that
       $(|z_i|, |w_i|) \in A^+(r, R)$.
4   **end for**
5    $\tilde{f} \leftarrow \varphi^{-1}(z_1, \ldots, z_{d/2}) \in \mathscr{K}_{\mathbb{R}}$
6    $\tilde{g} \leftarrow \varphi^{-1}(w_1, \ldots, w_{d/2}) \in \mathscr{K}_{\mathbb{R}}$
7    $f \leftarrow \lfloor \tilde{f} \rceil$
8    $g \leftarrow \lfloor \tilde{g} \rceil$
9 **until** $\big(|\varphi_i(f)|, |\varphi_i(g)|\big) \in A^+\big(\sqrt{q}/\alpha, \alpha\sqrt{q}\big)$ for all $i = 1, \ldots, d/2$
10 **return** (f, g)

---

r, R such that $\sqrt{q}/\alpha < r < R < \alpha\sqrt{q}$. This yields Algorithm 5, which is our proposed ANTRAG trapdoor generation algorithm.

Remark 2. One could consider carrying out the decoding to the ring differently, for example by sampling discrete Gaussians f and g in $\mathscr{R}$ centered at $\tilde{f}$ and $\tilde{g}$ respectively. The resulting algorithm would be simpler to analyze in some ways, and might be seen as better behaved in a certain sense, but it does have a major drawback: it introduces a much larger decoding error (on the order of the smoothing parameter $\eta_\varepsilon(\mathbb{Z})$ of $\mathbb{Z}$ on each coefficient, instead of the standard deviation $1/\sqrt{12}$ of the uniform distribution in $[-1/2, 1/2)$, so about 4 times larger). As a result, in this work, we focus on the rounding approach.

3.4 On the Distribution of Embeddings

We have mentioned above that taking the magnitudes of the embeddings of $\tilde{f}$ and $\tilde{g}$ in A_α^+ was very unlikely to result in f and g of the required quality α after rounding, but that the probability increased greatly when choosing $\tilde{f}$ and $\tilde{g}$ with embedding magnitudes in a narrower arc of annulus $A^+(r, R)$. We choose the bounds r and R as complementary convex combinations of $\alpha\sqrt{q}$ and $\sqrt{q}/\alpha$; in other words, we set:

$$r = \frac{1-\xi}{2}\alpha\sqrt{q} + \frac{1+\xi}{2} \cdot \frac{\sqrt{q}}{\alpha} \quad \text{and} \quad R = \frac{1+\xi}{2}\alpha\sqrt{q} + \frac{1-\xi}{2} \cdot \frac{\sqrt{q}}{\alpha} \quad (3)$$

for some constant $\xi \in (0, 1)$, so that $A^+(r, R)$ corresponds to the middle ξ-fraction of A_α^+. We will later specifically choose $\xi = 1/3$ (i.e., $A^+(r, R)$ as the "middle third" of A_α^+) to fix ideas, and because it yields the following expression for r and R with minimal coefficient height:

$$r = \left(\frac{1}{3}\alpha + \frac{2}{3} \cdot \frac{1}{\alpha}\right)\sqrt{q} \quad \text{and} \quad R = \left(\frac{2}{3}\alpha + \frac{1}{3} \cdot \frac{1}{\alpha}\right)\sqrt{q}.$$

In this section, we would like to provide a model allowing us to quantify the claim that sampling $\tilde{f}$ and $\tilde{g}$ in this $A^+(r,R)$ increases success probability. To that end, write $e = (e_f, e_g) = (f - \tilde{f}, g - \tilde{g}) \in \mathscr{K}_{\mathbb{R}}^2$ for the error term introduced by rounding. We would like to control the distribution of the embeddings of e_f and e_g in order to estimate the likelihood that the condition $(|\varphi_i(f)|, |\varphi_i(g)|)$ will be satisfied for all i.

In the polynomial basis, we write $e_f = \sum_{j=0}^{d-1} e_f^{(j)} x^j$ and similarly for e_g. Heuristically, we expect the coefficients $e_f^{(j)}$ and $e_g^{(j)}$ to behave essentially like independent uniform random variables in $[-1/2, 1/2)$.[4] This is well-supported by experiments (see the full version of this paper [17]).

Now consider a single embedding φ_θ, and recall that we are interested in an *a priori* arbitrary cyclotomic base ring, so that φ_θ is defined by the evaluation at some primitive m-th root of unity $\zeta = e^{i\theta}$. We therefore have:

$$\varphi_\theta(e_f) = x_\theta + iy_\theta \quad \text{with} \quad x_\theta = \sum_{j=0}^{d-1} e_f^{(j)} \cos(j\theta) \quad \text{and} \quad y_\theta = \sum_{j=0}^{d-1} e_f^{(j)} \sin(j\theta).$$

This expresses the real and imaginary parts x_θ, y_θ of $\varphi_\theta(e_f)$ as the sum of d independent random variables, with d relatively large, so by the central limit theorem, $\varphi_\theta(e_f)$ should essentially behave[5] like a normal random variable in $\mathbb{C}$, essentially determined by its expectation and covariance.

Now since $e_f^{(j)}$ has mean 0 and variance $1/12$ for all j, we obtain that $\mathbb{E}[x_\theta] = \mathbb{E}[y_\theta] = 0$. Therefore, the pair (x_θ, y_θ) has mean 0, and its covariance matrix is easily expressed as follows:

$$\Sigma_\theta = \frac{d}{24} \mathbf{I}_2 + E(\theta) \quad \text{where} \quad E(\theta) = \frac{1}{24} \begin{bmatrix} \operatorname{Re} S(\theta) & \operatorname{Im} S(\theta) \\ \operatorname{Im} S(\theta) & -\operatorname{Re} S(\theta) \end{bmatrix}.$$

Note that Σ_θ has eigenvalues $\lambda_+^\theta = \frac{d+|S(\theta)|}{24}$ and $\lambda_-^\theta = \frac{d-|S(\theta)|}{24}$. We thus expect that $\varphi_\theta(e_f)$ follows the normal distribution $\mathcal{N}(0, \Sigma_\theta)$, and the same argument applies to $\varphi_\theta(e_g)$ as well. Moreover, heuristically, those two normal distributions should be independent (this is again well-verified in practice), therefore, we can write

$$(\varphi_\theta(e_f), \varphi_\theta(e_g)) \sim \mathcal{N}\left(0, \begin{pmatrix} \Sigma_\theta & 0 \\ 0 & \Sigma_\theta \end{pmatrix}\right) \tag{4}$$

This leads us to model the distribution of the embeddings of secret keys as follows.

Heuristic 1. Let $(f, g) \in \mathscr{K}^2$ a pair output by Algorithm 5, corresponding to $(\tilde{f}, \tilde{g}) \in \mathscr{K}_{\mathbb{R}}^2$ obtained from the executions of Algorithm 4. For the embedding φ_θ

---

[4] This is equivalent to saying that the distribution of $\tilde{f}$ and $\tilde{g}$ is uniform modulo $\mathscr{R}$ in $\mathscr{K}_{\mathbb{R}}$, which should indeed happen as soon as we have sufficient width (i.e., if we exceed a regularity metric analogous to the smoothing parameters for Gaussians).

[5] This can in fact be made rigorous with the Berry–Esseen theorem.

corresponding to the primitive root of unity $e^{i\theta}$, $(\varphi_\theta(f), \varphi_\theta(g))$ is distributed as

$$(\varphi_\theta(f),\ \varphi_\theta(g)) \sim \mathcal{N}\big(\,(\varphi_\theta(\tilde{f}),\ \varphi_\theta(\tilde{g}))\,,\ \mathbf{I}_2 \otimes \Sigma_\theta\big).$$

Moreover, the pairs $(\varphi_\theta(f), \varphi_\theta(g))$ as φ_θ ranges through all the embeddings of $\mathscr{K}$ are independently distributed.

Note that this heuristic considers the pair $(\varphi_\theta(f), \varphi_\theta(g))$, which is actually supported on dense but countable subgroup of $\mathbb{C}^2$, as following a *continuous* distribution. This has the merit of allowing an analysis while being an accurate representation of the situation according to our experiments.

Under this heuristic we can express the expected length of the embeddings of secret keys and related elements, which will be useful in the security analysis. The proof is provided in the full version of this paper [17].

Proposition 1 (Heuristic). *Keeping the notation of Algorithm 5, let (f, g) be a random variable following the distribution of its output. Let θ be an argument of a primitive m-th root of unity, and let φ_θ be the corresponding embedding. Then:*

$$\mathbb{E}\big[|\varphi_\theta(f)|^2 + |\varphi_\theta(g)|^2\big] = \frac{d}{6} + \frac{r^2 + R^2}{2}.$$

Let $\|\cdot\|_\theta$ be the norm induced by the quadratic form Σ_θ. Then we also have:

$$\mathbb{E}\big[|\varphi_\theta(f)|^4 + |\varphi_\theta(g)|^4\big] = \frac{5}{8}(R^4 + r^4) + R^2 r^2 + \frac{d}{12}(R^2 + r^2) + \frac{d^2}{36} + T(\theta),$$

where $T(\theta) := |S(\theta)|^2/72 + 4 \cdot \mathbb{E}\big[\|\varphi_\theta(\tilde{f})\|_\theta^2 + \|\varphi_\theta(\tilde{g})\|_\theta^2\big]$.

4   Success Probability and Security Analysis

In this section, we first concentrate on the case of a power-of-two cyclotomic base ring, in which, under Heuristic 1, all the embeddings of f and g are simply modeled as independent and identically distributed isotropic normal variates, which simplifies the analysis somewhat. In this context, we analyze the success probability of Algorithm 5 as well as the security of the resulting scheme, which lets us derive concrete parameters.

At the end of the section, we also briefly describe how the analysis extends to the more general setting of cyclotomic rings with conductor $m = 2^k p^\ell$, with further details provided in the full version of this paper [17].

4.1   Success Probability over Power-of-Two Cyclotomics

Suppose that $\mathscr{K}$ is a cyclotomic field of conductor a power of two, and let $(\tilde{f}, \tilde{g}) \in \mathscr{K}_{\mathbb{R}}^2$ and $(f, g) \in \mathscr{R}^2$ be generated as in Steps 5–6 and Steps 7–8 of Algorithm 5 respectively.

We first fix one embedding $\varphi_\theta \colon \mathscr{K} \to \mathbb{C}$ of $\mathscr{K}$, and try to determine the probability with which the test of Step 10 of Algorithm 5 is satisfied with respect to that particular embedding. In other words, we want to estimate the probability that:

$$q/\alpha^2 \leqslant |\varphi_\theta(f)|^2 + |\varphi_\theta(g)|^2 \leqslant \alpha^2 q. \tag{5}$$

Now, according to Heuristic 1, the pair $(\varphi_\theta(f), \varphi_\theta(g)) \in \mathbb{C}^2$ follows a normal distribution centered at $(\varphi_\theta(\tilde{f}), \varphi_\theta(\tilde{g}))$ of scalar covariance $\frac{d}{24} \mathbf{I}_4$ (since over power-of-two cyclotomic fields, $E(\theta) = 0$ for all θ). Therefore, for fixed $(\tilde{f}, \tilde{g})$ and following the definitions of Sect. 2.3, the squared norm:

$$\| (\varphi_\theta(f), \varphi_\theta(g)) \|^2 = |\varphi_\theta(f)|^2 + |\varphi_\theta(g)|^2$$

follows a non central chi-squared distribution $\chi^2(4, \sigma^2; c)$ of degree 4, non-centrality $c = |\varphi_\theta(\tilde{f})|^2 + |\varphi_\theta(\tilde{g})|^2$ and scaling $\sigma^2 = d/24$. In particular, the probability that condition (5) does not depend on the exact position of the pair $(\varphi_\theta(\tilde{f}), \varphi_\theta(\tilde{g}))$, but only on its squared norm c, or equivalently on:

$$\beta := \frac{1}{\sqrt{q}} \| (\varphi_\theta(\tilde{f}), \varphi_\theta(\tilde{g})) \|.$$

We denote the probability that condition (5) is satisfied for a certain value β by $p_{\mathrm{succ}}(\beta)$. According to Lemma 3, the probability $p_{\mathrm{succ}}(\beta)$ can be expressed in terms of the Marcum Q-function Q_2 as follows:

$$p_{\mathrm{succ}}(\beta) = Q_2(\tau\beta, \tau/\alpha) - Q_2(\tau\beta, \tau\alpha) \quad \text{where} \quad \tau = \sqrt{\frac{24q}{d}}.$$

Based on this result, we will first provide a simple but loose lower bound of the success probability of Algorithm 5, and then derive a more complicated but tight estimate that we can use for numerical estimates and parameter selection.

Bounding the Success Probability Below. According to Lemma 4, the following bounds on the Marcum Q function hold for any $1/\alpha \leqslant \beta \leqslant \alpha$:

$$Q_2(\tau\beta, \tau/\alpha) \geqslant 1 - \frac{1}{2} \exp\left(-\frac{\tau^2}{2}(\beta - 1/\alpha)^2 \right)$$

$$Q_2(\tau\beta, \tau\alpha) \leqslant \left(1 + \frac{\alpha/\beta}{\pi} \right) \exp\left(-\frac{\tau^2}{2}(\alpha - \beta)^2 \right)$$

from which it follows that:

$$p_{\mathrm{succ}}(\beta) \geqslant 1 - \frac{1}{2} u_\tau(\beta - 1/\alpha) - \left(1 + \frac{\alpha/\beta}{\pi} \right) u_\tau(\alpha - \beta) \quad \text{where} \quad u_\tau(x) = \exp\left(-\frac{\tau^2}{2} x^2 \right). \tag{6}$$

We write $\beta = (\alpha + 1/\alpha)/2 + t(\alpha - 1/\alpha)/2$ for some $t \in (-1, 1)$. Recall furthermore from Eq. (3) that we have set:

$$\frac{r}{\sqrt{q}} = (\alpha + 1/\alpha)/2 - \xi(\alpha - 1/\alpha)/2 \quad \text{and} \quad \frac{R}{\sqrt{q}} = (\alpha + 1/\alpha)/2 + \xi(\alpha - 1/\alpha)/2$$

so that t actually varies in $[-\xi, \xi]$. In particular, we have:

$$\frac{\alpha}{\beta} \leqslant \frac{\alpha}{r} = \frac{\alpha}{\frac{1-\xi}{2}\alpha + \frac{1+\xi}{2}\frac{1}{\alpha}} = \frac{2}{1-\xi} \cdot \frac{1}{1 + \frac{1+\xi}{1-\xi}\frac{1}{\alpha^2}} \leqslant \frac{2}{1-\xi}.$$

Thus, inequality (6) becomes:

$$p_{\text{succ}}(\beta) \geqslant 1 - \frac{1}{2}u_\tau\big((1-t)\delta\big) - \Big(1 + \frac{2/\pi}{1-\xi}\Big)u_\tau\big((1+t)\delta\big)\Big) \quad \text{for} \quad \delta = \frac{\alpha - 1/\alpha}{2}.$$

Since u_τ is a decreasing function, both $u_\tau\big((1-t)\delta\big)$ and $u_\tau\big((1+t)\delta\big)$ are bounded above by $u_\tau\big((1-\xi)\delta\big)$, so that:

$$p_{\text{succ}}(\beta) \geqslant 1 - K_\xi u_\tau\big((1-\xi)\delta\big) \quad \text{with} \quad K_\xi = \frac{3}{2} + \frac{2/\pi}{1-\xi}$$

holds for all $\beta \in [r/\sqrt{q}, R/\sqrt{q}]$.

As a result, the *overall* success probability $p_{\text{succ-one}}$ for a single embedding (which is the probability that condition (5) holds when the starting embedding pair $\big(|\varphi_\theta(\tilde{f})|, |\varphi_\theta(\tilde{g})|\big)$ is sampled uniformly in $A^+(r, R)$) is similarly lower bounded as:

$$p_{\text{succ-one}} \geqslant 1 - K_\xi u_\tau\big((1-\xi)\delta\big) \tag{7}$$

and under our independence heuristic, the success probability $p_{\text{succ-all}}$ for all $d/2$ embeddings at the same time satisfies:

$$p_{\text{succ-all}} \geqslant \Big(1 - K_\xi u_\tau\big((1-\xi)\delta\big)\Big)^{d/2}.$$

To reach an overall success probability of $1/M$ (i.e., M repetitions on average), it therefore suffices to have:

$$\frac{d}{2}\log\Big(1 - K_\xi u_\tau\big((1-\xi)\delta\big)\Big) \geqslant -\log M.$$

Using the usual first order approximation $\log(1-x) \approx -x$, this yields $\frac{d}{2}K_\xi u_\tau\big((1-\xi)\delta\big) \lesssim \log M$, or equivalently:

$$\frac{\alpha - 1/\alpha}{2} \gtrsim \frac{d}{12(1-\xi)^2 q} \log\frac{K_\xi d}{2\log M}.$$

This shows that a quality α is achievable (with repetition rate up to M) as long as:

$$\alpha \geqslant \sqrt{A} + \sqrt{1+A} \quad \text{where} \quad A = \frac{d}{12(1-\xi)^2 q} \log\frac{K_\xi d}{2\log M}. \tag{8}$$

In particular, we see that, as long as $q = \Omega(d\log d)$, quality measures $\alpha = O(1)$ are achievable with any constant repetition rate. This is similar to FALCON and unlike MITAKA [14, Appendix C] and the original approach for the Peikert and hybrid samplers [32], where α increases as a power function of the dimension independently of q.

As discussed in the previous section, we choose $\xi = 1/3$ to fix ideas, so that the starting annulus becomes the "middle third" of the target annulus (we will see below that this choice is very safe). Condition (8) above with $M = 4$ and $q = 12289$ shows that one can reach quality at least $\alpha = 1.24$ in dimension 512 and $\alpha = 1.38$ in dimension 1024 with this modulus q and repetition rate up to 4. This is already much better than the quality parameters achievable by MITAKA, but since we have used loose inequalities throughout, these are actually rough lower bounds.

More Precise Expression of Success Probability. For concrete parameter selection, and also to test the validity of our heuristic assumptions, it is useful to write down the exact expression of success probability according to our model.

Recall that the success probability $p_{\text{succ-one}}$ for a single embedding is the probability that condition (5) holds when the starting embedding pair $(|\varphi_\theta(\tilde{f})|, |\varphi_\theta(\tilde{g})|)$ is sampled uniformly in $A^+(r, R)$. In other words, $p_{\text{succ-one}}$ is the expected value of $p_{\text{succ}}(\beta)$ for β^2 uniformly distributed in $[r^2/q, R^2/q]$. Therefore:

$$p_{\text{succ-one}} = \frac{q}{R^2 - r^2} \int_{r^2/q}^{R^2/q} p_{\text{succ}}(\sqrt{B})\, dB = \frac{2q}{R^2 - r^2} \int_{r/\sqrt{q}}^{R/\sqrt{q}} p_{\text{succ}}(\beta)\, \beta\, d\beta.$$

Carrying out the change of variables $\beta = (\alpha+1/\alpha)/2 + t(\alpha-1/\alpha)/2$ and plugging in the expression of $p_{\text{succ}}(\beta)$ in terms of Q_2, we finally get:

$$p_{\text{succ-one}} = \frac{1}{2\xi} \int_{-\xi}^{\xi} F(\alpha, t) \cdot \left(1 + t\frac{\alpha - \frac{1}{\alpha}}{\alpha + \frac{1}{\alpha}}\right) dt$$

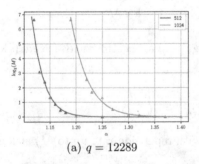

(a) $q = 12289$

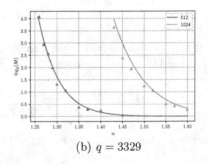

(b) $q = 3329$

Fig. 2. Base 2 logarithm of the repetition rate M of Algorithm 5 as a function of α, for $d \in \{512, 1024\}$ and $q \in \{12289, 3329\}$. The continuous lines are obtained based on our model, and the triangle data points are measured by simulations (averaging 100 iterations of the algorithm for each data point).

where

$$F(\alpha,t) = Q_2\left(\tau\left(\frac{\alpha+\frac{1}{\alpha}}{2} + t\frac{\alpha-\frac{1}{\alpha}}{2}\right), \tau/\alpha\right) - Q_2\left(\tau\left(\frac{\alpha+\frac{1}{\alpha}}{2} + t\frac{\alpha-\frac{1}{\alpha}}{2}\right), \tau\alpha\right),$$

and $1/M = p_{\text{succ-all}} = p_{\text{succ-one}}^{d/2}$. This makes it easy to solve numerically for α in order to reach a certain repetition rate. Again for $q = 12289$, we find that we reach repetition rate $M = 4$ for $\alpha \approx 1.143$ in dimension $d = 512$, and for $\alpha \approx 1.229$ for $d = 1024$. For $q = 3329$, the same repetition rate is reached for $\alpha \approx 1.290$ for $d = 512$ and $\alpha \approx 1.478$ for $d = 1024$. Moreover, this allows us to confirm that our model very closely matches experiments, as demonstrated on Fig. 2.

4.2   Security Analysis for Power-of-Two Cyclotomics

In order to assess the concrete security of the resulting signature scheme, we proceed using the usual cryptanalytic methodology of estimating the complexity of the best attacks against *key recovery attacks* on the one hand, and *signature forgery* on the other. In the hash-and-sign paradigm, the security of the forgery is a function of the standard deviation of the lattice Gaussian sampler used in the signature function, which itself depends on the quality α of the trapdoor. A first straightforward observation is that, since our work has only modified *which* trapdoors are used for signing, and not *how* they are used in signing, our modifications cannot have a negative impact on the resilience against forgery. On the contrary, we have shown how to increase the trapdoor quality, and therefore our new approach increases the security against forging attackers. As such our focus will now be the resilience to key recovery attacks.

In Sect. 4.2.1, we go through a short review of the general lattice reduction approach for key recovery, which is the current best attack when no additional information is provided to the attacker (seeing as combinatorial or hybrid attacks are irrelevant in our setting, with dense, non-ternary keys). Nevertheless, by changing the sampling of the good trapdoors, we might have restricted to a possibly smaller set of secret keys, or to a possibly much more geometrically constrained set of keys. Indeed, all their complex embeddings must lie in a publicly described annulus, so an adversary could use this additional information to gather more power for an attack.

In Sect. 4.2.2 we present a new approach exploiting this additional geometric information. It is reminiscent of the subfield attacks [1,6], however here we stop the descent in the subfields at the totally real subfield $\mathcal{K}^+$ (the set of elements satisfying $f = f^*$). Indeed, this subfield encodes the length information of the pair (f,g) in the elements (ff^*, gg^*) and its collection of embeddings. In the extreme (unlikely) case where the annulus would be a circle, an adversary would know this element exactly, and could use the Gentry-Szydlo attack [21] to recover f or g. Our situation could be summed-up as an "approximate" Gentry-Szydlo attack, where too much proximity of all the embeddings to a known circle could be exploited by an attacker through lattice reduction.

Our trapdoor generator could output keys with embeddings that would all be close to some circle, and we call these temporarily *potentially weak keys*. Our analysis will show that these potentially weak keys are in fact not so weak, or in other words, that we have some freedom for parametrization with respect to the available space $(\alpha - \alpha^{-1})\sqrt{q}$. This ensures a good success rate for ANTRAG. Ultimately, the attack will use lattice reduction but on a different lattice than in the direct, standard key-recovery context, and will try to recover (ff^*, gg^*).

For the context of Sect. 4.2.2, we need the expected length of (f, g) and (ff^*, gg^*). These two properties are gathered in the next result. The proof, a direct application of Proposition 1, is provided in the full version of this paper [17].

Corollary 1. *With the notation of Algorithm 5, let (f, g) be a random variable following the distribution of its output. Then we have* $\mathbb{E}[\|(f, g)\|^2] = \frac{d}{6} + \frac{R^2 + r^2}{2}$ *and* $\mathbb{E}[\|(ff^*, gg^*)\|^2] = \frac{5}{8}(R^4 + r^4) + R^2 r^2 + \frac{d}{6}(R^2 + r^2) + \frac{d^2}{36}$.

4.2.1   Classical Attack Against NTRU Keys

The key recovery in this context consists in constructing the algebraic lattice over $\mathscr{R}$ spanned by the vectors $(0, q)$ and $(1, h)$ (i.e. the public basis attached to the NTRU key) and retrieving the lattice vector $\mathbf{s} = (f, g)$ among all possible lattice vectors of norm bounded by $\|s\|$ (or a functionally equivalent vector, for instance $(\mu \cdot f, \mu \cdot g)$ for any unit μ of the ring of integer of the number field). From Corollary 1 we obtain $\mathbb{E}[\|\mathbf{s}\|^2] \leqslant qA$, where $A = \frac{d}{6q} + \frac{1}{9}\left(\frac{5\alpha^2}{2} + \frac{5}{\alpha^2} + 4\right)$. Since the attack is easier when the key to recover is longer, we take the value qA acting as $\mathbb{E}[\|\mathbf{s}\|^2]$. In order to avoid enumerating and testing all integer vectors in the sphere of radius $\sqrt{q}S$, which would contain a large number of vectors under the Gaussian heuristic[6], namely around $\left(\frac{qA}{q}\right)^d = A^d$, we make use of the projection trick (see also [15,18]). This technique involves reducing the public basis with some lattice reduction algorithm, and seeking for the projection of the secret key onto the lattice spanned by the few last Gram-Schmidt vectors of this reduced basis. If we find the projection of the secret key, we can retrieve the full key by using the Babai nearest plane algorithm to lift it to a lattice vector of the desired norm.

More precisely we proceed as follows. Set β to be the block size parameter of the DBKZ algorithm [28] and start by reducing the public basis with this latter algorithm. Call $[\mathbf{b}_1, \ldots, \mathbf{b}_{2d}]$ the resulting vectors. Then if we can recover the *projection* of the secret key onto $\mathcal{P}$, the orthogonal space to span$(\mathbf{b}_1, \ldots, \mathbf{b}_{2d-\beta-1})$, then we can retrieve in polynomial time the full key by *Babai nearest plane* algorithm to lift it to a lattice vector of the desired norm. Hence it suffices to be able find the projection of the secret key among the shortest vector of the

---

[6] The Gaussian heuristic predicts the number of vectors of length at most ℓ in a random lattice Γ of volume V to be a $v_\Gamma(\ell)/V + o(1)$ for large enough ℓ, where $v_\Gamma(\ell)$ is the volume of the sphere of radius ℓ for the measure induced by the inner product on Γ.

lattice generated by the last β vectors projected onto $\mathcal{P}$. Classically, sieving on this projected lattice will recover all vectors of norm smaller than $\sqrt{\frac{4}{3}}\ell$, where ℓ is the norm of the $2d - \beta$-th Gram-Schmidt vector $\widetilde{\mathbf{b}}_{2d-\beta}$ of the reduced basis.

The expected length of the projection is usually estimated under the *Geometric Series Assumption* (GSA). Instantiated on NTRU lattices, it states that the Gram-Schmidt vectors of the basis outputted by DBKZ with block-size β satisfy the relations (see Cor 2. of [28]):

$$\|\widetilde{\mathbf{b}}_i\| = \delta_\beta^{2(d-i)+1}\sqrt{q} \quad \text{where} \quad \delta_\beta = \left(\frac{(\pi\beta)^{1/\beta} \cdot \beta}{2\pi e}\right)^{\frac{1}{2(\beta-1)}}.$$

Therefore, we expect that $\ell = \delta_\beta^{-2(d-\beta)+1}\sqrt{q} \approx \sqrt{q} \cdot \left(\frac{\beta}{2\pi e}\right)^{1-\frac{d}{\beta-1}}$. Moreover, assuming that $\mathbf{s}$ behaves as a random vector, and using the GSA to bound the norm of the Gram-Schmidt vectors $[\widetilde{\mathbf{b}}_1, \dots, \widetilde{\mathbf{b}}_{2d-\beta}]$, the (squared) norm of its projection over $\mathcal{P}$ concentrates around $\frac{\beta}{2d} \cdot \mathbb{E}[\|\mathbf{s}\|^2] = \frac{Aq\beta}{2d}$. Hence, we will retrieve the projection among the sieved vectors if $\frac{Aq\beta}{2d} \leq \frac{4}{3}\ell^2$, that is if the following condition is fulfilled:

$$A \leq \frac{8d}{3\beta}\delta_\beta^{4(\beta-d)+2}. \tag{9}$$

Remark 3. On the Use of the GSA. In order to make a more accurate assessment of potential attacks, numerical models of the profile of the Gram-Schmidt length derived from simulations of the behavior of (D)BKZ can be utilized instead of relying solely on the Gaussian heuristic approximation (GSA). While this section focuses on using the GSA for the purpose of simplifying the formulae and presenting the information in a clear manner, it is important to note that predictive models that generate a "Z-shaped" profile are employed in the estimation scripts.

On the Size of the Enumeration Window. In the previous description we only considered the space $\mathcal{P}$, orthogonal to span $(b_1, \dots, b_{2d-\beta-1})$. It is natural to want to extend its dimension, and choose the optimal one. It appears that for the specific parameters of our work, this optimization would only result in a difference of less than a single bit of security. Besides, on the one hand, by using the exact block size beta we can extract the vectors we need to sieve for free from the preliminary run of DBKZ, avoiding the need for an additional sieving pass. On the other hand, using a larger dimension for the additional sieving pass adds a non-negligible cost. Note that this is a consequence of the Core-SVP methodology, which we discuss in more details in Sect. 4.3 which ignores the polynomial overhead cost of (D)BKZ.

4.2.2 Towards a Subfield Attack

Given the knowledge of the relative norm $M = ff^* + gg^*$, the structure of NTRU keys allows an attacker to determine both ff^* and gg^*. Note that (ff^*, gg^*) is in the NTRU lattice of hh^* over the totally real subfield $\mathcal{K}^+$, meaning that $ff^* \cdot hh^* \equiv gg^*$ (mod q). Thus, we deduce that $gg^* = \frac{Mhh^*}{1+hh^*}$ mod q and $fg^* = \frac{Mh^*}{1+hh^*}$ mod q over $\mathscr{R}$—a step we refer to as "algebra". As observed in [19], since f and g are chosen to be co-prime, the attacker can recover a $\mathbb{Z}$-basis of the principal ideal (g) in addition to gg^* through a greatest common divisor computation between the ideals (fg^*) and (gg^*). The attacker can finally retrieve g modulo units through the application of either the Gentry-Szydlo algorithm for power-of-two cyclotomic number fields or its extension for arbitrary cyclotomics, as demonstrated in the attack of Espitau et al. in [13].

Now if the attacker does not know the value of M exactly, but has a fairly good approximation of it, the preliminary "algebra" can be replaced by lattice reduction. Indeed, write $ff^* + gg^* = qN + E$ for a known[7] N and a small E, so that (ff^*, gg^*, E) is a rather short solution of the linear system

$$\begin{cases} HX - Y = 0 \bmod q, \\ X + Y - E = qN, \end{cases} \tag{10}$$

where $H = hh^*$. More precisely, this value would not correspond to an element of the ring R, but solving such a system amounts to finding a short vector inside the coset $(0, 0, qN) + \mathscr{L}$ (considered inside the extended NTRU lattice in $(\mathscr{K}^+)^3$ corresponding to $\{(u, v, w) | uH = v \pmod{q}\}$). A (row) basis of the lattice $\mathscr{L}$ corresponding to (10) is given by:

$$L = \begin{pmatrix} 1 & H & H+1 \\ 0 & q & q \end{pmatrix}.$$

and the most efficient known algorithms to solve this problem are essentially variations of lattice reduction and decoding (see for instance [16]), and amount in estimating the hardness of retrieving a vector of a given norm inside $\mathscr{L}$. We now give the details to find lower bound on the parameters of the key generation algorithm to make such attacks infeasible.

Distribution of the Relative Norm Vector. We now want to estimate the expected length of (ff^*, gg^*, E). By Corollary 1, we know already $\mathbb{E}[\|ff^*, gg^*\|^2]$. To determine the remaining term $\mathbb{E}[\|E\|^2]$, we must select a convenient value for qN. For this, fix an embedding φ_θ, and let $(F, G) = (\varphi_\theta(ff^*), \varphi_\theta(gg^*))$ and $(\tilde{F}, \tilde{G}) = (|\varphi_\theta(\tilde{f})|^2, |\varphi_\theta(\tilde{g})|^2)$ as in Proposition 1, so that $\mathbb{E}[F + G] = \frac{d}{6} + \frac{R^2 + r^2}{2}$. Since each embedding of $ff^* + gg^*$ averages around this (public!) value, we conveniently choose it for qN. From $ff^* + gg^* - qN = E$ and the definition of the variance, we obtain $\mathbb{E}[\|E\|^2] = \mathrm{Var}[F + G]$. It follows that (see the full version of this paper for details [17]):

---

[7] A typical "known" N would be the radius of a well-chosen circle inside the annulus. This value would not correspond to a ring element in general, but one can reduce to this case in a similar way as SIS and ISIS relate.

$$\mathbb{E}[\|E\|^2] = \text{Var}\left[\frac{d}{6} + \tilde{F} + \tilde{G}\right] + \mathbb{E}\left[\frac{d}{12}\left(\frac{d}{6} + 2\tilde{F} + 2\tilde{G}\right)\right]$$

$$= \frac{(R^2 - r^2)^2}{12} + \frac{d}{12}(R^2 + r^2) + \frac{d^2}{72}.$$

For convenience in the next paragraphs, we write $\mathbb{E}[\|ff^*, gg^*\|^2] = 2q^2 x$ and $\mathbb{E}[\|E\|^2] = q^2 y$, then:

$$x \cdot q^2 = \frac{5}{16}(R^4 + r^4) + \frac{1}{2}(R \cdot r)^2 + \frac{d}{12}(R^2 + r^2) + \frac{d^2}{72},$$

$$y \cdot q^2 = \frac{1}{12}\left(R^2 - r^2\right)^2 + \frac{d}{12}(R^2 + r^2) + \frac{d^2}{72}.$$

Mounting the Lattice Attack. In order to find a short solution for the system in Equation (10), it is known that $\|ff^*\|^2$ and $\|gg^*\|^2$ approximate to xq^2 and $\|E\|^2$ concentrates to yq^2. This results in the vector (ff^*, gg^*, E) being unbalanced with the first two coefficients being significantly larger than the third one. To address this issue, we can utilize a technique similar to the rescaling approach proposed in [4,18].

It has been observed that in the estimation procedure outlined in Sect. 4.2.1, the ratio of the length of the secret vector to the normalized volume of the lattice is the only relevant quantity. As such, we can run the same attack under any quadratic twist of the norm of the lattice, by replacing the ℓ_2 norm with any quadratic form of determinant 1, and selecting the one that minimizes the desired ratio. By following the proof technique in [18], we can restrict ourselves to quadratic forms corresponding to diagonal matrices.

Therefore, to view the corresponding lattice problem in a more suitable manner, we want to analyze it under the twisted (Euclidean) norm encoded by the Gram matrix (clearly of determinant 1) $G_\eta = \text{diag}(\eta, \eta, 1/\eta^2)$ with for $\eta = \left(\frac{y}{x}\right)^{\frac{1}{3}}$. Then under this new norm $\|\cdot\|_\eta$, we find that:

$$\mathbb{E}\left[\|(ff^*, gg^*, E)\|_\eta^2\right] = \eta\mathbb{E}\left[\|ff^*\|^2\right] + \eta\mathbb{E}\left[\|gg^*\|^2\right] + \frac{\mathbb{E}\left[\|E\|^2\right]}{\eta^2} = 3q^2\left(x^2 y\right)^{\frac{1}{3}}.$$

Under this norm the lattice $\mathscr{L}$ has $\mathscr{K}^+$-volume:

$$\det(LG_\eta L^T) = \left|\left|\begin{bmatrix} \eta H^2 + \eta + \frac{(H+1)^2}{\eta^2} & \eta Hq + \frac{(H+1)q}{\eta^2} \\ \eta Hq + \frac{(H+1)q}{\eta^2} & \eta q^2 + \frac{q^2}{\eta^2} \end{bmatrix}\right|\right| = q^2\left(\eta^2 + \frac{2}{\eta}\right),$$

giving a lattice of normalized volume being $\sqrt{q}(\eta^2 + \frac{2}{\eta})^{\frac{1}{4}}$ as of $\mathscr{K}^+$-rank 2. The attack is then similar as the one in Sect. 4.2.1 but where we want to recover a vector of squared norm $3q^2(x^2 y)^{\frac{1}{3}}$ in a $\mathbb{Z}$-lattice[8] of normalized (squared) volume $2q(\eta^2 + \frac{1}{\eta})^{\frac{1}{2}}$ of rank $2\frac{d}{2} = d$, yielding a condition of the form:

---

[8] The factor 2 accounting here for the normalized discriminant of the totally real subfield.

$$\frac{\beta}{d} 3q^2 \left(x^2 y\right)^{\frac{1}{3}} \leqslant 2q \left(\eta^2 + \frac{2}{\eta}\right)^{\frac{1}{2}} \delta_\beta^{2(2\beta-d+1)} \tag{11}$$

simplifying into:

$$q \leqslant \frac{2d}{3\beta} \sqrt{\frac{y+2x}{x^2 y}} \delta_\beta^{2(2\beta-d+1)}.$$

4.2.3 Further Optimizations

Beyond the projection trick and the rescaling, we can apply a final standard optimization to this lattice reduction part as there is an unbalance between the size of the secret vector we want to recover and the normalized volume of the lattice. Instead of working with the full lattice coming from the descent of $\mathscr{L}$ over $\mathbb{Z}$, we can instead consider the lattice spanned by a subset of the vectors of the public basis and perform the decoding within this sublattice. The only interesting subset seems to consists in forgetting the $k \leqslant \frac{d}{2}$ first vectors (dropping the so-called q-vectors would not be beneficial as it would actually sparsify the lattice, making the attack worst). Doing so, the rank is of course reduced by k, at the cost of working with a lattice with covolume proportionally $q^{\frac{k}{2(d-k)}}$ bigger. The condition of (11) updates into[9]:

$$\frac{\beta(d-k)}{(d-k)d} 3q^2 \left(x^2 y\right)^{\frac{1}{3}} \leqslant 2q^{\frac{n}{2n-2k}} \left(\eta^2 + \frac{2}{\eta}\right)^{\frac{1}{2}} \delta_\beta^{2(2\beta-d+k+1)},$$

for all $k \in \{0, \ldots, \frac{d}{2}\}$, which in turn simplifies to:

$$q \leqslant \min_{0 \leqslant k \leqslant \frac{n}{2}} \left(\frac{2d}{3\beta} \sqrt{\frac{y+2x}{x^2 y}} \delta_\beta^{2(2\beta-d+1)}\right)^{\frac{2n-2k}{n-2k}}. \tag{12}$$

The right-hand-side term increases as y becomes smaller making the attack easier and easier, recovering the intuition presented that knowing exactly the value of $ff^* + gg^*$) leads to a complete key recovery in polynomial time. However, because of the rounding to the ring of integer this term cannot be 0: it converges to a term which is greater than $\frac{d^2}{72} + \frac{dq}{6}$. Thus, the condition is *never* satisfied for cryptographically relevant parameters.

Remark 4 (On other subfield type attacks and related). We can also approach the problem as solving a *noisy-ring SIS* instance (namely $(1 + H)F = N + E$ (mod q)) or as solving a NTRU instance with a hint, in the spirit of [8]). In both cases, we are *in fine* decoding a lattice point at distance $\|E\|$ inside a lattice of normalized volume comparable to q. Up to some minor unessential constants, all three approaches give comparable results.

It is tempting to go further and try projection to other subfields, but the ratio secret size to normalized volume is increasing, worsening the attack. It indicates that we shall only focus on the plain NTRU and on the totally real subfield.

---

[9] This assumes the coefficients of s are balanced, which is a reasonable assumption after the rescaling by η.

Conclusion of Our Security Analysis. We presented two attacks on the distribution of the keys: the classical attack by reducing directly to an SVP instance form the (public) NTRU lattice and a more involved one which involves descending the problem to the totally real subfield and making use of the fact that the relative norm is somewhat close to a known integer. After careful optimization, it appears that this latter attack is *never* relevant in practice. Thus, the parameter selection only deals with the former attack, using the standard methodology, as we explain below.

4.3   Practical Security Assessment

This analysis translates into concrete bit-security estimates following the methodology of NEWHOPE [2] (so-called "core-SVP methodology"). In this model [5], the bit complexity of lattice sieving (which is asymptotically the best SVP oracle) is taken as $\lfloor 0.292\beta \rfloor$ in the classical setting and $\lfloor 0.259\beta \rfloor$ in the quantum setting in dimension β. Using the analysis presented, we can tailor the radius α of the final annulus to match the desired security level (NIST-I and NIST-V). The size of the signature is then derived similarly as in [18].

4.4   Extension to More General Cyclotomic Rings

As discussed at the beginning of this section, the analysis so far has concentrated on base fields $\mathcal{K}$ that are cyclotomic with power-of-two conductor for the sake of simplicity, but it extends with relatively few changes to a more general setting. Specifically, in the full version of this paper [17], we show that both the success probability estimates and the security analysis carry over to cyclotomic conductors of the form $m = 2^\ell p^k$ for some odd prime p. This setting encompasses in particular the case of 3-smooth conductors $m = 2^\ell 3^k$ for which parameters are proposed in the MITAKA paper [15] (and for which we also propose parameters below), and provides plenty of leeway to reach essentially any desired security level.[10]

While the analysis in this more general setting closely mimics the one presented so far, we briefly highlight the ways in which it does differ. The key change is that, for these conductors, the covariance matrix in Heuristic 1 is no longer scalar, making the estimation of the meaningful quantities more subtle. We give a high-level description of the situation here, referring to the full version of this paper [17] for details.

First, for the success probability of Algorithm 5, the conditional distribution of the embeddings of (f, g) becomes the sum of two non-central χ^2 distributions with different scaling parameters, each corresponding to the eigenvalues $\lambda_+^\theta, \lambda_-^\theta$

---

[10] One could in principle generalize the analysis even further (e.g., to arbitrary cyclotomic conductors), but this would introduce additional technicalities (such as the need to replace the power basis by the so-called powerful basis in order to obtain a well-behaved matrix for the canonical embedding), and would really be of theoretical interest at best.

of Σ_θ. This complicates the analysis somewhat, but counterparts to the results of Sect. 4.1 can still be obtained, either through numerical computations or by upper and lower bounding Σ_θ by scalar matrices independent of θ.

Second, regarding the security analysis with respect to key recovery attacks, the length of the secret keys is also impacted by the additional error term $T(\theta)$ in Proposition 1. Qualitatively speaking, the behavior in the case $m = 2^\ell p^k$ is however quite close to the power-of-two case, since for most embeddings, $|S(\theta)| = \left|\frac{\sin(d\theta)}{\sin\theta}\right|$ is small compared to d: only a handful of embeddings have a phase θ close to a multiple of π. We use the worst of these embeddings to bound from above the magnitude of $T(\theta)$, and find that even this pessimistic estimate only has negligible impact on the security level. Lastly, while we could rely on the identity $d\|x\|^2 = \|\varphi(x)\|^2$ in the power-of-two case, this is not true anymore for general conductors; we rely on upper bounds instead. Nevertheless, the geometry of the power basis for 3-smooth conductors remains quite good, acting at worst as an additional $\sqrt{2}$ factor.

5   ANTRAG in Practice

5.1   Optimization and Parameter Selection

In [18] new techniques to compress lattice-based hash-then-sign schemes were presented. Theoretically, they can all be applied to ANTRAG's signatures as well. One of these technique is a fine-tuned encoding approach for discrete Gaussian vectors, and is oblivious to the actual structure of the secret keys—we thus consider it done by default when estimating the bit size of signatures. The two other techniques are choosing a smaller modulus q than the popular choice $q = 12289$ on the one hand, and elliptical sampling on the other hand. They have more impact on the key generation step, and although they were shown somewhat equivalent when applied to scheme such as FALCON or MITAKA, the situation is different for ANTRAG.

We first discuss smaller moduli. From our analysis in Sect. 3 and Sect. 4, the annulus where candidate pairs are sampled becomes relatively smaller as q decreases, which noticeably impacts the success probability of Algorithm 5. To keep a small rejection rate in practice, we are led to decrease the quality of the key pairs, or in other words, to use a larger parameter α. Fortunately, it was pointed out in [18] that there is a range for such smaller q where, at fixed dimension, the key recovery becomes harder. This actually means that reducing q and increasing α does not necessarily translate to a substantially lower security level. We note however that q cannot be chosen arbitrarily small, as attacks exist for very small q.

The situation for elliptical sampling is less attractive for the following reason. Candidates should now be sampled in well-chosen elliptic annuli rather than circular ones. We can easily sample continuously uniformly in such annuli, but when carrying out the decoding back to the ring (e.g., by coefficient-wise rounding), we still incur an error term on embeddings that behaves like an isotropic normal distribution of standard deviation $\Omega(\sqrt{q})$. After the addition of the error term, embeddings sampled more towards the direction of the major axis of the ellipse are more likely than in a spherical case to end up in the target elliptical annulus, but embeddings sampled in the direction of the minor axis have much lower probability of success, and this has a much greater effect on overall success probability, constraining the choice of the quality parameter α. In the end, we find that rather than using elliptical sampling in our setting with a certain skewing factor γ, it is essentially just as effective to reduce the modulus q by the same factor γ instead (which additionally has the advantage of reducing public key size). As a result, we omit the detailed analysis of this less attractive approach.

We present our parameter selection in Table 2 for power-of-two cyclotomics, and Table 3 for the 3-smooth case. For all parameter sets, we set the quality α with two decimal places in such a way as to reach a repetition rate M of around 3 to 4. For the moduli, we give both the choices of q found in the literature as well as smaller candidates that also have close to optimal splitting in the ambient ring, should one wish to rely on NTT multiplication to slightly speed up verification.

Table 2. Practical parameter selection, power-of-two case

	$q = 12289$		$q = 3329$	
d	512	1024	512	1024
Quality α	1.15	1.23	1.23	1.48
Repetition rate M	3	4	4	4
Bit security (C/Q)	124/113	264/240	121/110	265/240
Verification key size (bytes)	896	1792	768	1536
Signature size (bytes)	646	1260	591	1176

Table 3. Practical parameter selection for ANTRAG, 3-smooth conductor case.

(a) Modulus $q = 12289$

d	648	768	864	972
Quality α	1.17	1.19	1.21	1.22
Repetition rate M	4	3	3	4
Bit security (C/Q)	166/151	196/178	222/201	251/227
Verification key size (bytes)	1134	1344	1512	1701
Signature size (bytes)	808	952	1069	1200

(b) Various moduli. For $d = 768, 864, 972$, the right column shows moduli of [15].

	$d = 648$		$d = 768$		$d = 864$		$d = 972$	
Modulus q	3889	9721	3329	18433	3727	10369	4373	17497
Quality α	1.32	1.19	1.39	1.16	1.40	1.23	1.40	1.18
Expected repetitions	4	4	4	3	4	3	4	4
Bit security (C/Q)	159/144	164/149	192/174	195/177	220/200	222/201	254/230	250/227
Verification key size (bytes)	972	1134	1152	1440	1296	1512	1580	1823
Signature size (bytes)	747	796	883	977	1000	1058	1133	1225

5.2 Implementation Results

We have implemented our trapdoor generation algorithm ANTRAG as well as the resulting complete signature scheme in portable C based on the source codes of FALCON and MITAKA. The code is publicly available on GitHub [36].

Since the signature scheme arising from ANTRAG is essentially identical to MITAKA for signing and verification, we largely reuse the code of MITAKA for those parts. Key generation consists of the original algorithm presented in this paper to generate the first basis vector (f, g), along with code to solve the NTRU equation in order to deduce (F, G), for which we basically reuse the code of FALCON, which follows the techniques presented in [31]. The Fast Fourier transform and the resulting code for ring arithmetic are similarly borrowed from FALCON.

We note that, since the C code of MITAKA itself did not include a key generation algorithm (only precomputed fixed keys obtained using separate Python scripts), our implementation constitutes, to the best of our knowledge, the first full C implementation of a hybrid sampler-based signature.

In view of the simplicity of our trapdoor generation, the code is fairly straightforward. In particular, since the floating point uniform distributions we generate for the absolute values of the embeddings are bounded away from zero, there is no subtlety related to precision loss for values close to zero (this is unlike the Box–Muller algorithm used in signing, for which we reuse MITAKA's code that behaves properly in that respect). The only trick worth mentioning is a check in the generation of (f, g) which rejects early the pairs such that the cyclotomic integer prime above 2 divides both f and g (this is a necessary condition for the later computation of F and G to succeed, so it saves some time to test it early).

As explained above, dimension 512 and 1024 are supported, and our `GoodPair` algorithm naturally extends to other conductors such as the 3-smooth

Table 4. Performance comparison with FALCON and MITAKA.

	FALCON [34]		MITAKA [15]		This paper	
d	512	1024	512	1024	512	1024
Quality α	1.17	1.17	2.04	2.33	1.15	1.23
Classical sec.	123	284	102	233	124	264
Key size (bytes)	896	1792	896	1792	896	1792
Sig. size (bytes)	666	1280	713	1405	646	1260
keygen speed (Mcycles)	—	—	—	—	9.5	33.2
keygen speed (ms)	4.2	12.4	1657*	6214*	3.5	12.3
sign speed (kcycles)	—	—	299	584	298	586
sign speed (μs)	184	371	111	217	111	218
verif speed (kcycles)	—	—	20	41	20	40
verif speed (μs)	18	36	8	16	8	15

* Timings for the optimized SageMath implementation (excluding NTRUSolve), since no C implementation exists.

cyclotomics considered in MITAKA to reach intermediate dimensions, as well as the signing and verification procedure. However, suitably optimized FFT code is needed for those intermediate rings, and more importantly, the NTRUSolve code of [31] needs to be adapted as well, in the spirit of, e.g., [27]. Neither of those steps are difficult in principle, but they represent a significant engineering effort left as future work.

A performance comparison with FALCON and MITAKA is provided in Table 4, using the same modulus $q = 12289$ for consistency. Compilation is carried out with gcc 13.2.1 with -O3 -march=native optimizations enabled. Timings are collected on a single core of an AMD Ryzen 7 PRO 6860Z @ 2.7 GHz laptop with hyperthreading and frequency scaling disabled. Cycle counts are not provided for FALCON, since the FALCON benchmarking tool only measures clock time.

As noted previously, the MITAKA C implementation does not include a key generation procedure. For reference, we provide the timings for the numpy-based SageMath implementation of the MITAKA key generation procedure instead, *not* including the cost of NTRUSolve, so that only the highly optimized GoodPair code is accounted for. As expected from the fact that MITAKA needs to explore a search space of millions of key candidates, the timings are orders of magnitude worse than FALCON and ANTRAG.

The running time of our key generation is close to that of FALCON. Signing speeds are basically identical to MITAKA since we mostly reuse that code (up to very minor optimizations). Verification is consistent across all three schemes.

Acknowledgments. We are indebted to Léo Ducas for the idea of the attack considered in Sect. 4.2.2, and for invaluable comments and discussions. We thank anonymous reviewers for numerous comments and suggestions for improvement.

Chao Sun was supported by the project "Research and development on new generation cryptography for secure wireless communication services" among "Research and Development for Expansion of Radio Wave Resources (JPJ000254)", which was supported by the Ministry of Internal Affairs and Communications, Japan. Thi Thu Quyen Nguyen and Alexandre Wallet were supported by the PEPR quantique France 2030 programme (ANR-22-PETQ-0008) and by the ANR ASTRID project AMIRAL (ANR-21-ASTR-0016).

References

1. Albrecht, M., Bai, S., Ducas, L.: A subfield lattice attack on overstretched NTRU assumptions. In: Robshaw, M., Katz, J. (eds.) CRYPTO 2016. LNCS, vol. 9814, pp. 153–178. Springer, Heidelberg (2016). https://doi.org/10.1007/978-3-662-53018-4_6

2. Alkim, E., Ducas, L., Pöppelmann, T., Schwabe, P.: Post-quantum key exchange - a new hope. In: Holz, T., Savage, S. (eds.) USENIX Security 2016, pp. 327–343. USENIX Association, August 2016

3. Annamalai, A., Tellambura, C.: Cauchy-Schwarz bound on the generalized Marcum-Q function with applications. Wirel. Commun. Mob. Comput. 1(2), 243–253 (2001)

4. Bai, S., Galbraith, S.D.: Lattice decoding attacks on binary LWE. In: Susilo, W., Mu, Y. (eds.) ACISP 2014. LNCS, vol. 8544, pp. 322–337. Springer, Cham (2014). https://doi.org/10.1007/978-3-319-08344-5_21

5. Becker, A., Ducas, L., Gama, N., Laarhoven, T.: New directions in nearest neighbor searching with applications to lattice sieving. In: Krauthgamer, R. (ed.) 27th SODA, pp. 10–24. ACM-SIAM, January 2016

6. Cheon, J.H., Jeong, J., Lee, C.: An algorithm for NTRU problems and cryptanalysis of the GGH multilinear map without a low-level encoding of zero. LMS J. Comput. Math. **19**, 255–266 (2016)

7. Chuengsatiansup, C., Prest, T., Stehlé, D., Wallet, A., Xagawa, K.: ModFalcon: compact signatures based on module-NTRU lattices. In: Sun, H.M., Shieh, S.P., Gu, G., Ateniese, G. (eds.) ASIACCS 20, pp. 853–866. ACM Press, October 2020

8. Dachman-Soled, D., Ducas, L., Gong, H., Rossi, M.: LWE with side information: attacks and concrete security estimation. In: Micciancio, D., Ristenpart, T. (eds.) CRYPTO 2020. LNCS, vol. 12171, pp. 329–358. Springer, Cham (2020). https://doi.org/10.1007/978-3-030-56880-1_12

9. Ducas, L., Lyubashevsky, V., Prest, T.: Efficient identity-based encryption over NTRU lattices. In: Sarkar, P., Iwata, T. (eds.) ASIACRYPT 2014. LNCS, vol. 8874, pp. 22–41. Springer, Heidelberg (2014). https://doi.org/10.1007/978-3-662-45608-8_2

10. Ducas, L., Nguyen, P.Q.: Learning a zonotope and more: cryptanalysis of NTRUSign countermeasures. In: Wang, X., Sako, K. (eds.) ASIACRYPT 2012. LNCS, vol. 7658, pp. 433–450. Springer, Heidelberg (2012). https://doi.org/10.1007/978-3-642-34961-4_27

11. Ducas, L., Prest, T.: A hybrid Gaussian sampler for lattices over rings. Cryptology ePrint Archive, Report 2015/660 (2015). https://eprint.iacr.org/2015/660

12. Ducas, L., Prest, T.: Fast Fourier orthogonalization. In: Abramov, S.A., Zima, E.V., Gao, X. (eds.) ISSAC 2016, pp. 191–198. ACM (2016)

13. Espitau, T., Fouque, P.A., Gérard, B., Tibouchi, M.: Side-channel attacks on BLISS lattice-based signatures: exploiting branch tracing against strongSwan and electromagnetic emanations in microcontrollers. In: Thuraisingham, B.M., Evans, D., Malkin, T., Xu, D. (eds.) ACM CCS 2017, pp. 1857–1874. ACM Press, October/November 2017

14. Espitau, T., et al.: MITAKA: a simpler, parallelizable, maskable variant of falcon. Cryptology ePrint Archive, Report 2021/1486 (2021). https://eprint.iacr.org/2021/1486

15. Espitau, T., et al.: MITAKA: a simpler, parallelizable, maskable variant of falcon. In: Dunkelman, O., Dziembowski, S. (eds.) EUROCRYPT 2022, Part III. LNCS, vol. 13277, pp. 222–253. Springer, Heidelberg (2022). https://doi.org/10.1007/978-3-031-07082-2_9

16. Espitau, T., Kirchner, P.: The nearest-colattice algorithm. Cryptology ePrint Archive, Report 2020/694 (2020). https://eprint.iacr.org/2020/694

17. Espitau, T., Nguyen, T.T.Q., Sun, C., Tibouchi, M., Wallet, A.: Antrag: annular NTRU trapdoor generation. Cryptology ePrint Archive, Paper 2023/1335 (2023). https://eprint.iacr.org/2023/1335

18. Espitau, T., Tibouchi, M., Wallet, A., Yu, Y.: Shorter hash-and-sign lattice-based signatures. In: Dodis, Y., Shrimpton, T. (eds.) CRYPTO 2022, Part II. LNCS, vol. 13508, pp. 245–275. Springer, Heidelberg (2022). https://doi.org/10.1007/978-3-031-15979-4_9

19. Fouque, P.-A., Kirchner, P., Tibouchi, M., Wallet, A., Yu, Y.: Key recovery from gram–Schmidt norm leakage in hash-and-sign signatures over NTRU lattices. In: Canteaut, A., Ishai, Y. (eds.) EUROCRYPT 2020. LNCS, vol. 12107, pp. 34–63. Springer, Cham (2020). https://doi.org/10.1007/978-3-030-45727-3_2

20. Gentry, C., Peikert, C., Vaikuntanathan, V.: Trapdoors for hard lattices and new cryptographic constructions. In: Ladner, R.E., Dwork, C. (eds.) 40th ACM STOC, pp. 197–206. ACM Press, May 2008

21. Gentry, C., Szydlo, M.: Cryptanalysis of the revised NTRU signature scheme. In: Knudsen, L.R. (ed.) EUROCRYPT 2002. LNCS, vol. 2332, pp. 299–320. Springer, Heidelberg (2002). https://doi.org/10.1007/3-540-46035-7_20

22. Goldreich, O., Goldwasser, S., Halevi, S.: Public-key cryptosystems from lattice reduction problems. In: Kaliski, B.S. (ed.) CRYPTO 1997. LNCS, vol. 1294, pp. 112–131. Springer, Heidelberg (1997). https://doi.org/10.1007/BFb0052231

23. Hoffstein, J., Howgrave-Graham, N., Pipher, J., Silverman, J.H., Whyte, W.: NTRUSign: digital signatures using the NTRU lattice. In: Joye, M. (ed.) CT-RSA 2003. LNCS, vol. 2612, pp. 122–140. Springer, Heidelberg (2003). https://doi.org/10.1007/3-540-36563-X_9

24. Lyubashevsky, V.: Fiat-Shamir with aborts: applications to lattice and factoring-based signatures. In: Matsui, M. (ed.) ASIACRYPT 2009. LNCS, vol. 5912, pp. 598–616. Springer, Heidelberg (2009). https://doi.org/10.1007/978-3-642-10366-7_35

25. Lyubashevsky, V.: Lattice signatures without trapdoors. In: Pointcheval, D., Johansson, T. (eds.) EUROCRYPT 2012. LNCS, vol. 7237, pp. 738–755. Springer, Heidelberg (2012). https://doi.org/10.1007/978-3-642-29011-4_43

26. Lyubashevsky, V., et al.: CRYSTALS-DILITHIUM. Technical report, National Institute of Standards and Technology (2022). https://csrc.nist.gov/Projects/post-quantum-cryptography/selected-algorithms-2022

27. Lyubashevsky, V., Seiler, G.: NTTRU: truly fast NTRU using NTT. IACR TCHES **2019**(3), 180–201 (2019). https://tches.iacr.org/index.php/TCHES/article/view/8293

28. Micciancio, D., Walter, M.: Practical, predictable lattice basis reduction. In: Fischlin, M., Coron, J.-S. (eds.) EUROCRYPT 2016. LNCS, vol. 9665, pp. 820–849. Springer, Heidelberg (2016). https://doi.org/10.1007/978-3-662-49890-3_31

29. Nguyen, P.Q., Regev, O.: Learning a parallelepiped: cryptanalysis of GGH and NTRU signatures. In: Vaudenay, S. (ed.) EUROCRYPT 2006. LNCS, vol. 4004, pp. 271–288. Springer, Heidelberg (2006). https://doi.org/10.1007/11761679_17

30. Peikert, C.: An efficient and parallel Gaussian sampler for lattices. In: Rabin, T. (ed.) CRYPTO 2010. LNCS, vol. 6223, pp. 80–97. Springer, Heidelberg (2010). https://doi.org/10.1007/978-3-642-14623-7_5

31. Pornin, T., Prest, T.: More efficient algorithms for the NTRU key generation using the field norm. In: Lin, D., Sako, K. (eds.) PKC 2019. LNCS, vol. 11443, pp. 504–533. Springer, Cham (2019). https://doi.org/10.1007/978-3-030-17259-6_17

32. Prest, T.: Gaussian sampling in lattice-based cryptography. Ph.D. thesis, École Normale Supérieure, Paris, France (2015)

33. Prest, T., et al.: FALCON. Technical report, National Institute of Standards and Technology (2017). https://csrc.nist.gov/projects/post-quantum-cryptography/post-quantum-cryptography-standardization/round-1-submissions

34. Prest, T., et al.: FALCON. Technical report, National Institute of Standards and Technology (2022). https://csrc.nist.gov/Projects/post-quantum-cryptography/selected-algorithms-2022

35. Simon, M., Alouini, M.S.: Exponential-type bounds on the generalized Marcum Q-function with application to error probability analysis over fading channels. IEEE Trans. Commun. **48**(3), 359–366 (2000)
36. Tibouchi, M.: Companion implementation of this paper. GitHub repository `mti/antrag` (2023). https://github.com/mti/antrag

G+G: A Fiat-Shamir Lattice Signature Based on Convolved Gaussians

Julien Devevey[1(✉)], Alain Passelègue[1,2,3], and Damien Stehlé[1,3]

[1] ENS de Lyon, Lyon, France
julien.devevey@ens-lyon.fr
[2] INRIA, Paris, France
[3] CryptoLab Inc., Lyon, France
{alain.passelegue,damien.stehle}@cryptolab.co.kr

Abstract. We describe an adaptation of Schnorr's signature to the lattice setting, which relies on Gaussian convolution rather than flooding or rejection sampling as previous approaches. It does not involve any abort, can be proved secure in the ROM and QROM using existing analyses of the Fiat-Shamir transform, and enjoys smaller signature sizes (both asymptotically and for concrete security levels).

1 Introduction

Schnorr's identification protocol [Sch91] allows secure authentication between a prover and a verifier based on the hardness on the discrete logarithm problem in a cyclic group of order p, generated by an element g. The prover's public verification key is simply a group element g^s, whose discrete logarithm s forms the prover's signing key. The identification protocol proceeds as follows: the prover first commits to some uniform $y \hookleftarrow U(\mathbb{Z}_p)$ by sending g^y to a verifier. The latter returns some challenge $c \in \mathbb{Z}_p$, to which the prover replies with a response z, namely $z = y + cs \bmod p$. Here, no information about s is revealed as z is still uniform modulo p. However, a verifier is convinced that the prover knows s as it can verify $g^z = g^y(g^s)^c$. This can be compiled into a signature scheme by using the Fiat-Shamir heuristic [FS86].

Adapting this protocol to the lattice setting has proved challenging. At a high-level, the approach adopted in [Lyu09,Lyu12] and subsequent works proceeds as follows. The discrete logarithms s is replaced with a short, tall matrix $\mathbf{S}$ in $\mathbb{Z}^{k \times m}$, whereas y and z are replaced with elements $\mathbf{y}$ and $\mathbf{z}$ of $\mathbb{Z}^k$ and the generator g is replaced with a uniform matrix $\mathbf{A} \in \mathbb{Z}_q^{m \times k}$. The challenge vector $\mathbf{c}$ belongs to a finite subset of $\mathbb{Z}^m$, typically designed to have the shortest possible vectors under the constraint that the challenge has sufficiently high min-entropy to prevent guessing. For security, one needs $\mathbf{z}$ and hence $\mathbf{y}$ to be short. Leaving things as they are described so far would make signatures leak the secret matrix $\mathbf{S}$, as $\mathbf{z}$ is centered around $\mathbb{E}[\mathbf{y}] + \mathbf{S}\mathbf{c}$ (see [ASY22] for a detailed key recovery). A solution could be to take a large enough standard deviation to "flood" this center (this is considered for example in [DPSZ12, Appendix A.1] in

J. Guo and R. Steinfeld (Eds.): ASIACRYPT 2023, LNCS 14444, pp. 37–64, 2023.
https://doi.org/10.1007/978-981-99-8739-9_2

the context of zero-knowledge proofs), but this results in very large signatures as the modulus then needs to grow exponentially with the security parameter λ (see the discussion in [ASY22]). The most efficient approach so far, introduced by Lyubashevsky [Lyu09,Lyu12] and notably leading to Dilithium [DKL+18], relies on rejection sampling to erase the center from $\mathbf{z}$. This comes at the cost of restarting the protocol multiple times before finally outputting an appropriately distributed response $\mathbf{z}$. This strategy still allows the identification protocol to be compiled into a signature, using a variant of the Fiat-Shamir heuristic called Fiat-Shamir with Aborts. To obtain shorter signatures, Ducas *et al.* [DDLL13] suggested to reject a bimodal Gaussian distribution against a Gaussian distribution. This was later argued in [DFPS22] to be essentially optimal among pairs of source and target distributions. Finally, we note that Fiat-Shamir with Aborts turns out to be complex to analyze, and flaws in many analyses have been recently discovered [DFPS23,BBD+23].

Removing rejection sampling while keeping similar signature sizes has been a long-standing open problem. Steps in this direction were made in [BCM21] for instance. The authors noticed that in the setting where $\mathbf{y}$ is sampled uniformly in a hypercube and one uses signature truncation [BG14], one rejection condition out of two is superfluous. They however argue that removing the second one is difficult.

Contribution. We introduce a new paradigm for adapting Schnorr's identification protocol to the lattice setting. It relies on Gaussian convolution, rather than flooding or rejection sampling. Our G + G (Gaussian Plus Gaussian) identification protocol can be compiled into a signature using the Fiat-Shamir heuristic (without aborts), in the Quantum Random Oracle Model (QROM). The resulting signature is asymptotically more compact than those based on rejection sampling and its analysis relies on the well-understood properties of the standard Fiat-Shamir transform. Finally, we provide concrete parameters which show that G + G is competitive with the state-of-the-art optimizations of Lyubashevsky's signature.

Technical Overview. G + G involves two Gaussians that are being summed. The first one is $\mathbf{y}$ and the second one corresponds to $\mathbf{Sc}$. The first difficulty that we face is that $\mathbf{S}$ is fixed and $\mathbf{c}$ is publicly known as part of the resulting signature and hence cannot be assumed random for the sake of studying the distribution of $\mathbf{z}$.

To introduce the required new randomness, we start from BLISS [DDLL13]. The verification key $\mathbf{A} \in \mathbb{Z}_{2q}^{m \times k}$ and the signing key $\mathbf{S} \in \mathbb{Z}^{k \times m}$ satisfy the relation $\mathbf{AS} = q\mathbf{I}_m \bmod 2q$. Among the variants of Lyubashesvky's signature, it is a specificity of BLISS to work modulo $2q$, which is particularly useful in our case. The commitment of the prover is $\mathbf{w} = \mathbf{Ay} \bmod 2q$, and upon receiving $\mathbf{c} \in \{0,1\}^m$, the prover replies with either $\mathbf{z} = \mathbf{y} + \mathbf{Sc}$ or $\mathbf{z} = \mathbf{y} - \mathbf{Sc}$ with probability $1/2$ each. The verifier checks that $\mathbf{z}$ is short and $\mathbf{Az} = \mathbf{w} + q\mathbf{c} \bmod 2q$. This check works for both values of $\mathbf{z}$ that the prover chose from. This can be explained by observing that the verification views $\mathbf{c}$ modulo 2, i.e., as a coset of $\mathbb{Z}^m / 2\mathbb{Z}^m$, and negating it does not change the coset. This observation was used in [Duc14] to take negations of individual coordinates of $\mathbf{c}$ to minimize the Euclidean norm of $\mathbf{Sc}$ and hence decrease the standard deviation of $\mathbf{y}$ necessary to hide $\mathbf{Sc}$ via rejection sampling. We go further and let the prover extend the coset $\mathbf{c}$ sent by the verifier to a Gaussian sample with support $2\mathbb{Z}^m + \mathbf{c}$ and center $\mathbf{0}$. The verification equation above still holds, and we now have our second Gaussian.

At this stage, the prover samples a Gaussian $\mathbf{y}$ over $\mathbb{Z}^k$, receives a uniform coset $\mathbf{c} \in \mathbb{Z}^m/2\mathbb{Z}^m$ from the verifier, produces a Gaussian sample $\mathbf{x}$ with support $2\mathbb{Z}^m + \mathbf{c}$ and computes $\mathbf{z} = \mathbf{y} + \mathbf{Sx}$. Equivalently, it samples $\mathbf{k}$ Gaussian with support $2\mathbf{S}\mathbb{Z}^m$ and center $-\mathbf{Sc}$, which will be used to cancel the center $\mathbf{Sc}$, and returns $\mathbf{z} = \mathbf{y} + \mathbf{k} + \mathbf{Sc}$. In order to obtain the zero-knowledge property (i.e., be able to simulate signatures without knowing the signing key), we aim to prove that the distribution of the Gaussian convolution $\mathbf{z}$ can be sampled from publicly. If $\mathbf{y}$ and $\mathbf{k}$ were continuous Gaussians, we would set their covariance matrices $\mathbf{\Sigma_y}$ and $\mathbf{\Sigma_k}$ such that $\mathbf{\Sigma_y} + \mathbf{\Sigma_k} = \mathbf{\Sigma_z}$ for a known covariance matrix $\mathbf{\Sigma_z}$ for $\mathbf{z}$. To fix the ideas, we could set $\mathbf{\Sigma_z} = \sigma^2\mathbf{I}$ for some $\sigma > 0$, i.e., the distribution of $\mathbf{z}$ is a spherical Gaussian, and set $\mathbf{\Sigma_y} = \sigma^2\mathbf{I} - \mathbf{\Sigma_k}$. If we sample $\mathbf{x}$ from a spherical Gaussian with standard deviation $s > 0$, then $\mathbf{\Sigma_k} = s^2\mathbf{SS}^\top$ and $\mathbf{\Sigma_y} = \sigma^2\mathbf{I} - s^2\mathbf{SS}^\top$ (by taking σ sufficiently large, the latter is indeed definite positive). This is the choice we actually make for $\mathsf{G} + \mathsf{G}$, but there is flexibility.

The above over-simplifies the situation as the Gaussians we manipulate are discrete rather than continuous. Further, their supports do not have the same dimensions. Indeed, the support of $\mathbf{y}$ is $\mathbb{Z}^k$ whereas the support of $\mathbf{k}$ is exactly $2\mathbf{S}\mathbb{Z}^m + \mathbf{Sc}$ whose span has dimension $m < k$: the second Gaussian lives in a smaller dimension and its support is sparser. This is illustrated in Fig. 1.

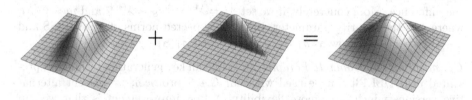

Fig. 1. The sum of two Gaussians with compensating covariance matrices is a spherical Gaussian, even when the second Gaussian is rank-deficient. In the $\mathsf{G} + \mathsf{G}$ identification protocol and signature, the first Gaussian corresponds to $\mathbf{y}$, the second Gaussian is associated to $\mathbf{Sc}$ and the resulting one corresponds to $\mathbf{z}$.

Thanks to the above, if the covariance matrices are set appropriately, then $\mathsf{G} + \mathsf{G}$ is honest-verifier zero-knowledge (HVZK). The proofs of completeness and soundness are adapted from [DDLL13].

Our final goal is to apply the Fiat-Shamir heuristic on this protocol to get a signature scheme. This heuristic replaces the uniform challenge with one derived from a hash function called on input the commitment and the message to be signed. The signature is then the whole transcript. As the commitment of $G + G$ can be recomputed from the challenge and its response, we actually exclude it from the signature for compactness. Then, as long as $G + G$ is complete, the resulting signature is correct. Moreover, the security reduction proceeds in two steps. First, it is shown that the EU-CMA security of the signature can be reduced to the EU-NMA security of the signature, where no signature query can be made. To do so, one shows that signatures queries can be answered with simulated ones (up to reprogramming the random oracle) from the HVZK property, as long as the commitment $\mathbf{Ay}$ has sufficiently high min-entropy. This is technically more complex than for Lyubashevsky's signatures as $\mathbf{y}$ is distributed from a skewed Gaussian. Second, computational soundness (resp. lossy-soundness) implies security against no-message attacks for different parametrizations.

Comparison with BLISS. Among variants of Lyubashevsky's signatures, BLISS provides the smallest $\mathbf{z}$: its expected norm can be as small as $\sigma_1(\mathbf{S})m/\sqrt{\log M}$ (up to a constant factor), where $\sigma_1(\mathbf{S})$ is the largest singular value of $\mathbf{S}$ and M is the expected number of repetitions (see [DFPS22, Appendix C]). Further, an argument is made in [DFPS22] that this is essentially optimal for Lyubashevsky's signatures, even if we allow to optimize over the choice of source and target distributions. In the case of $G + G$, the strongest constraint on parameters is essentially that the standard deviation σ of $\mathbf{z}$ be sufficiently large to "smooth out" the lattice $2S\mathbb{Z}^m$. By using a variant of the HVZK property based on the Rényi divergence rather than the statistical distance, which suffices for the signature application, it suffices that σ be above $\sigma_1(\mathbf{S})\sqrt{\log Q_S}$, up to a constant factor, where Q_S is the maximum number of signature queries that the adversary is allowed to make. As a result, the expected norm of $\mathbf{z}$ in $G + G$ is $\sigma_1(\mathbf{S})\sqrt{m \log Q_S}$. We conclude by observing that $\log Q_S$ is typically much smaller than m, and that the $\sqrt{\log M}$ term from BLISS cannot grow sufficiently to compensate for the difference. More concretely, if we set $M = \lambda^{\Theta(1)}$, $Q_S = \lambda^{\Theta(1)}$ and $m = \Theta(\lambda)$, where λ is the security parameter, then the expected norms of $\mathbf{z}$ in BLISS and $G + G$ respectively grow as $\sigma_1(\mathbf{S}) \cdot \lambda/\sqrt{\log \lambda}$ and $\sigma_1(\mathbf{S}) \cdot \sqrt{\lambda \log \lambda}$.

Optimization and Concrete Parameters. While all key generation techniques presented in [DDLL13] can be used with our $G + G$ protocol, we present alternative versions which offer more flexibility. A first improvement is that we can set $\mathbf{AS} = q\mathbf{J} \bmod 2q$, where $\mathbf{J} \in \mathbb{Z}_q^{m \times \ell}$ is only rectangular and full column-rank rather than set to the identity. When instantiating $G + G$ with the MLWE and MSIS hardness assumptions [BGV12,LS15] over a ring $\mathcal{R} = \mathbb{Z}[x]/(x^n + 1)$ with n a power of 2, we take $\mathbf{j} = (x^{n/2} + 1, 0, \ldots, 0)$. This allows us to replace the lattice $2s\mathcal{R}$ with $(x^{n/2} - 1)s\mathcal{R}$, and to decrease the standard deviation of $\mathbf{z}$ by a factor $\sqrt{2}$. Overall, we obtain signature sizes that are between 20% and 30% smaller than those in [DFPS22], or 35% to 45% smaller than Dilithium [DKL+18].

Related Work. As pointed out in [CLMQ21], GPV signatures [GPV08] can be seen as a special case of the lattice-based Fiat-Shamir signatures by considering a specific instance of the hash function and adapting parameters. This analysis can be extended to $G + G$, and we then recover the hash-and sign scheme described in [YJW23]. More details are provided in Appendix B.

2 Preliminaries

For any integers $k \geq m$, we let $\mathbf{I}_k$ denote the $k \times k$ identity matrix as well as $\mathbf{J}_{k,m} = (\mathbf{I}_m | \mathbf{0}^{m \times (k-m)})^\top$ denote the $k \times m$ matrix whose first m diagonal elements are 1 and all others are 0. The notations log and ln respectively refer to the base-2 and natural logarithms. The notation $\|\cdot\|$ refers to the Euclidean norm, while $\|\cdot\|_\infty$ refers to the infinity norm.

2.1 Probabilities

Let P, Q be two discrete random variables. The min-entropy of P is defined as

$$H_\infty(P) = - \log \max_{x \in \mathrm{Supp}(P)} \Pr[P = x] \ .$$

The conditional min-entropy of P on Q is defined as

$$H_\infty(P|Q) = - \log \sum_{y \in \mathrm{Supp}(Q)} \Pr[Q = y] \cdot \max_{x \in \mathrm{Supp}(P)} \Pr[P = x | Q = y] \ .$$

Let $\Omega = \mathrm{Supp}(P) \cup \mathrm{Supp}(Q)$. The statistical distance between P and Q is defined as $\Delta(P, Q) = \sum_{x \in \Omega} |\Pr[P = x] - \Pr[Q = x]| / 2$.

If $\mathrm{Supp}(P) \subseteq \mathrm{Supp}(Q)$, the Rényi divergence of infinite order between P and Q is defined as

$$R_\infty(P \| Q) = \sup_{x \in \mathrm{Supp}(P)} \frac{\Pr[P = x]}{\Pr[Q = x]} \in [1, +\infty] \ .$$

We will use the following properties of the Rényi divergence.

Lemma 1 ([vEH14]). *Let P and Q be two discrete random variables such that $\mathrm{Supp}(P) \subseteq \mathrm{Supp}(Q)$. Let $f : \mathrm{Supp}(Q) \to \mathcal{X}$ be a (possibly probabilistic) function. Let $E \subseteq \mathrm{Supp}(P)$ be an event. The Rényi divergence satisfies the probability preservation property:*

$$\Pr[P \in E] \leq R_\infty(P \| Q) \cdot \Pr[Q \in E] \tag{1}$$

and the data processing inequality:

$$R_\infty(f(P) \| f(Q)) \leq R_\infty(P \| Q) \ . \tag{2}$$

We will also use the following result.

Lemma 2. *Let $\varepsilon < 1$. Let P and Q be two random variables taking values in some countable set Ω. Let $c \in \mathbb{R}$ be a constant such that*

$$\forall a \in \Omega : \ \Pr[Q = a] = c(1 - \delta(a)) \Pr[P = a] \ ,$$

for some function $\delta : \Omega \to [0, \varepsilon]$. Then it holds that:

$$R_\infty(P\|Q) \leq \frac{1}{1-\varepsilon} \ , \quad R_\infty(Q\|P) \leq \frac{1}{1-\varepsilon} \quad and \quad \Delta(P, Q) \leq \frac{\varepsilon}{1-\varepsilon} \ .$$

Proof. Let us first note that $(1 - \varepsilon)c \leq 1 \leq c$, by summing the above equality over all $a \in \Omega$ and applying the bounds on $\delta(a)$. Then we have

$$R_\infty(P\|Q) = \sup_{a \in \Omega} \frac{\Pr[P = a]}{\Pr[Q = a]} = \sup_{a \in \Omega} \frac{1}{c(1 - \delta(a))} \leq \frac{1}{1-\varepsilon} \ .$$

We also have

$$R_\infty(Q\|P) = \sup_{a \in \Omega} \frac{\Pr[Q = a]}{\Pr[P = a]} = \sup_{a \in \Omega} c(1 - \delta(a)) \leq c \leq \frac{1}{1-\varepsilon} \ .$$

Finally, we refer to [BF11, Lemma A.2] for the third bound. $\qquad\square$

2.2 Lattice Gaussian Distributions

Let $k > 0, \mathbf{c} \in \mathbb{R}^k$ and $\boldsymbol{\Sigma} \in \mathbb{R}^{k \times k}$ be a positive-definite symmetric matrix. The Gaussian function with covariance parameter $\boldsymbol{\Sigma}$ and center parameter $\mathbf{c}$ is defined as

$$\rho_{\boldsymbol{\Sigma},\mathbf{c}} : \mathbf{x} \mapsto \exp\left(-\pi(\mathbf{x} - \mathbf{c})^\top \boldsymbol{\Sigma}^{-1}(\mathbf{x} - \mathbf{c})\right) \ .$$

The Gaussian distribution over the lattice $\Lambda \subseteq \mathrm{span}(\boldsymbol{\Sigma})$ with covariance parameter $\boldsymbol{\Sigma}$ and center parameter $\mathbf{c}$ is the distribution with support Λ and probability mass function

$$D_{\Lambda,\boldsymbol{\Sigma},\mathbf{c}} : \mathbf{x} \mapsto \frac{\rho_{\boldsymbol{\Sigma},\mathbf{c}}(\mathbf{x})}{\sum_{\mathbf{y} \in \Lambda} \rho_{\boldsymbol{\Sigma},\mathbf{c}}(\mathbf{y})} \ .$$

If $\boldsymbol{\Sigma} = \sigma^2 \mathbf{I}_k$, we write $\rho_{\sigma,\mathbf{c}}$ and $D_{\Lambda,\sigma,\mathbf{c}}$. We omit $\mathbf{c}$ when it is $\mathbf{0}$. We also define $D_{\Lambda+\mathbf{c},\boldsymbol{\Sigma}} = D_{\Lambda,\boldsymbol{\Sigma},-\mathbf{c}} + \mathbf{c}$. For convenience, we let $\rho_{\boldsymbol{\Sigma},\mathbf{c}}(S)$ denote the quantity $\sum_{\mathbf{y} \in S} \rho_{\boldsymbol{\Sigma},\mathbf{c}}(\mathbf{y})$ for any countable set S.

For spherical Gaussians, the upper and lower part of a vector are statistically independent. This is not the case anymore for general covariance matrices. The following lemma give the conditional distribution of the lower part of a Gaussian vector, given the upper part. The proof is adapted from the continuous setting and relies on writing the covariance as a 2×2 block matrix and inverting it using the Schur complement of the upper left matrix.

Lemma 3 (Conditional distribution). *Let $k \geq m > 0$, $\boldsymbol{\Sigma} \in \mathbb{R}^{k \times k}$ be a symmetric positive-definite matrix and $\mathbf{c} \in \mathbb{R}^k$. Write*

$$\mathbf{c} = \begin{pmatrix} \mathbf{c}_1 \\ \mathbf{c}_2 \end{pmatrix} \quad and \quad \boldsymbol{\Sigma} = \begin{pmatrix} \boldsymbol{\Sigma}_{11} & \boldsymbol{\Sigma}_{12} \\ \boldsymbol{\Sigma}_{21} & \boldsymbol{\Sigma}_{22} \end{pmatrix},$$

where $\mathbf{c}_1 \in \mathbb{R}^{k-m}$ and $\Sigma_{11} \in \mathbb{R}^{(k-m)\times(k-m)}$. Let $(Y_1^\top | Y_2^\top) \hookleftarrow D_{\mathbb{Z}^k, \Sigma, \mathbf{c}}$, where Y_1 takes values in $\mathbb{Z}^{k-m}$. Given any $\mathbf{y}_1 \in \mathbb{Z}^{k-m}$, the conditional distribution of Y_2 conditioned on $Y_1 = \mathbf{y}_1$ is $D_{\mathbb{Z}^m, \overline{\Sigma}, \overline{\mathbf{c}}}$, where

$$\overline{\mathbf{c}} = \mathbf{c}_2 + \Sigma_{21}\Sigma_{11}^{-1}(\mathbf{y}_1 - \mathbf{c}_1) \quad \text{and} \quad \overline{\Sigma} = \Sigma_{22} - \Sigma_{21}\Sigma_{11}^{-1}\Sigma_{12}.$$

Proof. As Σ is symmetric and positive-definite, both Σ_{11} and Σ_{22} are also symmetric and positive-definite and thus invertible. This is shown by considering vectors of the form $(\mathbf{x}^\top | (\mathbf{0}^m)^\top)^\top$ or $((\mathbf{0}^{k-m})^\top | \mathbf{y}^\top)^\top$. Let us write the block inverse of Σ as follows:

$$\Sigma^{-1} = \left(\begin{array}{c|c} \Sigma_{11}^{-1} + \Sigma_{11}^{-1}\Sigma_{12}\overline{\Sigma}^{-1}\Sigma_{21}\Sigma_{11}^{-1} & -\Sigma_{11}^{-1}\Sigma_{12}\overline{\Sigma}^{-1} \\ \hline -\overline{\Sigma}^{-1}\Sigma_{21}\Sigma_{11}^{-1} & \overline{\Sigma}^{-1} \end{array} \right) = \begin{pmatrix} \mathbf{S}_{11} & \mathbf{S}_{12} \\ \mathbf{S}_{21} & \mathbf{S}_{22} \end{pmatrix}.$$

This formula also ensures that $\overline{\Sigma}$ is invertible, as it is a diagonal block of the positive definite symmetric matrix Σ^{-1}.

Let $\mathbf{y}_2 \in \mathbb{Z}^m$. The probability that $Y_2 = \mathbf{y}_2$ conditioned on $Y_1 = \mathbf{y}_1$ is

$$\rho_{\Sigma, \mathbf{c}}\begin{pmatrix} \mathbf{y}_1 \\ \mathbf{y}_2 \end{pmatrix} \Big/ \sum_{\mathbf{y} \in \mathbb{Z}^m} \rho_{\Sigma, \mathbf{c}}\begin{pmatrix} \mathbf{y}_1 \\ \mathbf{y} \end{pmatrix}.$$

Let us then study $\rho_{\Sigma, \mathbf{c}}((\mathbf{y}_1^\top | \mathbf{y}^\top)^\top)$ by expanding it and completing the square.

$$\rho_{\Sigma, \mathbf{c}}\begin{pmatrix} \mathbf{y}_1 \\ \mathbf{y} \end{pmatrix} \sim \exp\left(-\pi\left((\mathbf{y} - \overline{\mathbf{c}})^\top \mathbf{S}_{22}(\mathbf{y} - \overline{\mathbf{c}})\right)\right) = \rho_{\overline{\Sigma}, \overline{\mathbf{c}}}(\mathbf{y}) \,,$$

where the notation $\sim$ hides terms that do not depend on $\mathbf{y}$. Using the fact that the probability mass sums to 1, we obtain that the distribution of Y_2 conditioned on $Y_1 = \mathbf{y}_1$ is $D_{\mathbb{Z}^m, \overline{\Sigma}, \overline{\mathbf{c}}}$. $\square$

As showed in [GPV08], Gaussian distributions can be sampled from by using Klein's algorithm [Kle00]. We will rely on the following variant.

Lemma 4 (Adapted from [BLP+13], Lemma 2.3). *There is a ppt algorithm that, given a basis $\mathbf{B} = (\mathbf{b}_1, \ldots, \mathbf{b}_\ell)$ of a full-rank ℓ-dimensional lattice Λ, a positive definite symmetric matrix Σ and $\mathbf{c} \in \mathbb{R}^\ell$ returns a sample from $D_{\Lambda, \Sigma, \mathbf{c}}$, assuming that $\sqrt{\ln(2\ell + 4)/\pi} \cdot \max_i \|\Sigma^{-1/2}\mathbf{b}_i\| \leq 1$.*

2.3 Smoothing Parameter

Given a k-dimensional lattice $\Lambda \subseteq \mathbb{R}^k$, its dual lattice Λ^* is defined as the set $\Lambda^* = \{\mathbf{x} \in \text{span}(\Lambda) \mid \mathbf{x}^\top \mathbf{y} \in \mathbb{Z}, \forall \mathbf{y} \in \Lambda\}$. If $\mathbf{B}$ is a basis of Λ, then $(\mathbf{B}^\dagger)^\top$ is a basis of Λ^*.

Given a lattice $\Lambda \subseteq \mathbb{R}^k$ and $\varepsilon > 0$, the smoothing parameter $\eta_\varepsilon(\Lambda)$ of the lattice Λ is defined as the smallest σ such that $\rho_{1/\sigma}(\Lambda^* \backslash \{\mathbf{0}\}) \leq \varepsilon$. The smoothing parameter satisfies the following two properties.

Lemma 5 ([ZXZ18],**Theorem 2**). *Let* $k > 1$ *and* $\varepsilon < 0.086k$. *Let* $\Lambda \subseteq \mathbb{R}^k$ *be a full-rank lattice with basis* $\mathbf{B} = (\mathbf{b}_1, \dots, \mathbf{b}_k)$. *It holds that*

$$\eta_\varepsilon(\Lambda) \leq \sqrt{\frac{\ln(k - 1 + 2k/\varepsilon)}{\pi}} \cdot \max_{i \leq k} \|\mathbf{b}_i\| \ .$$

Lemma 6 ([MR07]). *Let* Λ *be a* k-*dimensional full-rank lattice. Let* $\varepsilon > 0$ *and* $\boldsymbol{\Sigma} \in \mathbb{R}^{k \times k}$ *be a definite positive symmetric matrix with all singular values larger than* $\eta_\varepsilon(\Lambda)$ *and* $\mathbf{c} \in \mathbb{R}^k$. *We have*

$$\rho_{\boldsymbol{\Sigma},\mathbf{c}}(\Lambda) \ \in \ \frac{\sqrt{\det \boldsymbol{\Sigma}}}{\det \Lambda} \cdot [1 - \varepsilon, 1 + \varepsilon] \quad and \quad \frac{\rho_{\boldsymbol{\Sigma},\mathbf{c}}(\Lambda)}{\rho_{\boldsymbol{\Sigma}}(\Lambda)} \ \in \ \left[\frac{1 - \varepsilon}{1 + \varepsilon}, 1\right] \ .$$

The last upper bound holds for all $\boldsymbol{\Sigma}$.

The following lemma (adapted from [BMKMS22, Lemma 1]) is at the core of the completeness and zero-knowledge proofs. While [BMKMS22] does not give explicit statistical bounds, we note that Lemma 6 above, which is applied at the end of the proof from [BMKMS22], allows us to do so when combined with Lemma 2. A further adaptation is the use of the smoothing parameter bound from Lemma 5. Note that the dimension involved for this condition is ℓ rather than k, as this is the small-rank lattice that needs to be smoothed out (the corresponding condition from [BMKMS22, Lemma 1] is stronger than needed).

Lemma 7 (Gaussian decomposition, [BMKMS22], Lemma 1). *Let* $k \geq \ell$, $\varepsilon \in (0, 1)$ *and* $\mathbf{S} \in \mathbb{Z}^{k \times \ell}$. *Let* $s \geq \sqrt{2\ln(\ell - 1 + 2\ell/\varepsilon)/\pi}$ *and* $\sigma \geq \sqrt{8}\sigma_1(\mathbf{S}) \cdot s$. *Define*

$$\boldsymbol{\Sigma}(\mathbf{S}) = \sigma^2 \mathbf{I}_k - s^2 \mathbf{S}\mathbf{S}^\top \ ,$$

and let $\mathbf{y} \hookleftarrow D_{\mathbb{Z}^k, \boldsymbol{\Sigma}(\mathbf{S})}$ *and* $\mathbf{k} \hookleftarrow D_{\mathbb{Z}^\ell, s, -\mathbf{c}/2}$ *for any* $\mathbf{c} \in \mathbb{Z}^\ell$. *Then* $\boldsymbol{\Sigma}(\mathbf{S})$ *is positive definite and the distribution* $P_\mathbf{z}$ *of* $\mathbf{z} = \mathbf{y} + \mathbf{S}(2\mathbf{k} + \mathbf{c})$ *satisfies*

$$R_\infty(P_\mathbf{z} \| D_{\mathbb{Z}^k, \sigma}) \leq \frac{1 + \varepsilon}{1 - \varepsilon} \quad and \quad \Delta(P_\mathbf{z}, D_{\mathbb{Z}^k, \sigma}) \leq \frac{2\varepsilon}{1 - \varepsilon} \ .$$

Note that the matrix $\boldsymbol{\Sigma}(\mathbf{S})$ is positive definite since $\sigma \geq \sqrt{2}\sigma_1(\mathbf{S}) \cdot s$ ensures that all singular values of $\sigma^2 \mathbf{I}_k$ are larger than those of $s^2 \mathbf{S}\mathbf{S}^\top$.

2.4   Cryptographic Definitions

We recall the definition of an identification scheme and how such a scheme can be transformed into a digital signature via the Fiat-Shamir transform (see Fig. 6, p.25). For an identification scheme ID and a hash function H (modeled as a random oracle in the analysis), we let FS[ID, H] denote the resulting signature scheme. Details about correctness and security of FS[ID, H] are provided in Appendix A.

Definition 1 (Identification Scheme). *An identification scheme is a tuple of PPT algorithms* ID = (Igen, P, V) *such that:*

– Igen : *On input the security parameter* 1^λ, *algorithm* Igen *outputs a verification key* vk *and a signing key* sk. *We assume that* vk *defines the challenge space* $\mathcal{C}$.
– P : *The prover* P $= (P_1, P_2)$ *is split into two algorithms: given* sk, *algorithm* P_1 *produces a* commitment w *(first message sent to the verifier) and a state* st; *algorithm* P_2, *on input* (sk, w, st) *and a uniformly random* challenge $c \in \mathcal{C}$ *sent by the verifier in response to commitment* w, *outputs an answer* z.
– V : *On input* (vk, w, c, z), *the deterministic verifier* V *outputs* 1 *or* 0.

We let $P(sk, vk) \leftrightarrow V(vk)$ *denote the transcript* (w, c, z) *of an interaction between the prover and the verifier, as illustrated in Fig. 2.*

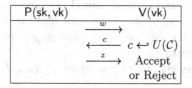

Fig. 2. Interaction Between P and V

We further define the following properties of identification schemes and recall their roles in the analysis of the signature obtained by applying the Fiat-Shamir transform to an identification protocol. We first recall *completeness* and *commitment-recoverability*, which allow to prove correctness of FS[ID, H].

Definition 2 (Completeness and commitment-recoverability).
An identification scheme ID $=$ (Igen, P, V) *is* ε-*complete for some* $\varepsilon > 0$ *if for any* $(vk, sk) \leftarrow$ Igen(1^λ), *for any challenge* $c \in \mathcal{C}$, *we have:*

$$\Pr\left[V(vk, (w, c, z)) = 0 \mid (w, c, z) \leftarrow (P(sk, vk) \leftrightarrow V(vk)) \right] \leq \varepsilon ,$$

where the randomness is taken over the random coins of P.

In addition, ID *satisfies* commitment-recoverability *if for any public key* vk, *challenge* $c \in \mathcal{C}$, *and answer* z, *there is at most one commitment* w *such that the transcript* (w, c, z) *is valid, and there exists a PPT algorithm* Rec *such that* $w = $ Rec(vk, c, z).

We then recall the definitions of *honest-verifier zero-knowledge* and *commitment min-entropy*, which allow to reduce EU-CMA security of FS[ID, H] to its EU-NMA security.

Definition 3 (HVZK and commitment min-entropy).] *An identification scheme* ID $=$ (Igen, P, V) *is Honest-Verifier Zero-Knowledge if there exists a PPT simulator* Sim *such that one of the following holds:*

• $\Delta((w, c, z) \leftarrow (P(sk, vk) \leftrightarrow V(vk))$, Sim$(c, vk)) \leq \varepsilon$. *In this case, we say that* ID *is* ε-HVZK.

- $R_\infty((w, c, z) \leftarrow (\mathsf{P}(\mathsf{sk}, \mathsf{vk}) \leftrightarrow \mathsf{V}(\mathsf{vk})) \parallel \mathsf{Sim}(c, \mathsf{vk})) \leq 1 + \varepsilon$. *In this case, we say that* ID *is* $(1 + \varepsilon)$-*divergence HVZK.*

Furthermore, we say that ID *satisfies* α-Min Entropy *or has* α *bits of commitment min-entropy if for any* $(\mathsf{vk}, \mathsf{sk})$ *in the range of* IGen*:*

$$H_\infty\Big(w|(w, c, z) \leftarrow (\mathsf{P}(\mathsf{sk}, \mathsf{vk}) \leftrightarrow \mathsf{V}(\mathsf{vk}))\Big) \geq \alpha .$$

Finally, we recall the notions of *lossiness* and *lossy-soundness*, which allow to prove EU-NMA security of $\mathsf{FS}[\mathsf{ID}, H]$ in the QROM.

Definition 4 (Lossiness and lossy-soundness). *An identification scheme* ID $= (\mathsf{Igen}, \mathsf{P}, \mathsf{V})$ *is lossy and* $\varepsilon_{\mathsf{ls}}$-*lossy sound for some* $\varepsilon_{\mathsf{ls}} > 0$ *if there exists a PPT lossy key generation algorithm* LossyIGen *that, on input a security parameter, outputs a verification key* $\mathsf{vk}_{\mathsf{ls}}$ *such that* $\mathsf{vk}_{\mathsf{ls}}$ *is indistinguishable from a verification key* vk *generated by* IGen.

Moreover, for any (unbounded) P^* *interacting with* V*, we have:*

$$\Pr\Big[\mathsf{V}(\mathsf{vk}_{\mathsf{ls}}, (w, c, z)) = 1 \mid (w, c, z) \leftarrow (\mathsf{P}^*(\mathsf{vk}_{\mathsf{ls}}) \leftrightarrow \mathsf{V}(\mathsf{vk}_{\mathsf{ls}}))\Big] \leq \varepsilon_{\mathsf{ls}} .$$

If we only consider classical adversaries, EU-NMA security of $\mathsf{FS}[\mathsf{ID}, H]$ can be argued by relying on the simpler notion of *special soundness*.

Definition 5 (Special soundness). *Let* ID $= (\mathsf{Igen}, \mathsf{P}, \mathsf{V})$ *be an identification scheme. It is* special sound *if for any PPT adversary* $\mathcal{A}$, *the quantity*

$$\Pr\Big[\mathsf{V}(\mathsf{vk}, (w, c_0, z_0)) = 1 \wedge \mathsf{V}(\mathsf{vk}, (w, c_1, z_1)) = 1 \mid (w, c_0, z_0, c_1, z_1) \leftarrow \mathcal{A}(\mathsf{vk})\Big]$$

is $\mathsf{negl}(\lambda)$, *where the probability is over the choice of* vk *and the coins of* $\mathcal{A}$.

We now briefly recall the formalism of digital signatures.

Definition 6. *A* signature scheme *is a tuple* $(\mathsf{KeyGen}, \mathsf{Sign}, \mathsf{Verify})$ *of PPT algorithms with the following specifications:*

- $\mathsf{KeyGen} : 1^\lambda \to (\mathsf{vk}, \mathsf{sk})$ *takes as input a security parameter* λ *and outputs a verification key* vk *and a signing key* sk.
- $\mathsf{Sign} : (\mathsf{sk}, \mu) \to \sigma$ *takes as inputs a signing key* sk *and a message* μ *and outputs a signature* σ.
- $\mathsf{Verify} : (\mathsf{vk}, \mu, \sigma) \to b \in \{0, 1\}$ *takes as inputs a verification key* vk, *a message* μ *and a signature* σ *and accepts* $(b = 1)$ *or rejects* $(b = 0)$.

We say that it is ε-*correct if for any pair* $(\mathsf{vk}, \mathsf{sk})$ *in the range of* KeyGen *and* μ,

$$\Pr\Big[\mathsf{Verify}(\mathsf{vk}, \mu, \mathsf{Sign}(\mathsf{sk}, \mu)) = 1\Big] \geq 1 - \mathsf{negl}(\lambda),$$

where the probability is taken over the random coins of Sign.

Finally, we recall the weak and strong Existential Unforgeability under Chosen Message Attack (EU-CMA and sEU-CMA) and the Existential Unforgeability under No Message Attack (EU-NMA) security game for digital signatures.

Definition 7. *Let $\delta > 0$. A signature scheme* (KeyGen, Sign, Verify) *is said to be δ-EU-CMA (resp. δ-EU-NMA) secure if no ppt adversary $\mathcal{A}$ given* vk *and access to a signing oracle (resp. without access to a signing oracle) has probability $\geq \delta$ over the choice of the signing and verification keys* (vk, sk) $\leftarrow$ KeyGen(1^λ) *and its random coins of outputting (μ^*, σ^*) such that*

1. *μ^* was not queried to the signing oracle,*
2. Verify(vk, μ^*, σ^*) $= 1$, *i.e., the forged signature must be accepted.*

The scheme is said δ-EU-CMA secure in the ROM if the above holds when the adversary can also make queries to a random oracle that models some hash function used in the scheme. The probability of forging a signature is also called the advantage of $\mathcal{A}$. If condition 1 is replaced with σ^* is not an answer of a signature query for μ^*, the scheme is instead said δ-sEU-CMA.

2.5 Hardness Assumptions

The security of our constructions relies on the hardness of two lattice problems, namely the decisional Learning with Errors problem and the Short Integer Solution problem.

Definition 8 (Learning With Errors). *Let $m, k > 0$ and $q \geq 2$. Let χ be a distribution over $\mathbb{Z}$. The* $\mathsf{LWE}_{m,k,\ell,q,\chi}$ *assumption states that no (quantum) adversary has non-negligible advantage in distinguishing $(\mathbf{A}, \mathbf{AS} + \mathbf{E})$ from $(\mathbf{A}, \mathbf{U})$, where $\mathbf{A} \hookleftarrow U(\mathbb{Z}_q^{m \times k})$, $\mathbf{U} \hookleftarrow U(\mathbb{Z}_q^{m \times \ell})$ and $(\mathbf{S}^\top | \mathbf{E}^\top)^\top \hookleftarrow \chi^{k+m \times \ell}$.*

Definition 9 (Short Integer Solution). *Let $m, k, \gamma > 0$ and $q \geq 2$ be a modulus. The* $\mathsf{SIS}_{m,k,q,\gamma}$ *assumption states that no (quantum) adversary has non-negligible probability of finding $\mathbf{s} \in \mathbb{Z}^k$ such that*

$$\mathbf{As} = \mathbf{0} \bmod q \quad and \quad 0 < \|\mathbf{s}\| \leq \gamma \, ,$$

when given $\mathbf{A} \hookleftarrow U(\mathbb{Z}_q^{m \times k})$ as input.

3 The G + G Identification Protocol

In this section, we first describe the G + G identification protocol, then prove the required properties to compile it into a signature using the Fiat-Shamir heuristic, and then discuss asymptotic parameters.

3.1 Description of the Scheme

Let us first introduce the parameters of the scheme as well as some notations. Let $m \geq \ell > 0$, $k > m + \ell$ and $\mathbf{J} = \mathbf{J}_{m,\ell}$. Let χ be a distribution over $\mathbb{Z}$. Let $\mathcal{C} \subseteq \mathbb{Z}_2^\ell$ be the challenge space, which we assume to be finite. Let $\sigma, s \geq 0$ and define $\mathbf{\Sigma} : \mathbb{Z}^{k \times \ell} \to \mathbb{R}^{k \times k}$ as

$$\mathbf{\Sigma} : \mathbf{S} \mapsto \sigma^2 \mathbf{I}_k - s^2 \mathbf{S} \mathbf{S}^\top.$$

The scheme is also parametrized by an odd modulus q and an acceptance bound γ.

The G + G identification protocol is described in Fig. 3. The instance generation algorithm samples a verification key $\mathbf{A} \in \mathbb{Z}_{2q}^{m \times k}$ and a signing key $\mathbf{S} \in \mathbb{Z}^{k \times \ell}$ with small-magnitude coefficients such that $\mathbf{A} \cdot \mathbf{S} = q\mathbf{J} \bmod 2q$. In the first phase of the interaction, the prover samples a vector $\mathbf{y}$ with well-crafted covariance matrix, and sends the commitment $\mathbf{w} = \mathbf{A}\mathbf{y} \bmod 2q$ to the verifier. The protocol is public-coin, i.e., the verifier just samples $\mathbf{c}$ uniformly in the challenge space and sends it to the prover. After receiving $\mathbf{c}$, the prover samples a Gaussian vector $\mathbf{k}$ over the lattice coset $2\mathbf{S}\mathbb{Z}^\ell + \mathbf{c}$. The covariance matrices of $\mathbf{y}$ and $\mathbf{k}$ are set so that the Gaussian plus Gaussian sum is statistically close to a spherical Gaussian distribution.

The first sampling that the prover has to perform is well-defined only if $\mathbf{\Sigma}(\mathbf{S})$ is definite positive, which we show thanks to Lemma 7. The first sampling is implemented using Lemma 4, which requires $\sigma^2 - s^2 \sigma_1(\mathbf{S})^2 \geq \sqrt{\ln(2\ell + 4)/\pi}$, where we let $\sigma_1(\mathbf{S})$ denote the largest singular value of $\mathbf{S}$. The protocol can then be executed in polynomial time.

$\mathsf{IGen}(1^\lambda)$:

1: $\mathbf{A}_1 \hookleftarrow U(\mathbb{Z}_q^{m \times (k-m-\ell)})$
2: $(\mathbf{S}_1, \mathbf{S}_2) \hookleftarrow \chi^{(k-m-\ell) \times \ell} \times \chi^{m \times \ell}$
3: $\mathbf{B} \leftarrow \mathbf{A}_1 \mathbf{S}_1 + \mathbf{S}_2 \bmod q$
4: $\mathbf{A} \leftarrow (q\mathbf{J} - 2\mathbf{B} | 2\mathbf{A}_1 | 2\mathbf{I}_m) \in \mathbb{Z}_{2q}^{m \times k}$
5: $\mathbf{S} \leftarrow (\mathbf{I}_\ell | \mathbf{S}_1^\top | \mathbf{S}_2^\top)^\top \in \mathbb{Z}^{k \times \ell}$
6: $\mathsf{vk} \leftarrow \mathbf{A}, \mathsf{sk} \leftarrow \mathbf{S}$
7: **return** $(\mathsf{vk}, \mathsf{sk})$

$P(\mathbf{A}, \mathbf{S})$	$V(\mathbf{A})$
$\mathbf{y} \hookleftarrow D_{\mathbb{Z}^k, \mathbf{\Sigma}(\mathbf{S})}$	
$\mathbf{w} \leftarrow \mathbf{A}\mathbf{y} \bmod 2q \quad \xrightarrow{\;\mathbf{w}\;}$	
$\xleftarrow{\;\mathbf{c}\;}$	$\mathbf{c} \hookleftarrow U(\mathcal{C})$
$\mathbf{k} \hookleftarrow D_{\mathbb{Z}^\ell, s, -\mathbf{c}/2}$	
$\mathbf{z} \leftarrow \mathbf{y} + 2\mathbf{S}\mathbf{k} + \mathbf{S}\mathbf{c} \quad \xrightarrow{\;\mathbf{z}\;}$	Accept if
	$\mathbf{A}\mathbf{z} = \mathbf{w} + q\mathbf{J}\mathbf{c} \bmod 2q$
	and $\|\mathbf{z}\| \leq \gamma$

Fig. 3. The G + G Identification Protocol.

Combining this identification protocol with the Fiat-Shamir (without aborts) paradigm, we then obtain a lattice-based signature $\mathsf{FS}[\mathsf{G}+\mathsf{G},H]$, as stated in the following Theorem. The correctness and security of the scheme are inherited from the properties of the underlying identification protocol.

Theorem 1. *Let $m \geq \ell > 0$, $k > m+\ell$, $\varepsilon \in (0,1/2]$, $s \geq \sqrt{2\ln(\ell-1+2\ell/\varepsilon)/\pi}$ and $\sigma \geq \sqrt{8}\sigma_1(\mathbf{S}) \cdot s$ for all $\mathbf{S} \in \mathbb{Z}^{k \times \ell}$ in the range of IGen. Let γ and ε_c be such that $\mathrm{Pr}_{\mathbf{z} \hookleftarrow D_{\mathbb{Z}^k,\sigma}}[\|\mathbf{z}\| > \gamma] \leq \varepsilon_c/3$. Let $q > \max(2\gamma, \sigma \cdot \eta_\varepsilon(\mathbb{Z}^m))$ be an odd modulus. Then the signature scheme $\mathsf{FS}[\mathsf{G}+\mathsf{G},H]$ is ε_c-correct and:*

- *EU-CMA-secure in the ROM under the $\mathsf{SIS}_{m,k,q,2\gamma}$ assumption. Namely, for any adversary $\mathcal{A}$ against the EU-CMA security of $\mathsf{FS}[\mathsf{G}+\mathsf{G},H]$ making at most Q_S sign queries and at most Q_H hash queries, there exists an adversary $\mathcal{B}$ against the $\mathsf{SIS}_{m,k,q,2\gamma}$ assumption such that:*

$$\mathsf{Adv}^{\mathsf{EU-CMA}}(\mathcal{A}) \leq \left(\frac{1+\varepsilon}{1-\varepsilon}\right)^{Q_S} \left[Q_H \cdot \left(\sqrt{\mathsf{Adv}^{\mathsf{SIS}_{m,k,q,2\gamma}}(\mathcal{B})} + \frac{2}{|\mathcal{C}|}\right)\right]$$
$$+ 3Q_S/2 \cdot \sqrt{(Q_H + Q_S + 1) \cdot s^{-m}} \; ;$$

- *EU-CMA-secure in the QROM under the $\mathsf{LWE}_{k-m-\ell,m,\ell,\chi,q}$ assumption, assuming that $1/|\mathcal{C}| + (|\mathcal{C}|^2(2\gamma+1)^{2k})/q^m$ is negligible. Namely, for any quantum adversary $\mathcal{A}$ against the EU-CMA security of $\mathsf{FS}[\mathsf{G}+\mathsf{G},H]$ making at most Q_S classical sign queries and at most Q_H quantum hash queries, there exists an adversary $\mathcal{B}$ against the $\mathsf{LWE}_{k-m-\ell,m,\ell,\chi,q}$ assumption such that:*

$$\mathsf{Adv}^{\mathsf{EU-CMA}}(\mathcal{A}) \leq \left(\frac{1+\varepsilon}{1-\varepsilon}\right)^{Q_S} \mathsf{Adv}^{\mathsf{LWE}_{k-m-\ell,m,\ell,\chi,q}}(\mathcal{B})$$
$$+ \left(\frac{1+\varepsilon}{1-\varepsilon}\right)^{Q_S} 8(Q_H + 1)^2 \cdot \left(\frac{1}{|\mathcal{C}|} + \frac{|\mathcal{C}|^2(2\gamma+1)^{2k}}{q^m}\right)$$
$$+ 3Q_S/2 \cdot \sqrt{(Q_H + Q_S + 1) \cdot s^{-m}} \; .$$

Moreover, these two bounds holds when $\mathcal{A}$ is an adversary against the sEU-CMA security of the scheme by adding an extra $+Q_S \cdot s^{-m}$ term on the right hand side.

The proof of Theorem 1 follows from Corollaries 1, 2, 3, and 4, which are derived from the properties of the underlying identification protocol proved in Sects. 3.2, 3.3, and 3.4, by applying the Fiat-Shamir transform. The Fiat-Shamir transform results are reminded in Appendix A.

3.2   Completeness and Commitment Recoverability

We first show that the $\mathsf{G}+\mathsf{G}$ protocol is complete and commitment recoverable. As a corollary, we obtain that the resulting Fiat-Shamir signature scheme $\mathsf{FS}[\mathsf{G}+\mathsf{G},H]$ is correct.

Theorem 2. *Let $m \geq \ell > 0$, $k > m+\ell$, $\varepsilon \in (0,1/2]$, $s \geq \sqrt{2\ln(\ell - 1 + 2\ell/\varepsilon)/\pi}$ and $\sigma \geq \sqrt{8}\sigma_1(\mathbf{S}) \cdot s$ for all $\mathbf{S} \in \mathbb{Z}^{k \times \ell}$ in the range of IGen. Let γ and ε_c be such that $\Pr_{\mathbf{z} \hookleftarrow D_{\mathbb{Z}^k,\sigma}}[\|\mathbf{z}\| > \gamma] \leq \varepsilon_c/3$. Let $q > 2\gamma$ be an odd modulus. Then the $\mathsf{G + G}$ identification protocol is ε_c-complete and achieves commitment-recoverability.*

Proof. First, we note that $\mathbf{AS} = q\mathbf{J} \bmod 2q$ holds for any matrix pair output by IGen. Then, in order to pass the first verification step, a transcript $(\mathbf{w}, \mathbf{c}, \mathbf{z})$ must satisfy:

$$\mathbf{Az} = \mathbf{A}(\mathbf{y} + 2\mathbf{Sk} + \mathbf{Sc}) = \mathbf{w} + \mathbf{0} + q\mathbf{Jc} \bmod 2q \ . \tag{3}$$

In particular, this defines a unique commitment $\mathbf{w} = \mathbf{Az} - q\mathbf{Jc} \bmod 2q$ such that $(\mathbf{w}, \mathbf{c}, \mathbf{z})$ can be a valid transcript, and $\mathbf{w}$ is efficiently recoverable, by defining Rec as $\mathsf{Rec}(\mathbf{A}, \mathbf{c}, \mathbf{z}) := \mathbf{Az} - q\mathbf{Jc} \bmod 2q$.

Now, we note that an honestly generated transcript $(\mathbf{w}, \mathbf{c}, \mathbf{z})$ always satisfies Eq. (3). The probability preservation property of the Rényi divergence (Eq. (1)) and Lemma 7 give the following bound:

$$\Pr_{(\mathbf{w},\mathbf{c},\mathbf{z})}[\|\mathbf{z}\| > \gamma] \leq R_\infty(P_\mathbf{z}\|D_{\mathbb{Z}^k,\sigma}) \cdot \Pr_{\mathbf{z} \hookleftarrow D_{\mathbb{Z}^k,\sigma}}[\|\mathbf{z}\| > \gamma]$$

$$\leq \frac{1+\varepsilon}{1-\varepsilon} \cdot \Pr_{\mathbf{z} \hookleftarrow D_{\mathbb{Z}^k,\sigma}}[\|\mathbf{z}\| > \gamma]$$

$$\leq \frac{1+1/2}{1-1/2} \cdot \Pr_{\mathbf{z} \hookleftarrow D_{\mathbb{Z}^k,\sigma}}[\|\mathbf{z}\| > \gamma].$$

Then the probability that an honest transcript $(\mathbf{w}, \mathbf{c}, \mathbf{z})$ be rejected at most $\leq 3 \cdot \Pr_{\mathbf{z} \hookleftarrow D_{\mathbb{Z}^k,\sigma}}[\|\mathbf{z}\| > \gamma]$. $\qquad \square$

We then obtain the following corollary.

Corollary 1. *Using the same assumptions as in Theorem 2, the resulting signature scheme $\mathsf{FS}[\mathsf{G + G}, H]$ is ε_c-correct.*

Note that correctness of $\mathsf{FS}[\mathsf{G + G}, H]$ does not require to assume that H is modeled as a random oracle, as Lemma 7 holds without relying on the randomness of $\mathbf{c}$. This is in contrast to Lemma 8 that generically considers completeness of signatures obtained using the Fiat-Shamir transform.

3.3   Honest-Verifier Zero-Knowledge and Commitment Min-Entropy

We now show that the $\mathsf{G + G}$ protocol is HVZK and has large commitment min-entropy. As a corollary, we obtain that the signature scheme $\mathsf{FS}[\mathsf{G + G}, H]$ is EU-CMA-secure provided it is EU-NMA-secure.

Theorem 3. *Let $m \geq \ell > 0$, $k > m+\ell$, $\varepsilon \in (0,1/2]$, $s \geq \sqrt{2\ln(\ell - 1 + 2\ell/\varepsilon)/\pi}$ and $\sigma \geq \sqrt{8}\sigma_1(\mathbf{S}) \cdot s$ for all $\mathbf{S} \in \mathbb{Z}^{k \times \ell}$ in the range of IGen. Let $q > \sigma \cdot \eta_\varepsilon(\mathbb{Z}^m)$ be an odd modulus. Then the $\mathsf{G + G}$ identification protocol satisfies:*

- $(1+\varepsilon)/(1-\varepsilon)$-*divergence HVZK,*
- $2\varepsilon/(1-\varepsilon)$-*HVZK.*

In addition, its commitment min-entropy is $\geq m \cdot \log(s/3)$.

Proof. We prove both properties separately. We start by proving HVZK, which is inherited from Lemma 7 and then focus on commitment min-entropy.

HVZK. The simulator on input a challenge $\mathbf{c} \in \mathcal{C}$ and a public matrix $\mathbf{A}$ samples $\mathbf{z} \hookleftarrow D_{\mathbb{Z}^k, \sqrt{2}\sigma}$, sets $\mathbf{w} = \mathbf{Az} - q\mathbf{Jc}$ and returns $(\mathbf{w}, \mathbf{c}, \mathbf{z})$ as a transcript. As everything here is a function of $\mathbf{z}$ and $\mathbf{c}$, we can rely on Lemma 7. The bounds from the above claim are immediately inherited from the latter lemma by applying the data processing inequalities (which we recall in Eq. (2) for the Rényi divergence – the same inequality holds replacing the Rényi divergence by the statistical distance). This completes the zero-knowledge analysis.

Commitment Min-Entropy. Let $\mathbf{w} \in \mathbb{Z}_{2q}^m$ and $(Y_1^\top, Y_2^\top)^\top \hookleftarrow D_{\mathbb{Z}^k, \Sigma(\mathbf{S})}$, where Y_1 takes values in $\mathbb{Z}^{k-m}$. Given a matrix $\mathbf{A} = (\mathbf{A}_0 | 2\mathbf{I}_m) \in \mathbb{Z}_{2q}^{m \times k}$, it holds that

$$\Pr_{(Y_1,Y_2)}[\mathbf{A}_0 Y_1 + 2Y_2 = \mathbf{w} \bmod 2q] = \Pr_{(Y_1,Y_2)}[2Y_2 = \mathbf{w} - \mathbf{A}_0 Y_1 \bmod 2q]$$

$$\leq \Pr_{(Y_1,Y_2)}[Y_2 = (\mathbf{w} - \mathbf{A}_0 Y_1)\zeta \bmod q] \ ,$$

where ζ is the modular inverse of 2 mod q. Hence, the min-entropy of the commitment is $\geq H_\infty(Y_2 \bmod q | Y_1)$ and we move on to bounding the latter quantity from below. Note that there exist $\sigma \geq \sigma_1 \geq \cdots \geq \sigma_m \geq (\sigma^2 - s^2 \sigma_1(\mathbf{S})^2)^{1/2}$ and $\mathbf{Q} \in \mathbb{R}^{m \times m}$ orthogonal such that

$$\Sigma(\mathbf{S}) = \mathbf{Q} \begin{pmatrix} \sigma_1^2 & & \\ & \ddots & \\ & & \sigma_m^2 \end{pmatrix} \mathbf{Q}^\top.$$

Let $\mathbf{y}_1 \in \mathbb{Z}^{k-m}$ be fixed. The distribution of Y_2 conditioned on $Y_1 = \mathbf{y}_1$ is exactly $D_{\mathbb{Z}^m, \overline{\Sigma}, \overline{\mathbf{c}}}$, as defined in Lemma 3 (with $\mathbf{c} = \mathbf{0}$). Let $\overline{\sigma}_1^2$ (resp. $\overline{\sigma}_m^2$) be the largest (resp. smallest) eigenvalue of $\overline{\Sigma}$ and $\overline{\mathbf{c}} = (\overline{c}_1, \ldots, \overline{c}_m)^\top$. We are interested in obtaining an upper bound on $\rho_{\overline{\Sigma}, \overline{\mathbf{c}}}(\mathbf{z} + q\mathbb{Z}^m)/\rho_{\overline{\Sigma}, \overline{\mathbf{c}}}(\mathbb{Z}^m)$ for all $\mathbf{z} \in (-q/2, q/2]^m$. Indeed, this quantity corresponds to all values taken by the probability mass function of the random variable $Y_2 \bmod q$ conditioned on $Y_1 = \mathbf{y}_1$, namely $\Pr_{Y_2|Y_1=\mathbf{y}_1}(Y_2 = \mathbf{z} \bmod q) = \sum_{\mathbf{u} \in q\mathbb{Z}^m} \rho_{\overline{\Sigma}, \overline{\mathbf{c}}}(\mathbf{z} + \mathbf{u})/\rho_{\overline{\Sigma}, \overline{\mathbf{c}}}(\mathbb{Z}^m)$.

As $\overline{\Sigma}^{-1}$ is the bottom right submatrix of Σ^{-1} of size $m \times m$, it holds that for any $\mathbf{y} \in \mathbb{R}^m$, we have $\mathbf{y}^\top \overline{\Sigma}^{-1} \mathbf{y} \in \|\mathbf{y}\|^2 \cdot [1/\sigma_1^2, 1/\sigma_m^2]$. Hence all singular values $\overline{\sigma}_i$ of $\overline{\Sigma}$ lie in $[(\sigma^2 - s^2 \sigma_1(\mathbf{S})^2)^{1/2}, \sigma]$. Thanks to the theorem assumptions, we obtain that all $\overline{\sigma}_i$'s are above $\eta_\varepsilon(\mathbb{Z}^m)$. Using Lemma 6, it holds that

$$\rho_{\overline{\Sigma}, \overline{\mathbf{c}}}(\mathbb{Z}^m) \geq (1-\varepsilon) \cdot \sqrt{\det \overline{\Sigma}} \geq (1-\varepsilon) \cdot \left(\sigma^2 - s^2 \sigma_1(\mathbf{S})^2\right)^{m/2} .$$

The latter is $\geq (1 - \varepsilon) \cdot (s\sigma_1(\mathbf{S}))^m$, by assumption on σ. For the numerator, we first use Lemma 6 once more, to obtain:

$$\rho_{\overline{\Sigma},\overline{c}}(\mathbf{z} + q\mathbb{Z}^m) \leq \rho_{\overline{\Sigma}}(q\mathbb{Z}^m) = 1 + \rho_{\overline{\Sigma}}(q\mathbb{Z}^m \setminus \{\mathbf{0}\}) \leq 1 + \rho_\sigma(q\mathbb{Z}^m \setminus \{\mathbf{0}\}) \ .$$

Rewriting the assumption on q we have $1/\sigma > \eta_\varepsilon((1/q)\mathbb{Z}^m)$. Note that the dual lattice of $(1/q)\mathbb{Z}^m$ is $q\mathbb{Z}^m$. Hence, we have $\rho_\sigma(q\mathbb{Z}^m \setminus \{\mathbf{0}\}) \leq \varepsilon$ by definition of the smoothing parameter. The result follows by noting that for any $\mathbf{S}$ in the range of IGen, we have $\sigma_1(\mathbf{S}) \geq 1$ as $\mathbf{S}$ includes an identity matrix. □

We then obtain the following corollary as an application of Theorem 6.

Corollary 2. *Using the same assumptions as in Theorem 3 the resulting signature scheme* FS$[G + G, H]$ *is EU-CMA-secure (and sEU-CMA-secure) in the QROM, provided it is EU-NMA-secure. Namely, for any (possibly quantum) adversary $\mathcal{A}$ against the EU-CMA security of* FS$[G + G, H]$ *making at most Q_S (classical) sign queries and at most Q_H (possibly quantum) hash queries, there exists an adversary $\mathcal{B}$ against the EU-NMA security of* FS$[G + G, H]$ *such that:*

$$\mathsf{Adv}^{\mathsf{EU-CMA}}(\mathcal{A}) \leq \left(1 + \frac{2\varepsilon}{1 - \varepsilon}\right)^{Q_S} \mathsf{Adv}^{\mathsf{EU-NMA}}(\mathcal{B})$$
$$+ 3Q_S/2 \cdot \sqrt{(Q_H + Q_S + 1) \cdot (s\sigma_1(\mathbf{S}))^{-m}} \ .$$

The bound holds with an extra $Q_S \cdot (s\sigma_1(\mathbf{S}))^{-m}$ term when $\mathcal{A}$ is an adversary against the sEU-CMA security of FS$[G + G, H]$.

3.4   Special Soundness and Lossy Soundness

To complete the analysis, we show that (i) $G + G$ is special-sound, and that (ii) $G + G$ is a lossy identification scheme with lossy-soundness. As a corollary, we obtain that the signature scheme FS$[G + G, H]$ is EU-NMA-secure in the ROM, and in the QROM under some parameters constraint.

Theorem 4. *Let $m \geq \ell > 0$, $k > m + \ell$, $\varepsilon \in (0, 1/2]$, $s \geq \sqrt{2\ln(\ell - 1 + 2\ell/\varepsilon)/\pi}$ and $\sigma \geq \sqrt{8}\sigma_1(\mathbf{S}) \cdot s$ for all $\mathbf{S} \in \mathbb{Z}^{k \times \ell}$ in the range of IGen. Let $\gamma > 0$ and $q > 2\gamma$ be an odd modulus. Then the $G + G$ identification protocol is:*

- *special-sound, under the* SIS$_{m,k,q,2\gamma}$ *assumption,*
- *lossy, under the* LWE$_{k-m-\ell,m,\ell,\chi,q}$ *assumption,*
- *$\varepsilon_{\mathsf{ls}}$-lossy sound for*

$$\varepsilon_{\mathsf{ls}} = \frac{1}{|\mathcal{C}|} + \frac{|\mathcal{C}|^2 (2\gamma + 1)^{2k}}{q^m} \ .$$

Proof. We first prove $G + G$ achieves special soundness, and then explain how to set our identification scheme in lossy mode.

Special Soundness. Assume there exists a PPT adversary $\mathcal{A}$ which, given the verification key vk $= \mathbf{A}$, produces two valid transcripts $(\mathbf{w}, \mathbf{c}_0, \mathbf{z}_0), (\mathbf{w}, \mathbf{c}_1, \mathbf{z}_1)$

with $c_0 \neq c_1$. It can be turned into an $\mathsf{SIS}_{m,k,q,2\gamma}$ solver. Indeed, by definition, such transcripts satisfy $\mathbf{A}(z_0 - z_1) = q\mathbf{J}(c_1 - c_0) \bmod 2q$.

Notice that we have $\mathbf{A}(z_0 - z_1) = \mathbf{0} \bmod q$, which implies that $z_0 - z_1$ is a solution to the SIS instance defined by $\mathbf{A}$. In addition, when reducing modulo 2, we also have $\mathbf{A}(z_0 - z_1) = \mathbf{J}(c_1 - c_0) \bmod 2$, which implies that $z_0 \neq z_1$. Finally, note that the condition on γ implies that $\|z_0 - z_1\| \leq 2\gamma$ (as transcript validity implies $\|z\| \leq \gamma$), and that $z_0 - z_1 \neq \mathbf{0} \bmod q$.

Hence, there exists an adversary $\mathcal{B}$ against the $\mathsf{SIS}_{m,k,q,2\gamma}$ problem such that:

$$\mathsf{Adv}(\mathcal{A}) \leq \mathsf{Adv}^{\mathsf{SIS}_{m,k,q,2\gamma}}(\mathcal{B}) \ .$$

Let us now focus on lossy-soundness. We first define a lossy key generation algorithm, and then argue about lossy-soundness.

Lossiness. The lossy key generation algorithm LossyIGen only modifies the generation of $\mathbf{B}$. Recall that in IGen, the latter is defined as $\mathbf{B} \leftarrow \mathbf{A}_1\mathbf{S}_1 + \mathbf{S}_2$, with $\mathbf{A}_1 \hookleftarrow U(\mathbb{Z}_q^{m \times (k-m-\ell)})$ and $(\mathbf{S}_1, \mathbf{S}_2) \hookleftarrow \chi_\eta^{(k-m-\ell) \times \ell} \times \chi_\eta^{m \times \ell}$. The lossy key generation algorithm LossyIGen samples it as $\mathbf{B} \hookleftarrow U(\mathbb{Z}_q^{m \times \ell})$. Lossy verification keys are computationally indistinguishable from non-lossy ones, under the $\mathsf{LWE}_{k-m-\ell,m,\ell,\eta,q}$ assumption.

$\varepsilon_{\mathsf{ls}}$-**lossy Soundness.** First note that, if the lossy verification key $\mathbf{A}$ is such that, for all commitment $\mathbf{w}$, there exists at most one challenge $\mathbf{c}$ such that there exists z with $(\mathbf{w}, \mathbf{c}, z)$ passing verification, then, as the challenge is sampled uniformly and independently of $\mathbf{w}$, an (unbounded) prover cannot pass verification, except with probability at most $1/|\mathcal{C}|$.

We then focus on proving that the above holds with overwhelming probability over the choice of the lossy key $\mathbf{A}$. By contradiction, assume there exists $\mathbf{w}, c_0, c_1, z_0, z_1$ with $\|z_0\|, \|z_1\| \leq \gamma$ and $c_0 \neq c_1 \in \mathcal{C}$, such that we have both $\mathbf{A}z_0 = \mathbf{w} + q\mathbf{J}c_0 \bmod 2q$ and $\mathbf{A}z_1 = \mathbf{w} + q\mathbf{J}c_1 \bmod 2q$. Then, we have:

$$\mathbf{A}(z_0 - z_1) = q\mathbf{J}(c_1 - c_0) \bmod 2q \ .$$

Recall that $\mathbf{A}$ is of the form $(q\mathbf{J} - 2\mathbf{B}|2\mathbf{A}_1|2\mathbf{I}_m)$, with $\mathbf{A}_1, \mathbf{B}$ uniform over $\mathbb{Z}_q$. Hence, the matrix $\mathbf{A} \bmod q$ is of the form $(\mathbf{B}|\mathbf{A}_1|\mathbf{I}_m)$, since q is odd. Then the above implies that $(\mathbf{B}|\mathbf{A}_1|\mathbf{I}_m)(z_0 - z_1) = \mathbf{0} \bmod q$ with $z_0 - z_1 \neq \mathbf{0} \bmod q$. This happens with probability at most $1/q^m$.

To conclude, note that there are at most $(2\gamma+1)^{2k} \cdot |\mathcal{C}|^2$ choices for z_0, z_1, c_0 and c_1. A union bound therefore implies that the probability over $\mathbf{A}$ that there is a commitment with at least two challenges permitting valid transcripts is at most $|\mathcal{C}|^2(2\gamma + 1)^{2k}/q^m$. Our lossy identification scheme is then $\varepsilon_{\mathsf{ls}}$-lossy-sound, with

$$\varepsilon_{\mathsf{ls}} \leq \frac{1}{|\mathcal{C}|} + \frac{|\mathcal{C}|^2(2\gamma + 1)^{2k}}{q^m} \ ,$$

which completes the proof of the theorem. $\qquad\qquad\qquad\qquad\qquad\qquad\qquad\square$

We then obtain the following corollary as an application of Lemma 10.

Corollary 3. *Using the same assumptions as in Theorem 4, the resulting signature scheme* FS[G + G, H] *is EU-NMA-secure, in the ROM. Namely, for any adversary $\mathcal{A}$ against the EU-NMA security of* FS[G + G, H], *there exists an adversary $\mathcal{B}$ against the* $\mathsf{SIS}_{m,k,q,2\gamma}$ *assumption such that:*

$$\mathsf{Adv}^{\mathsf{EU-NMA}}(\mathcal{A}) \leq Q_H \cdot \left(\sqrt{\mathsf{Adv}^{\mathsf{SIS}_{m,k,q,2\gamma}}(\mathcal{B})} + \frac{2}{|\mathcal{C}|} \right) .$$

We also obtain the following corollary as an application of Theorem 7.

Corollary 4. *Using the same assumptions as in Theorem 4, and if $\varepsilon_{\mathsf{ls}}$ is negligible, the signature scheme* FS[G + G, H] *is EU-NMA-secure, in the QROM. Namely, for any (possibly quantum) adversary $\mathcal{A}$ against the EU-NMA security of* FS[G + G, H] *making at most Q_H (possibly quantum) hash queries, there exists a quantum adversary $\mathcal{B}$ against the* $\mathsf{LWE}_{k-m-\ell,m,\ell,\chi,q}$ *assumption such that:*

$$\mathsf{Adv}^{\mathsf{EU-NMA}}(\mathcal{A}) \leq \mathsf{Adv}^{\mathsf{LWE}_{k-m-\ell,m,\ell,\chi,q}}(\mathcal{B}) + 8(Q_H+1)^2 \cdot \left(\frac{1}{|\mathcal{C}|} + \frac{|\mathcal{C}|^2(2\gamma+1)^{2k}}{q^m} \right) .$$

To conclude this section, we introduce an additional assumption of a similar flavour as the SelfTargetMSIS assumption [KLS18], which allows to directly prove EU-NMA-security of FS[G + G, H] in the QROM as it is (up to LWE) the EU-NMA security game of the resulting signature. As for SelfTargetMSIS, this problem can be related in the ROM to SIS, using the special soundness property of the scheme.

Definition 10 (GpGSelfTargetSIS). *Let $m \geq \ell > 0$, $k > m + \ell$. Let $\gamma > 0$ and $q > 2\gamma$ be an odd modulus. The* $\mathsf{GpGTargetSIS}_{m,k,\ell,\gamma,q}$ *states that given a matrix* $\mathbf{A} := (q\mathbf{J} - 2\mathbf{B}|2\mathbf{A}_1|2\mathbf{I}_m) \in \mathbb{Z}_{2q}^{m \times k}$, *where* $\mathbf{A}_1 \hookleftarrow U(\mathbb{Z}_q^{m \times (k-m-\ell)})$ *and* $\mathbf{B} \hookleftarrow U(\mathbb{Z}_q^{m \times \ell})$, *and oracle access to a hash function H, it is computationally hard to find $\mathbf{c} \in \mathcal{C}$, $\mathbf{z} \in \mathbb{Z}^k$ and $\mu \in \{0,1\}^*$ such that $H(\mathbf{Az} - q\mathbf{Jc}, \mu) = \mathbf{c}$ and $\|\mathbf{z}\| \leq \gamma$.*

3.5   Asymptotic Parameters Analysis

Our analysis above is applicable to the following instantiation of parameters, as a function of the security parameter λ and the number of signature queries Q_S. We assume Q_S to be a large polynomial in λ. We consider k, ℓ, m linear in λ. We set χ as $D_{\mathbb{Z}, \sqrt{k}}$ with tailcutting to get samples in $\{-k, \ldots, 0, \ldots, k\}$ with overwhelming probability. We let $\varepsilon = 1/Q_S$.

We make the security of the G + G scheme rely on the following two assumptions. First, the $\mathsf{LWE}_{k-m-\ell,k,\ell,q,\chi}$ assumption, where $\sqrt{k} = \alpha q$. This LWE parametrization is compatible with the reduction from worst-case lattice problems from [Reg09]. Second, the $\mathsf{SIS}_{m,k,\beta}$ assumption, where $\beta = O(\sqrt{k}\sigma)$. The SIS parametrization is compatible with the reductions from worst-case lattice problems from [MR07, GPV08] when $q \geq \Omega(\sqrt{k}\beta)$. The hardness of both problems is balanced out when $\alpha \approx 1/\beta$.

Further, the distribution of $\mathbf{z}$ is centered Gaussian with standard deviation $\sigma = 4\sigma_1(\mathbf{S})\sqrt{\ln(\ell - 1 + 2\ell/\varepsilon)/\pi}$, which is $O(\sigma_1(\mathbf{S})\sqrt{\log(Q_S\lambda)})$. Moreover as $\sigma_1(\mathbf{S}) = O(\lambda)$, the norm of $\mathbf{z}$ is at most $\beta = O(\lambda^{3/2}\log^{1/2}Q_S)$. Finally, we set $q = \Theta(\lambda^2\log^{1/2}Q_S)$.

The verification key and a signature respectively have bit-sizes $O(\lambda^2\log\lambda)$ and $O(\lambda\log\lambda)$.

4   Optimizations and Concrete Parameters

In order to decrease the sizes of a lattice-based scheme, a common approach is to replace $\mathbb{Z}$ with a cyclotomic polynomial ring of the form $\mathcal{R} = \mathbb{Z}[x]/(1 + x^n)$, where n is a power of 2, and to rely on the intractability of the module versions of SIS and LWE [BGV12, LS15]. Gaussian distributions are extended by considering the coefficients of the polynomials.

4.1   Description of the Module-Based Scheme

In this section, we propose parameters for an optimized, module version of the $\mathsf{G} + \mathsf{G}$ signature, that we present in Fig. 4.

As in Sect. 3, let $m > 0$, $k > m + 1$ and $\ell = 1$. Let $\mathbf{j} = (\zeta^*, 0, \ldots, 0) \in \mathcal{R}^m$, where $\zeta = 1 + x^{n/2}$ and $\zeta^* = 1 - x^{n/2}$ satisfy $\zeta^*\zeta = 2 \bmod 1 + x^n$. The challenge space is $\mathcal{R}/\zeta^*\mathcal{R}$. We let $\eta > 0$ and $\chi_\eta = U(\{y \in \mathcal{R} | \|y\|_\infty \leq \eta\})$. Given $s \in \mathcal{R}$, we define $\mathsf{rot}(s)$ as the $n \times n$ matrix whose (i, j)-th entry is the coefficient of degree $n - 1 - j$ of $x^i \cdot s \bmod 1 + x^n$. This matrix maps the coefficient embedding of a polynomial c to the coefficient embedding of sc. We extend this definition to vectors coordinate-wise and we define $\mathbf{\Sigma}(\mathbf{s}) = \mathbf{\Sigma}(\mathsf{rot}(\mathbf{s}))$, where $\mathbf{\Sigma}$ is borrowed from Sect. 3. This gives rise to the signature scheme presented in Fig. 4.

KeyGen(1^λ) :	Sign$(\mathbf{A}, \mathbf{s}, \mu)$:	Verify$(\mathbf{A}, \mu, \mathbf{z}, c)$:
1: $\mathbf{A}_0 \leftarrow U(\mathcal{R}_q^{m \times k - m - 1})$	1: $\mathbf{y} \leftarrow D_{\mathcal{R}^k, \mathbf{\Sigma}(\mathbf{s})}$	1: $\mathbf{w} \leftarrow \mathbf{A}\mathbf{z} - qc\mathbf{j} \bmod 2q$
2: do $(\mathbf{s}_1, \mathbf{s}_2) \leftarrow \chi_\eta^{k-m-1} \times \chi_\eta^m$	2: $\mathbf{w} \leftarrow \mathbf{A}\mathbf{y} \bmod 2q$	2: if $c = H(\mathbf{w}, \mu)$
3: $\mathbf{s} \leftarrow (1|\mathbf{s}_1^\top|\mathbf{s}_2^\top)^\top \in \mathcal{R}_{2q}^k$	3: $c \leftarrow H(\mathbf{w}, \mu)$	3: and $\|\mathbf{z}\| \leq \gamma$ then
4: while $\|\zeta\mathbf{s}\| \geq S$	4: $u \leftarrow D_{\mathcal{R}, s, -c/2}$	4: return 1
5: $\mathbf{b} \leftarrow \mathbf{A}_0\mathbf{s}_1 + \mathbf{s}_2 \bmod q$	5: $\mathbf{z} \leftarrow \mathbf{y} + (\zeta u + c)\mathbf{s}$	5: end if
6: $\mathbf{A} \leftarrow (-2\mathbf{b} + q\mathbf{j}|2\mathbf{A}_0|2\mathbf{I}_m)$	6: return $(\mathbf{z}, c)$	6: return 0
7: return $(\mathsf{vk}, \mathsf{sk}) = (\mathbf{A}, \mathbf{s})$		

Fig. 4. The Module $\mathsf{G} + \mathsf{G}$ Signature Scheme.

Beyond relying on polynomial rings, we consider various improvements and optimizations, which we discuss now.

KeyGen: The key generation step includes a rejection sampling step. The threshold S will be set such that about 50% of the keys will be rejected. This helps controlling the upper bound on the smoothing parameter of the secret lattice.

Sign: Instead of computing $\mathbf{z} = \mathbf{y} + (2u + c)\mathbf{s}$, we compute $\mathbf{z} = \mathbf{y} + (\zeta u + c)\mathbf{s}$. As $\mathbf{As} = \mathbf{j} \bmod 2q$, we have $\zeta \mathbf{As} = \mathbf{0} \bmod 2q$ by definition of $\mathbf{j}$. Thus, the identity $\mathbf{Az} - q c \mathbf{j} = \mathbf{Ay} \bmod 2q$ still holds. The main advantage of this modification is that the secret lattice is now $\zeta s \mathcal{R}$ instead of $2s\mathcal{R}$, whose smoothing parameter is a factor $\sqrt{2}$ smaller.

Verify: The verification bound is set to $\gamma = 1.01 \cdot \sqrt{nk}\sigma$, and the signer may verify that its signature is accepted before outputting it, up to restarting in the somewhat rare event that it is not.

An analysis similar to the one from the previous section would bring the following result. We omit the QROM analysis relying on the lossy-soundness, as the concrete parameters we propose in the next section are outside of the parameters range required for this analysis to hold.

Theorem 5. *Let $n > 0$ be a power of two defining a polynomial ring $\mathcal{R} = \mathbb{Z}[x]/(x^n + 1)$. Let $m > 0$, $k > m + 1$, $\varepsilon \in (0, 1/2]$, $s \geq \sqrt{2\ln(n - 1 + 2n/\varepsilon)/\pi}$ and $\sigma \geq \sqrt{2}\sigma_1(\mathbf{S}) \cdot s$ for all $\mathbf{S} \in \mathbb{Z}^{kn \times n}$ in the range of $\mathsf{rot}(\mathsf{IGen})$. Let γ and ε_c be such that $\Pr_{\mathbf{z} \hookleftarrow D_{\mathcal{R}^k, \sigma}}[\|\mathbf{z}\| > \gamma] \leq \varepsilon_c/3$. Let $q > \max(2\gamma, \sigma \cdot \eta_\varepsilon(\mathbb{Z}^{mn}))$ be an odd modulus.*

Then the signature scheme from Fig. 4 is ε_c-correct and EU-CMA-secure in the ROM under the $\mathsf{MSIS}_{n,m,k,q,2\gamma}$ assumption. Namely, for any adversary $\mathcal{A}$ against the EU-CMA security of $\mathsf{FS}[\mathsf{G} + \mathsf{G}, H]$ making at most Q_S sign queries and at most Q_H hash queries, there is an adversary $\mathcal{B}$ against the $\mathsf{MSIS}_{n,m,k,q,2\gamma}$ assumption such that:

$$\mathsf{Adv}^{\mathsf{EU-CMA}}(\mathcal{A}) \leq \left(\frac{1 + \varepsilon}{1 - \varepsilon}\right)^{Q_S} \left[Q_H \cdot \left(\sqrt{\mathsf{Adv}^{\mathsf{MSIS}_{n,m,k,q,2\gamma}}(\mathcal{B})} + \frac{2}{|\mathcal{C}|}\right)\right] + 3Q_S/2 \cdot \sqrt{(Q_H + Q_S + 1) \cdot s^{-mn}} \ .$$

This bound holds when $\mathcal{A}$ is an adversary against the sEU-CMA security of the scheme by adding an extra "$+Q_S \cdot s^{-m}$" term on the right hand side.

4.2 Concrete Parameters

We now give concrete parameters and estimates of the public key and signature sizes resulting from these optimizations in Table 1. This gives rise to the following estimates. The script we used is derived from the one provided with Dilithium [DKL+18] and is available as supplementary material. We made the following additional assumptions:

- We use the compression technique from [BG14] to get rid of the lower $\log \alpha$ bits of the signature, except the lowest.[1] The hint resulting from the compression technique is assumed to follow a Gaussian distribution whose standard

---

[1] As our key generation algorithm outputs a $\mathbf{A}$ with $2\mathbf{I}_m$, what we cut is cyclically bit-shifted.

Table 1. Parameter sets for the Module $G + G$ signature scheme. Numbers in parentheses for SIS security are for strong unforgeability.

Target Security	120	180	260
n	256	256	256
q	95233	50177	202753
S	23.33	27.59	32.97
s	14.22	14.22	14.22
σ	331.91	392.57	469.12
γ	13885.1830	18857.9404	33367.4202
$(m, k - m)$	(2,4)	(3,5)	(4,7)
η	1	1	1
α	128	128	1024
BKZ block-size b to break SIS	415 (338)	619 (512)	924 (777)
Best Known Classical bit-cost	121 (98)	181 (149)	270 (227)
Best Known Quantum bit-cost	106 (86)	159 (131)	237 (199)
BKZ block-size b to break LWE	411	615	895
Best Known Classical bit-cost	120	179	261
Best Known Quantum bit-cost	105	158	230
Signature size with rANS	1542	2033	2518
Expected public key size	1120	1568	2336
Sum	2662	3601	4854
Signature size [DFPS22]	1903	2473	3461
Public Key size	800	1056	1760
Sum	2703	3529	5221
Signature size [CCD+23]	1463	2337	2908
Public Key size	992	1472	2080
Sum	2455	3809	4988

deviation is $\sqrt{2}\sigma/\alpha$. The technique presented in [DKL+18] can be readily adapted to the mod $2q$ setting. This comes at the cost of increasing the verification bound to $\gamma = 1.01 \cdot \sqrt{nk}\sigma + \sqrt{nm}(1 + \alpha/4)$ to take into account the inaccuracy of the commitment recovered by the verifier.
- The final signature is compressed using range Asymmetric Numeral System, as explained in [ETWY22]. For simplicity, we assume that this gives expected bitsizes equal to the entropy of the compressed vector.

For comparison, we include in Table 1 a reminder on estimated sizes of optimized Lyubashevsky signatures from [DFPS22], in the hyperball setting, as well as the experimental sizes of Haetae [CCD+23], which implements the bimodal hyperball. As far as we are aware of, these are the lowest signatures and key sizes provided in the literature for Lyubashevsky's signatures (when using the core-SVP hardness methodology to estimate security). We note that the resulting signature sizes are 20% to 30% smaller than those from [DFPS22]. The asymptotic gain of our signature is observable when comparing the signature sizes with Haetae, as the tradeoff is first in their favor but ends up in our favor for the higher security level, up to 16% of savings. However, the sum of the public key and the signature sizes is somewhat similar across the three signatures. This is due to the fact that in the non-bimodal setting, a practical optimization due to [DKL+18] consists in truncating the low bits of the public key, at the cost of increasing the verification bound. While such a technique is also implemented in Haetae, its efficiency is relative in this setting, and we chose not to incorporate it in G + G for the sake of simplicity.

4.3   Optimized NTRU Key Generation Algorithm

We can alternatively use the NTRU-based key generation algorithm described in [DDLL13]. In our setting, it is possible to improve it, by relying on the aforementioned technique based on the divisibility of 2 by $(1 + x^{n/2})$. This leads to the key generation algorithm presented in Fig. 5.

KeyGen(1^λ) :
1: **do** $(f, g) \hookleftarrow U(\{\mathbf{x} \in \mathbb{R}^2[\|\mathbf{x}\|_\infty \leq \eta\})$
2: **while** $\|(\zeta f|2x^{n/2}g + \zeta)\| \geq S$ or f non-invertible mod q
3: $\mathbf{h} \leftarrow [\zeta g + 1]/f \bmod q$
4: $\mathbf{A} \leftarrow (\zeta^*(q-1)h \mid \zeta^*) \bmod 2q$
5: $\mathbf{s} \leftarrow (f \mid \zeta g + 1)^\top$
6: **return** vk = $\mathbf{A}$ and sk = $(\mathbf{A}, \mathbf{s})$

Fig. 5. NTRU KeyGen for G + G

The algorithm outputs keys $\mathbf{A}$ and $(\mathbf{A}, \mathbf{s})$ satisfying $\mathbf{As} = \zeta^* q \bmod 2q$ as it holds that $(q-1)hf = (q-1)(\zeta g + 1) \bmod 2q$ since $(q-1)$ is even. This implies that $\zeta \mathbf{As} = 0 \bmod 2q$, and the lattice that needs to be smoothed out is $\zeta \mathbf{s} \mathcal{R}$ where $\zeta \mathbf{s}^\top = (\zeta f|2x^{n/2}g + \zeta)$. We then propose two sets of parameters in Table 2, for ring dimensions 512 and 1024. The former leads to only around 90 bits of security, but the latter allows to reach NIST security level III. While the sum $|\mathsf{vk}| + |\mathsf{sig}|$ is similar to those of the other schemes, we note that the signature size is further decreased, compared to module G + G. The resulting signature is 40% smaller than [DFPS22] and 55% smaller than Dilithium.

Table 2. Parameter Sets for NTRU $G + G$.

Target Security	90	180
n	512	1024
q	32257	45569
S	43.73	36.11
KeyGen acceptance rate	0.25	0.5
s	14.32	14.42
σ	626.49	520.75
B	21719.152	40218.387
η	2	1
α	256	2048
BKZ block-size b to break SIS	314 (238)	740 (622)
Best Known Classical bit-cost	91 (69)	216 (181)
Best Known Quantum bit-cost	80 (61)	190 (159)
BKZ block-size b to break LWE	305	616
Best Known Classical bit-cost	89	180
Best Known Quantum bit-cost	78	158
Signature size with rANS	974	1497
Expected public key size	992	2080
Sum	1966	3577

Acknowledgment. This work was supported by the France 2030 ANR Project ANR-22-PECY-003 SecureCompute, the France 2030 ANR Project ANR-22-PETQ-0008 PQ-TLS and the AMIRAL ANR grant (ANR-21-ASTR-0016),

A   The Fiat-Shamir Transform

In this section, we recall the Fiat-Shamir transform, which allows to transform an identification scheme into a digital signature. It removes interaction by sampling the challenge as a hash function evaluation $H(w, \mu)$ with w being the prover's commitment and μ the signed message. The hash function is then modeled as a random oracle in the analysis. The signature is the pair (w, z), which is verified by checking validity of the transcript $(w, H(w, \mu), z)$.

As the challenge c being typically much shorter than w, it is desirable to replace w by c in the signature. This is possible if the underlying identification scheme is commitment-recoverable (see Definition 2). Verification simply starts by recovering $w \leftarrow \mathsf{Rec}(\mathsf{vk}, c, z)$. Our protocol satisfies this property, thus we describe the signature obtained applying this version of the Fiat-Shamir transform. See Fig. 6.

For the sake of completeness, we state the following lemma arguing correctness of the signature scheme $\mathsf{FS}[\mathsf{ID}, H]$, which immediately follows from the completeness and commitment-recoverability of the underlying identification scheme.

$\mathsf{KeyGen}(1^\lambda):$
  1: $(\mathsf{vk}, \mathsf{sk}) \leftarrow \mathsf{IGen}(1^\lambda)$
  2: **return** vk and sk

$\mathsf{Sign}(\mathsf{sk}, \mu):$
  1: $(w, \mathsf{st}) \leftarrow \mathsf{P}_1(\mathsf{sk})$
  2: $c \leftarrow H(w, \mu)$
  3: $z \leftarrow \mathsf{P}_2(\mathsf{sk}, \mathsf{st}, w, c)$
  4: **return** (c, z)

$\mathsf{Verify}(\mathsf{vk}, (c, z), \mu):$
  1: $w \leftarrow \mathsf{Rec}(\mathsf{vk}, c, z)$
  2: **if** $c \neq H(w, \mu)$ **then**
  3:     **return** 0
  4: **end if**
  5: **return** $\mathsf{V}(\mathsf{vk}, (w, c, z))$

Fig. 6. Fiat-Shamir Signature FS[ID, H].

Lemma 8. *Let* ID $=$ (IGen, P, V) *denote an identification scheme. Further assume that* ID *is ε-complete and commitment-recoverable. Then the signature scheme* FS[ID, H] *described in Fig. 6 is ε-correct in the ROM.*

Security of FS[ID, H] can be proven by successive claims. First, one can reduce EU-CMA security of FS[ID, H] to its EU-NMA security assuming ID has large commitment min-entropy and is honest-verifier zero-knowledge (see Definition 3). This can be shown by relying on the following theorem.

Theorem 6 (Adapted from [GHHM21], Theorem 3). *Let* ID *be an identification scheme which has α-min-entropy and satisfies ε-statistical HVZK. Let H a hash function modeled as a random oracle. Then, for any (possibly quantum) adversary $\mathcal{A}$ against the EU-CMA security of* FS[ID, H] *making at most Q_S (classical) sign queries and at most Q_H (possibly quantum) hash queries, there exists an adversary $\mathcal{B}$ against the EU-NMA security of* FS[ID, H] *such that:*

$$\mathsf{Adv}^{\mathsf{EU-CMA}}(\mathcal{A}) \leq \mathsf{Adv}^{\mathsf{EU-NMA}}(\mathcal{B}) + Q_S\varepsilon + 3\frac{Q_S}{2} \cdot \sqrt{(Q_H + Q_S + 1) \cdot 2^{-\alpha}} .$$

Furthermore, if ID *is $(1 + \varepsilon)$-divergence HVZK, the following bound applies:*

$$\mathsf{Adv}^{\mathsf{EU-CMA}}(\mathcal{A}) \leq (1 + \varepsilon)^{Q_S} \mathsf{Adv}^{\mathsf{EU-NMA}}(\mathcal{B}) + 3Q_S/2 \cdot \sqrt{(Q_H + Q_S + 1) \cdot 2^{-\alpha}} .$$

The result can be adapted to sEU-CMA security by adding $Q_S 2^{-\alpha}$ to the bounds.

It remains to prove EU-NMA-security to conclude the security analysis, which can be argued via the following statement for lossy identification schemes (see Definition 4).

Theorem 7 ([KLS18], Theorem 3.4). *Let* ID *be a lossy identification scheme satisfying $\varepsilon_{\mathsf{ls}}$-lossy soundness for some $\varepsilon_{\mathsf{ls}} > 0$. Let H a hash function modeled as a random oracle. For any (possibly quantum) adversary $\mathcal{A}$ against the EU-NMA security of* FS[ID, H] *making at most Q_H (possibly quantum) hash queries, there exists a quantum adversary $\mathcal{B}$ against the lossiness of* ID *such that*

$$\mathsf{Adv}^{\mathsf{EU-NMA}}(\mathcal{A}) \leq \mathsf{Adv}^{\mathsf{lossiness}}(\mathcal{B}) + 8(Q_H + 1)^2 \cdot \varepsilon_{\mathsf{ls}} .$$

Finally, we describe a reduction in the (classical) ROM which relies on weaker properties compared to the above QROM reduction. Various folklore reductions are known in this setting, and we consider a variant based on special soundness (see Definition 5), which is first reduced to the soundness as recalled below.

Definition 11 (Soundness). *Let* $\mathsf{ID} = (\mathsf{Igen}, \mathsf{P}, \mathsf{V})$ *be an identification scheme. It is* sound *if for any PPT adversary* $\mathcal{A}$, *the quantity*

$$\Pr\left[\mathsf{V}(\mathsf{vk}, (w, c, z)) = 1 \mid (w, c, z) \leftarrow \mathcal{A}(\mathsf{vk})\right]$$

is $\mathsf{negl}(\lambda)$, *where the probability is over the choice of* vk *and the coins of* $\mathcal{A}$.

We recall the Reset Lemma, which is a standard reduction between soundness and special soundness.

Lemma 9 (Reset Lemma [BP02]). *Let* $\mathsf{ID} = (\mathsf{Igen}, \mathsf{P}, \mathsf{V})$ *be an identification scheme. Given any adversary* $\mathcal{A}$ *against the soundness of* ID, *there exists an adversary* $\mathcal{B}$ *against the special soundness of* ID *such that*

$$\mathsf{Adv}^{\mathsf{special-sound}}(\mathcal{B}) \geq \left(\mathsf{Adv}^{\mathsf{sound}}(\mathcal{A}) - \frac{1}{|\mathcal{C}|}\right)^2.$$

While this result is folklore, we finally show that special soundness implies EU-NMA security in the ROM.

Lemma 10. *Let* ID *be an identification scheme and* H *a hash function modeled as a random oracle. For any adversary* $\mathcal{A}$ *against the EU-NMA security of* $\mathsf{FS}[\mathsf{ID}, H]$ *making* Q_H *classical hash queries, there exists an adversary* $\mathcal{B}$ *against the special soundness of* ID *such that:*

$$\mathsf{Adv}^{\mathsf{EU-NMA}}(\mathcal{A}) \leq Q_H \cdot \left(\sqrt{\mathsf{Adv}^{\mathsf{special-sound}}(\mathcal{B})} + \frac{2}{|\mathcal{C}|}\right).$$

Proof. We first reduce the soundness of ID to the EU-NMA security of $\mathsf{FS}[\mathsf{ID}, H]$. First, if $\mathcal{A}$ outputs a forgery $(\mu^*, (c^*, z^*))$ such that $H(\mathsf{Rec}(\mathsf{vk}, c^*, z^*), \mu^*)$ was never queried, it has probability at most $1/|\mathcal{C}|$ of outputting a valid forgery.

The reduction $\mathcal{B}'$ guesses the hash query $H(w^*, \mu^*)$ made by $\mathcal{A}$ which is used in $\mathcal{A}$'s forgery. When this query is made, $\mathcal{B}'$ answers it by running sending w^* as commitments to its challenger. The latter replies with a challenge c^* and $\mathcal{B}'$ programs $H(w^*, \mu^*)$ as c^*. With probability $1/Q_H$, $\mathcal{B}'$'s guess is correct and the adversary $\mathcal{A}$ halts with a forgery $(\mu^*, (c^*, z^*))$ with $\mathsf{Rec}(\mathsf{vk}, c^*, z^*) = w^*$. We then have

$$\mathsf{Adv}^{\mathsf{sound}}(\mathcal{B}') \geq \frac{1}{Q_H} \cdot \mathsf{Adv}^{\mathsf{EU-NMA}}(\mathcal{A}) - 1/|\mathcal{C}|.$$

Finally, Lemma 9 gives an adversary $\mathcal{B}$ against the special soundness such that

$$\mathsf{Adv}^{\mathsf{special-sound}}(\mathcal{B}) \geq \left(\mathsf{Adv}^{\mathsf{sound}}(\mathcal{B}') - \frac{1}{|\mathcal{C}|}\right)^2,$$

which completes the proof.   □

B   Related Work

In Fig. 7, we give a simplified version of the Eagle signature scheme described in [YJW23] (with our notations from Sect. 4 and an extra parameter $\gamma' > 0$). Minor differences with the scheme from Fig. 4 include the facts that Eagle works in the ring setting as opposed to the module setting, that a parameterizable integer p is considered while we work with $p = 2$, and that the RLWE sample from Eagle is computed modulo $Q = pq$, while we use MLWE samples computed modulo q. The exact signing algorithm from [YJW23] is omitting some elements of the final vector $\mathbf{z}$ to optimize compactness, but we do not consider this optimization to better illustrate the relationship with $\mathsf{G} + \mathsf{G}$. Moreover, as usual in hash-and-sign schemes, the message is padded using some salt, chosen as a uniform 320-bit long bitstring.

KeyGen(1^λ):	Sign($\mathbf{A}, \mathbf{s}, \mu$):	Verify($\mathbf{A}, \mu, \sigma$)
1: $\mathbf{a}_0 \hookleftarrow U(\mathcal{R}_q)$	1: $\mathsf{salt} \hookleftarrow U(\{0,1\}^{320})$	1: $\sigma = (\mathsf{salt}, \mathbf{z})$
2: $(\mathbf{s}_1, \mathbf{s}_2) \hookleftarrow \chi_\eta \times \chi_\eta$	2: $\mathbf{S} = \mathsf{rot}(\mathbf{s})$	2: $u \leftarrow H(\mu, \mathsf{salt})$
3: $\mathbf{s} \leftarrow (1|\mathbf{s}_1|\mathbf{s}_2)^\top \in \mathcal{R}_{2q}^3$	3: $\mathbf{y} \hookleftarrow D_{\mathcal{R}^3, \sigma^2 \mathbf{I}_{3n} - 4s^2 \mathbf{S}\mathbf{S}^\top}$	3: $z' \leftarrow u - \mathbf{A}\mathbf{z}$
4: $\mathbf{b} \leftarrow \mathbf{a}_0 \mathbf{s}_1 + \mathbf{s}_2 \bmod Q$	4: $u \leftarrow H'(\mu, \mathsf{salt})$	4: Accept if $\|\mathbf{z}\| \leq \gamma$
5: $\mathbf{A} \leftarrow (q - \mathbf{b}|\mathbf{a}_0|1)$	5: $u' \leftarrow u - \mathbf{A}\mathbf{y} \bmod Q$	and $\|z'\| \leq \gamma'$
6: **return** (vk, sk) = $(\mathbf{A}, \mathbf{s})$	6: $c \leftarrow \lfloor u' \rceil_q$	
	7: $k \leftarrow D_{\mathcal{R}, s, -c/2}$	
	8: $\mathbf{z} \leftarrow \mathbf{y} + \mathbf{S}c + p\mathbf{S}k$	
	9: **return** (salt, $\mathbf{z}$)	

Fig. 7. Simplified Eagle Signature Scheme.

We now explain how to decompose Eagle as an instance of $\mathsf{G} + \mathsf{G}$ with a specific hash function, as well as the differences that arise during verification due to this hash function, following the steps of [CLMQ21]. The instance of the hash function H that turns the signing algorithm of $\mathsf{G} + \mathsf{G}$ into a simplified version of Eagle is described in Steps 3, 4 and 5 of the signing algorithm from Fig. 7. It proceeds as follows. On input $w \in \mathcal{R}$, μ and salt, the function H computes a target $u = H'(\mu, \mathsf{salt})$ using another hash function H' and sets $u' = u - w$. The challenge is then $\lfloor u' \rceil_q$, i.e., a rounding of u' to the $q\mathcal{R}$ lattice.

The verification algorithm differs substantially due to the fact that Verify is aware of the inner workings of the hash function. It knows in particular that $\mathbf{A}\mathbf{z} = \mathbf{A}\mathbf{y} + qc \bmod Q \approx u$. However, the challenge c is omitted from the signature and instead of checking that $H(\mathbf{A}\mathbf{z} - qc, \mu, \mathsf{salt}) = c$, it checks that $u - \mathbf{A}\mathbf{z}$ is sufficiently short, i.e., has norm smaller than γ'. While this check is less accurate than recomputing the hash value, it allows one to omit c in the signature, hence reducing its size. Finally, the verification algorithm also checks that $\mathbf{z}$ has norm $\leq \gamma$, as in Fig. 4.

References

[ASY22]   Agrawal, S., Stehlé, D., Yadav, A.: Round-optimal lattice-based threshold signatures, revisited. In: ICALP (2022)

[BBD+23] Barbosa, M., et al.: Fixing and mechanizing the security proof of Fiat-Shamir with aborts and Dilithium. In: CRYPTO (2023)

[BCM21]   Behnia, R., Chen, Y., Masny, D.: On removing rejection conditions in practical lattice-based signatures. In: Cheon, J.H., Tillich, J.-P. (eds.) PQCrypto 2021 2021. LNCS, vol. 12841, pp. 380–398. Springer, Cham (2021). https://doi.org/10.1007/978-3-030-81293-5_20

[BF11]   Boneh, D., Freeman, D.M.: Linearly homomorphic signatures over binary fields and new tools for lattice-based signatures. In: Catalano, D., Fazio, N., Gennaro, R., Nicolosi, A. (eds.) PKC 2011. LNCS, vol. 6571, pp. 1–16. Springer, Heidelberg (2011). https://doi.org/10.1007/978-3-642-19379-8_1

[BG14]   Bai, S., Galbraith, S.D.: An improved compression technique for signatures based on learning with errors. In: Benaloh, J. (ed.) CT-RSA 2014. LNCS, vol. 8366, pp. 28–47. Springer, Cham (2014). https://doi.org/10.1007/978-3-319-04852-9_2

[BGV12]   Brakerski, Z., Gentry, C., Vaikuntanathan, V.: (Leveled) fully homomorphic encryption without bootstrapping. In: ITCS (2012)

[BLP+13] Brakerski, Z., Langlois, A., Peikert, C., Regev, O., Stehlé, D.: Classical hardness of learning with errors. In: STOC (2013)

[BMKMS22] Mera, J.M.B., Karmakar, A., Marc, T., Soleimanian, A.: Efficient lattice-based inner-product functional encryption. In: Hanaoka, G., Shikata, J., Watanabe, Y. (eds.) PKC 2022. LNCS, vol. 13178, pp. 163–193. Springer, Cham (2022). https://doi.org/10.1007/978-3-030-97131-1_6

[BP02]   Bellare, M., Palacio, A.: GQ and Schnorr identification schemes: proofs of security against impersonation under active and concurrent attacks. In: Yung, M. (ed.) CRYPTO 2002. LNCS, vol. 2442, pp. 162–177. Springer, Heidelberg (2002). https://doi.org/10.1007/3-540-45708-9_11

[CCD+23] Cheon, J.H., et al.: HAETAE: shorter lattice-based Fiat-Shamir signatures. Cryptology ePrint Archive (2023). https://ia.cr/2023/624

[CLMQ21] Chen, Y., Lombardi, A., Ma, F., Quach, W.: Does Fiat-Shamir require a cryptographic hash function? In: Malkin, T., Peikert, C. (eds.) CRYPTO 2021. LNCS, vol. 12828, pp. 334–363. Springer, Cham (2021). https://doi.org/10.1007/978-3-030-84259-8_12

[DDLL13] Ducas, L., Durmus, A., Lepoint, T., Lyubashevsky, V.: Lattice signatures and bimodal gaussians. In: Canetti, R., Garay, J.A. (eds.) CRYPTO 2013. LNCS, vol. 8042, pp. 40–56. Springer, Heidelberg (2013). https://doi.org/10.1007/978-3-642-40041-4_3

[DFPS22] Devevey, J., Fawzi, O., Passelègue, A., Stehlé, D.: On rejection sampling in Lyubashevsky's signature scheme. In: Agrawal, S., Lin, D. (eds.) ASIACRYPT 2022. LNCS, vol. 13794, pp. 34–64. Springer, Cham (2022)

[DFPS23] Devevey, J., Fallahpour, P., Passelègue, A., Stehlé, D.: A detailed analysis of Fiat-Shamir with aborts. In: CRYPTO (2023)

[DKL+18] Ducas, L., et al.: Crystals-Dilithium: a lattice-based digital signature scheme. IACR TCHES (2018)

[DPSZ12] Damgård, I., Pastro, V., Smart, N., Zakarias, S.: Multiparty computation from somewhat homomorphic encryption. In: Safavi-Naini, R., Canetti,

R. (eds.) CRYPTO 2012. LNCS, vol. 7417, pp. 643–662. Springer, Heidelberg (2012). https://doi.org/10.1007/978-3-642-32009-5_38

[Duc14] Ducas, L.: Accelerating Bliss: the geometry of ternary polynomials. Cryptology ePrint Archive (2014). https://ia.cr/2014/874

[ETWY22] Espitau, T., Tibouchi, M., Wallet, A., Yu, Y.: Shorter hash-and-sign lattice-based signatures. In: Dodis, Y., Shrimpton, T. (eds.) CRYPTO 2022. LNCS, vol. 13508, pp. 245–275. Springer, Cham (2022). https://doi.org/10.1007/978-3-031-15979-4_9

[FS86] Fiat, A., Shamir, A.: How to prove yourself: practical solutions to identification and signature problems. In: Odlyzko, A.M. (ed.) CRYPTO 1986. LNCS, vol. 263, pp. 186–194. Springer, Heidelberg (1987). https://doi.org/10.1007/3-540-47721-7_12

[GHHM21] Grilo, A.B., Hövelmanns, K., Hülsing, A., Majenz, C.: Tight adaptive reprogramming in the QROM. In: Tibouchi, M., Wang, H. (eds.) ASIACRYPT 2021. LNCS, vol. 13090, pp. 637–667. Springer, Cham (2021). https://doi.org/10.1007/978-3-030-92062-3_22

[GPV08] Gentry, C., Peikert, C., Vaikuntanathan, V.: Trapdoors for hard lattices and new cryptographic constructions. In: STOC (2008)

[Kle00] Klein, P.N.: Finding the closest lattice vector when it's unusually close. In: SODA (2000)

[KLS18] Kiltz, E., Lyubashevsky, V., Schaffner, C.: A concrete treatment of Fiat-Shamir signatures in the quantum random-oracle model. In: Nielsen, J.B., Rijmen, V. (eds.) EUROCRYPT 2018. LNCS, vol. 10822, pp. 552–586. Springer, Cham (2018). https://doi.org/10.1007/978-3-319-78372-7_18

[LS15] Langlois, A., Stehlé, D.: Worst-case to average-case reductions for module lattices. Designs, Codes and Cryptography (2015)

[Lyu09] Lyubashevsky, V.: Fiat-Shamir with aborts: applications to lattice and factoring-based signatures. In: Matsui, M. (ed.) ASIACRYPT 2009. LNCS, vol. 5912, pp. 598–616. Springer, Heidelberg (2009). https://doi.org/10.1007/978-3-642-10366-7_35

[Lyu12] Lyubashevsky, V.: Lattice signatures without trapdoors. In: Pointcheval, D., Johansson, T. (eds.) EUROCRYPT 2012. LNCS, vol. 7237, pp. 738–755. Springer, Heidelberg (2012). https://doi.org/10.1007/978-3-642-29011-4_43

[MR07] Micciancio, D., Regev, O.: Worst-case to average-case reductions based on Gaussian measures. SIAM J. Comput. $37(1)$, 267–302 (2007)

[Reg09] Regev, O.: On lattices, learning with errors, random linear codes, and cryptography. J. ACM $56(6)$, 1–40 (2009)

[Sch91] Schnorr, C.-P.: Efficient Signature Generation by Smart Cards. J. Cryptol. 4, 161–174 (1991)

[vEH14] van Erven, T., Harremos, P.: Rényi divergence and Kullback-Leibler divergence. IEEE T. Inform. Theory $60(7)$, 3797–3820 (2014)

[YJW23] Yu, Y., Jia, H., Wang, X.: Compact lattice gadget and its applications to hash-and-sign signatures. In: CRYPTO (2023)

[ZXZ18] Zheng, Z., Xu, G., Zhao, C.: Discrete Gaussian measures and new bounds of the smoothing parameter for lattices. Cryptology ePrint Archive (2018). https://ia.cr/2018/786

On Gaussian Sampling, Smoothing Parameter and Application to Signatures

Thomas Espitau[1] , Alexandre Wallet[2] , and Yang Yu[3,4,5]([✉])

[1] PQShield SAS, Paris, France
[2] Inria, IRISA, Univ. Rennes, CNRS, Rennes, France
[3] BNRist, Tsinghua University, Beijing, China
[4] Zhongguancun Laboratory, Beijing, China
[5] National Financial Cryptography Research Center, Beijing, China
yu-yang@mail.tsinghua.edu.cn

Abstract. We present a general framework for polynomial-time lattice Gaussian sampling. It revolves around a systematic study of the discrete Gaussian measure and its samplers under *extensions* of lattices; we first show that given lattices $\Lambda' \subset \Lambda$ we can sample efficiently in Λ if we know how to do so in Λ' and the quotient Λ/Λ', *regardless* of the primitivity of Λ'. As a direct application, we tackle the problem of domain extension and restriction for sampling and propose a sampler tailored for lattice *filtrations*, which can be seen as a broad generalization of the celebrated Klein's sampler. Then, we demonstrate how to sample using a change of bases, or even switching the ambient space, even when the target lattice is not represented as full-rank in the ambient space. We show how to correct the induced distortion with the "convolution-like" technique of Peikert (Crypto 2010) (which we encompass as a byproduct). Since our framework aims at modularity and leverage the combinations of smaller samplers to build new ones, we also propose ad-hoc samplers for the so-called *root lattices* A_n, D_n, E_n as base cases, extending the state-of-the-art for root lattice sampling, which was limited to $\mathbf{Z}^n$. We also show how our framework blends with the so-called $k$ing construction and provides a sampler for the remarkable Leech and Barnes-Wall lattices.

As a by-product, we obtain novel, quasi-linear samplers for prime and smooth conductor (as $2^\ell 3^k$) cyclotomic rings, achieving essentially optimal Gaussian width. In a practice-oriented application, we showcase the impact of our work on hash-and-sign signatures over NTRU lattices. In the best case, we can gain around 200 bytes (which corresponds to an improvement greater than 20%) on the signature size. We also improve the new gadget-based constructions (Yu, Jia, Wang, Crypto 2023) and gain up to 110 bytes for the resulting signatures.

Lastly, we sprinkle our exposition with several new estimates for the smoothing parameter of lattices, stemming from our algorithmic constructions and by novel methods based on series reversion.

© International Association for Cryptologic Research 2023
J. Guo and R. Steinfeld (Eds.): ASIACRYPT 2023, LNCS 14444, pp. 65–97, 2023.
https://doi.org/10.1007/978-981-99-8739-9_3

1   Introduction

For the last few decades, lattices have proved themselves to be a cornerstone of modern cryptography, allowing the development of feature-rich schemes, including digital signatures [9,15,29], identity-based encryption [18], functional encryption [2], (non-interactive) zero-knowledge proofs [27] and last but not least fully homomorphic encryption [4,17]. A common denominator of many such schemes revolves around the ability of sampling from the so-called *discrete Gaussian distribution* over a given lattice Λ. Given a center $\mathbf{c}$ in the ambient space $\Lambda_{\mathbf{R}}$ and a "width" s — which is essentially the standard deviation by analogy with the normal distribution — the distribution $\mathcal{D}_{\Lambda,\mathbf{c},s^2}$ assigns the vector $\mathbf{v} \in \Lambda$ the probability proportional to the Gaussian function $\exp(-\pi\|\mathbf{v} - \mathbf{c}\|^2/s^2)$. Remark that this distribution only depends on the lattice and not on the basis used to represent it. In this sense it does not leak any information about a possible secret basis: this "zero-knowledge" property accounts for its utility in cryptography.

For specific lattices such as $\mathbf{Z}^n$ or lattices stemming from some trapdoor sampling as in [23], *ad-hoc* approaches are commonly used. In comparison, to sample in an *a priori arbitrary* lattice, two polynomial time samplers are well-known and widely used in constructions and beyond: the so-called *Klein* sampler (or GPV sampler) [18] and the *Peikert* sampler [25], both having different advantages and drawbacks. The former is a *sequential* sampler: the algorithm performs adaptive iterations of sampling in projected lines, where the choices made in each iteration affect the values used in the next. It is rather costly and imposes to work with the Gram-Schmidt orthogonalization of the input basis. The latter is a naturally parallel sampler, reducing the problem of sampling in Λ to sample the coefficients of the desired sample on the input basis. This "change of basis" induces a distortion, blurred by convolving with a sufficiently wide perturbation. It is faster than Klein's sampler at the price of slightly worse quality, in the sense that the minimal sampleable width is larger. Note that these two algorithms correspond to the randomization of two famous polynomial time oracles for the (approximate) Closest Vector Problem from Babai [3]: the Klein sampler corresponds to the *nearest plane* algorithm and the Peikert sampler to the *rounding* algorithm. Fine-tuning such algorithms is one of the main tasks for designers of signatures in the hash-then-sign framework of [10,18].

On Hash-and-sign Digital Signatures. Designing, selecting, and analyzing quantum-resistant schemes is the main goal et Designing, selecting, and analyzing quantum-resistant schemes is the main goal of the ongoing NIST standardization effort for post-quantum cryptography. In July 2022, NIST eventually announced four post-quantum algorithms to be standardized. For signatures, two of the three selected algorithms are lattice-based, FALCON [29] and DILITHIUM [9], epitomizing two known classes of lattice signatures: hash-and-sign and Fiat-Shamir with aborts. Recently, Espitau et al. designed an alternative approach to FALCON, called MITAKA [15]. As an attractive advantage, MITAKA can be instantiated over arbitrary cyclotomic fields, conveniently allowing it to reach all NIST security levels. MITAKA relies on a so-called hybrid sampler [28], which acts as Klein's sampler at the level of the NTRU module and calls the Peikert sampler to sample within this ring. For power-of-two cyclotomics, this approach is sufficient, as the sampling of the ring of integers amounts to sampling in a square lattice $\mathbf{Z}^n$. However, for the other cyclotomic rings considered in [15], this induces a non-negligible quality loss, thus a slight degradation in security. Recently, the scheme Hawk [11] presented a new hash-and-sign signature tied to lattices, relying on a more recent—yet natural— cryptographic assumption, the so-called *lattice isomorphism problem*. This latter scheme raises the non-trivial question of the possibility of sampling efficiently in lattices with remarkable packing properties, such as the Leech or the Barnes-Walls lattices. Interestingly, the same question was also independently triggered in the new design of lattice gadgets of [31] to improve the efficiency and compactness of trapdoors. All in all, the quest for new efficient samplers, especially for remarkable lattices, has interesting consequences in the realm of cryptographic design.

Contributions. In this work, we aim at going beyond this Klein/Peikert dichotomy for polynomial time sampling. We showcase a general framework based on a systematic study of the discrete Gaussian distribution under *extensions*: algebraic extensions through short exact sequences and metric extensions through linear transformations. This framework allows us to build new samplers over extensions or restrictions of domains in which we already know how to sample. Our abstract samplers correspond to effective versions of general bounds on the smoothing parameter of lattices: this correspondence is a unifying thread in all our exposition. To complete our modular framework, we also provide ad-hoc samplers of essentially optimal widths for root lattices, to use them as fundamental blocks to instantiate more involved samplers. Optimality is deduced from a new theoretical bound on the smoothing parameter obtained from the relation between the Gaussian function over a lattice and its *theta* series. When the kissing number and minimum of the (dual) lattice are known, it gives a tighter bound on the smoothing, unconditionally on the value of ε — unfortunately, it is unlikely to get this information for an arbitrary lattice. As an application, we obtain novel, optimal, and efficient samplers over cyclotomic rings of prime and smooth conductors and optimized trapdoors in the spirit of [31]. The technical details of our contributions are as follows.

Exploiting the Decomposition over Short Exact Sequences. Given a lattice Λ and one of its sublattices Λ', we can associate the short exact sequence of $\mathbf{Z}$-modules:

$$0 \longrightarrow \Lambda' \longrightarrow \Lambda \longrightarrow \Lambda/\Lambda' \longrightarrow 0.$$

Note that in this sequence, the quotient Λ/Λ' is not necessarily a lattice[1] itself, and as such, Λ cannot be identified as a lattice to $\Lambda' \oplus \Lambda/\Lambda'$. We show how to deal with this extension of groups to extend samplers for Λ' and Λ/Λ' into a sampler for Λ, for standard deviations above the smoothing parameters of the Λ' component. In particular, we identify precisely the projection of the Gaussian measure onto the quotient, recovering the known situation where Λ' is either full-rank or primitive. This construction translates into a simple bound on the smoothing parameter, namely

$$\eta_{3\varepsilon}(\Lambda) \leqslant \max\left(\eta_\varepsilon(\Lambda'), \eta_\varepsilon\left(\Lambda/\Lambda'\right)\right),$$

where the notion of smoothing is generalized to accommodate non-lattice quotients. Note that the choice of the sublattice is arbitrary here. This suffices, for instance, to deal with the problem of domain extension and restriction of samplers: given a sampler over Λ, how can one extend it to an overlattice or restrict it to a sublattice?

A Filtered Sampler. A filtration of a lattice is an increasing sequence of lattices $0 \subset \Lambda_1 \subset \cdots \subset \Lambda_k = \Lambda$. Iterating the previous construction gives us a generic sampler for Λ. Namely, we have a first short exact sequence stemming from the filtration:

$$0 \longrightarrow \Lambda_1 \longrightarrow \Lambda \longrightarrow \Lambda/\Lambda_1 \longrightarrow 0,$$

and by our sampler over sequences, we can efficiently sample in Λ if we know how to sample in both Λ_1 and Λ/Λ_1. However, we can remark that quotienting by Λ_1 induces a filtration $0 \subset \Lambda_2/\Lambda_1 \subset \cdots \subset \Lambda_k = \Lambda/\Lambda_1$. Hence, we can recursively apply this technique and devise a sampler for Λ from samplers over $(\Lambda_{i+1}/\Lambda_i)_i$. This approach yields a natural generalization of Klein's sampler (as presented in [18]), which corresponds to the particular case where $\mathrm{rk}(\Lambda_i) = i$ for all $1 \leqslant i \leqslant \mathrm{rk}(\Lambda)$, and the successive quotients correspond to the Gram-Schmidt orthogonalization. Expectedly, we obtain a bound on the smoothing parameter of Λ in terms of the smoothing parameter of these quotients, generalizing that of [18]:

$$\eta_\varepsilon(\Lambda) \leqslant \max_{1\leqslant i\leqslant k} \eta_{\frac{\varepsilon}{k+1}}(\Lambda_i/\Lambda_{i-1}).$$

In a later section, we show how this abstract sampler and its designated bound can lead to significant improvements over the Klein-Peikert dichotomy on a concrete example.

A Linear Sampler. *Change of basis* is a natural technique in linear algebra allowing to re-express sets of linear equations in more congenial forms, by looking at the coordinates of a linear space under a different basis. It is a deep principle undertaking numerous aspects of numerical algorithm, whether by making incremental changes (like in Gaussian elimination or lattice reduction), or in one

---

[1] Generally, the quotient is a product of the *torsion part*, which is a finite abelian group and its *free part*, which corresponds to a lattice too. Even when the quotient is torsion-free, Λ does not identify to $\Lambda' \oplus \Lambda/\Lambda'$ as lattices in general.

take (e.g., computing the Discrete Fourier transform representation). Unsurprisingly, we can apply it to discrete Gaussian sampling as well[2]. Hence, from a high-level point of view, one can design a Gaussian sampler in a given lattice Λ as long as one can sample discrete Gaussians in the lattice spanned by a (fixed) congenial basis $\mathbf{C}$, which can even live in a different space. This process amounts to controlling the *distortion* on the Gaussian distribution induced by the change-of-basis procedure, and to smooth it out with a carefully chosen normal[3] perturbation. This algorithm encompasses the sampler of Peikert [25], which reduces sampling in a lattice Λ to sampling *spherically* in $\mathbf{Z}^{\mathrm{rk}\,\Lambda}$ — this can be done coordinate-wise. This construction yields a natural bound on the smoothing parameter, writing a basis $\mathbf{B}$ of Λ as the product $\mathbf{TC}$:

$$\eta_\varepsilon(\Lambda) \leqslant s_1(\mathbf{T}) \cdot \eta_\varepsilon(\mathcal{L}(\mathbf{C}))$$

for $s_1(\mathbf{T})$ being the largest singular value of $\mathbf{T}$. Again, note that the choice of the decomposition is arbitrary (as long as $\mathbf{C}$ is invertible). A generic sampler in tensor lattices $\Lambda_1 \otimes \Lambda_2$ follows almost immediately.

Sampling in Remarkable Lattices. The previous contributions aim at building a framework for efficient Gaussian sampling, by joining existing samplers through *extensions* (namely module extension for the exact sequence sampler, linear extension for the linear sampler and tensor extension for the tensor sampler). It means that we need to be able to sample in some base cases to fully instantiate these higher-order constructions. We thus introduce a set of ad-hoc samplers for some of the so-called root lattices (A_n lattices, the face-centered lattices D_n, the Gosset lattice E_8) emerging in many contexts. They are, for example, well-known for their outstanding geometric properties, e.g., enjoying quasi-linear decoding [5,6], or their appearance in more mathematical topics such as the classification of Lie algebras. In particular, our samplers rely on their well-understood structures and exceptional isomorphisms between them, coming from the latter topic, and we reach standard deviations quite close to the smoothing of these lattices. Generally, we add another tribute to the deep connexions of these remarkable lattices with coding theory, as we combine our algebraic framework with the *king* construction [8] to devise samplers in the Leech and low-dimensional Barnes-Wall lattices. The technique allows as a byproduct to construct samplers in parity-check-like lattices.

Cryptographic Impact. To showcase our framework in a cryptographic context, we demonstrate how to instantiate various samplers over some structured lattices. There are well-known identifications between certain ideals in prime cyclotomic rings and A_{p-1} lattices (or their duals), already subject to algorithmic works [13,20]. Cyclotomic rings of smooth conductors can also identify as (direct sums of) prime cyclotomic rings. We exploit our ad-hoc samplers to

---

[2] Of course, change of basis works very well for continuous Gaussians: it simply amounts to matrix-vector multiplication.

[3] What matters for proofs is that the perturbation distribution has good convolution properties with Gaussian kernels.

devise novel samplers in cyclotomic rings: our result combines quasi-linear efficiency and optimal Gaussian width. To our knowledge, all previous approaches reached worse Gaussian widths, and at best equivalent efficiency.

We also detail the implication for the design of hash-and-sign signatures, where the ability to sample efficiently and precisely is crucial for the security and bandwidth of the scheme. We compare our variations with the recently proposed and state-of-the-art Falcon [29] and Mitaka [15] signatures. In particular, we show how to design hash-and-sign signatures more tightly on smooth cyclotomic fields, giving more security (around 20 bits in both classical and quantum regimes) and slightly shorter signatures for free compared to [15] (although bitsize is not the focus of this work). More interestingly, we show how to implement them on *prime cyclotomics*, allowing a very tight choice of parameter selections. At a high-level, our results are also satisfying in the sense that they not only increase the security level for prime cyclotomics compared to [15], they also show a more regular growth and behavior of the ratio security level over cyclotomic-conductors compared to [15]. Then, we also give new instantiations of the recent framework of [31] for compact gadget-based sampling with a target lattice constructed as a tensor of the root E_8 and $\mathbf{Z}^n$. We again get slightly shorter signatures for free (110 bytes shorter) for higher security, both in the classical and quantum settings.

Organization of the Paper. After recalling some material about lattices and Gaussian measures in Sect. 2, we start with the first, central piece of our framework in Sect. 3: the sampling procedure over *short exact sequences* (Algorithm 1), and its natural recursive extension, the *filtered Sampler* (Algorithm 2). In Sect. 5, we present our *linear Sampler*; because of space constraints, its use for tensor sampling is only provided in the full version of this paper. Section 6 is devoted to our samplers remarkable lattices. Last, in Sect. 7 and Sect. 8, we instantiate many of our contributions into a hash-then-sign signature scheme with concrete parameters and analysis.

2   Algebraic and Computational Background

General Notation. The bold capitals $\mathbf{Z}$, $\mathbf{Q}$, and $\mathbf{R}$ refer respectively to the ring of integers, the field of rational and real numbers. Given a real number x, the integral roundings *floor*, *ceil* and *round to the nearest integer* are denoted respectively by $\lfloor x \rfloor, \lceil x \rceil, \lfloor x \rceil$. Let ln denote the natural logarithm. For a real-valued function f and a countable set S, we write generically $f(S) = \sum_{x \in S} f(x)$ assuming that this sum is absolutely convergent. Vectors and matrices are understood column-wise. For $\mathbf{A}, \mathbf{B}$ two matrices, we write $[\mathbf{A}, \mathbf{B}]$ for the concatenation of the columns from $\mathbf{A}$ and $\mathbf{B}$. The transpose of a matrix $\mathbf{T}$ is $\mathbf{T}^t$ and if $\mathbf{T}$ is non singular, its pseudo-inverse is $\mathbf{T}^\star = (\mathbf{T}^t \mathbf{T})^{-1} \mathbf{T}^t$.

2.1   Euclidean Lattices

A (real) *lattice* Λ is a finitely generated free $\mathbf{Z}$-module, endowed with a Euclidean norm $\|.\|$ on the real vector space $\Lambda_{\mathbf{R}} := \Lambda \otimes_{\mathbf{Z}} \mathbf{R}$. By definition, there exists a finite family $(\mathbf{b}_1, \ldots, \mathbf{b}_n) \in \Lambda^n$ of linearly independent elements such that $\Lambda = \bigoplus_{i=1}^{n} \mathbf{b}_i \mathbf{Z}$, and we write $\Lambda = \mathcal{L}(\mathbf{B})$, with the matrix $\mathbf{B} = [\mathbf{b}_1, \ldots, \mathbf{b}_n]$. It is called a *basis* of Λ. Every basis has the same number of elements $\mathrm{rk}(\Lambda)$, called the *rank* of the lattice. We let $\lambda_1(\Lambda)$ be the Euclidean norm of a shortest non-zero vector in Λ. The volume is $\det \Lambda = \sqrt{\det \mathbf{B}^t \mathbf{B}}$, for any basis $\mathbf{B}$ of Λ.

In this work, when dealing with lattices embedded in $\mathbf{R}^n$, we only consider the standard Euclidean norm, corresponding to the canonical inner product $\langle, \rangle$, but we stress that most of our algorithms are agnostic to the choice of the norm. The dual of a lattice Λ is the lattice $\Lambda^{\vee} = \{\mathbf{x} \in \Lambda_{\mathbf{R}} \mid \langle \mathbf{x}, \mathbf{v} \rangle \in \mathbf{Z}, \forall\, \mathbf{v} \in \Lambda\}$, and we always endow it with the same norm as Λ. If Λ is a full-rank lattice of basis $\mathbf{B}$, then $\mathbf{B}^{-t}$ is a basis of $\Lambda^{\vee}$; if it is not full rank, $\mathbf{B}(\mathbf{B}^t \mathbf{B})^{-1}$ is a basis of $\Lambda^{\vee}$.

Orthogonality. For a subspace $V \subset \Lambda_{\mathbf{R}}$, let $V^{\perp} = \{\mathbf{y} \in \Lambda_{\mathbf{R}} \mid \langle \mathbf{y}, \mathbf{v} \rangle = 0, \forall\, \mathbf{v} \in V\}$ be the orthogonal. Let $\pi_{V^{\perp}}$ denote the orthogonal projection onto $V^{\perp}$ equipped with the restriction of the norm to that space. If $\mathbf{P}$ is a matrix representation of $\pi_{V^{\perp}}$, we have $\mathbf{P}^2 = \mathbf{P}$ and $\mathbf{P}^t = \mathbf{P}$. Given a basis $\mathbf{B} = (\mathbf{b}_1, \ldots, \mathbf{b}_n)$ of a lattice Λ, we denote its Gram-Schmidt orthogonalization by $\mathbf{B}^* = (\mathbf{b}_1^*, \ldots, \mathbf{b}_n^*)$, where $\mathbf{b}_i^* = \pi_{(\mathbf{b}_1, \ldots, \mathbf{b}_{i-1})^{\perp}}(\mathbf{b}_i)$.

Sublattices, Quotient Lattices. Let $(\Lambda, \| \cdot \|)$ be a lattice, and let Λ' be a finitely generated submodule of Λ. The restriction of $\| \cdot \|$ to Λ' endows it with a lattice structure : $(\Lambda', \|\cdot\|)$ is called a *sublattice* of Λ. If any basis of Λ' extends into a basis of Λ, then Λ' is called *primitive*. In this case, the quotient Λ/Λ' is endowed with a canonical lattice structure by defining: $\|\mathbf{v} + \Lambda'\|_{\Lambda/\Lambda'} = \inf_{\mathbf{v}' \in \Lambda'_{\mathbf{R}}} \|\mathbf{v} - \mathbf{v}'\|$. Then, there is an isometry between $(\Lambda/\Lambda', \| \cdot \|_{\Lambda/\Lambda'})$ and $(\pi_{\Lambda'^{\perp}_{\mathbf{R}}}(\Lambda), \| \cdot \|)$. Effectively, this means we represent quotient lattices by computing the projection of a given basis for Λ. We write $\Lambda = \Lambda' \perp \Lambda''$ to highlight that Λ is the *orthogonal* direct sum of two lattices. In this case, $\pi_{\Lambda'^{\perp}_{\mathbf{R}}}(\Lambda) = \Lambda''$ and we have an *isometry* $\Lambda \cong \Lambda' \oplus \Lambda/\Lambda'$.

Whether Λ' is primitive or not, the quotient Λ/Λ' always decomposes as a product of its *torsion part* T (finite subgroup of torsion elements) and its *torsion-free* part. Torsion elements in the quotient represent $\mathbf{x} \in \Lambda$ such that $a\mathbf{x} \in \Lambda'$ for some $a \in \mathbf{Z}$, that is, the set $\Lambda \cap \Lambda'_{\mathbf{R}}$. The torsion-free part is itself a lattice: if $\overline{\Lambda'}$ is the (primitive) lattice generated by Λ' and a system of representative for T, it identifies to $\Lambda/\overline{\Lambda'}$, with the quotient norm. It is thus equivalent for Λ' to be primitive and for Λ/Λ' to be torsion-free. When Λ' has full-rank, Λ/Λ' is just the torsion group T. Usual solutions to perform the lift from a coset representative to a lattice point use *Babai's rounding* or *Babai's nearest plane* algorithm.

Filtrations. A *filtration* of a lattice Λ is an increasing sequence of sublattices $\{0\} = \Lambda_0 \subset \Lambda_1 \subset \Lambda_2 \subset \cdots \subset \Lambda_k = \Lambda$ where each Λ_i is a primitive sublattice of

Λ_{i+1}. Let $\mathrm{rk}(\Lambda_i) = d_i$, then $0 = d_0 < d_1 < d_2 < \cdots < d_k = \mathrm{rk}(\Lambda)$. A filtration is called *complete* if $d_i = i$ for all i: for example, any basis of Λ gives a complete filtration. Filtrations are compatible with quotienting: a filtration $(\Lambda_i)_i$ of Λ yields a filtration $(\Lambda_{i+j}/\Lambda_j)_i$ of Λ/Λ_j.

2.2 Discrete Gaussian Distributions

Let Σ be a positive definite matrix. We define $\rho_\Sigma(\mathbf{x}) = \exp(-\pi \mathbf{x}^t \Sigma^{-1} \mathbf{x})$ as the Gaussian kernel of covariance Σ. Equivalently, we could call it the standard Gaussian mass for the norm induced by Σ^{-1}. In that case, one sees that a Gaussian function is always *isotropic*, i.e., its value only depends on the designated norm of its input. When $\Sigma = s^2 \mathbf{I}_n$, the subscript Σ is shortened[4] in s^2 and s is called the *width*.

Let now $\Lambda \subset \mathbf{R}^m$ of rank $n \leqslant m$. The discrete Gaussian distribution over Λ with center $\mathbf{c} \in \Lambda_\mathbf{R}$ and covariance $\Sigma \in \mathbf{R}^{m \times m}$ is defined by the density

$$\mathcal{D}_{\Lambda, \mathbf{c}, \Sigma}(\mathbf{x}) = \frac{\rho_\Sigma(\mathbf{x} - \mathbf{c})}{\rho_\Sigma(\Lambda - \mathbf{c})}, \ \forall \mathbf{x} \in \Lambda.$$

When $\mathbf{c} = \mathbf{0}$, we omit the script $\mathbf{c}$.

Smoothing Parameter. For a lattice Λ and real parameter $\varepsilon > 0$, the *smoothing parameter* $\eta_\varepsilon(\Lambda)$ is the smallest $s > 0$ such that $\rho_{\frac{1}{s^2}}(\Lambda^\vee) \leqslant 1 + \varepsilon$. When the Gaussian width s exceeds the smoothing parameter, all the lattice cosets have roughly the same mass.

Lemma 1 ([25, Lemma 2.4]). *Given a lattice Λ, $\varepsilon \in (0,1)$ and $\Sigma \succ \eta_\varepsilon(\Lambda)^2 \mathbf{I}_n$, then, for any $\mathbf{c} \in \Lambda_\mathbf{R}$, $\rho_\Sigma(\Lambda + \mathbf{c}) \in [\frac{1-\varepsilon}{1+\varepsilon}, 1]\, \rho_\Sigma(\Lambda)$.*

The following result recalls that cosets' mass has exponential decay from the origin. A useful consequence is to express the Gaussian mass by means of a sublattice and its corresponding projection (for completeness, the full version of this paper will contain a proof).

Lemma 2. *Let $\Lambda \subset \mathbf{R}^m$ be a lattice and $\mathbf{x} \in \mathbf{R}^m$. For $\Sigma \succ 0$, let P be the orthogonal projection onto $\Lambda_\mathbf{R}^\perp$, where orthogonality is taken with respect to the inner product $\mathbf{x}^t \Sigma^{-1} \mathbf{y}$. Then we have $\rho_\Sigma(\mathbf{x}+\Lambda) \leqslant \rho_\Sigma(P(\mathbf{x})) \cdot \rho_\Sigma(\Lambda)$. If moreover Λ is primitive in Λ', we have $\rho_\Sigma(\Lambda') \leqslant \rho_\Sigma(\Lambda) \rho_\Sigma(P(\Lambda'))$. The equality case occurs when $\Lambda' = \Lambda \perp P(\Lambda')$.*

On Cyclotomic Rings. In Sect. 7, we need some background on cyclotomic rings and their geometry. Most of the used material is relatively standard. We have put these recalls in the full version for completeness.

---

[4] Most of the prior literature uses s or $\sqrt{\Sigma}$, that is, an analog of standard deviation instead of the covariance.

3 Algebraic Extensions and Sampling

3.1 Gaussian Measures over Short Sequences of Groups

For a lattice Λ, we want to study the behavior of the Gaussian measure $\mathcal{D} = \mathcal{D}_{\Lambda,\mathbf{c},\Sigma}$ with regards to exact sequences of $\mathbf{Z}$-modules[5]:

$$0 \longrightarrow \Lambda' \longrightarrow \Lambda \longrightarrow \Lambda/\Lambda' \longrightarrow 0. \tag{1}$$

Exactness means that the kernel of each arrow is exactly the image of the arrow preceding it. It implies that Λ' identifies to a submodule of Λ and that the map $\Lambda \to \Lambda/\Lambda'$ is surjective. We *do not assume* that Λ, Λ' have the same rank, nor that we have an exact sequence of *lattices*, nor that it splits (which would mean that $\Lambda \cong \Lambda' \times \Lambda/\Lambda'$ as $\mathbf{Z}$-modules).

Recall from Sect. 2 that Λ/Λ' decomposes as the direct sum $\mathrm{T} \oplus \Lambda'_f$ of its *torsion part* T and its free part. The free part can be seen as $\Lambda/\overline{\Lambda'}$, where $\overline{\Lambda'}$ is the lattice spanned by Λ' and a set of representative of T. This denser lattice can be understood as a "primitivation" of Λ'. Hence, $\Lambda/\overline{\Lambda'}$ identifies[6] to the lattice $\pi_{(\Lambda'_{\mathbf{R}})^\perp}(\Lambda)$. We detail an example in the full version of this manuscript.

$\mathcal{D}$ decomposes into two components measures, which can then be normalized to probability distributions:

- **the restriction** over the sublattice Λ', which identifies as $\mathcal{D}' = \rho/\rho(\Lambda')$.
- **the pushforward** $\pi_\star \mathcal{D}$ onto the quotient Λ/Λ'. By definition, for any witness $\mathbf{x}$ of a Λ'-coset in Λ, we have $\pi_\star \mathcal{D}(\mathbf{x}) = \mathcal{D}(\mathbf{x} + \Lambda')$.

Understanding the latter is the focus of the next lemma. In the lemma below, we distinguish the quotient map $\pi : \Lambda \to \Lambda/\Lambda'$ from the orthogonal projection $\overline{\pi} := \pi_{(\Lambda'_{\mathbf{R}})^\perp}$.

Lemma 3. *Let $\Lambda' \subset \Lambda$ be lattices and T the torsion part of Λ/Λ'. If $\Sigma \succ \eta_\varepsilon(\Lambda')$ and $\mathcal{D} = \mathcal{D}_{\Lambda,\mathbf{c},\Sigma}$, then the pushforward distribution proportional to $\pi_\star \mathcal{D}$ is at total variational distance $\frac{\varepsilon}{1-\varepsilon}$ of the distribution defined by $|\mathrm{T}|^{-1} \cdot \mathcal{D}_{\pi(\Lambda),\pi(\mathbf{c}),\Sigma}$, where $|\mathrm{T}|$ is the cardinality of T.*

For the sake of notational clarity, we restrict to the case of centered distributions but the proof readily adapts to the general case.

Proof. Our first goal is to describe the coset $\mathbf{x} + \Lambda'$, and recall that we denoted $\overline{\pi}$ the orthogonal projection from Λ to $\Lambda/\overline{\Lambda'}$. Consider a section[7] $s : \Lambda/\overline{\Lambda'} \to \Lambda$,

---

[5] We highlight that this is a short sequence of *groups* and not necessarily of *lattices*.

[6] The important catch here is about *which* orthogonality we are considering: in our proof, the orthogonality *must be* with respect to the norm induced by the covariance matrix of the target Gaussian, that is, $\mathbf{x} \mapsto \mathbf{x}^t \Sigma^{-1} \mathbf{x}$. This allows us to use that $\mathbf{x}, \mathbf{y} \in \Lambda_{\mathbf{R}}$ such that $\mathbf{x}^t \Sigma^{-1} \mathbf{y} = 0$, we have $\rho_\Sigma(\mathbf{x} + \mathbf{y}) = \rho_\Sigma(\mathbf{x}) \cdot \rho_\Sigma(\mathbf{y})$.

[7] Such a map always exists: indeed, as $\overline{\Lambda'}$ is primitive, one can always find a sublattice Λ_0 such that $\Lambda = \Lambda_0 \oplus \overline{\Lambda'}$ and the section can be defined by identifying the vectors of a basis of Λ_0 with their projections by $\overline{\pi}$.

that is, a linear map such that $\overline{\pi} \circ s = \mathrm{Id}$. From its properties, we see that $\mathbf{x} \in s(\overline{\pi}(\mathbf{x})) + \overline{\Lambda'}$. Let now $\mathrm{T} = \{\mathbf{t} + \Lambda'\}_{\mathbf{t}}$ be a system of representative of the torsion points. Since $\overline{\Lambda'}$ is the disjoint union of cosets $\mathbf{t} + \Lambda'$, there is a unique one such that $\mathbf{x} \in s(\overline{\pi}(\mathbf{x})) + \mathbf{t} + \Lambda'$, and it follows that $\mathbf{x} + \Lambda' = s(\overline{\pi}(\mathbf{x})) + \mathbf{t} + \Lambda'$. By definition and orthogonality, the pushforward of the discrete Gaussian under π therefore acts as

$$\mathcal{D}(\mathbf{x} + \Lambda') = \rho(s(\overline{\pi}(\mathbf{x})) - \overline{\pi}(\mathbf{x}) + \mathbf{t} + \Lambda') \cdot \mathcal{D}(\overline{\pi}(\mathbf{x})). \qquad (2)$$

Similarly, the total measure of the quotient Λ/Λ' can be written

$$\mathcal{D}\left(\pi^{-1}\left(\Lambda/\Lambda'\right)\right) = \sum_{(\mathbf{t}, \overline{\pi}(\mathbf{x}))} \rho(s(\overline{\pi}(\mathbf{x})) - \overline{\pi}(\mathbf{x}) + \mathbf{t} + \Lambda')\mathcal{D}(\overline{\pi}(\mathbf{x})). \qquad (3)$$

By assumption on the covariance parameter, we are above the smoothing of Λ', so all the Λ'-cosets have roughly the same Gaussian mass as Λ'. More precisely, taking ratio between Equalities (2) and (3) and using Lemma 1, we get our claim:

$$\frac{\pi_\star \mathcal{D}(\mathbf{x} \bmod \Lambda')}{\pi_\star \mathcal{D}(\Lambda/\Lambda')} \in \left[\frac{1-\varepsilon}{1+\varepsilon}, \frac{1+\varepsilon}{1-\varepsilon}\right] \cdot \frac{1}{|\mathrm{T}|} \cdot \frac{\rho(\overline{\pi}(\mathbf{x}))}{\rho(\overline{\pi}(\Lambda))}. \qquad (4)$$

■

Lemma 3 satisfyingly recovers the *extreme* cases which are frequently encountered in the literature:

- If Λ' is full-rank, we have $|\mathrm{T}| = [\Lambda : \Lambda']$ and the projection sends all points to 0, so that $\pi_\star \mathcal{D}$ is statistically close to the uniform distribution over the finite group of Λ'-cosets.
- If Λ' is primitive, the quotient is torsion-free, $\pi = \overline{\pi}$ and we recover that $\pi_\star \mathcal{D}$ is essentially the orthogonal projection of the discrete distribution, that is, a discrete Gaussian distribution over $\pi(\Lambda)$.

An interesting subcase happens when an *orthogonal* decomposition $\Lambda = \Lambda' \perp \Lambda''$ is known. We then have a short exact sequence $0 \to \Lambda' \to \Lambda \to \Lambda'' \to 0$. But now, the Gaussian measure splits perfectly, so that the pushforward is *exactly* the projected distribution.

Lemma 4. *Let Λ', Λ'' be two lattices, $\Lambda = \Lambda' \perp \Lambda''$, and π the orthogonal projection onto $\Lambda'^\perp_{\mathbf{R}}$. If $\mathcal{D} = \mathcal{D}_{\Lambda, \mathbf{t}, s^2}$, then we have $\pi_\star \mathcal{D} = \mathcal{D}_{\Lambda'', \pi(\mathbf{t}), s^2}$.*

Proof. The assumptions give $\pi(\Lambda) = \Lambda''$. Decompose $\mathbf{z} \in \Lambda$ as $\mathbf{z} = \mathbf{z}' + \pi(\mathbf{z})$ and similarly $\mathbf{t} = \mathbf{t}' + \pi(\mathbf{t})$. We use orthogonality twice: on the one hand, it gives $\rho_{s^2}(\pi(\mathbf{z}) - \mathbf{t} + \Lambda') = \rho_{s^2}(\pi(\mathbf{z}) - \pi(\mathbf{t}))\rho_{s^2}(\Lambda' - \mathbf{t}')$. On the other hand, it also gives $\rho_{s^2}(\Lambda - \mathbf{t}) = \rho_{s^2}(\Lambda' - \mathbf{t}')\rho_{s^2}(\Lambda'' - \pi(\mathbf{t}))$. Taking ratios gives the result. ■

Smoothing Parameter and Short Sequences. The decomposition induced by the quotient translates into a generic bound on the smoothing parameter:

Proposition 5 (Modularity of smoothing parameter). *Let Λ be a lattice and $0 < \varepsilon < \sqrt{17} - 4$, then*

$$\eta_{3\varepsilon}(\Lambda) \leqslant \min_{\Lambda' \subset \Lambda} \max\left(\eta_\varepsilon(\Lambda'), \eta_\varepsilon\left(\Lambda / \overline{\Lambda'}\right)\right),$$

where the minimum ranges over all possible sublattices of Λ.

The proof is detailed in the full version. Note that the bound makes appear $\overline{\Lambda'}$ and not Λ' itself in the quotient. The intuition behind this, maybe surprising, detail stems from the fact that the pushforward measure is driven only by Λ' and the torsion-free part of the quotient. Indeed, we can geometrically interpret the smoothing parameter to be the minimal width to *smooth out* the lattice structure i.e., the pushforward over $\Lambda_{\mathbf{R}}/\Lambda$ is the uniform distribution. But then remark that $(\Lambda/\Lambda')_{\mathbf{R}} = (\Lambda/\overline{\Lambda'})_{\mathbf{R}}$ as real spaces, making all the torsion elements geometrically irrelevant w.r.t. the smoothing.

Towards a Gaussian Sampler. The bound of Proposition 5 can be turned into a natural sampler built from given samplers over Λ/Λ' and Λ', or oracles for them. First, sample in the quotient with the appropriate distribution, lift the result to the full lattice, and sample around this point in the sublattice Λ'. Remark that all $\mathbf{x} \in \Lambda$ write uniquely as $\mathbf{x} = \overline{\mathbf{x}'} + \pi(\mathbf{x})$ with $\overline{\mathbf{x}'} \in \overline{\Lambda'}$ and $\overline{\mathbf{x}'} = \mathbf{t} + \mathbf{x}'$, since it also belongs to a unique coset $\mathbf{t} + \Lambda'$ with $\mathbf{t} \in \mathrm{T}$. Above the smoothing of Λ', sampling according to the pushforward selects such a coset and $\pi(\mathbf{x})$ with essentially the correct distribution. Similarly, above the smoothing of $\pi(\Lambda)$ we cannot really distinguish in which coset of $\pi(\Lambda)$ a Gaussian around $\pi(\mathbf{x})$ belongs.

All-in-all, this strategy leads to Algorithm 1, where we even allow sampling approximatively in the sets Λ' and Λ/Λ'—this will be proved useful to recursively chain calls of this sampler, as we do in Sect. 4.2.

The proof relies on Lemma 3 and the examination of the samples. Two smoothing arguments over Λ' are used: once to apply Lemma 3, and once to trade cosets for larger ε. The details are given in full version.

Theorem 6 (Correctness of the short exact sampler). *When $\Sigma \succ \eta_\varepsilon(\Lambda')$, Algorithm 1 is correct. Moreover, let $\mathcal{D}$ be the distribution of its output. For $\varepsilon < \frac{1}{2}$, we have*

$$\sup_{\mathbf{v} \in \Lambda} \left| \frac{\mathcal{D}(\mathbf{v})}{\mathcal{D}_{\Lambda, \mathbf{t}, \Sigma}(\mathbf{v})} - 1 \right| \leqslant 6(\delta + \varepsilon).$$

In particular, $\mathcal{D}$ is within statistical distance $3(\delta + \varepsilon)$ of $\mathcal{D}_{\Lambda, \mathbf{t}, \Sigma}$.

Algorithm 1: Short exact sequence sampler

Input:
- A sublattice $\Lambda' \subset \Lambda$, a centre $\mathbf{t}$
- an oracle $\mathcal{O}'$ for $\mathcal{D}_{\Lambda', *, \Sigma}$
- an oracle $\mathcal{O}_q$ over Λ/Λ', $\frac{1+\delta}{1-\delta}$-close to the pushforward of $\mathcal{D}_{\Lambda, *, \Sigma}$

Output: $\mathbf{v} \in \Lambda$ following distribution statistically close to $\mathcal{D}_{\Lambda, \mathbf{t}, \Sigma}$

1 **if** $\Lambda = \{0\}$ **then return** 0
2 Compute $\pi : \Lambda_{\mathbf{R}} \to \Lambda_{\mathbf{R}}/\Lambda'_{\mathbf{R}}$, the orthogonal projection onto $\Lambda'^{\perp}_{\mathbf{R}}$ for the norm induced by Σ^{-1}
3 $\mathbf{q} \leftarrow \mathcal{O}_q\left(\Lambda/\Lambda', \pi(\mathbf{t}), \Sigma\right)$; $\mathbf{u}_q \leftarrow \mathsf{Lift}(\mathbf{q}, \Lambda)$
4 $\mathbf{u}' \leftarrow \mathcal{O}'(\Lambda', (Id - \pi)(\mathbf{t} - \mathbf{u}_q), \Sigma)$
5 **return** $\mathbf{u}_q + \mathbf{u}'$

---

4 Generic Applications of the Short-Sequence Sampler

We now present two generic applications of this abstract sampler: domain extensions and restrictions, and a broad generalization of the so-called Klein/GPV sampler [18]. The formers are simple, elementary but important illustrations of the use of the pushforward distribution; the latter extends the toolbox for Gaussian sampling in cryptography. In Sect. 6, we will present several concrete samplers in remarkable lattices using these generic constructions, reaching closer to the smoothing than the approaches used previously.

4.1 Domain Extension and Restriction

Extension to an Overlattice. Let Λ' be a full-rank sublattice of Λ, so that the quotient Λ/Λ' is of torsion (i.e. the free part of this quotient is reduced to $\{0\}$) and suppose that we have access to an oracle $\mathcal{O}$ for $\mathcal{D}_{\Lambda', *, \Sigma}$ for a parameter $\Sigma \succ \eta_\varepsilon(\Lambda')$. By Lemma 3, the pushforward $\pi_* \mathcal{D}_{\Lambda, *, \Sigma}$ is at distance at most $\frac{\varepsilon}{1-\varepsilon}$ of the uniform distribution over Λ/Λ'. Hence specializing Algorithm 1 with $\mathcal{O}'$ and a uniform sampler for $\mathcal{O}_q$ yields the following:

Corollary 7 (Domain extension). *Let $\varepsilon > 0$ and Λ be a lattice, Λ' one of its sublattices of finite index. For any oracle $\mathcal{O}'$ realizing a discrete Gaussian sampling in Λ' at any center and covariance $\Sigma \succ \eta_\varepsilon(\Lambda')$, there exists an algorithm sampling at distance at most 6ε of $\mathcal{D}_{\Lambda, *, \Sigma}$ using at most one oracle call to $\mathcal{O}'$.*

In a nutshell, the ability to sample in Λ' and Λ/Λ' enables to reconstruct samples in Λ: we do a *domain extension* of the discrete Gaussian over Λ' to the overlattice Λ.

Restriction to a Sublattice. Conversely, it is easy to sample in a sublattice Λ' when we already know how to sample in Λ, and Λ' has finite index $[\Lambda : \Lambda']$: sample in Λ and reject all samples not landing in Λ'. The number of tries is of course driven by $[\Lambda : \Lambda']$, which can be proven when sampling above the smoothing of Λ'. In fact, it makes it a specific case of the *rejection sampling* technique, with trivial rejection probabilities. In the upcoming Sect. 6, we showcase some practical examples with root lattices.

Proposition 8 (Domain restriction). *Let $\varepsilon > 0$ and Λ be a lattice and Λ' one of its sublattices of finite index. For any oracle $\mathcal{O}$ realizing a discrete Gaussian sampling in Λ with covariance $\Sigma \succ \eta_\varepsilon(\Lambda')$, there exists a Gaussian sampler (for the same covariance) in Λ' using on expectation $[\Lambda : \Lambda']$ calls to $\mathcal{O}$.*

The proof is a routine computation stemming from Lemma 3 to compute the probability of rejection. Details are given in the full version of this paper.

Remark 1. We point out the possible connection with the averaging recombination technique used in [1], where a domain restriction is performed, and samples are then combined with a domain extension from 2Λ to Λ (using exponentially many vectors).

4.2 A Filtration Sampler

We now show how our short exact sequence sampler naturally extends to filtrations and allows to retrieve and generalize samplers appearing in cryptography, such as those in [15,18,28]. For example, in the most natural case where one would sample "coordinate-by-coordinate", our algorithm recovers Klein/GPV sampler. More generally it gives a family of new samplers for a given lattice, depending on how one decides to sort and "cut in subspaces" its input basis, offering larger freedom in the design of sampling algorithms[8].

Smoothing Parameter Bound over a Filtration. We first highlight a new smoothing parameter bound deduced from a given filtration $\{0\} = \Lambda_0 \subset \Lambda_1 \subset \cdots \subset \Lambda_k = \Lambda$ of a lattice Λ. It relies on repeatedly applying the splits of the smoothing parameter over the short sequences (Proposition 5) stemming from the filtration. Starting from the penultimate term Λ_{k-1}, we bound (ignoring here the exact values of ε to ease the exposition) the smoothing parameter of Λ by $\max(\eta(\Lambda_{k-1}), \eta(\Lambda/\Lambda_{k-1}))$. Applying Proposition 5 to Λ_{k-1}, we have $\eta(\Lambda_{k-1}) \leqslant \max(\eta(\Lambda_{k-1}/\Lambda_{k-2}), \eta(\Lambda_{k-2}))$. We go down in the filtration inductively until we reach Λ_1. All in all, the smoothing parameter is dominated by the biggest term appearing in the splitting.

---

[8] In the same way that Klein/GPV sampler is a randomized version of Babai's nearest plane algorithm, our technique can be interpreted as a randomized version of the nearest-colattice algorithm of Espitau and Kirchner [16].

Lemma 9. *Let $k \geqslant 1$ be an integer, Λ a lattice and $\varepsilon \leqslant \frac{2}{k}$. We have*

$$\eta_\varepsilon(\Lambda) \leqslant \min_{(\Lambda_i)_i} \max_i \eta_{\frac{\varepsilon}{k+1}} \left(\Lambda_i / \Lambda_{i-1} \right),$$

where the minimum is taken over all possible filtrations of length k of Λ.

The proof is provided in the full version of this work. The term $k + 1$ is chosen to obtain a compact, readable statement with an identical smoothing quality for each quotient lattice.[9] The idea behind the above bound allows to mildly relax the smoothness condition over lattice cosets: instead of the whole lattice, it is only needed to smooth the "worst" successive quotient deduced from the filtration for the cosets of the whole lattice to have essentially the same mass.

For example, it was shown[10] in [18], and subsequently used at the core of several practical constructions, that for any rank n lattice Λ,

$$\eta_\varepsilon(\Lambda) \leqslant \min_{\substack{(\mathbf{b}_1,\ldots,\mathbf{b}_n) \\ \text{basis of } \Lambda}} \max_{1 \leqslant i \leqslant n} \eta_{\frac{\varepsilon}{n}}(\mathbf{Zb}_i^*),$$

where the $\mathbf{b}_i^*$'s are the Gram-Schmidt vector of the corresponding basis. This bound corresponds to restricting Lemma 9 to filtrations of length n stemming from the $\mathbf{b}_i$'s as $\Lambda_i = \mathcal{L}(\mathbf{b}_1, \ldots, \mathbf{b}_i)$. Indeed, we have that for any $0 \leqslant i < n$, Λ_{i+1}/Λ_i is isometric to $\mathbf{Zb}_i^*$ (see also Sect. 2.1). While it could seems more likely that such a fine-grained filtration would give in general better smoothing bounds, we actually show that there are practical cryptographic cases where one can improve the situation by carefully selecting a different and *a priori* coarser-grained filtration.

The Filtered Sampler. Following our motto — smoothing bounds and sampling are built on the same underlying principles — we can transform Lemma 9 into a Gaussian sampler. In essence, the process corresponds to k successive calls of Algorithm 1, recursively progressing along the filtration.

Assume that we are given approximate oracles to sample discrete Gaussians in the sequence of lattices $(\Lambda_{i+1}/\Lambda_i)_i$, and a deterministic lift the first call considers the short exact sequence

$$0 \to \Lambda_1 \to \Lambda \to \Lambda/\Lambda_1 \to 0.$$

Algorithm 1 requires a pushforward oracle on Λ/Λ_1, so since we do not have *a priori* an explicit access to it, we instantiate it as a recursive call over the quotient filtration $\{0\} = \Lambda_1/\Lambda_1 \subset \Lambda_2/\Lambda_1 \subset \cdots \subset \Lambda/\Lambda_1$. Hence the callee now deals with the sequence $0 \to \Lambda_2/\Lambda_1 \to \Lambda/\Lambda_1 \to \Lambda/\Lambda_2 \to 0$. This is done until we reach the trivial sequence. Then, the algorithm climbs its way back in the recursion tree, providing samples in the lattices Λ_{i+1}/Λ_i.

---

[9] What matters in the proof is that $\prod_i (1 + \varepsilon_i) \leqslant 1 + \varepsilon$, where ε_i is a given smoothing quality for Λ_i/Λ_{i-1} and ε is the target quality for Λ.

[10] In its usual form for a fixed basis, the bound is $\eta_\varepsilon(\Lambda) \leqslant \max_{1 \leqslant i \leqslant n} \|\mathbf{b}_i^*\| \cdot \eta_\varepsilon(\mathbf{Z}^n)$.

Algorithm 2: Filtered sampler

Input: A filtration $\{0\} \subset \Lambda_1 \subset \cdots \subset \Lambda_k = \Lambda$, a parameter
$$\Sigma > \max_{0 \leqslant i < k} \eta_\varepsilon \left(\Lambda_{i+1}/\Lambda_i \right) \text{ and a center } \mathbf{t} \in \Lambda \otimes \mathbf{R}.$$
Output: $\mathbf{v} \in \Lambda$ following distribution statistically close to $\mathcal{D}_{\Lambda, \mathbf{t}, \Sigma}$

1   **if** $\Lambda = \{0\}$ **then return** 0
2   Compute $\pi : \Lambda \to \Lambda/\Lambda_1$
3   $\mathbf{z} \leftarrow$ **FilteredSampler** $\left(\left(\Lambda_i/\Lambda_1 \right)_i, \pi(\mathbf{t}), \Sigma \right)$
4   $\mathbf{u} \leftarrow$ **Lift**$(\mathbf{z}, V_1)$
5   $\mathbf{u}' \leftarrow \mathcal{D}_{\Lambda_1, (\mathrm{Id}-\pi)(\mathbf{t} \neg \mathbf{u}), \Sigma}$
6   **return** $\mathbf{u} + \mathbf{u}'$

Theorem 10. (Correctness of the filtered sampler). *Algorithm 2 is correct. Moreover, let $\mathcal{D}$ be the distribution of its output. For any $\varepsilon < 1/k^2$,, we have*

$$\sup_{\mathbf{v} \in \Lambda} \left| \frac{\mathcal{D}(\mathbf{v})}{\mathcal{D}_{\Lambda, \mathbf{t}, \Sigma}(\mathbf{v})} - 1 \right| \leqslant (2k+1)\varepsilon.$$

In particular, $\mathcal{D}$ is within statistical distance $(k+1)\varepsilon$ of $\mathcal{D}_{\Lambda, \mathbf{t}, \Sigma}$.

It suffices to proceed by induction along the filtration repeatedly calling Algorithm 2. The detailed proof can be found in full version.

4.3 Recovering Some Known Samplers

Klein/GPV sampler. As we saw, this sampler corresponds to taking the full filtration associated to a lattice basis $(\mathbf{b}_1, \ldots, \mathbf{b}_n)$ giving a lower bound on the width in $\max_i \eta_\varepsilon (\Lambda_{i+1}/\Lambda_i) = \max_i \eta_\varepsilon (\mathbf{b}_i^* \mathbf{Z}) = \eta_\varepsilon(\mathbf{Z}) \cdot \max_i (\|\mathbf{b}_i^*\|)$.

Klein/GPV Sampler over a Ring. This sampler works at the ring level of a module over some ring of integer $\mathcal{O}_\mathbf{K}$ in a number field $\mathbf{K}$ (for example on NTRU lattices which are rank two module over a cyclotomic ring). More precisely given a module basis $(\mathbf{m}_1, \ldots, \mathbf{m}_d)$ over $\mathcal{O}_\mathbf{K}$, we make use of the full filtration[11]
$\mathbf{m}_1\mathcal{O}_\mathbf{K} \subset \mathbf{m}_1\mathcal{O}_\mathbf{K} \oplus \mathbf{m}_2\mathcal{O}_\mathbf{K} \subset \cdots$. Each recursive call thus consists in calling the oracles over the quotients $\mathbf{m}_{i+1}\mathcal{O}_\mathbf{K}/\mathbf{m}_i\mathcal{O}_\mathbf{K}$, which are scaling by an algebraic number of $\mathcal{O}_\mathbf{K} \cong \mathbf{Z}^{\deg \mathbf{K}}$. When instantiating this oracle with subsequently described Algorithm 3 (or Peikert's [25] for instance), it retrieves the so-called *hybrid sampler* used in [15].

---

[11] We make a slight abuse of notations here by silently identifying a submodule with the corresponding sublattice of the lattice attached to the module. To be perfectly formal, we shall understand the elements of the filtration as viewed under the canonical embedding map, see also the full version.

Fast Fourier Orthogonalization Sampler. Introduced in [12,29], this sampler reaches the same quality as Klein's sampler but run in quasi-linear time in the dimension, by exploiting the structure of tower of subfields in power-of-two cyclotomic fields. It is retrieved as the filtered sampler where the oracle over the ring is the sampler itself, called recursively. More precisely given a basis $\mathbf{m}_1, \mathbf{m}_2$ of a module Λ over the ring of integers $\mathcal{O}_\mathbf{K}$ of the cyclotomic field of conductor 2^k, we have the short exact sequence:

$$0 \longrightarrow \mathbf{m}_1\mathcal{O}_\mathbf{K} \longrightarrow \Lambda \longrightarrow {}^\Lambda\!/_{\mathbf{m}_1\mathcal{O}_\mathbf{K}} \longrightarrow 0$$

where once again the submodule $\mathbf{m}_1\mathcal{O}_\mathbf{K}$ shall be understood as a sublattice through the canonical embedding map. Now remark that an oracle call is made on the modules of rank 1 $\mathbf{m}_1\mathcal{O}_\mathbf{K}$ and $\Lambda/\mathbf{m}_1\mathcal{O}_\mathbf{K}$. However, these modules are also modules of rank 2 over the cyclotomic field of conductor 2^{k-1}. As such, for each of them we can apply the same technique recursively, requiring samples in modules of rank 2 over smaller and smaller fields, until we eventually reach $\mathbf{Q}$, where we know how to sample.

A Filtered Tensor Sampler. Let A be a lattice given with a complete filtration $\{0\} \subset A_1 \subset \ldots \subset A_\ell \subset A$ and another lattice B. Suppose that we have a gaussian sampler $\mathcal{O}$ in B. Then remark that the tensor filtration $\{0\} \subset A_1 \otimes B \subset \otimes \subset A_\ell \otimes B \subset A \otimes B$ is a filtration of $A \otimes B$ and that since each quotient A_{i+1}/A_i is of dimension 1, the quotients $(A_{i+1} \otimes B)/(A_i \otimes B)$ are actually isometrics to scalings of B — the scaling factor being exactly the covolume of the line $A_{i+1} \otimes /A_i$. Hence, from the sampler $\mathcal{O}$, we can sample in $A \otimes B$ by the ℓ calls generated when applying the **Filtered Sampler** to our filtration.

5   The Linear Sampler

5.1   Smoothing Parameters and Linear Transformations

The algorithms presented in Sect. 3 sample without leaving the ambient space of the lattice. However, in certain cases, it is of interest to transfer the problem to another space — where the local geometry eases the sampling process — and transfer the result back to the original lattice. In a sense, as all lattices can be seen as a transformation of the integer lattice $\mathbf{Z}^n$, and as most practical Gaussian samplers rely on the ability to sample integral Gaussians, this observation is already implicit in previous works. As expected, such back and forth between different spaces will generate bias because of the *distortion* incurred by the underlying linear transformation. To enforce the correctness of the output distribution, it must be corrected. For example, the filtered sampler of Sect. 4.2 *iteratively* corrects the transformation to the space attached to the filtration one subspace at a time. A *global* approach to the problem consists in considering any lattice as a linear transformation of another lattice, but not always $\mathbf{Z}^n$. This gives the following bound on the smoothing parameter, possibly implicit in previous works. We provide a proof in the full version of this paper.

Lemma 11. *Let Λ be a lattice of rank n in $\mathbf{R}^m$, then $\eta_\varepsilon(\Lambda) \leqslant \inf s_1(\mathbf{T}) \cdot \eta_\varepsilon(\mathcal{L}(\mathbf{C}))$, where the infimum is taken over all pair $(\mathbf{T}, \mathbf{C})$ such that $\Lambda = \mathcal{L}(\mathbf{TC})$ and $\mathbf{C} \in \mathbf{R}^n$ is invertible.*

5.2 Sampling by Linear Transformation

The global approach is an algorithmic formulation of the proposition of Peikert [25, Theorem 3.1]. For the sake of simplicity, we will restrict ourselves to the case of *continuous* perturbations in our presentation. As explained, on a high level the transformation of a *fixed* lattice distorts the geometry in the initial space and consequently any ellipsoid in that space. The bias can be corrected to any target ellipsoidal shape by adding a large enough perturbation, and up to rescaling.

Going formal, one can prove the correctness of the approach thanks to the nice properties of Gaussian distributions, and the scaling factor appears implicitly as a condition of positive-definiteness involving the smoothing parameter of the initial lattice.

Theorem 12. (Correctness of the linear sampler). *Let $r \geqslant \eta_\varepsilon(\Lambda(\mathbf{C}))$. If $s_n(\Delta) > r^2 \cdot s_1(\mathbf{T})^2$, then Algorithm 3 is correct. Moreover, let $\mathcal{D}$ be the distribution of its output. For $\varepsilon < 1/2$, we have*

$$\sup_{\mathbf{v} \in \Lambda} \left| \frac{\mathcal{D}(\mathbf{v})}{\mathcal{D}_{\Lambda,\mathbf{t},\Delta}(\mathbf{v})} - 1 \right| \leqslant 4\varepsilon.$$

In particular, $\mathcal{D}$ is within statistical distance 2ε of $\mathcal{D}_{\Lambda,\mathbf{t},\Delta}$.

──────────────── Algorithm 3: Linear sampler ────────────────

Input:
- Two matrices $\mathbf{T} \in \mathbf{R}^{m \times n}, \mathbf{C} \in \mathbf{R}^{n \times n}$ with $m \geqslant n$ and $\mathbf{C}$ invertible such that $\mathbf{TC} = \mathbf{B}$ is a basis of a lattice Λ;
- a center $\mathbf{t} \in \Lambda \otimes \mathbf{R}$;
- a parameter $r \geqslant 0$ and a positive definite matrix $\Delta \in \mathbf{R}^{m \times m}$ such that $\Sigma := (\mathbf{T}^t \Delta^{-1} \mathbf{T})^{-1} \succ r^2 \mathbf{I}_n$;

Output: $\mathbf{y} \in \Lambda$ with distribution statistically close to $\mathcal{D}_{\Lambda,\mathbf{t},\Delta}$.

1 $\Sigma_{\mathbf{p}} \leftarrow \Sigma - r^2 \mathbf{I}$
2 $\mathbf{p} \leftarrow \mathcal{N}_{\Sigma_{\mathbf{p}}}$
3 $\mathbf{x} \leftarrow \mathcal{D}_{\mathcal{L}(\mathbf{C}),\mathbf{T}^*\mathbf{t}+\mathbf{p},r^2}$ /* $\mathbf{T}^*$ is the pseudo-inverse   */
4 ; **return** $\mathbf{y} := \mathbf{Tx}$

Remark 2. This sampler also relies on a continuous Gaussian sampler, but fundamentally, the required property is that the product of the density functions of the perturbation and the lattice sampler can be understood: this is the core fact used to ensure the correctness of the output.

The proof is very similar in spirit of [15,25], and amounts to a marginal distribution calculation combined with the nice properties of Gaussian functions with respect to multiplication (see e.g. [25, Fact 2.1]). It is therefore only in the full version.

Many matrix decompositions can be exploited by the linear sampler, such as SVD or QR decompositions. Due to space constraints, these illustrative examples are presented in the full version of this work.

5.3   Application: Sampling in Tensor Lattices

A lattice $\mathcal{L}(\mathbf{A}) \otimes \mathcal{L}(\mathbf{B})$ is generated by the matrix $\mathbf{A} \otimes \mathbf{B}$ which can be rewritten as a matrix product involving $\mathbf{A}$ and $\mathbf{B}$. Therefore Algorithm 3 instantiates very well over such lattices. This gives (up to our knowledge) a novel and *parallel*[12] way to sample in $\mathcal{L}(\mathbf{A}) \otimes \mathcal{L}(\mathbf{B})$, and a corresponding smoothing parameter bound. The details are deferred to the full version due to space constraints.

6   Sampling in Remarkable Lattices

This section collects various approaches to efficiently sample Gaussian in the remarkable lattices A_n, D_n and E_8 (i.e., root lattices) and the Barnes-Walls, Leech, and Nebe lattices. On the one hand, some of them will appear to be important building blocks for sampling cyclotomic integers, be incorporated in cryptographic gadget constructions, and can be seen as *base cases* or elementary functions to construct samplers on arbitrary lattices by combination (in the same way Klein's and Peikert's samplers are built around one-dimensional samplers). On the other hand, they are also a good way to illustrate practical use cases of our generic samplers from the previous sections.

6.1   Sampling in Low Dimensional Root Lattices.

Our ad-hoc samplers for the root lattices rely on exceptional orthogonal decompositions involving such lattices, and their close relationship in general.

On Root Lattices. So-called *root lattices* are families of special lattices with nice geometry deriving from root systems. They enjoy, for instance, good decoding properties (see [5,6], or more recently and closely related to this work, see [13,30]). Most of their fundamental quantities are well-understood, and general exposition can be found in [22, Chapter 4] or [7]. We only recall here the definitions of three types of root lattices $(A_n, E_n$ and $D_n)$, and highlight some properties of the A_n family.

---

[12] Indeed, similarly to the Klein sampler being inherently sequential and Peikert sampler being parallelizable, our filtered tensor sampler of Sect. 4.3 requires to wait for the result of each sample in the filtration, while this linear sampler allows performing all operations in parallel.

Definition 1 (Root lattices). *For integer $n > 0$, the root lattices A_n, D_n, E_n of rank n are respectively defined as*

$$A_n = \{\mathbf{v} \in \mathbf{Z}^{n+1} \mid v_1 + \cdots + v_{n+1} = 0\}, \qquad D_n = \{\mathbf{v} \in \mathbf{Z}^n \mid v_1 + \cdots + v_n \in 2\mathbf{Z}\},$$

$$E_n = \left\{ \mathbf{v} \in \mathbf{Z}^n \cup \left(\mathbf{Z} + \frac{1}{2}\right)^n \mid v_1 + \cdots + v_n \in 2\mathbf{Z} \right\}.$$

Sampling in Roots. We will particularly focus on the A_n lattices. If $(\mathbf{e}_i)_{i \leqslant n+1}$ denotes the canonical basis of $\mathbf{R}^{n+1}$, they are generated by $(\mathbf{e}_i - \mathbf{e}_{i+1})_{1 \leqslant i \leqslant n}$ and span the hyperplane $\mathbf{1}^\perp$, where $\mathbf{1} = (1, \ldots, 1)$. Their volume is $\sqrt{n+1}$, and $\lambda_1(A_n) = \sqrt{2}$. Their dual is $A_n^\vee = \pi_{\mathbf{1}^\perp}(\mathbf{Z}^{n+1})$, with $\lambda_1(A_n^\vee) = \sqrt{n/(n+1)}$, and A_n has index $n+1$ in $A_n^\vee$. Noticeably, A_2 identifies with the famous hexagonal lattice. We start with samplers for the root lattices of small dimensions, as well as the D_n family. They are based on the ability to juggle between restrictions and extensions of lattices using Proposition 8 and Corollary 7, and exceptional isometries and geometric relations between them [22, Chap. 4.6].

Theorem 13. *We can sample efficiently and at a standard deviation right above the smoothing parameter in the following root lattices: D_n for all $n > 1$, A_2, A_3, A_4, $A_5, A_6, A_8, E_6, E_7, E_8$.*

Below, we only give the high-level ideas of the samplers used in Sect. 7. All remaining proofs and details[13] can be found in the full version.

D_n **samplers:** The D_n lattice can be described as the vectors of $\mathbf{Z}^n$ which coordinates in the canonical basis $(\mathbf{e}_i)_{i \leqslant n}$ sum to an even number, so that $[\mathbf{Z}^n : D_n] = 2$. This congenial definition leads to a domain extension approach form as in Proposition 8: a sample either belongs to D_n or either to its non-zero coset (with almost equiprobability above $\eta_\varepsilon(D_n)$).

E_8 **sampler:** the E_8 lattice is an unimodular lattice in $\mathbf{R}^8$ so in particular its determinant is 1. We have the exact sequence $0 \to D_8 \to E_8 \to \mathbf{Z}/2\mathbf{Z} \to 0$ by the covering of cosets $E_8 = D_8 \cup (1/2, \ldots, 1/2) + D_8$. Combining our D_n sampler with Algorithm 1 this provide an algorithm to sample in E_8: flip a coin to decide the coset, sample a Gaussian in D_8, output the sum. See the full version for more details.

A_2 **sampler:** We rely on the index 3 containment $E_8 \supset L_1 \perp E_6$, where L_1 is isometric to A_2 and the decomposition defines E_6 (see also [7, 22]). The sampler combines Lemma 4 with Proposition 8: map the target center with the isometry $A_2 \simeq L_1$, sample in E_8 around that center until the output belongs to $L_1 \perp E_6$ and project it onto L_1. Still, we rely on a sampler in E_8 that reaches standard deviation at least $\eta_\varepsilon(D_8)$, as seen from Lemma 3. The smoothing of $L_1 \perp E_6$ is at most that of A_2 by Lemma 2, which turns out to be larger than $\eta_\varepsilon(D_8)$: we can sample exactly at the smoothing of A_2. Although very simple, it is not

---

[13] One can also sample in $A_n = \mathbf{Z}^{n+1} \cap \mathbf{1}^\perp$, checking when the sum of coordinates vanishes. This is clearly inefficient when n grows. In the next section, we propose a far more efficient algorithm, when $n \geqslant 9$.

efficiently using its randomness coins. We show in the full version of this paper how to somewhat amortize this process.

A_8 **sampler:** from [22, Theorem 4.6.7 and 4.6.12], A_8 is isometric to a lattice of index 3 in E_8. Combining the E_8 sampler and Proposition 8 in the natural way gives the algorithm. See the full version for pseudo-code.

An Exact Calculation of the Smoothing Parameter. As we are dealing with remarkable lattices, it is often possible to have a very accurate understanding of their meaningful quantities. The smoothing parameter is no exception and is the topic of this subsection. Our main ingredient here is the general identification of the Gaussian mass with the *theta series* of a lattice:

$$\rho_{1/s^2}(\Lambda^\vee) = 1 + \kappa(\Lambda^\vee) \cdot \exp(-\pi s^2)^{\lambda_1(\Lambda^\vee)^2} + \kappa_2 \exp(-\pi s^2)^{n_2^2} + \cdots$$
$$= \theta_{\Lambda^\vee}(\exp(-\pi s^2)), \tag{5}$$

where we have sorted the vectors of $\Lambda^\vee$ by their increasing squared norm[14], and $\kappa(\Lambda^\vee)$ is the *kissing number* of $\Lambda^\vee$. Let now $q = \exp(-\pi s^2)$, then determining the smoothing parameter of a lattice amounts to find q such that $\theta_{\Lambda^\vee}(q) - 1 = \varepsilon$. This can always be done by *series reversion*: there exists a series S such that $S(\theta_{\Lambda^\vee}(q) - 1) = q$. Routine calculations then show

$$s = \sqrt{\frac{1}{\pi} \ln\left(\frac{1}{S(\varepsilon)}\right)}.$$

Note that this is an *exact* expression, and formulae from formal series theory even give the coefficients of S. Of course, calculating the actual value for some lattice Λ requires knowing those of $\theta_{\Lambda^\vee}$. Thankfully, for all exceptional lattices, the first terms of the theta series are well-known (details are given in the full version and the minima and kissing numbers of remarkable lattices are often found in [7], among others).

Lemma 14. *For any lattice Λ, we have the following estimate, valid for $\varepsilon > 0$:*

$$\eta_\varepsilon(\Lambda) = \frac{1}{\lambda_1(\Lambda^\vee)} \cdot \sqrt{\frac{1}{\pi} \ln\left(\frac{\kappa(\Lambda^\vee)}{\varepsilon}(1 + o(1))\right)}.$$

In particular, we have the following approximations:

- $\eta_\varepsilon(\mathbf{Z}^n) \approx \sqrt{\frac{1}{\pi} \ln(\frac{2n}{\varepsilon})}$ *and for* $n \geq 5$, $\eta_\varepsilon(D_n) \approx \sqrt{\frac{1}{\pi}(\ln(\frac{2n}{\varepsilon}))}$;

- $\eta_\varepsilon(A_n) \approx \frac{1}{\lambda_1(A_n^\vee)} \cdot \sqrt{\frac{1}{\pi} \ln\left(\frac{2(n+1)}{\varepsilon}\right)} \approx \sqrt{\frac{n+1}{n}} \cdot \eta_\varepsilon(\mathbf{Z}^n)$;

- $\eta_\varepsilon(E_8) \approx \frac{1}{\sqrt{2}} \cdot \sqrt{\frac{1}{\pi} \ln(\frac{240}{\varepsilon})}$ *and* $\eta_\varepsilon(\mathcal{L}) \approx \frac{1}{2} \cdot \sqrt{\frac{1}{\pi} \ln(\frac{196560}{\varepsilon})}$, *where $\mathcal{L}$ is the Leech lattice.*

---

[14] The parameters κ_2 and n_2 are placeholders for the number κ_2 of vectors of norm n_2, the smallest possible norm in the lattice that is larger than λ_1.

The second result can be understood intuitively as follows: $D_n^\vee$ is the disjoint union of $\mathbf{Z}^n$ and $\mathbf{Z}^n + \frac{1}{2}\mathbf{1}$. It tells us that D_n and $\mathbf{Z}^n$ have almost equivalent smoothing, as the first term in the theta series of their duals is the same. Additionally, $\lambda_1^\infty(D_n^\vee) = \frac{1}{2}$, so that the usual bound[15] obtained from the shortest vector of the dual *in the* ℓ_∞ *norm* would give an overestimate by a factor ≈ 2.

6.2   Sampling in $\mathbf{A}_n$ Lattices.

We now study the Gaussian sampling problem for arbitrary $\mathbf{A}_n$ lattices. The generic case is trickier, as there is no known direct isomorphisms or decompositions involving other exceptional lattices. A possible approach consists in instantiating our framework of Sect. 4.2 and Sect. 5.2 using the base cases we just constructed. As a point of comparison, we first briefly give the results given by the generic use of standard Klein and Peikert samplers.

Trivial Instantiations: Peikert and Klein Samplers. Unrolling the Cholesky algorithm on the Gram-matrix[16] G_n of the standard basis $(\mathbf{e}_i - \mathbf{e}_{i+1})_{1 \leqslant i \leqslant n}$ of $\mathbf{A}_n$ is reveals that the maximal value of its diagonal coefficients is achieved on its first element, which value is $\sqrt{2}$. Hence, the Klein sampler allows performing Gaussian sampling at standard deviation above $\sqrt{2}\eta_\varepsilon(\mathbf{Z})$. As G_n is a tridiagonal Toeplitz matrix with pattern $(-1, 2, -1)$, its eigenvalues are of the form $2 + 2\cos(k\pi/(n+1))$ for $1 \leqslant k \leqslant n$ [19]. Consequently, the largest singular value of this basis is $(2 + 2\cos(\pi/(n+1)))^{1/2} \geqslant 2\sqrt{1 - \frac{\pi^2}{2n^2}}$, a worse reachable standard deviation. The other classic basis $(\mathbf{e}_1 - \mathbf{e}_i)_{2 \leqslant i \leqslant n+1}$ of $\mathbf{A}_n$ has a largest singular value of $\sqrt{n+1}$, which has an even worse geometry.

Constructing a Better Filtration. To showcase possible trade-offs using Algorithm 2, we now describe different filtrations for $\mathbf{A}_n$ lattices. Our approach here is to rely on samplers in larger exceptional lattices from the previous section as subroutines. This new family of algorithms allows sampling very close to the smoothing parameter of the $\mathbf{A}_8$. These improvements also stem from an additional ingredient: the filtrations we highlight are close to being block-orthogonal. A practical benefit yielded by such filtrations is the more parallelizable nature of the resulting processes. While the next result is straightforward, we highlight it for the sake of reusability.

Proposition 15. *Let $n > k$ be integers and $n = (k+1)q + r$ the euclidean division of n by $(k+1)$. Then $\mathbf{A}_n$ admits a filtration as $0 = \Lambda_0 \subset \Lambda_1 \subset \Lambda_2 \subset$*

---

[15] From e.g. [24, Lemma 3.5], we have $\eta_\varepsilon(\Lambda) \leqslant \lambda_1^\infty(\Lambda^\vee)^{-1} \cdot \eta_\varepsilon(\mathbf{Z}^n)$ for all rank n lattices. While out of the scope of the present paper, it is possible to give a bound depending on $\lambda_1(\Lambda^\vee)$ in the ℓ_2-norm instead, *without* a $\sqrt{n}$ loss as in [24, Lemma 3.5], *unconditionnally* on ε contrary to [26, Lemma 2.6], but involving the kissing number of the dual.

[16] Due to space constraints, the Gram matrices of the standard bases for $\mathbf{A}_n$ and its dual are moved to the full version for space savings.

$\cdots \subset \Lambda_q \subset \mathsf{A}_n$, *where for all* $1 \leqslant i \leqslant q$, Λ_i *is isometric to an orthogonal direct sum of* i *copies of* A_k.

The proof amounts to identifying several copies of smaller A_k lattices, *orthogonal to each other*, in the standard basis of A_n, by appropriately permuting the columns (for instance the first two vectors in the usual basis of A_3 generate a copy of A_2) and packing the remaining vectors all together in the final part of the filtration. All details are presented in the full version.

The remaining vectors have to be dealt with, but it turns out not to impact what follows. This allows to sample over the A_n lattice using Algorithm 2. Let us call $\mathbf{B}_n$ the basis corresponding to the filtration of Proposition 15. At the deepest level of recursion, we sample in the lattice Λ/Λ_q, using for example Klein sampler, or equivalently, Algorithm 2 with the filtration corresponding to the projection of the last $q+r$ columns of $\mathbf{B}_n$ orthogonally to $V_q^\perp = \mathrm{Span}(\Lambda_q)^\perp$. Then, all subsequent samplings happen in (a copy of) A_k, and for example, when $k = 8$, one calls the E_8 sampler for these last q steps. For the sake of clarity, we restrict ourselves to $k = 8$ and give an equivalent *iterative* algorithm. The result is proved in the full version of this work.

Theorem 16. *Let* $n > 8$ *be an integer and* $n = 9q + r$ *the Euclidean division of* n *by* 9. *Let* $t \in \mathbf{R}^n$ *and* $\mathcal{D}$ *be the distribution of the* A_n **sampler**, *for* $\sigma \geqslant \max\{\sqrt{9/8} \cdot \eta_\varepsilon(\mathbf{Z}^8), \eta_\varepsilon(\mathsf{A}_8)\}$. *Then for a small enough* ε, *the statistical distance between* $\mathcal{D}$ *and* $\mathcal{D}_{\mathsf{A}_n, t, \sigma^2}$ *is at most* $(q+1)\varepsilon$.

Algorithm 4: A_n sampler

Input: $\sigma \geqslant \max\left\{\sqrt{\frac{9}{8}}\eta_\varepsilon(\mathbf{Z}^8), \eta_\varepsilon(\mathsf{A}_8)\right\}$, a center $t \in \mathrm{Span}_{\mathbf{R}}(\mathsf{A}_n)$, a filtration $(\Lambda_i)_i$ of A_n in the form of $\mathbf{B}_n$, as in Proposition 15.
Output: $\mathbf{v}$ following distribution statistically close to $\mathcal{D}_{\mathsf{A}_n, t, \sigma^2}$

1 Compute $\mathbf{c}_i = \pi_{V_q^\perp}(\mathbf{b}_{i+kq})$ for $1 \leqslant i \leqslant q+r$
2 $\mathbf{t}_{q+1} \leftarrow \pi_{V_q^\perp}(\mathbf{t})$
3 $\mathbf{x}_{q+1} \leftarrow$ *Algorithm 2*$(\{\mathbf{c}_1, \ldots, \mathbf{c}_{q+r}\}, \sigma, \mathbf{t}_{q+1})$
4 $\mathbf{u} \leftarrow$ **Lift**$(\mathbf{x}_{q+1}, V_q)$
5 $\mathbf{t}' \leftarrow \mathbf{t} - \mathbf{x}_{q+1}$
6 Compute the orthogonal projections $\mathbf{t}'_j$ of $\mathbf{t}'$ on $\mathrm{Span}(\mathbf{b}_{jk+1}, \ldots \mathbf{b}_{jk})$ for $0 \leqslant j < q$
7 $\mathbf{x}_1, \ldots, \mathbf{x}_q \leftarrow \mathsf{E}_8 - sampler(\sigma, \mathbf{t}'_1), \ldots, \mathsf{E}_8 - sampler(\sigma, \mathbf{t}'_q)$ /* can be done in parallel */
8 **return** $\mathbf{x}_1 + \cdots + \mathbf{x}_q + \mathbf{x}_{q+1}$

6.3   The *king* Sampler

The Iterated Parity-Check Construction. In [8], a unifying construction is introduced to generalize the parity-check lattices. Notably, this so-called *king-construction* recovers some constructions of famous remarkable lattices, including the Barnes-Walls, Leech and Nebe lattices. By leveraging a recursive combination of the conventional parity-check construction, this technique provides a convenient coset decomposition, which the authors turn into novel decoding algorithms. In line with the philosophy that a Gaussian sampler serves as a randomized decoding algorithm, we further demonstrate how our domain extension techniques blend into the creation of new samplers for the *king*-based lattices.

The *king* construction starts from a double inclusion $L \subset M \subset N$ of full-rank lattices. Fixing coset representatives to identify the quotients $A = N/M$ and $B = M/L$, define the *king* construction $\Gamma(L, A, B, k)$ as follows, starting from its parity check sublattice is:

$$\Gamma(L, B, k)_P = \left\{ (t_1, \ldots, t_k) \,\middle|\, t_i \in L + B, \sum_i t_i \in L \right\}. \tag{6}$$

and its definition as the coset decomposition:

$$\Gamma(L, A, B, k) = \bigcup_{m \in A} \left\{ \Gamma(L, B, k)_P + (m, \ldots, m) \right\} \tag{7}$$

Towards a Sampler.

Reduction to sublattice sampling. This decomposition then translates to a sampler, by plugging the bricks described in Sect. 4.1: if we denote by Γ_0 the quotient of the *king* construction by its parity-check sublattice, the short sequence $0 \to \Gamma(L, B, k)_P \to \Gamma(L, A, B, k) \to \Gamma_0 \to 0$ underlying the decomposition of Equation (7) allows with the results of Sect. 3 to reduce the problem to sampling in the parity-check $\Gamma(L, B, k)_P$.

Sampling in parity check lattices. To leverage the extension results presented in Sect. 3 once again, we will now focus on describing $M^k / \Gamma(L, B, k)_P$ in a concise manner. By considering the map $\mathrm{tr} : (x_1, \ldots, x_k) \mapsto \sum_i x_i$ over B, we can express this quotient as $B^k / \ker(\mathrm{tr})$. The proof is a matter of elementary commutative algebra and is provided in the full version of this work as it is not directly relevant to the subsequent developments. Consequently, by utilizing the short exact sampler (Algorithm 1), we can effectively reduce the task of sampling within the parity check lattice $\Gamma(L, B, k)_P$ to two main steps: sampling a uniform element in $B / \ker(\mathrm{tr})$ and sampling an element in L. It is worth noting that sampling within the aforementioned group is equivalent to sampling a uniform k-tuple of elements with a zero-sum. This particular distribution can be accurately simulated by independently and uniformly sampling the first $k - 1$ elements, followed by setting the final element to be the negation of the sum of these previously sampled elements.

Algorithm 5: $king$ sampler

Input:
- A chain of (full-rank) lattices $L \subsetneq M \subsetneq N$
- Sets of representatives for $A = N/L$ and $B = M/L$
- A sampler $\mathcal{D}_{L,\cdot,\Sigma}$ at covariance $\Sigma > \eta_\varepsilon(N)$.
- a center $\mathbf{c} \in N^k \otimes \mathbf{R}$

Output: $\mathbf{v}$ following a distribution close to $\mathcal{D}_{\Gamma(L,A,B,k),\mathbf{c},\Sigma}$

1 $\alpha \leftarrow \mathcal{U}(A)$
2 $\mathbf{m} \leftarrow (\alpha, \ldots, \alpha)$
3 **for** $i = 1$ *to* $k - 1$ **do** $t_i \leftarrow \mathcal{U}(B)$
4 $t_k \leftarrow - \sum_{i=1}^{k-1} t_i$
5 $\mathbf{t} \leftarrow (t_1, \ldots, t_k)$
6 $u \leftarrow \mathcal{D}_{L^k, \mathbf{c}-\mathbf{t}-\mathbf{m}, \Sigma}$
7 **return** $(\mathbf{u} + \mathbf{t} + \mathbf{m})$

Putting all together. By these two steps, we reduced the sampling in the $king$ construction to samples in the small sublattice L. The complete pseudo-code is given in Algorithm 5 when expanding all steps of the short exact sequence technique and using direct set of representatives to avoid lifting:

The correctness of the **$king$ sampler** can be derived from the proven correctness of the short exact sampler (Theorem 6). It is important to note that in this context, the selection of a suitable covariance Σ greater than the smoothing of the first lattice in the chain is mandatory (L) However, an interesting observation is that if we possess a direct sampler for the parity check lattice $\Gamma(L, B, k)_P$, we have the opportunity to optimize lines 3-4-5-6 by directly sampling from this lattice, centered at the vector $\mathbf{c} - \mathbf{m}$. By employing this optimization, the condition can be weakened, requiring only that Σ exceeds the smoothing of the parity check lattice. This modification not only simplifies the algorithm but also enhances its precision.

Recovering Remarkable Lattices Following [8] we have recursive descriptions when $k = 2, 3$, with a slight abuse on notation where we allow the lattices in the chain to be rotated or scaled. The corresponding decoding/sampling algorithms are adapted *mutatis mutendis*[17].

- *Barnes-Walls*: This family can be defined as $BW_{2n} = \Gamma(\phi \cdot BW_n, B, 2)$ for $B = BW_n/(1 + i)BW_n$ and the bootstrap $BW_2 = \mathbf{Z}[i] \cong \mathbf{Z}^2$, where ϕ repre-

---

[17] We don't describe the construction of the Nebe here as it will not be used in the following practical applications. However, we point out that it is based also on 3-ing construction upon the Leech lattice, and as such our framework readily applies.

sents the multiplication by $(1+i)$ (which translates to a rotation and scaling, when looking at the underlying $\mathbf{Z}$-lattice.

- *Leech*: The celebrated Leech lattice can be constructed as a 3-construction (also called Turyn construction) from the $\mathsf{E_8}$ root lattice. For this, we select the chain $2\mathsf{E_8} \subseteq T_\theta \subset T$ where $T_\theta \cong T \cong \mathsf{E_8}$, for a phase such that $\sqrt{2}e^{i\theta} = \frac{1}{2}(1 + i\sqrt{7})$ (see [8] for a complete description). Other variants of the same approach exist.

7 Application I: Improved Samplers for Mitaka

MITAKA [15] is a variant of FALCON offering simpler implementations and flexible parameters. It can be theoretically instantiated over *arbitrary* cyclotomic fields. While concrete parameters and security estimates are provided, the preliminary implementation of MITAKA only covers the case of power-of-2 cyclotomics. The instantiation over other cyclotomic rings $\mathcal{R}_m$ relies on how the Gaussian sampling over $\mathcal{R}_m$ is performed. This is non-trivial as the canonical basis of these rings of integers fails to be orthogonal when the conductor m is not a power-of-2.

In this section, we present two novel approaches relying on our ad-hoc, explicit samplers for root lattices: one for cyclotomic rings with *prime* conductor, one for *smooth* conductor $m = 2^\ell 3^k$. We believe that the techniques introduced in this section could find further use in designs, providing more flexible parameters, more efficient samplers, and tighter security.

7.1 Hybrid Sampling and Representation of Cyclotomic Numbers

MITAKA is an NTRU-based instantiation of the GPV framework [18]. Its secret key is a short basis $\mathbf{b}_0 = (f,g)^t, \mathbf{b}_1 = (F,G)^t \in \mathcal{R}_m^2$ of the NTRU module $\mathcal{M}_{\text{ntru}} = (f,g)^t \mathcal{R}_m \oplus (F,G)^t \mathcal{R}_m$. The signing amounts to sampling a discrete Gaussian in $\mathcal{M}_{\text{ntru}}$ close to an arbitrary target (a hashed message), which is accomplished by the *hybrid sampler* [12,28]. Let σ_{sig} be the standard deviation of the sampled lattice Gaussian. For better sizes and security against forgery, one wants to minimize σ_{sig}.

As seen in Sect. 4.3, the hybrid sampler leverages the filtration $\{0\} \subset \psi(\mathbf{b}_0 \mathcal{R}_m) \subset \psi(\mathcal{M}_{\text{ntru}})$, where ψ denotes the canonical embedding extended to vectors. The calls to Algorithm 3 consider $\mathbf{b}_0 \mathcal{R}_m$ and $\mathcal{M}_{\text{ntru}}/\mathbf{b}_0 \mathcal{R}_m$ as linear transformations[18] of $\mathcal{R}_m$. Under this identification, Lemma 9 and Lemma 11 show that the sampler of MITAKA reaches standard deviation as

$$\sigma_{sig} \geqslant \max\left(s_1(\psi(\mathbf{b}_0)), s_1(\psi(\mathbf{b}_1^*))\right) \cdot \alpha \cdot \eta_\varepsilon\left(\psi(\mathcal{R}_m)\right),$$

where $\alpha > 1$ encodes how close we are able to sample from the smoothing parameter of the base ring $\mathcal{R}_m$. For Algorithm 2 to reach the stated covariance,

---

[18] In practice, this second call is encoded by the orthogonalization $\mathbf{b}_1^*$ of $\mathbf{b}_1$ *in the cyclotomic field*; such details are not our focus here, we let the interested reader refer to the full version of this paper for a complete presentation.

it requires two *elliptic* samples in $\mathcal{R}_m$. In [15], this is handled by Peikert's sampler in $\psi(\mathcal{R}_m)$, or equivalently, Algorithm 3 with $\mathbf{C}$ being the (canonical embedding of) the power basis — equivalently, the Fourier domain of this basis. This choice comes from the use of a well-chosen continuous perturbation, which has diagonal covariance in this representation so that its square root can be computed in quasi-linear time, avoiding costly Cholesky decompositions.

The next requirement of Algorithm 3 is a *spherical, discrete* sample in $\mathcal{R}_m$. For *power-of-two* cyclotomics, the canonical embedding $\psi(\mathcal{R}_m)$ is essentially a scaling of $\mathbf{Z}^{m/2}$, and so $\alpha = 1$. The situation is less favorable for more general cyclotomic rings. For example in prime cyclotomic, sampling directly the coefficients of $x = \sum_j x_j \zeta^j$ as spherical Gaussians means that $\psi(x)$ has covariance (proportional to) $V_p \overline{V_p}^t$, a matrix far from being diagonal. In other words, going back and forth the canonical embedding distorts severely the resulting sample in $\mathcal{M}_{ntru}$. Another approach is to sample directly in the Fourier domain; for prime or smooth conductors, the current best approaches yield $\alpha = \sqrt{p-1}$ and $\alpha = \sqrt{2}$ losses, respectively [15].

Changing the construction of the basis of $\mathcal{M}_{ntru}$ is not the topic of this paper. We focus instead on decreasing the contribution of α. Our goal is to show that *a different representation* of $\mathcal{R}_m$ can significantly reduce this parameter. The hero of the story is the principal ideal[19] $\langle 1 - \zeta_p \rangle$. Using Algorithm 2 over the filtration induced by the so-called *decoding basis* [20] $\zeta_p^i - \zeta_p^{i+1}$ of the ideal $\langle 1 - \zeta_p \rangle$, one can achieve generally, $\alpha = \sqrt{2}$, which is the length of the largest Gram-Schmidt vector of this basis. We leverage this observation thanks to the next result.

Proposition 17 (Adapted from [30, Chap. 1]). *Let p be a prime, ζ_p a primitive p-th root of 1, and ψ the canonical embedding of $\mathcal{R}_p$. There exists a linear map $\phi : \langle 1 - \zeta_p \rangle \longrightarrow A_{p-1}$ such that we have $\|\psi(x)\|^2 = p\|\phi(x)\|^2$, for all $x \in \langle 1 - \zeta_p \rangle$.*

The map ϕ is not the one described in [30], but they are very related; see the full version for details. Recall that ψ can be computed using the Vandermonde matrix V_p associated with the p-th primitive roots of 1. We have $s_1(V_p) = \sqrt{p}$ and $s_{p-1}(V_p) = 1$, where s_{p-1} is the smallest singular value. This implies $\frac{1}{p}\|x\|^2 \leqslant \|\phi(x)\|^2 \leqslant \|x\|^2$ for all $x \in \langle 1 - \zeta_p \rangle$.

7.2 Sampling over Cyclotomic Fields of Conductor $2^\ell \cdot 3^k$

Here, we work in $\mathcal{R}_m = \mathbf{Z}[\zeta_m]$ with $m = 2^\ell \cdot 3^k$ and $\ell, k > 0$, as suggested in [15]. To our knowledge, very few works focus[20] on such conductors. From e.g. [20,30] or the full version, the tensor decomposition $\mathcal{R}_m = \mathcal{R}_{2^\ell} \otimes \mathcal{R}_{3^k}$ leads to an *orthogonal* decomposition (tied to the *powerful basis* [20]) $\mathcal{R}_m \cong \mathbf{Z}^{\frac{\ell}{2}} \otimes$

---

[19] It is also known as (a scaling of) the co-different ideal.

[20] FALCON showcased an FFO-style sampler over cyclotomic rings of conductor $3 \cdot 2^\ell$ in the round 1 of the NIST call. It was abandoned because of its high technicality. Such rings are also the focus of the implementation in [21].

$(\bigoplus_{i=1}^{3^{k-1}} \mathcal{R}_3) \cong \bigoplus_{i=1}^{\frac{m}{6}} \mathcal{R}_3$. Alternatively, we have an orthogonal decomposition

$$\langle 1 - \zeta_m^{m/3} \rangle = \frac{m}{2} \mathcal{R}_m^{\vee} \cong \bigoplus_{i=1}^{m/6} \langle 1 - \zeta_3 \rangle. \tag{8}$$

(see also [20, Cor. 2.18]). We can use our A_2 sampler with this decomposition: sampling in $\mathcal{R}_3$ is done by $m/6$ independent sampling in A_2, by orthogonality.

Efficiency and Signature Quality From the A_2 sampler algorithm, we obtain samples in A_2 of width at least $\eta_\varepsilon(D_8)$, for some chosen ε.

We observe using the estimates of Lemma 14 that $\eta_\varepsilon(D_8) \leqslant \eta_\varepsilon(A_2)$, so we can sample each component in the decomposition (8) *at the smoothing of A_2*. Taking into account the entire filtration, the resulting sampler reaches standard deviation starting

$$\sigma' = \eta_{6\varepsilon/m}(A_2) \approx \cdot \sqrt{\frac{3}{2}} \cdot \eta_{2\varepsilon/3}(\mathbf{Z}^{\frac{m}{3}}). \tag{9}$$

The running time is linear in the conductor m. As we need large batches of samples, the alternate approach[21] of the A_2 sampler that amortizes randomness is a good choice here. While still a bit randomness-hungry, the resulting sampler is completely parallelizable and also memory-efficient: we only need to store a table for integer Gaussians of small width. Moreover, thanks to the small Gaussian parameter, the constant-time implementation is easy and efficient.

Comparisons with Other Methods. On the one hand, the basis b_0, b_1 is not changed between our methods and the previous ones. On the other hand, previous approaches such as [15] could only sample representants of $\mathcal{R}_m$ to a standard deviation of $\sigma' \geqslant \sqrt{2} \cdot \eta_\varepsilon(\mathbf{Z}^{m/3})$. This translates quantitatively into a NIST security[22] level-up for each 3-smooth conductors parameter sets proposed in [15], as reported in Table 1.

Another generic method for low-dimensional lattices with a small width is *tabulated sampling*. Concretely, one precomputes a CDT-like table for all short vectors of A_2 and then outputs the sample through table look-up. However, the size of the table for $\mathcal{D}_{A_2,\sigma'^2}$ is much larger than the one for $\mathcal{D}_{\mathbf{Z},\sigma'^2/3}$ in our algorithm, which significantly lowers the speed of the constant-time implementation.

7.3 Sampling over Prime Cyclotomic Fields

The sampler results from a combination of Proposition 17 with our efficient Algorithm 4 instantiated over A_{p-1}.

---

[21] See the full version.

[22] We use here the same security estimates as in [15], in the so-called Core-SVP model for a fair comparison. We point out that the recent work of Ducas et al. on small modulus SIS [14] doesn't apply for these modulus choices.

Table 1. Concrete values for forgery compared to Mitaka base sampler.

	MITAKA			This work		
	Classical	Quantum	NIST Level	Classical	Quantum	NIST Level
$d = 648$	117	103	I$^-$	137	121	II
$d = 768$	147	129	II	170	150	III
$d = 864$	168	148	III	195	171	IV
$d = 972$	194	170	IV	224	197	V

Efficiency and Signature Quality. Both approaches are linear in p, with Algorithm 4's main cost coming from the sampling in A_8, achieving a width $\max(\eta_\varepsilon(\mathsf{D}_8), \eta_\varepsilon(\mathsf{A}_8))$. Using the approximation of Lemma 14, we see that $\eta_\varepsilon(\mathsf{D}_8) \leqslant \eta_\varepsilon(\mathsf{A}_8)$: we can sample the components at the smoothing of A_8. The resulting standard deviation in Algorithm 4 is thus

$$\sigma' = \eta_{\varepsilon/q}(\mathsf{A}_8) \approx \sqrt{\frac{9}{8}} \cdot \eta_{2\varepsilon/9}(\mathbf{Z}^{8q}) \quad \text{with} \quad q = \lfloor p/9 \rfloor. \tag{10}$$

The isochronous implementation for both approaches is easy and efficient, as the involved algorithms only rely on an integer sampler of a fixed width and simple rejection samplings. They are both highly parallelizable, thanks to the filtration shown in Proposition 15; and memory-efficient, as the base sampling has small width $\sqrt{9/8} \cdot \eta_\varepsilon(\mathbf{Z})$ and it does not need to store many intermediate values due to the parallelism.

Comparisons with Other Methods. In [20, Sec. 6.3], the ideal $\langle 1 - \zeta_p \rangle$ and the identification of prime-power cyclotomic rings were used to sample *continuous* Gaussians, by mean of the so-called "decoding basis", which is the $\mathbf{Z}$-basis of the ideal. From the map ϕ, we can directly identify the Gram matrix of $\mathcal{R}_p$ as a scaling by p of that of $\mathsf{A}_{p-1}^{\vee}$ to be the circulant matrix G_p of first line $(p-1, -1, \ldots, -1)$. The largest element in the diagonal of the Cholesky of G_p is $\sqrt{p-1}$, which drives the quality of a Klein/GPV approach (as done in [15]). An approach *à la Peikert* with Algorithm 3 is driven by the Vandermonde matrix V_p, and we have $s_1(V_p) = \sqrt{p}$. Considering now the decoding basis as a matrix A_p with Gram matrix G_p (equivalently, using the map ϕ), we have identified the meaningful quantities in Sect. 6.2. Comparisons between all approaches are displayed in Table 2, showing that our filtration choice improves on the state-of-the-art.

Practical Impact. The improvement over MITAKA is significant, as seen in Table 3. On the one hand, we can use finely tailored conductors to match the requirements of the NIST level, which allows working in smaller dimensions. But we can also use NTT-friendly moduli q that are smaller than the traditional $q = 12289$ used for power-of-two cyclotomics, which also allows for reducing both

Table 2. Comparisons with other samplers over prime cyclotomics.

	Quality	Running time
Peikert, canonical basis	$\sqrt{p} \cdot \eta_\varepsilon(\mathbf{Z}^{p-1})$	$O(p^2)$
Klein, canonical basis	$\sqrt{p-1} \cdot \eta_\varepsilon(\mathbf{Z}^{p-1})$	$O(p^2)$
Peikert, decoding basis	$\approx 2\sqrt{1 - \frac{\pi}{2p^2}} \cdot \eta_\varepsilon(\mathbf{Z}^{p-1})$	$O(p)$
Klein, decoding basis	$\sqrt{2} \cdot \eta_\varepsilon(\mathbf{Z}^{p-1})$	$O(p)$
Coefficient embedding	$\eta_\varepsilon(\mathbf{Z}^{p-1})$	$O(p)$
Ours (ϕ)	$\eta_{\varepsilon/q}(A_8) \approx \sqrt{\frac{9}{8}} \cdot \eta_{2\varepsilon/9}(\mathbf{Z}^{8q})$	$O(p)$

Table 3. Intermediate parameters and security levels for prime-Mitaka.

	Conductor $m : \varphi(m)$	Modulus q	Quality α	Security (C/Q/NIST level)
MITAKA	2304 : 768	18433	2.20	167/151/NIST-II
This work	683 : 682	1367	2.125	**157/138/NIST-II**
MITAKA	2592 : 864	10369	2.25	192/174/NIST-III
This work	857 : 856	6857	2.215	**207/182/NIST-III**
MITAKA	2916 : 972	17497	2.30	220/199/NIST-IV
This work	919 : 918	3677	2.247	**223/196/NIST-IV**
FALCON	2048 : 1024	12289	1.17	285/258/NIST-V
MITAKA	2048 : 1024	12289	2.33	233/211/NIST-V
This work	1009 : 1008	10091	2.30	**250/219/NIST-V**

the public key and signature sizes — however the improvement is mild, therefore we focus on the security.

8 Application II: New Compact Lattice Gadgets

Lattice gadgets are an important ingredient to build efficient lattice trapdoors. Very recently, Yu, Jia, and Wang developed a new gadget framework [31] and proposed practical signature schemes based on it. In their scheme, the gadget can be in principle any square matrix supporting efficient decoding and Gaussian sampling. However, the concrete instantiations only use the simplest (scaled) integer lattice $\mathbb{Z}^n$ as the gadget. To design more efficient gadgets, one is not only required to explore new lattice structures but also to develop specialized decoding and/or sampling algorithms.

This section showcases a new practical construction based on the E_8 lattice. We have shown that the E_8 lattice has an efficient sampler achieving the Gaussian width $\eta_\varepsilon(\mathsf{E}_8) < \eta_\varepsilon(\mathbb{Z}^8)$, which allows better size and security than the $\mathbb{Z}^n$-based instantiation.

8.1 The Yu-Jia-Wang Compact Gadget Framework

In a general gadget-based trapdoor scheme, the preimage sampling is converted to the gadget sampling by using the trapdoor, following the idea of the Micciancio-Peikert trapdoor [23]. In the Yu-Jia-Wang framework, the gadget is a square matrix $\mathbf{G} \in \mathbb{Z}^{n \times n}$ along with $\mathbf{H} \in \mathbb{Z}^{n \times n}$ such that $\mathbf{GH} = q\mathbf{I}_n$, and the gadget sampling is implemented by the so-called *semi-random* sampler. Given a target $\mathbf{u}$, the semi-random sampler outputs a Gaussian preimage $\mathbf{v}$ such that $\mathbf{Gv} = \mathbf{u} - \mathbf{e} \mod q$ for a small error $\mathbf{e}$. The sampler proceeds in two steps:

1. *Deterministic decoding over* $\mathcal{L}(\mathbf{G})$. The sampler first computes an error $\mathbf{e}$ such that $\mathbf{u} - \mathbf{e} \in \mathcal{L}(\mathbf{G})$. Let $\mathbf{u} - \mathbf{e} = \mathbf{Gc}$ for some $\mathbf{c} \in \mathbb{Z}^n$.
2. *Gaussian sampling over* $\mathcal{L}(\mathbf{H})$. The sampler then samples $\mathbf{v} \leftarrow D_{\mathcal{L}(\mathbf{H})+\mathbf{c},r}$ with $r \geqslant \eta_\varepsilon(\mathcal{L}(\mathbf{H}))$. It holds that $\mathbf{Gv} = \mathbf{u} - \mathbf{e} \mod q$.

Note that either shorter $\mathbf{e}$ or shorter $\mathbf{v}$ can be beneficial to the security. The concrete instantiations in [31] choose the simplest gadget $(\mathbf{G}, \mathbf{H}) = (p\mathbf{I}_n, (q/p)\mathbf{I}_n)$. In this setting, $\|\mathbf{e}\|$ is around $p\sqrt{n/12}$ and $\|\mathbf{v}\|$ is around $(q/p) \cdot \eta_\varepsilon(\mathbb{Z}^n)$.

8.2 Compact Gadget from the E_8 Lattice

The E_8 lattice has a good basis with well-structured inverse as follows

$$\mathbf{B} = \begin{pmatrix} 1 & 1 & 0 & 0 & 0 & 0 & 0 & 1/2 \\ -1 & 1 & 1 & 0 & 0 & 0 & 0 & 1/2 \\ 0 & 0 & 1 & 1 & 0 & 0 & 0 & 1/2 \\ 0 & 0 & 0 & 1 & 1 & 0 & 0 & 1/2 \\ 0 & 0 & 0 & 0 & 1 & 1 & 0 & 1/2 \\ 0 & 0 & 0 & 0 & 0 & 1 & 1 & 1/2 \\ 0 & 0 & 0 & 0 & 0 & 0 & 1 & 1/2 \\ 0 & 0 & 0 & 0 & 0 & 0 & 0 & 1/2 \end{pmatrix} \quad \mathbf{B}^{-1} = \frac{1}{2} \cdot \begin{pmatrix} 1 & -1 & 1 & -1 & 1 & -1 & 1 & -1 \\ 1 & 1 & -1 & 1 & -1 & 1 & -1 & -1 \\ 0 & 0 & 2 & -2 & 2 & -2 & 2 & -2 \\ 0 & 0 & 0 & 2 & -2 & 2 & -2 & 0 \\ 0 & 0 & 0 & 0 & 2 & -2 & 2 & -2 \\ 0 & 0 & 0 & 0 & 0 & 2 & -2 & 0 \\ 0 & 0 & 0 & 0 & 0 & 0 & 2 & -2 \\ 0 & 0 & 0 & 0 & 0 & 0 & 0 & 4 \end{pmatrix}.$$

In our E_8-based instantiation, the gadget $(\mathbf{G}, \mathbf{H}) = (p \cdot \mathbf{B}^{-1} \otimes \mathbf{I}_{n/8}, (q/p) \cdot \mathbf{B} \otimes \mathbf{I}_{n/8})$.

The lattice $\mathcal{L}(\mathbf{B}^{-1})$ has an orthogonal basis

$$\mathbf{D} = \frac{1}{2} \cdot \begin{pmatrix} 1 & -1 & & \\ 1 & 1 & & \\ & & 2 \cdot \mathbf{I}_6 & \\ & & & 4 \end{pmatrix}$$

that offers fast decoding. The error size is around $\sqrt{\frac{n}{8}} \cdot \sqrt{\frac{1}{24} + \frac{6}{12} + \frac{1}{3}} \approx 0.33\sqrt{n}$ slightly larger than $\sqrt{n/12} \approx 0.29\sqrt{n}$ the one in the $\mathbb{Z}$-based instantiation. The sampling on $\mathcal{L}(\mathbf{H})$ is tighter than that in the $\mathbb{Z}$-base gadget: by using the ad-hoc sampler for E_8, one can sample with a Gaussian width $\eta_\varepsilon(\mathsf{E}_8) \approx \frac{1}{\sqrt{2}} \cdot \eta_\varepsilon(\mathbb{Z}^8)$ (scaled by q/p). As shown in Table 4, the E_8 gadget gains 56 (resp. 113) bytes of the signature size and 3 (resp. 9) bits of security against forgery for Eagle (the Ring-LWE-based scheme). The comparisons follow the suggested parameters in [31] where the secret standard deviation is $\sqrt{1/2}$. We note that the presented parameters may not be optimal: there seems a few bits of gap between the

Table 4. Parameters for the compact gadget-based signatures.

	$(p, q/p)$	Forgery security (C/Q)	|Sig.| (bytes)
$\mathbb{Z}$-based Eagle-512	$(2000, 8)$	83 / 75	1406
E_8-based Eagle-512	$(2000, 8)$	86 / 78	1350
$\mathbb{Z}$-based Eagle-1024	$(2700, 12)$	189 / 172	3052
E_8-based Eagle-1024	$(2700, 12)$	198 / 179	2939

key recovery and the forgery security. Finding optimal parameters and closing this gap could be interesting future work.

Acknowledgements. We thank anonymous reviewers for numerous comments and suggestions for improvement.

Yang Yu is supported by the National Natural Science Foundation of China (No. 62102216), the Mathematical Tianyuan Fund of the National Natural Science Foundation of China (Grant No. 12226006), the National Key Research and Development Program of China (Grant No. 2018YFA0704701, 2022YFB2702804), the Major Program of Guangdong Basic and Applied Research (Grant No. 2019B030302008), Major Scientific and Technological Innovation Project of Shandong Province, China (Grant No. 2019JZZY010133), and Shandong Key Research and Development Program (Grant No. 2020ZLYS09). Alexandre Wallet was supported by PEPR quantique France 2030 programme (ANR-22-PETQ-0008) and by the ANR ASTRID project AMIRAL (ANR-21-ASTR-0016).

References

1. Aggarwal, D., Stephens-Davidowitz, N.: Just take the average! an embarrassingly simple $2^{\cdot}$ n-time algorithm for SVP (and CVP). In: 1st Symposium on Simplicity in Algorithms (SOSA 2018). Schloss Dagstuhl-Leibniz-Zentrum fuer Informatik (2018)
2. Agrawal, S.: Stronger security for reusable garbled circuits, general definitions and attacks. In: Katz, J., Shacham, H. (eds.) CRYPTO 2017. Part I, volume 10401 of LNCS, pp. 3–35. Springer, Heidelberg (2017)
3. Babai, L.: On lovasz' lattice reduction and the nearest lattice point problem. Combinatorica **6**(1), 1–13 (1986)
4. Chillotti, I., Gama, N., Georgieva, M., Izabachène, M.: TFHE: fast fully homomorphic encryption over the torus. J. Cryptol. **33**(1), 34–91 (2020)
5. Conway, J., Sloane, N.: Fast quantizing and decoding and algorithms for lattice quantizers and codes. IEEE Trans. Inf. Theory **28**(2), 227–232 (1982)
6. Conway, J., Sloane, N.: A fast encoding method for lattice codes and quantizers. IEEE Trans. Inf. Theory **29**(6), 820–824 (1983)
7. Conway, J., Sloane, N.J.A.: Sphere Packings, Lattices and Groups. Grundlehren der Mathematischen Wissenschaften 290. Springer-Verlag, New York (1988). https:// doi.org/10.1007/978-1-4757-6568-7
8. Corlay, V., Boutros, J.J., Ciblat, P., Brunel, L.: On the decoding of lattices constructed via a single parity check. IEEE Trans. Inf. Theory **68**, 2961–2963 (2022)

9. Léo Ducas, E.K., et al.: CRYSTALS-dilithium: a lattice-based digital signature scheme. IACR TCHES. **2018**(1), 238–268 (2018). https://tches.iacr.org/index.php/TCHES/article/view/839

10. Ducas, L., Lyubashevsky, V., Prest, T.: Efficient identity-based encryption over NTRU lattices. In: Sarkar, P., Iwata, T. (eds.) ASIACRYPT 2014. Part II, volume 8874 of LNCS, pp. 22–41. Springer, Heidelberg (2014)

11. Ducas, L., Postlethwaite, E.W., Pulles, L.N., van Woerden, W.P.J.: Hawk: Module LIP makes lattice signatures fast, compact and simple. IACR Cryptol. ePrint Arch., p. 1155 (2022)

12. Ducas, L., Prest, T.: Fast Fourier Orthogonalization. In: ISSAC 2016, pp. 191–198 (2016)

13. Ducas, L., van Woerden, W.P.J.: The closest vector problem in tensored root lattices of type a and in their duals. Des. Codes Crypt. **86**(1), 137–150 (2018)

14. Ducas, L., Espitau, T., Postlethwaite, E.W.: Finding short integer solutions when the modulus is small. In: Handschuh, H., Lysyanskaya, A. (eds.) Advances in Cryptology. CRYPTO 2023. LNCS, vol. 14083, pp. 150–176. Springer, Cham (2023). https://doi.org/10.1007/978-3-031-38548-3_6

15. Espitau, et al.: MITAKA: a simpler, parallelizable, maskable variant of FALCON. In: Dunkelman, O., Dziembowski, S. (eds.) Advances in Cryptology. EUROCRYPT 2022. Lecture Notes in Computer Science, vol. 13277, pp. 222–223. Springer, Cham (2022). https://doi.org/10.1007/978-3-031-07082-2_9

16. Espitau, T., Kirchner, P.: The nearest-colattice algorithm. ANTS 2020 (2020)

17. Gentry, C.: Fully homomorphic encryption using ideal lattices. In: Mitzenmacher, M., (ed.) 41st ACM STOC, pp. 169–178. ACM Press, May/June 2009

18. Gentry, C., Peikert, C., Vaikuntanathan, V.: Trapdoors for hard lattices and new cryptographic constructions. In: Ladner, R.E., Dwork, C., (ed.) 40th ACM STOC, pp. 197–206. ACM Press, May 2008

19. Gover, M.J.C.: The eigenproblem of a tridiagonal 2-Toeplitz matrix. Linear Algebra Appl. **198**, 63–78 (1994)

20. Lyubashevsky, V., Peikert, C., Regev, O.: A toolkit for ring-LWE cryptography. In: Johansson, T., Nguyen, P.Q. (eds.) EUROCRYPT 2013. LNCS, vol. 7881, pp. 35–54. Springer, Heidelberg (2013). https://doi.org/10.1007/978-3-642-38348-9_3

21. Lyubashevsky, V., Seiler, G.: NTTRU: truly fast NTRU using NTT. IACR TCHES. **2019**(3), 180–201 (2019). https://tches.iacr.org/index.php/TCHES/article/view/8293

22. Martinet, J.: Perfection and Eutaxy, pp. 67–108 (2003)

23. Micciancio, D., Peikert, C.: Trapdoors for lattices: simpler, tighter, faster, smaller. In: Pointcheval, D., Johansson, T. (eds.) EUROCRYPT 2012. LNCS, vol. 7237, pp. 700–718. Springer, Heidelberg (2012)

24. Peikert, C.: Limits on the hardness of lattice problems in l_p norms (2008)

25. Peikert, C.: An efficient and parallel gaussian sampler for lattices. In: Rabin, T. (ed.) CRYPTO 2010. LNCS, vol. 6223, pp. 80–97. Springer, Heidelberg (2010). https://doi.org/10.1007/978-3-642-14623-7_5

26. Peikert, C., Regev, O., Stephens-Davidowitz, N.: Pseudorandomness of ring-LWE for any ring and modulus. In: Hatami, H., McKenzie, P., King, V., (ed.) 49th ACM STOC, pp. 461–473. ACM Press, June 2017

27. Peikert, C., Shiehian, S.: Noninteractive zero knowledge for NP from (plain) learning with errors. In: Boldyreva, A., Micciancio, D. (eds.) CRYPTO 2019. Part I, volume 11692 of LNCS, pp. 89–114. Springer, Heidelberg (2019). https://doi.org/10.1007/978-3-030-26948-7_4

28. Prest, T.: Gaussian Sampling in Lattice-Based Cryptography. Ph.D. thesis, École Normale Supérieure, Paris, France (2015)
29. Prest, T., et al.: Falcon: Submission to the NIST's post-quantum cryptography standardization process. https://csrc.nist.gov/Projects/post-quantum-cryptography/round-3-submissions
30. van Woerden, W.P.J.: The closest vector problem in cyclotomic lattices. Ph.D. thesis, Leiden University (2016)
31. Yu, Y., Jia, H., Wang, X.: Compact lattice gadget and its applications to hash-and-sign signatures. In: Handschuh, H., Lysyanskaya, A. (eds.) Advances in Cryptology. CRYPTO 2023. LNCS, vol. 14085, pp. 390–420. Springer, Cham (2023). https://doi.org/10.1007/978-3-031-38554-4_13

FESTA: Fast Encryption
from Supersingular Torsion Attacks

Andrea Basso[1]([📧])[iD], Luciano Maino[1], and Giacomo Pope[1,2]

[1] University of Bristol, Bristol, UK
{andrea.basso,luciano.maino}@bristol.ac.uk, giacomo.pope@nccgroup.com
[2] NCC Group, Cheltenham, UK

Abstract. We introduce FESTA, an efficient isogeny-based public-key
encryption (PKE) protocol based on a constructive application of the
SIDH attacks.

At its core, FESTA is based on a novel trapdoor function, which uses
an improved version of the techniques proposed in the SIDH attacks to
develop a trapdoor mechanism. Using standard transformations, we construct an efficient PKE that is IND-CCA secure in the QROM. Additionally, using a different transformation, we obtain the first isogeny-based
PKE that is IND-CCA secure in the standard model.

Lastly, we propose a method to efficiently find parameters for FESTA,
and we develop a proof-of-concept implementation of the protocol. We
expect FESTA to offer practical performance that is competitive with
existing isogeny-based constructions.

Keywords: Isogeny-based Cryptography · Public-key Encryption ·
Trapdoor Function

1 Introduction

Over the last decade, isogeny-based cryptography has become one of the major
candidates to develop cryptographic protocols that are resistant against attacks
from quantum computers. Isogeny-based solutions often offer practical execution
times, and, despite being significantly slower than their lattice-based counterparts, they usually benefit from small bandwidth requirements.

The Supersingular Isogeny Diffie-Hellman (SIDH) protocol by De Feo, Jao,
and Plût [22] has been the most well-known and efficient encryption protocol

Author list in alphabetical order; see https://www.ams.org//profession/leaders/
CultureStatement04.pdf. The first author has been supported in part by EPSRC via
grant EP/R012288/1, under the RISE (http://www.ukrise.org) programme. The second author has been supported by the UK Engineering and Physical Sciences Research
Council (EPSRC) Centre for Doctoral Training (CDT) in Trust, Identity, Privacy and
Security in Large-scale Infrastructures (TIPS-at-Scale) at the Universities of Bristol
and Bath.

© International Association for Cryptologic Research 2023
J. Guo and R. Steinfeld (Eds.): ASIACRYPT 2023, LNCS 14444, pp. 98–126, 2023.
https://doi.org/10.1007/978-981-99-8739-9_4

based on isogenies. However, recent attacks [9,36,48] broke the security guarantees of the protocol. Fouotsa, Moriya, and Petit [26] proposed two countermeasures to these attacks, but the result requires significantly larger parameters which make the protocols impractically slow for most applications. Further countermeasures have been suggested by Basso and Fouotsa [3]; these countermeasures achieve better performance and smaller keys compared to [26].

The attacks on SIDH significantly altered the landscape of isogeny-based protocols: they similarly affected the security of other protocols that revealed torsion point information, such as SÉTA [21]. Other isogeny-based encryption schemes, such as CSIDH [10] and pSIDH [35], are unaffected; however, they are vulnerable to a quantum subexponential attack [42] and a quantum polynomial-time attack [12], respectively. This makes it hard to estimate the quantum security of a given parameter set; nonetheless, according to the conservative estimates in [42], CSIDH requires very large primes, which would increase the running time of a single key exchange to several seconds [14].

In this work, we aim to fill the gap by proposing a novel PKE protocol that is practical and efficient; we call it FESTA, for *Fast Encryption from Supersingular Torsion Attacks*. We first develop a trapdoor function, where the SIDH attacks are used to invert the one-way function. Then, we use the proposed trapdoor function to build a IND-CCA secure PKE.

In the trapdoor formulation, the trapdoor key is an isogeny $\varphi_A \colon E_0 \to E_A$ and a random special matrix $\mathbf{A}$; the public parameters are the codomain E_A, together with the image of a large torsion basis (P_b, Q_b) under φ_A. The image points, before being revealed, are scaled by the matrix $\mathbf{A}$, which protects the isogeny φ_A from the SIDH attacks. The one-way function receives as input two isogenies $\varphi_1 \colon E_0 \to E_1$, $\varphi_2 \colon E_A \to E_2$, and a random special matrix $\mathbf{B}$. Evaluating the function then consists in computing the images of the torsion basis on E_0 and E_A under φ_1 and φ_2, respectively, and scaling them both with the matrix $\mathbf{B}$; see Fig. 1. The matrices $\mathbf{A}$ and $\mathbf{B}$ are special in the sense that they commute; this is the case, for instance, for diagonal matrices. Commutativity of the matrices is what enables the trapdoor inversion: applying the inverse matrix $\mathbf{A}^{-1}$ to scale the points on E_2 yields the correct images of the torsion points on E_1 under the isogeny $\psi := \varphi_2 \circ \varphi_A \circ \widehat{\varphi}_1$. Hence, the SIDH attacks allow the trapdoor holder to recover the function input φ_1, φ_2, and the matrix $\mathbf{B}$, while the attacks are infeasible to anyone who does not know the secret matrix $\mathbf{A}$.

Related Work. FESTA can be considered a successor of SÉTA [21]: both protocols constructively use torsion-point attacks to develop a trapdoor function, which is then the foundation of a IND-CCA PKE. Despite the similarities, the two protocols rely on different techniques, and the efficiency of the SIDH attacks [41], compared to the torsion-point attacks used by SÉTA [44], allows us to obtain a practical encryption protocol.

In terms of techniques used, key generation and encryption in FESTA rely on similar computations as those in SIDH, with the key difference that the revealed torsion images are scaled to prevent the SIDH attacks. Unlike the scaling pro-

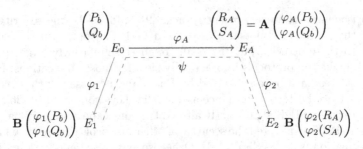

Fig. 1. The FESTA trapdoor function. The parameter generation computes the isogeny φ_A, while the trapdoor function evaluation consists of evaluating the isogenies φ_1 and φ_2. The inversion algorithm recovers the isogeny $\psi = \varphi_2 \circ \varphi_A \circ \widehat{\varphi}_1$.

posed in [26], the two points are scaled by different values, which provides higher security and allows us to use significantly smaller parameters. The decryption algorithm in FESTA recovers two secret isogenies at once by adapting techniques used for SIDH attacks: this is one of the first protocols to use this cryptanalytic tool constructively. A different application of similar techniques has been proposed in [19,24].

Contributions. In this work, we make the following contributions:

1. We propose the FESTA trapdoor function, which constructively uses the SIDH attacks to invert a one-way function.
2. We assess the security of the proposed trapdoor functions. The security proofs rely on novel security assumptions, for which we provide a comprehensive discussion on potential classical and quantum attacks.
3. Relying on the new trapdoors, we apply the OAEP transform [25] to obtain an efficient PKE that is IND-CCA secure in the QROM. We call this the FESTA PKE, or just FESTA. We also derive the first isogeny-based PKE to be IND-CCA secure in the standard model, using a generic transform by Hohenberger, Koppula, and Waters [30].
4. We describe a novel technique to find parameters that lead to a fast computation of the SIDH attacks. In particular, we leverage scalar endomorphisms to obtain an efficient SIDH attack in dimension two that recovers isogenies between supersingular elliptic curves whose endomorphism ring is unknown.
5. Lastly, we implement the proposed FESTA PKE in SageMath: while this is a proof of concept, it demonstrates the feasibility of our protocol. Given these preliminary results, we expect that an optimised implementation of FESTA can offer practical running times that are competitive with existing isogeny-based constructions.

Organisation. In Sect. 2, we cover the necessary background of cryptographic one-way functions and isogenies between abelian varieties. In Sect. 3, we introduce the FESTA family of trapdoor functions, and its security is analysed in

Sect. 4. Then, we build upon the proposed trapdoor functions to obtain a PKE that is IND-CCA secure in the QROM model in Sect. 5. Section 6 gives a precise and concrete description of the FESTA PKE, which is supported by the proof-of-concept implementation detailed in Sect. 7.

Notation. Throughout this paper, we denote the security parameter as λ, and we say a function $f(x)$ is negligible if, for all positive integers c, there exists an integer N such that $|f(x)| < x^{-c}$, for all $x > N$. We write $\mathsf{negl}(\cdot)$ to say a negligible function and $\mathbb{Z}_{>0}$ to represent the set of positive integers. Given a $t \in \mathbb{Z}_{>0}$, we denote its square-free part by t_{sf}. We also write $x \xleftarrow{\$} \mathcal{X}$ to denote that x is sampled uniformly at random among the elements of $\mathcal{X}$.

We also define TorGen to be a *deterministic* algorithm that, given a supersingular elliptic curve E and an integer n, outputs two generators of the n-torsion on E, denoted by $E[n]$. Given four isogenies $\varphi_{i,j} \colon E_i \to E_j$ and two points $P_i \in E_i$, for $i = 1, 2$ and $j = 3, 4$, evaluating the isogeny

$$\begin{pmatrix} \varphi_{1,3} & \varphi_{2,3} \\ \varphi_{1,4} & \varphi_{2,4} \end{pmatrix} : E_1 \times E_2 \to E_3 \times E_4$$

at $\begin{pmatrix} P_1 & P_2 \end{pmatrix}^T$ amounts to

$$\begin{pmatrix} \varphi_{1,3} & \varphi_{2,3} \\ \varphi_{1,4} & \varphi_{2,4} \end{pmatrix} \begin{pmatrix} P_1 \\ P_2 \end{pmatrix} = \begin{pmatrix} \varphi_{1,3}(P_1) + \varphi_{2,3}(P_2) \\ \varphi_{1,4}(P_1) + \varphi_{2,4}(P_2) \end{pmatrix}.$$

In particular, we can view the action of scaling points P_1, Q_1 by a matrix $\mathbf{A}$ just as above, by interpreting the matrix coefficients $\alpha, \beta, \gamma, \delta$ to be scalar endomorphisms:

$$\begin{pmatrix} \alpha & \beta \\ \gamma & \delta \end{pmatrix} \begin{pmatrix} P_1 \\ P_2 \end{pmatrix} = \begin{pmatrix} [\alpha]P_1 + [\beta]P_2 \\ [\gamma]P_1 + [\delta]P_2 \end{pmatrix}.$$

2 Preliminaries

In this section, we summarise some background knowledge about public-key encryption schemes and isogenies.

2.1 Cryptographic Preliminaries

For the sake of being self-contained, we briefly recall some cryptographic notions we will use in the rest of the paper; we refer to [7] for background material. The main ingredient in FESTA is the notion of a *trapdoor function*. Roughly speaking, trapdoor functions can be seen as one-way functions with the property of being easily invertible if one has access to additional secret information. While definitions in the literature vary, throughout this paper we restrict ourselves to injective trapdoor functions. Formally, trapdoor functions form a family of functions indexed by the public parameters, but when the context allows it, we may refer to a trapdoor function to denote the entire family for ease of notation.

Definition 1 (Family of trapdoor functions). *Let $\mathcal{X}$ and $\mathcal{Y}$ be two finite sets. A family of trapdoor functions is a triple of algorithms* $(\mathsf{KeyGen}, f, f^{-1})$ *such that:*

- $\mathsf{KeyGen}(\lambda) \xrightarrow{\$} (\mathsf{sk}, \mathsf{pk})$: KeyGen *is a probabilistic key generation algorithm that outputs a secret key* sk *and a public key* pk *for a given security parameter* λ;
- $f(\mathsf{pk}, x) \to y$: f *is a deterministic algorithm that, on input a public key* pk *and* $x \in \mathcal{X}$, *outputs* $y \in \mathcal{Y}$;
- $f^{-1}(\mathsf{sk}, y) \to x$: f^{-1} *is a deterministic algorithm that, on input the secret key* sk *and* $y \in \mathcal{Y}$, *outputs* $x \in \mathcal{X}$.

Trapdoor functions need to be correct, *i.e. for all possible outputs* $(\mathsf{pk}, \mathsf{sk})$ *of* KeyGen *and for all* $x \in \mathcal{X}$, $f^{-1}(\mathsf{sk}, f(\mathsf{pk}, x)) = x$. *Moreover, they should also be* one-way, *which means that given a valid output* $y \in \mathcal{Y}$, *computed using* $(\mathsf{sk}, \mathsf{pk})$, *and the public key* pk, *any probabilistic polynomial-time adversary cannot compute* $x \in \mathcal{X}$ *such that* $f(\mathsf{pk}, x) = y$ *with probability greater than* $\mathsf{negl}(\lambda)$.

In this work, we rely on a stronger version of trapdoor functions: *partial-domain trapdoor function* [25]. Informally, this means that not only recovering the entire input is hard, but also the same holds if one tries to recover a part of it.

Definition 2 (Quantum partial-domain one-way function). *Let $\mathcal{X}_0, \mathcal{X}_1$ and $\mathcal{Y}$ be three finite sets. A function $f : \mathcal{X}_0 \times \mathcal{X}_1 \to \mathcal{Y}$ is a quantum partial-domain one-way function if, for any polynomial-time quantum adversary $\mathcal{A}$, the following holds:*

$$P\left(s' = s \;\middle|\; s \xleftarrow{\$} \mathcal{X}_0, t \xleftarrow{\$} \mathcal{X}_1, s' \leftarrow \mathcal{A}(f(s, t))\right) < \mathsf{negl}(\lambda).$$

In Sect. 5.1, we show how to derive a Public-key Encryption (PKE) scheme from a quantum partial-domain one-way function.

Definition 3 (Public-key Encryption). *A public-key encryption scheme is a triple of efficient algorithms* $(\mathsf{KeyGen}, \mathsf{Enc}, \mathsf{Dec})$ *such that:*

- $\mathsf{KeyGen}(\lambda) \xrightarrow{\$} (\mathsf{sk}, \mathsf{pk})$: KeyGen *is a probabilistic key generation algorithm that outputs a secret key* sk *and a public key* pk *for a given security parameter* λ;
- $\mathsf{Enc}(\mathsf{pk}, m) \to \mathsf{ct}$: Enc *is a probabilistic algorithm that, given a public key* pk *and a message* m, *returns a ciphertext* ct;
- $\mathsf{Dec}(\mathsf{sk}, \mathsf{ct}) \to m$: Dec *is a deterministic algorithm that returns a message* m *having a ciphertext* ct *and a secret key* sk *as input.*

A public-key encryption scheme is correct *if, for all possible outputs* $(\mathsf{sk}, \mathsf{pk})$ *of* KeyGen *and for all messages* m, $\mathsf{Dec}(\mathsf{sk}, \mathsf{Enc}(\mathsf{pk}, m)) = m$.

Mainly, there are two notions of indistinguishability security for PKEs: security against a chosen plaintext attack (CPA), and security against a chosen ciphertext attack (CCA). The FESTA PKE we will introduce in Sect. 5 verifies the strongest notion of IND-CCA: roughly speaking, given two messages, any probabilistic polynomial-time adversary cannot distinguish which message has been encrypted even if they can ask to decrypt some ciphertexts different from the challenge ciphertext at any point during the attack.

2.2 Isogenies

Most of the existing isogeny-based cryptosystems rely on the computation of isogenies between elliptic curves. For details on these, we refer the reader to [20,49]. We recall here some results about isogenies between abelian varieties, while keeping in mind our main application: recovering isogenies between elliptic curves from isogenies between abelian varieties.

Implicitly, elliptic curves come equipped with an additional structure: the *principal polarisation*. Principal polarisations can be seen as special isomorphisms between the curve itself and its Jacobian. Thus, the correct generalisation of elliptic curves to higher dimension is *principally polarised abelian varieties*; that is, abelian varieties endowed with a principal polarisation. An abelian variety of dimension two is called *abelian surface*. Up to isomorphisms over the algebraic closure of their field of definition, principally polarised abelian surfaces come into two flavors: either Jacobians of genus-2 hyperelliptic curves or products of two elliptic curves. This property allows us to compute certain polarised isogenies between abelian surfaces efficiently; polarised isogenies are isogenies that are compatible with the principal polarisations on the two abelian surfaces. We refer to [39] for more thorough background and to [36, Section 2] for an introduction to principally polarised abelian surfaces from a cryptographic perspective.

Products of supersingular elliptic curves are the main ingredient underlying the recent attacks on SIDH. Given the description of some torsion under a secret isogeny, it is possible to recover such an isogeny using the following result, which is proved in [36, Theorem 1] and is a corollary of Kani's criterion [32].

Theorem 4. *Let E_0, E_1 and E_2 be three elliptic curves defined over $\overline{\mathbb{F}}_p$ such that there exist two isogenies $\varphi_{N_1}\colon E_0 \to E_1$ and $\varphi_{N_2}\colon E_0 \to E_2$ of coprime degrees $\deg(\varphi_{N_1}) = N_1$ and $\deg(\varphi_{N_2}) = N_2$. Then, the subgroup*

$$\langle([N_2]\varphi_{N_1}(P), [N_1]\varphi_{N_2}(P)), ([N_2]\varphi_{N_1}(Q), [N_1]\varphi_{N_2}(Q))\rangle \subset E_1 \times E_2,$$

where $\langle P, Q \rangle = E_0[N_1 + N_2]$, is the kernel of a $(N_1 + N_2, N_1 + N_2)$-polarised isogeny Φ having product codomain. Furthermore, the matrix form of Φ is given by

$$\begin{pmatrix} \widehat{\varphi}_{N_1} & -\widehat{\varphi}_{N_2} \\ g_{N_2} & \widehat{g}_{N_1} \end{pmatrix},$$

where g_{N_i} are N_i-isogenies such that $\varphi_{N_2} \circ \widehat{\varphi}_{N_1} = g_{N_1} \circ g_{N_2}$.

In the context of the SIDH attacks, Kani's criterion is used to learn information about either Alice or Bob's secret isogeny. In [9], whether the (N_1+N_2, N_1+N_2)-isogeny splits into the product of supersingular elliptic curves is used as an oracle to determine if a guess of a step along the secret isogeny path was correct. In [36], the entire secret isogeny is recovered from Kani's criterion by noticing that up to isomorphism, the dual of the secret isogeny $-\widehat{\varphi}_{N_2}$ can be recovered from one element of the matrix representation of the

$(N_1 + N_2, N_1 + N_2)$-isogeny. In [48], this strategy is generalised to higher dimension to allow provable polynomial-time attacks in the general case.

In the high-level description of FESTA, we write TorAtk to denote a generic attack that can be implemented with different techniques. In other words, given the points $P' = \psi(P)$ and $Q' = \psi(Q)$, for some unknown d-isogeny $\psi \colon E \to E'$, points P, Q such that $E[2^b] = \langle P, Q \rangle$ and $b \in \mathbb{Z}_{>0}$, TorAtk(E, P, Q, E', P', Q', d) outputs a description of the isogeny $\psi \colon E \to E'$. The concrete description of the attack used for our tailored parameter set is introduced in Sect. 6.

As in the case of elliptic curves, isogenies between principally polarised abelian surfaces can be computed as a chain of (ℓ, ℓ)-isogenies, where ℓ is prime. There exist some algorithms to compute (ℓ, ℓ)-isogenies, where ℓ is an odd prime (see, for instance, [16]). Some recent work has improved existing algorithms for the case $\ell = 3$ [23]. However, for $\ell = 2$, a classical result of Richelot provides an efficient algorithm to compute $(2, 2)$-polarised isogenies between Jacobians of genus-2 hyperelliptic curves [47,50]. For this reason, we will restrict ourselves to N_i-isogenies between elliptic curves such that $N_1 + N_2 = 2^b$, for some $b \in \mathbb{Z}_{>0}$, when searching for parameter sets. This choice allows to implement our protocol only with $(2, 2)$-isogenies in dimension two.

3   The **FESTA** Trapdoor Function

In this section, we introduce FESTA: a family of quantum-resistant trapdoor functions. The function evaluation consists of computing two isogenies starting from two curves, linked by a secret isogeny: the outputs of the function are then the image curves, together with some scaled torsion images. Roughly speaking, the one-wayness depends on scaling the torsion points, which makes the SIDH attacks unapplicable. The secret trapdoor information is a matrix that undoes the scaling action on the torsion points, which enables the inverter to apply the SIDH attacks and extract the input.

More formally, let E_0 be a supersingular elliptic curve defined over $\mathbb{F}_{p^2}$, and fix a basis $\langle P_b, Q_b \rangle = E_0[2^b]$. These values, together with the isogeny degrees, form the parameters common to each function in the trapdoor family. The public key of each trapdoor function is generated by computing a secret d_A-isogeny from E_0 to E_A and consist of the curve E_A, together with the torsion images of P_b, Q_b, scaled by a matrix $\mathbf{A}$ of special form. We write $\mathcal{M}_b$ to denote the set of possible matrices $\mathbf{A}$, and we postpone a precise definition of it until after we introduce the trapdoor inversion procedure.

The public keys are defined by the following set:

$$
\mathcal{A}^{\mathsf{pk}} := \left\{ (E_A, R_A, S_A) \;\middle|\; \begin{array}{l} \varphi_A \colon E_0 \to E_A, \ \deg(\varphi_A) = d_A, \\ \mathbf{A} \in \mathcal{M}_b, \ \begin{pmatrix} R_A \\ S_A \end{pmatrix} = \mathbf{A} \begin{pmatrix} \varphi_A(P_b) \\ \varphi_A(Q_b) \end{pmatrix} \end{array} \right\}.
$$

For each $(E_A, R_A, S_A) \in \mathcal{A}^{\mathsf{pk}}$, we highlight the dependence of the trapdoor function f on the public key (E_A, R_A, S_A) by using the notation $f_{(E_A, R_A, S_A)}$.

Evaluating the trapdoor function $f_{(E_A,R_A,S_A)}$ consists of computing the d_1-isogeny $\varphi_1 : E_0 \to E_1$ and the d_2-isogeny $\varphi_2 : E_A \to E_2$. The output of the function is the curves E_1, E_2, together with the torsion images of P_b, Q_b under φ_1 and the images of R_A, S_A under φ_2, both scaled by the matrix $\mathbf{B} \in \mathcal{M}_b$. These computations are summarised in Algorithm 1, and we denote its output by $(E_1, R_1, S_1, E_2, R_2, S_2)$.

Algorithm 1. $f_{(E_A,R_A,S_A)}(\langle K_1 \rangle, \langle K_2 \rangle, \mathbf{B})$

Input: Two cyclic subgroups $\langle K_1 \rangle \subset E_0[d_1]$ and $\langle K_2 \rangle \subset E_A[d_2]$ of order d_1 and d_2, respectively, and $\mathbf{B} \in \mathcal{M}_b$.
Output: $(E_1, R_1, S_1, E_2, R_2, S_2)$.
1: Compute the d_1-isogeny $\varphi_1 \colon E_0 \to E_1$ having kernel $\langle K_1 \rangle$.
2: Compute the d_2-isogeny $\varphi_2 \colon E_A \to E_2$ having kernel $\langle K_2 \rangle$.
3: Acting with scalar multiplication compute

$$\begin{pmatrix} R_1 \\ S_1 \end{pmatrix} = \mathbf{B} \begin{pmatrix} \varphi_1(P_b) \\ \varphi_1(Q_b) \end{pmatrix} \qquad \begin{pmatrix} R_2 \\ S_2 \end{pmatrix} = \mathbf{B} \begin{pmatrix} \varphi_2(R_A) \\ \varphi_2(S_A) \end{pmatrix}.$$

4: **return** $(E_1, R_1, S_1, E_2, R_2, S_2)$.

To invert the function, we would like to scale the torsion points R_2, S_2 on E_2 to undo the scaling-by-$\mathbf{A}$ transform that was applied during the public-key generation. However, the public points on E_2 have already been scaled by $\mathbf{B}$; we thus need that $\mathbf{A}$ and $\mathbf{B}$ commute. In practice, we require that the matrices are diagonal:[1] applying the matrices then becomes scaling the two torsion points by two independent scalars.

Given diagonal matrices $\mathbf{A}, \mathbf{B}$, we can recover the images of the points R_1, S_1 on E_1 under the composition isogeny $\psi := \varphi_2 \circ \varphi_A \circ \widehat{\varphi}_1$. Note that

$$d_1 \begin{pmatrix} R_2 \\ S_2 \end{pmatrix} = \mathbf{B} \cdot \mathbf{A} \cdot \mathbf{B}^{-1} \begin{pmatrix} \psi(R_1) \\ \psi(S_1) \end{pmatrix} = \mathbf{A} \begin{pmatrix} \psi(R_1) \\ \psi(S_1) \end{pmatrix}.$$

Hence, after scaling $d_1 \begin{pmatrix} R_2 & S_2 \end{pmatrix}^T$ by $\mathbf{A}^{-1}$, we can apply the torsion-point attacks on E_1 and E_2 to recover the isogeny ψ, from which we can reconstruct the kernels of φ_1 and φ_2, denoted $\langle K_1 \rangle$, $\langle K_2 \rangle$ respectively, along with the scaling matrix $\mathbf{B}$. In other words, we have that $\mathsf{TorAtk}(E_1, R_1, S_1, E_2, R'_2, S'_2, d_1 d_A d_2) = \psi$, where the points R'_2, S'_2 are computed by scaling the points $[d_1]R_2, [d_1]S_2$ by the matrix $\mathbf{A}^{-1}$. The procedure to invert $f_{(E_A,R_A,S_A)}$ is summarised in Algorithm 2. Note that our trapdoor can be inverted using any torsion-point attack that works with a starting curve of unknown endomorphism ring. We detail the specifics of the attack algorithm we use in Sect. 6.

---

[1] This is not the only option: for instance, circulant matrices, i.e. those of the form $\left[\begin{smallmatrix} a & b \\ b & a \end{smallmatrix}\right]$, form a commutative algebra. However, using such matrices does not seem to have any major advantage over diagonal matrices.

The torsion-point attacks can only recovery isogenies up to automorphisms, and, in our setting, the automorphism groups of the curves E_1 and E_2 coincides with $\langle -\mathrm{id} \rangle$.[2] Hence, we define $\mathcal{M}_b$, the set from which the matrices $\mathbf{A}$ and $\mathbf{B}$ are sampled, to be the commutative subset of invertible diagonal matrices over $(\mathbb{Z}/2^b\mathbb{Z})^\times$ modulo $\langle -\mathbf{I}_2 \rangle$, where $\mathbf{I}_2$ represents the 2×2 identity matrix. The modulo $\langle -I_2 \rangle$ condition translates to picking a canonical choice in each equivalence class. For instance, the canonical representative $\mathbf{A}$ of an equivalence class can be the matrix $\mathbf{A}$ that verifies $\mathbf{A}_{1,1} < -\mathbf{A}_{1,1}$, where the comparison is over the integers. Throughout this paper, we always implicitly fix a canonical representative in any equivalence class; as such, we identify the equivalent classes in $\mathcal{M}_b$ with their canonical representatives. We can extend the definition to the more general case by $\mathcal{M}_n$ to denote the commutative subset of invertible diagonal matrices over $(\mathbb{Z}/n\mathbb{Z})^\times$ modulo $\langle -\mathbf{I}_2 \rangle$, for any smooth integer n.

Algorithm 2. $f^{-1}_{(E_A, R_A, S_A)}(E_1, R_1, S_1, E_2, R_2, S_2)$

Input: A tuple $(E_1, R_1, S_1, E_2, R_2, S_2)$, the trapdoor $(\mathbf{A} \in \mathcal{M}_b, \varphi_A \colon E_0 \to E_A)$.
Output: $(\langle K_1 \rangle, \langle K_2 \rangle, \mathbf{B})$ such that $f_{(E_A, R_A, S_A)}(\langle K_1 \rangle, \langle K_2 \rangle, \mathbf{B}) = (E_1, R_1, S_1, E_2, R_2, S_2)$.
1: Recover R'_2, S'_2 by inverting $\mathbf{A}$ and acting with scalar multiplication:

$$\begin{pmatrix} R'_2 \\ S'_2 \end{pmatrix} = d_1 \mathbf{A}^{-1} \begin{pmatrix} R_2 \\ S_2 \end{pmatrix}.$$

2: Compute $\psi = \varphi_2 \circ \varphi_A \circ \widehat{\varphi}_1 \colon E_1 \to E_2$ via $\mathsf{TorAtk}(E_1, R_1, S_1, E_2, R'_2, S'_2, d_1 d_A d_2)$.
3: Recover the kernel $\langle K_1 \rangle$ of the d_1-isogeny $\varphi_1 \colon E_0 \to E_1$ from ψ using φ_A.
4: Recover the kernel $\langle K_2 \rangle$ of the d_2-isogeny $\varphi_2 \colon E_A \to E_2$ from ψ using φ_A.
5: Compute $\mathbf{B} \in \mathcal{M}_b$ such that

$$\begin{pmatrix} R_1 \\ S_1 \end{pmatrix} = \mathbf{B} \begin{pmatrix} \varphi_1(P_b) \\ \varphi_1(Q_b) \end{pmatrix}.$$

6: **return** $(\langle K_1 \rangle, \langle K_2 \rangle, \mathbf{B})$.

Remark 5. As in SIDH, upon choosing a canonical basis $\langle P, Q \rangle$ of $E[d]$, we can restrict ourselves to isogenies whose kernels are cyclic subgroups of the form $\langle P + [x]Q \rangle$, without affecting the security of the protocol. This makes it possible to represent every isogeny with an element in $\mathbb{Z}/d\mathbb{Z}$. This representation is injective if the automorphisms on the curve E are only $\pm\mathrm{id}$: to avoid such issues, we choose the starting curve E_0 to have j-invariant $\neq 0, 1728$.

Hence, the domain of $f_{(E_A, R_A, S_A)}$ is $\mathbb{Z}/d_1\mathbb{Z} \times \mathbb{Z}/d_2\mathbb{Z} \times \mathcal{M}_b$. Additionally, we denote its codomain by $\mathcal{S}$.

The trapdoor function we are proposing is correct, i.e. the inversion algorithm produces the original function input. The isogeny ψ is uniquely determined by

---

[2] Unless either $j(E_1)$ or $j(E_2) \in \{0, 1728\}$, which happens with negligible probability.

its action on the 2^b torsion [37, Section 4]; in other words, there is only one isogeny of degree $d_1 d_A d_2$ that maps R_1 and S_1 to R_2' and S_2'. Hence, the function TorAtk recovers the unique isogeny up to automorphisms. If all the automorphism groups of the curves E involved in the protocol are trivial (i.e. $\mathrm{Aut}(E) = \langle -\mathrm{id} \rangle$), which is the case for all curves with j-invariant $\notin \{0, 1728\}$, the kernels are uniquely defined and the images of torsion points are defined up to inversions. This is because the matrix $\mathbf{B}$ is a canonical representative of the equivalence class modulo $\langle -\mathbf{I}_2 \rangle$. Additionally, the matrix $\mathbf{B}$ is invertible, and thus the torsion-point scaling is also an injection. Hence, the inversion algorithm produces the correct output with overwhelming probability, which also implies that the function is injective.

4   Security of the **FESTA** Trapdoor

In this section, we analyse the security of the FESTA trapdoor. We first introduce a computational and a decisional variant of the problem that asks to either compute an isogeny or distinguish whether an isogeny exists between two curves, given the image of torsion points scaled by a matrix $\mathbf{A} \in \mathcal{M}_b$.[3] These problems can be seen as a generalisation of the classic isogeny problems [22] to the scaled-torsion setting.

Problem 6 (Decisional isogeny with scaled-torsion (DIST) problem). Let E_0 be a supersingular elliptic curve, and P_0, Q_0 be two points spanning $E_0[n]$, for some smooth order n. Fix a smooth degree d, coprime with n, and given an elliptic curve E_1 and two points P_1, Q_1, sampled with probability $1/2$ from either distribution:

- $\mathcal{D}_0 = \{E_1, P_1, Q_1\}$, where E_1 is the codomain of a d-isogeny $\varphi : E_0 \to E_1$, and the points P_1, Q_1 are given by $(P_1\ Q_1)^T = \mathbf{A}(\varphi(P_0)\ \varphi(Q_0))^T$, where the matrix $\mathbf{A} \xleftarrow{\$} \mathcal{M}_n$,
- $\mathcal{D}_1 = \{E_1, P_1, Q_1\}$, where E_1 is a random supersingular elliptic curve with the same order as E_0, and (P_1, Q_1) is a random basis of $E_1[n]$,

distinguish from which distribution the values were sampled.

Problem 7 (Computational isogeny with scaled-torsion (CIST) problem). Let $\varphi : E_0 \to E_1$ be an isogeny of smooth degree d between supersingular elliptic curves defined over $\mathbb{F}_{p^2}$, and let n be a smooth integer coprime with d.

Given the curves E_0 with a basis P_0, Q_0 of $E_0[n]$ and the curve E_1 with a basis $\mathbf{A}(\varphi(P_0)\ \varphi(Q_0))^T$, where $\mathbf{A} \xleftarrow{\$} \mathcal{M}_n$, compute the isogeny φ.

Problem 6 is the decisional variant of Problem 7, and as such it is at least as hard as Problem 7. The converse is also partially true: given an oracle that solves Problem 6 for any degree, it is possible to solve Problem 7 using the search-to-decision reduction for classic isogeny problems [29].

---

[3] The problem definitions can easily be extended to the case of circulant matrices.

The CIST assumption guarantess the hardness of extracting the trapdoor information from the public parameters of a FESTA trapdoor function. However, the output of the FESTA one-way function produces two pairs of curves and torsion points, scaled by the same matrix. The correlated scaling can potentially make inverting the one-way function easier than solving Problem 7. Thus, to guarantee the one-wayness of the FESTA function, we need to introduce the following problem.

Problem 8 (Computational isogeny with double scaled-torsion (CIST^2) problem). Let E_0 be a supersingular elliptic curve defined over $\mathbb{F}_{p^2}$, and let E_0' be a random supersingular elliptic curves defined over the same field. Consider two isogenies $\varphi : E_0 \to E_1$ and $\varphi' : E_0' \to E_1'$ of smooth degrees d and d', respectively. Let n be a smooth integer coprime with d and d', and let $\mathbf{A}$ be a matrix sampled as $\mathbf{A} \xleftarrow{\$} \mathcal{M}_n$.

Given the curves E_0, E_1, E_0', E_1', two bases P, Q of $E_0[n]$ and P', Q' of $E_0'[n]$, and the points $\mathbf{A}(\varphi(P)\ \varphi(Q))^T$ and $\mathbf{A}(\varphi'(P')\ \varphi'(Q'))^T$, compute the isogenies φ and φ'.

Since this problem provides additional information (two sets of torsion images, scaled by the same matrix), the hardness of Problem 7 is implied by the CIST^2 assumption, whereas the converse may not be true.

Having introduced the relevant computational assumptions, we can now prove the one-wayness of the FESTA trapdoor function.

Theorem 9. *The function $f_{(E_A, R_A, S_A)} : \mathbb{Z}/d_1\mathbb{Z} \times \mathbb{Z}/d_2\mathbb{Z} \times \mathcal{M}_b \to \mathcal{S}$, defined in Algorithm 1, is a one-way function, assuming the hardness of Problem 6 for $d = d_A$ and $n = 2^b$ and of Problem 8 for $d = d_1$, $d' = d_2$ and $n = 2^b$.*

Proof. In the definition of one-wayness (see Definition 1), the attacker $\mathcal{A}$ receives the FESTA public parameters, including the d_A-isogenous curves E_0 and E_A, and the FESTA output comprising of the curves E_0, E_1 and the points P_0, Q_0, P_1, Q_1, computed as in Algorithm 1, and produces the isogenies φ_1, φ_2 and the matrix $\mathbf{B}$.

Through a hybrid argument, we can replace curve E_A, which is the d_A-isogenous to E_0, with a random starting curve. Any attacker that can distinguish between the two cases can be used as a distinguisher for Problem 6. Now, any attacker that can invert the FESTA trapdoor function when the curves E_0 and E_1 are randomly generated can be used to solve Problem 8, since the input and outputs are the same.   □

Under the strong assumption that an attacker that can solve Problem 6 can do so for any degree d, Problem 6 and 7 are equivalent, and the hardness of Problem 7 is implied by that of Problem 8. In that case, Theorem 9 can thus be simplified to rely only on the CIST^2 assumption.

Hardness Analysis. We now discuss potential strategies that an attacker may employ to solve the presented problems and introduce several arguments to justify the presumed hardness of the corresponding computational assumptions.

First, let us consider the torsion point attacks [9,36,48]: as argued in [48, Section 6.4], given a d-isogeny φ, it is possible to recover φ if the image of the n-torsion is available, provided $n^2 > 4d$. While FESTA does reveal torsion point images of sufficiently large order, these are scaled by a random invertible diagonal matrix. An attacker may recover the determinant of such a matrix through pairing computations since $e([\alpha]\varphi(P), [\beta]\varphi(Q)) = e(P,Q)^{\alpha\beta \deg \varphi}$ and P, Q and $\deg \varphi$ are known. This information can be used to remove one variable: given $P' = [\alpha]\varphi(P)$, $Q' = [\beta]\varphi(Q)$ and $\alpha\beta$, scaling Q' by $(\alpha\beta)^{-1} \pmod{n}$ yields the point $Q'' = [1/\alpha]\varphi(Q)$. Thus, P' and Q'' are the images of P, Q scaled by a random diagonal matrix of determinant one, where the scaling depends uniquely on the value α. While this change reduces the number of variables, it does not affect security because α is randomly sampled from an exponentially large set. Due to this reduction, in the rest of the paper we can restrict the matrices to those with unitary determinant without affecting the security of the protocol.

If the attacks on SIDH do not apply to FESTA, it is natural to wonder whether the attacks could be extended to cover the case of scaled torsion points. This seems unlikely, because the torsion information revealed by FESTA is significantly less than that in SIDH, or even the variants of SIDH called M-SIDH and MD-SIDH [26] that are believed to be secure—we compare FESTA to M-SIDH and MD-SIDH at the end of this section.

Another attack strategy consists of guessing (or brute forcing) the scaling value α. While the scaling values are sampled from an exponentially large set, the attacker can also focus on recovering only part of α. Given the scaled points $P' = [\alpha]\varphi(P)$ and $Q' = [\alpha^{-1}]\varphi(Q)$, the attacker can scale them by a power of two and obtain

$$2^{b-j}P' = [\alpha \bmod 2^j]\varphi([2^{b-j}]P), \quad 2^{b-j}Q' = [\alpha^{-1} \bmod 2^j]\varphi([2^{b-j}]Q).$$

This means that it is possible to guess only $\alpha \bmod 2^j$ if the images of points of order 2^j is enough to apply the SIDH attacks on the secret isogeny. However, FESTA uses isogenies of degree $2^{2\lambda}$, which implies this guessing attack requires $j = \lambda$ and has thus a computational cost of 2^λ. Thus, as long as the isogenies have degree at least $2^{2\lambda}$, the best known attack against Problem 6 and 7 is a simple meet-in-the-middle attack that ignores the additional torsion information.

Remark 10. Some isogeny protocols have been known to be vulnerable when the starting curve has known endomorphism ring [4,6], when the known endomorphism ring contains small endomorphisms [26], or when the starting curve (and potentially the underlying prime) is maliciously chosen [45]. In many of these cases, a trusted setup is a necessary countermeasure [2]. This does not appear to be the case in FESTA, where Problem 7 remains hard even when the starting curve E_0 is a special curve with known endomorphism ring, such as the case $j(E_0) = 1728$ or a close neighbour. Nonetheless, any potential future attack that exploits unknown endomorphism ring can be avoided by generating E_0 during key generation and including its description in the public key.

Very recent analysis [11] has shown that it is possible to recover an isogeny given its scaled action, i.e. efficiently solve Problem 7 when the attacker knows an endomorphism on E_0 (or an endomorphism composed with the Frobenius map from E_0 to its Frobenius conjugate) that acts as scalar multiplication on the starting basis P, Q. However, a random basis, such as that deterministically generated from its curve, is subject to such an attack only with probability negligible in the security parameter. The parameters chosen in the implementation described in Sect. 7 are thus not affected by this attack.

Up until now, we focused on the hardness of the CIST assumption. However, the security of FESTA relies on the CIST^2 assumption, which might be easier to break. This is because the attacker has access to two CIST samples, where the scaling matrix $\mathbf{A}$ is the same. This may be useful, for instance, because an attacker that successfully recovers the isogeny in one of the CIST samples can obtain the correct torsion images in the other sample by scaling by $\mathbf{A}^{-1}$, recovered in the first sample. Applying the SIDH attacks then yields the second isogeny in polynomial time. However, this approach relies on one CIST instance being already broken. More generally, it seems that the correlated scaling matrix does not reveal significantly more information: the correlation between the instances is very tenuous, as the two samples have different starting curves and use isogenies of different large degrees (usually, the two degrees are coprime). Thus, it is unclear how an attacker may exploit the correlation to devise a strategy to break either CIST instance.

If we consider quantum-enabled adversaries, the security profile of FESTA remains mostly unchanged. Similarly to the classical case, it appears to be hard for a quantum attacker to exploit the scaled torsion images. Thus, such an attacker would be limited to attempting to solve the torsionless version of the isogeny problem, i.e. recover the secret isogeny given only the end curves and the isogeny degree. In this setting, we can rely on the quantum security analysis of SIDH [31], which shows that sufficiently long isogenies are hard to recover even with a quantum computer.

Comparison with Existing Protocols. In SIDH, and M-SIDH and MD-SIDH [26], the parties reveal the scaled action $[\alpha]\varphi(P), [\alpha]\varphi(Q)$ of a secret isogeny φ on a torsion basis P, Q (in SIDH, $\alpha = 1$), but crucially the scaling value is the same for both points. This information is sufficient to compute the images of exponentially-many full-order subgroups: for any subgroup $\langle [x]P + [y]Q \rangle$, its image under the secret isogeny is $\langle [x]([\alpha]\varphi(P)) + [y]([\alpha]\varphi(Q)) \rangle$. This is not the case in FESTA: since the torsion images are scaled by different values, only the pushforward of two subgroups of full order is revealed: the pushforward of $\langle P \rangle$ is $\langle [\alpha]\varphi(P) \rangle$ and that of $\langle Q \rangle$ is $\langle [1/\alpha]\varphi(Q) \rangle$. Hence, FESTA reveals significantly less information about its secret isogenies than SIDH, M-SIDH, and MD-SIDH, which makes an extension of the SIDH attacks to FESTA unlikely.

We can also compare FESTA to other isogeny-based protocols. In binSIDH and terSIDH [3], the parties also reveal the images of two torsion points scaled by different values, similarly to what happens in FESTA. Indeed, Problem 7 is very similar to [3, Problem 5 (SSIP-A)]; however, the torsion points in binSIDH and terSIDH have highly composite order. This means that the pushforward of exponentially many subgroups of full order is still available, although the number is much smaller than if the points were scaled by the same value. Thus, FESTA uses torsion points of prime power order, and thus also reveals less information than binSIDH and terSIDH.

Lastly, if we consider CSIDH (in its many variants), we see that CSIDH also implicitly reveals the images of some subgroups: the image of the subgroup $\ker(\pi - 1) \cap E_0[\ell]$ under a secret isogeny from E_0 to E_1 is $\ker(\pi - 1) \cap E_1[\ell]$, and the image of $\ker(\pi + 1) \cap E_0[\ell]$ is $\ker(\pi + 1) \cap E_1[\ell]$. While this suggests a relationship between the CSIDH assumption and the hardness of Problem 7, the isogenies used in CSIDH are $\mathbb{F}_p$-rational. This may be a small difference, but it makes the two assumptions different enough that they cannot be compared. For instance, consider the attack by Castryck and Vercauteren [11]: while it applies to specially crafted instances of FESTA, the attack cannot be extended to CSIDH.

5   The FESTA Public-Key Encryption Protocol

In this section, we show how the FESTA trapdoor function can be used to build public-key encryption protocols with different security guarantees.

5.1   IND-CCA Encryption in the QROM

Given an injective partial-domain trapdoor function, Ebrahimi [25] showed it is possible to obtain a IND-CCA PKE, secure in the Quantum Random Oracle Model (QROM) by using the OAEP transform.

To use the OAEP transform in our construction, we first need to prove that the FESTA function is indeed a partial-domain trapdoor function.

Theorem 11. *The function* $f_{(E_A, R_A, S_A)} : \mathbb{Z}/d_1\mathbb{Z} \times (\mathbb{Z}/d_2\mathbb{Z} \times \mathcal{M}_b) \to \mathcal{S}$ *defined in Algorithm 1 is a quantum partial one-way function, under the hardness of Problem 7 and 8.*

Proof. We show a stronger statement, i.e. that recovering any of three inputs is as hard as full-domain inversion: given the isogeny φ_1, the matrix $\mathbf{B}$ can be obtained by computing the change-of-basis matrix between $\varphi_1(P_b), \varphi_1(Q_b)$ and R_1, S_1. The remaining input, the isogeny φ_2, can be computed as the output of $\mathsf{TorAtk}(E_A, R_A, S_A, E_2, R_2^\star, S_2^\star, d_2)$, where the points $R_2^\star, S_2^\star$ are obtained by scaling the points R_2, S_2 by $\mathbf{B}^{-1}$. $\square$

After applying the OAEP transform, we obtain the following PKE protocol: the prime p, the curve E_0, the values d_1, d_2, d_A, b, and a description of the set $\mathcal{M}_b$ form the PKE parameters. We also rely on two random oracles, $G : \mathbb{Z}/d_2\mathbb{Z} \times \mathcal{M}_b \to \mathbb{Z}/d_1\mathbb{Z}$, and $H : \mathbb{Z}/d_1\mathbb{Z} \to \mathbb{Z}/d_2\mathbb{Z} \times \mathcal{M}_b$. The KeyGen algorithm is similar to that in the trapdoor function, and it produces the trapdoor public parameters E_A, R_A, S_A.

To encrypt, we first evaluate G at a randomly sampled input (r, R), and we use its output, combined with the message m, to determine the kernel of the isogeny φ_1. The isogeny φ_2 and the matrix $\mathbf{B}$, which are the remaining part of the input for the trapdoor function, are deterministically derived from the randomness (r, R) and the kernel of φ_1 via H. The output of the trapdoor function determines the ciphertext of the encryption algorithm.

During decryption, the trapdoor information is used to recover the isogenies φ_1, φ_2 and the matrix $\mathbf{B}$, from which the message can be extracted. These procedures are formalised in Algorithms 3 and 4.

Note that, unlike the trapdoor definition used in [25], the input and output spaces of our trapdoor function are not binary strings; thus, the xor operation used in the transform presented in [25] would not produce correct results. We replaced it with ring addition for the values representing kernel generators and matrix multiplications for the scaling matrix, without affecting the security of the transform.

Algorithm 3. FESTA.Enc(pk, m)

Input: The public key pk $= (E_A, R_A, S_A)$ and the message m to be encrypted.
Output: The ciphertext $(E_1, R_1, S_1, E_2, R_2, S_2)$.

1: Sample $r \xleftarrow{\$} \mathbb{Z}/d_2\mathbb{Z}$ and $R \xleftarrow{\$} \mathcal{M}_b$.
2: Write $m' = m \,||\, 0^k \bmod d_1$ and compute $s = m' + G(r, R)$.
3: Write $(x, X) = H(s)$ and compute $t = x + r$, $T = XR$.
4: Compute ct $= f_{(E_A, R_A, S_A)}(s, t, T)$.   ▷ Using Algorithm 1
5: **return** ct $= (E_1, R_1, S_1, E_2, R_2, S_2)$.

Algorithm 4. FESTA.Dec(sk, ct)

Input: The secret key sk $= (\mathbf{A}, \varphi_A)$ and the ciphertext ct $= (E_1, R_1, S_1, E_2, R_2, S_2)$.
Output: The decrypted message m or $\perp$ on failure.
1: Compute $(s, t, T) = f^{-1}_{(E_A, R_A, S_A)}(\text{sk}, \text{ct})$.   ▷ Using Algorithm 2
2: Write $(x, X) = H(s)$ and compute $r = t - x$, $R = X^{-1}T$.
3: Compute $m' = s - G(r, R)$ and write $m \,||\, m_k = m'$, where $|m_k| = k$.
4: **if** $m_k = 0^k$ **then**
5:     **return** m.
6: **else**
7:     **return** $\perp$.

Remark 12. Most post-quantum encryption protocols attain IND-CCA security using the Fujisaki-Okamoto transform [27], which requires re-evaluating the encryption procedure during decryption. Besides the computational overhead, the re-evaluation check has enabled a wide range of side-channel attacks [52]. These issues are entirely avoided by FESTA: decryption does not require to run the encryption algorithm, which reduces the latency of the decryption algorithm and brings a significant advantage in the development of side-channel-resistant implementations.

Partial-Input Extraction. The OAEP transform requires that the entire input is computed in Line 1 of Algorithm 4. This is necessary to avoid trivial CCA attacks: in the case of FESTA, if the matrix $\mathbf{B}$ is not recovered, an attacker may scale all torsion points by the same diagonal matrix to obtain a different but valid ciphertext. However, recovering all inputs limits our choice of parameters (as we will show in Sect. 6, extracting both isogenies φ_1 and φ_2 requires d_1, d_2, and d_A to be pairwise coprime) and reduces the efficiency of the inversion algorithm.

In the Random Oracle Model, we can modify the trapdoor function with a technique similar to the Fujisaki-Okamoto transform [28]. The new function f receives as input only the kernel corresponding to φ_1: the isogeny φ_2 and the matrix $\mathbf{B}$ are obtained deterministically from φ_1 through a random oracle. The inversion function also needs to be modified to extract the isogeny φ_1 and $\mathbf{B}$. Then, from the knowledge of $\ker(\varphi_1)$, we check that the kernel of φ_2 is correct to ensure that the output matches what an honest evaluator would have computed. If we only need to recover φ_1 during inversion, we would not require d_2 to be coprime with d_A; this would translate in a prime p that is about λ bits shorter than the prime currently proposed.

The parameters proposed in Sect. 7.3 and the implementation discussed in Sect. 7 consider a full inversion and do not integrate this optimisation. This is to keep FESTA simple and maintain a cleaner security proof. We leave a thorough analysis of the benefits of this optimisation for future work.

5.2 IND-CCA Encryption in the Standard Model

While trapdoor functions from group actions are known in the literature [1], FESTA is currently the only secure trapdoor function based on non-group-action isogenies. Besides enabling efficient encryption, as described in the previous section, this allows us to apply the techniques presented in [30] to obtain a PKE protocol that is IND-CCA secure in the standard model. To the best of our knowledge, this is the first PKE based on non-group-action isogenies to be IND-CCA secure in the standard model.

The construction relies upon two building blocks: a randomness-recoverable IND-CPA PKE and a tagged set commitment protocol. The first can be built from an *almost-all-keys injective trapdoor function*. This requires that for nearly all private/public key pairs, the trapdoor inversion function outputs precisely the same input that the function was evaluated at for *all* inputs. This is generally not the case in FESTA since for a large class of public keys, it may be possible that a specific input produces an output curve with j-invariant in $\{0, 1728\}$. In that case, the function may not be injective because the target curve has additional automorphisms. However, in FESTA, whether the inversion is correct depends entirely on public information: hence, we can check whether an input may lead to issues by evaluating the trapdoor function and checking the j-invariant of the output. We can thus satisfy the almost-all-keys injective property by redefining the function input to exclude the particular inputs that may be problematic.

The construction of tagged set commitment protocol requires, besides a trapdoor function, a strongly secure one-time signature. Such a signature can be constructed from any one-way function [33]: we can thus use the FESTA function to construct all the elements needed to obtain an isogeny-based PKE that is IND-CCA secure in the standard model.

6   Concrete Instantiation

In this section, we propose concrete parameter sets for FESTA. Such parameters are specifically tailored to make the recovery of the d_i-isogenies as fast as possible via Theorem 4.

6.1   Recovering an Isogeny from Torsion Point Images

We now describe how to invert the trapdoor functions proposed in Sect. 3. Let $\varphi_1\colon E_0 \to E_1$, $\varphi_A\colon E_0 \to E_A$ and $\varphi_2\colon E_A \to E_2$ be three isogenies between supersingular elliptic curves having odd degrees d_1, d_A and d_2, respectively, such that $\gcd(d_1, d_A) = \gcd(d_1, d_2) = \gcd(d_2, d_A) = 1$. The isogeny φ_A is computed as the composition of two isogenies $\varphi_{A,1}\colon E_0 \to \tilde{E}_A$ and $\varphi_{A,2}\colon \tilde{E}_A \to E_A$ of coprime degrees $d_{A,1}$ and $d_{A,2}$, respectively. Graphically, we have

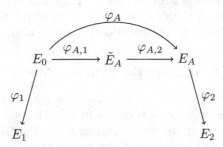

Suppose now we have found $m_1, m_2, b \in \mathbb{Z}_{>0}$ such that

$$m_1^2 d_{A,1} d_1 + m_2^2 d_{A,2} d_2 = 2^b, \tag{1}$$

for some odd m_i coprime to d_1, d_2 and d_A. Specialising Theorem 4 to the case where $\varphi_{N_1} = [m_1] \circ \varphi_1 \circ \widehat{\varphi}_{A,1}$ and $\varphi_{N_2} = [m_2] \circ \varphi_2 \circ \varphi_{A,2}$, the isogeny Φ with kernel

$$\langle([m_2 d_{A,2} d_2]\varphi_1(P_b), [d_1 m_1]\varphi_2 \circ \varphi_A(P_b)), ([m_2 d_{A,2} d_2]\varphi_1(Q_b), [d_1 m_1]\varphi_2 \circ \varphi_A(Q_b))\rangle,$$

where the points P_b, Q_b form a basis of $E_0[2^b]$, has matrix form

$$\Phi = \begin{pmatrix} [m_1] \circ \varphi_{A,1} \circ \widehat{\varphi}_1 & -[m_2] \circ \widehat{\varphi}_{A,2} \circ \widehat{\varphi}_2 \\ [m_2] \circ g_{d_2 d_{A,2}} & [m_1] \circ \widehat{g}_{d_{A,1} d_1} \end{pmatrix}.$$

Additionally, we have that $\varphi_2 \circ \varphi_A \circ \widehat{\varphi}_1 = g_{d_{A,1}d_1} \circ g_{d_2 d_{A,2}}$, $\deg(g_{d_{A,1}d_1}) = d_{A,1}d_1$ and $\deg(g_{d_2 d_{A,2}}) = d_2 d_{A,2}$.

Given a security parameter λ, we define

$$\mathsf{params}_\lambda = (m_1, m_2, b, p, d_1, d_{A,1}, d_{A,2}, d_2, E_0)$$

to be a parameter set, where E_0 is a supersingular curve whose j-invariant $\neq$ $0, 1728$ and $E_0(\mathbb{F}_{p^2}) \simeq \mathbb{Z}/(p+1)\mathbb{Z} \times \mathbb{Z}/(p+1)\mathbb{Z}$, the prime p is of the form $f 2^b d_1 (d_{A,1}d_{A,2})_{\mathsf{sf}} d_2 - 1$ for some small $f > 0$, and $m_1^2 d_{A,1}d_1 + m_2^2 d_{A,2}d_2 = 2^b$.

On input params_λ, we give a precise description of the trapdoor evaluation algorithm (Algorithm 1) in Algorithm 5. The kernels, which are cyclic subgroups $\langle K_1 \rangle \subset E_0[d_1]$ and $\langle K_2 \rangle \subset E_A[d_2]$, are chosen such that they are generated by an element of the form $P + [x]Q$, for some basis (P, Q): thus, they can respectively be represented by $s_1 \in [0, d_1 - 1]$ and $s_2 \in [0, d_2 - 1]$, given two bases (P_{d_1}, Q_{d_1}) of $E_0[d_1]$ and $(P_{d_2}^A, Q_{d_2}^A)$ of $E_A[d_2]$.

Since d_1 and d_2 both divide $p + 1$, the d_1-torsion of E_0 and the d_2-torsion of E_A are defined over $\mathbb{F}_{p^2}$. This choice allows us to compute d_i-isogenies using points that are $\mathbb{F}_{p^2}$-rational, making the entire computation faster. As for the d_A-isogeny, only $(d_A)_{\mathsf{sf}}$ is included as a factor in $p + 1$ as we need not represent the kernel of φ_A explicitly.

Algorithm 5. $f_{(E_A, R_A, S_A)}(s_1, s_2, \mathbf{B})$

Input: Two integers $s_1 \in [0, d_1 - 1]$ and $s_2 \in [0, d_2 - 1]$, and $\mathbf{B} \in \mathcal{M}_b$.
Output: $(E_1, R_1, S_1, E_2, R_2, S_2)$.
1: Compute the bases $(P_{d_1}, Q_{d_1}) \leftarrow \mathsf{TorGen}(E_0, d_1)$ and $(P_{d_2}^A, Q_{d_2}^A) \leftarrow \mathsf{TorGen}(E_A, d_2)$.
2: Compute the d_1-isogeny $\varphi_1 \colon E_0 \to E_1$ having kernel $\langle P_{d_1} + [s_1]Q_{d_1} \rangle$.
3: Compute the d_2-isogeny $\varphi_2 \colon E_A \to E_2$ having kernel $\langle P_{d_2}^A + [s_2]Q_{d_2}^A \rangle$.
4: Acting with scalar multiplication compute

$$\begin{pmatrix} R_1 \\ S_1 \end{pmatrix} = \mathbf{B} \begin{pmatrix} \varphi_1(P_b) \\ \varphi_1(Q_b) \end{pmatrix} \qquad \begin{pmatrix} R_2 \\ S_2 \end{pmatrix} = \mathbf{B} \begin{pmatrix} \varphi_2(R_A) \\ \varphi_2(S_A) \end{pmatrix}.$$

5: **return** $(E_1, R_1, S_1, E_2, R_2, S_2)$.

To invert $f_{(E_A, R_A, S_A)}$, given the tuple $(E_1, R_1, S_1, E_2, R_2, S_2)$, we compute the points

$$\begin{pmatrix} R_2' \\ S_2' \end{pmatrix} = \mathbf{A}^{-1} \begin{pmatrix} R_2 \\ S_2 \end{pmatrix}.$$

Thus, as we explained above, the isogeny Φ with kernel

$$\langle ([m_2 d_{A,2}d_2]R_1, [d_1 m_1]R_2'), ([m_2 d_{A,2}d_2]S_1, [d_1 m_1]S_2') \rangle,$$

has matrix form

$$\Phi = \begin{pmatrix} [m_1] \circ \varphi_{A,1} \circ \widehat{\varphi}_1 & -[m_2] \circ \widehat{\varphi}_{A,2} \circ \widehat{\varphi}_2 \\ [m_2] \circ g_{d_2 d_{A,2}} & [m_1] \circ \widehat{g}_{d_{A,1}d_1} \end{pmatrix}.$$

If F is the image curve of $g_{d_2 d_{A,2}} \colon E_1 \to F$, then Φ maps $E_1 \times E_2$ onto $\tilde{E}_A \times F$, up to polarised isomorphisms.

Let $(P^1_{d_1}, Q^1_{d_1}) \leftarrow \mathsf{TorGen}(E_1, d_1)$ and $(P^2_{d_2}, Q^2_{d_2}) \leftarrow \mathsf{TorGen}(E_2, d_2)$. Then, we have

$$\begin{pmatrix} L \\ - \end{pmatrix} := \Phi \begin{pmatrix} P^1_{d_1} + R_1 \\ P^2_{d_2} \end{pmatrix} = \begin{pmatrix} [m_1]\varphi_{A,1} \circ \widehat{\varphi}_1(P^1_{d_1} + R_1) - [m_2]\widehat{\varphi}_{A,2} \circ \widehat{\varphi}_2(P^2_{d_2}) \\ \underline{\hspace{2cm}} \end{pmatrix},$$

from which we can compute

$$[2^b d_2 m_1]\varphi_{A,1} \circ \widehat{\varphi}_1(P^1_{d_1}) = [2^b d_2] L,$$
$$[2^b d_1 m_2]\widehat{\varphi}_{A,2} \circ \widehat{\varphi}_2(P^2_{d_2}) = -[2^b d_1] L,$$
$$[d_1 d_2 m_1]\varphi_{A,1} \circ \widehat{\varphi}_1(R_1) = [d_1 d_2] L.$$

Similarly, we evaluate $\Phi \begin{pmatrix} Q^1_{d_1} + S_1 & Q^2_{d_2} \end{pmatrix}^T$ to obtain $[2^b d_2 m_1]\varphi_{A,1} \circ \widehat{\varphi}_1(Q^1_{d_1})$, $[2^b d_1 m_2]\widehat{\varphi}_{A,2} \circ \widehat{\varphi}_2(Q^2_{d_2})$ and $[d_1 d_2 m_1]\varphi_{A,1} \circ \widehat{\varphi}_1(S_1)$.

Using the knowledge of $\varphi_{A,i}$, we can extract the images $\widehat{\varphi}_1(P^1_{d_1})$, $\widehat{\varphi}_1(Q^1_{d_1})$, $\widehat{\varphi}_2(P^2_{d_2})$ and $\widehat{\varphi}_2(Q^2_{d_2})$. With these, we compute s_1 and s_2 such that $\ker(\varphi_1) = \langle P_{d_1} + [s_1]Q_{d_1} \rangle$ and $\ker(\varphi_2) = \langle P^A_{d_2} + [s_2]Q^A_{d_2} \rangle$. This is slightly more complicated than the more common case when d_1 is a prime power and can be done following Algorithm 6.

Algorithm 6. ComputeCanonicalKernel$(\widehat{\varphi}(P'), \widehat{\varphi}(Q'), d)$

Input: $\widehat{\varphi}(P')$ and $\widehat{\varphi}(Q')$, where $\varphi \colon E \to E'$ is a d-isogeny and $\langle P', Q' \rangle = E'[d]$.
Output: $s \in [0, d-1]$ such that $\ker(\varphi) = \langle P + [s]Q \rangle$, where $(P, Q) \leftarrow \mathsf{TorGen}(E, d)$.[4]
1: Compute the canonical basis $(P, Q) \leftarrow \mathsf{TorGen}(E, d)$, and let $d = \prod_{i=1}^n \ell_i^{e_i}$.
2: Compute $a_1, b_1 \in [0, d-1]$ such that $\widehat{\varphi}(P') = [a_1]P + [b_1]Q$.
3: Compute $a_2, b_2 \in [0, d-1]$ such that $\widehat{\varphi}(Q') = [a_2]P + [b_2]Q$.
4: **for** $i = 1, \ldots, n$ **do**
5:     **if** $a_1 = 0 \pmod{\ell_i}$ **then**
6:         Impose $t_1 = 0 \pmod{\ell_i^{e_i}}$ and $t_2 = a_2^{-1} \pmod{\ell_i^{e_i}}$.
7:     **else**
8:         Impose $t_1 = a_1^{-1} \pmod{\ell_i^{e_i}}$ and $t_2 = 0 \pmod{\ell_i^{e_i}}$.
9: Lift t_1 and t_2 in $\mathbb{Z}/d\mathbb{Z}$, and define $s \leftarrow t_1 b_1 + t_2 b_2$.
10: **return** s.

Finally, we highlight that

$$\begin{pmatrix} \widehat{\varphi}_1(R_1) \\ \widehat{\varphi}_1(S_1) \end{pmatrix} = d_1 \mathbf{B} \begin{pmatrix} P_b \\ Q_b \end{pmatrix},$$

which implies we can recover the matrix $\mathbf{B}$ by solving a discrete logarithm problem, which is efficient as the order of our points is a power of two. To ensure

---

[4] We highlight that we already know that $\ker(\varphi)$ can be expressed as $\langle P + [s]Q \rangle$, for some $s \in \mathbb{Z}/d\mathbb{Z}$.

that the inversion input was computed as the correct output of the FESTA trap-door function, we check that $\mathbf{B} \in \mathcal{M}_b$: if not, the inversion algorithm fails and returns $\perp$. We summarise the inversion procedure in Algorithm 7.

Algorithm 7. $f^{-1}_{(E_A, R_A, S_A)}(E_1, R_1, S_1, E_2, R_2, S_2)$

Input: TDF output $y := (E_1, R_1, S_1, E_2, R_2, S_2)$, and $\mathsf{sk} = (\mathbf{A}, \varphi_{A,1}, \varphi_{A,2})$.
Output: The TDF input $x := (s_1, s_2, \mathbf{B})$ such that $f_{(E_A, R_A, S_A)}(x) = y$.

1: Compute $\begin{pmatrix} R'_2 \\ S'_2 \end{pmatrix} = \mathbf{A}^{-1} \begin{pmatrix} R_2 \\ S_2 \end{pmatrix}$.

2: Define Φ to be the isogeny with kernel

$$\langle ([m_2 d_{A,2} d_2] R_1, [m_1 d_1] R'_2), ([m_2 d_{A,2} d_2] S_1, [m_1 d_1] S'_2) \rangle.$$

3: **if** The codomain of Φ does not split **then return** $\perp$.

4: Set $(P^1_{d_1}, Q^1_{d_1}) \leftarrow \mathsf{TorGen}(E_1, d_1)$ and $(P^2_{d_2}, Q^2_{d_2}) \leftarrow \mathsf{TorGen}(E_2, d_2)$.

5: Evaluate

$$\begin{pmatrix} L_1 \\ - \end{pmatrix} = \Phi \begin{pmatrix} P^1_{d_1} + R_1 \\ P^2_{d_2} \end{pmatrix} \quad \text{and} \quad \begin{pmatrix} L_2 \\ - \end{pmatrix} = \Phi \begin{pmatrix} Q^1_{d_1} + S_1 \\ Q^2_{d_2} \end{pmatrix}.$$

6: Unpack L_1 to obtain $\varphi_{A,1} \circ \widehat{\varphi}_1(P^1_{d_1})$, $\varphi_{A,1} \circ \widehat{\varphi}_1(R_1)$ and $\widehat{\varphi}_{A,2} \circ \widehat{\varphi}_2(P^2_{d_2})$.

7: Unpack L_2 to obtain $\varphi_{A,1} \circ \widehat{\varphi}_1(Q^1_{d_1})$, $\varphi_{A,1} \circ \widehat{\varphi}_1(S_1)$ and $\widehat{\varphi}_{A,2} \circ \widehat{\varphi}_2(Q^2_{d_2})$.

8: Set $s_1 \leftarrow \mathsf{ComputeCanonicalKernel}(\widehat{\varphi}_1(P^1_{d_1}), \widehat{\varphi}_1(Q^1_{d_1}), d_1)$.   ▷ Via Algorithm 6

9: Set $s_2 \leftarrow \mathsf{ComputeCanonicalKernel}(\widehat{\varphi}_2(P^2_{d_2}), \widehat{\varphi}_2(Q^2_{d_2}), d_2)$.   ▷ Via Algorithm 6

10: Compute $\mathbf{B} \in \mathcal{M}_b$ such that

$$\begin{pmatrix} \widehat{\varphi}_1(R_1) \\ \widehat{\varphi}_1(S_1) \end{pmatrix} = d_1 \mathbf{B} \begin{pmatrix} P_b \\ Q_b \end{pmatrix}.$$

11: **if** $\mathbf{B} \notin \mathcal{M}_b$ **then**
12:     **return** $\perp$.
13: **else**
14:     **return** $(s_1, s_2, \mathbf{B})$.

Remark 13. To compute the images

$$\widehat{\varphi}_1(P^1_{d_1}) = [d_{A,1}]^{-1} \widehat{\varphi}_{A,1} \left(\varphi_{A,1} \circ \widehat{\varphi}_1(P^1_{d_1}) \right), \quad \text{and}$$

$$\widehat{\varphi}_1(Q^1_{d_1}) = [d_{A,1}]^{-1} \widehat{\varphi}_{A,1} \left(\varphi_{A,1} \circ \widehat{\varphi}_1(Q^1_{d_1}) \right),$$

we need to evaluate the isogeny $\widehat{\varphi}_{A,1}$ on points of order d_1. We can avoid such a computation by precomputing the image of the isogeny on a basis of $E_A[d_1]$ during KeyGen and expressing the points in terms of such a basis.

The same approach can be used to compute the points $\widehat{\varphi}_2(P^2_{d_2})$ and $\widehat{\varphi}_2(Q^2_{d_2})$, where we precompute the action of φ_{A_2} on a basis of $\tilde{E}_A[d_2]$, and the points $\widehat{\varphi}_1(R_1)$ and $\widehat{\varphi}_1(S_1)$ used to recover the matrix $\mathbf{B}$.

6.2 Computing Parameters

We propose a method to generate solutions of Eq. (1), i.e. finding parameters that allow us to efficiently run the trapdoor inversion algorithm. Given the security analysis of Sect. 4, we also have several additional requirements on the solutions we can use. In particular, we want all the solution values, i.e. $m_1, d_1, m_2, d_2, d_{A,1}, d_{A,2}$, to be odd, so that the isogenies have degree coprime with the torsion points order. Moreover, we require that isogeny degrees d_1, $d_A = d_{A,1}d_{A,2}$ and d_2 are pairwise coprime and sufficiently long, i.e. $\log(d_1), \log(d_A), \log(d_2) \geq 2\lambda$, to prevent meet-in-the-middle and torsion-guessing attacks.

The number of solutions and the corresponding protocol efficiency crucially depends on the smoothness of the degrees of the isogenies we are using. Let us denote our smoothness bound as B. Let c be a positive integer such that the number $T := 2^c - 1$ is B-smooth. We start by finding primitive solutions, i.e. solutions $(x, y) \in \mathbb{Z} \times \mathbb{Z}$ with $\gcd(x, y) = 1$, for the equation

$$x^2 + y^2 T = 2^b. \tag{2}$$

We do so by ranging the value b within a reasonable interval, and finding solutions of Eq. (2) via Cornacchia's algorithm [15]. Given a primitive solution (x, y) for some even $b > 0$, we have

$$y^2 T = (2^{b/2} - x)(2^{b/2} + x).$$

Define T_1 to be the B-smooth part of $2^{b/2} - x$ and T_2 to be the B-smooth part of $2^{b/2} + x$. Then, there exist $m_1, m_2 \in \mathbb{Z}_{>0}$ such that $m_1^2 T_1 = 2^{b/2} - x$ and $m_2^2 T_2 = 2^{b/2} + x$. In particular, we have

$$m_1^2 T_1 + m_2^2 T_2 = 2^{b/2+1}.$$

If $T_1 T_2$ and T_i are sufficiently large to guarantee security (we need $T_1 T_2 > 2^{6\lambda}$ and $T_i > 2^{2\lambda}$), we define d_i to be the smoothest factor of T_i such that $d_i \sim 2^{2\lambda}$ for $i = 1, 2$. Additionally, we define $d_{A,i}$ to be the smoothest part of T_i/d_i such that $d_{A,1}d_{A,2} > 2^{2\lambda}$ and multiply m_i by $\sqrt{T_i/(d_i d_{A,i})}$, ensuring that the values d_1, $d_{A,1}$, $d_{A,2}$, d_2, m_1, m_2 are pairwise coprime. We thus have found solutions of Eq. (1) that guarantee our size requirements, i.e. a valid set of parameters.

To find parameter sets, we perform an exhaustive search ranging over different values of b and c within a reasonable interval. Experimentally, this approach is highly efficient, and it is easy to generate parameter sets for any security level. Ideally, to have a small prime p, we look for small b's satisfying the conditions above. Allowing for a larger smoothness bound B, it is possible to find smaller b's and in turn smaller primes p. This comes with a potential slowdown in performances. Different trade-offs between efficiency and bandwidth can be achieved: if bandwidth is a more valuable asset, then one could allow larger smoothness bound. Note that as well as reducing the size of the base field characteristic, reducing the size of b shortens the length of the $(2^b, 2^b)$-isogeny, which in turn speeds up the decryption algorithm.

6.3 Further Optimisations

We designed FESTA and chose its parameters to obtain an optimal trade-off between the performance of the three PKE algorithms (KeyGen, Enc, Dec), the size of public keys and ciphertexts, the hardness of the security assumptions, and the simplicity of the protocol. Many other options are possible: for instance, increasing the smoothness bound for the solutions of Eq. (2) leads to smaller primes (and thus smaller ciphertexts), at the cost of slower isogeny computations.

In this section, we discuss further optimisations that may lead to different trade-offs or that require further work to investigate.

Using Larger (ℓ, ℓ)-Isogenies. In the search for parameters, we restrict ourselves to torsion points of order a power of two. There is no fundamental reason why torsion points of odd order cannot be used; however, the inversion function needs to compute (ℓ, ℓ)-isogenies for any ℓ dividing the order of the torsion points. Currently, the formulae to compute (ℓ, ℓ)-isogenies are most practical for $\ell = 2$. However, future developments in the computation of isogenies between principally polarised abelian surfaces may render new parameter sets feasible.

The method we propose to find parameters in Sect. 6.2 generalises to any prime power. In other words, it appears that analysing the equation $x^2 + y^2 T = \ell^b$, when T is of the form $T = \ell^c - 1$ for increasing $b \in \mathbb{Z}_{>0}$, leads to smooth solutions of $m_1^2 d_1 d_{A,1} + m_2^2 d_2 d_{A,2} = \ell^{b/2+1}$. However, the same method does not appear to generalise for products of prime powers; for those parameters, it may be necessary to develop new tools to efficiently find parameter sets.

Higher-Dimensional Trapdoor Inversion. In [48, Section 6.4], Robert proposed a method that relies on isogenies in dimension four (heuristically, eight otherwise) to recover a d-isogeny from the map of the m-torsion under such an isogeny for $m^2 > 4d$. This method could be employed to obtain smaller parameters. For instance, given a security parameter λ, we define e_1, e_2 and e_3 such that $\ell_i^{e_i} > 2^{2\lambda}$ for some distinct odd small prime ℓ_i; then, we can use isogenies φ_1, φ_A and φ_2 with degrees $\ell_1^{e_1}$, $\ell_2^{e_2}$ and $\ell_3^{e_3}$, respectively. We can also choose b such that $2^b > 2\sqrt{\ell_1^{e_1} \ell_2^{e_2} \ell_3^{e_3}}$. With such parameters, we obtain a significantly smaller prime (roughly, $p \approx 2^{7\lambda}$) since the isogeny φ_A does not need to be rational. We expect a major improvement in the protocol bandwidth, as well as the running times of key generation and encryption. This would come at the cost of decryption efficiency, which would require the computation of higher dimensional isogenies.

It is also possible to introduce even more extreme trade-offs: by using irrational isogenies φ_1 and φ_2,[5] one can achieve very small primes that further improve the compactness of the protocol and the efficiency of the key generation

---

[5] The isogenies φ_i are irrational in the sense that each prime-degree isogeny factoring φ_i has kernel defined over $\mathbb{F}_{p^2}$, but the kernel of φ_i is not necessarily defined over $\mathbb{F}_{p^2}$.

and encryption procedures; however, this requires computing higher dimensional isogenies several times, which slows down the decryption algorithm even more.

7   Implementation

We provide a proof-of-concept implementation of FESTA in SageMath [51] and make it available at:

https://github.com/FESTA-PKE/FESTA-SageMath

We designed our implementation to be modular to facilitate translation into a high-performance language. In particular, we aimed to explicitly implement the algorithms for both the isogenies between elliptic curves and abelian varieties, without relying on the generic Sagemath implementations. In what follows, we explain some of the techniques we employed, and we propose concrete parameters.

7.1   Montgomery Curve x-Only Isogenies

To compute isogenies between elliptic curves, we leverage the efficient x-only formulae between Montgomery curves [17,46]. Additionally, we include $\sqrt{\text{élu}}$ [5] to evaluate isogenies of large prime degree and the formula using twisted Edwards curves in [38] for the computation of the codomain curves. Working with the x-only isogenies allows a significant improvement in performance, however, the y-coordinates of image points must eventually be recovered in order to compute the chain of $(2,2)$-isogenies between elliptic products. We use the following method to reconstruct the valid y-coordinates from the x-only point evaluation.

Let $E\colon y^2 = x^3 + Ax^2 + x$ and $E'\colon y^2 = x^3 + A'x^2 + x$ be two elliptic curves in Montgomery form connected by a d-isogeny $\varphi\colon E \to E'$ and suppose we want to evaluate the action of φ on P, Q generating the n-torsion, where $n \neq d$. Using the x-only isogeny formulae, we compute $x(\varphi(P))$ and $x(\varphi(Q))$. Then, we lift the x-coordinates onto the curve by computing y_P and y_Q, which we allow to be any square root of $x(\varphi(P))^3 + A'x(\varphi(P))^2 + x(\varphi(P))$ and $x(\varphi(Q))^3 + A'x(\varphi(Q))^2 + x(\varphi(Q))$. From this lifting, we effectively recover $\varphi(P) = \pm(x(\varphi(P)), y_P)$ up to an overall sign.

Although we cannot recover the correct sign for one point, we can recover a relative sign such that we recover the tuple $\pm(\varphi(P), \varphi(Q))$. To do this, we use the Weil pairing and compare

$$e_n^E(P, Q)^d \stackrel{?}{=} e_n^{E'}\big((x(\varphi(P)), y_P), (x(\varphi(Q)), y_Q)\big).$$

If the equality holds, then the lifted points can be used as the image, otherwise we flip a sign such that $\varphi(Q) = (x(\varphi(Q)), -y_Q)$. In this way, we evaluate the action of either φ or $-\varphi$ on the torsion basis. Given that we use canonical representations of the scaling matrices in $\mathcal{M}_b$, evaluating either of these isogenies does not represent a problem for the trapdoor. Overall, this allows us to perform two isogeny evaluations using x-only formula with the additional cost of two square-roots and two Weil pairings.

7.2   Optimisations of the (2, 2)-Isogeny Chain

The most expensive step of decryption is the evaluation of the $(2,2)$−isogeny chain between elliptic products. Of this computation, the majority of the cost is spent computing the isogenies via the Richelot correspondence between Jacobians of genus-2 hyperelliptic curves. The computational cost, just as in the elliptic case, is split between doubling to recover divisors of order two, and the evaluation of the isogenies themselves.

One optimisation, which we can borrow from our experience with elliptic curve isogenies, is to employ the optimal strategies introduced in [22] to minimise the cost of long isogeny chains. The generalisation of this problem to higher dimensional isogeny chains was recently studied in [13]. By measuring the relative cost of divisor doubling and isogeny evaluations, we can compute an optimal strategy using identical methods to the elliptic case.

Another performance improvement we made comes from deriving explicit addition and doubling algorithms for divisors of Jacobians of genus-2 hyperelliptic curves using only base field operations. Previously in the literature, effort was made to derive low cost genus-2 addition and doubling for the context of hyperelliptic Diffie-Hellman [8,18,34]. In this case, the hyperelliptic curve is fixed, and isomorphisms can be used to minimise the number of non-zero coefficients of the hyperelliptic curve model, effectively reducing the cost of divisor arithmetic.

For our implementation, the curve model of the codomain when computed via the Richelot correspondence is some generic (non-monic) sextic polynomial and the previously derived efficient formula are unsuitable for our doubling chains. To recover efficient formula, we generalise the work of [18] by using similar methods without restricting the hyperelliptic curve model to a friendly form. Ultimately, what is required is to solve linear equations to express the arithmetic in the polynomial ring $\mathbb{F}_q[X]$ as operations of the base field and pass as arguments to the addition and doubling formula the coefficients of the curve equation as well as the reduced Mumford coordinates.

Representing the cost of $\mathbb{F}_{p^2}$ inversion, multiplication and squaring as $\mathbf{I}, \mathbf{M}$ and $\mathbf{S}$, we have derived affine addition at a cost of $25\mathbf{M} + 4\mathbf{S} + 1\mathbf{I}$ and affine doubling at a cost of $32\mathbf{M} + 6\mathbf{S} + 1\mathbf{I}$. Practically, we find that our formulae are about four-times faster than the in-built SageMath divisor arithmetic and two-times faster than the optimised formula used in the SageMath implementation of the Castryck-Decru attack on SIDH [41]. We consider further improving these formulae to be future work.

7.3   Parameters

Following the approach in Sect. 6.2, we generated parameter sets for FESTA. We highlight that the proposed techniques allow for different trade-offs between the smoothness of the isogeny degrees and the length b of the chain of $(2,2)$-isogenies.

For FESTA-128, we define the following parameter set:

$$b := 632,$$
$$d_1 := (3^3 \cdot 19 \cdot 29 \cdot 37 \cdot 83 \cdot 139 \cdot 167 \cdot 251 \cdot 419 \cdot 421 \cdot 701 \cdot 839 \cdot 1009 \cdot$$
$$1259 \cdot 3061 \cdot 3779)^2,$$
$$d_2 := 7 \cdot (5^2 \cdot 7 \cdot 11 \cdot 13 \cdot 17 \cdot 41 \cdot 43 \cdot 71 \cdot 89 \cdot 127 \cdot 211 \cdot 281 \cdot 503 \cdot 631 \cdot$$
$$2309 \cdot 2521 \cdot 2647 \cdot 2729)^2,$$
$$d_{A,1} := (59 \cdot 6299 \cdot 6719 \cdot 9181)^2,$$
$$d_{A,2} := (3023 \cdot 3359 \cdot 4409 \cdot 5039 \cdot 19531 \cdot 22679 \cdot 41161)^2,$$
$$m_1 := 1492184945093476592520242083925044182103921,$$
$$m_2 := 25617331336429939300166693069,$$
$$f := 107.$$

The values d_1 and d_2 are 2^{12}-smooth, while $d_A = d_{A,1}d_{A,2}$ is 2^{16}-smooth. The corresponding prime, defined as $p = 2^b d_1 (d_{A,1}d_{A,2})_{\mathsf{sf}} d_2 f - 1$, is 1292-bit long. The public key and ciphertext sizes are, respectively, 561 and 1,122 bytes. The same approach can be used to produce parameter sets for higher security levels.

To reduce the bandwidth of FESTA, we compress the torsion points by expressing them in terms of linear coefficients of canonical bases, as proposed in [40,43]. Unlike in SIDH, however, our protocol needs the exact torsion images. This means the points cannot be scaled, and their compressed representation requires four coefficients of size equal to their order. However, since an attacker can always reconstruct the determinant of the scaling matrices, we can restrict ourselves to unitary matrices in $\mathcal{M}_b$. Then, given three of the four coefficients representing the scaled points, it is possible to retrieve the fourth one via the compatibility of the Weil pairing with isogenies. We remark the bandwidth of FESTA is affected by the choice of parameters: future developments may lead to smaller parameters, which would translate to significantly smaller public keys and ciphertexts.

We benchmarked our proof-of-concept implementation on an Apple M1 PRO CPU clocked at 3.2 GHz using a single performance core. Averaging 100 executions, we obtained that KeyGen, Enc and Dec run in 4.47, 3.09 and 9.14 s, respectively. The slowness of Dec compared to the other components is mainly caused by the computation of $(2,2)$-isogenies. Due to the lack of research on optimizing such computations in the past, we expect future work to significantly improve on this aspect, leading to a much faster decryption algorithm.

8   Conclusion

In this paper, we have introduced FESTA, an efficient isogeny-based public-key encryption (PKE) protocol that constructively relies on an application of the SIDH attacks. Preliminary experimental results show that our proof-of-concept implementation is competitive with optimised implementations of other isogeny-based PKEs. We are also currently working on an optimised implementation of FESTA, and we are looking forward to obtaining concrete running times.

The efficiency of the protocol is highly dependent on the smoothness bounds and size of the parameter sets: in future work, we will investigate different approaches to find more efficient parameters. In particular, our current choice of parameters is limited by the requirement of ensuring a fast decryption: a more optimised implementation of $(2, 2)$-isogenies will allow us to use smoother values. An interesting project for future work is to compare the performance of isogenies via the Richelot correspondence against those computed using theta functions.

Additionally, we chose a conservative approach when imposing the security requirements: we believe a more detailed analysis of the cost of certain attacks may lead to better parameter sets. Moreover, we highlight that FESTA can inherently benefit from advancements in computations of higher dimensional isogenies: new developments in those areas could lead to both smaller field characteristics and faster encryption.

Lastly, we believe that the flexible design of FESTA and the new techniques proposed in this work may lead to new mechanics that can be exploited to develop new advanced protocols, such as digital signatures and oblivious pseudorandom functions.

Acknowledgments. The authors are indebted to Tako Boris Fouotsa for fruitful feedback on a preliminary version of this paper that led to a more complete security analysis. The authors would also like to thank Ross Bowden, James Clements, Péter Kutas, and Chloe Martindale for useful discussions regarding the parameter generation, and Yan Bo Ti for an interesting discussion on potential adaptive attacks.

References

1. Alamati, N., De Feo, L., Montgomery, H., Patranabis, S.: Cryptographic group actions and applications. In: Moriai, S., Wang, H. (eds.) ASIACRYPT 2020, Part II. LNCS, vol. 12492, pp. 411–439. Springer, Cham (2020). https://doi.org/10.1007/978-3-030-64834-3_14
2. Basso, A., et al.: Supersingular curves you can trust. In: Hazay, C., Stam, M. (eds.) Advances in Cryptology - EUROCRYPT 2023. LNCS, vol. 14005, pp. 405–437. Springer, Cham (2023). https://doi.org/10.1007/978-3-031-30617-4_14
3. Basso, A., Fouotsa, T.B.: New SIDH countermeasures for a more efficient key exchange. Cryptology ePrint Archive, Paper 2023/791, To appear in "Asiacrypt 2023" (2023). https://eprint.iacr.org/2023/791
4. Basso, A., Kutas, P., Merz, S.-P., Petit, C., Sanso, A.: Cryptanalysis of an oblivious PRF from supersingular isogenies. In: Tibouchi, M., Wang, H. (eds.) ASIACRYPT 2021, Part I. LNCS, vol. 13090, pp. 160–184. Springer, Cham (2021). https://doi.org/10.1007/978-3-030-92062-3_6
5. Bernstein, D.J., de Feo, L., Leroux, A., Smith, B.: Faster computation of isogenies of large prime degree. In: Proceedings of the Fourteenth Algorithmic Number Theory Symposium, pp. 39–55. THE OPEN BOOK SERIES 4 (2020). https://doi.org/10.2140/obs.2020.4.39

6. Boneh, D., Kogan, D., Woo, K.: Oblivious pseudorandom functions from isogenies. In: Moriai, S., Wang, H. (eds.) ASIACRYPT 2020, Part II. LNCS, vol. 12492, pp. 520–550. Springer, Cham (2020). https://doi.org/10.1007/978-3-030-64834-3_18

7. Boneh, D., Shoup, V.: A Graduate Course in Applied Cryptography. Version 0.6 (2023). http://toc.cryptobook.us/

8. Bos, J.W., Costello, C., Hisil, H., Lauter, K.: Fast cryptography in genus 2. J. Cryptol. **29**(1), 28–60 (2016). https://doi.org/10.1007/s00145-014-9188-7

9. Castryck, W., Decru, T.: An efficient key recovery attack on SIDH. In: Hazay, C., Stam, M. (eds.) Advances in Cryptology - EUROCRYPT 2023. LNCS, vol. 14008, pp. 423–447. Springer, Cham (2023). https://doi.org/10.1007/978-3-031-30589-4_15

10. Castryck, W., Lange, T., Martindale, C., Panny, L., Renes, J.: CSIDH: an efficient post-quantum commutative group action. In: Peyrin, T., Galbraith, S. (eds.) ASIACRYPT 2018, Part III. LNCS, vol. 11274, pp. 395–427. Springer, Cham (2018). https://doi.org/10.1007/978-3-030-03332-3_15

11. Castryck, W., Vercauteren, F.: A polynomial time attack on instances of M-SIDH and FESTA. In: Guo, J., Steinfeld, R. (eds.) ASIACRYPT 2023. LNCS, vol. 14444, pp. 127–156. Springer, Singapore (2023). https://doi.org/10.1007/978-981-99-8739-9_5

12. Chen, M., Imran, M., Ivanyos, G., Kutas, P., Leroux, A., Petit, C.: Hidden stabilizers, the isogeny to endomorphism ring problem and the cryptanalysis of pSIDH. Cryptology ePrint Archive, Paper 2023/779, To appear in "Asiacrypt 2023" (2023). https://eprint.iacr.org/2023/779

13. Chi-Domínguez, J.J., Pizarro-Madariaga, A., Riquelme, E.: Computing quotient groups of smooth order with applications to isogenies over higher-dimensional abelian varieties. Cryptology ePrint Archive, Paper 2023/508 (2023). https://eprint.iacr.org/2023/508

14. Chávez-Saab, J., Chi-Domínguez, J.J., Jaques, S., Rodríguez-Henríquez, F.: The SQALE of CSIDH: sublinear Vélu quantum-resistant isogeny action with low exponents. J. Cryptogr. Eng., 349–368 (2022). https://doi.org/10.1007/s13389-021-00271-w

15. Cornacchia, G.: Su di un metodo per la risoluzione in interi dell'equazione $\sum_{h=0}^{n} x^{n-h}y^h$. In: Giornale di Matematiche di Battaglini 46, pp. 33–90 (1908)

16. Cosset, R., Robert, D.: Computing (ℓ, ℓ)-isogenies in polynomial time on Jacobians of genus 2 curves. Math. Comput. **84**, 1953–1975 (2015). https://doi.org/10.1090/S0025-5718-2014-02899-8

17. Costello, C., Hisil, H.: A simple and compact algorithm for SIDH with arbitrary degree isogenies. In: Takagi, T., Peyrin, T. (eds.) ASIACRYPT 2017, Part II. LNCS, vol. 10625, pp. 303–329. Springer, Cham (2017). https://doi.org/10.1007/978-3-319-70697-9_11

18. Costello, C., Lauter, K.: Group law computations on Jacobians of hyperelliptic curves. In: Miri, A., Vaudenay, S. (eds.) SAC 2011. LNCS, vol. 7118, pp. 92–117. Springer, Heidelberg (2012). https://doi.org/10.1007/978-3-642-28496-0_6

19. Dartois, P., Leroux, A., Robert, D., Wesolowski, B.: SQISignHD: new dimensions in cryptography. Cryptology ePrint Archive, Paper 2023/436 (2023). https://eprint.iacr.org/2023/436

20. De Feo, L.: Mathematics of isogeny based cryptography. arXiv (2017). http://arxiv.org/abs/1711.04062

21. De Feo, L., et al.: Séta: supersingular encryption from torsion attacks. In: Tibouchi, M., Wang, H. (eds.) ASIACRYPT 2021, Part IV. LNCS, vol. 13093, pp. 249–278. Springer, Cham (2021). https://doi.org/10.1007/978-3-030-92068-5_9

22. De Feo, L., Jao, D., Plût, J.: Towards quantum-resistant cryptosystems from super-singular elliptic curve isogenies. J. Math. Cryptol. **8**(3), 209–247 (2014). https://doi.org/10.1515/jmc-2012-0015

23. Decru, T., Kunzweiler, S.: Efficient computation of $(3^n, 3^n)$-isogenies. In: El Mrabet, N., De Feo, L., Duquesne, S. (eds.) Progress in Cryptology - AFRICACRYPT 2023, pp. 53–78. Springer, Cham (2023). https://doi.org/10.1007/978-3-031-37679-5_3

24. Decru, T., Maino, L., Sanso, A.: Towards a quantum-resistant weak verifiable delay function. In: Aly, A., Tibouchi, M. (eds.) Progress in Cryptology – LATINCRYPT 2023. LATINCRYPT 2023. LNCS, vol. 14168. Springer, Cham (2023). https://doi.org/10.1007/978-3-031-44469-2_8

25. Ebrahimi, E.: Post-quantum security of plain OAEP transform. In: Hanaoka, G., Shikata, J., Watanabe, Y. (eds.) PKC 2022, Part I. LNCS, vol. 13177, pp. 34–51. Springer, Heidelberg (2022). https://doi.org/10.1007/978-3-030-97121-2_2

26. Fouotsa, T.B., Moriya, T., Petit, C.: M-SIDH and MD-SIDH: countering SIDH attacks by masking information. In: Hazay, C., Stam, M. (eds.) Advances in Cryptology - EUROCRYPT 2023, pp. 282–309. Springer, Cham (2023). https://doi.org/10.1007/978-3-031-30589-4_10

27. Fujisaki, E., Okamoto, T.: Statistical zero knowledge protocols to prove modular polynomial relations. In: Kaliski, B.S. (ed.) CRYPTO 1997. LNCS, vol. 1294, pp. 16–30. Springer, Heidelberg (1997). https://doi.org/10.1007/BFb0052225

28. Fujisaki, E., Okamoto, T.: Secure integration of asymmetric and symmetric encryption schemes. In: Wiener, M. (ed.) CRYPTO 1999. LNCS, vol. 1666, pp. 537–554. Springer, Heidelberg (1999). https://doi.org/10.1007/3-540-48405-1_34

29. Galbraith, S.D., Vercauteren, F.: Computational problems in supersingular elliptic curve isogenies. Quantum Inf. Process. **17**(10), 265 (2018). https://doi.org/10.1007/s11128-018-2023-6

30. Hohenberger, S., Koppula, V., Waters, B.: Chosen ciphertext security from injective trapdoor functions. In: Micciancio, D., Ristenpart, T. (eds.) CRYPTO 2020, Part I. LNCS, vol. 12170, pp. 836–866. Springer, Cham (2020). https://doi.org/10.1007/978-3-030-56784-2_28

31. Jaques, S., Schanck, J.M.: Quantum cryptanalysis in the RAM model: claw-finding attacks on SIKE. In: Boldyreva, A., Micciancio, D. (eds.) CRYPTO 2019, Part I. LNCS, vol. 11692, pp. 32–61. Springer, Cham (2019). https://doi.org/10.1007/978-3-030-26948-7_2

32. Kani, E.: The number of curves of genus two with elliptic differentials (1997). https://doi.org/10.1515/crll.1997.485.93

33. Lamport, L.: Constructing digital signatures from a one way function. Technical report, SRI International (1979)

34. Lange, T.: Efficient arithmetic on genus 2 hyperelliptic curves over finite fields via explicit formulae. Cryptology ePrint Archive, Paper 2002/121 (2002). https://eprint.iacr.org/2002/121

35. Leroux, A.: A new isogeny representation and applications to cryptography. In: Agrawal, S., Lin, D. (eds.) ASIACRYPT 2022, Part II. LNCS, vol. 13792, pp. 3–35. Springer, Heidelberg (2022). https://doi.org/10.1007/978-3-031-22966-4_1

36. Maino, L., Martindale, C., Panny, L., Pope, G., Wesolowski, B.: A direct key recovery attack on SIDH. In: Hazay, C., Stam, M. (eds.) Advances in Cryptology - EUROCRYPT 2023, pp. 448–471. Springer, Cham (2023). https://doi.org/10.1007/978-3-031-30589-4_16

37. Martindale, C., Panny, L.: How to not break SIDH. Cryptology ePrint Archive, Report 2019/558 (2019). https://eprint.iacr.org/2019/558

38. Meyer, M., Reith, S.: A faster way to the CSIDH. In: Chakraborty, D., Iwata, T. (eds.) INDOCRYPT 2018. LNCS, vol. 11356, pp. 137–152. Springer, Cham (2018). https://doi.org/10.1007/978-3-030-05378-9_8

39. Milne, J.S.: Arithmetic Geometry. Springer, New York (1986). https://doi.org/10.1007/978-1-4613-8655-1_5

40. Naehrig, M., Renes, J.: Dual isogenies and their application to public-key compression for isogeny-based cryptography. In: Galbraith, S.D., Moriai, S. (eds.) ASIACRYPT 2019, Part II. LNCS, vol. 11922, pp. 243–272. Springer, Cham (2019). https://doi.org/10.1007/978-3-030-34621-8_9

41. Oudompheng, R., Pope, G.: A note on reimplementing the Castryck-Decru attack and lessons learned for SageMath. Cryptology ePrint Archive, Paper 2022/1283 (2022). https://eprint.iacr.org/2022/1283

42. Peikert, C.: He gives C-sieves on the CSIDH. In: Canteaut, A., Ishai, Y. (eds.) EUROCRYPT 2020, Part II. LNCS, vol. 12106, pp. 463–492. Springer, Cham (2020). https://doi.org/10.1007/978-3-030-45724-2_16

43. Pereira, G.C.C.F., Doliskani, J., Jao, D.: x-only point addition formula and faster compressed SIKE. J. Cryptogr. Eng. **11**(1), 57–69 (2021). https://doi.org/10.1007/s13389-020-00245-4

44. Petit, C.: Faster algorithms for isogeny problems using torsion point images. In: Takagi, T., Peyrin, T. (eds.) ASIACRYPT 2017, Part II. LNCS, vol. 10625, pp. 330–353. Springer, Cham (2017). https://doi.org/10.1007/978-3-319-70697-9_12

45. de Quehen, V., Kutas, P., Leonardi, C., Martindale, C., Panny, L., Petit, C., Stange, K.E.: Improved torsion-point attacks on SIDH variants. In: Malkin, T., Peikert, C. (eds.) CRYPTO 2021, Part III. LNCS, vol. 12827, pp. 432–470. Springer, Cham (2021). https://doi.org/10.1007/978-3-030-84252-9_15

46. Renes, J.: Computing isogenies between montgomery curves using the action of (0, 0). In: Lange, T., Steinwandt, R. (eds.) PQCrypto 2018. LNCS, vol. 10786, pp. 229–247. Springer, Cham (2018). https://doi.org/10.1007/978-3-319-79063-3_11

47. Richelot, F.: Ueber die Integration eines merkwürdigen Systems Differentialgleichungen (1842)

48. Robert, D.: Breaking SIDH in polynomial time. In: Hazay, C., Stam, M. (eds.) Advances in Cryptology - EUROCRYPT 2023, pp. 472–503. Springer, Cham (2023). https://doi.org/10.1007/978-3-031-30589-4_17

49. Silverman, J.H.: The Arithmetic of Elliptic Curves, Graduate Texts in Mathematics, vol. 106. Springer, New York (1986). https://doi.org/10.1007/978-1-4757-1920-8

50. Smith, B.: Explicit endomorphisms and correspondences. Ph.D. thesis, The University of Sydney (2005). http://hdl.handle.net/2123/1066

51. The Sage Developers: SageMath, the Sage Mathematics Software System (Version 9.8) (2023). https://www.sagemath.org

52. Ueno, R., Xagawa, K., Tanaka, Y., Ito, A., Takahashi, J., Homma, N.: Curse of re-encryption: a generic power/EM analysis on post-quantum KEMs. IACR Trans. Cryptogr. Hardw. Embed. Syst. **2022**(1), 296–322 (2021). https://doi.org/10.46586/tches.v2022.i1.296-322

A Polynomial Time Attack on Instances of M-SIDH and FESTA

Wouter Castryck[(✉)] and Frederik Vercauteren

COSIC, KU Leuven, Leuven, Belgium
{wouter.castryck,frederik.vercauteren}@esat.kuleuven.be

Abstract. The recent devastating attacks on SIDH rely on the fact that the protocol reveals the images $\varphi(P)$ and $\varphi(Q)$ of the secret isogeny $\varphi : E_0 \to E$ on a basis $\{P, Q\}$ of the N-torsion subgroup $E_0[N]$ where $N^2 > \deg(\varphi)$. To thwart this attack, two recent proposals, M-SIDH and FESTA, proceed by only revealing the images upto unknown scalars $\lambda_1, \lambda_2 \in \mathbb{Z}_N^\times$, i.e. only $\lambda_1\varphi(P)$ and $\lambda_2\varphi(Q)$ are revealed, where $\lambda_1 = \lambda_2$ for M-SIDH and $\lambda_1 = \lambda_2^{-1}$ for FESTA. Similar information is leaked in CSIDH since φ maps the eigenspaces of Frobenius on E_0 to the corresponding eigenspaces on E.

In this paper, we introduce a new polynomial time attack that generalizes the well known "lollipop" attack and analyze how it applies to M-SIDH, FESTA and CSIDH. We show that M-SIDH can be broken in polynomial time whenever E_0 or E is $\mathbb{F}_p$-rational, even when the endomorphism rings of E_0 and E are unknown. This can be generalized to the case where the starting (or end) curve is not $\mathbb{F}_p$-rational, but is connected to its Frobenius conjugate by an isogeny of small degree.

For FESTA, where the curve E_0 is already $\mathbb{F}_p$-rational, we obtain a polynomial time attack under the added requirement that at least one of the basis points P, Q spans an eigenspace of Frobenius, of an endomorphism of low degree, or of a composition of both. We note that the current implementation of FESTA does not choose such a basis. Since it is always possible to construct an endomorphism, typically of large degree, with either P, Q an eigenvector, we conclude that FESTA with overstretched parameters is insecure.

Although the information leaked in CSIDH is very similar to FESTA, we show that our attack does not reveal any new information about the secret isogeny, i.e. we only learn that it is $\mathbb{F}_p$-rational, which is a priori knowledge.

Finally, we analyze if and how it would be possible to backdoor M-SIDH and FESTA by choosing system parameters that look inconspicuous, but in fact reduce to the special cases above via a secret isogeny chosen by the adversary.

Keywords: Isogeny-based cryptography · Frobenius · M-SIDH · FESTA · CSIDH

This work was supported in part by the European Research Council (ERC) under the European Union's Horizon 2020 research and innovation programme (grant agreement ISOCRYPT - No. 101020788) and by CyberSecurity Research Flanders with reference number VR20192203. Date of this document: 9th November 2023.

© International Association for Cryptologic Research 2023
J. Guo and R. Steinfeld (Eds.): ASIACRYPT 2023, LNCS 14444, pp. 127–156, 2023.
https://doi.org/10.1007/978-981-99-8739-9_5

1   Introduction

The Supersingular Isogeny Diffie-Hellman (SIDH) protocol [16] and the corresponding key encapsulation mechanism SIKE [1] were once considered to be the pinnacle of isogeny-based cryptography, due to their efficiency and compactness. A recent series of papers [4,19,21] resulted in a practical polynomial time attack, exploiting the extra information about the secret isogeny given out by the SIDH-/SIKE protocols. In particular, let $\varphi : E_0 \to E$ be a secret isogeny of known degree d, then SIDH/SIKE also reveals the images $\varphi(P)$ and $\varphi(Q)$ of a basis $\{P, Q\}$ for $E[N]$ where N is a large power of a small prime with $\gcd(N, d) = 1$. Given these images, as long as $N^2 > d$ and d is known, the above attack allows to recover the secret isogeny φ in polynomial time. Since the attack really requires the exact knowledge of $\varphi(P)$ and $\varphi(Q)$, it is natural to look for countermeasures that do not reveal such information. However, building an actual functioning SIDH-like protocol seems to be impossible without revealing at least some partial information.

The first approach in this direction was devised by Fouotsa, Moriya and Petit [15] resulting in two protocols: M-SIDH (Masked torsion points SIDH) and MD-SIDH (Masked Degree SIDH). In M-SIDH the degree of the secret isogeny is known, but the images of the torsion points are scaled by a random secret integer $\lambda \in \mathbb{Z}_N^\times$, i.e. the protocol only reveals $\lambda\varphi(P)$ and $\lambda\varphi(Q)$. In MD-SIDH, not only the images of the points are scaled, but the degree of the secret isogeny is also hidden. As shown by the authors in [15], the MD-SIDH problem reduces to the M-SIDH problem, so in the remainder of the paper we will only deal with M-SIDH. The reason why both scalars have to be the same is that the protocol requires that the subgroup $\langle \alpha\lambda\varphi(P) + \beta\lambda\varphi(Q)\rangle$ for random $\alpha, \beta \in \mathbb{Z}_N^\times$ is exactly the same subgroup as $\langle \alpha\varphi(P) + \beta\varphi(Q)\rangle$.

By bilinearity and compatibility of the Weil pairing e_N with isogenies, we can in fact derive $\lambda^2 \bmod N$ via a single discrete logarithm (which is easy since N is smooth):

$$e_N(\lambda\varphi(P), \lambda\varphi(Q)) = e_N(P, Q)^{\lambda^2 d}.$$

As such we can always reduce to the case where $\lambda^2 = 1 \bmod N$, so for M-SIDH to be s-bit secure we require at least 2^s square roots of unity. This requires N to have at least s small distinct prime factors, and as shown in [15] one really requires $2s$ factors. Furthermore, since the N_A used by Alice needs to be coprime with the N_B used by Bob, we end up with a prime p such that $p+1$ is divisible by at least $4s$ small distinct primes. In particular, even for 128-bit security, the prime p is close to 6000 bits, which makes M-SIDH much slower than SIDH.

The second such approach is called FESTA [3] by Basso, Maino and Pope. Here the authors reveal $\lambda_1\varphi(P)$ and $\lambda_2\varphi(Q)$ where λ_1 can be different from λ_2.[1] However, as explained above, this blocks a straightforward adaptation of the SIDH protocol. To circumvent this problem, the authors construct a trapdoor one-way function, where knowledge of the secret λ_i allows to invert the one-way function. Furthemore, using the same Weil paring trick as above we can derive $\lambda_1\lambda_2 \bmod N$, so we can always reduce to the case where $\lambda_2 = \lambda_1^{-1} \bmod N$.

Although CSIDH [6] does not explicitly reveal torsion point information, there is an implicit leak: since the isogenies used in CSIDH are $\mathbb{F}_p$-rational, we have $\varphi \circ \pi_0 = \pi \circ \varphi$, where π_0, π denote the Frobenius endomorphisms on E_0 and E. Since the characteristic polynomial of these Frobenius endomorphisms is given by $x^2 + p$, we conclude that for N a power of an odd prime ℓ with $\left(\frac{-p}{\ell}\right) = 1$, they will have two different eigenvalues modulo N, say $\mu_1 \neq \mu_2 \bmod N$. Note that using the Chinese Remainder Theorem we are not limited to N being powers of a small prime, but we can deal with any odd N as long as for each prime factor ℓ_i of N we have $\left(\frac{-p}{\ell_i}\right) = 1$. Now assume $P \in E_0[N]$ is an eigenvector with eigenvalue μ_1, i.e. $\pi_0(P) = \mu_1 P$, then applying φ to both sides and using commutativity with Frobenius shows that $\pi(\varphi(P)) = \mu_1\varphi(P)$, so $\varphi(P)$ lies in the μ_1-eigenspace of π on $E[N]$. Therefore if $S \in E[N]$ is an eigenvector of π on $E[N]$ with eigenvalue μ_1, we know there exists some λ_1 such that $S = \lambda_1\varphi(P)$ (and similarly for the other eigenspace). As such, at first glance, the CSIDH case looks very similar to the FESTA case.

The main security argument for both M-SIDH and FESTA is that the polynomial time attack on SIDH no longer applies since the exact images of the torsion points are not revealed and thus it is impossible to recover $\varphi : E_0 \to E$. Although this reasoning is correct when one focuses on the isogeny φ itself, it does not rule out other polynomial time attacks when considering a different, but related isogeny, in particular an isogeny that does not map from E_0 to E. The main idea underlying our attack (which is a generalization of the "lollipop attack" from [15, Sects. 4.2–4.3]) is as follows: since we do not know the exact images of the torsion points due to the presence of the λ_i, we will construct a new isogeny ψ (related to φ) from E to some other curve E' that is oblivious to the unknown λ_i.

To illustrate this idea, assume we are attacking M-SIDH where E_0 is $\mathbb{F}_p$-rational. Then consider the following diagram:

---

[1] We note that the authors consider a slightly more general setting where

$$\mathbf{A} \cdot \begin{pmatrix} \varphi(P) \\ \varphi(Q) \end{pmatrix}$$

is revealed, with $\mathbf{A}$ sampled from a commutative subgroup $X \subseteq \mathrm{GL}_2(\mathbb{Z}_N)$. However, as also stated by the authors, there seems little advantage over using diagonal matrices.

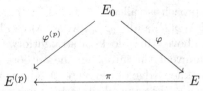

Here $E^{(p)}$ denotes the Frobenius conjugate of E, i.e. the curve obtained by raising all coefficients of E to the p-th power, and $\pi : E \to E^{(p)}$ the connecting Frobenius isogeny. The isogeny $\varphi^{(p)}$ is the Frobenius conjugate of φ and satisfies $\varphi^{(p)} \circ \pi_0 = \pi \circ \varphi$ with π_0 the Frobenius endomorphism on E_0 (recall that E_0 is assumed to be $\mathbb{F}_p$-rational).

Consider now the isogeny $\psi = \varphi^{(p)} \circ \hat{\varphi}$ from E to $E^{(p)}$ of degree d^2. Denote with $T = \lambda\varphi(P)$ and $S = \lambda\varphi(Q)$ the points revealed by the M-SIDH protocol, then an easy calculation (see Lemma 3) shows that in this case

$$\psi \begin{pmatrix} S \\ T \end{pmatrix} = d \cdot \mathbf{M}_{\pi_0}^{-1} \cdot \pi \begin{pmatrix} S \\ T \end{pmatrix}, \tag{1}$$

where $\mathbf{M}_{\pi_0}$ is such that

$$\pi_0 \begin{pmatrix} P \\ Q \end{pmatrix} = \mathbf{M}_{\pi_0} \begin{pmatrix} P \\ Q \end{pmatrix},$$

i.e., it is the transpose of the matrix of π_0 acting on $E_0[N]$ with respect to the basis $\{P, Q\}$. Since all quantities in Eq. (1) are known, we can compute the exact images of S, T under ψ and thus the polynomial time attack on SIDH (see Theorem 1) can be applied to recover ψ since in M-SIDH we have $N > d$ and thus $N^2 > \deg(\psi) = d^2$. If ψ is cyclic, we can recover the kernel of $\hat{\varphi}$ since in this case $\ker(\hat{\varphi}) = \ker(\psi)[d]$. Even if ψ is not fully cyclic, it typically remains possible to derive almost all information about φ; see Sect. 3.2.

A similar attack applies to FESTA with the main difference being that (1) is generalized to

$$\psi \begin{pmatrix} S \\ T \end{pmatrix} = d \cdot \mathbf{D} \cdot \mathbf{M}_{\pi_0}^{-1} \cdot \mathbf{D}^{-1} \cdot \pi \begin{pmatrix} S \\ T \end{pmatrix}, \tag{2}$$

with $\mathbf{D}$ the diagonal matrix with λ_1, λ_2 as entries. Since now $\lambda_1 \neq \lambda_2$ we are faced with the problem that in general the matrix product $\mathbf{D} \cdot \mathbf{M}_{\pi_0}^{-1} \cdot \mathbf{D}^{-1}$ does not simplify to $\mathbf{M}_{\pi_0}^{-1}$ unless $\mathbf{M}_{\pi_0}$ itself is a diagonal matrix; or to put it differently, P, Q need to be eigenvectors of π_0.

Since the information revealed in CSIDH is similar to FESTA, we arrive at the same Eq. (2) above, where P, Q are now indeed eigenvectors of Frobenius, so we will be able to recover the isogeny $\psi = \varphi^{(p)} \circ \hat{\varphi}$ (assuming we know the degree d of φ which is required in (2) but also in the polynomial time attack on SIDH). However, since φ is $\mathbb{F}_p$-rational by construction, we have that $\varphi^{(p)} = \varphi$ and we simply recover the isogeny $\psi = \varphi \circ \hat{\varphi} = [d]$, so the attack reveals no new information.

Contributions

– We formalize the above attack strategy resulting in a polynomial time attack on the M-SIDH protocol when E_0 is $\mathbb{F}_p$-rational and similarly on the FESTA protocol when E_0 is $\mathbb{F}_p$-rational, but with the added constraint that at least one of P or Q is an eigenvector of π_0. Of course, by focusing on $\hat{\varphi} : E \to E_0$ rather than on φ, the same conclusions apply in case E is $\mathbb{F}_p$-rational.
– We generalize this attack (see Fig. 1 for a pictorial representation) to cases where E_0 is not $\mathbb{F}_p$-rational and where we allow for different maps than Frobenius. Furthermore, we also deal with the more general case of non-diagonal matrices, where we are given

$$\begin{pmatrix} S \\ T \end{pmatrix} = \mathbf{A} \begin{pmatrix} \varphi(P) \\ \varphi(Q) \end{pmatrix}$$

with $\mathbf{A}$ sampled from some public set $X \subseteq \mathrm{GL}_2(\mathbb{Z}_N)$. This generalized attack encompasses known constructions such as the "lollipop endomorphism" from [14] and the corresponding polynomial time attacks on M-SIDH from [15, Sects. 4.2–4.3]. Furthermore, we show that this generalized attack results in many more weak bases for FESTA than just eigenspaces of Frobenius (but still a negligible number, so the probability of hitting such bases via random sampling is low) and that it also applies to FESTA with over-stretched parameters, i.e. where the order N is artificially larger than what is used in FESTA.
– We analyze the impact of our attack on CSIDH and conclude that there is no impact, i.e. the only information we learn from the attack is a priori knowledge.
– We discuss the possibilities for an attacker to backdoor systems such as M-SIDH and FESTA by using a secret isogeny that reduces the system parameters to the weak instances above and analyze if and how such a backdoor can be detected.

2   Background

We assume some basic familiarity with elliptic curves and isogenies; for a self-contained overview we refer the reader to the excellent notes of De Feo [12].

We briefly recall how the different protocols such as SIDH [16], M-SIDH [15], FESTA [3] and CSIDH [6] reveal partial information about a secret isogeny $\varphi : E_0 \to E$. We refer to the corresponding papers for the full protocols; here we focus only on which partial information is revealed and how the degree of the secret isogeny relates to the order of the points on which said partial information is leaked.

These protocols work with supersingular elliptic curves over $\mathbb{F}_p$, in the case of CSIDH, or over $\mathbb{F}_{p^2}$, for the other protocols. An elliptic curve $E/\mathbb{F}_q$ with $q = p^n$ is called supersingular if its trace of Frobenius $t = q + 1 - \#E(\mathbb{F}_q)$ satisfies $p \mid t$. In the cryptographic setting, p is a large prime, so for a supersingular elliptic curve E over $\mathbb{F}_p$ we have $\#E(\mathbb{F}_p) = p + 1$ since $|t| \leq 2\sqrt{q}$, and consequently $\#E(\mathbb{F}_{p^2}) = (p + 1)^2$. The protocols that work with supersingular curves E over

$\mathbb{F}_{p^2}$ all start an isogeny walk from a curve over $\mathbb{F}_p$ and for such curves we thus have $\#E(\mathbb{F}_{p^2}) = (p+1)^2$ via Tate's isogeny theorem. Furthermore, their group structure is given by

$$E(\mathbb{F}_{p^2}) \cong \mathbb{Z}_{p+1} \times \mathbb{Z}_{p+1}.$$

To speed-up isogeny computations it is advantageous to work with curves that have many small rational subgroups, and as such the primes used have a specific form $p = fN - 1$ where f is a small co-factor and N is a smooth number. When $N = \ell_1^n \ell_2^m$ for small primes ℓ_i we call p an SIDH-prime; when $N = \prod \ell_i^{e_i}$ for many different small primes ℓ_i and small e_i, we call p a CSIDH-prime.

2.1 SIDH

SIDH [16] is a Diffie-Hellman type key exchange where partial information is revealed to allow the participants in the protocol to complete the following commutatitive diagram:

$$E_0, P_A, Q_A, P_B, Q_B \xrightarrow{\varphi_A} E_A = E/\langle G_A\rangle, \varphi_A(P_B), \varphi_A(Q_B)$$
$$\downarrow{\varphi_B} \qquad\qquad\qquad\qquad\qquad \downarrow{\varphi'_B}$$
$$E_B = E/\langle G_B\rangle, \varphi_B(P_A), \varphi_B(Q_A) \xrightarrow{\varphi'_A} E_{AB} \cong E_{BA} \cong E_0/\langle G_A, G_B\rangle.$$

Here, $\{P_A, Q_A\}$ (resp. $\{P_B, Q_B\}$) are public torsion bases for $E_0[A]$ (resp. $E_0[B]$), G_A (resp. G_B) is a generator of a secret subgroup of $E[A]$ (resp. $E[B]$) chosen by Alice (resp. Bob) and $\varphi'_A = \varphi_{B*}\varphi_A$ (resp. $\varphi'_B = \varphi_{A*}\varphi_B$) is the pushforward of φ_A under φ_B (resp. of φ_B under φ_A). In particular, we have $\ker(\varphi'_B) = \varphi_A(\ker(\varphi_B))$, which is the reason why $\varphi_A(P_B)$ and $\varphi_A(Q_B)$ are revealed by Alice (and similarly for Bob).

The prime used is an SIDH prime typically of the form $p = f2^n 3^m - 1$ where $2^n \approx 3^m$, and the degrees of the secret isogenies are 2^n and 3^m respectively, so $A = 2^n$ and $B = 3^m$.

To attack SIDH, we can therefore either look at Alice's key, i.e. a secret degree A isogeny where we are given the images of a basis of the B-torsion or Bob's key, i.e. a secret degree B isogeny where we are given the images of a basis of the A-torsion. As such, the degree of the secret isogeny and torsion point order are (A, B) or (B, A) respectively.

Unfortunately, this extra information can be exploited to recover the secret isogenies of both Alice and Bob in polynomial time [4,19,21] by application of the following theorem.

Theorem 1 ([21, Sect. 6.4]). *Let $\varphi : E_0 \to E$ be a secret degree d isogeny (where d is known) and assume we are given the images of φ on a basis $\{P, Q\}$ of $E_0[N]$, where N and d are assumed smooth and coprime, and $N^2 > 4d$. Let $\mathbb{F}_q$ be the smallest field over which $E_0[N], E_0[d]$ and φ are defined, then the kernel of φ can be computed in a polynomial number of operations in $\mathbb{F}_q$.*

Remark 2. The attack in fact runs as soon as $N^2 > d$, but the output may be ambiguous because $\ker(\varphi)$ may not be uniquely determined by how φ acts on $E_0[N]$. E.g., if E_0 has j-invariant 0 and $\omega \in \mathrm{End}(E_0)$ denotes an automorphism such that $\omega^2 + \omega + 1 = 0$, then the isogenies $1 \pm \omega : E_0 \to E_0$ both have degree $d = 3$, have different kernels, yet they agree on $E_0[2]$. The bound $N^2 > 4d$ guarantees that φ and hence also $\ker(\varphi)$ is uniquely determined [17, Lemma 3.1].

2.2 M-SIDH

To make the above SIDH-diagram commute, it is sufficient for Bob to know the subgroup $\varphi_A(\ker(\varphi_B))$ and as such it is not necessary to know the exact image of the chosen generator G_B of $\ker(\varphi_B)$. In M-SIDH [15], SIDH is therefore adapted by revealing $\lambda_A \varphi_A(P_B), \lambda_A \varphi_A(Q_B)$ for some secret $\lambda_A \in \mathbb{Z}_B^\times$ chosen by Alice. However, it is not sufficient to just make this simple change, since by the Weil pairing trick mentioned in the introduction it is possible to recover $\lambda_A^2 \bmod B$, which allows to reduce to the case $\lambda_A^2 = 1 \bmod B$. To prevent exhaustive search, this requires to choose a B (similarly for A) such that there are at least 2^s roots of unity with s the security parameter. Using a divide and conquer approach [15], it is even required for both A and B to have $2s$ different prime factors. As such the primes used in M-SIDH are of CSIDH type $p = 4f \prod_{i=1}^{4s} \ell_i - 1$ where the ℓ_i are consecutive odd small primes and one lets

$$ A = \prod_{i=1}^{2s} \ell_{2i-1}, \qquad B = \prod_{i=1}^{2s} \ell_{2i} . $$

Due to the large number of small primes required, the total size of p is much larger than for SIDH, e.g. the suggested 128-bit parameter set has p of size 5911 bits. The degree of the secret isogeny and torsion point order are (A, B) or (B, A) respectively.

2.3 FESTA

In FESTA [3] the approach is to construct a trapdoor one-way function from the following (somewhat different) commutative diagram:

$$
\begin{array}{ccc}
E_0, \begin{pmatrix} P_B \\ Q_B \end{pmatrix} & \xrightarrow{\ \varphi_A\ } & E_A, \begin{pmatrix} S \\ T \end{pmatrix} = \mathbf{A} \begin{pmatrix} \varphi_A(P_B) \\ \varphi_A(Q_B) \end{pmatrix} \\
\Big\downarrow{\scriptstyle \varphi_1} & & \Big\downarrow{\scriptstyle \varphi_2} \\
E_1, \mathbf{B} \begin{pmatrix} \varphi_1(P_B) \\ \varphi_1(Q_B) \end{pmatrix} & & E_2, \mathbf{B} \begin{pmatrix} \varphi_2(S) \\ \varphi_2(T) \end{pmatrix} .
\end{array}
$$

The system parameters contain the curve E_0 together with a basis $\{P_B, Q_B\}$ of $E[B]$ where for efficiency reasons $B = 2^b$. The public key of a user consists of the curve E_A and the tuple

$$\begin{pmatrix} S \\ T \end{pmatrix} = \mathbf{A} \begin{pmatrix} \varphi_A(P_B) \\ \varphi_A(Q_B) \end{pmatrix}$$

where $\mathbf{A}$ (part of the private key) is sampled from a commutative subgroup $X \subseteq$ $\mathrm{GL}_2(\mathbb{Z}_B)$. The input to the one-way function then consists of two isogenies φ_1 and φ_2 and a matrix $\mathbf{B}$ which is also sampled from X. The output of the one-way function are the evaluations of the bases $\{P_B, Q_B\}$ under φ_1 and $\{S, T\}$ under φ_2 both multiplied by $\mathbf{B}$. Using the trapdoor information $\mathbf{A}$ and Theorem 1, it is possible to recover the isogeny $\psi = \varphi_2 \circ \varphi_A \circ \hat{\varphi}_1$ from which φ_1, φ_2 and $\mathbf{B}$ follow. The authors of FESTA propose to use for X the group of invertible 2×2 diagonal matrices over $\mathbb{Z}_B$. In particular, $\mathbf{A} = \mathrm{diag}(\lambda_1, \lambda_2)$, and by using the same Weil pairing trick as before, one can reduce to the case $\lambda_2 = \lambda_1^{-1} \bmod B$.

To make the protocol efficient, the authors suggest $B = 2^b$, but also the degrees of $\varphi_A, \varphi_1, \varphi_2$ are taken smooth and coprime. Furthermore, $\deg(\varphi_A) = v^2$ for a smooth v. This results in a CSIDH-type prime of the form $p = f2^b v d_1 d_2 - 1$. For the 128-bit parameter set, the authors suggest $b = 623$, v has 137 bits, d_1 has 257 bits and d_2 has 260 bits, resulting in a prime of size 1292 bits.

Note that to attack FESTA we can consider two scenarios: either we try to recover the private key φ_A (or equivalently $\mathbf{A}$) or we try to invert the one way function by recovering $\varphi_1, \varphi_2, \mathbf{B}$. Both cases are instances of the same problem, where only the degrees of the secret isogenies are slightly different. In particular, in the first case we have to recover a secret degree v^2 isogeny given 2^b-torsion information, where in the second, we need to recover a secret degree d_1 or d_2 isogeny, again given 2^b-torsion information. Note that once $\mathbf{B}$ is derived, the second isogeny follows immediately.

2.4   CSIDH

Unlike the previous protocols, CSIDH works with $\mathbb{F}_p$-rational curves and $\mathbb{F}_p$-rational isogenies. More in detail, CSIDH works on the set of supersingular elliptic curves over $\mathbb{F}_p$ whose ring of $\mathbb{F}_p$-rational endomorphisms is isomorphic to a fixed order $\mathcal{O}$ in the imaginary quadratic field $\mathbb{Q}(\sqrt{-p})$. It is possible to define a group action of the ideal class group of $\mathcal{O}$ on this set as follows: let $[\mathfrak{a}] \in \mathrm{Cl}(\mathcal{O})$ be an ideal class, represented by an ideal $\mathfrak{a} \subseteq \mathcal{O}$ of norm coprime to p. Then the $\mathfrak{a}$-torsion subgroup on a curve E_0 is defined as

$$E_0[\mathfrak{a}] = \bigcap_{\alpha \in \mathfrak{a}} \ker(\alpha),$$

which is finite of order $N(\mathfrak{a}) = \#(\mathcal{O}/\mathfrak{a})$. Thus there exists an elliptic curve E and a separable isogeny $\varphi_\mathfrak{a} : E_0 \to E$ with $\ker(\varphi_\mathfrak{a}) = E_0[\mathfrak{a}]$, which is unique up to post-composition with an isomorphism. The isomorphism class of E is independent of the choice of the representing ideal $\mathfrak{a}$ and we denote this isomorphism class with $[\mathfrak{a}]E_0$. This approach can be extended to more general oriented curves [11, 20].

To speed-up isogeny computations, p is chosen to be of CSIDH-type, in particular, $p = 4f \prod_{i=1}^{t} \ell_i - 1$ where the ℓ_i are small odd primes. To achieve classical 128-bit security it is sufficient to take p of size 512 bits; however, for post-quantum security p needs to be much larger, e.g. for 128-bit post-quantum security p needs to be of size 4096 bits [9].

As we described in the introduction, CSIDH implicitly leaks a lot of information. Indeed for any $P \in E_0[N]$ that is an eigenvector of π_0 with eigenvalue $\mu \in \mathbb{Z}_N$, we have that $\varphi(P)$ is also an eigenvector of π with eigenvalue μ. So as long as the eigenspace in $E_0[N]$ corresponding to μ is one-dimensional, we obtain $\lambda\varphi(P)$. Note that this reasoning holds for any N for which there is a unique one-dimensional eigenspace with eigenvalue μ, which will be the case as long as N is odd and for each prime factor $\ell \mid N$ we have $\left(\frac{-p}{\ell}\right) = 1$ since the characteristic polynomial of Frobenius is $x^2 + p$. This shows we can take N arbitrary large, and in particular, we are always in the overstretched case.

3   Generalized Lollipop Attacks

3.1   Strategy

We now detail and generalize the attack strategy from the introduction. Our goal is to recover a secret cyclic isogeny $\varphi : E_0 \to E$ of known degree d, when given bases $\{P, Q\} \subseteq E_0[N]$ and $\{S, T\} \subseteq E[N]$ such that

$$\begin{pmatrix} S \\ T \end{pmatrix} = \mathbf{A} \cdot \varphi \begin{pmatrix} P \\ Q \end{pmatrix}$$

for some secret matrix $\mathbf{A}$ sampled from a public set $X \subseteq \mathrm{GL}_2(\mathbb{Z}_N)$; here, and always from now on, it is assumed that $p \nmid N$. In M-SIDH the set X consists of all invertible scalar matrices, while for the standard instantiation of FESTA it consists of all invertible diagonal matrices. We make use of two auxiliary inputs:

- an isogeny $\sigma_0 : E_0 \to E_0'$ (we denote its degree by s) whose push-forward

$$\sigma := \varphi_* \sigma_0 : E \to E'$$

under φ is known; equivalently, we know $\varphi(\ker(\sigma_0))$ as a subgroup scheme of E,
- another isogeny $\omega : E_0 \to E_0'$ having the same codomain, of small degree w,

as depicted in Fig. 1.

For simplicity, we assume throughout that N, d, s, w are pairwise coprime and that $p \nmid dw$. It is allowed that $p \mid s$: indeed, an important special case is where σ_0 is the Frobenius isogeny.

Under suitable "compatibility" conditions, which are discussed in more detail in Sect. 3.2 below, the attack returns an oracle for evaluating the degree-wd^2 isogeny

$$\psi := \varphi' \circ \omega \circ \hat{\varphi} : E \to E'$$

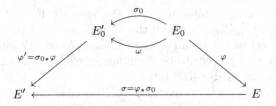

Fig. 1. Generalized attack diagram.

at any given point. Here φ' denotes the push-forward isogeny $\sigma_{0*}\varphi : E_0' \to E'$, i.e., the isogeny with kernel $\sigma_0(\ker(\varphi))$ normalized such that $\varphi' \circ \sigma_0 = \sigma \circ \varphi$. If ψ is cyclic then this can be used to recover $\ker(\varphi)$. But even in the non-cyclic case, this typically reveals non-trivial information about φ; see again Sect. 3.2 for a discussion. The key ingredient is the following lemma, which describes the images of S and T under ψ.

Lemma 3. *Using the above notation, assume that the matrix* $\mathbf{M}$ *such that*

$$(\hat{\sigma}_0 \circ \omega)\begin{pmatrix} P \\ Q \end{pmatrix} = \mathbf{M} \cdot \begin{pmatrix} P \\ Q \end{pmatrix}$$

commutes with every element of X. *Then we have*

$$s \cdot \psi\begin{pmatrix} S \\ T \end{pmatrix} = d \cdot \mathbf{M} \cdot \sigma\begin{pmatrix} S \\ T \end{pmatrix}.$$

Proof. Since $\begin{pmatrix} S \\ T \end{pmatrix} = \mathbf{A} \cdot \varphi\begin{pmatrix} P \\ Q \end{pmatrix}$ and $\hat{\varphi} \circ \varphi = [d]$ we have that

$$\hat{\varphi}\begin{pmatrix} S \\ T \end{pmatrix} = d \cdot \mathbf{A} \cdot \begin{pmatrix} P \\ Q \end{pmatrix}.$$

Furthermore, we have $\varphi' \circ \sigma_0 = \sigma \circ \varphi$ which implies that $[s] \circ \varphi' = \sigma \circ \varphi \circ \hat{\sigma}_0$ and therefore

$$s \cdot (\varphi' \circ \omega \circ \hat{\varphi})\begin{pmatrix} S \\ T \end{pmatrix} = d \cdot \mathbf{A} \cdot (\sigma \circ \varphi \circ \hat{\sigma}_0 \circ \omega)\begin{pmatrix} P \\ Q \end{pmatrix} = d \cdot \mathbf{A} \cdot \mathbf{M} \cdot (\sigma \circ \varphi)\begin{pmatrix} P \\ Q \end{pmatrix}$$

We thus see that

$$s \cdot \psi\begin{pmatrix} S \\ T \end{pmatrix} = d \cdot \mathbf{A} \cdot \mathbf{M} \cdot \mathbf{A}^{-1} \cdot \sigma\begin{pmatrix} S \\ T \end{pmatrix}, \tag{3}$$

and the lemma follows because $\mathbf{M}$ commutes with every matrix in X, in partic- ular it commutes with $\mathbf{A}$. $\qquad\square$

One sees that, whenever the lemma applies, we obtain full knowledge of $\psi(S)$ and $\psi(T)$, because it is assumed that $\gcd(s, N) = 1$. If we then assume that N

is smooth and $N^2 > \deg(\psi) = wd^2$, then an application of Theorem 1 yields the desired oracle for evaluating ψ.

Our assumption on σ_0, namely that we know its push-forward by the unknown isogeny φ, is obviously very restrictive. Nevertheless, there are two natural candidates for σ_0, both of which lead to interesting instantiations of our attack strategy:

1. the identity map $\mathrm{id} : E_0 \to E_0$, with push-forward the identity map on E,
2. the Frobenius isogeny

$$\pi_0 : E_0 \to E_0^{(p)},$$

   whose push-forward is the Frobenius isogeny from E to $E^{(p)}$,

Other examples are obtained by composing one of the above examples with an isogeny of small degree: then its push-forward can be guessed with a reasonable success probability, which is good enough for our purposes.

Remark 4. If X consists of diagonal matrices,[2] then there is another natural family of isogenies whose push-forwards under φ are known. Indeed, isogenies of the form $E_0 \to E_0/\langle \mu P \rangle$ or $E_0 \to E_0/\langle \mu Q \rangle$ for some $\mu \in \mathbb{Z}$ are pushed-forward to $E \to E/\langle \mu S \rangle$ and $E \to E/\langle \mu T \rangle$, respectively. If X is the set of scalar matrices, as in the case in M-SIDH, then we can even take any isogeny $\sigma_0 : E_0 \to E_0'$ with $\ker(\sigma_0) \subseteq E_0[N]$. However, in these cases s and N are never coprime and Lemma 3 bears only partial information about $\psi(S)$ and $\psi(T)$.

Likewise, for $\mathbf{M}$ to have a reasonable chance of commuting with every matrix in X, the centralizer of X in $\mathrm{GL}_2(\mathbb{Z}_N)$ has to be sufficiently large, and this puts severe restrictions on X. We discuss a few special cases:

1. if $X = \{$ scalar matrices $\}$ as is the case in M-SIDH, then the centralizer is all of $\mathrm{GL}_2(\mathbb{Z}_N)$; in other words this condition is void,
2. if $X = \{$ diagonal matrices $\}$ as in standard FESTA, then X is its own centralizer. In this case the condition is equivalent to P, Q being eigenvectors of $\hat{\sigma}_0 \circ \omega$ acting on $E_0[N]$,
3. if $X = \{$ circulant matrices $\}$, as has also been proposed for use in FESTA [3, Footnote 3], then again X is its own centralizer.

The latter two examples are instances of maximal commutative subgroups of $\mathrm{GL}_2(\mathbb{Z}_N)$. Many further examples can be found in Appendix A, where we give a partial classification of such subgroups.

Remark 5. In the case of diagonal matrices,[3] the condition on $\mathbf{M}$ can be relaxed at the expense of a stronger condition on N. Namely, if P is an eigenvector of $\hat{\sigma}_0 \circ \omega$ then it remains possible to determine $\psi(S)$, even in cases where Q is not an eigenvector. If N is smooth and $N > wd^2$ then this still allows us to obtain

---

[2] More generally, a variant of this remark applies whenever X is a so-called *split Cartan subgroup* of $\mathrm{GL}_2(\mathbb{Z}_N)$; see Appendix A.

[3] Here too, a variant of this remark applies if X is a split Cartan subgroup of $\mathrm{GL}_2(\mathbb{Z}_N)$.

the desired evaluation oracle; e.g., if N is a smooth square[4] then one can use a reduction by De Feo et al. [13], the details of which can be found in [5, p. 22]. Of course, the analogous remark applies if Q is an eigenvector, but P not necessarily is.

3.2   Information Retrieved from the Attack

Let us sum up the requirements for the attack strategy from Sect. 3.1 to reveal (at least partial) information about the secret isogeny φ:

- Firstly, the basis $\{P, Q\}$, the isogenies σ_0, ω and the set X should be such that the matrix $\mathbf{M}$ belongs to the centralizer of X in $\mathrm{GL}_2(\mathbb{Z}_N)$, so that Lemma 3 applies.
- Secondly, N should be smooth and larger than wd^2, so that we can invoke Theorem 1.
- Thirdly and most subtly, the isogeny $\psi = \varphi' \circ \omega \circ \hat{\varphi}$ should encode non-trivial information about φ.

We discuss this third point in more detail. The ideal scenario is where ψ is cyclic, in which case we simply recover $\ker(\hat{\varphi})$ as $\ker(\psi)[d]$. A worst case scenario is where $\hat{\sigma}_0 \circ \omega \in \mathbb{Z}$. Indeed, if we assume that σ_0 is cyclic then this implies that $\omega = \sigma_0$ and therefore

$$\psi = \varphi' \circ \omega \circ \hat{\varphi} = \varphi' \circ \sigma_0 \circ \hat{\varphi} = \sigma \circ \varphi \circ \hat{\varphi} = \sigma \circ [d],$$

leaving us clueless about φ (if σ_0 is not cyclic then a similar conclusion applies).

Let us henceforth assume that $\hat{\sigma}_0 \circ \omega$ is cyclic and make a more systematic analysis. Let $d' \mid d$ be maximal such that

$$E[d'] \subseteq \ker(\psi). \tag{4}$$

Let P be a generator of the (as yet unknown) kernel of $\hat{\varphi}$. Because $(\ker(\psi))[d] \cong \mathbb{Z}_{d'} \times \mathbb{Z}_d$, we can compute $d'P$ up to an invertible scalar by taking any order-d point in $\ker(\psi)$ and scaling it by d'. This reveals a degree-d/d' component of $\hat{\varphi}$ emanating from E, and one's task is to close the remaining gap of degree d', as illustrated in Fig. 2.

Equivalently, the goal is to find $\ker(\varphi)[d']$. Notice that the case $\ker(\psi)$ cyclic corresponds to $d' = 1$.

To proceed, observe that Eq. (4) is equivalent to

$$\omega(\ker(\varphi))[d'] = \ker(\varphi')[d'] = \sigma_0(\ker(\varphi))[d'],$$

which in turn can be rewritten as

$$(\hat{\sigma}_0 \circ \omega)(\ker(\varphi))[d'] = \ker(\varphi)[d'].$$

---

[4] The general case, i.e. N need not be a square, was solved recently at the workshop "Isogeny Graphs in Cryptography", Banff (Canada) and Bristol (UK), 20–25 August 2023.

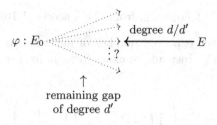

Fig. 2. Extracting φ from ψ.

Thus from (4) we learn that $(\ker(\varphi))[d']$ is an invariant subspace of $\hat{\sigma}_0 \circ \omega$ acting on $E_0[d']$. This strongly narrows down the options, and we proceed by guessing. For example, if $d = \ell^e$ is a power of an odd prime ℓ, then necessarily $d' = \ell^{e'}$ for some $0 \le e' \le e$. Then

- if ℓ splits in $\mathbb{Z}[\hat{\sigma}_0 \circ \omega]$ then possibly $e' > 0$, in which case we are left with exactly two options for $(\ker(\varphi))[d']$, namely the two eigenspaces of $\hat{\sigma}_0 \circ \omega$ acting on $E_0[d']$,
- if ℓ is inert in $\mathbb{Z}[\hat{\sigma}_0 \circ \omega]$, then necessarily $e' = 0$, i.e., $d' = 1$.

Remark 6. In order to avoid too many technicalities, we have ignored the (exceptional) ramified case in our analysis: there we may be left with anything between 0 and $\ell^e + \ell^{e-1}$ options for $(\ker(\varphi))[d']$. For a similar reason, we have omitted the case $\ell = 2$, where there are up to 4 options for $(\ker(\varphi))[d']$ in the split case.

More generally, the number of options for $(\ker(\varphi))[d']$ grows roughly as $O(2^{r'})$ with r' denoting the number of distinct prime factors of d'. So, in the worst case, our strategy involves an exponential number of guesses (e.g. this is the main bottleneck when applying it to CSIDH, we refer to Sect. 6 for a more elaborate discussion). However, for fixed φ and varying $\hat{\sigma}_0 \circ \omega$, we typically expect r' to be very small. This is based on the following heuristic reasoning. Write

$$d = \ell_1^{e_1} \cdots \ell_r^{e_r}, \qquad d' = \ell_1^{e_1'} \cdots \ell_r^{e_r'} \quad (0 \le e_i' \le e_i)$$

as products of distinct prime powers and assume for simplicity that all prime factors ℓ_i are odd. Then r' equals the number of indices i for which $e_i' > 0$, which holds if and only if $(\ker \varphi)[\ell_i]$ happens to be an eigenspace of $\hat{\sigma}_0 \circ \omega$. If ℓ_i splits in $\mathbb{Z}[\hat{\sigma}_0 \circ \omega]$ then there are two such eigenspaces and we estimate the probability for this to happen by $2/(\ell_i + 1)$. If ℓ_i is inert in $\mathbb{Z}[\hat{\sigma}_0 \circ \omega]$, then this cannot happen. Altogether we arrive at an estimated probability of

$$\frac{1}{2} \cdot \frac{2}{\ell_i + 1} + \frac{1}{2} \cdot 0 = \frac{1}{\ell_i + 1}$$

that $e_i' > 0$. So the expected value of r' is

$$\sum_{i=1}^{r} \frac{1}{\ell_i + 1} \le \sum_{\substack{\text{primes} \\ \ell \le d}} \frac{1}{\ell} = O(\log \log d), \tag{5}$$

where the last estimate follows e.g. from [23, Theorem 1.10].

Remark 7. A priori, the expected number of guesses is not given by $2^{r'}$ with r' the estimate from (5). Instead, an exact formula for the expected number of guesses is:

$$\sum_{\mathbf{b} \in \{0,1\}^r} 2^{\#\{i \mid \mathbf{b}_i = 1\}} \left(\prod_{\substack{i=1 \\ \mathbf{b}_i = 0}}^{r} \frac{\ell_i}{\ell_i + 1} \right) \left(\prod_{\substack{i=1 \\ \mathbf{b}_i = 1}}^{r} \frac{1}{\ell_i + 1} \right) = \prod_{i=1}^{r} \frac{\ell_i + 2}{\ell_i + 1}.$$

This can be estimated as

$$\prod_{\substack{\text{primes} \\ \ell \le d}} \frac{\ell + 2}{\ell + 1} \le \prod_{\substack{\text{primes} \\ \ell \le d}} \frac{\ell}{\ell - 1} = O(\log d)$$

by Mertens' formula [23, Theorem 1.12].

3.3   Comparison to Lollipop Attack

If $\sigma_0 : E_0 \to E_0$ is just the identity map, then ω must be an endomorphism and

$$\psi = \varphi \circ \omega \circ \hat{\varphi}$$

is the corresponding "lollipop endomorphism" on E; this nomenclature was popularized by [14]. For $X = \{\text{scalar matrices}\}$ we recover the attack on M-SIDH as outlined in [15, Sects. 4.2–4.3]. Therefore, the strategy from Sect. 3.1 should be viewed as a generalization of this lollipop attack to arbitrary sets X and arbitrary instances of σ_0.

Let us highlight the role of σ_0. In theory, it would also be possible to just apply the lollipop attack to the endomorphism

$$\omega' = \hat{\sigma}_0 \circ \omega \in \mathrm{End}(E_0).$$

But then we would need that $N^2 > swd^2$, rather than just $N^2 > wd^2$. So the crucial observation is that components of ω' whose push-forward under φ are known (σ_0 in this case) do not contribute to the degree of ψ and thereby lead to an improvement on the lower bound on N.

Example 8. One clear instance where one can take $\sigma_0 = \pi_0$ is when the starting curve E_0 is defined over $\mathbb{F}_p$. In this case π_0 is an endomorphism and one can simply take $\omega = \mathrm{id}$, so that

$$\psi = \varphi^{(p)} \circ \hat{\varphi}.$$

Note that, when compared to the lollipop attack applied to $\omega = \pi_0$, the degree of ψ drops from pd^2 to d^2. This corresponds to the attack strategy described in the introduction. In turn, the insertion of an endomorphism ω is a special case of the more general situation where E_0 is not necessarily defined over $\mathbb{F}_p$ but is connected to its Frobenius conjugate via a small-to-moderate degree isogeny ω:

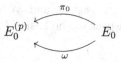

Such curves were considered, for instance, in [10].

4 M-SIDH

In this section we apply our attack to M-SIDH, where we analyze the different choices for σ_0. Recall that $S = \lambda\varphi(P)$ and $T = \lambda\varphi(Q)$ for a basis $\{P, Q\}$ of $E[N]$ with $\lambda \in \mathbb{Z}_N^\times$ and $d = \deg(\varphi)$.

4.1 Case $\sigma_0 = \mathrm{id}$

Let ω be an endomorphism on E_0 and set $\psi = \varphi \circ \omega \circ \hat{\varphi}$, then Lemma 3 implies

$$\psi\begin{pmatrix}S\\T\end{pmatrix} = d \cdot \mathbf{M}\begin{pmatrix}S\\T\end{pmatrix}$$

with $\mathbf{M}$ the (transpose of the) matrix of ω acting on $E_0[N]$ with respect to the basis $\{P, Q\}$. Using our attack we obtain an oracle for evaluating ψ as soon as $N > d\sqrt{w}$. If w is sufficiently small, then this condition is likely satisfied for either Alice's or Bob's secret isogeny. Unless $\omega \equiv [\lambda] \bmod [N]$ in $\mathrm{End}(E_0)$ for some $\lambda \in \mathbb{Z}$, the oracle can then be used to extract non-trivial information about φ. In general, one simply expects that ψ is a cyclic isogeny revealing all of $\ker(\hat{\varphi})$ and hence $\ker(\varphi)$. Thus as soon as E_0 comes equipped with a small non-scalar endomorphism then one should consider M-SIDH broken. This is precisely the attack described in [15, Sects. 4.2–4.3]. Similarly, by focusing on $\hat{\varphi} : E \to E_0$ rather than on $\varphi : E_0 \to E$, the same conclusion applies if E carries a small non-scalar endomorphism.

Remark 9. If the endomorphism ring of E_0 (resp. E) is known and we are in the overstretched case where $N/d \gtrsim p^{1/3}$, then we can run the attack with a non-scalar endomorphism ω on E_0 (resp. on E) of degree about $p^{2/3}$, which exists in view of [18, Proposition B.5] and can be computed using lattice reduction.[5]

4.2 Case $\sigma_0 = \pi_0$

If the curve E_0 is $\mathbb{F}_p$-rational, we can take $\omega = \mathrm{id}$ and consider $\psi = \varphi^{(p)} \circ \hat{\varphi}$. Since $p \nmid N$ by assumption, Lemma 3 implies

$$\psi\begin{pmatrix}S\\T\end{pmatrix} = (p^{-1}d \bmod N) \cdot \mathbf{M} \cdot \pi\begin{pmatrix}S\\T\end{pmatrix}$$

---

[5] A similar remark is made in [15, Sect. 4.3] but their claim that ω can be taken of degree about $p^{1/2}$ seems slightly overoptimistic.

with $\pi : E \to E^{(p)}$ the Frobenius isogeny and $\mathbf{M}$ the (transpose of the) matrix of $\hat{\pi}_0$ acting on $E_0[N]$ with respect to the basis $\{P, Q\}$. Note that

$$p^{-1}\mathbf{M} = \mathbf{M}_{\pi_0}^{-1},$$

so this confirms Eq. (1). As above, we thus obtain an oracle for evaluating ψ as soon as $N > d$; recall that in M-SIDH this condition is satisfied for either Alice's or Bob's secret isogeny. In general, one expects that ψ is a cyclic isogeny revealing all of $\ker(\varphi)$. Consequently, one should consider M-SIDH insecure as soon as E_0 is defined over $\mathbb{F}_p$. Again, by focusing on $\hat{\varphi} : E \to E_0$ instead, the same conclusion applies in case E is defined over $\mathbb{F}_p$.

More general, we can consider the case where E_0 is not $\mathbb{F}_p$-rational, but such that there exists a low degree isogeny $\omega : E_0 \to E_0^{(p)}$. The attack then results in an oracle to evaluate $\psi = \varphi^{(p)} \circ \omega \circ \hat{\varphi}$ as long as $N > d\sqrt{w}$. As such, if E_0 is close to its Frobenius conjugate $E_0^{(p)}$, i.e. w is small enough, then M-SIDH is also insecure. Once again, we arrive at the same conclusion in case E and $E^{(p)}$ are connected by a small-degree isogeny.

4.3 Backdoors

In this section we analyze how easy it would be for an attacker to backdoor M-SIDH by generating rigged system parameters and whether these backdoors can be detected or avoided altogether. The general idea is to generate system parameters E_0, P_B, Q_B which are a short distance removed, i.e. via a somewhat low degree isogeny ϵ, from one of the weak instances described above. Note that due to the symmetry of M-SIDH, i.e. by looking at the dual, the domain and co-domain are swapped, the same checks have to be performed for the co-domain curve E.

In [15, Sect. 7.1] the authors analyzed the requirements on the starting curve E_0 for M-SIDH to be secure and concluded that any curve E_0 without a small endomorphism is sufficient. Since a random $\mathbb{F}_p$-rational supersingular elliptic curve will not admit small endomorphisms, but still succumbs to our attack, this is clearly not sufficient. Furthermore, since the starting curve is part of the system parameters, for efficiency reasons, it might be tempting to organize a distributed random walk in the $\mathbb{F}_p$-isogeny graph. As we have shown, this is a bad idea.

Given a starting curve E_0 which is generated by a third party (trusted or not), detecting a possible backdoor amounts to verifying that E_0 and $E_0^{(p)}$ are not close in the $\mathbb{F}_{p^2}$-isogeny graph. Let $\theta : E_0 \to E_0^{(p)}$ be a connecting isogeny of degree t, then the composition $\hat{\pi}_0 \circ \theta$ is an endomorphism on E_0 of degree $t \cdot p$. Unfortunately, we are not aware of an efficient test for the existence of such endomorphism. The only (trivial) possibility seems to be to test whether $\Phi_k(j(E_0), j(E_0)^p) = 0$ for all $k = 1, \ldots, U$. The bound U depends on the difference between the degree of the isogenies φ_A (resp. φ_B) and the order of P_B, Q_B (resp. P_A, Q_A). To illustrate, if we are trying to recover φ_A, then the isogeny

$\psi = \varphi_A^{(p)} \circ \theta \circ \varphi_A$ has degree $A^2 t$ with $A = \deg(\varphi_A)$ and we thus require $B^2 > A^2 t$ or equivalently, $(B/A)^2 > t$. As such, we require to test at least up to

$$U \geq \max\{\frac{A^2}{B^2}, \frac{B^2}{A^2}\}.$$

To make this test efficient, it is therefore beneficial to take A as close to B as possible, which corresponds to the parameter selection in [15]. In particular, for the largest M-SIDH parameter set, we need to test existence of isogenies up to degree $U < 823$.

Finally, the authors suggest that the curve is generated using an MPC protocol as in [2], where a random supersingular curve is generated by n parties in a round-robin manner, i.e. party i executes a secret isogeny walk from E_{i-1} to E_i, where party 1 starts from a known supersingular elliptic curve E_0. Furthermore, each party needs to prove that they really know a path from E_{i-1} to E_i. The question now becomes whether the last party can force the walk to go through a curve E which is close to its Frobenius conjugate $E^{(p)}$. Since we assume at least one honest party preceding the last one, it is clear that for party n the curve E_{n-1} is a random supersingular elliptic curve. According to [8, Lemma 6], the number of (isomorphism classes of) supersingular elliptic curves such that E and $E^{(p)}$ are connected by an isogeny of degree up to d is bounded by $\tilde{O}(\sqrt{d^3 p})$. The probability of party n being able to force such a curve is therefore negligible.

In conclusion: using an MPC protocol as in [2] to execute an isogeny walk in the full $\mathbb{F}_{p^2}$-isogeny graph, will result in a non-backdoored curve with overwhelming probability. As an added measure, one can run the explicit test described above.

5   FESTA

To apply our attack to FESTA, in view of Remark 5 we require at least one of the basis points to be an eigenvector of $\hat{\sigma}_0 \circ \omega$ where σ_0 is either the identity or Frobenius and ω is a small degree endomorphism. Recall that in FESTA the torsion point order is given by $B = 2^b$ and our attack recovers $\psi = \sigma_{0*} \varphi \circ \omega \circ \hat{\varphi}$ as long as $B > d\sqrt{w}$, in case we know the images of a full basis, or $B > d^2 w$, in case we only know the image of a single point.

In this section we analyze how many such ω and *different* eigenspaces can exist for the curve $E_0 : y^2 = x^3 + 6x^2 + x$ over $\mathbb{F}_p$ used in the FESTA implementation [3]. Since E_0 is 2-isogenous to the elliptic curve $E_1 : y^2 = x^3 + x$ via an isogeny θ with $\ker \theta = \langle (0,0) \rangle$, and since the endomorphism ring of E_1 is well-known,[6] we can compute the following $\mathbb{Z}$-module basis of $\mathrm{End}(E_0)$:

$$\mathrm{id}, \quad \frac{\pi_0 - [1]}{2}, \quad \mathbf{i} - \mathbf{i}\pi_0, \quad \frac{\mathbf{i} + \mathbf{i}\pi_0}{4},$$

---

[6] See e.g. Sect. 6 for an explicit basis.

where $i = \sqrt{-1}$ and π_0 the Frobenius endomorphism. Note that i itself is not an endomorphism on E_0, but is an endomorphism on E_1. As such we obtain the endomorphism $2i = \hat{\theta} \circ i \circ \theta$ on E_0.

To simplify matters we will work with the subring generated by $\mathrm{id}, \pi_0, 2i, 2i\pi_0$, which has index 16 in $\mathrm{End}(E_0)$. Since $\deg(\pi_0) = p$ and we require $w = \deg(\omega)$ to be of moderately small degree (note that in the overstretched case we can allow for combinations with π_0), we are thus limited to choosing ω of the form $a + 2bi$ which has degree $a^2 + 4b^2$.

To illustrate this for the 128-bit secure parameter set, we have $B = 2^{632}$ and d has 273 bits, which allows ω of degree up to 2^{718} assuming we know images of a full basis and ω of degree up to 2^{86} if we only know the image of a single point.

5.1   Case $\sigma_0 = \mathrm{id}$

We have to analyze the eigenspaces of $\omega = \alpha + 2\beta i$ with $\alpha, \beta \in \mathbb{Z}$. However it is easy to see that if P is an eigenvector of such ω with eigenvalue μ, then if $\gcd(\beta, B) = 1$, P is also an eigenvector of $2i$ with eigenvalue $(\mu - \alpha)/\beta \bmod B$. As such the different choices for ω do not result in distinct eigenspaces, and only the eigenspaces of $2i$ are weak.

5.2   Case $\sigma_0 = \pi_0$

We have to analyze the eigenspaces of $\hat{\pi}_0 \circ \omega = \hat{\pi}_0 \circ (\alpha + 2\beta i)$. Since $\pi_0^2 = [-p]$ on E_0, we have $\hat{\pi}_0 = -\pi_0$, so it suffices to analyze the eigenspaces of $\pi_0 \circ (\alpha + 2\beta i)$.

Assume for now that B is odd (the case $B = 2^n$ is analyzed below). Let $\{U, V\}$ be a basis of eigenvectors of π_0 on $E_0[B]$, i.e. $\pi_0(U) = U$ and $\pi_0(V) = -V$ (here we used $p \equiv -1 \bmod B$ as in FESTA). Since π_0 and $2i$ anti-commute, we can in fact take $V = 2i(U)$, which indeed satisfies $\pi_0(V) = -V$ and has the same order as U (here we use B odd). Note that we also have the equality $2i(V) = -4U$.

Assume that $P \in E_0[B]$ is an eigenvector of $\pi_0 \circ (\alpha + 2\beta i)$ of exact order B, then using the basis $\{U, V\}$ of $E[B]$, we can express $P = cU + dV$ with $c, d \in \mathbb{Z}_B$ and at least one of c, d is a unit in $\mathbb{Z}_B$. Assume without loss of generality that this is c, then after rescaling by $c^{-1} \bmod B$, we can assume P is of the form $P = U + aV$ with $a \in \mathbb{Z}_B$. Note that by rescaling we are now counting different eigenspaces instead of eigenvectors, in particular, each a gives rise to a whole different eigenspace (and thus $\phi(B)$ different eigenvectors of exact order B, where ϕ denotes the Euler-phi function). To deal with the case that P has order $B' | B$ with $B' < B$, we can simply replace B by B', U by $(B/B')U$ and V by $(B/B')V$.

Assume that the eigenvalue corresponding to P is μ then using $V = 2i(U)$ and $2i(V) = -4U$ we have

$$\pi_0 \circ (\alpha + 2\beta i)(P) = (\alpha - 4a\beta)U + (-a\alpha - \beta)V = \mu(U + aV).$$

This is equivalent with

$$4a^2\beta - 2a\alpha - \beta \equiv 0 \bmod B.$$

For every choice of α and β we therefore get a quadratic equation for a with discriminant $\Delta = 4\alpha^2 + 16\beta^2$.

Case $B = \ell^n$ with ℓ an Odd Prime. Assume first that $B = \ell^n$ for an odd prime ℓ, then for β a unit in $\mathbb{Z}_B$, this equation will have two different solutions for a exactly when $\left(\frac{\Delta}{\ell}\right) = 1$ which are given by

$$a_\pm = \frac{\alpha \pm \sqrt{\alpha^2 + 4\beta^2}}{4\beta} = \frac{(\alpha/2\beta) \pm \sqrt{(\alpha/2\beta)^2 + 1}}{2} \bmod B.$$

Note that the solutions for a result in two different eigenspaces, one corresponding to a_+ and one corresponding to a_- and that the one fully determines the other. In particular, the eigenspaces come in pairs corresponding to $\{a_+, a_-\}$.

Assume we now consider the attack where the images of a full basis are required, then w is bounded by $w = \deg(\omega) = \alpha^2 + 4\beta^2 < (B/d)^2$. To estimate the total number of pairs of weak eigenspaces, we therefore simply need to compute the number of *different* values for a above where α, β vary *inside* the ellipse $x^2 + 4y^2 = (B/d)^2$. Ignoring (small) constants, the number of such pairs is given by $(B/d)^2$. However, as shown above, the value of a is really determined by $\alpha/2\beta \bmod B$. As such we need to distinguish 2 cases: if $d > \sqrt{B}$, then up to a small constant, the number of values for a really is $(B/d)^2$, however, when $d < \sqrt{B}$ the number of values for a is simply B. This shows that the total number of weak eigenspaces is, up to a small constant, given by

$$\min\{\frac{B^2}{d^2}, B\}.$$

Since the total number of eigenspaces is given by B^2, we conclude that the proportion of weak eigenspaces for FESTA in the full basis attack scenario is $O(\min\{\frac{1}{d^2}, \frac{1}{B}\})$.

We can do a similar analysis for the case where we want to run the attack with the image of only a single point, following Remark 5. The main difference is now that the bound on w is changed to $w = \deg(\omega) = \alpha^2 + 4\beta^2 < B/d^2$. Instead of counting the number of pairs of eigenspaces, we now simply count the number of eigenspaces. As before, we need to compute the number of *different* values for a above where α, β vary *inside* the ellipse $x^2 + 4y^2 = B/d^2$ (note the right hand side is different from before). Up to a small constant, this number is given by B/d^2. Note that for $d > \sqrt{B}$ there are no solutions, and otherwise there are B/d^2 (up to a small constant). Given that there are B different eigenspaces in total, the proportion of weak eigenspaces for FESTA in the single image point attack scenario is $O(1/d^2)$.

Case $B = 2^n$ with $n > 3$. The overall reasoning remains exactly the same, with a few small changes. The first change is that since $E[2]$ is already rational over $\mathbb{F}_p$ in FESTA, we will only be able to select U of order $B/2$. Furthermore, by construction $V = 2i(U)$ only has order $B' = B/8$ (note that the $\deg(2i) = 4$, so this is the worst that can happen). We thus consider the basis $U' = 4U$ and

V for $E[B']$. Note that we now have the equality $2\mathbf{i}(V) = -U'$. Considering eigenvectors of the form $P = U' + aV \in E[B']$ with eigenvalue μ, we get

$$\pi_0 \circ (\alpha + 2\beta\mathbf{i})(P) = (\alpha - a\beta)U' + (-a\alpha - 4\beta)V = \mu(U' + aV).$$

The quadratic equation for a thus also changes slightly, in that a now has to satisfy:

$$a^2\beta - 2a\alpha - 4\beta = 0 \bmod B'.$$

For β a unit, i.e. $\beta \not\equiv 0 \bmod 2$, it is easy to verify that the above equation will have no solutions. For $\beta \equiv 0 \bmod 2$, we can set $\beta' = \beta/2$ and obtain the equivalent equation:

$$a^2\beta' - a\alpha - 4\beta' = 0 \bmod B'/2.$$

It is easy to check that this equation will have 2 solutions modulo $B'/2$ whenever $\beta' \equiv \alpha \bmod 2$ and no solutions otherwise.

The remainder of the analysis now remains exactly the same, since the different solutions are fully determined by α/β, so up to a small constant, it suffices to compute the number of such tuples inside the ellipses $x^2 + 4y^2 = B'^2/d^2$ and $x^2 + 4y^2 = B'/d^2$ exactly as before. As such, also for $B = 2^n$, the proportion of weak eigenspaces for FESTA is again $O(\min\{\frac{1}{d^2}, \frac{1}{B}\})$ in the full basis attack scenario and $O(1/d^2)$ in the single image point attack scenario.

5.3   Backdoors

The general approach of introducing a backdoor into FESTA is similar to the M-SIDH case in that an attacker generates system parameters E_0, P_B, Q_B which are obtained as the image under a low degree isogeny ε of one of the weak instances identified above. In particular, let E_w, P_w, Q_w be a weak instance for FESTA, then $E_0 = \varepsilon(E_w)$, $P_B = \varepsilon(P_w)$ and $Q_B = \varepsilon(Q_w)$. The attack then proceeds to recover $\varepsilon \circ \varphi$, which is possible as long as $B^2 > e^2 d^2 w$ with $e = \deg(\varepsilon)$. Assuming that the weak basis is optimal, i.e. eigenvectors of Frobenius, we have $w = 1$ and so the backdoor can tolerate isogenies ε up to degree B/d which in FESTA is very large. If the endomorphism ring of E_0 is known or given, then one can proceed exactly as above to test whether the basis is weak; however, when the endomorphism ring of E_0 is unknown, then it is near impossible to verify whether FESTA has been backdoored since the degree of ε can be so large.

A possible, easy solution however is the following: as shown above, the proportion of weak bases for a given curve is on the order of $O(1/d^2)$ which is very small. Therefore, given system parameters E_0, P_B, Q_B it suffices to publicly rerandomize the basis, which with overwhelming probability will result in a basis which no longer is weak. Another possible solution, as done in the FESTA implementation, is to obtain P_B, Q_B deterministically using a hash function to the elliptic curve E_0 such as described in [24]. The paranoid user can rerandomize the basis themselves and include these as part of their public key.

Finally, we note that due to the symmetry of FESTA, i.e. by looking at the dual, the domain and co-domain are swapped, the same checks/countermeasures have to be performed for the co-domain curve E.

5.4   Overstretched FESTA

It is natural to ask whether, given any two points P and Q, it is always possible to construct an endomorphism ω such that P and Q become eigenvectors, and what the expected degree of such ω would be. To analyze this, we consider what can be expected for E_0 a sufficiently general supersingular elliptic curve over $\mathbb{F}_{p^2}$ with known endomorphism ring and $\{P, Q\}$ a sufficiently general basis of $E_0[B]$. Using lattice reduction we can find a $\mathbb{Z}$-basis

$$\mathrm{id}, \omega_1, \omega_2, \omega_3 \in \mathrm{End}(E_0)$$

with $\deg(\omega_i) \approx p^{2/3}$ for all i; see [18, Proposition B.5]. Writing $\mathbf{M}_i$ for the matrix of ω_i acting on $E_0[B]$ with respect to $\{P, Q\}$, we hope to find scalars $\lambda_i \in \mathbb{Z}$ such that

$$\lambda_1 \mathbf{M}_1 + \lambda_2 \mathbf{M}_2 + \lambda_3 \mathbf{M}_3 \qquad (6)$$

is diagonal (and non-scalar). The proportion of diagonal matrices in $\mathbb{Z}_B^{2 \times 2}$ is $1/B^2$, so we expect that we can take $|\lambda_i| \leq B^{2/3}$, and then $w = \deg(\omega) = \deg(\lambda_1 \omega_1 + \lambda_2 \omega_2 + \lambda_3 \omega_3)$ is in $O(p^{2/3} B^{4/3})$. In conclusion, as soon as $B \gtrsim pd^3$, we expect being able to find a degree-w endomorphism ω of which P and Q are eigenvectors and such that $B > d\sqrt{w}$, as required for the attack. Note that the condition $B \gtrsim pd^3$, implies that the B-torsion cannot be $\mathbb{F}_{p^2}$-rational as done in FESTA, so this attack really only concerns an overstretched case and does not apply to FESTA itself.

6   CSIDH

We now discuss CSIDH in its known-degree variant (e.g., the dummy-free variant from [7, Sect. 5] with $m = 1$). Concretely, our secret isogeny φ is a horizontal isogeny of known degree d connecting two supersingular elliptic curves E_0, E over $\mathbb{F}_p$. As discussed before, for bases $\{P, Q\} \subseteq E_0[N]$, $\{S, T\} \subseteq E[N]$ consisting of Frobenius eigenvectors we know that

$$\begin{pmatrix} S \\ T \end{pmatrix} = \mathbf{D} \cdot \varphi \begin{pmatrix} P \\ Q \end{pmatrix}$$

for some unknown diagonal matrix $\mathbf{D} \in \mathrm{GL}_2(\mathbb{Z}_N)$, where N can be taken arbitrarily large. Note that the eigenvalues corresponding to P, Q are necessarily of the form $\mu, -\mu$ since the characteristic polynomial of Frobenius is $x^2 + p$.

In order to apply our attack strategy, we wish to find $\sigma_0 \in \{\mathrm{id}, \pi_0\}$ and $\omega \in \mathrm{End}(E_0)$ such that:

– the matrix $\mathbf{M}$ of $\hat{\sigma}_0 \circ \omega$ acting on $E_0[N]$ with respect to the basis $\{P, Q\}$ is diagonal,
– $N^2 > wd^2$, where $w = \deg(\omega)$.

We will show that for

$$E_0 : y^2 = x^3 + x \text{ over } \mathbb{F}_p \text{ with } p \equiv 3 \text{ mod } 8 \tag{7}$$

(as is the setting for the original CSIDH proposal [6]) these conditions imply

$$(\hat{\sigma}_0 \circ \omega)(\ker(\varphi)) = \ker(\varphi) \tag{8}$$

so that, using the notation from Sect. 3.2, we are always in the case $d' = d$. Consequently, our attack strategy comes with $O(2^r)$ guesses, where r denotes the number of distinct prime factors of d, and therefore does not offer any improvement over existing attacks.

Our belief is that the same conclusions apply to any starting curve over any finite prime field,[7] but the discussion becomes more technical. The two features of (7) that make life easier are:

- N is odd, because 2 does not split in $\mathbb{Q}(\sqrt{-p})$,
- the endomorphism ring of E_0 is easy to handle; namely as a $\mathbb{Z}$-module it is generated by

$$[1], \frac{\mathbf{i} + \pi_0}{2}, \pi_0, \frac{[1] + \mathbf{i}\pi_0}{2}$$

with $\mathbf{i} : (x, y) \mapsto (-x, \sqrt{-1}y)$ such that $\mathbf{i}^2 = [-1]$.

It suffices to concentrate on the case $\sigma_0 = \text{id}$. Indeed, the matrix of an endomorphism ω with respect to $\{P, Q\}$ is diagonal if and only if the matrix of $\hat{\pi}_0 \circ \omega = -\pi_0 \circ \omega$ with respect to $\{P, Q\}$ is diagonal. Similarly, the equality from (8) holds for $\sigma_0 = \pi_0$ if and only if it holds for $\sigma_0 = \text{id}$.

Then the main observation is that $\mathbf{i}$ swaps the eigenspaces $\langle P \rangle$ and $\langle Q \rangle$. Indeed, this follows from

$$\pi_0(\mathbf{i}(P)) = -\mathbf{i}(\pi_0(P)) = -\mu\mathbf{i}(P).$$

Consequently, the matrix of $\mathbf{i}$ with respect to $\{P, Q\}$ is anti-diagonal. Likewise, also the matrix of $\mathbf{i}\pi_0$ with respect to $\{P, Q\}$ is anti-diagonal. This means that if we want the matrix of

$$\omega = a_1 + a_2\frac{\mathbf{i} + \pi_0}{2} + a_3\pi_0 + a_4\frac{1 + \mathbf{i}\pi_0}{2} = a_1 + \frac{a_4}{2} + \frac{a_2}{2}\mathbf{i} + (a_3 + \frac{a_2}{2})\pi_0 + \frac{a_4}{2}\mathbf{i}\pi_0$$

with respect to $\{P, Q\}$ to be diagonal, then

$$a_2\mathbf{i} + a_4\mathbf{i}\pi_0 = (a_2 - a_4\pi_0)\mathbf{i}$$

should act as the zero map on $\langle P, Q \rangle = E_0[N]$. By construction π_0 has distinct eigenvalues modulo every prime factor of N, so this can only happen if $a_2 \equiv a_4 \equiv 0 \text{ mod } N$. If $a_2 = a_4 = 0$ then ω is a linear combination of 1 and π_0, from

---

[7] Or even more generally: to arbitrary orientations.

which it readily follows that $\omega(\ker(\varphi)) = \ker(\varphi)$. On the other hand, as soon as one of a_2, a_4 is non-zero, we find that

$$w \geq \frac{\deg(a_2\mathbf{i} + a_4\mathbf{i}\pi_0)}{4} = \frac{a_2^2 + pa_4^2}{4} \geq N^2/4$$

and therefore $N^2 \leq wd^2$: a contradiction (here we have used that $d > 1$, which can of course be assumed without loss of generality).

Remark 10. According to Remark 5, an alternative strategy is to look for $\omega \in \mathrm{End}(E_0)$ such that P is an eigenvector of $\hat{\sigma}_0 \circ \omega$, but Q not necessarily is; recall that the bound $N^2 > wd^2$ strengthens to $N > wd^2$ in this case. The analysis is similar, except that now we run into the conclusion that $(a_2 - a_4\pi_0)\mathbf{i}$ should vanish on $\langle P \rangle$, rather than on all of $E_0[N]$. Equivalently, this means that $a_2 - a_4\pi_0$ should vanish on $\langle Q \rangle$, or in other words that $a_2 + a_4\mu \equiv 0 \bmod N$. As before, we have

$$w \geq \frac{a_2^2 + pa_4^2}{4}$$

where now we observe that the numerator of the right-hand side is divisible by N because $a_2^2 + pa_4^2 \equiv (\mu^2 + p)a_4^2 \equiv 0 \bmod N$. Here we have used that $\mu^2 + p \equiv 0 \bmod N$ because μ is an eigenvalue of Frobenius mod N. We conclude: if $a_2 = a_4 = 0$ then $\omega \in \mathbb{Z}[\pi_0]$, else $w \geq N/4$ and therefore $N \leq wd^2$.

Acknowledgments. We thank the anonymous reviewers and the shepherd for the many suggestions for improving our exposition. We also thank Boris Fouotsa, Chenfeng He, Péter Kutas, Guido Lido, Simon-Philipp Merz, Christophe Petit Antonio Sanso and Benjamin Wesolowski for helpful discussions.

A   Maximal Commutative Subgroups of $\mathrm{GL}_2(\mathbb{Z}_N)$

This appendix contains a partial classification of the maximal commutative subgroups of $\mathrm{GL}_2(\mathbb{Z}_N)$. The classification seems classical in case N is a prime number, but we could not find a reference that deals with the general case, where various subtleties arise, see for instance Example 12 below. Maximal commutative subgroups of $\mathrm{GL}_2(\mathbb{Z}_N)$ are natural candidates for the set X from Sect. 3.1, and they can also be used as substitutes for $X = \{\text{diagonal matrices}\}$ in FESTA [3]. By the Chinese Remainder Theorem, it suffices to concentrate on the case $N = \ell^e$ for some prime number ℓ.

Free Maximal Commutative Subalgebras

We first study maximal commutative sub*algebras* $\mathcal{A} \subset \mathrm{M}_2(\mathbb{Z}_{\ell^e})$, by which we mean that $\mathcal{A}$ equals its own centralizer, i.e., there is no matrix in $\mathrm{M}_2(\mathbb{Z}_{\ell^e}) \backslash \mathcal{A}$ that commutes with every element of $\mathcal{A}$. As an additive group, $\mathcal{A}$ must be isomorphic to

$$\mathbb{Z}_{\ell^{e_1}} \oplus \cdots \oplus \mathbb{Z}_{\ell^{e_r}}, \qquad 2 \leq r \leq 4$$

for certain exponents $e = e_1 \geq \ldots \geq e_r$, just because

- it concerns a subgroup of $M_2(\mathbb{Z}_{\ell^e}) \cong (\mathbb{Z}_{\ell^e})^4$,
- it contains I_2, which has additive order ℓ^e,
- it contains at least one non-scalar matrix.

The following useful lemma implies that if $e_2 = e$, then necessarily $r = 2$ and as a result $\mathcal{A}$ is free when viewed as a $\mathbb{Z}_{\ell^e}$-module. We can indeed apply the lemma, because it is easy to see that if a matrix $M = (m_{ij})$ is $\mathbb{Z}_{\ell^e}$-linearly independent of I_2, then at least one of $m_{12}, m_{21}, m_{11} - m_{22}$ is a unit.

Lemma 11. *Let* $M = (m_{ij}) \in M_2(\mathbb{Z}_{\ell^e})$ *be such that* $\{m_{12}, m_{21}, m_{11} - m_{22}\}$ *contains a unit. Then the centralizer*

$$C_{M_2(\mathbb{Z}_{\ell^e})}(M) = \{\, X \in M_2(\mathbb{Z}_{\ell^e}) \mid MX = XM \,\},$$

when considered as a $\mathbb{Z}_{\ell^e}$-*module, is free of rank 2.*

Proof. Through the use of one of the conjugations

$$\begin{pmatrix} 0 & 1 \\ 1 & 0 \end{pmatrix} \cdot \begin{pmatrix} m_{11} & m_{12} \\ m_{21} & m_{22} \end{pmatrix} \cdot \begin{pmatrix} 0 & 1 \\ 1 & 0 \end{pmatrix}^{-1} = \begin{pmatrix} m_{22} & m_{21} \\ m_{12} & m_{11} \end{pmatrix},$$

$$\begin{pmatrix} 1 & 0 \\ 1 & 1 \end{pmatrix} \cdot \begin{pmatrix} m_{11} & m_{12} \\ m_{21} & m_{22} \end{pmatrix} \cdot \begin{pmatrix} 1 & 0 \\ 1 & 1 \end{pmatrix}^{-1} = \begin{pmatrix} m_{11} - m_{12} & m_{12} \\ m_{11} - m_{12} + m_{21} - m_{22} & m_{12} + m_{22} \end{pmatrix}$$

we can reduce to the case where m_{21} is a unit. Expressing that a matrix $X = (x_{ij})$ commutes with M leads to a system of equations

$$\begin{pmatrix} -m_{21}x_{12} + m_{12}x_{21} & -m_{12}x_{11} + (m_{11} - m_{22})x_{12} + m_{12}x_{22} \\ m_{21}x_{11} + (-m_{11} + m_{22})x_{21} - m_{21}x_{22} & m_{21}x_{12} - m_{12}x_{21} \end{pmatrix}$$

$$= \begin{pmatrix} m_{11} & m_{12} \\ m_{21} & m_{22} \end{pmatrix} \begin{pmatrix} x_{11} & x_{12} \\ x_{21} & x_{22} \end{pmatrix} - \begin{pmatrix} x_{11} & x_{12} \\ x_{21} & x_{22} \end{pmatrix} \begin{pmatrix} m_{11} & m_{12} \\ m_{21} & m_{22} \end{pmatrix} = \begin{pmatrix} 0 & 0 \\ 0 & 0 \end{pmatrix}$$

which can be checked to reduce to

$$\begin{cases} x_{11} = (m_{22} - m_{11})x_{21}/m_{21} + x_{22}, \\ x_{12} = m_{12}x_{21}/m_{21}. \end{cases}$$

From this the lemma follows. □

We call such a maximal commutative subalgebra *free*. Let us recall that this is a maximal commutative subalgebra $\mathcal{A} \subseteq M_2(\mathbb{Z}_{\ell^e})$ whose additive group is isomorphic to

$$\mathbb{Z}_{\ell^e} \oplus \mathbb{Z}_{\ell^e},$$

and that this is automatically satisfied as soon as $\mathcal{A}$ admits an additive subgroup of this form.

Example 12. An example of a *non-free* maximal commutative subalgebra is the algebra of matrices of the form

$$\alpha I_2 + \beta \ell M \in M_2(\mathbb{Z}_{\ell^2})$$

whose additive group structure is given by

$$\mathbb{Z}_{\ell^2} \oplus \mathbb{Z}_\ell \oplus \mathbb{Z}_\ell \oplus \mathbb{Z}_\ell.$$

Observe that its number of elements ℓ^5 is *larger* than $\ell^{2e} = \ell^4$ in this case!

Note that freeness comes for free if $e = 1$, i.e., when working over the field $\mathbb{F}_\ell$. In that case the following theorem is likely well-known.

Theorem 13. *Up to conjugation, the free maximal commutative subalgebras of* $M_2(\mathbb{Z}_{\ell^e})$ *are given by*

$$\mathcal{A}_{c,d} = \{\, \mathbf{M}_{c,d}(ax + b) \mid a, b \in \mathbb{Z}_{\ell^e} \,\}$$

with $c, d \in \mathbb{Z}_{\ell^e}$. *Here* $\mathbf{M}_{c,d}(ax + b)$ *denotes the matrix of multiplication by* $ax + b$ *in the ring*

$$\frac{(\mathbb{Z}_{\ell^e})[x]}{(x^2 + cx + d)}$$

with respect to the basis $1, x$. *Moreover, writing* $\Delta_{c,d} = c^2 - 4d$, *two such subalgebras are conjugate if and only if*

$$\Delta_{c,d} = u^2 \Delta_{c',d'}$$

for some $u \in \mathbb{Z}_{\ell^e}^\times$.

Proof. It is easy to see that the algebras $\mathcal{A}_{c,d}$ are maximal commutative and free. Indeed, it is immediate that they are commutative and that their additive group structure is isomorphic to $\mathbb{Z}_{\ell^e} \oplus \mathbb{Z}_{\ell^e}$ (one can choose $\mathbf{I}_2 = \mathbf{M}_{c,d}(1)$ and $\mathbf{M}_{c,d}(x)$ as generators). Maximality then follows from the foregoing discussion.

To prove that every free maximal commutative subalgebra $\mathcal{A} \subseteq M_2(\mathbb{Z}_{\ell^e})$ is conjugate to an algebra of the form $\mathcal{A}_{c,d}$, it suffices to show:

Claim. Every matrix in $M_2(\mathbb{Z}_{\ell^e})$ is conjugate to a matrix

$$\mathbf{M} \in \mathcal{A}_{c,d}$$

for some $c, d \in \mathbb{Z}_{\ell^e}$.

Indeed, recall that $\mathcal{A}$ is additively generated by $\mathbf{I}_2$ and some non-scalar matrix $\mathbf{M}$. By the claim, we can assume that $\mathbf{M} \in \mathcal{A}_{c,d}$ for certain c, d. Every matrix in $\mathcal{A}_{c,d}$ commutes with $\mathbf{M}$ and therefore it commutes with every matrix in $\mathcal{A}$. Hence it follows from the maximal commutativity of $\mathcal{A}$ that $\mathcal{A}_{c,d} \subseteq \mathcal{A}$. But since $\mathcal{A}_{c,d}$ is maximal commutative, equality must hold.

To prove the claim, we argue that every matrix in $M_2(\mathbb{Z}_{\ell^e})$ is conjugate to a matrix $\mathbf{M} = (m_{ij})$ satisfying

$$\nu_\ell(m_{21}) \leq \nu_\ell(m_{12}), \qquad \nu_\ell(m_{21}) \leq \nu_\ell(m_{22} - m_{11}).$$

This follows from the conjugations that were used in the proof of Lemma 11. Using a conjugation of the first kind we can ensure that $\nu_\ell(m_{21}) \leq \nu_\ell(m_{12})$.

Once this is established, a conjugation of the second kind ensures that $\nu_\ell(m_{21}) \leq \nu_\ell(m_{22} - m_{11})$, as wanted. Consequently, there exist c, d such that

$$\mathbf{M} = \begin{pmatrix} m_{11} & -m_{21}d \\ m_{21} & m_{11} - m_{21}c \end{pmatrix},$$

but this is nothing else than $\mathbf{M}_{c,d}(m_{21}x + m_{11})$. Therefore $\mathbf{M} \in \mathcal{A}_{c,d}$.

Next, assume that two multiplication algebras $\mathcal{A}_{c,d}$ and $\mathcal{A}_{c',d'}$ are conjugates of each other, i.e., $\mathcal{A}_{c',d'} = \mathbf{T}\mathcal{A}_{c,d}\mathbf{T}^{-1}$ for some $\mathbf{T} \in \mathrm{GL}_2(\mathbb{Z}_{\ell^e})$. Let $\mathbf{M}$ be any matrix which along with $\mathbf{I}_2$ additively generates $\mathcal{A}_{c,d}$; then necessarily $\mathbf{M} = \mathbf{M}_{c,d}(ax + b)$ for some unit a. We also have that $\mathbf{T}\mathbf{M}\mathbf{T}^{-1}$ is a generator of $\mathcal{A}_{c',d'}$ along with $\mathbf{I}_2$, hence it is of the form $\mathbf{M}_{c',d'}(a'x + b')$ for some unit a'. Now it is straightforward to check the identity

$$\mathrm{disc}(\mathrm{charpol}(\mathbf{M}_{c,d}(ax + b))) = a^2\Delta_{c,d},$$

but since $\mathbf{M}$ and $\mathbf{T}\mathbf{M}\mathbf{T}^{-1}$ have the same characteristic polynomial this also equals $a'^2\Delta_{c',d'}$. We conclude that $\Delta_{c,d} = u^2\Delta_{c',d'}$ with $u = a'/a$.

Conversely, assume that $\Delta_{c,d} = u^2\Delta_{c',d'}$ for some unit u. One then checks that

$$\varphi : \frac{(\mathbb{Z}_{\ell^e})[x]}{(x^2 + cx + d)} \rightarrow \frac{(\mathbb{Z}_{\ell^e})[x]}{(x^2 + c'x + d')} : x \mapsto ux + \frac{uc' - c}{2}$$

is an isomorphism of rings; this is also true for $\ell = 2$, where we note that our assumption $\Delta_{c,d} = u^2\Delta_{c',d'}$ implies that $uc' - c$ has positive valuation, so that division by 2 makes sense. Writing $\mathbf{T}$ for the matrix of φ with respect to the bases $\{1, x\}$ and $\{1, x\}$, it readily follows that

$$\mathbf{M}_{c',d'}(\varphi(ax + b)) = \mathbf{T}\mathbf{M}_{c,d}(ax + b)\mathbf{T}^{-1},$$

showing that the algebras $\mathcal{A}_{c,d}$ and $\mathcal{A}_{c',d'}$ are conjugates of each other. $\square$

Extrapolating from the case $e = 1$, the following nomenclature is natural; see also [22, Appendix A5]:

- The *split Cartan case* corresponds to $\Delta_{c,d}$ being a square unit. This case is unique up to conjugation. Taking $c = -1, d = 0$, we see that $\mathbf{M}_{c,d}$ consists of matrices of the form

$$\begin{pmatrix} b & 0 \\ a & a + b \end{pmatrix},$$

where we note that

$$\begin{pmatrix} 1 & 0 \\ 1 & 1 \end{pmatrix} \cdot \begin{pmatrix} b & 0 \\ a & a + b \end{pmatrix} \cdot \begin{pmatrix} 1 & 0 \\ 1 & 1 \end{pmatrix}^{-1} = \begin{pmatrix} b & 0 \\ 0 & a + b \end{pmatrix}$$

so, up to conjugation, the split Cartan case corresponds to the subalgebra of diagonal matrices.

- The *non-split Cartan cases* correspond to $\Delta_{c,d}$ being a non-square unit. Usually this case is also unique up to conjugation: this is true as soon as $\ell > 2$ or $b < 3$; e.g. if $\ell \equiv 3 \bmod 4$ then we can realize it as the subalgebra of anticirculant matrices

$$\begin{pmatrix} b & -a \\ a & b \end{pmatrix}.$$

by taking $c = 0$ and $d = 1$. If $\ell = 2$ and $b \geq 3$ then there are three non-split Cartan cases, corresponding to whether $\Delta_{c,d} \bmod 8$ is 3, 5, or 7.
- The *ramified Cartan cases* correspond to $\Delta_{c,d}$ being a non-unit. These can be classified according to the valuation $v = \nu_\ell(\Delta_{c,d})$ and the class of the unit

$$\Delta_{c,d}/\ell^v \in \frac{\mathbb{Z}_{\ell^{e-v}}^*}{\mathbb{Z}_{\ell^{e-v}}^{*2}},$$

for which there are
  - 1 option if $v = e$ — this is the *totally ramified case*, corresponding to matrices of the form

$$\begin{pmatrix} b & 0 \\ a & b \end{pmatrix}$$

    (e.g., take $c = d = 0$), up to conjugation — or also if $\ell = 2$ and $v = e - 1$,
  - 2 options if $\ell > 2$ and $v < e$ or if $\ell = 2$ and $v = e - 2$,
  - 4 options if $\ell = 2$ and $v < e - 2$.

Example 14. The subalgebra of circulant matrices

$$\begin{pmatrix} b & a \\ a & b \end{pmatrix},$$

which have also been proposed for use in FESTA [3, Footnote 3], is precisely $\mathcal{A}_{0,-1}$, with discriminant 4. If $\ell > 2$ then this is the split Cartan case, while if $\ell = 2$ we are *almost* in the split Cartan case (we have $v = 2$ and $\Delta_{0,-1}/2^2 = 1$).

Subgroups

We now proceed to the study of maximal commutative subgroups of $\mathrm{GL}_2(\mathbb{Z}/\ell^e\mathbb{Z})$. Of course, by a maximal commutative subgroup we mean a subgroup that is equal to its own centralizer, but now considered inside $\mathrm{GL}_2(\mathbb{Z}/\ell^e\mathbb{Z})$. Note that we have commutativity-preserving maps

$$\mathcal{A} \mapsto \mathcal{A} \cap \mathrm{GL}_2(\mathbb{Z}_{\ell^e}) \subseteq \mathrm{GL}_2(\mathbb{Z}_{\ell^e}), \qquad G \mapsto \langle G \rangle_{\mathbb{Z}_{\ell^e}} \subseteq \mathrm{M}_2(\mathbb{Z}_{\ell^e})$$

between the set of subalgebras of $\mathrm{M}_2(\mathbb{Z}_{\ell^e})$ and the set of subgroups of $\mathrm{GL}_2(\mathbb{Z}_{\ell^e})$. To see that $\mathcal{A} \cap \mathrm{GL}_2(\mathbb{Z}_{\ell^e})$ is indeed a subgroup, it suffices to observe that if $\mathbf{M} \in \mathcal{A}$ is invertible, then also $\mathbf{M}^{-1} = (\det \mathbf{M})^{-1}(\mathrm{tr}(\mathbf{M})\mathbf{I}_2 - \mathbf{M}) \in \mathcal{A}$ by Cayley–Hamilton.

Lemma 15. *Every maximal commutative subgroup of $\mathrm{GL}_2(\mathbb{Z}_{\ell^e})$ is of the form $\mathcal{A} \cap \mathrm{GL}_2(\mathbb{Z}_{\ell^e})$ with $\mathcal{A}$ a maximal commutative subalgebra of $\mathrm{M}_2(\mathbb{Z}_{\ell^e})$.*

Proof. Let $G \subseteq \mathrm{GL}_2(\mathbb{Z}_{\ell^e})$ be a maximal commutative subgroup. Since $\langle G \rangle_{\mathbb{Z}_{\ell^e}}$ is commutative, we have that G is contained in a maximal commutative algebra $\mathcal{A}$. But then $G \subseteq \mathcal{A} \cap \mathrm{GL}_2(\mathbb{Z}_{\ell^e})$ and by the maximality of G, equality holds. $\square$

The converse to this statement is slightly more subtle. But here is a special case where things work out:

Lemma 16. *If $\ell > 2$ then for any free maximal commutative subalgebra $\mathcal{A} \subseteq M_2(\mathbb{Z}_{\ell^e})$ we have that $\mathcal{A} \cap \mathrm{GL}_2(\mathbb{Z}_{\ell^e})$ is a maximal commutative subgroup of $\mathrm{GL}_2(\mathbb{Z}_{\ell^e})$.*

Proof. Recall that $\mathcal{A}$ is additively generated by $\mathbf{I}_2$ and another matrix $\mathbf{M}$. We claim that $\mathbf{M}$ can be chosen to be an invertible matrix. To this end, consider

$$\det(\mathbf{M} + x\mathbf{I}_2) \bmod \ell \in \mathbb{F}_\ell[x]. \tag{9}$$

This polynomial has at most two roots, so since $\ell > 2$ we can find $\lambda \in \mathbb{Z}_{\ell^e}$ which does not reduce to a root of (9) modulo ℓ. If we then replace $\mathbf{M}$ with $\mathbf{M} + \lambda\mathbf{I}_2$ we find a generator that is invertible, as wanted.

Now the proof is easy. Let $\mathbf{N} \in \mathrm{GL}_2(\mathbb{Z}_{\ell^e})$ be a matrix that commutes with every matrix in $\mathcal{A} \cap \mathrm{GL}_2(\mathbb{Z}_{\ell^e})$. Then it commutes with $\mathbf{M}$, and therefore it commutes with every matrix in $\mathcal{A}$. From the maximality of $\mathcal{A}$ it follows that $\mathbf{N} \in \mathcal{A}$. $\square$

In the foregoing lemma the condition $\ell > 2$ is necessary. Indeed, an easy counterexample is the split Cartan subalgebra

$$\mathcal{A} = \left\{ \begin{pmatrix} * & 0 \\ 0 & * \end{pmatrix} \right\},$$

which is generated by

$$\mathbf{I}_2 = \begin{pmatrix} 1 & 0 \\ 0 & 1 \end{pmatrix} \quad \text{and} \quad \mathbf{M} = \begin{pmatrix} 1 & 0 \\ 0 & 0 \end{pmatrix}.$$

Note that none of the matrices $\mu\mathbf{M} + \lambda\mathbf{I}_2$ with μ odd is invertible. Therefore $\mathcal{A} \cap \mathrm{GL}_2(\mathbb{Z}_{2^e})$ is contained in the index-2 subalgebra $\langle 2\mathbf{M}, \mathbf{I}_2 \rangle$. Every matrix in this subalgebra commutes with the invertible matrix

$$\begin{pmatrix} 1 & 2^{e-1} \\ 0 & 1 \end{pmatrix}$$

which is not contained in $\mathcal{A}$. Therefore $\mathcal{A} \cap \mathrm{GL}_2(\mathbb{Z}_{\ell^e})$ is not maximal commutative.

Remark 17. We end by remarking that with $\mathcal{A} \subseteq M_2(\mathbb{Z}_{\ell^2}\mathbb{Z})$ the non-free maximal commutative subalgebra from Example 12, the resulting commutative subgroup $\mathcal{A} \cap \mathrm{GL}_2(\mathbb{Z}_{\ell^2})$ still contains $\ell^4(\ell-1)$ matrices, which is strictly larger than ℓ^4 as soon as $\ell > 2$. So this is still larger than what could be attained using free maximal commutative subalgebras.

References

1. Azarderakhsh, R., et al.: Supersingular isogeny key encapsulation. In: Submission to the NIST Post-Quantum Standardization Project, vol. 152, pp. 154–155 (2017)
2. Basso, A., et al.: Supersingular curves you can trust. In: Hazay, C., Stam, M. (eds.) EUROCRYPT 2023. LNCS, vol. 14005, pp. 405–437. Springer, Cham (2023). https://doi.org/10.1007/978-3-031-30617-4_14
3. Basso, A., Maino, L., Pope, G.: FESTA: fast encryption from supersingular torsion attacks. Asiacrypt 2023. https://eprint.iacr.org/2023/660
4. Castryck, W., Decru, T.: An efficient key recovery attack on SIDH. In: Hazay, C., Stam, M. (eds.) EUROCRYPT 2023. LNCS, vol. 14008, pp. 423–447. Springer, Cham (2023). https://doi.org/10.1007/978-3-031-30589-4_15
5. Castryck, W., Houben, M., Merz, S.-P., Mula, M., Buuren, S. van, Vercauteren, F.: Weak instances of class group action based cryptography via self-pairings. In: Handschuh, H., Lysyanskaya, A. (eds.) CRYPTO 2023. LNCS, vol. 14083, pp. 762–792. Springer, Cham (2023). https://doi.org/10.1007/978-3-031-38548-3_25
6. Castryck, W., Lange, T., Martindale, C., Panny, L., Renes, J.: CSIDH: an efficient post-quantum commutative group action. In: Peyrin, T., Galbraith, S. (eds.) ASIA-CRYPT 2018. LNCS, vol. 11274, pp. 395–427. Springer, Cham (2018). https://doi.org/10.1007/978-3-030-03332-3_15
7. Cervantes-Vázquez, D., et al.: Stronger and faster side-channel protections for CSIDH. In: Schwabe, P., Thériault, N. (eds.) LATINCRYPT 2019. LNCS, vol. 11774, pp. 173–193. Springer, Cham (2019). https://doi.org/10.1007/978-3-030-30530-7_9
8. Charles, D.X., Lauter, K.E., Goren, E.Z.: Cryptographic hash functions from expander graphs. J. Cryptol. 22(1), 93–113 (2009)
9. Chávez-Saab, J., Chi-Domínguez, J.-J., Jaques, S., Rodríguez-Henríquez, F.: The SQALE of CSIDH: sublinear Vélu quantum-resistant isogeny action with low exponents. J. Cryptogr. Eng. 12(3), 349–368 (2022)
10. Chenu, M., Smith, B.: Higher-degree supersingular group actions. Math. Cryptol. 1(2), 85–101 (2022)
11. Colò, L., Kohel, D.: Orienting supersingular isogeny graphs. J. Math. Cryptol. 14(1), 414–437 (2020)
12. De Feo, L.: Mathematics of isogeny based cryptography (2017)
13. De Feo, L., et al. Modular isogeny problems. Private communication
14. de Quehen, V., et al.: Improved torsion-point attacks on SIDH variants. In: Malkin, T., Peikert, C. (eds.) CRYPTO 2021. LNCS, vol. 12827, pp. 432–470. Springer, Cham (2021). https://doi.org/10.1007/978-3-030-84252-9_15
15. Fouotsa, T.B., Moriya, T., Petit, C.: M-SIDH and MD-SIDH: countering SIDH attacks by masking information. In: Hazay, C., Stam, M. (eds.) EUROCRYPT 2023. LNCS, vol. 14008, pp. 282–309. Springer, Cham (2023). https://doi.org/10.1007/978-3-031-30589-4_10
16. Jao, D., De Feo, L.: Towards quantum-resistant cryptosystems from supersingular elliptic curve isogenies. In: Yang, B.-Y. (ed.) PQCrypto 2011. LNCS, vol. 7071, pp. 19–34. Springer, Heidelberg (2011). https://doi.org/10.1007/978-3-642-25405-5_2
17. Jao, D., Urbanik, D.: SOK: the problem landscape of SIDH. In: Proceedings of the 5th ACM on ASIA Public-Key Cryptography Workshop, pp. 53–60. ACM (2018)
18. Love, J., Boneh, D.: Supersingular curves with small non-integer endomorphisms. In: ANTS-XIV. Open Book Series, vol. 4, pp. 7–22. MSP (2020)

19. Maino, L., Martindale, C., Panny, L., Pope, G., Wesolowski, B.: A direct key recovery attack on SIDH. In: Hazay, C., Stam, M. (eds.) EUROCRYPT 2023. LNCS, vol. 14008, pp. 448–471. Springer, Cham (2023). https://doi.org/10.1007/978-3-031-30589-4_16

20. Onuki, H.: On oriented supersingular elliptic curves. Finite Fields Their Appl. **69**, 101777 (2021)

21. Robert, D.: Breaking SIDH in polynomial time. In: Hazay, C., Stam, M. (eds.) EUROCRYPT 2023. LNCS, vol. 14008, pp. 472–503. Springer, Cham (2023). https://doi.org/10.1007/978-3-031-30589-4_17

22. Serre, J.-P.: Lectures on the Mordell-Weil Theorem. In: Aspects of Mathematics, 3rd edn., vol. E15. Springer, Fachmedien Wiesbaden (1997). (orig. Vieweg & Sohn)

23. Tenenbaum, G.: Introduction to Analytic and Probabilistic Number Theory, 3rd edn. Graduate Studies in Mathematics, vol. 163. American Mathematical Society (2015)

24. Zanon, G.H., Simplicio, M.A., Pereira, G.C., Doliskani, J., Barreto, P.S.: Faster key compression for isogeny-based cryptosystems. IEEE Trans. Comput. **68**(5), 688–701 (2019)

NEV: Faster and Smaller NTRU Encryption Using Vector Decoding

Jiang Zhang[✉] , Dengguo Feng , and Di Yan

State Key Laboratory of Cryptology, P.O. Box 5159, Beijing 100878, China
{zhangj,yand}@sklc.org, fengdg@263.net

Abstract. In this paper, we present NEV – a faster and smaller NTRU Encryption using Vector decoding, which is provably IND-CPA secure in the standard model under the decisional NTRU and RLWE assumptions over the cyclotomic ring $R_q = \mathbb{Z}_q[X]/(X^n + 1)$. Our main technique is a novel and non-trivial way to integrate a previously known plaintext encoding and decoding mechanism into the provably IND-CPA secure NTRU variant by Stehlé and Steinfeld (Eurocrypt 2011). Unlike the original NTRU encryption and its variants which encode the plaintext into the least significant bits of the coefficients of a message polynomial, we encode each plaintext bit into the most significant bits of multiple coefficients of the message polynomial, so that we can use a vector of noised coefficients to decode each plaintext bit in decryption, and significantly reduce the size of q with a reasonably negligible decryption failure.

Concretely, we can use $q = 769$ to obtain public keys and ciphertexts of 615 bytes with decryption failure $\leq 2^{-138}$ at NIST level 1 security, and 1229 bytes with decryption failure $\leq 2^{-152}$ at NIST level 5 security. By applying the Fujisaki-Okamoto transformation in a standard way, we obtain an IND-CCA secure KEM from our basic PKE scheme. Compared to NTRU and Kyber in the NIST Round 3 finalists at the same security levels, our KEM is 33–48% more compact and 5.03–29.94X faster than NTRU in the round-trip time of ephemeral key exchange, and is 21% more compact and 1.42–1.74X faster than Kyber.

We also give an optimized encryption scheme NEV' with better noise tolerance (and slightly better efficiency) based on a variant of the RLWE problem, called Subset-Sum Parity RLWE problem, which we show is polynomially equivalent to the standard decisional RLWE problem (with different parameters), and maybe of independent interest.

1 Introduction

The NTRU encryption proposed by Hoffstein, Pipher and Silverman [24] is one of the first publicly known practical public key encryptions (PKEs) on lattices. The security of NTRU encryption was originally stated as its own assumption, but after more than 25 years of studies, there is no significant algorithmic progress against it (except for overstretched parameters [17,29]). Now, it is more natural

© International Association for Cryptologic Research 2023
J. Guo and R. Steinfeld (Eds.): ASIACRYPT 2023, LNCS 14444, pp. 157–189, 2023.
https://doi.org/10.1007/978-981-99-8739-9_6

to view NTRU encryption as a cryptosystem based on two hardness assumptions [18,43]: the decisional NTRU assumption which roughly says that the quotient $h = g/f$ of two small polynomials g, f is pseudorandom, and the RLWE assumption [32,44] which says that it is hard to recover e from $(h, hr + e)$ when h is uniformly random, and r, e are randomly chosen small polynomials. It is worth to note that the first assumption can be removed for appropriately chosen (but very inefficient) parameters [43].

In NIST post-quantum cryptography (PQC) standardization process [36], NTRU was one of the four PKEs/KEMs in NIST Round 3 finalists [37], but it was not selected for standardization by NIST in the end [38]. One main reason is that it is neither the fastest nor the smallest among the lattice KEM finalists [38]. In particular, compared to Kyber which was selected as the NIST KEM standard, NTRU has 8.3–18.6% larger public key and ciphertext sizes (see Table 1) and 8.21–45.34X slower key generation (see Table 2). Several recent efforts [18,20,33] have been made to improve the performance of NTRU.

Lyubashevsky and Seiler [33] proposed a NTRU variant, called NTTRU, over the specific cyclotomic ring $\mathbb{Z}_{7681}[x]/(x^{768} - x^{384} + 1)$ that supports Number Theory Transform (NTT), and obtained significant speedup over the original NTRU that uses rings (e.g., $\mathbb{Z}_q[x]/(x^n - 1)$) do not support NTT. Later, Duman et al. [18] extended the idea of [33] to other NTT-friendly rings of the same form $\mathbb{Z}_q[x]/(x^n - x^{n/2} + 1)$, and obtained comparable efficiency improvement for flexible choices of parameters. Note that given an NTRU public key $h = pg/f$ for some plaintext modulus p, the message m in the original NTRU encryption $c = hr + m$ will be multiplied by the secret f in decryption. Thus, purposefully choosing a "bad" m can significantly increase the decryption failure (by more than 2^{100} times for standard parameter choices [18]), which might be utilized by the adversary in a decryption failure attack to obtain information of f. To resist this attack, the authors [18] also provide three transformations to detach the decryption failure from the message. One of their main transformation called NTRU-A (that is used in comparison with related works in [18, Table 3]) requires a new assumption called RLWE2, which is closely related to the RLWE problem, but the authors only provide heuristic arguments to the equivalence of RLWE2 and RLWE [18]. Despite of the efficiency improvement, the sizes of [18,33] are still larger than that of Kyber at the same security levels (see Table 3).

Fouque et al. [20] proposed another NTRU variant, called BAT, with a GGH-like encryption and decryption paradigm over the power of 2 cyclotomic ring $\mathbb{Z}_q[x]/(x^n + 1)$, which requires a very complex trapdoor inversion algorithm. Compared to other NTRU schemes, BAT has the smallest sizes (see Table 3). But it has a very slow key generation, which is 266-2131X slower than Kyber, and is even 7-104X slower than NTRU (see Tables 2 and 5). Moreover, BAT needs a strong RLWR with binary secret assumption.

1.1 Our Results

We present a faster and smaller NTRU-like Encryption using Vector decoding, called NEV-PKE, which is provably IND-CPA secure under the decisional NTRU and RLWE assumptions over the cyclotomic ring $R_q = \mathbb{Z}_q[X]/(X^n + 1)$ in the standard model, and thus can be directly used as a passively secure key exchange without resorting to the (quantum) random oracle model. Our main technique is a novel way to non-trivially integrate a previously known plaintext encoding and decoding mechanism [4,41] into the provably secure NTRU variant [43], which allows us to use a very small modulus q and obtain smaller public key and ciphertext sizes with a reasonably negligible decryption failure (see Sect. 1.2).

Concretely, the small modulus $q = 769$ can be used to achieve a decryption failure $\leq 2^{-138}$ for NIST level 1 security and $\leq 2^{-152}$ for NIST level 5 security. With a compressed representation of R_q elements (see Sect. 6.5), we can obtain public keys and ciphertexts of 615 and 1229 bytes respectively at the two security levels, which is 33–48% more compact than NTRU, and is 21% more compact than Kyber (see Table 1). By applying the Fujisaki-Okamoto transformation to NEV-PKE, we obtain an IND-CCA secure KEM called NEV-KEM. We implement our schemes using reference C language and AVX2 instructions in experiment. Due to the use of (partial) NTT multiplications and inversions in R_q (see Sects. 6.1 and 6.2), our NEV-KEM is 5.03–29.94X faster than NTRU and 1.42–1.74X faster than Kyber in the round-trip time of ephemeral key exchange.

We also give an optimized NTRU encryption called NEV-PKE′ with better noise tolerance based on a variant of the RLWE problem, called Subset-Sum Parity RLWE (sspRLWE) problem, which can also be seen as a generalization of the RLWE2 problem in [18]. We show that the sspRLWE problem is polynomially equivalent to the decisional RLWE problem (with different parameters), which partially solves the problem of proving the equivalence of RLWE2 and RLWE in [18]. By assuming that the concrete hardness of sspRLWE is equal to RLWE with the same parameters as for RLWE2 in [18], NEV-PKE′ can achieve a smaller decryption failure and slightly better performance than NEV-PKE. Concretely, we can use the same modulus $q = 769$ to achieve a decryption failure $\leq 2^{-200}$ at both NIST levels 1 and 5 security.

One nice feature which is worth to mention is that our schemes NEV-PKE and NEV-PKE′ are more robust than NTRU to a decryption failure attack because the plaintext has little contribution to the decryption noise in NEV-PKE, and the plaintext in NEV-PKE′ will essentially be masked using a random secret share algorithm (see Sect. 1.2 below). Similar to Newhope [4] that uses the power of 2 cyclotomic ring $\mathbb{Z}_q[x]/(x^n + 1)$, one possible limitation for our schemes is that we cannot find a proper parameter set for NIST level 3 security, but since our performance at NIST level 5 security is already comparable with existing schemes at NIST level 3 security (see Tables 1 and 2), we believe this would not be a real problem in practice.

1.2 Technical Overview

We begin by first recalling the original NTRU encryption. Formally, let n, q, p be three positive integers, and p coprime to q. Let $R_q = \mathbb{Z}_q/(x^n - 1)$. The public key h and ciphertext c of NTRU has forms of:

$$h = pg/f, \qquad c = hr + m,$$

where g, f, r are polynomials with small coefficients, m is the message polynomial. The decryption is done by first computing $u = fc = pgr + fm \in R_q$, and then computing $m = f^{-1}u \in R_p$. The decryption requires the ℓ_∞ norm of $pgr + fm$ to be smaller than $\frac{q-1}{2}$ (i.e., $\|pgr + fm\|_\infty < \frac{q-1}{2}$), and f invertible in both R_q and R_p for correctness, where p is typically equal to 3 for ternary message polynomial m. To simplify the decryption, f is usually set to have the form of $f = pf'+1$ such that $f^{-1} \bmod p = 1$. In this case, we have $u = pgr+pf'm+m$, where the decryption noise $pgr + pf'm$ essentially has the same form to that of RLWE-based encryptions (except that m in the term $pf'm$ is replaced with a random error polynomial). There are two main reasons why NTRU has larger public keys and ciphertexts sizes than its RLWE-based counterparts: 1) when fixing all other parameters, the decryption noise with $p = 3$ in NTRU is 1.5X larger than that of its RLWE counterparts where $p = 2$ is typically used; and 2) the decryption failure for NTRU is more subtle because the term $pf'm$ in the decryption noise usually has the same magnitude as pgr, which may be utilized by the adversary in a decryption failure attack with a purposefully chosen "bad" message m. This is why NTRU [11] submitted to NIST PQC standardization sets its parameters to have no decryption failure.

Our basic idea is to use the plaintext encoding and decoding mechanism in [4,41] to increase the noise tolerance of NTRU, which basically encodes each plaintext bit into the most significant bit of multiple coefficients of the message polynomial, so that a vector of noised coefficients can be used to decode each plaintext bit in decryption. We note that this mechanism was, to the best of our knowledge, not used in NTRU and its variants before, because it is not quite compatible with the central features of NTRU: 1) m is required to be a random polynomial for the security of the ciphertext $c = hr+m$ (since m is directly used as the RLWE error); and 2) fm is required to be small for decryption correctness. We solve the above two technical issues by slightly modifying the key generation and the plaintext encoding/decoding of the provably IND-CPA secure NTRU variant [43] (whose security is independent from the message polynomial) with a small polynomial $v = (1 - x^{n/k})$, where n/k is the plaintext length and is fixed to be 256 for our interest.[1] Our construction crucially relies on the power of 2 cyclotomic ring $R_q = \mathbb{Z}_q[X]/(X^n + 1)$. In particular, $v = (1 - x^{n/k})$ has a nice inverse $v^{-1} = \frac{q+1}{2}(1 + x^{n/k} + \cdots + x^{(k-1)n/k}) \in R_q$, which will serve as our plaintext encoding polynomial. The public key and ciphertext of our NEV-PKE has forms of:

$$h = g/(vf' + 1), \qquad c = hr + e + v^{-1}m,$$

where g, f', r, e are small polynomials, and m is the plaintext polynomial only having non-zero binary coefficients in the first 256 coordinates. For decryption, we first compute $u = (vf' + 1)c = gr + vf'e + f'm + e + v^{-1}m$. Since $v^{-1}m \in R_q$ essentially copies $k = n/256$ times the first 256 coefficients of m to obtain n coefficients, we can use k coefficients in u to decode each plaintext bit in decryption (if $\|gr + vf'e + f'm + e\|_\infty \leq \frac{q-1}{4}$ holds with high probability) as

---

[1] We note that a 256-bit session key is sufficient for most real applications, and that the NIST PQC standard Kyber also only supports a 256-bit plaintext [9].

in [4, 41]. The major reason that we can obtain a reasonably negligible decryption failure with very small modulus is because: 1) the magnitude of the major noise term $vf'e$ in our NEV-PKE is at least $\sqrt{2}$ times smaller than that of using $p = 2, 3$ or $x + 2$ in NTRU and its provable version [43]; 2) m has at most 256 non-zero binary coefficients; and 3) the use of vector decoding will lower the decryption failure (using a single coefficient) by roughly k times in the exponent.

We clarify that the slight modification of the public key in NEV-PKE will not require a stronger NTRU assumption because 1) the use of a polynomial $v = x+2$ was recommended by the authors of NTRU as early as 2000 [25] (note that $vf'+1$ is small if f' is small) and was investigated in [6, 22, 23, 27, 35, 43]; 2) by replacing $v = (1-x^{n/k})$ with $v = p$ we recover the provably IND-CPA secure NTRU in [43], and the proof for the public key uniformity in [43, Theorem 3] mainly depends on the properties of the distributions of g and f', which essentially applies to any invertible $v \in R_q$ (even without changing any other parameters); and 3) the currently concrete security estimation also only cares about the distributions of g and f', since $v = (1 - x^{n/k})$ (or $v = p$) is invertible and publicly known which can be somehow removed in lattice attacks (see Sect. 5.1).

One nice feature of our NEV-PKE is that the magnitude of $f'm$ is much smaller than that of $gr + vf'e + e$ because m only has non-zero binary coefficients in the first 256 coordinates. This means that our NEV-PKE is more robust than NTRU to a decryption failure attack with maliciously chosen bad messages in generating ciphertexts. Experimentally, the best choice for the adversary to obtain a failure decryption in NEV-PKE is to use a message polynomial with all ones in the first 256 coordinates, which will only increase the decryption failure by a factor of 2^{21} and 2^{14} for parameters NEV-512 and NEV-1024, respectively (in contrast, NTRU has a factor more than 2^{100} for standard parameter choices [18]), which means that the resulting decryption failure (i.e., 2^{-117} for NEV-512 and 2^{-138} for NEV-1024) is still sufficiently small for a common restriction of at most 2^{64} decryption queries. We note that one can further remove this dependence on m by using the generic transformation (say, NTRU-C) with a small price of an extra 32 bytes in ciphertexts in [18].

An Optimization Based on the sspRLWE Assumption. Based on the observation that in the application of using PKEs as KEMs, the session key is randomly chosen and not necessarily known in advance, we also provide an optimized construction NEV-PKE′ which essentially merges the sampling of the encryption noise and the random session key in a single step: one can roughly think that the encryption noise is a random secret share of a random session key. Specifically, the public key and ciphertext of NEV-PKE′ has forms of

$$h = vg/(vf' + 1) = g/(f' + v^{-1}), \qquad c = hr + e,$$

where g, f', r, e are randomly chosen small polynomials. Note that by setting $v = p$, the above construction is essentially the same as the original NTRU encryption. For decryption, we first compute $u = (f' + v^{-1})c = gr + f'e + v^{-1}e$. Let $\bar{v} = 1 + x^{n/k} + \cdots + x^{(k-1)n/k}$, $e_0 = \bar{v}e \bmod 2$, and $2e_1 = \bar{v}e - e_0$, we have

$$v^{-1} = \frac{q+1}{2}\bar{v}, \quad v^{-1}e = e_1 + \frac{q+1}{2}e_0 \in R_q, \text{ and } u = gr + f'e + e_1 + \frac{q+1}{2}e_0 \in R_q.$$

Let m be a polynomial only having $n/k = 256$ non-zero coefficients that are equal to the first 256 coefficients of e_0. By the nice property of $R_q = \mathbb{Z}_q[x]/(x^n + 1)$ and the choice of $\bar{v}$ (and v^{-1}), it is easy to check that e_0 is essentially a polynomial which copies $k = n/256$ times the first 256 coefficients of m (and thus itself) to obtain n coefficients. Hence, we can use the vector decoding technique [4, 41] again to recover m from u, and output m as the session key. Clearly, the decryption noise $gr + f'e + e_1$ in NEV-PKE' is much smaller than that of NEV-PKE.

To obtain an IND-CCA secure KEM, we have to convert NEV-PKE' into a PKE where m (or equivalently $\bar{v}e \bmod 2$) is determined before e. Since $\bar{v}e$ essentially adds k coefficients (with $\pm$ signs) of e to a single coefficient, we can easily achieve the goal of "inverting $\bar{v}e \bmod 2$ to obtain e" by using binomial noise distribution B_η. Take $\eta = 1$ and $k = 2$ as an example, we can "invert" a plaintext bit $b^* \in \{0, 1\}$ to 2 samples from B_1 as follows: randomly choose $b_1, b_2, b_3 \leftarrow \{0, 1\}$, set $b_0 = b^* \oplus b_1 \oplus b_2 \oplus b_3$, and output $e_0 = b_0 - b_1, e_1 = b_2 - b_3$. It is easy to check that $e_0 \pm e_1 \bmod 2 = b^*$, and $e_0, e_1 \sim B_1$ if b^* is random.

One problem is that we do not know how to directly prove the IND-CPA, or even OW-CPA security of NEV-PKE' under the RLWE assumption. For this, we introduce a variant of the RLWE problem, called subset-sum parity RLWE problem (sspRLWE), which basically says that it is hard to compute $\bar{v}e \bmod 2$ given an RLWE tuple $(h, hr + e)$ as input. We note that our sspRLWE can also be seen as a generalization of the RLWE2 problem in [18], which essentially asks to compute $\bar{v}e \bmod 2$ for $\bar{v} = 1$ (or equivalently $k = 1$). At first glance, one might think that sspRLWE is hard if its corresponding RLWE is hard. Unfortunately, even in the special RLWE2 setting, the authors [18] only provide heuristic arguments for its equivalence to RLWE.

In Sect. 4.3, we show that the sspRLWE problem with discrete Gaussian noise distribution is polynomially equivalent to the DRLWE problem (with different Gaussian parameters), which can be extended to the binomial distribution by a standard argument using Rényi divergence [5]. Our proof is based on a very simple observation: $\bar{v}(2e_1 + e_0) = \bar{v}e_0 \bmod 2$, and one can naturally convert a DRLWE instance $(h, b = hr + e_1)$ to an sspRLWE instance $(h' = 2h, b' = 2b + e_0)$ (note that when both e_1 and e_0 follow discrete Gaussian distributions, so does $2e_1 + e_0$ [39]). Then, if (h, b) is computationally indistinguishable from uniform, the adversary can obtain no information about $\bar{v}e_0 \bmod 2$ from (h', b'). Since this proof also applies to $\bar{v} = 1$, we partially solve the problem of connecting RLWE2 to RLWE (for sufficiently large parameters). We also provide two concrete theorems for basing sspRLWE with $k = 1$ (namely, RLWE2) and $k = 2$ on the RLWE problem with binomial noise distribution B_1 and uniform binary noise distribution, respectively. The two proofs are mainly based the fact that $e \bmod 2 = 0 \Leftrightarrow e = 0$ for any variable $e \in \{-1, 0, 1\}$. Note that our parameter set NEV'-512 exactly corresponds to the case of $k = 2$. We believe that those proofs provide a good confidence to make the reasonable assumption: the concrete hardness of sspRLWE is equal to RLWE with the same parameters. For those who is unsatisfying with this assumption, we recommend to use NEV-PKE, which is provably IND-CPA secure under the standard NTRU and RLWE assumptions, and only has slightly worse decryption failure and performance.

Table 1. Comparison between our NEV-KEMs, NTRU and Kyber in sizes

Schemes	$\|pk\|$ (Bytes)	$\|sk\|$ (Bytes)	$\|C\|$ (Bytes)	Dec Failure	LWE Estimator	NIST Security	Improv. Ratio
Kyber-512	800	1632	768	2^{-178}	140	Level 1	21.56%
NTRU-HPS2048677	930	1234	930	–	170		33.87%
NTRU-HRSS701	1138	1450	1138	–	158		45.96%
Our NEV-512	615	1294	615	2^{-138}	141		–
Our NEV'-512	615	1294	615	2^{-200}	145		–
Kyber-768	1184	2400	1088	2^{-164}	201	Level 3	$-8.19\%^{\dagger}$
NTRU-HPS4096821	1230	1590	1230	–	199		$0.08\%^{\dagger}$
Kyber-1024	1568	3168	1568	2^{-174}	270	Level 5	21.62%
NTRU-HPS40961229	1842	2366	1842	–	296		33.28%
NTRU-HRSS1373	2401	2983	2401	–	300		48.81%
Our NEV-1024	1229	2522	1229	2^{-152}	281		–
Our NEV'-1024	1229	2522	1229	2^{-200}	292		–

1.3   Comparison to the State of the Art

We give a detailed comparison between our KEMs, NTRU and Kyber in Tables 1 and 2. The column "LWE estimator" in Table 1 presents the concrete security estimates obtained by using the LWE estimator script [1]. The columns "Improv. Ratio" in Table 1 and "Speedup" in Table 2 are obtained by dividing the total sizes/timings of the corresponding schemes in an ephemeral key exchange by that of our NEV-KEM (i.e., NEV-512 and NEV-1024) at the same security levels, except that we obtain the figures (marked with †) for Kyber768 and NTRU-HPS4096821 at NIST level 3 security by dividing that of our KEMs at NIST level 5 security (i.e., NEV-1024). One can see that our NEV-KEM using NEV-1024 has the same public key and ciphertext sizes as that of NTRU-HPS4096821, but is still 4.10–11.05X faster: because our ring allows (partial) NTT. Compared to Kyber768, our NEV-KEM using NEV-1024 has size 8.19% larger but is 1.2X faster: because we do not have to expand a seed to a random matrix.

In Table 3, we compare our KEMs with three recent NTRU variants in sizes, where the figures in the column "LWE estimator" for schemes based on RLWE2, RLWR and sspRLWE problems are all obtained by using the assumption that the concrete hardness of those problems are equal to their corresponding RLWE problems with the same parameters. In Sect. 7, we will also compare the concrete

Table 2. Comparison between our NEV-KEMs, NTRU and Kyber in efficiency

Schemes	KeyGen (Ref)	Encap (Ref)	Decap (Ref)	KeyGen (AVX2)	Encap (AVX2)	Decap (AVX2)	Speedup (Ref/AVX2)
Kyber-512	132 334	167 834	195 024	32 996	47 514	34 816	1.67/1.42X
NTRU-HPS2048677	4 957 166	220 554	293 126	320 234	82 991	62 907	18.46/5.74X
NTRU-HRSS701	5 469 959	125 559	309 743	287 524	54 270	66 801	19.92/5.03X
Our NEV-512	95 007	88 131	113 268	21 192	33 694	26 297	–
Our NEV′-512	89 154	83 978	110 463	20 620	30 787	23 841	–
Kyber-768	217 023	263 971	303 945	54 789	72 268	53 822	1.21/1.19X[†]
NTRU-HPS4096821	6 645 818	251 935	280 318	450 336	96 475	78 522	11.05/4.10X[†]
Kyber-1024	329 555	377 541	421 837	73 562	97 756	76 454	1.74/1.62X
NTRU-HPS40961229	14 944 617	484 755	654 931	–	–	–	24.76/-X
NTRU-HRSS1373	18 366 972	313 188	769 187	–	–	–	29.94/-X
Our NEV-1024	208 045	183 977	257 489	37 636	64 046	50 807	–
Our NEV′-1024	205 719	171 669	251 303	37 805	60 411	45 851	–

Table 3. Comparison between our NEV-KEMs and recent NTRU variants in Size

Schemes	$|pk|$ (Bytes)	$|C|$ (Bytes)	Dec Failure	Hardness Assumption	LWE Estimator
NTRU-A$_{2593}^{576}$ [18]	864	864	2^{-150}	NTRU + RLWE2 $R_q = \mathbb{Z}_q[x]/(x^n - x^{n/2} + 1)$	154
NTRU-A$_{2917}^{648}$ [18]	972	972	2^{-170}		171
NTRU-A$_{3457}^{768}$ [18]	1152	1152	2^{-202}		200
NTRU-A$_{3457}^{864}$ [18]	1296	1296	2^{-182}		225
NTRU-A$_{3889}^{972}$ [18]	1458	1458	2^{-206}		252
NTRU-A$_{3457}^{1152}$ [18]	1728	1728	2^{-140}		305
NTRU-A$_{3889}^{1296}$ [18]	1944	1944	2^{-158}		341
NTTRU-768 [33]	1248	1248	2^{-1217}	NTRU + RLWE $R_q = \mathbb{Z}_q[x]/(x^n - x^{n/2} + 1)$	170
BAT-512 [20]	521	473	2^{-146}	NTRU + RLWR	144
BAT-1024 [20]	1230	1006	2^{-166}	$R_q = \mathbb{Z}_q[x]/(x^n + 1)$	273
Our NEV-512	615	615	2^{-138}	NTRU + RLWE	141
Our NEV-1024	1229	1229	2^{-152}	$R_q = \mathbb{Z}_q[x]/(x^n + 1)$	281
Our NEV′-512	615	615	2^{-200}	NTRU + sspRLWE	145
Our NEV′-1024	1229	1229	2^{-200}	$R_q = \mathbb{Z}_q[x]/(x^n + 1)$	292

performance of our schemes with BAT in Table 5 and NTTRU in Table 6 (we do not have the source code of NTRU-A, but it was reported having comparable performance with NTTRU [18, Table 3]). In summary, our KEMs have comparable efficiency as NTRU-A, but have sizes at least 28% more compact. The sizes of BAT are 19.19% (resp., 9.03%) smaller than our Π_{KEM} at NIST level 1 (resp., 5) security (note that BAT uses a strong RLWR with binary secret assumption, which allows to compress the ciphertexts almost for free), but our NEV-KEM is 140-973X (resp., 334-2648X) faster than BAT.

Most recently, Micciancio and Schultz [34] provide a framework to capture the encoding of the message and the compression/quantization of the ciphertext, which aims at improving the ratio of the size of a plaintext to the size of a LWE-based ciphertext. As a NTRU-like ciphertext only contains a single ring element which will be multiplied by the secret key (namely, f) in decryption, one cannot directly apply their framework to improve the encryption rate of our schemes.

2 Preliminaries

2.1 Notation

Let n be a power of 2, and q a prime. We denote by R the ring $R = \mathbb{Z}[X]/(X^n+1)$ and by R_q the ring $R_q = \mathbb{Z}_q[X]/(X^n + 1)$. The regular font letters (e.g., a, b) represent elements in R or R_q (including elements in $\mathbb{Z}$ or $\mathbb{Z}_q$), and bold lower-case letters (e.g., $\mathbf{a}, \mathbf{b}$) denote vectors of R or $\mathbb{Z}$ elements. For a positive integer $\ell \in \mathbb{Z}$, by $[\ell]$ we denote the set $\{0, \ldots, \ell - 1\}$. By $r' = r \bmod^{\pm} q$ we denote the unique element in the range $[-\frac{q-1}{2}, \frac{q-1}{2}]$ such that $r' = r \bmod q$. For an element $w \in \mathbb{Z}_q$, we write $\|w\|_\infty$ to mean $|w \bmod^{\pm} q|$. The ℓ_∞ and ℓ_2 norms of a ring element $w \in R_q$ is defined as that of its coefficient vector $\mathbf{w} \in \mathbb{Z}_q^n$.

By $x \leftarrow \mathcal{D}$ we denote sampling x according to a distribution $\mathcal{D}$ and by $\mathcal{U}(S)$ we denote the uniform distribution over a finite set S. When we write that sampling a polynomial $g \leftarrow \mathcal{D}$ from a distribution $\mathcal{D}$ over $\mathbb{Z}$, we mean that sampling each coefficient of g from $\mathcal{D}$ individually. We use $\log_b$ to denote the logarithm function in base b (e.g., 2 or natural constant e) and $\log$ to represent $\log_e$. We say that a function $f : \mathbb{N} \to [0, 1]$ is *negligible*, if for every positive c and all sufficiently large κ it holds that $f(\kappa) < 1/\kappa^c$. We denote by $\mathsf{negl} : \mathbb{N} \to [0, 1]$ an (unspecified) negligible function.

Binomial Distribution. The centered binomial distribution B_η with some positive $\eta \in \mathbb{Z}$ is defined as follows:

$$B_\eta = \left\{ \sum_{i=0}^{\eta-1} (a_i - b_i) : (a_0, \ldots, a_{\eta-1}, b_0, \ldots, b_{\eta-1}) \leftarrow \{0, 1\}^{2\eta} \right\}$$

Ternary Distribution. The ternary distribution $\mathcal{T}_\sigma$ with some positive real $\sigma \in (0, 1/2)$ denotes the distribution of sampling a variable $x \in \{-1, 0, 1\}$ with $\Pr[x = 1] = \Pr[x = -1] = \sigma$, and $\Pr[x = 0] = 1 - 2\sigma$. By this notation, we have $\mathcal{T}_{1/3} = \mathcal{U}(\{-1, 0, 1\})$ is the uniform ternary distribution, and $\mathcal{T}_{1/4} = B_1$ is the centered binomial distribution with $\eta = 1$.

Gaussian Distribution. The Gaussian function $\rho_{s,\mathbf{c}}(\mathbf{x})$ over $\mathbb{R}^m$ centered at $\mathbf{c} \in \mathbb{R}^m$ with parameter $s > 0$ is defined as $\rho_{s,\mathbf{c}}(\mathbf{x}) = \exp(-\pi \|\mathbf{x} - \mathbf{c}\|^2 / s^2)$. For lattice $\Lambda \subseteq \mathbb{R}^m$, let $\rho_{s,\mathbf{c}}(\Lambda) = \sum_{\mathbf{x} \in \Lambda} \rho_{s,\mathbf{c}}(\mathbf{x})$, and define the discrete Gaussian distribution over Λ as $D_{\Lambda,s,\mathbf{c}}(\mathbf{y}) = \frac{\rho_{s,\mathbf{c}}(\mathbf{y})}{\rho_{s,\mathbf{c}}(\Lambda)}$, where $\mathbf{y} \in \Lambda$. We omit the subscript $\mathbf{c}$ in the above notations if $\mathbf{c} = \mathbf{0}$.

Lemma 1 ([7,30]). *For any real $s, t > 0$, $c \geq 1$, $C = c \cdot \exp(\frac{1-c^2}{2}) < 1$, integer $m > 0$, and any $\mathbf{y} \in \mathbb{R}^m$ we have that $\Pr_{\mathbf{x} \leftarrow D_{\mathbb{Z}^m, s}}[\|\mathbf{x}\|_\infty > t \cdot s] \leq 2e^{-\pi t^2}$.*

Lemma 2 (Special case of [39, Theorem 3.1]). *Let $\alpha, \beta, \gamma > 0$ be reals such that $\alpha \geq \omega(\sqrt{\log n})$, $\gamma = \sqrt{\alpha^2 + \beta^2}$ and $\alpha\beta/\gamma > 2 \cdot \omega(\sqrt{\log n})$. Consider the following probabilistic experiment:*

$$\text{Choose } \mathbf{x}_2 \leftarrow D_{2\mathbb{Z}^n, \beta}, \text{ then choose } \mathbf{x}_1 \leftarrow \mathbf{x}_2 + D_{\mathbb{Z}^n, \alpha}.$$

Then, the marginal distribution of $\mathbf{x}_1$ is statistically close to $D_{\mathbb{Z}^n, \gamma}$.

2.2 Public-Key Encryption

A public-key encryption (PKE) Π_{PKE} with plaintext space $\mathcal{M}$ consists of three PPT algorithms (KeyGen, Enc, Dec):

- KeyGen(1^κ): given a security parameter κ as input, output a pair of public and secret keys (pk, sk), denoted as $(pk, sk) = \text{KeyGen}(1^\kappa)$.
- Enc($pk, M; r$): given the public key pk, a plaintext $M \in \mathcal{M}$ and a randomness r (which might be an empty string) as inputs, output a ciphertext C, denoted as $C = \text{Enc}(pk, M; r)$ or $C = \text{Enc}(pk, M)$ in brief.
- Dec(sk, C): given the secret key sk and a ciphertext C as inputs, output a plaintext M' (which might be $\perp$), denoted as $M' = \text{Dec}(sk, C)$.

We say that a PKE scheme $\Pi_{\text{PKE}} = (\text{KeyGen}, \text{Enc}, \text{Dec})$ is δ-correct, if for any $M \in \mathcal{M}$, $(pk, sk) = \text{KeyGen}(1^\kappa)$ and $C = \text{Enc}(pk, M)$, the probability that $\text{Dec}(sk, C) \neq M$ is at most δ over the random coins used in KeyGen and Enc. For our interest, we recall the OW-CPA and IND-CPA security for PKEs from [8], which is modeled by games between a challenger $\mathcal{C}$ and an adversary $\mathcal{A}$ in Fig. 1.

Definition 1 (OW-CPA PKE). *We say that a PKE scheme Π_{PKE} is OW-CPA secure if for any PPT adversary $\mathcal{A}$, its advantage*

$$\text{Adv}_{\Pi_{\text{PKE}}, \mathcal{A}}^{\text{ow-cpa}}(\kappa) = \Pr[M' = M^*]$$

in the OW-CPA security game in Fig. 1 is negligible in security parameter κ.

Definition 2 (IND-CPA PKE). *We say that a PKE scheme Π_{PKE} is IND-CPA secure if for any PPT adversary $\mathcal{A} = (\mathcal{A}_1, \mathcal{A}_2)$, its advantage*

$$\text{Adv}_{\Pi_{\text{PKE}}, \mathcal{A}}^{\text{ind-cpa}}(\kappa) = \left| \Pr[\mu' = \mu^*] - \frac{1}{2} \right|$$

in the IND-CPA security game in Fig. 1 is negligible in security parameter κ.

Algorithm OW-CPA:	**Algorithm IND-CPA:**
1 $(pk, sk) = \Pi_{\text{PKE}}.\text{KeyGen}(1^\kappa)$;	1 $(pk, sk) = \Pi_{\text{PKE}}.\text{KeyGen}(1^\kappa)$;
2 $M^* \leftarrow \mathcal{M}$;	2 $(M_0, M_1, st) = \mathcal{A}_1(pk)$;
3 $C^* = \Pi_{\text{PKE}}.\text{Enc}(pk, M^*)$;	3 $\mu \leftarrow \{0, 1\}$;
4 $M' = \mathcal{A}(pk, C^*)$;	4 $C^* = \Pi_{\text{PKE}}.\text{Enc}(pk, M_\mu)$;
5 **return** $M' = M^*$;	5 $\mu' = \mathcal{A}_2(C^*, st)$;
	6 **return** $\mu' = \mu^*$;

Fig. 1. Games for OW-CPA and IND-CPA Security of PKEs

2.3 Key Encapsulation Mechanism

A key encapsulation mechanism (KEM) Π_{KEM} with session key space $\mathcal{K}$ consists of three PPT algorithms (KeyGen, Encap, Decap):

- KeyGen(1^κ): given a security parameter κ as input, output a pair of public and secret keys (pk, sk), denoted as $(pk, sk) = \text{KeyGen}(1^\kappa)$.
- Encap($pk; r$): given the public key pk, and a randomness r as inputs, output a ciphertext C and a session key $K \in \mathcal{K}$, denoted as $(C, K) = \text{Encap}(pk; r)$, or $(C, K) = \text{Encap}(pk)$ in brief.
- Decap(sk, C): given a secret key sk and a ciphertext C as inputs, output a key K' (which might be a failure symbol $\perp$), denoted as $K' = \text{Decap}(sk, C)$.

We say that a KEM scheme $\Pi_{\text{KEM}} = (\text{KeyGen}, \text{Encap}, \text{Decap})$ is δ-correct, if for any $(pk, sk) = \text{KeyGen}(1^\kappa)$ and $(C, K) = \text{Encap}(pk)$, the probability that $\text{Decap}(sk, C) \neq K$ is at most δ over the random coins used in KeyGen and Enc. We now recall the chosen-ciphertext security for KEMs from [12], which is modeled by the game between a challenger $\mathcal{C}$ and an adversary $\mathcal{A}$ in Fig. 2.

Algorithm IND-CCA:	**Oracle** $\mathcal{O}_{\text{Dec}}(C)$:
1 $(pk, sk) = \Pi_{\text{KEM}}.\text{KeyGen}(1^\kappa)$;	1 **if** $C = C^*$ **then**
2 $\mu \leftarrow \{0, 1\}$;	2 **return** $\perp$;
3 $(C^*, K_0^*) = \Pi_{\text{KEM}}.\text{Encap}(pk)$;	3 **end**
4 $K_1^* \leftarrow \mathcal{K}$;	4 $K = \text{Decap}(sk, C)$;
5 $\mu' = \mathcal{A}^{\mathcal{O}_{\text{Dec}}(\cdot)}(pk, C^*, K_\mu^*)$;	5 **return** K;
6 **return** $\mu' = \mu^*$;	

Fig. 2. Game for IND-CCA Security of KEMs

Definition 3 (IND-CCA KEM). *We say that a KEM scheme* Π_{KEM} *is IND-CCA secure if for any PPT adversary* $\mathcal{A}$, *its advantage*

$$\text{Adv}_{\Pi_{\text{KEM}}, \mathcal{A}}^{\text{ind-cca}}(\kappa) = \left| \Pr[\mu' = \mu^*] - \frac{1}{2} \right|$$

in the IND-CCA security game in Fig. 2 is negligible in security parameter κ.

2.4 Hard Problems

Let n be a power of 2, and q a prime. Let $R_q = \mathbb{Z}_q[x]/(x^n+1)$. Let R_q^* denote all invertible ring elements in R_q. Let $\chi_f, \chi_g, \chi_r, \chi_e$ be four probability distributions over R. Let $v \in R_q^*$ be a publicly known small ring element.

The NTRU Assumption. The computational NTRU problem $\text{NTRU}_{n,q,\chi_f,\chi_g,v}$ asks an algorithm, given $h = g/f \in R_q$ as input, to output f', where $f' \leftarrow \chi_f, g \leftarrow \chi_g$ and $f = vf' + 1 \in R_q^*$. The decisional NTRU problem $\text{DNTRU}_{n,q,\chi_f,\chi_g,v}$ asks an algorithm to distinguish the following two distributions:

$$\{h = g/f \mid f' \leftarrow \chi_f, g \leftarrow \chi_g, \text{ and } f = vf' + 1 \in R_q^*\} \text{ and } \{u \mid u \leftarrow R_q\}.$$

The computational (resp., decisional) NTRU assumption says that it is hard for any PPT algorithms to solve $\text{NTRU}_{n,q,\chi_f,\chi_g,v}$ (resp., $\text{DNTRU}_{n,q,\chi_f,\chi_g,v}$) with non-negligible advantage over a random guess.

Remark 1. The above definition generalizes the common NTRU assumption with $v = p \in R_q^*$ for some integer p (e.g., $p = 3$ in [11,24,25,43]) with a publicly known ring element $v \in R_q^*$. We note that this generalization is mild up to the choices of the secret key distribution χ_f, because $\text{NTRU}_{n,q,\chi_f,\chi_g,v}$ is essentially equivalent to the standard NTRU problem $\text{NTRU}_{n,q,\chi_f',\chi_g,p}$ with $\chi_f' = p^{-1}v\chi_f$ (or $\chi_f = pv^{-1}\chi_f'$). In fact, the polynomial $v = x + 2$ was recommended by the authors of the original NTRU cryptosystem as early as 2000 [25], and was investigated in [6,22,23,27,35,43].

Since its introduction [24], the NTRU problem has been studied more than 25 years, and there is no significant algorithmic progress. The decisional NTRU (DNTRU) assumption over the cyclotomic ring $R = \mathbb{Z}_q[x]/(x^n+1)$, which is also known as the decisional small polynomial ratio (DSPR) assumption, has been extensively used and investigated in [10,16,19,31,40,43]. Notably, Stehlé and Steinfeld [43] showed that the DNTRU assumption indeed holds unconditionally if χ_f, χ_g are discrete Gaussian distributions of standard deviation $\sigma = \omega(n\sqrt{q})$ (We note that their proof mainly focuses on the special case $v = 3$, but it essentially applies to any invertible $v \in R_q^*$). For small secret distributions, a variant of the NTRU problem over $R_q = \mathbb{Z}_q[x]/(x^n + 1)$ is also shown to be at least as hard as the worst-case approximate SVP problem on ideal lattices [40].

The RLWE Assumption. The computational RLWE problem $\text{RLWE}_{n,q,\chi_r,\chi_e}$ asks an algorithm, given a polynomial number of samples from the distribution $\{(a, b = ar + e) \mid a \leftarrow R_q, e \leftarrow \chi_e\}$ as inputs, to output the secret $r \in R_q$, where $r \leftarrow \chi_r$. The decisional RLWE problem $\text{DRLWE}_{n,q,\chi_r,\chi_e}$ asks an algorithm, given a polynomial number of samples to distinguish the following two distributions:

$$\{(a, b = ar + e) \mid a \leftarrow R_q, e \leftarrow \chi_e\} \text{ and } \{(a, u) \mid a \leftarrow R_q, u \leftarrow R_q\}.$$

The computational (resp., decisional) RLWE assumption says that it is hard for any PPT algorithms to solve $\text{RLWE}_{n,q,\chi_r,\chi_e}$ (resp., $\text{DRLWE}_{n,q,\chi_r,\chi_e}$) with non-negligible advantage over a random guess.

As an extension of the LWE problem [42], the RLWE problem was first considered in [32,44], and was provably as hard as some hard lattice problems such as the Shortest Vectors Problem (SVP) on ideal lattices.

The Subset-Sum Parity RLWE Assumption. We introduce a variant of the RLWE problem which we call subset-sum parity RLWE (sspRLWE) problem. Formally, the sspRLWE problem sspRLWE$_{n,q,\chi_r,\chi_e,v}$ asks an algorithm, given an RLWE instance $(a, b = ar + e) \in R_q$ as input, to output $ve \bmod 2 \in R_2$ for some fixed ring element $v \in R_2$. This name comes from the fact that for $R = \mathbb{Z}[X]/(x^n + 1)$, the i-th coefficient of $ve \bmod 2 \in R_2$ is essentially equal to the parity of the subset sum $\sum_{v_j=1} e_{(i-j) \bmod n}$ of the coefficient vector $\mathbf{e} = (e_0, \ldots, e_{n-1})$ of $e \in R_q$. The sspRLWE assumption says that it is hard for any PPT algorithms to solve sspRLWE$_{n,q,\chi_r,\chi_e,v}$ with non-negligible advantage over a random guess according to the distribution $\chi' = v\chi_e \bmod 2$.

Remark 2. Our sspRLWE problem can be seen as a generalization of the RLWE2 problem [18] from a special choice of $v = 1$ to a general chosen $v \in R_2$. On the first hand, the sspRLWE$_{n,q,\chi_r,\chi_e,v}$ problem is not harder than the corresponding RLWE problem RLWE$_{n,q,\chi_r,\chi_e}$. On the other hand, if the DRLWE problem DRLWE$_{n,q,\chi_r,\chi_e}$ is hard, it seems that a RLWE sample $(a, b = ar+e)$ essentially hides all the information about e, and that the best way for a PPT algorithm to solve the sspRLWE problem is to make a random guess on $ve \bmod 2$ according to the distribution $\chi' = v\chi_e \bmod 2$. Moreover, the problem of reducing DRLWE$_{n,q,\chi_r,\chi_e}$ to sspRLWE$_{n,q,\chi_r,\chi_e,v}$ can be seen as the problem of solving DRLWE$_{n,q,\chi_r,\chi_e}$ with modular hints $ve \bmod 2$, and an efficient algorithm to solve sspRLWE$_{n,q,\chi_r,\chi_e,v}$ may directly lead to a new and better algorithm to solve RLWE$_{n,q,\chi_r,\chi_e}$ according to the study in [13].

However, we cannot expect a general reduction that bases the hardness of sspRLWE$_{n,q,\chi_r,\chi_e,v}$ on that of DRLWE$_{n,q,\chi_r,\chi_e}$ for arbitrary choices of v and noise distribution χ_e, because $ve \bmod 2$ may loose too much information about e and may be of little help to solve DRLWE$_{n,q,\chi_r,\chi_e}$. Note that the authors [18] only present heuristic arguments for the equivalence of RLWE and sspRLWE$_{n,q,\chi_r,\chi_e,v}$ even for the special case $v = 1$. Moreover, it is easy to show that DRLWE$_{n,q,\chi_r,\chi'_e}$ for $\chi'_e = 2\chi_e$ is equivalent to DRLWE$_{n,q,\chi_r,\chi_e}$, but we always have $v\chi'_e = 0 \bmod 2$ for the sspRLWE$_{n,q,\chi_r,\chi'_e,v}$ problem. For our purpose, we are particularly interested in the sspRLWE problem sspRLWE$_{n,q,\chi_r,\chi_e,\bar{v}}$ satisfying the following two conditions:

- $\bar{v} = 1 + x^{n/k} + x^{2n/k} + \cdots + x^{(k-1)n/k} \in R_2$ for integers $n/k = 256$;
- χ_e is the binomial distribution.

Looking ahead, we will use this kind of sspRLWE assumption to construct a OW-CPA secure encryption NEV-PKE′ with better noise tolerance in Sect. 4.2, and will show that for appropriate choices of parameters, the sspRLWE problem is at least as hard as the standard RLWE problem (with slightly different parameters) in Sect. 4.3 (and thus partially solves the problem of reducing the RLWE2 problem to the standard RLWE problem in [18]).

3 NTRU Encryption Using Vector Decoding

In this section, we first give a provably secure IND-CPA PKE scheme called NEV-PKE from the standard DNTRU and DRLWE assumptions, then we transform it into a IND-CCA KEM called NEV-KEM using the generic Fujisaki-Okamoto (FO) transformation [21]. We begin by describing our plaintext encoding and decoding algorithms.

3.1 Plaintext Encoding and Decoding

Our way of encoding and decoding plaintext is inspired by the method for RLWE-based encryption in [41], which essentially encodes a single plaintext bit into multiple coefficients of a ring element, and is also used in Newhope [2,4] submitted to NIST PQC competition. We adapted this idea to the NTRU setting. Formally, let n be a power of 2, and q be a prime. Let $R = \mathbb{Z}[x]/(x^n + 1)$ and $R_q = \mathbb{Z}_q[x]/(x^n + 1)$. Let $\mathcal{M} = \{0,1\}^\ell$ be the plaintext space. Let k be the largest integer satisfying $k|n$ and $n/k \geq \ell$. Let $v = (1 - x^{n/k}) \in R_q^*$ be a ring element, whose inverse is $v^{-1} = \frac{q+1}{2}(1 + x^{n/k} + \cdots + x^{(k-1)n/k}) \in R_q^*$. We define the following two algorithms Pt2poly and Poly2Pt for encoding and decoding:

- Pt2poly(M) : given a plaintext $M \in \{0,1\}^\ell$ as input, return a polynomial $m = M_0 + M_1 x + \cdots + M_{\ell-1} x^{\ell-1} \in R_q$, where $M_i \in \{0,1\}$ is the i-th bit of M, denoted as $m = \mathsf{Pt2poly}(M)$.
- Poly2Pt(w) : given a polynomial $w = w_0 + w_1 x + \cdots + w_{n-1} x^{n-1} \in R_q$ as input, first compute $\tilde{w}_i = w_i - \frac{q+1}{2} \bmod^{\pm} q$ for all $i \in [n]$. Then, compute $t_j = \sum_{i=j \bmod n/k} |\tilde{w}_i|$ for all $j \in [\ell]$. Finally, set

$$M_j = \begin{cases} 1, & \text{if } t_j < \frac{k \cdot (q-1)}{4}; \\ 0, & \text{otherwise}, \end{cases}$$

and return the plaintext $M = (M_0, \ldots, M_{\ell-1}) \in \{0,1\}^\ell$.

We have the following lemma for the above two algorithms.

Lemma 3. *Let $n, q, k, \ell \in \mathbb{Z}$ and $v \in R_q^*$ be defined as above. Then, for any $M \in \{0,1\}^\ell$, $m = \mathsf{Pt2poly}(M) \in R_q$ and any polynomial $e = e_0 + e_1 x + \cdots + e_{n-1} x^{n-1} \in R_q$ satisfying the following condition*

$$\left(\sum_{i=j \bmod n/k} |e_i \bmod^{\pm} q| \right) < \frac{k \cdot (q-1)}{4} \text{ for } i \in [n] \text{ and } j \in [\ell] \quad (1)$$

we always have $\mathsf{Poly2Pt}(v^{-1}m + e) = M$.

Proof. Let $m = \mathsf{Pt2poly}(M) \in R_q$. By the definition of $\mathsf{Pt2poly}(M)$, we have that m only has non-zero binary coefficients at the first $\ell \leq n/k$ coordinates. Thus, multiplying m with $v^{-1} = \frac{q+1}{2}(1 + x^{n/k} + \cdots + x^{(k-1)n/k})$ is essentially equal to first multiply m by $\frac{q+1}{2}$ and then copy $k - 1$ times the first n/k coefficients as a block to the next $(k-1)n/k$ coordinates. In other words, for all $u = v^{-1}m \in R_q$, we always have $u_i = M_j \frac{q+1}{2}$ for all $i = j \bmod n/k$ for $i \in [n]$ and $j \in [\ell]$, where $u = u_0 + u_1 x + \cdots + u_{n-1}x^{n-1}$ and $M = (M_0, \ldots, M_{\ell-1})$. Let $w = u + e = v^{-1}m + e \in R_q$, it suffices to show that $\mathsf{Poly2Pt}(w)$ will always correctly recover each bit of M. Formally, let $w = w_0 + w_1 x + \cdots + w_{n-1}x^{n-1}$, we continue the proof by considering the value of each $M_j \in \{0,1\}$ for $j \in [\ell]$:

- $M_j = 1$: we have that $w_i = u_i + e_i = \frac{q+1}{2} + e_i$ for all $i = j \bmod n/k$, and that $\tilde{w}_i = w_i - \frac{q+1}{2} = e_i \bmod^{\pm} q$. This means that

$$t_j = \sum_{i=j \bmod n/k} |\tilde{w}_i| = \sum_{i=j \bmod n/k} |e_i \bmod^{\pm} q| < \frac{k \cdot (q-1)}{4},$$

  and that $\mathsf{Poly2Pt}(w)$ will output $M_j = 1$;
- $M_j = 0$: we have that $w_i = e_i$ for all $i = j \bmod n/k$, and that $\tilde{w}_i = w_i - \frac{q+1}{2} = e_i - \frac{q+1}{2} \bmod^{\pm} q$. Since we have either $e_i = |e_i \bmod^{\pm} q|$ or $e_i = q - |e_i \bmod^{\pm} q|$, it is easy to check that $|\tilde{w}_i| \geq \frac{q-1}{2} - |e_i \bmod^{\pm} q|$. This means that

$$t_j = \sum_{i=j \bmod n/k} |\tilde{w}_i| \geq \sum_{i=j \bmod n/k} \left(\frac{q-1}{2} - |e_i \bmod^{\pm} q|\right) > \frac{k \cdot (q-1)}{4},$$

  and that $\mathsf{Poly2Pt}(w)$ will output $M_j = 0$.

This completes the proof.

Remark 3. There is a tradeoff between the plaintext length ℓ and the decoding capacity. A smaller k (e.g., $k = 1$) allows to support longer plaintext length (as we require $\ell \leq n/k$) but has worse noise tolerance. In particular, if each coefficient of e is chosen from a distribution such that the probability of $|e_i \bmod^{\pm} q| < \frac{q-1}{4}$ for all $i \in [n]$ is $1 - p$, then the probability that $\mathsf{Poly2Pt}(v^{-1}m + e) = M$ is roughly about $1 - p^k$. This is why we prefer to choose the largest integer k such that $n/k \geq \ell$. For the typical application of PKE in encrypting a session key $\ell = 128$ or 256, one could fix $k = n/\ell$ to obtain the best noise tolerance.

3.2   A Provably Secure IND-CPA NTRU Encryption

Let $n, q, k, \ell \in \mathbb{Z}$ and $v \in R_q^*$ be defined as above. Let $\chi_f, \chi_g, \chi_r, \chi_e$ be four probability distributions over R. Our PKE scheme NEV-PKE consists of the following three algorithms (KeyGen, Enc, Dec):

- NEV-PKE.KeyGen(κ): given the security parameter κ as input, randomly choose $f' \leftarrow \chi_f$ and $g \leftarrow \chi_g$ such that $f = vf' + 1 \in R_q^*$ is invertible. Then, return the public and secret key pair $(pk, sk) = (h = g/f, f) \in R_q \times R_q$.

- NEV-PKE.Enc(pk, M): given the public key $pk = h \in R_q$ and a plaintext $M \in \{0,1\}^\ell$ as inputs, randomly choose $r \leftarrow \chi_r, e \leftarrow \chi_e$, compute $m = $ Pt2poly$(M) \in R_q$ and $c = hr + e + v^{-1}m$. Return the ciphertext $c \in R_q$.
- NEV-PKE.Dec(sk, c): given the secret key $sk = f = vf' + 1 \in R_q^*$ and a ciphertext $c \in R_q$ as inputs, compute $w = fc$, and $M' = $ Poly2Pt(w). Finally, return the message $M' \in \{0,1\}^\ell$.

Remark 4. Our above PKE scheme can be easily adapted to support other choices of $v \in R_q^*$, e.g., $v = 3$, but it seems that $v = (1 - x^{n/k})$ might be the optimal one in reducing the decryption failure (see below).

Since we have the following decryption formula

$$w = fc = gr + (vf' + 1)(e + v^{-1}m) = \underbrace{gr + vf'e + f'm + e}_{= \tilde{e}} + v^{-1}m = \tilde{e} + v^{-1}m.$$

the decryption is correct as long as we set the parameters such that $\tilde{e}$ satisfies the condition (1) in Lemma 3. It is worth to note the following three nice properties about our decryption formula, which are very important for our scheme to choose practical (and small) parameters:

1. Multiplying $v = (1 - x^{n/k})$ will only increase the size of $vf'e$ from that of $f'e$ in a very mild way when taking account of the distributions of f' and e: the standard deviation of $vf'e$ is about $\sqrt{2}$ times larger than that of $f'e$;
2. The size of $f'm$ is far smaller than that of gr and $vf'e$ because m only has non-zero binary coefficients at the first $\ell \leq n/k$ coefficients.
3. The contribution of g, r to the size of $\tilde{e}$ is much less than that of (f', e), and we can utilize this asymmetric property to obtain a better balance between security and decryption failure as in [45].

In Sect. 5.2, we will choose concrete parameters such that the decryption failure is negligibly small. For security, we have the following theorem.

Theorem 1. *Let $n, q \in \mathbb{Z}$, $v \in R_q^*$ and distributions $\chi_f, \chi_g, \chi_r, \chi_e$ be defined as above. Then, under the $\text{DNTRU}_{n,q,\chi_f,\chi_g,v}$ and $\text{DRLWE}_{n,q,\chi_r,\chi_e}$ assumption, our PKE scheme NEV-PKE is provably IND-CPA secure in the standard model.*

Proof. We prove Theorem 1 by using a sequence of games $G_0 \sim G_2$, where G_0 is the standard IND-CPA game, and G_2 is a random one. The security is established by showing that G_0 and G_2 are computationally indistinguishable in the adversary's view. Let $\mathcal{A} = (\mathcal{A}_1, \mathcal{A}_2)$ be an adversary which can break the IND-CPA security of our PKE with advantage ϵ. Let F_i be the event that $\mathcal{A}$ correctly guesses $\mu' = \mu^*$ in game $i \in \{0, \ldots, 2\}$. By definition, the adversary's advantage $\text{Adv}_{\text{NEV-PKE},\mathcal{A}}^{\text{ind-cpa}}(\kappa)$ in game i is exactly $|\Pr[F_i] - 1/2|$.

Game G_0. This game is the real IND-CPA security game defined in Fig. 1. Formally, the challenger $\mathcal{C}$ works as follows:

KeyGen. randomly choose $f' \leftarrow \chi_f$ and $g \leftarrow \chi_g$ such that $f = vf' + 1 \in R_q^*$, compute $h = g/f$. Then, return the public key $pk = h$ to the adversary $\mathcal{A}_1$, and keep the secret key f private.

Challenge. Upon receiving two challenge plaintexts $(M_0, M_1) \in \{0,1\}^\ell \times \{0,1\}^\ell$ from the adversary $\mathcal{A}_1$, first randomly choose $\mu^* \leftarrow \{0,1\}, r^* \leftarrow \chi_r, e^* \leftarrow \chi_e$, compute $m^* = \mathsf{Pt2poly}(M_{\mu^*}) \in R_q$ and $c^* = hr^* + e^* + v^{-1}m^*$. Finally, return the challenge ciphertext c^* to $\mathcal{A}_2$.

Finalize. Upon receiving a guess $\mu' \in \{0,1\}$ from $\mathcal{A}_2$, return 1 if $\mu' = \mu^*$, otherwise return 0.

By definition, we have the following lemma.

Lemma 4. $|\Pr[F_0] - 1/2| = \epsilon$.

Game G_1. This game is similar to game G_0 except that the challenger $\mathcal{C}$ changes the KeyGen phase as follows:

KeyGen. randomly choose $h \leftarrow R_q$, and return the public key $pk = h$ to the adversary $\mathcal{A}_1$.

Lemma 5. *Under the* $\mathrm{DNTRU}_{n,q,\chi_f,\chi_g}$ *assumption, we have that Games G_1 and G_0 are computationally indistinguishable in the adversary's view. Moreover, $|\Pr[F_1] - \Pr[F_0]| \leq \mathsf{negl}(\kappa)$.*

Proof. This lemma directly follows from that the only difference between Games G_0 and G_1 is that $\mathcal{C}$ replaces $h = g/f$ in G_0 with a random one $h \leftarrow R_q$ in G_1.

Game G_2. This game is similar to game G_1 except that the challenger $\mathcal{C}$ changes the Challenge phase as follows:

Challenge. Upon receiving two challenge plaintexts $(M_0, M_1) \in \{0,1\}^\ell \times \{0,1\}^\ell$ from the adversary $\mathcal{A}_1$, first randomly choose $\mu^* \leftarrow \{0,1\}$ and $b \leftarrow R_q$, compute $m^* = \mathsf{Pt2poly}(M_{\mu^*}) \in R_q$ and $c^* = b + v^{-1}m^*$. Finally, return the challenge ciphertext c^* to $\mathcal{A}_2$.

Lemma 6. *Under the* $\mathrm{DRLWE}_{n,q,\chi_r,\chi_e}$ *assumption, we have that Games G_2 and G_1 are computationally indistinguishable in the adversary's view. Moreover, $|\Pr[F_2] - \Pr[F_1]| \leq \mathsf{negl}(\kappa)$.*

Proof. This lemma follows from that the only difference between Games G_1 and G_2 is that $\mathcal{C}$ replaces $b = hr^* + e^*$ in G_1 with a random one $b \leftarrow R_q$ in G_2.

Lemma 7. $|\Pr[F_2] - \frac{1}{2}| \leq \mathsf{negl}(\kappa)$.

Proof. This lemma directly follows from that b in Game G_2 is uniformly random, and statistically hides the information of m^* in $c^* = b + v^{-1}m^*$.

By Lemmas 4–7, we have that $\epsilon = |\Pr[F_0] - \frac{1}{2}| \leq \mathsf{negl}(\kappa)$. This completes the proof of Theorem 1.

3.3   An IND-CCA NTRU KEM from FO-Transformation

Let NEV-PKE $=$ (KeyGen, Enc, Dec) be defined in the above subsection. Let $H_1 : \{0,1\}^* \to \{0,1\}^\kappa$, $H_2 : \{0,1\}^{\ell+\kappa} \to \{0,1\}^\kappa \times \{0,1\}^\kappa$ and $H_3 : \{0,1\}^* \to \{0,1\}^\kappa$ be three hash functions, which will be modeled as random oracles in the security proof. We now transform NEV-PKE into a IND-CCA secure KEM NEV-KEM $=$ (KeyGen, Encap, Decap) following the generic FO-transformation.

- NEV-KEM.KeyGen(κ): given the security parameter κ as input, compute $(pk', sk') =$ NEV-PKE.KeyGen(1^κ) and randomly choose $s \leftarrow \{0,1\}^\kappa$. Then, return the public key $pk = pk'$, and secret key $sk = (sk', pk, H_1(pk), s)$.
- NEV-KEM.Encap(pk, M): given the public key pk as input, randomly choose $M \leftarrow \{0,1\}^\ell$, and compute

$$(\bar{K}, \rho) = H_2(M, H_1(pk)), c = \text{NEV-PKE.Enc}(pk, M; \rho) \text{ and } K = H_3(\bar{K}, c).$$

  Then, return the ciphertext and session key pair (c, K).
- NEV-KEM.Decap(sk, c): given the secret key $sk = (sk', pk, H_1(pk), s)$ and a ciphertext c as inputs, compute $M' =$ NEV-PKE.Dec(sk', c), $(\bar{K}', \rho') = H_2(M', H_1(pk))$ and $c' =$ NEV-PKE.Enc(pk, M', ρ'). If $c' = c$, return $K = H_3(\bar{K}', c)$, otherwise, return $K = H_3(s, c)$.

Since NEV-KEM is obtained by a standard application of the FO transformation (with implicit rejection) to NEV-PKE, the correctness of NEV-KEM directly follows from that of NEV-PKE. Moreover, we have the following security theorem for NEV-KEM according to the studies in [15,18,26,28].

Theorem 2. *Let $n, q \in \mathbb{Z}$, $v \in R_q^*$ and distributions $\chi_f, \chi_g, \chi_r, \chi_e$ be defined as in Theorem 1. Then, under the $\text{DNTRU}_{n,q,\chi_f,\chi_g,v}$ and $\text{DRLWE}_{n,q,\chi_r,\chi_e}$ assumption, our KEM scheme NEV-KEM is provably IND-CCA secure in the (quantum) random oracle model.*

4   An Optimized NTRU Encryption from sspRLWE

Since in the typical application of using PKEs as KEMs, the session key is randomly chosen and not necessarily known in advance, one might wonder if we can somehow simplify the construction of NEV-PKE based on the assumption that the plaintext is random. In this section, we give an optimized NTRU encryption called NEV-PKE', which essentially merges the sampling of the noise and the plaintext in a single step: one can roughly think that the noise is the output of a random secret share algorithm with a random plaintext as input.

4.1   Randomized Plaintext Encoding and Decoding

Let n be a power of 2, and q be a prime. Let $R = \mathbb{Z}[x]/(x^n + 1)$ and $R_q = \mathbb{Z}_q[x]/(x^n+1)$. Let $\mathcal{M} = \{0,1\}^{n/k}$ be the plaintext space. Let $v = (1-x^{n/k}) \in R_q^*$ be a ring element, whose inverse is $v^{-1} = \frac{q+1}{2}(1 + x^{n/k} + \cdots + x^{(k-1)n/k}) \in R_q^*$. Let B_η be the binomial distribution with parameter $\eta \in \mathbb{Z}$. We define a pair of encoding and decoding algorithm (Pt2noise, Noise2Pt) as follows:

- Pt2noise(M, η) : given a plaintext $M \in \{0,1\}^{n/k}$ and an integer η as inputs, first randomly choose $s \leftarrow \{0,1\}^{2n\eta - n/k}$, and parse $s = (s_0, \ldots, s_{2k\eta - 2})$ as $(2k\eta - 1)$ blocks of n/k bits (i.e., $s_i \in \{0,1\}^{n/k}$ for all $i \in [2k\eta - 1]$). Then, set $s_{2k\eta - 1} = M \oplus (\oplus_{i=0}^{2k\eta - 2} s_i) \in \{0,1\}^{n/k}$, arrange the bit string $(s_0, \ldots, s_{2k\eta - 1}) \in \{0,1\}^{2n\eta}$ as a bit array with 2η rows and n columns, and use the 2η bits in the i-th column as the randomness to sample the i-th coefficient of a polynomial $m \in R_q$ from B_η, as depicted in Fig. 3. Finally, return $m = m_0 + m_1 x + \cdots + m_{n-1} x^{n-1} \in R_q$, where

$$m_{in/k+j} = \sum_{t=0}^{\eta - 1} (s_{2i\eta+t,j} - s_{2i\eta+\eta+t,j}) \text{ for } i \in [k], j \in [n/k].$$

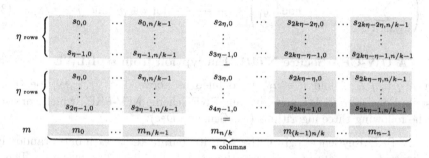

Fig. 3. The bit array for randomized encoding of a plaintext

- Noise2Pt(w) : given a ring element $w \in R_q$ as input, compute and return $M = \text{Poly2Pt}(w)$.

We have the following lemma for the above two algorithms.

Lemma 8. *Let $n, q, k, \eta \in \mathbb{Z}$ and $v \in R_q^*$ be defined as above. If M is uniformly chosen from $\{0,1\}^{n/k}$, then the coefficient distribution of $m = \text{Pt2noise}(M, \eta)$ is identical to the binomial distribution B_η. Moreover, if $k\eta < \frac{q}{2}$, then for any $m = \text{Pt2noise}(M, \eta)$ and any polynomial $e = e_0 + e_1 x + \cdots + e_{n-1} x^{n-1} \in R_q$ satisfying the following condition*

$$\left(\sum_{i=j \bmod n/k} |e_i \bmod^{\pm} q| \right) < \frac{k \cdot (q-1)}{4} - k \frac{k\eta + 1}{2} \text{ for } i \in [n] \text{ and } j \in [n/k]$$

(2)

we always have $\text{Noise2Pt}(v^{-1} m + e) = M$.

Proof. The first claim directly follows from the fact that $(s_0, \ldots, s_{2k\eta - 2})$ are uniformly chosen from $\{0,1\}^{2n\eta - n/k}$, and given $(s_0, \ldots, s_{2k\eta - 2})$, $s_{2k\eta - 1}$ is also uniformly distributed over $\{0,1\}^{n/k}$. Let $\bar{m} = \text{Pt2poly}(M)$. By Lemma 3, it suffices to show that $v^{-1}m = v^{-1}\bar{m} + e' \in R_q$ for some $\|e'\|_\infty \leq \frac{k\eta+1}{2}$. Formally, let $\bar{v} = (1 + x^{n/k} + \cdots + x^{(k-1)n/k})$, and $u = u_0 + u_1 x + \cdots + u_{n-1} x^{n-1} = \bar{v}m$, we have that $u_{in/k+j} = \sum_{t \leq i} m_{tn/k+j} - \sum_{t>i}^{k-1} m_{tn/k+j}$ for all $i \in [k], j \in [n/k]$. By the assumption that $k\eta < \frac{q}{2}$, we have that $u_{in/k+j} \in [-\frac{q-1}{2}, \frac{q-1}{2}]$ for all $i \in [k], j \in [n/k]$. Moreover, using a routine calculation one can check that $u_{in/k+j} = \sum_{t=0}^{k-1} m_{tn/k+j} = M_j \bmod 2$ for all $i \in [k], j \in [n/k]$ by the definition of m, and that there exists a polynomial e' such that $u = 2e' + \bar{v}\bar{m}$ and $\|e'\|_\infty \leq \frac{k\eta+1}{2}$ by the definition of $\bar{m}$. We immediately have $v^{-1}m = v^{-1}\bar{m} + e'$ using the fact that $v^{-1} = \frac{q+1}{2}\bar{v}$. This completes the proof.

Remark 5. Since $v^{-1}m + e = v^{-1}\bar{m} + e + e'$, the condition (2) in Lemma 8 can actually be relaxed to the following condition:

$$\left(\sum_{i=j \bmod n/k} |e_i + e'_i \bmod^\pm q| \right) < \frac{k \cdot (q-1)}{4} \text{ for } i \in [n] \text{ and } j \in [n/k]. \quad (3)$$

4.2   A OW-CPA Secure NTRU Encryption from sspRLWE

Let $n, q, k, \eta \in \mathbb{Z}$ and $v \in R_q^*$ be defined as above. Let χ_f, χ_g, χ_r be three distributions over R. We now give our PKE scheme NEV-PKE$'$, which consists of the following three algorithms (KeyGen, Enc, Dec):

- NEV-PKE$'$.KeyGen(κ): given the security parameter κ as inputs, randomly choose $f' \leftarrow \chi_f$ and $g \leftarrow \chi_g$ such that $f = f' + v^{-1} \in R_q^*$ is invertible. Then, return the public key and secret key pair $(pk, sk) = (h = g/f, f) \in R_q \times R_q$.
- NEV-PKE$'$.Enc(pk, M): given the public key $pk = h \in R_q$ and a plaintext $M \in \{0,1\}^{n/k}$ as inputs, sample $r \leftarrow \chi_r$ and $m \leftarrow \text{Pt2noise}(M, \eta) \in R_q$. Then, compute and return the ciphertext $c = hr + m$.
- NEV-PKE$'$.Dec(sk, C): given the secret key $sk = f = f' + v^{-1} \in R_q^*$ and a ciphertext $c \in R_q$ as inputs, compute $u = fc$, and $M' = \text{Noise2Pt}(u)$. Finally, return the plaintext $M' \in \{0,1\}^{n/k}$.

Remark 6. Note that if one wants to use NEV-PKE$'$ as a passively secure KEM, the encryption algorithm can be further simplified to directly sample a noise m from the binomial distribution B_η, and then derive a pre-session key $\bar{K}$ from the first n/k coefficients of $\bar{v}m \bmod 2$. By Lemma 8, this is actually equivalent to first randomly choose a prekey $\bar{K} \leftarrow \{0,1\}^{n/k}$ and then compute $m = \text{Pt2noise}(\bar{K})$. We prefer to describe it as a PKE scheme because it supports the generic FO transformation in Sect. 3.3 to obtain an IND-CCA secure KEM.

Since we have the following decryption formula

$$w = fc = gr + (f' + v^{-1})m = \underbrace{gr + f'm}_{= \tilde{e}} + v^{-1}m = \tilde{e} + v^{-1}m.$$

the decryption is correct as long as $\tilde{e}$ satisfies the condition (2) in Lemma 8. We will choose concrete parameters such that the decryption failure is negligibly small in Sect. 5.2. For security, we have the following theorem.

Theorem 3. *Let $n, q, k, \eta \in \mathbb{Z}$ and $v = 1 - x^{n/k}, \bar{v} = (1 + x^{n/k} + \cdots + x^{(k-1)n/k}) \in R_q$ be defined as above. Let χ_f, χ_g, χ_r be three probability distributions over R_q. Then, under the $\mathrm{DNTRU}_{n,q,\chi_f,\chi_g,v}$ and $\mathrm{sspRLWE}_{n,q,\chi_r,B_\eta,\bar{v}}$ assumption, the above PKE scheme NEV-PKE′ is provably OW-CPA secure in the standard model.*

This proof is very similar to that of Theorem 1, we omit the details. By applying the same FO transformation in Sect. 3.3 to NEV-PKE′, we can obtain an IND-CCA secure KEM NEV-KEM′ in the (quantum) random oracle model.

4.3   On the Hardness of the SspRLWE Problem

In this subsection, we provide more evidences on the hardness of the problem $\mathrm{sspRLWE}_{n,q,\chi_r,B_\eta,\bar{v}}$ for binomial distribution B_η and $\bar{v} = (1 + x^{n/k} + \cdots + x^{(k-1)n/k}) \in R_2$. Specifically, we will first show that for discrete Gaussian noise distributions, the $\mathrm{sspRLWE}_{n,q,\chi_r,D_{\mathbb{Z}^n,\gamma},\bar{v}}$ problem is at least as hard as its standard decisional RLWE problem $\mathrm{DRLWE}_{n,q,\chi_r,D_{\mathbb{Z}^n,\beta}}$ for sufficiently large parameters $\gamma > \beta$, which can be extended to binomial distributions (with sufficiently large η) by a standard argument using Rényi divergence [5]. We will also prove two theorems for special cases of $\mathrm{sspRLWE}_{n,q,\chi_r,B_\eta,\bar{v}}$, which apply to η that is as small as 1. Formally, we have that following three theorems. A high-level intuition of the proofs for the theorems is already given in Sect. 1.2.

Theorem 4. *Let n, q, k, χ_r and $\bar{v}$ be defined as above. Let α, β, γ be three positive reals satisfying $\alpha \geq \omega(\sqrt{\log n}), \gamma = \sqrt{\alpha^2 + 4\beta^2}, 2\alpha\beta/\gamma \geq \sqrt{2} \cdot \omega(\sqrt{\log n})$ and $\gamma\sqrt{n} < q/2$. Let $D_{\mathbb{Z}^n,\beta}, D_{\mathbb{Z}^n,\gamma}$ be two discrete Gaussian distributions with parameter β and γ, respectively. If there is a PPT algorithm $\mathcal{A}$ solving the $\mathrm{sspRLWE}_{n,q,\chi_r,D_{\mathbb{Z}^n,\gamma},\bar{v}}$ problem (with probability negligibly close to 1), then there is another PPT algorithm $\mathcal{B}$ solving the $\mathrm{DRLWE}_{n,q,\chi_r,D_{\mathbb{Z}^n,\beta}}$ problem.*

Proof. It is sufficient to give the description of $\mathcal{B}$. Formally, given a DRLWE tuple $(a, b) \in R_q \times R_q$ as input, $\mathcal{B}$ first randomly chooses a polynomial $e' \in R_q$ from the distribution $D_{\mathbb{Z}^n,\alpha}$, and sets $(a', b') = (2a, 2b + e') \in R_q \times R_q$. Then, it runs algorithm $\mathcal{A}$ with input (a', b'), and obtains $w \in R_2$ from $\mathcal{A}$. Finally, $\mathcal{B}$ returns 1 if $w = \bar{v}e' \bmod 2$, otherwise returns 0.

We now analyze the behavior of algorithm $\mathcal{B}$. First, if $(a, b = ar + e)$ is a real $\mathrm{DRLWE}_{n,q,\chi_r,D_{\mathbb{Z}^n,\beta}}$ tuple, then we have that the coefficients of e are chosen from $D_{\mathbb{Z}^n,\beta}$, which means that the coefficient distribution of $2e$ follows the distribution of $D_{2\mathbb{Z}^n,2\beta}$. By Lemma 2, we have that the distribution of $\hat{e} = 2e + e'$ is statistically close to $D_{\mathbb{Z}^n,\gamma}$. Since $\gamma\sqrt{n} < q/2$, we have that $\|\hat{e}\|_\infty < q/2$ with probability negligibly close to 1 by Lemma 1, which means that $\hat{e} \bmod q = \hat{e}$ holds with probability negligibly close to 1. Thus, the distribution of $(a' = 2a, b' = 2ar + \hat{e}) \in R_q \times R_q$ is statistically close to an $\mathrm{sspRLWE}_{n,q,\chi_r,D_{\mathbb{Z}^n,\gamma},\bar{v}}$ tuple. Using the fact that $w = \bar{v}\hat{e} = \bar{v}e' \bmod 2$, we have that $\mathcal{B}$ will return 1 with probability negligibly close to 1. Second, if (a, b) is randomly chosen from $R_q \times R_q$, we have that $(a' = 2a, b' = 2b + e')$ is also randomly distributed over $R_q \times R_q$. This means that the probability for any $\mathcal{A}$ to output $w \in R_2$ such that $w = \bar{v}e' \bmod 2$ is negligible in n/k by our choice of $e' \leftarrow D_{\mathbb{Z}^n,\alpha}$ with $\alpha \geq \omega(\sqrt{\log n})$. In all, we have shown that $\mathcal{B}$ is a valid distinguisher for $\mathrm{DRLWE}_{n,q,\chi_r,D_{\mathbb{Z}^n,\beta}}$ problem. This completes the proof.

Remark 7. As commonly seen in lattice-based cryptography, Theorem 4 does not provide concrete guarantee for practical parameters with typically small η. In the following, we show that for any $\eta \geq 1$, the $\mathrm{sspRLWE}_{n,q,\chi_r,B_\eta,\bar{v}}$ problem for $k = 1$ (resp., $k = 2$) is at least as hard as the standard $\mathrm{RLWE}_{n,q,\chi_r,\chi_e}$ problem with binomial distribution $\chi_e = B_1$ (resp., uniform binary distribution $\chi_e = U(R_2)$), where the case $k = 2$ essentially corresponds to our concrete parameter set NEV'-512.

Theorem 5. *Let $n, q, k, \chi_r, \eta, \bar{v}$ be defined as above, and $\eta < \frac{q}{2}$. If there is a PPT algorithm $\mathcal{A}$ solving the $\mathrm{sspRLWE}_{n,q,\chi_r,B_\eta,\bar{v}}$ problem for $k = 1$ (with probability negligibly close to 1), then there is another PPT algorithm $\mathcal{B}$ solving the $\mathrm{RLWE}_{n,q,\chi_r,B_1}$ problem.*

Proof. We now give the description of $\mathcal{B}$. Formally, given an $\mathrm{RLWE}_{n,q,\chi_r,B_1}$ instance $(a, b = ar + e)$ as input, $\mathcal{B}$ first randomly chooses a polynomial $e' \in R_q$ with coefficients sampling from the distribution $B_{\eta-1}$, and sets $b' = b + e' \in R_q$. Since $\eta \leq \frac{q-1}{2}$, it is easy to check that the coefficients of $\hat{e} = e + e' \bmod q = e + e'$ follows the distribution B_η, and that $(a, b' = ar + \hat{e})$ is an $\mathrm{sspRLWE}_{n,q,\chi_r,B_\eta,\bar{v}}$ instance. Then, it runs algorithm $\mathcal{A}$ with input (a, b'), which is expected to return $\bar{v}\hat{e} \bmod 2$ in polynomial time. Next, $\mathcal{B}$ computes $\bar{v}\hat{e} + \bar{v}e' = \bar{v}e \bmod 2$. Note that $\bar{v} = 1$ for $k = 1$. Let $u = \bar{v}e = e$, where $u = u_0 + u_1 + \cdots + u_{n-1}x^{n-1}$ and $e = e_0 + e_1x + \cdots + e_{n-1}x^{n-1}$. Since $e_i \in \{-1, 0, 1\}$, we have that $u_i \bmod 2 = 0$ if and only if $e_i = 0$. Thus, $\mathcal{B}$ can expect to obtain $n/2$ equations on the n variables consisting of the coefficients of the secret r from $(a, b = ar + e)$. Let d be the order of q modulo $2n$, we have that $x^n + 1$ modulo q factors into n/d irreducible polynomials of the same degree d, the probability that a random $a \leftarrow R_q$ is invertible is $(1 - \frac{1}{q^d})^{n/d} \geq 1/2$. Thus, with probability greater than $1/2$ we have that those obtained equations are linearly independent. By repeating the above process using fresh $\mathrm{RLWE}_{n,q,\chi_r,B_1}$ instances at most a polynomial number of times, $\mathcal{B}$ can collect n linearly independent equations to recover all the n coefficients of r by using Gaussian elimination. In all, $\mathcal{B}$ can solve the $\mathrm{RLWE}_{n,q,\chi_r,B_1}$ problem in polynomial time. This completes the proof.

Theorem 6. *Let $n, q, k, \chi_r, \eta, \bar{v}$ be defined as above, and $\eta < \frac{q}{2}$. If there is a PPT algorithm $\mathcal{A}$ solving the $\mathrm{sspRLWE}_{n,q,\chi_r,B_\eta,\bar{v}}$ problem for $k = 2$ (with probability negligibly close to 1), then there is another PPT algorithm $\mathcal{B}$ solving the $\mathrm{RLWE}_{n,q,\chi_r,U(R_2)}$ problem.*

Proof. In order to prove Theorem 6, it suffices to prove the following two claims:

Claim 1. $\mathrm{sspRLWE}_{n,q,\chi_r,U(R_2),\bar{v}} \Rightarrow \mathrm{sspRLWE}_{n,q,\chi_r,B_\eta,\bar{v}}$: If there is a PPT algorithm $\mathcal{A}$ solving $\mathrm{sspRLWE}_{n,q,\chi_r,B_\eta,\bar{v}}$, then there is another PPT algorithm $\bar{\mathcal{A}}$ solving $\mathrm{sspRLWE}_{n,q,\chi_r,U(R_2),\bar{v}}$.

Claim 2. $\text{RLWE}_{n,q,\chi_r,\mathcal{U}(R_2)} \Rightarrow \text{sspRLWE}_{n,q,\chi_r,\mathcal{U}(R_2),\bar{v}}$: If there is a PPT algorithm $\bar{\mathcal{A}}$ solving $\text{sspRLWE}_{n,q,\chi_r,\mathcal{U}(R_2),\bar{v}}$, then there is another PPT algorithm $\mathcal{B}$ solving $\text{RLWE}_{n,q,\chi_r,\mathcal{U}(R_2)}$.

For Claim 1, we construct an algorithm $\bar{\mathcal{A}}$ as follows. Formally, given an $\text{sspRLWE}_{n,q,\chi_r,\mathcal{U}(R_2),\bar{v}}$ instance $(a, b = ar + e) \in R_q \times R_q$ as input, $\bar{\mathcal{A}}$ first randomly chooses a polynomial $e' \in R_q$ with coefficients sampling from the following distribution

$$B'_\eta = \left\{ \sum_{i=0}^{\eta-1} (a_i - b_i) : (a_0, \ldots, a_{\eta-2}, b_0, \ldots, b_{\eta-1}) \leftarrow \{0,1\}^{2\eta-1} \right\}$$

in time $O(n\eta)$ and computes $(a, b' = b + e') = as + (e + e') \in R_q$. Since $\eta \leq \frac{q-1}{2}$, it is easy to check that the coefficients of $\hat{e} = e + e' \bmod q = e + e'$ follows the distribution B_η, and that (a, b') is an $\text{sspRLWE}_{n,q,\chi_r,B_\eta,\bar{v}}$ instance. Then, it runs algorithm $\mathcal{A}$ with input (a, b'), which is expected to return $\bar{v}\hat{e} \bmod 2$ in polynomial time. Finally, it returns $\bar{v}\hat{e} + \bar{v}e' = \bar{v}e \bmod 2$. This shows that $\bar{\mathcal{A}}$ can output $\bar{v}e \bmod 2$ in polynomial time. This completes the proof of Claim 1.

We now define an algorithm $\mathcal{B}$ for Claim 2 as follows. Formally, given an $\text{RLWE}_{n,q,\chi_r,\mathcal{U}(R_2)}$ instance $(a, b = as + e)$ as input, it first runs algorithm $\bar{\mathcal{A}}$ with input (a, b), which is expected to return $\bar{v}e \bmod 2$ in polynomial time. Note that $\bar{v} = 1 + x^{\frac{n}{2}}$ for $k = 2$. Let $u = \bar{v}e$, we have

$$u_j = \begin{cases} e_j - e_{\frac{n}{2}+j} \in \{-1,0,1\}, & \text{if } j \in [\frac{n}{2}] \\ e_j + e_{j-\frac{n}{2}} \in \{0,1,2\}, & \text{otherwise,} \end{cases}$$

where $u = u_0 + u_1 + \cdots + u_{n-1}x^{n-1}$ and $e = e_0 + e_1 x + \cdots + e_{n-1}x^{n-1} \in R_2$. Thus, we have that $u_j \bmod 2 = 0$ if and only if $u_j = 0$ for all $j \in [\frac{n}{2}]$ and that $u_j \bmod 2 = 1$ if and only if $u_j = 1$ for all $j \geq \frac{n}{2}$. Thus, $\mathcal{B}$ can expect to obtain $n/2$ equations on the n variables consisting of the coefficients of secret s from $(\bar{v}a, \bar{v}b = \bar{v}as + \bar{v}e)$. Let d be the order of q modulo $2n$, we have that $x^n + 1$ modulo q factors into n/d irreducible polynomials of the same degree d, the probability that a random $a \leftarrow R_q$ is invertible is $(1 - \frac{1}{q^d})^{n/d} \geq 1/2$. Thus, with probability greater than $1/2$ we have that those obtained equations are linearly independent. By repeating the above process using fresh $\text{RLWE}_{n,q,\chi_r,\mathcal{U}(R_2)}$ instances a polynomial number of times, $\mathcal{B}$ can collect n linearly independent equations to recover all the n coefficients of s by using Gaussian elimination. In all, $\mathcal{B}$ can solve the $\text{RLWE}_{n,q,\chi_r,\mathcal{U}(R_2)}$ problem in polynomial time. This completes the proof. $\square$

5 Concrete Attacks and Parameters

As discussed in [18], the most efficient known attacks against the NTRU and RLWE problems are lattice attacks. In this section, we mainly show how to apply lattice attacks to our (variants of) NTRU and RLWE problems, and take account of other relevant attacks by directly using the LWE estimator script [1] to obtain the concrete security estimates for our recommended parameters.

5.1   Lattice Attacks Against NTRU and (ssp)RLWE

In general, the lattice attacks against NTRU and RLWE problems work by defining the same set

$$\mathcal{L}_c^{\perp}(h) = \{(u, w) \in R_q = \mathbb{Z}[x]/(x^n + 1) : hu + w = c \in R_q\}.$$

The NTRU problem correspond to the special case $c = 0$, and $\mathcal{L}_0^{\perp}(h)$ essentially forms a lattice. To solve the decisional NTRU problem, namely, to distinguish the quotient $h = g/(vf' + 1) \in R_q$, where f', g have small coefficients noticeably less than $\sqrt{q/3}$, from a uniformly-random $h \in R_q$, an algorithm can try to find a good approximation to the shortest vector in $\mathcal{L}_0^{\perp}(h)$ [18]. This is because the vector $(f = vf' + 1, -g)$ will be a short vector significantly less than $\sqrt{nq}$ for $h = g/f$ (recall that $v = 1 - x^{n/k}$ is small in our case), while a vector of ℓ_2-norm less than $\Omega(\sqrt{nq})$ is very unlikely to exist in $\mathcal{L}_0^{\perp}(h)$ for a random $h \in R_q$.

For RLWE problems, we have $c \neq 0$ for $(h, c = hr + e)$, and $\mathcal{L}_c^{\perp}(h)$ is a shift of the lattice $\mathcal{L}_0^{\perp}(h)$. Finding the shortest vector in it is known as the Bounded Distance Decoding (BDD) problem, which in turn can be solved by finding the short vector $(e, r, 1) \in \mathbb{Z}^{2n+1}$ in an embedding lattice with dimension $2n + 1$ and basis

$$\mathbf{B} = \begin{pmatrix} qI_n & \text{Rot}(h) & \mathbf{c} \\ 0 & I_n & 0 \\ 0 & 0 & 1 \end{pmatrix} \in \mathbb{Z}^{(2n+1) \times (2n+1)},$$

where $\text{Rot}(h) \in \mathbb{Z}_q^n \times \mathbb{Z}_q^n$ is the anti-circular matrix corresponding ring multiplication in R_q, and $\mathbf{c} \in \mathbb{Z}_q^n$ is the coefficient vector of $c \in R_q$ in column form. For the same secret and noise distributions, the complexity of attacking the NTRU and RLWE problems are typically identical for modulus $q = O(n)$. Since for RLWE problems we can directly use the LWE estimator to obtain concrete security estimates, it suffices to how to use the LWE estimator to obtain concrete security estimates for our NTRU and sspRLWE problems.

On the DNTRU$_{n,q,\chi_f,\chi_g,v}$ *Problem with* $v = 1 - x^{n/k}$ *over* $R_q = \mathbb{Z}[x]/(x^n + 1)$. First, as discussed in Sect. 2.4, for the setting that $v = 1 - x^{n/k} \in R_q$ is invertible, our NTRU problem DNTRU$_{n,q,\chi_f,\chi_g,v}$ is essentially equivalent to the standard NTRU problem (with $v = 3$) up to the choices of the secret key distribution. Second, the ℓ_2-norm of $vf' + 1$ is only roughly about $\sqrt{2}$ times larger than that of f', which is small as long as f' is chosen from a small distribution. Thus, one can either solve the NTRU problem by taking $f = vf' + 1$ as whole just as in the standard lattice attacks against the NTRU problem with secret distributions $(\chi_f' = v\chi_f, \chi_g)$ in lattice $\mathcal{L}_0^{\perp}(h)$ for $h = g/f$, or solve the BDD problem on the shifted lattice $\mathcal{L}_h^{\perp}(-vh)$ by treating it as an RLWE instance $(vh, h = -vhf' + g)$ with secret distribution χ_f and noise distribution χ_g. We use the latter for concrete estimates for our NTRU problems in the LWE estimator because the norm of the short vector $(g, f', 1)$ in the latter case (which is independent from v) is smaller than that of $(f = vf' + 1, -g)$ in the former case.

Table 4. Practical Parameters Sets for Our KEM Schemes

Parameters	(n, q)	Key Dist (χ_f, χ_g)	Enc Dist (χ_r, χ_e)	Size (PK, CT)	Dec Failure	BKZ Sizes (SK, CT)	LWE Estimator (SK, CT)
NEV-512	$(512, 769)$	(B_1, B_1)	$(B_1, T_{1/6})$	(615,615)	2^{-138}	(426, 413)	(145, 141)
NEV'-512	$(512, 769)$	(B_1, B_1)	(B_1, B_1)	(615,615)	2^{-200}	(426, 426)	(145, 145)
NEV-1024	$(1024, 769)$	(B_1, B_1)	$(B_1, T_{1/6})$	(1229,1229)	2^{-152}	(953, 929)	(292, 281)
NEV'-1024	$(1024, 769)$	(B_1, B_1)	(B_1, B_1)	(1229,1229)	2^{-200}	(953, 953)	(292, 292)

On the $\text{sspRLWE}_{n,q,\chi_r,B_\eta,v}$ *Problem over* $R_q = \mathbb{Z}[x]/(x^n + 1)$. In Sect. 4.3, we have shown that the $\text{sspRLWE}_{n,q,\chi_r,B_\eta,v}$ problem is polynomially equivalent to the standard RLWE problem (with different parameters). Although those reductions are too loose to estimate concrete estimates on practical parameters, we believe it is very reasonable to assume that the concrete hardness of the $\text{sspRLWE}_{n,q,\chi_r,B_\eta,v}$ problem with $v = 1+x^{n/k}+\cdots+x^{(k-1)n/k}$ is the same as that of $\text{RLWE}_{n,q,\chi_r,B_\eta}$. Note that similar assumption for RLWE2 is also made in [18]. Thus, we estimate the concrete hardness of the $\text{sspRLWE}_{n,q,\chi_r,B_\eta,v}$ problem by treating it as a standard RLWE problem $\text{RLWE}_{n,q,\chi_r,B_\eta}$ in the LWE estimator.

5.2 Recommended Parameters

In Table 4, we present two parameter sets NEV-512 and NEV-1024 for NEV-PKE and NEV-KEM, along with two parameter sets NEV'-512 and NEV'-1024 for NEV-PKE' and NEV-KEM', aiming at NIST levels 1 and 5 security, respectively. The fifth column gives the corresponding sizes of public key (PK) and ciphertext (CT). The sixth column presents the decryption failure probability, which is computed by using a python script adapted from the python script for Kyber [9]. Note that we make the same choice as Kyber [9] to set our decryption failure probabilities $< 2^{-128}$ with some margin so that it is infeasible to obtain a single decryption failure using at most 2^{64} decryption queries (see the directional failure boosting attacks [14]). The seventh column gives the BKZ blocksizes needed to break the security of the secret key (SK) and ciphertext (CT) for each parameter set in the core-SVP model [3]. The last column presents concrete security estimates obtained by running the LWE estimator [1]. As known schemes using the power of 2 cyclotomic ring for both security and performance considerations such as Newhope [3], we cannot find a proper parameter set for NIST level 3 security. Fortunately, as shown in Tables 1 and 2, the performance of our schemes using the parameter sets at NIST level 5 security is already comparable to that of known schemes using parameter sets aiming at NIST level 3 security. For example, in the application of ephemeral key exchanges, our NEV-KEM using the parameter set NEV-1024 has the same size as that of NTRU4096821 and is 4.10–11.05X faster. Compared to Kyber768, our NEV-KEM using NEV-1024 has size about 8.19% larger but is 1.2X faster. Thus, we do not think this security gaps for our parameter sets will be a real problem for practical use: one can simply use NEV-1024 (or NEV'-1024) for applications requiring NIST level 3 security.

6   Implementations

We made two implementations of our schemes: one uses the reference C language, and the other is (partially) optimized by using AVX2 instructions. In the following, we provide some implementation details that heavily affect the performance of our schemes.

6.1   Partial NTT Multiplication

One costly arithmetic operation in our schemes is to do polynomial multiplication in R_q. Since the use of small modulus $q = 769$, we cannot apply full NTT multiplications in $R_q = \mathbb{Z}[x]/(x^n + 1)$ for both $n = 512$ and 1024. But because $q - 1 \bmod 256 = 1$, we can still speedup polynomial multiplications by first splitting the polynomials in R_q to a set of sub-polynomials in $R'_q = \mathbb{Z}_q[y]/(y^{128} + 1)$ and then realize a single polynomial multiplication in R_q by using a number of polynomial multiplications in $R'_q = \mathbb{Z}_q[y]/(y^{128} + 1)$, which in turn can be done efficiently using full NTT multiplications. Taking $n = 512$ as an example, by letting $y = x^4$ we can split any two polynomials $a, b \in R_q = \mathbb{Z}[x]/(x^{512} + 1)$ as follows:

$$a(x) = a_0(y) + xa_1(y) + x^2a_2(y) + x^3a_3(y)$$
$$b(x) = b_0(y) + xb_1(y) + x^2b_2(y) + x^3b_3(y),$$

where all the a_i's and b_i's are polynomials in $R'_q = \mathbb{Z}_q[y]/(y^{128} + 1)$. Since multiplications between a_i's and b_j's can be done using full NTT multiplications in R'_q, we can realize the multiplication between $a(x)$ and $b(x)$ by roughly using 16 NTT multiplications in $R'_q = \mathbb{Z}_q[y]/(y^{128} + 1)$ as follows:

$$\begin{aligned} a(x) \cdot b(x) = &(a_0b_0 + y(a_1b_3 + a_2b_2 + a_3b_1)) \\ &+x(a_0b_1 + a_1b_0 + y(a_2b_3 + a_3b_2)) \\ &+x^2(a_0b_2 + a_1b_1 + a_2b_0 + ya_3b_3) \\ &+x^3(a_0b_3 + a_1b_2 + a_2b_1 + a_3b_0). \end{aligned}$$

We can further save 6 NTT multiplications in R'_q by using the Karatsuba method as observed in [46]. For example, to compute the term $a_1b_3 + a_3b_1$ in the first row, we only need a single NTT multiplication by computing $a_1b_3 + a_3b_1 = (a_1 + a_3)(b_1 + b_3) - a_1b_1 - a_3b_3$ given as inputs a_1b_1 and a_3b_3, which will be computed in the third row.

To facilitate the above polynomial multiplications, we directly represent each polynomial in $R_q = \mathbb{Z}[x]/(x^n + 1)$ by simply concatenating the coefficient vectors of its split sub-polynomials, which are almost for free when all the coefficients are identically chosen from the same distribution. Moreover, we will keep the split sub-polynomials for the public key, secret key and ciphertext in their NTT forms to save some forward and inverse NTT operations in $R'_q = \mathbb{Z}_q[y]/(y^{128} + 1)$.

6.2   Partial NTT Inversion

The other costly arithmetic operation is to do polynomial inversion in R_q to generate the public key. Note that if we can do full NTT multiplications in R_q, this operation can be simply done by using n inversions in $\mathbb{Z}_q$ using the NTT representation. Fortunately, we can still speedup this operation by making full use of partial NTT multiplications given above as shown in [20]. Specifically, given a polynomial $f \in R_q = \mathbb{Z}_q[x]/(x^n + 1)$, by letting $z = x^2$ we can first use Karatsuba with an even/odd split to obtain two sub-polynomials in $\hat{R}_q = \mathbb{Z}_q[z]/(z^{n/2} + 1)$:

$$f(x) = f_0(z) + xf_1(z).$$

Then, the inversion of f in R_q can be done using one polynomial multiplication in R_q and one polynomial inversion in $\hat{R}_q$ because

$$\frac{1}{f(x)} = \frac{f_0(z) - xf_1(z)}{(f_0(z) + xf_1(z))(f_0(z) - xf_1(z))} = \frac{f_0(z) - xf_1(z)}{f_0^2(z) - zf_1^2(z)}.$$

By repeating this process, we can finally reduce the inversion of f to a few polynomial multiplications in R_q and a single polynomial inversion in $R_q' = \mathbb{Z}_q[y]/(y^{128} + 1)$, which in turn can be done using 128 inversions in $\mathbb{Z}_q$. Since $q = 769$ is very small, we can simply precompute the inversion table for all the elements in $\mathbb{Z}_q$. This is main reason why the key generation algorithm is much faster than NTRU (and some of its variants not using NTT).

6.3   Symmetric Primitives

In our default implementations, we use SHA3 and SHAKE256 as the hash function and the pseudorandom generator (PRG), respectively, which are the same as that of NTRU and Kyber in the NIST PQC submissions. Since the arithmetic operation of our KEMs is so fast that the use of SHA3 and SHAKE256 become the main bottleneck of our schemes: we actually observe a 1.82–2.27X speedup in experiment by replacing SHA3 and SHAKE256 with BLAKE2 and AES256CTR in the AVX2 implementation. For a fair comparison, we will use the same hash and PRG functions as that of BAT and NTTRU in the comparison with them (see Tables 5 and 6): BLAKE2 is used as both the hash and PRG functions in the open source code of BAT [20]; SHA3 and AES256CTR are used as the hash and PRG functions respectively in the open source code of NTTRU [33].

6.4   Multi-target Countermeasure

In the description of our IND-CCA transform in Sect. 3.3, we follow the strategy of Kyber to hash the public key into a prekey $\bar{K}$ and the random coins ρ, aiming at improving the security against multi-target attacks. We also hash the prekey together with the ciphertext into the final session key to make sure that our KEMs are contributory. The above two countermeasures are applied in our default implementations and in efficiency comparison with NTRU and Kyber (see Table 2). Since the performance of symmetric primitives is a major bottleneck of our schemes, those countermeasures will significantly reduce the performance: we observe a 2.25–2.54X speedup in experiment by removing the two countermeasures in the AVX2 implementation using SHA3 and SHAKE256 as the hash function and the pseudorandom generator (PRG), respectively. Since both BAT [20] and NTTRU [33] do not apply those countermeasures, we turned off the countermeasures in the comparison with them (see Tables 5 and 6).

6.5 Compressed Representation of R_q Elements

We apply the strategy of [20] to store an element in R_q in the compressed form. In particular, we encode coefficients by groups of 5 in 48 bits: each coefficient is split into a low 3 bits and a high 7 bits (value 0 to 96, inclusive); 5 "high bits" are encoded using 33 bits in base 97. For $n = 512$ (resp., 1024), this will lead to a reduction of 25 (resp., 51) bytes in storing a polynomial in R_q. The encoding can be done very efficiently using about 300 (resp., 600) CPU cycles, but the decoding is really costly, and will take about 1200 (resp., 2400) CPU cycles, which is about 3.1X (resp., 1.6X) slower than a polynomial multiplication in the same dimension. Thus, for applications that the few reduction in size is not very crucial, we highly recommend to remove this encoding/decoding optimization, and to obtain significantly speedup in efficiency especially when fast symmetric primitives are used (see Table 6).

7 Benchmarks and Comparisons

We run the codes of our schemes and several related works on the same 64-bit CentOS Linux 7.6 system (equipped with an Intel Core-i7 4790 3.6 GHz CPU and 4 GB memory), and present the average number of CPU cycles (over 100000 times) for running the corresponding algorithms in Tables 2, 5 and 6. All the codes are complied using the same optimization flags "-O3 -march=native -mtune=native -fomit-frame-pointer".

In Table 2, we give an efficiency comparison between our NEV-KEMs, NTRU and Kyber. The timings for our KEMs are obtained using our default implementations. In particular, we use SHA3 and SHAKE256 as the hash and PRG functions, which are the same as that in the code of Kyber and NTRU, submitted to the NIST PQC standardizations. We also use the multi-target countermeasures to hash the public key to generate the prekey and the random coins, and hash the ciphertext to generate the final session key. From Table 2, one can see that our scheme NEV-KEM (which is based on NEV-PKE from the standard NTRU and RLWE assumption) is 5.03–29.94X faster than NTRU (with key generation being 13.56–88.28X faster, encapsulation being 1.42–2.63X faster, and decapsulation being 2.39–2.99X faster) and 1.42–1.74X faster than Kyber, in the round-trip time of ephemeral key exchange at the same security levels. The efficiency improvement over Kyber is mainly because we do not have to expand a random coins to a uniform matrix over R_q, which needs many calls to the underlying symmetric primitives for rejection sampling. It is also worth to note that our NEV-KEM using the parameter set NEV-1024 at NIST level 5 security has the same public key and ciphertext size as that of NTRU-HPS4096821 at NIST level 3 security, but is 4.10–11.05X faster (with key generation being 11.96–31.94X faster, encapsulation being 1.36–1.51X faster, and decapsulation being 1.08–1.55X faster). The main reason that our KEMs is much faster than NTRU is that we allow (partial) NTT multiplications and inversions in R_q.

Table 5. Comparison between our NEV-KEMs and BAT in efficiency (CPU Cycles)

Schemes	KeyGen (Ref)	Encap (Ref)	Decap (Ref)	KeyGen (AVX2)	Encap (AVX2)	Decap (AVX2)	Speedup (Ref/AVX2)
BAT-512	35 249k	55 930	297 472	33 305k	10 191	68 795	140.5/973.6X
NEV-512	79 465	69 244	104 760	8 202	12 661	13 424	–
NEV'-512	79 220	62 261	101 367	8 224	9 017	10 272	–
BAT-1024	182 931k	111 694	818 690	156 811k	20 387	144 357	334.7/2648.3X
NEV-1024	182 198	144 157	223 059	16 001	18 844	24 429	–
NEV'-1024	182 619	134 622	225 169	15 938	16 109	21 274	–

In Table 5, we give a comparison between our NEV-KEMs and BAT. The timings for our KEMs are obtained using BLAKE2 as the hash and PRG functions without multi-target countermeasures, which are the same as that in the public available code of BAT. The size of BAT is about 19.19% (resp., 9.03%) than our Π_{KEM} at NIST level 1 (resp., 5) security (see Table 3), but our NEV-KEM is about 140-973X (resp., 334-2648X) faster than BAT, with key generation being 443-4060X (resp., 1004-9800X) faster, and decapsulation being 2.84–5.12X(resp., 3.67–5.90X) faster. Our encapsulation is slightly slower than that of BAT (especially in the reference implementation) mainly because BAT uses the strong RLWR assumption with binary secret and only needs to generate a few random bits in encapsulation. The efficiency improvement over BAT is mainly because we do not use the heavy trapdoor inversion algorithm, which requires very complex key generation and decryption operations.

Table 6. Comparison between our NEV schemes and NTTRU in efficiency (CPU Cycles)

Schemes	KeyGen (PKE)	Encap (PKE)	Decap (PKE)	KeyGen (KEM)	Encap (KEM)	Decap (KEM)
NEV-512	4 439	3 636	1 378	5 107 (4 881)	6 419 (5 289)	9 612 (6 675)
NEV'-512	4 453	3 112	1 399	5 201 (4 800)	6 167 (4 683)	9 382 (6 565)
NTTRU-768	8 199	2 976	2 675	9 640	6 586	8 603
NEV-1024	9 467	7 595	3 484	10 715 (9 891)	11 534 (9 841)	19 340 (12 955)
NEV'-1024	9 211	6 733	3 275	10 887 (10 195)	10 281 (8 864)	17 803 (11 531)

In Table 6, we give a comparison with NTTRU using the AVX2 instructions. The columns 2–4 present the timings for the corresponding OW/IND-CPA PKEs, while columns 4–7 give the timings for the final IND-CCA KEMs. The timings for our schemes are obtained using SHA3 and AES256CTR as the hash and PRG functions without multi-target countermeasures, which are the same as that in the public available code of NTTRU. The figures in the brackets give the timings of our NEV-KEMs without using the compressed representation of R_q elements. We note that NTTRU only supports the parameter of $n = 768, q = 7681$ in the cyclotomic ring $\mathbb{Z}_q[x]/(x^n - x^{n/2} + 1)$, aiming at NIST level 3 security. A recent paper [18] presents more parameter sets (see NTRU-A in Table 3) with reported comparable efficiency over the same ring as NTTRU, but their implementation is not publicly available. From Tables 3 and 6, we can expect that our schemes would have comparable computational efficiency with NTTRU and NTRU-A, but is at least 28% more compact, at the same security levels.

Acknowledgements. We thank the anonymous reviewers of ASIACRYPT 2023 for their helpful comments and suggestions on earlier version of our paper. This paper is supported by the National Natural Science Foundation of China (Grant Nos. 62022018, 61932019), and by the National Key Research and Development Program of China (Grant No. 2022YFB2702000).

References

1. Albrecht, M.R., Player, R., Scott, S.: On the concrete hardness of learning with errors. J. Math. Cryptol. **9**, 169–203 (2015)
2. Alkim, E., et al.: Newhope - submission to the NIST post-quantum project (2020)
3. Alkim, E., Ducas, L., Pöppelmann, T., Schwabe, P.: Post-quantum key exchange-a new hope. In: USENIX Security Symposium 2016 (2016)
4. Alkim, E., Ducas, L., Pöppelmann, T., Schwabe, P.: NewHope without reconciliation. Cryptology ePrint Archive, Report 2016/1157 (2016)
5. Bai, S., Langlois, A., Lepoint, T., Stehlé, D., Steinfeld, R.: Improved security proofs in lattice-based cryptography: using the Rényi divergence rather than the statistical distance. In: Iwata, T., Cheon, J.H. (eds.) ASIACRYPT 2015. LNCS, vol. 9452, pp. 3–24. Springer, Heidelberg (2015). https://doi.org/10.1007/978-3-662-48797-6_1
6. Bailey, D.V., Coffin, D., Elbirt, A., Silverman, J.H., Woodbury, A.D.: NTRU in constrained devices. In: Koç, Ç.K., Naccache, D., Paar, C. (eds.) CHES 2001. LNCS, vol. 2162, pp. 262–272. Springer, Heidelberg (2001). https://doi.org/10.1007/3-540-44709-1_22
7. Banaszczyk, W.: New bounds in some transference theorems in the geometry of numbers. Math. Ann. **296**, 625–635 (1993)
8. Bindel, N., Hamburg, M., Hövelmanns, K., Hülsing, A., Persichetti, E.: Tighter proofs of CCA security in the quantum random oracle model. In: Hofheinz, D., Rosen, A. (eds.) TCC 2019. LNCS, vol. 11892, pp. 61–90. Springer, Cham (2019). https://doi.org/10.1007/978-3-030-36033-7_3
9. Bos, J., et al.: Crystals - Kyber: a CCA-secure module-lattice-based KEM. In: 2018 IEEE European Symposium on Security and Privacy (EuroS P), pp. 353–367 (2018)

10. Brakerski, Z., Döttling, N.: Lossiness and entropic hardness for ring-LWE. In: Pass, R., Pietrzak, K. (eds.) TCC 2020. LNCS, vol. 12550, pp. 1–27. Springer, Cham (2020). https://doi.org/10.1007/978-3-030-64375-1_1

11. Chen, C., et al.: NTRU - submission to the NIST post-quantum project (2019)

12. Cramer, R., Shoup, V.: A practical public key cryptosystem provably secure against adaptive chosen ciphertext attack. In: Krawczyk, H. (ed.) CRYPTO 1998. LNCS, vol. 1462, pp. 13–25. Springer, Heidelberg (1998). https://doi.org/10.1007/BFb0055717

13. Dachman-Soled, D., Ducas, L., Gong, H., Rossi, M.: LWE with side information: attacks and concrete security estimation. In: Micciancio, D., Ristenpart, T. (eds.) CRYPTO 2020. LNCS, vol. 12171, pp. 329–358. Springer, Cham (2020). https://doi.org/10.1007/978-3-030-56880-1_12

14. D'Anvers, J.-P., Rossi, M., Virdia, F.: *(One) failure is not an option*: bootstrapping the search for failures in lattice-based encryption schemes. In: Canteaut, A., Ishai, Y. (eds.) EUROCRYPT 2020. LNCS, vol. 12107, pp. 3–33. Springer, Cham (2020). https://doi.org/10.1007/978-3-030-45727-3_1

15. Don, J., Fehr, S., Majenz, C., Schaffner, C.: Online-extractability in the quantum random-oracle model. In: Dunkelman, O., Dziembowski, S. (eds.) EUROCRYPT 2022. LNCS, vol. 13277, pp. 677–706. Springer, Cham (2022). https://doi.org/10.1007/978-3-031-07082-2_24

16. Ducas, L., Lyubashevsky, V., Prest, T.: Efficient identity-based encryption over NTRU lattices. In: Sarkar, P., Iwata, T. (eds.) ASIACRYPT 2014. LNCS, vol. 8874, pp. 22–41. Springer, Heidelberg (2014). https://doi.org/10.1007/978-3-662-45608-8_2

17. Ducas, L., van Woerden, W.: NTRU fatigue: how stretched is overstretched? In: Tibouchi, M., Wang, H. (eds.) ASIACRYPT 2021. LNCS, vol. 13093, pp. 3–32. Springer, Cham (2021). https://doi.org/10.1007/978-3-030-92068-5_1

18. Duman, J., Hövelmanns, K., Kiltz, E., Lyubashevsky, V., Seiler, G., Unruh, D.: A thorough treatment of highly-efficient NTRU instantiations. Cryptology ePrint Archive, Paper 2021/1352 (2021)

19. Fouque, P.A., et al.: Falcon: fast-Fourier lattice-based compact signatures over NTRU (2016)

20. Fouque, P.A., Kirchner, P., Pornin, T., Yu, Y.: BAT: small and fast kem over NTRU lattices. IACR Trans. Cryptograph. Hardw. Embed. Syst. **2022**(2), 240–265 (2022)

21. Fujisaki, E., Okamoto, T.: Secure integration of asymmetric and symmetric encryption schemes. In: Wiener, M. (ed.) CRYPTO 1999. LNCS, vol. 1666, pp. 537–554. Springer, Heidelberg (1999). https://doi.org/10.1007/3-540-48405-1_34

22. Gama, N., Nguyen, P.Q.: New chosen-ciphertext attacks on NTRU. In: Okamoto, T., Wang, X. (eds.) PKC 2007. LNCS, vol. 4450, pp. 89–106. Springer, Heidelberg (2007). https://doi.org/10.1007/978-3-540-71677-8_7

23. Hermans, J., Vercauteren, F., Preneel, B.: Speed records for NTRU. In: Pieprzyk, J. (ed.) CT-RSA 2010. LNCS, vol. 5985, pp. 73–88. Springer, Heidelberg (2010). https://doi.org/10.1007/978-3-642-11925-5_6

24. Hoffstein, J., Pipher, J., Silverman, J.H.: NTRU: a ring-based public key cryptosystem. In: Buhler, J.P. (ed.) ANTS 1998. LNCS, vol. 1423, pp. 267–288. Springer, Heidelberg (1998). https://doi.org/10.1007/BFb0054868

25. Hoffstein, J., Silverman, J.H.: Optimizations for NTRU. In: Buhler, J.P. (ed.) Proceedings of the Conference on Public Key Cryptography and Computational Number Theory, pp. 77–88. Springer, Cham (2000)

26. Hofheinz, D., Hövelmanns, K., Kiltz, E.: A modular analysis of the Fujisaki-Okamoto transformation. In: Kalai, Y., Reyzin, L. (eds.) TCC 2017. LNCS, vol. 10677, pp. 341–371. Springer, Cham (2017). https://doi.org/10.1007/978-3-319-70500-2_12

27. Howgrave-Graham, N., et al.: The impact of decryption failures on the security of NTRU encryption. In: Boneh, D. (ed.) CRYPTO 2003. LNCS, vol. 2729, pp. 226–246. Springer, Heidelberg (2003). https://doi.org/10.1007/978-3-540-45146-4_14

28. Jiang, H., Zhang, Z., Chen, L., Wang, H., Ma, Z.: IND-CCA-secure key encapsulation mechanism in the quantum random oracle model, revisited. In: Shacham, H., Boldyreva, A. (eds.) CRYPTO 2018. LNCS, vol. 10993, pp. 96–125. Springer, Cham (2018). https://doi.org/10.1007/978-3-319-96878-0_4

29. Kirchner, P., Fouque, P.-A.: Revisiting lattice attacks on overstretched NTRU parameters. In: Coron, J.-S., Nielsen, J.B. (eds.) EUROCRYPT 2017. LNCS, vol. 10210, pp. 3–26. Springer, Cham (2017). https://doi.org/10.1007/978-3-319-56620-7_1

30. Lindner, R., Peikert, C.: Better key sizes (and attacks) for LWE-based encryption. In: Kiayias, A. (ed.) CT-RSA 2011. LNCS, vol. 6558, pp. 319–339. Springer, Heidelberg (2011). https://doi.org/10.1007/978-3-642-19074-2_21

31. López-Alt, A., Tromer, E., Vaikuntanathan, V.: On-the-fly multiparty computation on the cloud via multikey fully homomorphic encryption. In: STOC '12, pp. 1219–1234 (2012)

32. Lyubashevsky, V., Peikert, C., Regev, O.: On ideal lattices and learning with errors over rings. In: Gilbert, H. (ed.) EUROCRYPT 2010. LNCS, vol. 6110, pp. 1–23. Springer, Heidelberg (2010). https://doi.org/10.1007/978-3-642-13190-5_1

33. Lyubashevsky, V., Seiler, G.: NTTRU: truly fast NTRU using NTT. Cryptology ePrint Archive, Paper 2019/040 (2019)

34. Micciancio, D., Schultz, M.: Error correction and ciphertext quantization in lattice cryptography. In: Handschuh, H., Lysyanskaya, A. (eds.) CRYPTO 2023. LNCS, vol. 14085, pp. 648–681. Springer Nature Switzerland, Cham (2023). https://doi.org/10.1007/978-3-031-38554-4_21

35. Nguyen, P.Q., Pointcheval, D.: Analysis and improvements of NTRU encryption paddings. In: Yung, M. (ed.) CRYPTO 2002. LNCS, vol. 2442, pp. 210–225. Springer, Heidelberg (2002). https://doi.org/10.1007/3-540-45708-9_14

36. NIST: Post-Quantum Cryptography Standardization. http://csrc.nist.gov/groups/ST/post-quantum-crypto/submission-requirements/index.html

37. NIST: Status report on the second round of the NIST post-quantum cryptography standardization process (2020). https://doi.org/10.6028/NIST.IR.8309

38. NIST: Status report on the third round of the NIST post-quantum cryptography standardization process (2022). https://doi.org/10.6028/NIST.IR.8413-upd1

39. Peikert, C.: An efficient and parallel gaussian sampler for lattices. In: Rabin, T. (ed.) CRYPTO 2010. LNCS, vol. 6223, pp. 80–97. Springer, Heidelberg (2010). https://doi.org/10.1007/978-3-642-14623-7_5

40. Pellet-Mary, A., Stehlé, D.: On the hardness of the NTRU problem. In: Tibouchi, M., Wang, H. (eds.) ASIACRYPT 2021. LNCS, vol. 13090, pp. 3–35. Springer, Cham (2021). https://doi.org/10.1007/978-3-030-92062-3_1

41. Pöppelmann, T., Güneysu, T.: Towards practical lattice-based public-key encryption on reconfigurable hardware. In: Lange, T., Lauter, K., Lisoněk, P. (eds.) SAC 2013. LNCS, vol. 8282, pp. 68–85. Springer, Heidelberg (2014). https://doi.org/10.1007/978-3-662-43414-7_4

42. Regev, O.: On lattices, learning with errors, random linear codes, and cryptography. In: STOC '05, pp. 84–93. ACM (2005)

43. Stehlé, D., Steinfeld, R.: Making NTRU as secure as worst-case problems over ideal lattices. In: Paterson, K.G. (ed.) EUROCRYPT 2011. LNCS, vol. 6632, pp. 27–47. Springer, Heidelberg (2011). https://doi.org/10.1007/978-3-642-20465-4_4

44. Stehlé, D., Steinfeld, R., Tanaka, K., Xagawa, K.: Efficient public key encryption based on ideal lattices. In: Matsui, M. (ed.) ASIACRYPT 2009. LNCS, vol. 5912, pp. 617–635. Springer, Heidelberg (2009). https://doi.org/10.1007/978-3-642-10366-7_36

45. Zhang, J., Yu, Yu., Fan, S., Zhang, Z., Yang, K.: Tweaking the asymmetry of asymmetric-key cryptography on lattices: KEMs and signatures of smaller sizes. In: Kiayias, A., Kohlweiss, M., Wallden, P., Zikas, V. (eds.) PKC 2020. LNCS, vol. 12111, pp. 37–65. Springer, Cham (2020). https://doi.org/10.1007/978-3-030-45388-6_2

46. Zhu, Y., Liu, Z., Pan, Y.: When NTT meets Karatsuba: preprocess-then-NTT technique revisited. In: Gao, D., Li, Q., Guan, X., Liao, X. (eds.) ICICS 2021. LNCS, vol. 12919, pp. 249–264. Springer, Cham (2021). https://doi.org/10.1007/978-3-030-88052-1_15

Cryptographic Smooth Neighbors

Giacomo Bruno[1]($\boxtimes$), Maria Corte-Real Santos[2], Craig Costello[3],
Jonathan Komada Eriksen[4], Michael Meyer[5], Michael Naehrig[3],
and Bruno Sterner[6]

[1] IKARUS Security Software, Vienna, Austria
giako13@gmail.com
[2] University College London, London, UK
maria.santos.20@ucl.ac.uk
[3] Microsoft Research, New York , USA
{craigco,mnaehrig}@microsoft.com
[4] Norwegian University of Science and Technology, Trondheim, Norway
jonathan.k.eriksen@ntnu.no
[5] University of Regensburg, Regensburg, Germany
michael@random-oracles.org
[6] Surrey Centre for Cyber Security, University of Surrey, Guildford, UK
b.sterner@surrey.ac.uk

Abstract. We revisit the problem of finding two consecutive B-smooth integers by giving an optimised implementation of the Conrey-Holmstrom-McLaughlin "smooth neighbors" algorithm. While this algorithm is not guaranteed to return the complete set of B-smooth neighbors, in practice it returns a very close approximation to the complete set but does so in a tiny fraction of the time of its exhaustive counterparts. We exploit this algorithm to find record-sized solutions to the pure twin smooth problem, and subsequently to produce instances of cryptographic parameters whose corresponding isogeny degrees are significantly smoother than prior works. Our methods seem well-suited to finding parameters for the SQISign signature scheme, especially for instantiations looking to minimise the cost of signature generation. We give a number of examples, among which are the first parameter sets geared towards efficient SQISign instantiations at NIST's security levels III and V.

Keywords: Post-quantum cryptography · isogeny-based
cryptography · twin smooth integers · smooth neighbors · Pell
equation · SQISign

1 Introduction

In recent years the tantalising problem of finding two large, consecutive, smooth integers has emerged in the context of instantiating efficient isogeny-based

Supported by EPSRC grant EP/S022503/1.

Supported by the German Federal Ministry of Education and Research (BMBF) under the project QuantumRISC (ID 16KIS1039).

Supported by EPSRC grant EP/R513350/1.

The original version of the chapter has been revised. The second author name was displayed incorrectly due to a tagging error. This has been corrected. A correction to this chapter can be found at https://doi.org/10.1007/978-981-99-8739-9_13

J. Guo and R. Steinfeld (Eds.): ASIACRYPT 2023, LNCS 14444, pp. 190–221, 2023.
https://doi.org/10.1007/978-981-99-8739-9_7

public key cryptosystems. Though the problem was initially motivated in the context of key exchange [9], a wave of polynomial time attacks [6,22,23] has completely broken the isogeny-based key exchange scheme SIDH [19], leaving post-quantum signatures as the most compelling cryptographic application of isogenies at present. In terms of practical potential, the leading isogeny-based signature scheme is SQISign [16]; it boasts the smallest public keys and signatures of all post-quantum signature schemes (by far!), at the price of a signing algorithm that is orders of magnitude slower than its post-quantum counterparts. Finding secure parameters for SQISign is related to the twin smooth problem mentioned above[1], with a large contributing factor to the overall efficiency of the protocol being the smoothness bound, B, of the rational torsion used in isogeny computations. This bound corresponds to the degree of the largest prime-degree isogeny computed in the protocol, for which the fastest algorithm runs in $\tilde{O}(\sqrt{B})$ field operations [4]. Part of the reason for SQISign's performance drawback is that the problem of finding parameters with small B is difficult: the fastest implementation to date targets security comparable to NIST Level I [27, §4.A] and has $B = 3923$ [17]. Additionally, methods for finding efficient SQISign parameters have to date not been able to obtain suitable primes reaching NIST Level III and V security. In view of NIST's recent call for additional general purpose post-quantum signature schemes that are not based on structured lattices [28], it is important to find methods of generating efficient isogeny-based signature parameters beyond those that have been proposed thus far at NIST Level I.

The CHM Algorithm. In this work we introduce new ways of finding large twin smooth instances based on the Conrey-Holmstrom-McLaughlin (CHM) "Smooth neighbors" algorithm [8]. For a fixed smoothness bound B, the CHM algorithm starts with the set of integers $S = \{1, 2, \ldots, B - 1\}$ representing the smooth neighbors $(1, 2), (2, 3), \ldots, (B - 1, B)$, and recursively grows this set by constructing new twin smooth integers from unordered pairs in $S \times S$ until a full pass over all such pairs finds no new twins, at which point the algorithm terminates. Although the CHM algorithm is not guaranteed to find the set of all B-smooth twins, for moderate values of B it converges with the set S containing *almost all* such twins. The crucial advantage is that, unlike the algorithm of Lehmer [20] that exhaustively solves $2^{\pi(B)}$ Pell equations to guarantee the full set of B-smooth twins, the CHM algorithm terminates much more rapidly. For example, in 2011 Luca and Najman [21] used Lehmer's approach with $B = 100$ to compute the full set of 13,374 twin smooths in 15 days (on a quad-core 2.66 GHz processor) by solving $2^{\pi(B)} = 2^{25}$ Pell equations, the solutions of which can have as many as 10^{10^6} decimal digits. The largest pair of 100-smooth twins they found

---

[1] SQISign is instantiated over large primes p such that $p^2 - 1$ is divisible by a large, B-smooth factor. If, for example, we find B-smooth twins r and $r + 1$ whose sum is a prime $p = 2r + 1$, then $p^2 - 1$ is immediately B-smooth.

were the 58-bit integers

$$166055401586083680 = 2^5 \cdot 3^3 \cdot 5 \cdot 11^3 \cdot 23 \cdot 43 \cdot 59 \cdot 67 \cdot 83 \cdot 89, \text{ and}$$
$$166055401586083681 = 7^2 \cdot 17^{10} \cdot 41^2.$$

In 2012, Conrey, Holmstrom and McLaughlin ran *their* algorithm on a similar machine to find 13,333 (i.e. all but 41) of these twins in 20 min [8]. Subsequently, they set $B = 200$ and found a list of 346,192 twin smooths in about 2 weeks, the largest of which were the 79-bit integers

$$589864439608716991201560 = 2^3 \cdot 3^3 \cdot 5 \cdot 7^2 \cdot 11^2 \cdot 17 \cdot 31 \cdot 59^2 \cdot 83 \cdot 139^2$$
$$\cdot 173 \cdot 181, \text{ and}$$
$$589864439608716991201561 = 13^2 \cdot 113^2 \cdot 127^2 \cdot 137^2 \cdot 151^2 \cdot 199^2.$$

Exhausting the full set of 200-smooth twins would have required solving $2^{\pi(200)} = 2^{46}$ Pell equations, which is pushing the limit of what is currently computationally feasible. The largest run of Lehmer's algorithm reported in the literature used $B = 113$ [9, §5.3], which required solving 2^{30} Pell equations and a significant parallelised computation that ran over several weeks. The largest set of 113-smooth twins found during that computation were the 75-bit integers

$$19316158377073923834000 = 2^4 \cdot 3^6 \cdot 5^3 \cdot 7 \cdot 23^2 \cdot 29 \cdot 47 \cdot 59 \cdot 61 \cdot 73 \cdot 97 \cdot 103,$$
$$19316158377073923834001 = 13^2 \cdot 31^2 \cdot 37^2 \cdot 43^4 \cdot 71^4.$$

Remark 1. The above examples illustrate some important phenomena that are worth pointing out before we move forward. Observe that, in the first and third examples, the largest prime not exceeding B is not found in the factors of the largest twins. The largest 89-smooth twins are the same as the largest 97-smooth twins, and the largest 103-smooth twins are the same as the largest 113-smooth twins. In other words, increasing B to include more primes necessarily increases the size of the set of B-smooth twins, but it does not mean we will find any new, larger twins. This trend highlights part of the difficulty we face in trying to find optimally smooth parameters of cryptographic size: increasing the smoothness bound B makes the size of the set of twins grow rapidly, but the growth of the largest twins we find is typically painstakingly slow. The set of 100-smooth twins has cardinality 13,374, with the largest pair being 58 bits; increasing B to 200 gives a set of cardinality (at least) 345,192, but the largest pair has only grown to be 79 bits. In fact, most of this jump in the bitlength of the largest twins occurs when increasing $B = 97$ (58 bits) to include two more primes with $B = 103$ (76 bits). Including the 19 additional primes up to 199 only increases the bitlength of largest twins with $B = 199$ by 3 (79 bits), and this is indicative of what we observe when B is increased even further.

Our Contributions. We give an optimised implementation of CHM that allows us to run the algorithm for much larger values of B in order to find larger sized twins. For example, the original CHM paper reported that the full algorithm with $B = 200$ terminated in approximately 2 weeks; our implementation did the same computation in around 943 s on a laptop. Increasing the smoothness bound to $B = 547$, our implementation converged with a set of 82,026,426 pairs of B-smooth twins, the largest of which are the 122-bit pair $(r, r + 1)$ with

$$r = 5^4 \cdot 7 \cdot 13^2 \cdot 17^2 \cdot 19 \cdot 29 \cdot 41 \cdot 109 \cdot 163 \cdot 173 \cdot 239 \cdot 241^2 \cdot 271 \cdot 283$$
$$\cdot 499 \cdot 509, \qquad \text{and}$$
$$r + 1 = 2^8 \cdot 3^2 \cdot 31^2 \cdot 43^2 \cdot 47^2 \cdot 83^2 \cdot 103^2 \cdot 311^2 \cdot 479^2 \cdot 523^2. \tag{1}$$

Although it remains infeasible to increase B to the point where the twins found through CHM are large enough to be used out-of-the-box in isogeny-based schemes (i.e. close to 2^{256}), we are able to combine the larger twins found through CHM with techniques from the literature in order to find much smoother sets of SQISign parameters. In this case we are aided by the requirements for SQISign, which permit us to relax the size of the smooth factor that divides $p^2 - 1$. The current state-of-the-art instantiation [17] uses primes p such that

$$\ell^f \cdot T \mid (p^2 - 1),$$

where ℓ is a small prime (typically $\ell = 2$), where f is as large as possible, and where $T \approx p^{5/4}$ is both coprime to ℓ and B-smooth. For example, the original SQISign implementation [16] used a 256-bit prime p such that

$$p^2 - 1 = 2^{34} \cdot T_{1879} \cdot R,$$

where T_{1879} is an odd 334-bit integer[2] whose largest prime factor is $B = 1879$, and R is the *rough* factor; a 144-bit integer containing no prime factors less than or equal to B. As another example, De Feo, Leroux and Wesolowski [17, §5] instead use a 254-bit prime p with

$$p^2 - 1 = 2^{66} \cdot T_{3923} \cdot R,$$

where T_{3923} is an odd 334-bit integer whose largest prime factor is $B = 3923$, and where all of R's prime factors again exceed B.

During the search mentioned above that found the record 547-smooth twins in (1), over 82 million other pairs of smaller sized twins were found. One such pair was the 63-bit twins $(r - 1, r)$ with $r = 8077251317941145600$. Taking $p = 2r^4 - 1$ gives a 253-bit prime p such that

$$p^2 - 1 = 2^{49} \cdot T_{479} \cdot R,$$

where T_{479} is an odd 328 bit integer that is 479-smooth. This represents a significant improvement in smoothness over the T values obtained in [16] and [17]. Although the smoothness of T is not the only factor governing the efficiency of

---

[2] The initial SQISign requirements [16] had $T \approx p^{3/2}$, but T_{1879} corresponds to the new requirements.

the scheme, our analysis in Sect. 6 suggests that the parameters found in this paper are interesting alternatives to those currently found in SQISign implementations, giving instantiations with a significantly lower expected signing cost, but with a modest increase in verification cost.

Just as we transformed a pair of 85-bit twins into a 255-bit prime by taking $p = 2r^3 - 1$, we combine the use of twins found with CHM and primes of the form $p = 2r^n - 1$ with $n \geq 3$ to obtain several SQISign-friendly primes that target higher security levels. For example, with some 64-bit twins $(r, r + 1)$ found through CHM, we give a 382-bit prime $p = 2r^6 - 1$ such that $p^2 - 1 = 2^{80} \cdot T_{10243} \cdot R$, where T is an odd 495-bit integer that is 10243-smooth; this prime would be suitable for SQISign signatures geared towards NIST Level III security. As another example, with some 85-bit twins $(r, r + 1)$, we give a 508-bit prime $p = 2r^6 - 1$ such that $p^2 - 1 = 2^{86} \cdot T_{150151} \cdot R$, where T is a 639-bit integer that is 150151-smooth; this prime would be suitable for SQISign signatures targeting NIST Level V security.

Our implementation of the CHM algorithm is written in C/C++ and is found at

https://github.com/GiacomoBruno/TwinsmoothSearcher.

Remark 2. In a recent paper [15], it was shown that computing the constructive Deuring correspondence, which is the heavy computation that SQISign needs to perform as part of its signature generation algorithm, is feasible to compute without choosing a specific characteristic p beforehand. However, the paper further confirms (comparing [15, Figure 3] with [15, Table 2]) that the efficiency of this computation depends heavily on the factorisation of $p^2 - 1$ (or more generally $p^k - 1$ for small k). In a setting that allows to freely choose a fixed characteristic p, for instance in the SQISign setting, it is clear that one should choose p carefully for optimal performance.

Remark 3. Another recent work introduces SQISignHD [11], a variant of SQISign in higher dimensions. Although the signature generation could be significantly faster in SQISignHD, the verification algorithm requires computing 4-dimensional isogenies. Since the research of implementing practical 4-dimensional isogenies has mainly only begun since the SIDH attacks, there is no implementation of SQISignHD yet. While breakthroughs in this area of research could change the picture of the field, it remains unclear whether the verification algorithm can be implemented efficiently enough to consider SQISignHD for practical applications, or to reach similar performance as SQISign verification.

Organisation. Sect. 2 reviews prior methods for generating large instances of twin smooths. In Sect. 3, we recall the CHM algorithm and give a generalisation of it that may be of independent interest. Section 4 details our implementation of the CHM algorithm and presents a number of optimisations that allowed us to run it for much larger values of B. In Sect. 5, we discuss the combination of CHM with primes of the form $p = 2x^n - 1$ to give estimates on the probabilities of finding SQISign parameters at various security levels. Section 6 presents our results, giving record-sized twin smooth instances and dozens of SQISign-friendly primes that target NIST's security levels I, III, and V.

2   Preliminaries and Prior Methods

We start by fixing some definitions and terminology.

Definition 1. *A positive integer n is called B-smooth for some real number $B > 0$ if all prime divisors of n are at most B. An integer n generates a B-smooth value of a polynomial $f(X)$ if $f(n)$ is B-smooth. In this case we call n a B-smooth value of $f(X)$. We call two consecutive integers B-smooth twins if their product is B-smooth. An integer n is called B-rough if all of its prime factors exceed B.*

We now review prior methods of searching for twin smooth integers by following the descriptions of the three algorithms reviewed in [10, §2] and including the method introduced in [10] itself.

Solving Pell Equations. Fix B, let $\{2, 3, \ldots, q\}$ be the set of primes up to B with cardinality $\pi(B)$, and consider the B-smooth twins $(r, r+1)$. Let $x = 2r+1$, so that $x - 1$ and $x + 1$ are also B-smooth, and let D be the squarefree part of their product $(x - 1)(x + 1)$, i.e. $x^2 - 1 = Dy^2$ for some $y \in \mathbb{Z}$. It follows that Dy^2 is B-smooth, which means that

$$D = 2^{\alpha_2} \cdot 3^{\alpha_3} \cdots \cdot q^{\alpha_q}$$

with $\alpha_i \in \{0, 1\}$ for $i = 2, 3, \ldots, q$. For each of the $2^{\pi(B)}$ squarefree possibilities for D, Størmer [24] reverses the above argument and proposes to solve the $2^{\pi(B)}$ Pell equations

$$x^2 - Dy^2 = 1,$$

finding *all* of the solutions for which y is B-smooth, and in doing so finding the complete set of B-smooth twins.

The largest pair of 2-smooth integers is $(1, 2)$, the largest pair of 3-smooth integers is $(8, 9)$, and the largest pair of 5-smooth integers is $(80, 81)$. Unfortunately, solving $2^{\pi(B)}$ Pell equations becomes infeasible before the size of the twins we find is large enough (i.e. exceeds 2^{200}) for our purposes. As we saw in Sect. 1, [9] reports that with $B = 113$ the largest twins $(r, r + 1)$ found upon solving all 2^{30} Pell equations have $r = 19316158377073923834000 \approx 2^{75}$.

The Extended Euclidean Algorithm. The most naïve way of searching for twin smooth integers is to compute B-smooth numbers r until either $r - 1$ or $r + 1$ also turns out to be B-smooth. A much better method [9,16] is to instead choose two coprime B-smooth numbers α and β that are both of size roughly the square root of the target size of r and $r + 1$. On input of α and β, Euclid's extended GCD algorithm outputs two integers (s, t) such that $\alpha s + \beta t = 1$ with $|s| < |\beta/2|$ and $|t| < |\alpha/2|$. We can then take $\{m, m+1\} = \{|\alpha s|, |\beta t|\}$, and the probability of m and $m+1$ being B-smooth is now the probability that $s \cdot t$ is B-smooth. The reason this performs much better than the naïve method above is that $s \cdot t$ with $s \approx t$ is much more likely to be B-smooth than a random integer of similar size.

Searching with $r = x^n - 1$. A number of works [9, 16, 17] have found performant parameters by searching for twins of the form $(r, r+1) = (x^n - 1, x^n)$, for relatively small $n \in \mathbb{Z}$. For example, suppose we are searching for b-bit twins $(r, r+1)$ and we take $n = 4$ so that $r = (x^2 + 1)(x - 1)(x + 1)$. Instead of searching for two b-bit numbers that are smooth, we are now searching for three smooth $(b/4)$-bit numbers (i.e. $x - 1$, x, and $x + 1$) and one smooth $(b/2)$-bit number, which increases the probability of success (see [10]).

Searching with PTE Solutions. The approach taken in [10] can be viewed as an extension of the method above, where the important difference is that for $n > 2$ the polynomial $x^n - 1$ does not split in $\mathbb{Z}[x]$, and the presence of higher degree terms (like the irreducible quadratic $x^2 + 1$ above) significantly hampers the probability that values of $x^n - 1 \in \mathbb{Z}$ are smooth. Instead, the algorithm in [10] takes $(r, r+1) = (f(x), g(x))$, where $f(x)$ and $g(x)$ are both of degree n and are comprised entirely of linear factors. This boosts the success probability again, but one of the difficulties facing this method is that polynomials $f(x)$ and $g(x)$ that differ by a constant and are completely split are difficult to construct for $n \geq 4$. Fortunately, instances of these polynomials existed in the literature prior to [10], since they can be trivially constructed using solutions to the Prouhet-Tarry-Escott (PTE) problem (see [10]).

3   The CHM Algorithm

In this section, we first recall the Conrey, Holmstrom, and McLaughlin (CHM) algorithm [8], a remarkably simple algorithm that generates twin smooth integers (or *smooth neighbors* as they are called in [8]), i.e. smooth values of the polynomial $X(X + 1)$. We then present a generalisation of this algorithm, which generates smooth values of any monic quadratic polynomial. The algorithm generalises the CHM algorithm, as well as another algorithm in the literature by Conrey and Holmstrom [7], which generates smooth values of the polynomial $X^2 + 1$. In the end, we are primarily interested in the CHM algorithm, but present the generalised algorithm here, as it may be of independent interest.

3.1   Finding Smooth Twins with the CHM Algorithm

Conrey, Holmstrom, and McLaughlin [8] present the following algorithm for producing many B-smooth values of $X(X + 1)$. It starts with the initial set

$$S^{(0)} = \{1, 2, \ldots, B - 1\}$$

of all integers less than B, representing the B-smooth twins $(1, 2)$, $(2, 3)$, $\ldots$, $(B-1, B)$. Next, it iteratively passes through all pairs of distinct $r, s \in S^{(0)}, r < s$ and computes

$$\frac{t}{t'} = \frac{r}{r+1} \cdot \frac{s+1}{s},$$

writing $\frac{t}{t'}$ in lowest terms. If $t' = t + 1$, then clearly t also represents a twin smooth pair. The next set $S^{(1)}$ is formed as the union of $S^{(0)}$ and the set of all solutions t such that $t' = t + 1$. Now the algorithm iterates through all pairs of distinct $r, s \in S^{(1)}$ to form $S^{(2)}$ and so on. We call the process of obtaining $S^{(d)}$ from $S^{(d-1)}$ the d-th CHM iteration. Once $S^{(d)} = S^{(d-1)}$, the algorithm terminates.

Example: We illustrate the algorithm for $B = 5$, i.e. with the goal to generate 5-smooth twin integers. The starting set is

$$S^{(0)} = \{1, 2, 3, 4\}.$$

Going through all pairs $(r, s) \in S^{(0)}$ with $r < s$, we see that the only ones that yield a new twin smooth pair $(t, t+1)$ via Eq. (2) with t not already in $S^{(0)}$ are $(2, 3)$, $(2, 4)$ and $(3, 4)$, namely,

$$\frac{2}{2+1} \cdot \frac{3+1}{3} = \frac{8}{9}, \quad \frac{2}{2+1} \cdot \frac{4+1}{4} = \frac{5}{6}, \quad \text{and} \quad \frac{3}{3+1} \cdot \frac{4+1}{4} = \frac{15}{16}.$$

Hence, we add 5, 8 and 15 to get the next set as

$$S^{(1)} = \{1, 2, 3, 4, 5, 8, 15\}.$$

The second and third CHM iterations give

$$S^{(2)} = \{1, 2, 3, 4, 5, 8, 9, 15, 24\} \text{ and } S^{(3)} = \{1, 2, 3, 4, 5, 8, 9, 15, 24, 80\}.$$

The fourth iteration does not produce any new numbers, i.e. we have $S^{(4)} = S^{(3)}$, the algorithm terminates here and returns $S^{(3)}$. This is indeed the full set of twin 5-smooth integers as shown in [24], see also [20, Table 1A].

Remark 4. The CHM check that determines whether a pair (r, s) yields an integer solution t to the equation

$$\frac{t}{t+1} = \frac{r}{r+1} \cdot \frac{s+1}{s} \tag{2}$$

can be rephrased by solving this equation for t, which yields

$$t = \frac{r(s+1)}{s - r}. \tag{3}$$

This shows that in order for (r, s) to yield a new pair, $s - r$ must divide $r(s+1)$ and in particular, must be B-smooth as well.

3.2 Generalising the CHM Algorithm

We now present a generalisation of the CHM algorithm, which finds smooth values of any monic quadratic polynomial $f(X) = X^2 + aX + b \in \mathbb{Z}[X] \subseteq \mathbb{Q}[X]$. The algorithm works with elements in the $\mathbb{Q}$-algebra $A = \mathbb{Q}[X]/\langle f(X) \rangle$. Let $\bar{X}$ denote the residue class of X in A. The generalisation closely follows the idea of the CHM algorithm and is based on the observation that for any $r \in \mathbb{Q}$, we have that

$$N_{A/\mathbb{Q}}(r - \bar{X}) = f(r),$$

where $N_{A/\mathbb{Q}}(\alpha)$ denotes the algebraic norm of $\alpha \in A$ over $\mathbb{Q}$. The algorithm now starts with an initial set

$$S^{(0)} = \{r_1 - \bar{X}, \ldots, r_d - \bar{X}\},$$

where r_i are smooth integer values of $f(X)$ (Definition 1), which means that the element $r_i - \bar{X}$ has smooth non-zero norm. Next, in the d-th iteration of the algorithm, given any two $\alpha, \beta \in S^{(d-1)}$, compute

$$\alpha \cdot \beta^{-1} \cdot N_{A/\mathbb{Q}}(\beta) = r - s\bar{X}$$

for integers r, s (notice that β is invertible, since it has non-zero norm). Now, if s divides r, we obtain an integer $t = \frac{r}{s}$. It follows that

$$
\begin{aligned}
f(t) &= N_{A/\mathbb{Q}}\left(\frac{r}{s} - \bar{X}\right) \\
&= N_{A/\mathbb{Q}}(r - s\bar{X})s^{-2} \\
&= N_{A/\mathbb{Q}}(\alpha \cdot \beta^{-1} \cdot N_{A/\mathbb{Q}}(\beta))s^{-2} \\
&= N_{A/\mathbb{Q}}(\alpha)N_{A/\mathbb{Q}}(\beta)s^{-2}.
\end{aligned}
$$

Since both $N_{A/\mathbb{Q}}(\alpha)$ and $N_{A/\mathbb{Q}}(\beta)$ are B-smooth and s is an integer, it follows that t is a B-smooth value of $f(X)$. The set $S^{(d)}$ is then formed as the union of $S^{(d-1)}$ and the set of all such integral solutions. Finally, we terminate when $S^{(d)} = S^{(d-1)}$.

3.3 Equivalence with Previous Algorithms

We now show that the CHM algorithm, as well as another algorithm by Conrey and Holmstrom [7], are special cases of the generalised algorithm, for the polynomials $f(x) = X^2 + X$, and $f(X) = X^2 + 1$ respectively.

Smooth values of $X^2 + X$. To see that the CHM algorithm (see Sect. 3.1) is indeed a special case of the generalised algorithm above, we show how the generalised algorithm works for $f(X) = X(X + 1) = X^2 + X$. Consider the algebra $A = \mathbb{Q}[X]/\langle X^2 + X \rangle$. This embeds into the matrix algebra $M_{2\times 2}(\mathbb{Q})$ via

$$\psi : r + s\bar{X} \rightarrow \begin{pmatrix} r & 0 \\ s & r - s \end{pmatrix}.$$

Instead of working with elements in A, we will work with elements in $\psi(A) \subseteq M_{2 \times 2}(\mathbb{Q})$ since this simplifies the argument. In this case, for $\alpha \in A$, we have

$$N_{A/\mathbb{Q}}(\alpha) = \det(\psi(\alpha)).$$

The set corresponding to the initial set in the CHM algorithm is

$$S^{(0)} = \left\{ \left(\begin{smallmatrix} 1 & 0 \\ -1 & 2 \end{smallmatrix} \right), \left(\begin{smallmatrix} 2 & 0 \\ -1 & 3 \end{smallmatrix} \right), \dots, \left(\begin{smallmatrix} B-1 & 0 \\ -1 & B \end{smallmatrix} \right) \right\}.$$

All these elements clearly have B-smooth norm. The d-th CHM iteration proceeds as follows: For all $\left(\begin{smallmatrix} r & 0 \\ -1 & r+1 \end{smallmatrix} \right), \left(\begin{smallmatrix} s & 0 \\ -1 & s+1 \end{smallmatrix} \right)$ in $S^{(d-1)}$, we try

$$\begin{pmatrix} r & 0 \\ -1 & r+1 \end{pmatrix} \begin{pmatrix} s & 0 \\ -1 & s+1 \end{pmatrix}^{-1} s(s+1) = \begin{pmatrix} r & 0 \\ -1 & r+1 \end{pmatrix} \left(\begin{pmatrix} s+1 & 0 \\ 1 & s \end{pmatrix} \frac{1}{s(s+1)} \right) s(s+1)$$

$$= \begin{pmatrix} r(s+1) & 0 \\ -(s-r) & (r+1)s \end{pmatrix}.$$

Finally, we transform this matrix into the right form, i.e. into a matrix corresponding to an element of the form $\tau = t - \bar{X}$, which means that $\psi(\tau)$ has a -1 in the lower left corner. So, we divide by $s - r$ and end up with the matrix

$$\begin{pmatrix} \frac{r(s+1)}{s-r} & 0 \\ -1 & \frac{(r+1)s}{s-r} \end{pmatrix} = \begin{pmatrix} \frac{r(s+1)}{s-r} & 0 \\ -1 & \frac{r(s+1)}{s-r} + 1 \end{pmatrix}.$$

Now if $\frac{r(s+1)}{s-r}$ is an integer, we add this matrix to the next set $S^{(d+1)}$.

As we have seen in Remark 4, this integer indeed corresponds to the solution (3) of Eq. (2) and therefore, the generalised algorithm in the case $f(X) = X^2 + X$ is equivalent to the original CHM algorithm.

Smooth Values of $X^2 + 1$. Conrey and Holmstrom later presented a method to generate smooth values of $X^2 + 1$ [7]. Similar to the CHM algorithm, it starts with an initial set $S^{(0)}$ of positive smooth values of $X^2 + 1$. Again, for $d > 0$ and given $r, s \in S^{(d-1)}, r < s$, they compute

$$\frac{rs - 1}{s + r}.$$

The next set $S^{(d)}$ is then again formed as the union of $S^{(d-1)}$ and the set of all such values that are integers.

It is equally straightforward to verify that this algorithm is also a special case of the generalised CHM algorithm described above in Sect.3.2. We could again work with matrices in $M_{2 \times 2}(\mathbb{Q})$, but here, we are actually working in the number field $K = \mathbb{Q}[X]/\langle X^2 + 1 \rangle$, which is isomorphic to $\mathbb{Q}(i)$, where $i^2 = -1$. The product of the elements $\alpha = r - i$ and $\beta = s - i$ is given as

$$\alpha\beta = (r - i)(s - i) = (rs - 1) - (r + s)i.$$

Conrey and Holmstrom's method then simply tries all such products $\alpha\beta$. However, a possibly better choice could be to use

$$\alpha\beta^{-1}N_{K/\mathbb{Q}}(\beta) = \alpha\bar{\beta} = (r - i)(s + i) = (rs + 1) - (s - r)i$$

as described in our generalisation. This is due to the fact that the new denominator, $s - r$, is smaller and hence

$$\frac{rs + 1}{s - r}$$

is more likely to be an integer[3] (assuming that the numerator follows a random, uniform distribution). As a result, we can expect the algorithm to converge faster.

Whichever option is chosen, one tries to divide by $r + s$ resp. $s - r$, and if the result is an element in $\mathbb{Z}[i]$, it is added to the next set $S^{(d)}$ of smooth values of $X^2 + 1$. Conrey and Holmstrom's method is therefore another special case of the generalised algorithm.

Remark 5. We note that neither the generalised CHM algorithm, nor any of the previous special cases give any guarantees to what proportion of B-smooth values of $f(X)$ it finds. However, for the previous special case algorithms, certain conjectural results have been stated, based on numerical evidence, which suggests that the algorithm returns all but a small fraction of all smooth values of the respective quadratic polynomials. We make no similar claims for the general case algorithm.

4   Searching for Large Twin Smooth Instances: CHM in Practice

Ideally, the CHM algorithm could be run as described in [8] with a large enough smoothness bound B to find twin smooths of cryptographic sizes. However, experiments suggest that this is not feasible in practice. We report on data obtained from an implementation of the pure CHM algorithm in Sect. 4.1, present several optimisations in Sect. 4.2 and details on our optimised implementation in Sect. 4.3.

4.1   Running CHM in Practice

In order to collect data and assess the feasibility of finding large enough twin smooths, we implemented a somewhat optimised version of the pure CHM algorithm. In particular, this implementation is parallelised, and avoids multiple checks of the same pairs of twin smooths (r, s). Furthermore, we iterate

---

[3] Another alternative is to include both positive and negative values in the inital set $S^{(0)}$. Observe that in this case, it does not matter whether one uses $(rs + 1)/(s - r)$ or $(rs - 1)/(s + r)$, as $(rs + 1)/(s - r) = -(s(-r) + 1)/(s + (-r)))$.

through smoothness bounds: We start with a small bound B_1 and the initial set $S_1^{(0)} = \{1, \ldots, B_1 - 1\}$, and use the CHM algorithm to iteratively compute sets $S_1^{(i)}$ until we reach some d_1 such that $S_1^{(d_1)} = S_1^{(d_1-1)}$. In the next iteration, we increase the smoothness bound to $B_2 > B_1$ and define the initial set $S_2^{(0)} = S_1^{(d_1)} \cup \{B_1, \ldots, B_2 - 1\}$. Again we compute CHM iterations until we find d_2 such that $S_2^{(d_2)} = S_2^{(d_2-1)}$, where we avoid checking pairs (r, s) that have been processed in earlier iterations. Ideally, we could repeat this procedure until we reach a smoothness bound B_i for which the CHM algorithm produces large enough twin smooths for cryptographic purposes. However, our data suggests that this is infeasible in practice due to both runtime and memory limitations.

In particular, we ran this approach up to the smoothness bound $B = 547$, and extrapolating the results gives us rough estimations of the largest possible pair and number of twin smooths per smoothness bound.

After the $B = 547$ iteration, the set of twin smooths contains 82,026,426 pairs, whose bitlength distribution roughly resembles a normal distribution centered around bitlength 58. The largest pair has a bitlength of 122 bits. An evaluation of the obtained set is shown in Fig. 1. Figure 1a shows the distribution of bitsizes in the full set, while Fig. 1b shows that of the subset of all 199-smooth twins obtained in this run. Figure 1c shows the bitsize of the largest q-smooth twin pairs for each prime q between 3 and 547. And Figs. 1d and 1e show the number of q-smooth twins for each such q.

Using the data of these experiments, we can attempt to estimate at which smoothness bound B this approach can be expected to reach twin smooths of cryptographic sizes, and how much memory is required to run iterations to reach this B. The data indicates that the bound necessary for the largest twin smooth pair obtained by running CHM with this bound to reach a bitlength of 256 lies in the thousands, possibly larger than 5,000. Similarly, it shows how quickly the number of B-smooth twins increases with B. Given that the effort for CHM iterations grows quadratically with the set size, these estimates indicate that it is not feasible to reach cryptographically sized smooth twins with the original CHM algorithm.

4.2   Optimisations

One major issue with running the plain CHM algorithm for increasing smoothness bound is the sheer size of data that needs to be dealt with. The sets $S_i^{(d_i)}$ grow very rapidly and the quadratic complexity of checking all possible pairs (r, s) leads to a large runtime. The natural question that arises is whether CHM can be restricted to checking only a certain subset of such pairs without losing any or too many of the new smooth neighbors. Furthermore, if the purpose of running the CHM algorithm is not to enumerate all twin smooth pairs for a given smoothness bound but instead, to produce a certain number of pairs of a given size or to obtain some of the largest pairs, it might even be permissible to omit a fraction of pairs.

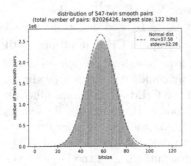 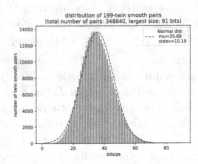

(a) Distribution of bitsizes for the full set of 547-twin smooth pairs.

(b) Distribution of bitsizes for the subset of 199-twin smooth pairs.

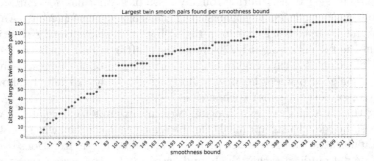

(c) Bitsizes of the largest q-smooth twins for all primes q between 3 and 547.

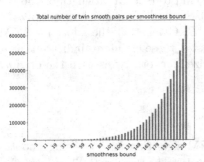 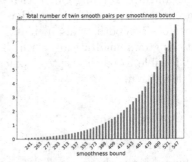

(d) Number of q-smooth twins for all primes q between 3 and 233.

(e) Number of q-smooth twins for all primes q between 239 and 547.

Fig. 1. Evaluation of the set of 547-smooth twins obtained by running the original CHM algorithm with smoothness bound $B = 547$. The bitsize of a pair $(r, r+1)$ is $\lfloor \log r \rfloor + 1$. Data for the number of q-smooth twins for all primes q up to 547 has been split into two histograms of different scale.

To find a sensible way to restrict to a smaller set, we next discuss which pairs (r, s), $r < s$ result in a given twin smooth pair $(t, t+1)$ via

$$\frac{r}{r+1} \cdot \frac{s+1}{s} = \frac{t}{t+1}. \tag{4}$$

This is discussed in [8, §3], but we elaborate on it in a slightly different way here. Let $t > 0$, let u be any divisor of t and v any divisor of $t+1$. Let $h, x \in \mathbb{Z}$ be given by $t = uh$ and $t+1 = vx$ (where $u, v, h, x > 0$). Therefore, $v/u = h/x + 1/(ux)$. If $u < v$ then $h > x$ and if $u > v$ then $h < x$. We therefore fix $u < v$ (otherwise switch the roles of u, v and h, x). Since $u < v$, the pair

$$(r, s) = (t - \frac{u}{v}(t+1), \; \frac{v}{u}t - (t+1) = \frac{v}{u}r) \tag{5}$$

satisfies Equation (4) and it follows that

$$r = u(h - x), \; r + 1 = x(v - u), \; s = v(h - x), \; s + 1 = h(v - u). \tag{6}$$

Therefore, $s/r = v/u$ and $(s+1)/(r+1) = h/x$, $u < v$, $h > x$ and $0 < r < s$. This also means that $s = r+(v-u)(h-x)$, $t = r+ux$ and that $\gcd(r(s+1), s(r+1)) = s - r = (v - u)(h - x)$ (note that $\gcd(uh, vx) = \gcd(t, t+1) = 1$).

Conversely, given (r, s) with $r > 0$ that satisfy Eq. 4, define $u = r/\gcd(r, s)$ and $v = s/\gcd(r, s)$, then $s > r$, $u < v$ and $u \mid t$, $v \mid (t+1)$. Hence we have the correspondence between the set of pairs (r, s) with $r < s$ that yield a new twin pair $(t, t+1)$ via Eq. (4) and the set of pairs of divisors of t and $t+1$ described in [8, §3] as follows:

$$\{(r, s) \mid r < s \text{ and } r(s + 1)(t + 1) = s(r + 1)t\}$$
$$\longleftrightarrow \{(u, v) \mid u < v \text{ and } u \mid t, \; v \mid (t + 1)\}. \tag{7}$$

However, this correspondence does not identify the pairs (r, s) corresponding to twin smooths, i.e. given (u, v) there is no guarantee that any of $r, r + 1, s, s + 1$ are B-smooth. This is not discussed in [8, §3]. The next lemma fills this gap by stating an explicit condition on the divisors u, v, h, x.

Lemma 1. *Let $t \in \mathbb{Z}$ such that $t(t + 1)$ is B-smooth. Let (u, v) be a pair of divisors such that $t = uh$, $t + 1 = vx$ and let (r, s) be defined as in Eq. (5).*
Then $r(r + 1)s(s + 1)$ is B-smooth if and only if $(v - u)(h - x) = s - r$ is B-smooth.

Proof. As divisors of t and $t + 1$, u and v as well as h and x are all B-smooth. The statement follows from the Eqs. (6). □

Using Similar Sized Pairs. We next consider the following condition to restrict the visited pairs (r, s) in CHM as a mechanism to reduce the set size and runtime. Let $k > 1$ be a constant parameter. We then only check pairs (r, s) if they satisfy

$$0 < r < s < kr. \tag{8}$$

Assume that (r, s) results in a pair $(t, t + 1)$ through satisfying Eq. (4). As seen above, $\frac{s}{r} = \frac{v}{u}$ for $u \mid t$, $v \mid (t+1)$, so we can use (u, v) to determine which values k are useful. Since $\frac{v}{u} < k$, it follows $s = \frac{v}{u} t - (t + 1) < (k - 1)t$. If we are only interested in obtaining a new t from a pair (r, s) such that $s < t$, we can take $k \leq 2$, overall resulting in $1 < k \leq 2$.

This k seems to be a good quantity to study as we can relate it to the factors of $v - u$. Indeed, $v - u = u(\frac{v}{u} - 1) = u(\frac{s}{r} - 1)$ and we have $s < kr$.

Definition 2. *Let $(r, r+1)$ and $(s, s+1)$ be twin smooths with $r < s$ and $k \in \mathbb{R}$ with $1 < k \leq 2$. We call the pair (r, s) k-balanced if $r < s < k \cdot r$.*

We want to find a k such that a k-balanced pair (u, v) subject to the above conditions will yield a balanced r, s such that $r, r + 1, s, s + 1$ are B-smooth, or equivalently that $v - u$ and $h - x$ are.

Running the CHM algorithm only with 2-balanced pairs (r, s) then guarantees that any t produced by Eq. 4 will be larger than the inputs r and s. Although we sacrifice completeness of the set of twin B-smooths with this approach, we can significantly reduce the runtime.

We can even push this approach further. Recall that we require $\gcd(r(s + 1), (r + 1)s) = s - r$ in order to generate a new pair of twin smooths $(t, t + 1)$. By Lemma 1, this can only hold if $\Delta = s - r$ is B-smooth. Hence, only checking pairs (r, s) for which Δ is likely to be smooth increases the probability for a successful CHM step. Heuristically, the smaller Δ is, the better the chances for Δ to be smooth. Furthermore, if Δ contains small and only few prime factors, the probability for the condition $\Delta = \gcd(r(s + 1), (r + 1)s)$ is relatively high. We can summarise this in the following heuristic.

Heuristic 1. *Let $k_1, k_2 \in \mathbb{R}$ with $1 < k_1 < k_2 \leq 2$, and (r_1, s_1) resp. (r_2, s_2) a k_1- resp. k_2-balanced pair of twin smooths. Then the probability for (r_1, s_1) to generate new twin smooths via the CHM equation is larger than that for (r_2, s_2).*

In order to save additional runtime, we can thus pick k closer to 1, and only check the pairs (r, s) that are most likely to generate new twin smooths. Therefore, we can still expect to find a significant portion of all twin B-smooths for a given smoothness bound B. We expand on the choice of k and different ways of implementing this approach in Sect. 4.3.

Thinning Out Between Iterations. Another approach to reduce both runtime and memory requirement is to thin out the set of twin smooths between iterations. In particular, once we finished all CHM steps for a certain smoothness bound B_i, we can remove twins from the set $S_i^{(d_i)}$ based on their likeliness to produce new twin smooths before moving to the next iteration for B_{i+1}.

One possible condition for removing twins is to look at their smoothness bounds. Let $(r, r+1)$ be B_1-smooth, $(s, s+1)$ be B_2-smooth (but not B-smooth for any $B < B_2$), and $B_1 \ll B_2$. Since $(s, s + 1)$ contains (multiple) prime factors larger than B_1, they cannot be contained in $(r, r + 1)$, which makes the requirement $\gcd(r(s+1),(r+1)s) = s-r$ heuristically less likely to be satisfied. However, in practice it turns out that the differences between the smoothness bounds we are concerned with are not large enough for this heuristic to become effective.

In our experiments, it turned out to be more successful to keep track of how many new twin smooths each r produces. We can then fix some bound m, and discard twins that produced less then m twins after a certain number of iterations. Our experiments suggest that using this approach with carefully chosen parameters yields a noticeable speedup, but fails completely at reducing the memory requirements, as we still need to keep track of the twins we already found. Furthermore, in practice the approach of only using k-balanced twins turned out to be superior, and hence we focus on this optimisation in the following.

4.3 Implementation

We implemented the CHM algorithm with several of the aforementioned optimisations in C++, exploiting the fact that it parallelises perfectly. Note that some of our approaches require the set of twin smooths to be sorted with respect to their size. Hence, an ordered data structure is used for storing the twins set. We used the following techniques and optimisations.

CHM Step. For each pair (r, s) considered by the implementation, we have to check if Eq. (4) holds. As mentioned in Sect. 4.2, this requires that $\gcd(r(s + 1), (r + 1)s) = s - r$ is satisfied. However, we can completely avoid the gcd calculation by observing that we require $r \cdot (s+1) \equiv 0 \mod (s-r)$. Only if this is the case we perform a division to compute t, which represents the new pair of twin smooths $(t, t + 1)$. Therefore, we only perform one modular reduction per considered pair (r, s), followed by one division if the CHM step is successful. This is significantly cheaper than a naïve implementation of Equation (4) or a gcd computation.

Data Structure. Initially the set of twins was organised in a standard C array, that each time an iteration completed was reallocated to increase its size, and reordered.

To avoid the overall inefficiency of this method we moved to use the C++ standard library std::set. This data structure is implemented with a Red Black tree, guarantees $O(\log N)$ insertion and search, while keeping the elements always ordered.

We then moved to use B+Trees [5], that have the same guarantees for insertion, search, and ordering, but are more efficient in the memory usage. Because the elements of a B+Tree are stored close to each other in memory it becomes much faster to iterate through the set, an operation that is necessary for creating the pairs used in each computation.

Implemented Optimisations. As discussed in Sect. 4.2, we focus on the case of k-balanced pairs (r, s), which satisfy $r < s < k \cdot r$. Compared to the full CHM algorithm, this leads to a smaller set of twin smooths, but allows for much faster running times. We implemented the k-balanced approach in various different flavours.

Global-k. In the simplest version - the `global-k` approach - we initially pick some k with $1 < k \leq 2$, and restrict the CHM algorithm to only check k-balanced pairs (r, s). The choice of k is a subtle manner: Picking k too close to 1 may lead to too many missed twin smooths, such that we cannot produce any meaningful results. On the other hand, picking k close to 2 may result in a relatively small speedup, which does not allow for running CHM for large enough smoothness bounds B. Unfortunately, there seems to be no theoretical handle on the optimal choice of k, which means that it has to be determined experimentally. We note that when picking an aggressive bound factor $k \approx 1$, small numbers r in the set of twins S may not have any suitable $s \in S$ they can be checked with. Thus, we pick a different bound, e.g. $k = 2$, for numbers below a certain bound, e.g. for $r \leq 2^{20}$.

Iterative-k. Instead of iterating through smoothness bounds B_i as described in Sect. 4.1 and using the `global-k` approach, we can switch the roles of B and k if we are interested in running CHM for a fixed smoothness bound B. We define some initial value k_0, a target value $k_{\max}$, and a step size $k_{\text{step}} > 0$. In the first iteration, we run CHM as in the `global-k` approach, using k_0. The next iteration then increases to $k_1 = k_0 + k_{\text{step}}$, and we add the condition to not check pairs (r, s) if they were already checked in previous iterations. We repeat this iteration step several times until we reach $k_{\max}$. Compared to the `global-k` approach, this allows us to generate larger B-smooth twins faster, since we restrict to the pairs (r, s) first that are most likely to generate new twins. However, the additional checks if previous pairs have been processed in earlier iterations add a significant runtime overhead. Thus, this method is more suitable for finding well-suited choices of k, while actual CHM searches benefit from switching to the `global-k` approach.

Constant-Range. In both the `global-k` and `iterative-k` approach, the checks if a pair (r, s) is k-balanced, or has been processed in earlier iterations, consumes a significant part of the overall runtime. Therefore, we can use constant ranges to completely avoid these checks. Since we always keep the set of twins S sorted by size, the numbers s closest to r (with $s > r$) are its neighbors in S. Thus, we can sacrifice the exactness of the k-balanced approaches above, and instead fix a range R and for each r check (r, s) with the R successors s of r in S. As shown below, this method significantly outperforms the `global-k` approach due to the elimination of all checks for k-balance. This is true even when R is large enough to check more pairs than are considered in the `global-k` approach for a given k.

Table 1. Performance results for different variants of our CHM implementation for smoothness bound $B = 300$. Speedup factors refer to the full CHM variant.

Variant	Parameter	Runtime	Speedup	#twins	#twins from largest 100
Full CHM	-	4705 s	1	2300724	100
global-k	$k = 2.0$	364 s	13	2289000	86
	$k = 1.5$	226 s	21	2282741	82
	$k = 1.05$	27 s	174	2206656	65
constant-range	$R = 10000$	82 s	57	2273197	93
	$R = 5000$	35 s	134	2247121	87
	$R = 1000$	16 s	294	2074530	75

Variable-Range. Similar to the `constant-range` approach, we can adapt the range R depending on the size of r. For instance, choosing r at the peak of the size distribution will lead to many possible choices of s such that (r, s) are balanced. Hence, we can choose a larger range R whenever more potential pairs exist, while decreasing R otherwise. In practice, the performance of this method ranks between `global-`k and `constant-range` by creating roughly the same pairs that `global-`k creates without any of the overhead of the balance checks. If R is chosen large enough such that the `constant-range` approach ends up generating more pairs than `global-`k, then `variable-range` performs better. Realistically, the size of the range R increases by (very) roughly 3% for each prime number smaller than the smoothness bound B, and slows down the algorithm drastically at higher smoothness, similarly to the k-based approaches.

Remark 6. Similar to the `variable-range` approach, we experimented with a variant of the `global-`k approach, which adjusts k according to the size of r to find suitable s for the CHM step. However, the `constant-range` and `variable-range` approaches turned out to be superior in terms of performance, and therefore we discarded this `variable-`k variant.

Performance Comparison. In order to compare the implications of the optimisations in practice, we ran different variants of the CHM implementation for the fixed smoothness bound $B = 300$. All experiments ran on a machine configured with 4 x Xeon E7-4870v2 15C 2.3 GHz, 3072 GB of RAM. The total amount of parallel threads available was 120. As described above, the `global-`k and `constant-range` approach significantly outperform their respective variants, hence we focus on different configurations of these two methods.

The results are summarised in Table 1. For both the `global-`k and the `constant-range` approach we measured the results for conservative and more aggressive instantiations, where smaller values of k and R are considered more aggressive. It is evident that already for the conservative instantiations, we gain significant performance speedup, while still finding almost the full set of twin smooths, and most of the 100 largest 300-smooth twins. For the more aggressive instantiations, we miss more twins, yet still find a significant amount of large twins.

As discussed above, the `constant-range` approach outperforms the `global-k` approach in terms of runtime, due to the elimination of all checks for k-balance of twins. Interestingly, while very aggressive instantiations of `constant-range` miss more twin smooths, they find a larger share of the largest 100 twins than their `global-k` counterpart. Therefore, we conclude that for larger smoothness bounds B, for which we cannot hope to complete the full CHM algorithm, `constant-range` is the most promising approach for obtaining larger twin smooths within feasible runtimes.

Remark 7. While all optimisations lose a small proportion of the largest twin smooths, they are not necessarily lost permanently. In practice, when iterating to larger smoothness bounds B_i, we often also find some B_j-smooth twins for bounds $B_j < B_i$. Thus, the size of the set of 300-smooth twins usually increases in the optimised variants when moving to larger B.

Remark 8. In the following sections, we will require twin smooths of a certain (relatively small) bitlength. This can easily be incorporated into all implemented variants by removing all twins above this bound after each iteration. This means that we cut off the algorithm at this size, and do not attempt to obtain larger twins, which significantly improves the runtime and memory requirements.

5   Fantastic p's and Where to Find Them: Cryptographic Primes of the Form $p = 2r^n - 1$

This section focuses on finding primes suitable for isogeny-based cryptographic applications. As discussed in the previous sections, the pure CHM method does not allow for us to directly compute twins of at least 256 bits as required for this aim. However, some cryptographic applications, for example the isogeny-based signature scheme SQISign, do not need twins $(r, r + 1)$ that are fully smooth. Indeed, the current incarnation of SQISign requires a prime p that satisfies $2^f T \mid p^2 - 1$, where f is as large as possible, and $T \approx p^{5/4}$ is smooth and odd [17]. This flexibility allows us to move away from solely using CHM and, instead, to use CHM results as inputs to known methods for finding such primes. At a high level, we will find fully smooth twins of a smaller bit-size via CHM and boost them up using the polynomials $p_n(x) = 2x^n - 1$ (for carefully chosen n). Hence, if $r, r + 1$ are fully smooth integers and n is not too large, we can guarantee a large proportion of $p_n(r)^2 - 1$ to be smooth.

Notation. For a variable x, we will denote $2x^n - 1$ by $p_n(x)$, and the evaluated polynomial $p_n(r)$ by p, emphasising that it is an integer.

General Method. In this section, we will give a more in-depth description of the approach to obtaining cryptographic sized primes p, such that $p^2 - 1$ has

Table 2. Factorisation of $p_n(x)^2 - 1$ for $n = 2, 3, 4, 5, 6$, where $p_n(x) = 2x^n - 1$

n	$p_n(x)^2 - 1$
2	$4x^2(x-1)(x+1)$
3	$4x^3(x-1)(x^2+x+1)$
4	$4x^4(x-1)(x+1)(x^2+1)$
5	$4x^5(x-1)(x^4+x^3+x^2+x+1)$
6	$4x^6(x-1)(x+1)(x^2-x+1)(x^2+x+1)$

$\log T'$ bits of B-smoothness, where $T' = 2^f T$. We recall that for our SQISign application, we have $\log p \in \{256, 384, 512\}$ for NIST Level I, III and V (respectively), $T \approx p^{5/4}$ and f as large as possible. In the current implementation of SQISign, $f \approx \lfloor \log(p^{1/4}) \rfloor$ (i.e., $T' \approx p^{3/2}$), and therefore, we aim for this when finding primes.

Fix a smoothness bound B and let $p_n(x) = 2x^n - 1$. We have $p_n(x)^2 - 1 = 4x^n(x-1)f(x)$ for some polynomial $f(x)$, as shown in Table 2.

We observe that for n even, both $x+1$ and $x-1$ appear in the factorisation of $p_n(x)^2 - 1$. In this case, for twin smooths $(r, r \pm 1)$, evaluating $p_n(x)$ at r guarantees that we have a smooth factor $4x^n(x \pm 1)$ in $p^2 - 1$. For n odd, we will only have that $x - 1$ appears in the factorisation, and therefore only consider twins $(r, r-1)$ to guarantee we have B-smooth factor $4x^n(x-1)$.

The first step is to use our implementation of the CHM algorithm, described in Sects. 3 and 4, to obtain B-smooth twins $(r, r \pm 1)$ of bitsize approximately $(\log p - 1)/n$. We then obtain primes of suitable sizes via computing $p = p_n(r)$ for all candidate r, as described above. By construction, $p^2 - 1$ has guaranteed $\frac{n+1}{n}(\log(p) - 1) + 2$ bits of smoothness. We then require that the remaining factors have at least

$$\max\left(0, \frac{3}{2}\log p - \left(\frac{n+1}{n}(\log p - 1) + 2\right)\right)$$

bits of B-smoothness. In Sect. 5.2, we will discuss the probability obtaining this smoothness from the remaining factors.

5.1   Choosing n

For small n, we require CHM to find twin smooths of *large* bit size. For certain bit sizes, running full CHM may be computationally out of reach, and therefore we use a variant that may not find all twins. In this case, however, we have more guaranteed smoothness in $p^2 - 1$ and so it is more likely that the remaining factors will have the required smoothness. For large n, we can obtain more twin smooths from CHM (in some cases, we can even exhaustively search for all twin smooths), however we have less guaranteed smoothness in $p^2 - 1$. Finding values of n that balance these two factors will be the focus of this section.

$n = 2$. Let $(r, r \pm 1)$ be twin smooth integers and let $p = 2r^2 - 1$. In this case, $2r^2(r \pm 1) \mid T'$, meaning that $\log T' \geq \frac{3}{2} \log p$, and we have all the required smoothness. Write $T' = 2^f T = 2r^2(r \pm 1)$ where T is odd. If $f < \lfloor \log(p^{1/4}) \rfloor$, we have $T > p^{5/4}$, and we do not have to rely on a large power of 2 dividing $r - 1$. Otherwise, we turn to Sect. 5.2 to estimate the probability of $r \mp 1$ having enough small factors to make up for this difference.

Suppose we target primes with λ bits of classical security, i.e., we need a prime of order $p \approx 2^{2\lambda}$. For $n = 2$, this corresponds to finding twin smooths of size $\approx 2^{\lambda - \frac{1}{2}}$, and so is only suitable for finding NIST Level I parameters due to the limitations of the CHM method (see Sect. 4). One could instead use other techniques for finding large enough twins for $n = 2$, such as the PTE sieve [10], at the cost of significantly larger smoothness bounds. Alternatively, we can move to higher n, which comes at the cost of loosing guaranteed smoothness. Another challenge here is that, given the relatively large size of the twins, it appears difficult to find enough twins for obtaining primes with a large power of two.

$n = 3$. Let $(r, r - 1)$ be twin smooth integers and let $p = 2r^3 - 1$. Here, we can guarantee that the smooth factor T' of $p^2 - 1$ is at least of size $\approx p^{4/3}$. If $f < \lfloor \log_2(p^{1/12}) \rfloor$, we have $T > p^{5/4}$. Otherwise, we require that there are enough smooth factors in $r^2 + r + 1$ to reach this requirement.

Here, for λ bits of classical security, we need to target twin smooth integers of size $\approx 2^{\frac{2\lambda - 1}{3}}$. In this case, the CHM method will (heuristically) allow us to reach both NIST Level I and III parameters.

$n = 4$. Let $(r, r \pm 1)$ be twin smooth integers and $p = 2r^4 - 1$. Here we can only guarantee a factor of size $\approx p^{5/4}$ of $p^2 - 1$ to be smooth. When accounting for the power of two, we must hope for other smooth factors. As $p_n(x) - 1$ splits into (relatively) small degree factors, namely $p_n(x) - 1 = 2(x-1)(x+1)(x^2+1)$, the probability of having enough B-smooth factors is greater (than if there was, for example, a cubic factor).

In contrast to the previous cases, this setting should be suitable for targeting all necessary security parameters. However, for the NIST Level I setting, the work by De Feo, Leroux and Wesolowski [17][§5.2] showed that the best one could hope for here while maximising the power of two gives SQISign parameters with a smoothness bound of ≈ 1800. While this is a better smoothness bound than the NIST Level I prime with the best performance for SQISign, it does not perform as well in practice. Indeed, most of the odd primes less than 1800 that appear in $p^2 - 1$ are relatively large, making isogeny computation relatively slow. In the best performing prime, however, a large power of 3 divides $p^2 - 1$, and most of its other odd prime divisors are fairly small. We note that the authors of [17] only searched for parameters that maximise the power of two, and hence there could be some scope to find parameters that have slightly smaller powers of two.

Other n. For larger n, the amount of guaranteed smoothness decreases, and thus the probability that the remaining factors have the required smoothness is small. Indeed, we find that only $n = 6$ has the correct balance of requiring small twin smooths while still having a reasonable probability of success. This is primarily due to the factorisation of $p_6(x) - 1 = 2(x - 1)(x + 1)(x^2 - x + 1)(x^2 + x + 1)$, having factors of degree at most 2, which improves the probability that we have enough smooth factors. In contrast, $n = 5$ results in more guaranteed smoothness than $n = 6$, but requires the quartic factor in $p_5(x) - 1$ to provide the necessary smoothness, which is relatively unlikely.

While one could use $n = 6$ to find NIST Level I parameters, this larger n shines in its ability to give us both NIST Level III and V parameters.

5.2   Probability of Sufficient Smoothness

In this section, we determine the probability of obtaining cryptographic primes with sufficient smoothness using the methods outlined above. We follow Banks and Shparlinski [1] to determine the probability of $p^2 - 1$ being sufficiently smooth for some prime p. More precisely, given that the factor $r(r \pm 1) \mid p^2 - 1$ is already fully smooth, we want to calculate the probability of $p^2 - 1$ having $\log T'$-bits of B-smoothness.

First, we find the probability that the factor $r(r \pm 1) \mid p^2 - 1$ is fully smooth, i.e., the probability of finding fully B-smooth twins $(r, r \pm 1)$. To do so, we use the following counting function:

$$\Psi(X, B) = \#\{N \leq X : N \text{ is } B\text{-smooth}\}.$$

For a large range of X and B, it is known that

$$\Psi(X, B) \sim \rho(u)X,$$

where $u = (\log X)/(\log B)$ and ρ is the Dickman function [12,14]. The Dickman function is implemented in most computational algebra packages, including SageMath, which allows us to evaluate $\Psi(X, B)$ for various X and B. In practice, we find B-smooth twins $(r, r \pm 1)$ using our implementation of the CHM algorithm as described in 4.

Next, we calculate the probability of $p^2 - 1$ having $\log T'$-bits of B-smoothness. As $p^2 - 1$ may only be partially smooth, we will use the following counting function

$$\Theta(X, B, D) = \#\{N \leq X : D < \text{ largest } B\text{-smooth divisor of } N\}.$$

The value $\Theta(X, B, D)$ will give the number of positive integers $N \leq X$ for which there exists a divisor $d \mid N$ with $d > D$ and such that d is B-smooth. This function has been previously studied in the literature, for example [25,26]. For X, B, D varying over a wide domain, Banks and Shparlinski [1, Theorem 1] derive the first two terms of the asymptotic expansion of $\Theta(X, B, D)$. By implementing this expansion, we are able to estimate the value of Θ at various X, B, D in the correct range.

As discussed in the section above, we restrict to $n = 2, 3, 4, 6$. Recall that $p_n(x)^2 - 1 = 4x^n(x - 1)f(x)$, as given in Table 2 for each $2 \leq n \leq 6$. Write $f(x) = f_1(x) \cdots f_k(x)$, where each f_i is irreducible of degree $d_i = \deg(f_i)$ and $d = \deg(f)$. To calculate the probabilities, we require that the probability of $f(x)$ having at least $\log_2 D$-bits of B-smoothness is the product of the probabilities of each of its factors f_i having at least $\log_2 D_i$-bits of B-smoothness where $\log_2 D = \sum_{i=1}^{k} \log_2 D_i$. We can view this as an extension of [10, Heuristic 1]. Note that the only constraint on how the smoothness is distributed between the factors $f_i(x)$ is that the total bit size of B-smooth factors must equal $\log_2 D$. We could, for example, sum over all the possible distributions of smoothness using the inclusion-exclusion principle. However, in distributions where one of the factors has a very small amount of smoothness, we fall out of the ranges allowed as input into Θ determined by [1, Theorem 1]. Therefore, for simplicity, we will assume that smoothness is distributed evenly between the remaining factors (weighted by the degree), i.e., $\log_2 D_i = (d_i \log_2 D)/d$. In reality, this only gives us a lower bound for the probability, but this will suffice for our purposes. Obtaining a more theoretical and accurate grasp on these probabilities is left as an avenue for future research.

In Table 3, we give an overview of the relevant probabilities for NIST Level I, III, and V parameters, calculated as described above. Our code for computing these probabilities is available in the code package attached to this submission. We observe that as n gets larger, the probability of finding B-smooth integers of the appropriate bitsize increases. In contrast, for bigger n we are guaranteed less smoothness in $p^2 - 1$. As a result, given B-smooth twins, the probability of finding a SQISign prime p decreases as n increases. For each NIST level, we predict that the n that balance these two contrasting probabilities have a higher chance of finding a p satisfying our requirements. As discussed in the next section, this trend is reflected in practice.

6 Results and Comparisons

In this section we give the concrete results that were obtained from our experiments with the CHM algorithm, and analyse the various twins in relation to SQISign in accordance with the relevant bitsizes mentioned in Table 3.

6.1 Record Twin Smooth Computations

We ran the optimised full CHM algorithm with $B = 547$ and found a total of 82,026,426 pairs of B-smooth twins. Among these pairs, we found 2,649 additional 200-smooth twins that were not found by the original authors of the algorithm [8]. This showcases the validity of Remark 5 that the algorithm does not guarantee us to find all B-smooth twins. Furthermore, there is no guarantee

Table 3. Assuming that $(r, r \pm 1)$ are twin smooth integers and p has $\log p$ bits, calculates the probability of having a B-smooth divisor $T' \mid p^2 - 1$ of size $\approx p^{3/2}$. More details in text.

	n	$\log_2(r)$	Probability of B-smooth $(r, r \pm 1)$	Probability of $p^2 - 1$ $\log T'$-bits B-smooth given $(r, r \pm 1)$ twin smooth	Extra Smoothness Needed
NIST-I $B = 2^9$ $\log p = 256$ $\log T' = 384$	2	≈ 127.5	$2^{-58.5}$	1	0
	3	≈ 85.0	$2^{-32.1}$	$2^{-8.4}$	42
	4	≈ 63.8	$2^{-20.5}$	$\approx 2^{-12.7}$	63.3
	6	≈ 42.5	$2^{-10.4}$	$\approx 2^{-16.8}$	84.5
NIST-III $B = 2^{14}$ $\log p = 384$ $\log T' = 576$	2	≈ 191.5	$2^{-55.7}$	1	0
	3	≈ 127.7	$2^{-30.5}$	$2^{-8.2}$	63.3
	4	≈ 95.8	$2^{-19.4}$	$\approx 2^{-12.4}$	95.3
	6	≈ 63.8	$2^{-9.7}$	$\approx 2^{-16.2}$	127.2
NIST-V $B = 2^{17}$ $\log p = 512$ $\log T' = 768$	2	≈ 255.5	$2^{-63.7}$	1	0
	3	≈ 170.3	$2^{-35.2}$	$2^{-9.6}$	84.7
	4	≈ 127.8	$2^{-22.6}$	$\approx 2^{-14.5}$	127.3
	6	≈ 85.2	$2^{-11.5}$	$\approx 2^{-19.2}$	169.8

that running CHM with $B = 547$ will produce all 200-smooth twins. As mentioned in the introduction, the only way to see how far away we are from the exact number of 200-smooth twins is to solve all 2^{46} Pell equations.

For the application mentioned in the previous section, we only need twins of a certain bitsize. Within this set of twins, 9,218,648 pairs $(r, r + 1)$ fall in the range $2^{60} < r < 2^{64}$; 1,064,249 pairs fall in the range $2^{81} < r < 2^{85}$; 31,994 pairs fall in the range $2^{92} < r < 2^{96}$; and, only 1 pair falls in the range $2^{120} < r < 2^{128}$. This pair in the final interval is the largest pair found in this run, with $r = 401203124184886652642416579604774\,9375$, and factorisations:

$$r = 5^4 \cdot 7 \cdot 13^2 \cdot 17^2 \cdot 19 \cdot 29 \cdot 41 \cdot 109 \cdot 163 \cdot 173 \cdot 239 \cdot 241^2 \cdot 271 \cdot 283$$
$$\cdot 499 \cdot 509, \text{ and}$$

$$r + 1 = 2^8 \cdot 3^2 \cdot 31^2 \cdot 43^2 \cdot 47^2 \cdot 83^2 \cdot 103^2 \cdot 311^2 \cdot 479^2 \cdot 523^2.$$

As we will see later, the number of 64-bit and 85-bit twins we found in this run is enough to find attractive parameters for SQISign. The 96-bit twins will give us parameters with the required smoothness, however we do not have enough pairs to hope to find a prime p where $p^2 - 1$ is divisible by a large power of two.

Table 3 shows that finding many twins of around 128 bits in size is likely to be fruitful in the search for SQISign-friendly parameters, so we ran the algorithm for $B = 1300$ using the `constant-range` optimisation with a range $R = 5000$, in order to specifically target twins $(r, r+1)$ with $r > 2^{115}$. In this run we found 1,091 such pairs - the largest of these pairs is the following 145-bit twin $(r, r+1)$ with $r = 36132012096025817587153962195378848686084640$, where

$$r = 2^5 \cdot 5 \cdot 7 \cdot 11^2 \cdot 13 \cdot 23 \cdot 53 \cdot 71 \cdot 109 \cdot 127 \cdot 131 \cdot 193 \cdot 251 \cdot 283 \cdot 307$$
$$\cdot 359 \cdot 367 \cdot 461 \cdot 613 \cdot 653 \cdot 1277, \text{ and}$$
$$r+1 = 3^2 \cdot 29^2 \cdot 31^2 \cdot 43^2 \cdot 59^2 \cdot 61^2 \cdot 73^2 \cdot 79^2 \cdot 89^2 \cdot 167^2 \cdot 401^2 \cdot 419^2.$$

Among the 1,091 twins CHM found, 184 pairs fall in the range $2^{120} < r < 2^{128}$, which was sufficient to find some SQISign-friendly parameters (though not at all NIST security levels).

In addition, we also ran CHM with $B = 2^{11}$ to obtain a large number of twin smooth integers in the range $2^{55} < r < 2^{100}$ (see Remark 8 in the setting where we want to find twins in such an interval). This run was performed using the `constant-range` optimisation with a range $R = 2500$, and produced 608,233,761 pairs of twins lying in this range. Compared with the $B = 547$ run, the yield from this run gave ample twins with $2^{92} < r < 2^{96}$, which was sufficient to find SQISign parameters with the desirable large power of two.

All of these searches were done using the machine specified in Sect. 4.3 - each search took between 1 and 2 days to run.

6.2 Concrete Parameters for SQISign

We now turn to giving a list of SQISign-friendly primes that target NIST Level I, III, and V. Recall from Sect. 1 that this means that we need to find primes p with $2^f \cdot T \mid p^2 - 1$. We need the exponent f to be as large as possible and the cofactor $T \approx p^{5/4}$ to be B-smooth, aiming to keep the ratio $\sqrt{B}/f$ as small as possible; this quantity is a rough cost metric for the performance of the signing algorithm in SQISign [17, §5.1]. To complement this, the exponent f controls the performance of the verification of SQISign; the larger this exponent is the faster the verification is. We may run into circumstances where the signing cost metric is minimised, but the power of two is not large enough or vice-versa. We aim to balance these as much as possible, thus finding parameters that maximise the power of two while minimising the signing cost metric. We refer to Sect. 6.3 for more details on the practicability of our parameters.

Though we need $T \approx p^{5/4}$, if this cofactor is too close to $p^{5/4}$, then the underlying heuristics within the generalised KLPT algorithm might fail and one cannot guarantee a successful signature in SQISign [17, §3.2]. Thus, in practice we need $T \approx p^{5/4+\epsilon}$ for some small ϵ (e.g., $0.02 < \epsilon < 0.1$).

We find parameters for NIST Level I, III and V by searching for 256, 384 and 512-bit primes, respectively. For those primes targeting the higher security levels, these are the first credible SQISign-friendly primes. In what follows, we look at each security level and analyse the most noteworthy primes found in our searches. When stating the factorisations of $p \pm 1$ for the mentioned primes, the underlined factors are the smooth factors of T, while factors in violet are the rough factors which are not needed for SQISign. A full collection of our best SQISign-friendly primes that were found using the CHM machinery is showcased in Table 4.

Remark 9. We note that in all of the forthcoming searches, the post-processing of the CHM twins to find the SQISign-friendly parameters can be made reasonably efficient with straightforward techniques. In particular, the runtime is negligible in comparison to running the CHM searches mentioned in Sect. 6.1 and can be done using naive trial division.

NIST I Parameters. We targeted 256-bit primes using $n = 2, 3$ and 4. Given that our CHM runs produced a lot more twins of smaller bit-size compared to the 128-bit level, we expect to find more primes using $n = 3, 4$, which was indeed the case. It is worth noting that some primes found with $n = 2$ gave rise to $p^2 - 1$ being divisible by a relatively large power of two. However, in these cases, most of the primes dividing $p^2 - 1$ are relatively large and would therefore give rise to slower isogeny computations during the SQISign protocol [17].

Through the experimentation with the 85-bit twins produced from CHM with $B = 547$, we found the following 254-bit prime $p = 2r^3 - 1$ with $r = 2046144912550037474885632$. All the specific criteria that we need for a SQISign parameter set are met, while obtaining an attractively small signing cost metric $\sqrt{B}/f$. For this prime, we have

$$p + 1 = 2^{46} \cdot 5^3 \cdot 13^3 \cdot 31^3 \cdot 73^3 \cdot 83^3 \cdot 103^3 \cdot 107^3 \cdot 137^3 \cdot 239^3 \cdot 271^3 \cdot 523^3, \text{ and}$$

$$p - 1 = 2 \cdot 3^3 \cdot 7 \cdot 11^2 \cdot 17^2 \cdot 19 \cdot 101 \cdot 127 \cdot 149 \cdot 157 \cdot 167 \cdot 173 \cdot 199 \cdot 229 \cdot 337$$
$$\cdot 457 \cdot 479 \cdot 141067 \cdot 3428098456843 \cdot 484047594531861479165862.$$

While the associated cofactor T here exceeds $p^{5/4}$, it does not exceed it by much. As we mentioned earlier, it might therefore be prone to signing failures and hence might not currently be suitable for SQISign. The next 255-bit prime of mention, $p = 2r^3 - 1$ with $r = 2660668240363446474895360$, is very similar to the previous prime, however the cofactor T exceeds $p^{5/4}$ by a larger margin, so would be less prone to these failures. In this case we have

$$p + 1 = 2^{40} \cdot 5^6 \cdot 11^3 \cdot 47^3 \cdot 67^6 \cdot 101^3 \cdot 113^3 \cdot 137^3 \cdot 277^3 \cdot 307^3 \cdot 421^3, \text{ and}$$

$$p - 1 = 2 \cdot 3^2 \cdot 19^3 \cdot 37 \cdot 59 \cdot 61 \cdot 97 \cdot 181^2 \cdot 197 \cdot 223 \cdot 271 \cdot 281 \cdot 311 \cdot 397 \cdot 547$$
$$\cdot 1015234718965008560203 \cdot 3143438922304814418457.$$

We additionally ran experiments with the 64-bit twins produced from CHM with $B = 547$ and found a 253-bit prime $p = 2r^4 - 1$ with $r = 8077251317941145600$, where we have

$$p + 1 = 2^{49} \cdot 5^8 \cdot 13^4 \cdot 41^4 \cdot 71^4 \cdot 113^4 \cdot 181^4 \cdot 223^4 \cdot 457^4, \text{ and}$$

$$p - 1 = 2 \cdot 3^2 \cdot 7^5 \cdot 17 \cdot 31 \cdot 53 \cdot 61 \cdot 73 \cdot 83 \cdot 127 \cdot 149 \cdot 233 \cdot 293 \cdot 313 \cdot 347 \cdot 397$$
$$\cdot 467 \cdot 479 \cdot 991 \cdot 1667 \cdot 19813 \cdot 211229 \cdot 107155419089$$
$$\cdot 295288804621$$

Among all the primes that we found for NIST I security, this appears to be the best. It has both a larger power of two compared to the primes mentioned above found with $n = 3$ and a smaller smoothness bound, thus making the signing cost metric attractively small. Additionally, the cofactor T is large enough to be practical for SQISign without any failures. We note once again that this prime would have been out of scope for the authors of [17] to find since they constrained their search to only find primes for which the power of two is larger than the one found here.

NIST III Parameters. We targeted 384-bit primes using $n = 3, 4$ and 6. The challenge in all three of these scenarios is finding enough twins whose product is divisible by a large power of two. With the limited yield of 128-bit twins, finding such primes is not straightforward; the example with $n = 3$ in Table 4 is the only such instance that we managed to find. The picture is somewhat similar with the 96-bit twins: while we have more of them, the success probabilities in Table 3 suggest that we need a lot more twins with a large power of two in order to produce any SQISign-friendly instances. One exceptional prime that was found in this search was the following 375-bit prime, $p = 2r^4 - 1$ with $r = 1232621228336746350727292 5184$. Here we have

$$p + 1 = \underline{2^{77} \cdot 11^4 \cdot 29^4 \cdot 59^4 \cdot 67^4 \cdot 149^4 \cdot 331^4 \cdot 443^4 \cdot 593^4 \cdot 1091^4 \cdot 1319^4}, \text{ and}$$
$$p - 1 = 2 \cdot \underline{3 \cdot 5 \cdot 13 \cdot 17 \cdot 31 \cdot 37 \cdot 53 \cdot 83 \cdot 109 \cdot 131 \cdot 241 \cdot 269 \cdot 277 \cdot 283 \cdot 353 \cdot 419}$$
$$\underline{\cdot 499 \cdot 661 \cdot 877 \cdot 1877 \cdot 3709 \cdot 9613 \cdot 44017 \cdot 55967} \cdot 522673 \cdot 3881351$$
$$\cdot 4772069 \cdot 13468517 \cdot 689025829 \cdot 30011417945673766253.$$

Of the NIST Level III primes listed in Table 4, the prime that shows the most promise is the 382-bit prime $p = 2r^6 - 1$ with $r = 11896643388662145024$. Not only is the power of two particularly large but also the smoothness bound of the cofactor T is quite small, reflected in its small signing cost metric (when compared to other p where $p^2 - 1$ is divisible by a large power of 2). We have the factorisations

$$p + 1 = \underline{2^{79} \cdot 3^6 \cdot 23^{12} \cdot 107^6 \cdot 127^6 \cdot 307^6 \cdot 401^6 \cdot 547^6}, \text{ and}$$
$$p - 1 = 2 \cdot \underline{5^2 \cdot 7 \cdot 11 \cdot 17 \cdot 19 \cdot 47 \cdot 71 \cdot 79 \cdot 109 \cdot 149 \cdot 229 \cdot 269 \cdot 283 \cdot 349 \cdot 449}$$
$$\underline{\cdot 463 \cdot 1019 \cdot 1033 \cdot 1657 \cdot 2179 \cdot 2293 \cdot 4099 \cdot 5119 \cdot 10243} \cdot 381343$$
$$\cdot 19115518067 \cdot 740881808972441233 \cdot 83232143791482135163921.$$

NIST V Parameters. We targeted 512-bit primes using $n = 4$ and 6. Once again, combining our CHM runs with $n = 6$ proved to be the best option for finding SQISign parameters at this level. None of the twins found at the 128-bit level combined with $n = 4$ to produce any SQISign friendly primes. From the set of 85-bit twins found in the $B = 547$ CHM run, the 510-bit prime $p = 2r^6 - 1$

with $r = 3192974042794487000652185$ is particularly attractive. The power of two here is the largest found from this run. Here we have

$$p + 1 = 2^{91} \cdot 19^6 \cdot 61^6 \cdot 89^6 \cdot 101^6 \cdot 139^6 \cdot 179^6 \cdot 223^6 \cdot 239^6 \cdot 251^6 \cdot 281^6, \text{ and}$$

$$p - 1 = 2 \cdot \underline{3^2 \cdot 5 \cdot 7 \cdot 13 \cdot 23 \cdot 29 \cdot 31 \cdot 41 \cdot 53 \cdot 109 \cdot 149 \cdot 157 \cdot 181 \cdot 269 \cdot 317 \cdot 331}$$
$$\cdot \underline{463 \cdot 557 \cdot 727 \cdot 10639 \cdot 31123 \cdot 78583 \cdot 399739 \cdot 545371 \cdot 550657} \cdot 4291141$$
$$\cdot 32208313 \cdot 47148917 \cdot 69050951 \cdot 39618707467 \cdot 220678058317$$
$$\cdot 107810984992771213 \cdot 1779937809321608257.$$

The 85-bit twins found in the CHM run with $B = 2^{11}$ were used to try and find NIST V parameters. The largest power of two that was found in this run which is suitable for SQISign was $f = 109$. The prime with smallest signing cost metric while having a relatively large power of two is the following 508-bit prime, $p = 2r^6 - 1$ where $r = 266979739004466483680608256$. Here we have

$$p + 1 = 2^{85} \cdot 17^{12} \cdot 37^6 \cdot 59^6 \cdot 97^6 \cdot 233^6 \cdot 311^{12} \cdot 911^6 \cdot 1297^6, \text{ and}$$

$$p - 1 = 2 \cdot \underline{3^2 \cdot 5 \cdot 7 \cdot 11^2 \cdot 23^2 \cdot 29 \cdot 127 \cdot 163 \cdot 173 \cdot 191 \cdot 193 \cdot 211 \cdot 277 \cdot 347 \cdot 617}$$
$$\cdot \underline{661 \cdot 761 \cdot 1039 \cdot 4637 \cdot 5821 \cdot 15649 \cdot 19139 \cdot 143443 \cdot 150151} \cdot 3813769$$
$$\cdot 358244059 \cdot 992456937347 \cdot 35324048178196536982389750$$
$$\cdot 860102006951457440137165889140302.$$

6.3   Performance Estimates

We would ideally implement our primes using the SQISign code provided in [17] to determine how well these parameters perform in practice. However, the current implementation is specifically tailored towards the particular primes that are being used, and is limited to NIST I parameter sizes. Including our NIST I primes from Table 4 results in failures during key generation, which seem to stem from using parameters with different powers of two. Thus, implementing and benchmarking our parameters would require a major rework of the provided code, which is out of the scope of this work.

NIST I. The state-of-the-art implementation of SQISign uses a 254-bit prime that was found using the extended Euclidean algorithm (XGCD) [9,16] (see Sect. 2). With this method, it is possible to, for example, force $p \pm 1$ and $p \mp 1$ to be divisible by a large power of 2 and 3 (respectively). Indeed, with this approach, a smooth factor of size $\approx \sqrt{p}$ comes for free in both $p \pm 1$.

Concretely, the prime p_{3923} used in [17] has

$$p + 1 = 2^{65} \cdot 5^2 \cdot 7 \cdot 11 \cdot 19 \cdot 29^2 \cdot 37^2 \cdot 47 \cdot 197 \cdot 263 \cdot 281 \cdot 461 \cdot 521 \cdot 3923 \cdot 62731$$
$$\cdot \underline{96362257} \cdot 3924006112952623, \text{ and}$$

$$p - 1 = 2 \cdot \underline{3^{65} \cdot 13 \cdot 17 \cdot 43 \cdot 79 \cdot 157 \cdot 239 \cdot 271 \cdot 283 \cdot 307 \cdot 563 \cdot 599 \cdot 607 \cdot 619}$$
$$\cdot \underline{743 \cdot 827 \cdot 941 \cdot 2357} \cdot 10069.$$

Table 4. A table of SQISign parameters $p = p_n(r)$ for twin-smooth integers $(r, r \pm 1)$ found using CHM at each security level. The f is the power of two dividing $(p^2 - 1)/2$ and B is the smoothness bound of the odd cofactor $T \approx p^{5/4}$. It also includes existing primes in the literature including the state-of-the-art.

NIST security level	p		$\lceil \log_2(p) \rceil$	f	B	$\sqrt{B}/f$	$\log_p(T)$
	p_{3923} [17]		254	65	3923	0.96	1.32
	n	r					
NIST I	2	1211460311716772790566574529001 291776 2091023014142971802357816084152 713216	241 243	49 49	1091 887	0.67 0.61	1.28 1.28
	3	3474272816789867297357824 10227318375788227199589376 21611736033260878876800000 20461449125500374748856320 26606682403634464748953600	246 251 254 254 255	43 31 31 46 40	547 383 421 523 547	0.54 0.63 0.66 0.50 0.58	1.29 1.31 1.28 1.26 1.28
	4	1466873880764125184 8077251317941145600 12105439990105079808 [17] 13470906659953016832 [17]	243 253 255 256	49 49 61 61	701 479 1877 1487	0.54 0.45 0.71 0.63	1.28 1.30 1.31 1.30
NIST III	3	1374002035005713149550405343373 848576	362	37	1277	0.97	1.25
	4	5139734876262390964070873088 12326212283367463507272925184 18080754980295452456023326720 27464400309146790228660255744	370 375 377 379	45 77 61 41	11789 55967 95569 13127	2.41 3.07 5.07 2.79	1.26 1.31 1.26 1.29
	6	2628583629218279424 5417690118774595584 11896643388662145024	369 375 382	73 79 79	13219 58153 10243	1.58 3.05 1.28	1.27 1.27 1.30
	12	5114946480 [13]	389	49	31327	3.61	1.30
NIST V	6	9469787780580604464332800 12233468605740686007808000 26697973900446483680680256 31929740427944870006521856 41340248200900819056793600	499 502 508 510 512	109 73 85 91 67	703981 376963 150151 550657 224911	7.70 8.41 4.56 8.15 7.08	1.25 1.28 1.26 1.25 1.28

The primes from Table 4 provide various alternatives for NIST I parameters, and we can give simplified estimates for their performance in comparison to p_{3923}. As an example, we will consider p_{479}, the 253-bit prime from Table 4 having $B = 479$. With $f = 49$, it features a slightly smaller power of two compared to p_{3923} with $f = 65$. This means that we would have to verify the signature isogeny in 21 chunks of 2^{49}-isogenies, instead of 16 chunks of 2^{65}-isogenies for p_{3923}. Given that the computational bottleneck for this is the generation of the respective kernel points per chunk, and ignoring the savings of computing 2^{49}-isogenies instead of 2^{65}-isogenies and the relatively cheap recomputation of the challenge isogeny, this results in an estimated slowdown of roughly $21/16 \approx 1.31$. Thus, we expect a modest slowdown from a verification time of 6.7ms (see [17]) to roughly 8.8ms on a modern CPU.

However, we expect a significant speedup for signing: The computational bottleneck during the signature generation is the repeated computation of T-isogenies; one computes two T isogenies per chunk of 2^f-isogenies in the verification. Since the T-isogeny computation is dominated by its largest prime factor B, and its cost can be estimated by $\sqrt{B}$, the ratio of the signing cost metrics $\sqrt{B}/f$ from Table 4 reflects the overall comparison. Given this metric, we expect a speedup factor of roughly $0.45/0.96 \approx 0.47$. For the running time, this would mean an improvement from 424ms (see [17]) to roughly 199ms on a modern CPU.

We can also consider a different cost-estimate, given by summing the cost $\sqrt{\ell_i}$ for the five biggest (not necessarily distinct) prime factors $\ell_i \mid T$, before dividing by f. The advantage of considering more factors of T is that it constitutes a larger portion of the time it takes to compute a T-isogeny, while the disadvantage is that the cost $\sqrt{\ell}$ becomes increasingly inaccurate for smaller prime factors ℓ. In this metric, the speedup is smaller, but is still significant. Specifically, we expect a speedup factor of roughly $2.19/3.04 \approx 0.72$, which would result in an improvement from 424ms to roughly 305ms.

In a nutshell, even though we can only give rough estimates for running times, we expect our NIST I parameters to achieve much better signing times due to the smaller smoothness bounds B, at the cost of a very modest slowdown for verification due to slightly smaller values of f. In the light of the relatively slow signing times in SQISign, this option seems worthwhile for applications that require faster signing.

NIST III and V. As mentioned earlier, our work showcases the first credible primes for SQISign at the NIST III and NIST V security level. A beneficial feature about most of the primes found in Table 4 is that the majority of the smooth factors are relatively small (e.g. $B < 2^{10}$). In comparison, we expect the XGCD method to scale worse for larger security levels, i.e., requiring much larger smoothness bounds. This is similar to the analysis in [10], which shows that while the XGCD approach has reasonable smoothness probabilities for NIST I parameters, other methods become superior for larger sizes.

We note that there are other 384 and 512-bit primes in the literature for which $p^2 - 1$ is smooth [10,13]. None of the primes from [10] have a large enough power of two for a suitable SQISign application. Some primes were found in the context of the isogeny-based public-key encryption scheme Séta [13] that could be suitable for SQISign. As part of their parameter setup, they required finding $\approx$ 384-bit primes[4]. Of the 7 primes that they found, the 389-bit prime, $p = 2r^{12} - 1$ with $r = 5114946480$ appears to be somewhat SQISign-friendly to achieve NIST III security (see Table 4). However, in addition to its worse signing metric, representations of $\mathbb{F}_p$-values require an additional register in this case compared to our primes of bitlengths slightly below 384. Thus, we can expect implementations of $\mathbb{F}_p$-arithmetic to perform significantly worse for this prime.

Remark 10. The requirement we impose on $p^2 - 1$ being divisible by $2^f \cdot T$ is to ensure that it fits within the current implementation of SQISign. At present, the SQISign implementation has a fine-grained optimisation of their ideal to isogeny algorithm to the setting with $\ell = 2$. In general, one could instead allow $p^2 - 1$ to be divisible by $L \cdot T$, for a smooth number L with $\gcd(L, T) = 1$. This could open new avenues to find SQISign-friendly primes, but would require a

---

[4] That satisfy some mild conditions outside of just requiring $p^2 - 1$ to be smooth.

reconfiguration of the SQISign code. For example, using the prime found with $r = 2091023014142971802357816084152713216$ from Table 4, we could use $L = 2^{49} \cdot 3^4 \cdot 5 \mid p^2 - 1$ and still have a large enough smooth factor T to exceed $p^{5/4}$, thereby further minimising the expected slowdown for verification.

Remark 11. The focus of this work has been on finding parameters for SQISign but there are other isogeny-based cryptosystems that could benefit from such quadratic twist-style primes. While traditional SIDH [19] is now broken, there have been proposed countermeasures [2,3,18] that aim to thwart the attacks from [6,22,23]. Currently, these countermeasures use SIDH-style primes, but could potentially benefit from quadratic twist-style primes like those explored in this work for SQISign. However, these countermeasure require primes of larger sizes, so it is unclear if our CHM-based approach scales to these sizes, especially when aiming to balance the size of the smooth cofactors of $p + 1$ and $p - 1$. Nevertheless, our techniques might give a good starting point for future research in this direction.

Acknowledgements. We thank Joost Renes for several helpful discussions about the CHM algorithm, and Luca De Feo for helpful comments on SQISign prime requirements during the preparation of this work as well as the anonymous reviewers for their constructive feedback.

References

1. Banks, W.D., Shparlinski, I.E.: Integers with a large smooth divisor. arXiv preprint math/0601460 (2006)
2. Basso, A., Fouotsa, T.B.: New sidh countermeasures for a more efficient key exchange. Cryptology ePrint Archive, Paper 2023/791 (2023). https://eprint.iacr.org/2023/791
3. Basso, A., Maino, L., Pope, G.: FESTA: fast encryption from supersingular torsion attacks. Cryptology ePrint Archive, Paper 2023/660 (2023). https://eprint.iacr.org/2023/660
4. Bernstein, D.J., De Feo, L., Leroux, A., Smith, B.: Faster computation of isogenies of large prime degree. Open Book Series 4(1), 39–55 (2020)
5. Bingmann, T.: TLX: collection of sophisticated C++ data structures, algorithms, and miscellaneous helpers (2018). https://panthema.net/tlx. Accessed 7 Oct 2020
6. Castryck, W., Decru, T.: An efficient key recovery attack on SIDH. In: EURO-CRYPT. LNCS, vol. 14008, pp. 423–447. Springer (2023)
7. Conrey, J.B., Holmstrom, M.A.: Smooth values of quadratic polynomials. Exp. Math. **30**(4), 447–452 (2021)
8. Conrey, J.B., Holmstrom, M.A., McLaughlin, T.L.: Smooth neighbors. Exp. Math. **22**(2), 195–202 (2013)
9. Costello, C.: B-SIDH: supersingular isogeny Diffie-Hellman using twisted torsion. In: Moriai, S., Wang, H. (eds.) ASIACRYPT 2020. LNCS, vol. 12492, pp. 440–463. Springer, Cham (2020). https://doi.org/10.1007/978-3-030-64834-3_15
10. Costello, C., Meyer, M., Naehrig, M.: Sieving for twin smooth integers with solutions to the prouhet-tarry-escott problem. In: Canteaut, A., Standaert, F.-X. (eds.) EUROCRYPT 2021. LNCS, vol. 12696, pp. 272–301. Springer, Cham (2021). https://doi.org/10.1007/978-3-030-77870-5_10

11. Dartois, P., Leroux, A., Robert, D., Wesolowski, B.: SQISignHD: New dimensions in cryptography. Cryptology ePrint Archive, Paper 2023/436 (2023). https://eprint.iacr.org/2023/436

12. de Bruijn, N.G.: On the number of positive integers $\leq$ x and free of prime factors $> y$, ii. Indag. Math. **38**, 239–247 (1966)

13. De Feo, L., Delpech de Saint Guilhem, C., Fouotsa, T.B., Kutas, P., Leroux, A., Petit, C., Silva, J., Wesolowski, B.: Séta: supersingular encryption from torsion attacks. In: Tibouchi, M., Wang, H. (eds.) ASIACRYPT 2021. LNCS, vol. 13093, pp. 249–278. Springer, Cham (2021). https://doi.org/10.1007/978-3-030-92068-5_9

14. Dickman, K.: On the frequency of numbers containing prime factors of a certain relative magnitude. Arkiv for matematik, astronomi och fysik **22**(10), A-10 (1930)

15. Komada Eriksen, J., Panny, L., Sotáková, J., Veroni, M.: Deuring for the people: Supersingular elliptic curves with prescribed endomorphism ring in general characteristic. Cryptology ePrint Archive (2023)

16. De Feo, L., Kohel, D., Leroux, A., Petit, C., Wesolowski, B.: SQISign: Compact Post-quantum Signatures from Quaternions and Isogenies. In: Moriai, S., Wang, H. (eds.) ASIACRYPT 2020. LNCS, vol. 12491, pp. 64–93. Springer, Cham (2020). https://doi.org/10.1007/978-3-030-64837-4_3

17. De Feo, L., Leroux, A., Longa, P., Wesolowski, B.: New algorithms for the deuring correspondence - towards practical and secure sqisign signatures. In: EUROCRYPT, vol. 14008, pp. 659–690. Springer (2023)

18. T. B. Fouotsa, T. Moriya, and C. Petit. M-SIDH and MD-SIDH: Countering sidh attacks by masking information. In: EUROCRYPT, vol. 14008, pp. 282–309. Springer (2023). doi: https://doi.org/10.1007/978-3-031-30589-4_10

19. Jao, D., De Feo, L.: Towards quantum-resistant cryptosystems from supersingular elliptic curve isogenies. In: Yang, B.-Y. (ed.) PQCrypto 2011. LNCS, vol. 7071, pp. 19–34. Springer, Heidelberg (2011). https://doi.org/10.1007/978-3-642-25405-5_2

20. Lehmer, D.H.: On a problem of Störmer. Ill. J. Math. **8**(1), 57–79 (1964)

21. Luca, F., Najman, F.: On the largest prime factor of x^2-1. Math. Comput. **80**(273), 429–435 (2011)

22. Maino, L., Martindale, C., Panny, L., Pope, G., Wesolowski, B.: A direct key recovery attack on SIDH. In: EUROCRYPT. LNCS, vol. 14008, pp. 448–471. Springer (2023). https://doi.org/10.1007/978-3-031-30589-4_16

23. Robert, D.: Breaking SIDH in polynomial time. In: EUROCRYPT. LNCS, vol. 14008, pp. 472–503. Springer (2023). https://doi.org/10.1007/978-3-031-30589-4_17

24. Størmer, C.: Quelques théorèmes sur l'équation de Pell $x^2 - dy^2 = \pm 1$ et leurs applications. Christiania Videnskabens Selskabs Skrifter, Math. Nat. Kl (2), 48 (1897)

25. Tenenbaum, G.: Integers with a large friable component. Acta Arith **124**, 287–291 (2006)

26. Tenenbaum, G.: Introduction to analytic and probabilistic number theory, volume 163. American Mathematical Soc. (2015)

27. The National Institute of Standards and Technology (NIST). Submission requirements and evaluation criteria for the post-quantum cryptography standardization process, December 2016

28. The National Institute of Standards and Technology (NIST). Call for additional digital signature schemes for the post-quantum cryptography standardization process, October 2022

Non-interactive Commitment
from Non-transitive Group Actions

Giuseppe D'Alconzo[1]([✉]) [ID], Andrea Flamini[2] [ID], and Andrea Gangemi[2] [ID]

[1] Department of Mathematical Sciences, Politecnico di Torino, Corso Duca degli
Abruzzi 24, 10129 Torino, Italy
giuseppe.dalconzo@polito.it
[2] Department of Mathematics, University of Trento, Povo, 38123 Trento, Italy
{andrea.flamini,andrea.gangemi}@unitn.it

Abstract. Group actions are becoming a viable option for post-quantum cryptography assumptions. Indeed, in recent years some works have shown how to construct primitives from assumptions based on isogenies of elliptic curves, such as CSIDH, on tensors or on code equivalence problems. This paper presents a bit commitment scheme, built on non-transitive group actions, which is shown to be secure in the standard model, under the decisional Group Action Inversion Problem. In particular, the commitment is computationally hiding and perfectly binding, and is obtained from a novel and general framework that exploits the properties of some orbit-invariant functions, together with group actions. Previous constructions depend on an interaction between the sender and the receiver in the commitment phase, which results in an interactive bit commitment. We instead propose the first non-interactive bit commitment based on group actions. Then we show that, when the sender is honest, the constructed commitment enjoys an additional feature, i.e., it is possible to tell whether two commitments were obtained from the same input, without revealing the input. We define the security properties that such a construction must satisfy, and we call this primitive *linkable commitment*. Finally, as an example, an instantiation of the scheme using tensors with coefficients in a finite field is provided. In this case, the invariant function is the computation of the rank of a tensor, and the cryptographic assumption is related to the Tensor Isomorphism problem.

Keywords: Cryptographic group actions · Non-transitive group actions · Bit commitments · Linkable commitments · Tensors

1 Introduction

Group Actions in Cryptography. Recent developments in quantum computing make the advent of a quantum machine suitable for cryptanalysis purposes a threat. Many cryptographic algorithms that are used nowadays can no longer be considered secure against a quantum attacker. Primitives relying on the hardness of the Discrete Logarithm or the Factorization problem are broken by the

© International Association for Cryptologic Research 2023
J. Guo and R. Steinfeld (Eds.): ASIACRYPT 2023, LNCS 14444, pp. 222–252, 2023.
https://doi.org/10.1007/978-981-99-8739-9_8

well known Shor's algorithm [33]. This leads to the birth of the Post-Quantum Cryptography, that aims to find and study protocols based on cryptographic assumptions that appear to be resistant to attacks performed by quantum computers. The most promising ones are based on lattices, multivariate polynomials, hash functions, error correcting codes and isogenies of elliptic curves. However, in order to increase the variety of probably secure assumptions, it is necessary to find new problems with useful features to build new cryptographic protocols. A recent line of study concerns equivalence problems and cryptographic group actions. The most known reference is given by Couveignes in 2006 [11] and was used in the setting of isogeny-based cryptography. Moreover, the explicit use of group actions can be found in the 1991 article of Brassard and Young [8]. More recently, the framework has been studied by Grigoriev and Shpilrain, [15], Alamati, De Feo, Montgomery and Patranabis [1] and Ji, Qiao, Feng and Yun [20], introducing some formal cryptographic assumptions. There are many group actions suitable for post-quantum cryptography, arising from different areas of mathematics and computer science. Some examples can be the class group action of CSIDH [9], the one induced by the general linear group on various objects [20,30,35], the action acting on polynomials [26] or the ones concerning linear codes [3,30]. In the last years, cryptographic group actions have been employed to design many primitives such as sigma protocols and signature schemes (via the GMW scheme for Graph Isomorphism [14]), ring and group signatures [4,5], key exchanges [9] and updatable encryption schemes [22].

Commitment Schemes. A commitment scheme is a cryptographic protocol between two parties, a sender and a receiver. The sender wants to commit to a value b without revealing it to the other party. To do this, he binds b to a commitment C that is sent to the receiver. In a second moment, the sender wants to reveal b and the receiver must be able to verify that it was the committed value behind C. A commitment must satisfy two security properties: it must not reveal any information about the committed value (hiding property), and the sender cannot reveal a different $b' \neq b$ that opens to the same commitment (binding property).

Commitment schemes are widely used, both as stand-alone protocols and as atomic parts of more involved mechanisms. For example, they are used in Zero-Knowledge proofs [23], digital auctions [25], signature schemes [21], multi-party computation [13], e-voting [12] and confidential transactions [29]. In this work, we will mainly focus on *bit* commitments, where the committed value b can be 1 or 0.

Related Works. Bit commitments schemes are a component of many cryptographic algorithms. In 1991, Naor [24] showed how to obtain a bit commitment protocol starting from a pseudorandom generator. Bit committments from group actions are known in literature. In 1991 Brassard and Young [8] present an interactive scheme from certified and uncertified group actions. In 2019 Ji, Qiao, Song and Yun [20] present, among other construction, two interactive bit commitment schemes relying on cryptographic assumptions on non-abelian group actions.

Finally, another famous commitment, which is however based on a pre-quantum assumption, is the *Pedersen commitment* [27]. This scheme has an interesting property: it can be shown that two commitments are created starting from the same value, without opening the commitments [29].

Our Contribution. We present a bit commitment scheme that is non-interactive, perfectly binding and computationally hiding in the standard model. This scheme is based on a group action framework that makes use of certain invariant functions. One of the innovative aspects of our proposal is that it concerns *non-transitive* group actions, while known cryptographic applications use transitive actions or they restrict to one orbit. The non-transitivity of the action used in this paper is crucial and necessary; in fact, we need to be able to exhibit two elements that are in two different orbits. Such elements are generated with the aid of the new group action framework, in which we endow the group action with a function that is constant inside the orbits. Given the group G acting on the set X via the action $\star$, an *invariant function* $f : X \to T$, with T be a set, has the following property

$$f(g \star x) = f(x), \quad \forall x \in X, g \in G.$$

The key point is that evaluating this function on a randomly chosen element is hard, while, for a particular subset of elements that we call *canonical elements*, it is easy to compute. Also, the fact that the function is constant inside the orbits guarantees that, if we consider two elements with distinct image, they must live in (and generate under the action of G) distinct orbits. This observation is crucial to prove our commitment scheme is perfectly binding. We call *Group Action with Canonical Elements* (GACE) a group action with the above properties. Moreover, the existence of decision problems about whether an element is randomly picked from a specific orbit or not enables us to prove that our commitment scheme is computationally hiding.

The structure of our construction enables an additional property that is shared with the Pedersen commitment. An honest sender generating two commitments of the same value b can prove to the receiver that they are in fact linked to the same message, without revealing it. We call this scheme a *linkable commitment* and we formally define the security properties that enable the adoption of such a primitive in cryptography. However, using some techniques from ring signature schemes [5], we show how to extend this property to the case of a possibly malicious sender in the Random Oracle Model.

This work is organized as follows: Sect. 2 recaps all the cryptographic tools that will be used in the rest of the paper, while Sect. 3 introduces the framework that we will use to design a non-interactive commitment scheme starting from cryptographic group actions. In particular, we introduce the concept of Group Action with Canonical Elements. Section 4 shows how to design a bit commitment starting from canonical elements, and its security is proved under the decisional Group Action Inversion Problem assumption, while in Sect. 5 we introduce the notion of linkable commitments and we show how our protocol is indeed a linkable one. Section 6 shows an instantiation of the framework with tensors, and finally, Sect. 7 concludes the work and gives some idea for further research.

2   Preliminaries

In the course of this paper, with $\Pr[A]$ we denote the probability of the event A. Let λ denote the security parameter, this means that the parameters of the cryptographic schemes instantiated with security parameter λ are chosen in such a way that the best known attack would break the scheme using at least 2^λ operations. A function $\mu(\lambda)$ is *negligible* in λ if for every positive integer c there exists a λ_0 such that for each $\lambda > \lambda_0$ we get $\mu(\lambda) < \frac{1}{\lambda^c}$.

Finally, in the pseudocode " $\leftarrow\$$ " denotes the random sampling, " $\leftarrow$ " is a variable assignment and "$=$" is the equality check.

2.1   Group Actions

This section introduces group actions, along with the complexity assumptions that must be made in order to use them in cryptographic protocols. Definitions reported here are mostly taken from [1]. We point out that through this work we do not need the action to be abelian, contrary to what is required in [11] or [1]. All the following definitions and constructions are meaningful also in the non-abelian case.

Definition 1. *A group G is said to act on a set X if there is a map $\star : G \times X \to X$ that satisfies the following properties:*

- Identity: *if e is the identity element of the group G, then $e \star x = x$ for every x in X.*
- Compatibility: *given g and h in G and x in X, we have that $(gh) \star x = g \star (h \star x)$.*

In this case, we say that the triple $(G, X, \star)$ is a group action.

A group action $(G, X, \star)$ may satisfy some algebraic properties that lead to the definition of classes of group actions, namely the action is *transitive* if for all x_1, x_2 in X there exists an element g in G such that $x_1 = g \star x_2$; moreover, the action is said *free* when the following holds: g is the identity element of G if and only if there is an x in X such that $g \star x = x$. Finally, we say that the action is *regular* if it is both free and transitive.

Note that, if the group action $(G, X, \star)$ is regular and the group G is finite, then for every x in X the map $g \mapsto g\star x$ is a bijection and $|G| = |X|$. Furthermore, if the group action is regular, then we can define the element $\delta(x, y)$ of G as the unique element for which $x = \delta(x, y) \star y$. If the action is not transitive, instead, then there exist x and y in X such that $\delta(x, y)$ does not exist.

Alamati, De Feo, Montgomery and Patranabis also define the concept of *effective group action*: a formal definition can be found in [1], here we just report the key points.

Definition 2. *A group action $(G, X, \star)$ is* effective *if:*

- *the group G is finite and there exists a probabilistic polynomial time* (PPT) *algorithm for executing membership and equality testing, sampling, and for computing the group operation and the inverse of an element;*
- *the set X is finite and there exist* PPT *algorithms for computing membership testing and the unique representation of any element in X;*
- *there exists an efficient algorithm to compute $g \star x$, for each g in G and x in X.*

Informally, a group action is said effective if it can be manipulated easily and it can be computed in practical time. An example of non-effective group actions is the set of polynomials in m variables of bounded degree n over a finite field, with the symmetric group $\mathcal{S}_m$, permuting the variables. It can be seen that the unique representation is given by the algebraic normal form, but it cannot be computed in polynomial time in n and m.

In the rest of this work, even when not explicitly written, we will consider effective group actions.

2.2 Cryptographic Assumptions on Group Actions

The presented definition leads to efficient group actions, which can be used to build cryptographic protocols. However, in order to use them in cryptography we need to define some suitable computational assumptions. In [1], the authors report some computational assumptions on group actions, for instance the following embraces the fact that, given two random elements $x, y \in X$ in the same orbit, then it must be intractable to compute $\delta(x, y)$.

Definition 3. *Let λ be a parameter indexing G and X. Being $\mathcal{D}_G$ and $\mathcal{D}_X$ two distributions over G and X respectively, then the group action $(G, X, \star)$ is $(\mathcal{D}_G, \mathcal{D}_X)$-one-way if for all* PPT *adversaries $\mathcal{A}$ there is a negligible function $\mu(\lambda)$ such that*

$$\Pr[\mathcal{A}(x, g \star x) \star x = g \star x] \leq \mu(\lambda),$$

where x is sampled according to $\mathcal{D}_X$ and g according to $\mathcal{D}_G$.

In this paper, we assume that $\mathcal{D}_G$ and $\mathcal{D}_X$ are the uniform distributions over G and X, and we refer to this assumption as *One-way group action assumption*.

Another assumption that can be used when working with group actions is the *Group Action Pseudo Randomness* (GA-PR) problem, defined in [20]. It can be seen as a generalisation of the Decisional Diffie-Hellman assumption. An equivalent assumption can be found in [1], and a group action with this property is called *weakly pseudorandom*. For example, in [20], the authors state that it can be applied to the general linear group action on tensors. Let us now define more formally the problem on which the GA-PR assumption is based.

Definition 4. *Let $\mathcal{G}$ be a group action family such that for a security parameter λ, $\mathcal{G}(1^\lambda)$ returns an effective group action $(G, X, \star)$ with $\log(|G|) = \mathsf{poly}(\lambda)$ and $\log(|X|) = \mathsf{poly}(\lambda)$. Denote the triple as a public parameter $\mathsf{pp} = (G, X, \star)$.*

The group action pseudo random game (GA-PR) is given in Fig. 1. We define the advantage of an adversary $\mathcal{A}$ of GA-PR as

$$\mathsf{Adv}(\mathcal{A}, \textit{GA-PR}) = \left| \Pr[\mathcal{A} \text{ wins GA-PR}(\mathsf{pp})] - \frac{1}{2} \right|.$$

The GA-PR assumption states that for all PPT adversaries $\mathcal{A}$ there is a negligible function $\mu(\lambda)$, with λ being the security parameter, such that

$$\mathsf{Adv}(\mathcal{A}, \textit{GA-PR}) \leq \mu(\lambda),$$

GA-PR(pp)

Adversary $\mathcal{A}$		**Challenger $\mathcal{C}$**
		$b \leftarrow\!\!\$\ \{0,1\},\ s \leftarrow\!\!\$\ X$
		if $b = 1$ then
		$g \leftarrow\!\!\$\ G,\ t \leftarrow g \star s$
		if $b = 0$ then
	$\xleftarrow{\quad s, t \quad}$	$t \leftarrow\!\!\$\ X$
Guess b'	$\xrightarrow{\quad b' \quad}$	$\mathcal{A}$ wins if $b = b'$

Fig. 1. Group Action Pseudo Random game.

For the bit commitment scheme, we will refer to the GA-PR assumption when the set X consists of only two orbits. We call this new assumption and the relative game 2GA-PR.

We remark that the adversary of the GA-PR game must be able to distinguish whether the challenger has picked the element t uniformly at random inside the orbit of s or inside the set X. However, when t is picked inside X, it is still possible that t is picked inside the orbit of s as well; therefore, even a computationally unbounded adversary would not be able to win the game with probability 1.

In particular, if we consider the 2GA-PR game, and we suppose that the two orbits have the same cardinality, the event that t is picked uniformly at random inside the set X and t results to be an element in the orbit of s is $\frac{1}{4}$. Therefore, even an adversary with unbounded computational power, who can distinguish whether t lives in the same orbit of s or not, cannot win the game with probability greater than $\frac{3}{4}$.

The observation above motivates the introduction of an assumption which we refer to as *decisional Group Action Inversion Problem* (dGA-IP). The dGA-IP problem, also known as Isomorphism Problem [20], is the decisional variant of the group action inversion problem presented in [34], applied to the case in which the set X is given by only two orbits. If the restriction on the two orbits is removed, a large number of similar problems can be found in literature [16,17,28].

Definition 5. *The* dGA-IP *game is presented in Fig. 2, where* pp *is given by the tuple* $(G, X, \star, t_0, t_1)$, *with* t_0 *and* t_1 *elements that lie in distinct orbits under the action of* G. *We define the advantage of an adversary* $\mathcal{A}$ *of dGA-IP as*

$$\mathsf{Adv}(\mathcal{A}, dGA\text{-}IP) = \left| \Pr[\mathcal{A} \text{ wins } dGA\text{-}IP(\mathsf{pp})] - \frac{1}{2} \right|.$$

The dGA-IP *assumption states that for all* PPT *adversaries* $\mathcal{A}$ *there is a negligible function* $\mu(\lambda)$, *with* λ *being the security parameter, such that*

$$\mathsf{Adv}(\mathcal{A}, dGA\text{-}IP) \leq \mu(\lambda),$$

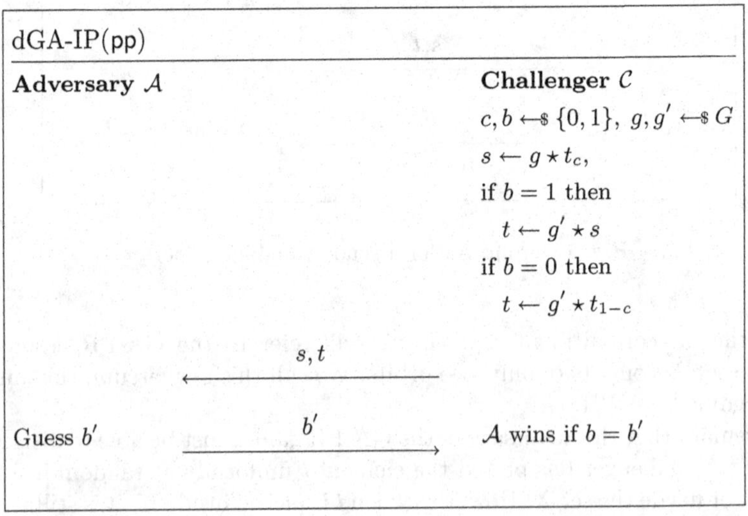

---

dGA-IP(pp)

Adversary $\mathcal{A}$ **Challenger $\mathcal{C}$**

$c, b \leftarrow\!\!\$\ \{0,1\}, \ g, g' \leftarrow\!\!\$\ G$

$s \leftarrow g \star t_c,$

if $b = 1$ then

$t \leftarrow g' \star s$

if $b = 0$ then

$t \leftarrow g' \star t_{1-c}$

$\xleftarrow{\qquad s, t \qquad}$

Guess b' $\xrightarrow{\qquad b' \qquad}$ $\mathcal{A}$ wins if $b = b'$

Fig. 2. decisional Group Action Inversion Problem game.

This game, compared to 2GA-PR, reflects more clearly the fact that it is hard to distinguish whether two elements in X live in the same orbit or not, and an adversary with unbounded computational power would win this game with probability 1.

2.3 Commitment Schemes

A commitment scheme is a cryptographic scheme that allows one party to commit to a value m by sending a commitment com, and then to reveal m by opening the commitment at a later point in time.

Definition 6. *A* commitment scheme *on a message space* $\mathcal{M}$ *is a triple of* PPT *algorithms* (PGen, Commit, Open) *such that:*

1. PGen(1^λ) *takes as input a security parameter* λ *in unary and returns public parameters* pp*;*
2. Commit(pp, m) *takes as input the public parameters* pp*, a message* m *in* $\mathcal{M}$ *and returns the commitment* com *and the* opening material *r;*
3. Open(pp, m, com, r) *takes as input the public parameters* pp*, the message* m*, the commitment* com *and the opening material* r *and returns* **accept** *if* com *is the commitment of* m *or* **reject** *otherwise.*

In the rest of this work we omit the public parameters pp in the inputs of Commit and Open.

To be suitable in cryptography, commitment schemes must satisfy the *hiding* and *binding* properties. Hiding means that com reveals nothing about m and binding means that it is not possible to create a commitment com that can be opened in two different ways. These properties are formally defined.

Definition 7. *Let* $\Pi_{\mathsf{Com}} = $ (PGen, Commit, Open) *be a commitment scheme and let* $\mathrm{Hiding}(\Pi_{\mathsf{Com}})$ *be the hiding game represented in Fig. 3. We define the advantage of an adversary* $\mathcal{A}$ *of* $\mathrm{Hiding}(\Pi_{\mathsf{Com}})$ *as*

$$\mathrm{Adv}(\mathcal{A}, \mathrm{Hiding}(\Pi_{\mathsf{Com}})) = \left| \Pr[\mathcal{A} \text{ wins } \mathrm{Hiding}(\Pi_{\mathsf{Com}})] - \frac{1}{2} \right|.$$

A commitment scheme Π_{Com} *is computationally hiding if for all* PPT *adversaries* $\mathcal{A}$ *there is a negligible function* $\mu(\lambda)$*, with* λ *being the security parameter, such that*

$$\mathrm{Adv}(\mathcal{A}, \mathrm{Hiding}(\Pi_{\mathsf{Com}})) \leq \mu(\lambda),$$

If, for every pair m_0, m_1*, the commitments* com_0 *and* com_1 *have the same distribution, where* $(\mathsf{com}_i, r_i) = $ Commit(m_i) *for* $i = 0, 1$*, we say that the commitment is perfectly hiding.*

Note that, in the case of a bit commitment, the adversary does not send m_0 and m_1, and the bit chosen by the challenger is the committed bit in com.

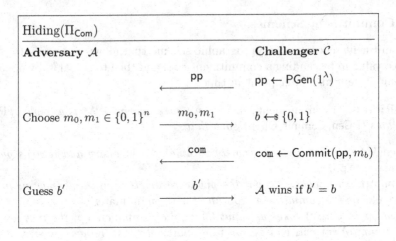

Fig. 3. Hiding game for commitment schemes.

Definition 8. *A commitment scheme* $\Pi_{\mathsf{Com}} = (\mathsf{PGen}, \mathsf{Commit}, \mathsf{Open})$ *is computationally binding if for all* PPT *adversaries* $\mathcal{A}$ *there is a negligible function* $\mu(\lambda)$, *with* λ *being the security parameter, such that*

$$\Pr\left[\begin{array}{l} \mathsf{pp} \leftarrow \mathsf{PGen}(1^{\lambda}), \\ (\mathsf{com}, m_0, r_0, m_1, r_1) \leftarrow \mathcal{A}(\mathsf{pp}) \end{array} \middle| \begin{array}{l} m_0 \neq m_1, \\ \mathsf{Open}(m_0, \mathsf{com}, r_0) = \mathbf{accept}, \\ \mathsf{Open}(m_1, \mathsf{com}, r_1) = \mathbf{accept} \end{array}\right] \leq \mu(\lambda).$$

If for every adversary $\mathcal{A}$ *it holds that* $\mu(\lambda) = 0$, *we say that the commitment scheme is* perfectly binding.

Commitment Schemes from Group Actions. Previous commitments were known from cryptographic group actions. Brassard and Young [8] propose two kind of bit commitments from what they call *certified* and *uncertified* group actions. A certified group action is an action from the group G over the set X such that checking that two elements are in the same orbit is an easy task. On the contrary, the same verification could not be polynomial-time for an uncertified group action. Since the problem of deciding whether two elements of X are in the same orbit is assumed to be hard in this work, we will focus on the latter case. Given a group action from G on X, the computationally binding and perfectly hiding bit commitment presented in [8] is as follows.

- The receiver randomly generates x_0 from X and g from G. Then sets x_1 as $g \star x_0$. He sends to the sender the pair (x_0, x_1) and a proof π that they are in the same orbit.
- The sender wants to commit to the bit b. First, he checks that the proof π is valid, then he picks h from G and sends $\mathsf{com} = h \star x_b$ to the receiver, keeping secret h.

- To open the committed bit b, the sender reveals b and h to the receiver, which checks that com is equal to $h \star x_b$.

The first thing to notice is that this is an interactive bit commitment, since the sender needs the receiver's cooperation for the creation of the commitment. Secondly, the communication cost is at least as big as the proof of the statement that x_0 and x_1 are in the same orbit. This is an NP-statement (the witness is given by g) and hence admits an interactive proof (even a non-interactive one, using the Fiat-Shamir heuristic and the Random Oracle Model), but it can be very large in communication.

In [20], Ji, Qiao, Song and Yun propose two bit commitment protocols. The first is a slight generalization of the protocol from [8], using non-abelian group actions. The obtained protocol has the same drawbacks noticed above: it is interactive and has a large communication cost. The second proposal concerns the use of the following pseudorandom function

$$f : X \times G \to X \times X, \quad (x, g) \mapsto (x, g \star x)$$

and, after applying the Blum-Micali amplification [7], the authors build an interactive bit commitment scheme using the construction from [24]. In this construction it is needed that $|X| \geq |G|$, and the obtained bit commitment is statistically binding and computationally hiding.

3   Our Framework

The goal of this section is to design a non-interactive commitment scheme using assumptions from cryptographic group actions. We will focus on non-abelian and non-transitive actions. To develop such a commitment scheme, we first analyze the issues arising from an initial construction, then we define a framework that we use to circumvent these problems.

3.1   A First Attempt

Based on the non-transitivity of the group action $(G, X, \star)$, we can do a first attempt in building a *non-interactive* bit commitment scheme. We give its description using a trusted third party (TTP), and then we analyze how to remove it.

Given the action $(G, X, \star)$, the TTP chooses and publishes two elements x_0 and x_1 of X lying in different orbits. The sender, to commit a bit b, generates a random g in G and sets as the commitment of b the value com $= g \star x_b$. The opening material is g. In other words, the sender picks a random element in the orbit of x_b. In the opening phase, given b, com and g, the receiver accepts if com is equal to $g \star x_b$ and rejects otherwise. Informally, the hiding property is given by the fact that checking whether com is in the orbit of x_0 or x_1 is hard, while the binding property follows from the impossibility of going from an orbit to another via the action of G.

In the following we try to remove the TTP and analyze some possible scenarios.

1. **The sender generates and publishes x_0 and x_1.** In this case we can see that a malicious sender can generate x_0 and x_1 in the same orbit via $x_1 = h \star x_0$. He commits to $g \star x_0$ and, during the opening phase, he could open to both 0 and 1 using g or gh^{-1}. In this case, the binding property does not hold.

2. **The sender generates and publishes x_0, x_1 together with a proof π that they are in different orbits.** Given a proof π that x_0 and x_1 are not in the same orbit, we obtain that the protocol is hiding and binding, under the assumption that deciding whenever two elements share the orbit is hard. In this scenario, the hard task is the generation of the proof π. In fact, the language

$$L = \{(y_0, y_1) \in X \times X \mid y_0 \text{ and } y_1 \text{ are in different orbits}\}$$

is in coNP. Unless we have a computationally unbounded prover [14] (and this is not the case), it means that known techniques fails to generate a short non-interactive proof for L which would enable the design of a non-interactive commitment scheme. Since interactive bit commitments based on group actions are known [8,20], we do not further study this case.

3. **The receiver generates and publishes x_0 and x_1.** We are again in the case of interactive bit commitments, and we remand to the known schemes based on group actions.

With such techniques, we have seen that there are some tricky aspects that are hard to deal with. For example, we need to build a proof for a language in coNP, and the absence of a witness (as we are used to, when we work in NP) is the first obstacle. To overcome such difficulties, we introduce a general framework on group actions that ease the design of the non-interactive bit commitment sketched above. The trick is the definition of an invariant function that is constant inside the orbits and hard to compute for a randomly chosen element. However, we assume that there is a set of representative elements for which the computation of such a function is easy. This avoids the need of a proof for the above language L. These concepts will be formalized in the next subsection.

3.2   Group Actions with Canonical Elements

In this section, we introduce the concepts of invariant functions and canonical elements, and we present the cryptographic assumptions linked to them.

Definition 9. *Given a group action $(G, X, \star)$ and a function $f : X \to T$, we say that f is* invariant *under the action of G if $f(g \star x) = f(x)$ for every g in G and every x in X. We say that f is* fully invariant *if $f(x) = f(y)$ if and only if there exists g in G such that $y = g \star x$.*

In the following, we can assume that f is surjective, restricting the set T to the image $f(X)$. To exploit the properties of invariant functions while keeping the dGA-IP hard, we want the function f to be hard to compute on a large class of elements of X. At the same time, we want to define particular elements of X on which the computation of f is feasible.

Definition 10. *Let $f : X \to T$ be a surjective invariant function for the action $(G, X, \star)$ and let $T' \subset T$. Suppose that there exists a polynomial-computable map*

$$\langle \cdot \rangle : T' \to X, \quad t \mapsto \langle t \rangle$$

such that the function $f \circ \langle \cdot \rangle$ is the identity on the subset T' of T. We call $\langle \cdot \rangle$ the canonical representation of T' in X and $\langle t \rangle$ the canonical t-element (with respect to f and $\langle \cdot \rangle$). If $T' = T$, we say that $\langle \cdot \rangle$ is complete. Moreover, we say that $(G, X, \star, f, \langle \cdot \rangle)$ is a Group Action with Canonical Element (GACE) if the following hold:

1. *if $O(z)$ is the orbit of z in X, then for any PPT adversary $\mathcal{A}$ there is a negligible function μ such that*

$$\Pr[\mathcal{A}(x) = f(x)] \leq \frac{1}{|T'|} + \mu(|x|),$$

   where x is sampled uniformly random from $\bigsqcup_{t \in T'} O(\langle t \rangle)$;
2. *there is a PPT algorithm that for any t in T' computes $f(\langle t \rangle)$.*

In other words, the definition above says that, for every t in T', we have $f(\langle t \rangle) = t$ and the function f is hard to compute in general, but is instead easy to calculate on canonical elements. Moreover, the construction of such $\langle t \rangle$ is a polynomial-time task.

In the following constructions, whenever a random element of X is needed, we pick a random canonical element $\langle t \rangle$, a random g from G and compute $g \star \langle t \rangle$. In this way, instead of using the whole X, we always work with the union of the orbits of the canonical elements. In other words, the set on which the group G acts becomes

$$X' = \bigsqcup_{t \in T'} O(\langle t \rangle).$$

This implies that the GACE $(G, X', \star, f, \langle \cdot \rangle)$ has a fully invariant function f and the canonical representation $\langle \cdot \rangle$ is complete. Given a fully invariant function f, the problem of determining whether two elements have the same image under f is equivalent to deciding whether they lie in the same orbit (dGA-IP).

4   The Commitment Scheme

4.1   Bit Commitment Scheme from a GACE

The first application of our framework is a bit commitment scheme. Given a Group Action with Canonical Elements, we design the commitment scheme described in Fig. 4, following the attempts shown in Subsect. 3.1. The bit commitment is proven secure under both the dGA-IP assumption that we have introduced in this paper and the 2GA-PR assumption; the security proof under the latter assumption can be found in Appendix A.

Theorem 1. *The bit commitment scheme in Fig. 4 is perfectly binding.*

$$\text{PGen } (1^\lambda)$$

1 :   choose $(G, X, \star, f, \langle \cdot \rangle)$

2 : $t_0 \leftarrow\!\!{\$}\, T'$

3 : $t_1 \leftarrow\!\!{\$}\, T' \setminus \{t_0\}$

4 :   **return** $(G, X, \star, f, \langle \cdot \rangle, t_0, t_1)$

Commit (b)

1 : $g \leftarrow\!\!{\$}\, G$

2 : $c \leftarrow g \star \langle t_b \rangle$

3 :   **return** (c, g)

Open (b, c, g)

1 :   **if** $g^{-1} \star c = \langle t_b \rangle$

2 :   **return accept**

3 :   **else return reject**

Fig. 4. Bit commitment scheme from a GACE.

Proof. Without loss of generality, we can assume $m_0 = 0$ and $m_1 = 1$. Suppose there exists an adversary $\mathcal{A}$ that on input $\mathsf{pp} = (G, X, \star, f, \langle \cdot \rangle, t_0, t_1)$ returns the tuple com, r_0, r_1 such that

$$\mathsf{Open}(0, \mathsf{com}, r_0) = \mathsf{Open}(1, \mathsf{com}, r_1) = \mathbf{accept}$$

with positive probability. This means that $r_0 \star \langle t_0 \rangle = \mathsf{com} = r_1 \star \langle t_1 \rangle$, and then $r_1^{-1} r_0 \star \langle t_0 \rangle = \langle t_1 \rangle$. Therefore, $\langle t_0 \rangle$ and $\langle t_1 \rangle$ are in the same orbit, but this is a contradiction and such an adversary $\mathcal{A}$ cannot exist.

Theorem 2. *The bit commitment scheme in Fig. 4 is computationally hiding under the decisional Group Action Inversion Problem assumption.*

Proof. The dGA-IP assumption states that every adversary of the dGA-IP game has at most negligible advantage. We prove that the existence of an adversary of the game $\mathsf{Hiding}(\varPi_{\mathsf{Com}})$ with advantage at least $\epsilon(\lambda)$, where $\epsilon(\lambda)$ is a non-negligible function, implies the existence of an adversary $\mathcal{A}$ of the dGA-IP game with advantage $2\epsilon^2(\lambda)$, which is non-negligible.

The proof is divided in 3 parts: firstly, we describe our adversary $\mathcal{A}$ of the dGA-IP game. It will exploit two instances of an adversary of the $\mathsf{Hiding}(\varPi_{Com})$ game, therefore we must show that it correctly simulates the challenger of such a game. Finally, we quantify a lower bound to the advantage of the adversary $\mathcal{A}$.

1. *Reduction description.*

   The adversary $\mathcal{A}$ of the dGA-IP game (see Fig. 5) receives from the challenger two set elements s and t, generated according to the dGA-IP game. $\mathcal{A}$ creates two instances of the adversary of $\mathsf{Hiding}(\varPi_{\mathsf{Com}})$ game having non-negligible advantage, namely $\mathcal{A}_1$ and $\mathcal{A}_2$. Then, the adversary $\mathcal{A}$ provides $\mathcal{A}_1$ with s

and $\mathcal{A}_2$ with t separately. The two hiding commitment adversaries $\mathcal{A}_1$ and $\mathcal{A}_2$ return respectively the bits b_0 and b_1 as outputs of their internal routine. Finally, the dGA-IP adversary $\mathcal{A}$ returns to the challenger the bit b' which is set to 1 if $b_0 = b_1$, otherwise it is set to 0.

2. $\mathcal{A}$ *correctly simulates the* $\text{Hiding}(\Pi_{\text{Com}})$ *challenger.*

   We show that $\mathcal{A}$ correctly simulates the challenger of the $\text{Hiding}(\Pi_{\text{Com}})$ game, so that it is possible to quantify the probability of success of the adversaries $\mathcal{A}_1$ and $\mathcal{A}_2$. The elements s and t which $\mathcal{A}$ uses as input to $\mathcal{A}_1$ and $\mathcal{A}_2$ are generated as follows:

   - s is a random element in the orbit generated by $\langle t_c \rangle$, with c chosen uniformly at random in $\{0, 1\}$;
   - when $b = 1$, t is chosen uniformly at random in the same orbit of s (note that $g' \star s = g'g \star \langle t_c \rangle$ is random as long as $g' \leftarrow_\$ G$), otherwise, if $b = 0$, t is chosen at random in the orbit of $\langle t_{1-c} \rangle$.

   In particular, the orbit of s is chosen uniformly at random via the selection of c; then, given c, the orbit of t is chosen uniformly at random via b. This guarantees that $\mathcal{A}$ correctly simulates the challenger of the $\text{Hiding}(\Pi_{Com})$ game, who must choose, in the first step, whether to create a commitment to 0 or to 1. Therefore, the adversaries $\mathcal{A}_1, \mathcal{A}_2$ win their games with probability greater than $\frac{1}{2} + \epsilon(\lambda)$.

3. *Measurement of* $\mathcal{A}$'s *advantage.*

   Finally, we compute a lower bound to the probability of success of $\mathcal{A}$ that we have described in the dGA-IP game.

   We observe that the adversaries $\mathcal{A}_1$ and $\mathcal{A}_2$ do not interact, so the events that they win their games can be considered independent as long as their inputs are also independent.

   It is possible to show that the selection of the inputs is independent, since the selection process of s and t is performed picking at random the orbit $O(s)$ of s by sampling the bit c, and the orbit $O(t)$ of t by sampling the bit b (actually the bit that determines the orbit of t is interpreted according to the value of s, but this is not relevant as long as the bit b is chosen at random).

   Then, the canonical elements of the sampled orbits are randomized by sampling two random group elements $g, g' \in G$ and computing the action of such elements (or of the element $g'g$ instead of g', if $b = 1$, which is a random element as long as g' is random) on the canonical elements.

   Given that the inputs to $\mathcal{A}_1$ and $\mathcal{A}_2$ are independent and that the two adversaries perform their operations regardless of the existence of each other, the events that $\mathcal{A}_1$ wins its game and $\mathcal{A}_2$ wins its game are independent.

   For the sake of brevity, we refer to the event that $\mathcal{A}_1$ wins or loses its game as ($\mathcal{A}_1$ wins) or ($\mathcal{A}_1$ loses) and we do the same for $\mathcal{A}_2$ and $\mathcal{A}$: the game they are playing will be clear from the context.

   Finally, we compute the lower bound of the probability of advantage of $\mathcal{A}$. To do that, we observe that $\mathcal{A}$ wins the game when $b' = b$ and this happens either when both $\mathcal{A}_1$ and $\mathcal{A}_2$ win, or when they both lose.

   In fact, when $b = 0$ then $O(t) \neq O(s)$; therefore, $b_0 \neq b_1$ happens if and only if both $\mathcal{A}_1$ and $\mathcal{A}_2$ win or when they both lose. The same holds when $b = 1$.

Therefore,

$$\Pr[\mathcal{A} \text{ wins}] =$$
$$\Pr[(\mathcal{A}_1 \text{ wins} \wedge \mathcal{A}_2 \text{ wins}) \vee (\mathcal{A}_1 \text{ loses} \wedge \mathcal{A}_2 \text{ loses})] =$$
$$\Pr[(\mathcal{A}_1 \text{ wins} \wedge \mathcal{A}_2 \text{ wins})] + \Pr[(\mathcal{A}_1 \text{ loses} \wedge \mathcal{A}_2 \text{ loses})] =$$
$$\Pr[(\mathcal{A}_1 \text{ wins})]\Pr[(\mathcal{A}_2 \text{ wins})] + \Pr[(\mathcal{A}_1 \text{ loses})]\Pr[\mathcal{A}_2 \text{ loses}] \geq$$
$$\left(\frac{1}{2} + \epsilon(\lambda)\right)^2 + \left(\frac{1}{2} - \epsilon(\lambda)\right)^2 = \frac{1}{2} + 2\epsilon(\lambda)^2.$$

Since $\epsilon(\lambda)$ is a non-negligible function, we have defined an adversary $\mathcal{A}$ of the dGA-IP game that has a non-negligible advantage. This contradicts the dGA-IP assumption, therefore the adversary of Hiding(Π_{Com}) with non-negligible advantage does not exist and the commitment scheme Π_{Com} satisfies the hiding property.

The two previous results can be summarized in the following corollary.

Corollary 1. *The bit commitment scheme in Fig. 4 is secure under the decisional Group Action Inversion Problem assumption.*

We also have expanded the security analysis of the hiding property of the commitment scheme under to the 2GA-PR assumption requiring that the two orbits O_0 and O_1 used to instantiate the bit commitment have *similar size*, i.e.

$$|\Pr[x \in O_0] - \Pr[x \in O_1]| = \nu(\lambda)$$

for a randomly chosen x in $O_0 \cup O_1$ and a negligible function $\nu(\lambda)$.

We have proved the following theorem.

Theorem 3. *If the bit commitment scheme in Fig. 4 is instantiated using two orbits of similar size, it is secure under the 2GA-PR assumption.*

Proof. The commitment scheme satisfies the property of perfect binding, as shown in Theorem 1. The proof of the computationally hiding property can be found in Appendix A.

Finally, Appendix B shows that Hiding(Π_{Com}) reduces to dGA-IP, also. This allows us describe the relation between the dGA-IP and 2GA-PR assumptions.

Corollary 2. *The 2GA-PR problem reduces to dGA-IP when it is instantiated with two orbits of similar size.*

We summarize the reductions between the hiding game of the commitment scheme and the two assumptions in Fig. 6.

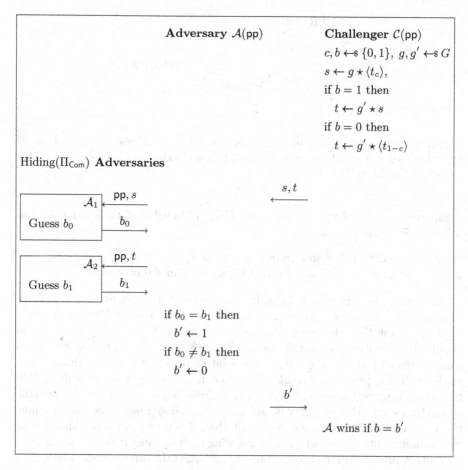

Fig. 5. Reduction from dGA-IP(pp) to the hiding game for the bit commitment scheme.

5   Linkable Commitments

The proposed bit commitment has the following additional feature. Given two commitments com_0 and com_1, if we suppose that the sender is honest, there is a way to prove that their committed value is the same. Based on this notion, we define the concept of *linkable commitment*. We require that the sender is honest to be assured that the commitments lie either in the orbit of $\langle t_0 \rangle$ or $\langle t_1 \rangle$. To the best of our knowledge, this property has not been formally defined before. However it is well known that, for example, Pedersen commitments enjoy this property which is used, among other things, in the Monero's RingCT protocol [29].

Definition 11. *Let $\Pi_{\mathsf{Com}} = (\mathsf{PGen}, \mathsf{Commit}, \mathsf{Open})$ be a commitment scheme. Let m_0 and m_1 be two messages and let $(\mathsf{com}_0, r_0) = \mathsf{Commit}(m_0)$ and*

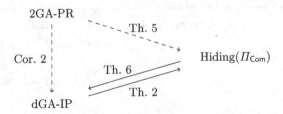

Fig. 6. Reductions between games and problems. "$A \to B$" means that solving B implies solving A. The reductions represented by a dashed line require the extra hypothesis about the similarity of the orbits.

$(\mathsf{com}_1, r_1) = \mathsf{Commit}(m_1)$. *We say that* $\varPi_{\mathsf{Com}}$ *is* linkable *if there exist the two following* PPT *algorithms:*

1. $\mathsf{LinkMaterial}(r_0, r_1)$, *whose output is a value* r_L;
2. $\mathsf{Link}(\mathsf{com}_0, \mathsf{com}_1, r_L)$, *that returns 1 if* $m_0 = m_1$ *and 0 otherwise.*

In order to be secure, a linkable bit commitment must satisfy some security properties for these two additional algorithms Link and LinkMaterial as well. First, we want that the linking material r_L does not reveal any information about the committed value. This means that an adversary that has access to two commitments of m and the linking material r_L does not learn anything about m. We call this property *linkable-hiding*. Then, it must not be possible to link two commitments that are obtained starting from two distinct values. A linkable commitment with this property is said *linkable-binding*. Finally, we focus on how the value r_L can be generated. We want that, if a user (somehow) knows that two commitments are linked without knowing their opening material, he can not generate a proof of that (via the linking material). In other words, being m a message, and being $(\mathsf{com}_0, r_0) = \mathsf{Commit}(m)$ and $(\mathsf{com}_1, r_1) = \mathsf{Commit}(m)$, no one can generate a value r_L such that $\mathsf{Link}(\mathsf{com}_0, \mathsf{com}_1, r_L) = 1$ without knowledge of any information regarding the opening materials r_0 and r_1. This additional property is called *link secrecy*.

We formalize these new properties in the following definition.

Definition 12. *Let* $\mathsf{HidingLink}(\varPi_{\mathsf{Com}})$ *be the game described in Fig. 7. We define the advantage of an adversary* $\mathcal{A}$ *of the game* $\mathsf{HidingLink}(\varPi_{\mathsf{Com}})$ *as*

$$\mathsf{Adv}(\mathcal{A}, \mathsf{HidingLink}(\varPi_{\mathsf{Com}})) = \left| \Pr[\mathcal{A} \text{ wins } \mathsf{HidingLink}(\varPi_{\mathsf{Com}})] - \frac{1}{2} \right|.$$

Let λ *be the security parameter. A linkable bit commitment* $\varPi_{\mathsf{Com}} = (\mathsf{PGen}, \mathsf{Commit}, \mathsf{Open}, \mathsf{LinkMaterial}, \mathsf{Link})$ *is said*

- *computationally linkable-hiding if for all* PPT *adversaries* $\mathcal{A}$ *there is a negligible function* $\mu(\lambda)$ *such that*

$$\mathsf{Adv}(\mathcal{A}, \mathsf{HidingLink}(\varPi_{\mathsf{Com}})) \le \mu(\lambda);$$

– *computationally* linkable-binding *if for all* PPT *adversaries* $\mathcal{A}$ *there is a negligible function* $\mu(\lambda)$ *such that*

$$\Pr\left[\begin{array}{c|c} \text{pp} \leftarrow \text{PGen}(1^\lambda), & m_0 \neq m_1, \\ (m_0, \text{com}_0, m_1, \text{com}_1, r_L) \leftarrow \mathcal{A}(\text{pp}) & \text{Link}(\text{com}_0, \text{com}_1, r_L) = 1 \end{array}\right] \leq \mu(\lambda);$$

– *computationally* link secret *if for all* PPT *adversaries* $\mathcal{A}$ *there is a negligible function* $\mu(\lambda)$ *such that*

$$\Pr[\mathcal{A} \text{ wins LinkSecrecy}(\Pi_{\text{Com}})] \leq \mu(\lambda),$$

where $\text{LinkSecrecy}(\Pi_{\text{Com}})$ *is the linking secrecy game in Fig. 8.*

In the above definitions, whenever $\mu(\lambda) = 0$, *we say that the property is* perfect.

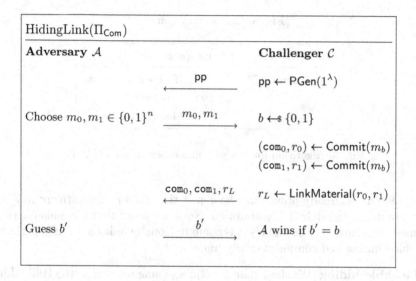

Fig. 7. Linkable-hiding game.

5.1 Linkable Bit Commitment from GACE

Using the bit commitment shown in Subsect. 4.1, we can endow the scheme to obtain a linkable bit commitment. This extension is natural, since the commitments of a chosen message are in the orbit of that message, and showing that they are linked reduces to exhibit a group element which sends one into the other.

Theorem 4. *The bit commitment scheme in Fig. 4 endowed with the algorithms in Fig. 9 is a secure linkable bit commitment scheme under the One-Way Group Action and dGA-IP assumptions.*

LinkSecrecy(Π_{Com})	
Adversary $\mathcal{A}$	**Challenger** $\mathcal{C}$
	$\mathsf{pp} \leftarrow \mathsf{PGen}(1^\lambda)$
	$m \leftarrow_{\$} \mathcal{M}$
	$(\mathsf{com}_0, r_0) \leftarrow \mathsf{Commit}(m)$
$\xleftarrow{\quad \mathsf{pp}, \mathsf{com}_0, \mathsf{com}_1 \quad}$	$(\mathsf{com}_1, r_1) \leftarrow \mathsf{Commit}(m)$
Choose r_L $\xrightarrow{\quad r_L \quad}$	$\mathcal{A}$ wins if
	$\mathsf{Link}(\mathsf{com}_0, \mathsf{com}_1, r_L) = 1$

Fig. 8. Link secrecy game.

LinkMaterial (m, r_0, r_1)	Link($\mathsf{com}_0, \mathsf{com}_1, r_L$)
1 : **return** $r_0 r_1^{-1}$	1 : **if** $r_L \star \mathsf{com}_1 = \mathsf{com}_0$
	2 : **return** 1
	3 : **else return** 0

Fig. 9. Algorithm for linking commitment from a GACE.

Proof. We have already proven in Theorem 1 that the bit commitment in Fig. 4 is secure under the dGA-IP assumption. Now, we prove that the linkable commitment scheme is secure, namely it is computationally linkable-hiding, perfectly linkable-binding and computationally link secret.

- **Linkable-hiding.** We show that the Hiding game reduces to the HidingLink game. The idea is to let the adversary of the Hiding(Π_{Com}) game to simulate the HidingLink game challenger by creating a new random commitment (and the linking material) to the same message of the commitment it has received from its challenger. Now we explain it in greater detail.
  Let $\mathcal{A}'$ be an adversary that wins the *cLink* game with non-negligible advantage $\epsilon(\lambda)$. We can define an adversary $\mathcal{A}$ for the Hiding game that wins with a non-negligible advantage. Since we are in the binary case, the challenger $\mathcal{C}$ picks a message b and sends to $\mathcal{A}$ the commitment com of b. Now $\mathcal{A}$ picks a random element g in G and computes $\mathsf{com}' = g \star \mathsf{com}$, that is a valid and randomly generated commitment to b. $\mathcal{A}$ queries to $\mathcal{A}'$, the adversary of the HidingLink game, the commitments com, com' and the linking material g. Note that $\mathcal{A}$ correctly simulates the challenger of the HidingLink game since the bit b and com are chosen at random from $\mathcal{C}$, com' is chosen at random from $\mathcal{A}$ and the linking material is valid.

$\mathcal{A}'$ returns a bit b' which $\mathcal{A}$ sends to $\mathcal{C}$ as its guess. If $\mathcal{A}'$ correctly guesses the bit committed to in com and com' then clearly also $\mathcal{A}$ wins its game. Therefore the advantage of $\mathcal{A}$ is the same of the one of $\mathcal{A}'$ and is non-negligible.

We can conclude that, since the commitment Π_{Com} is computationally hiding under the dGA-IP assumption, it is also computationally linkable-hiding.

- **Perfectly linkable-binding.** Suppose that an adversary returns with positive probability a tuple $(m_0, m_1, \mathsf{com}_0, \mathsf{com}_1, r_L)$ such that $m_0 \neq m_1$ and $\mathsf{Link}(\mathsf{com}_0, \mathsf{com}_1, r_L) = 1$. By construction, there exist two elements g_0 and g_1 in G such that

$$\mathsf{com}_0 = g_0 \star \langle m_0 \rangle \text{ and } \mathsf{com}_1 = g_1 \star \langle m_1 \rangle$$

From $\mathsf{Link}(\mathsf{com}_0, \mathsf{com}_1, r_L) = 1$ we have that $r_L \star \mathsf{com}_1 = \mathsf{com}_0$, and hence com_0 and com_1 are in the same orbit. Since $m_0 = f(\mathsf{com}_0) = f(\mathsf{com}_1) = m_1$, where f is the invariant function in the GACE, we have a contradiction. Hence, there are no adversaries that can output such a tuple with positive probability.

- **Computationally link secret.** We show that, if a PPT adversary $\mathcal{A}$, on input com_0 and com_1, can find r_L such that $\mathsf{Link}(\mathsf{com}_0, \mathsf{com}_1, r_L) = 1$, then it contradicts the One-way group action assumption. Essentially, if com_0 and com_1 are commitments to m_0, then they are in the same orbit of $\langle m_0 \rangle$. Finding an r_L in G such that $\mathsf{Link}(\mathsf{com}_0, \mathsf{com}_1, r_L) = 1$ means finding an element of G sending com_1 to com_0, and this is intractable by hypothesis.

Remark 1. Observe that, if an inadmissible value is committed, for instance an element x that is not in the orbit of $\langle t_0 \rangle$ nor $\langle t_1 \rangle$, then the linkability continues to work. In fact, two commitments of the above x can be linked. Therefore we refer to the above scheme as a *honest sender* linkable commitment. To cover even the case where the sender may commit to an inadmissible value, some techniques from ring signature schemes can be used. Using the framework of Beullens, Katsumata and Pintore [5], a proof of the legitimacy of the commitment can be generated in the random oracle model. In the commit phase, the sender generates (com, r) from $\mathsf{Commit}(b)$, then attaches to com a non-interactive proof of the OR-relation

$$\{(\mathsf{com}, g) \mid \mathsf{com} = g \star \langle t_0 \rangle \text{ or } \mathsf{com} = g \star \langle t_1 \rangle\}.$$

We refer to [5] for the details. However, this proof needs many repetitions to achieve a reasonable security level, leading to a huge cost in communication.

6   An Instantiation with Tensors

6.1   3-Tensors and Group Actions

Let n be a positive integer and let $\mathbf{V}$ be the tensor space given by $\mathbb{F}_q^n \otimes \mathbb{F}_q^n \otimes \mathbb{F}_q^n$. Let $\{e_1, \ldots, e_n\}$ be a base of $\mathbb{F}_q^n$, hence an element M of $\mathbf{V}$ can be written as

$$M = \sum_{i,j,k} M(i,j,k) e_i \otimes e_j \otimes e_k, \tag{1}$$

where $M(i, j, k)$ are elements in $\mathbb{F}_q$. A *rank one* (or *decomposable*) tensor is an element of the form $a \otimes b \otimes c$, where a, b, c are in $\mathbb{F}_q^n$. Given a tensor M, its *rank* is the minimal non-negative integer r such that there exist $M_1, \ldots, M_r$ rank one tensors for which $M = \sum_{i=1}^r M_i$, and we write $\mathrm{rk}(M) = r$. In general, computing the rank of a tensor is an hard task [18,31,32].

A group action can be defined on the vector space $\mathbf{V}$ of tensors from the group $G = \mathrm{GL}(n) \times \mathrm{GL}(n) \times \mathrm{GL}(n)$ as follows:

$$\star : G \times \mathbf{V} \to \mathbf{V},$$

$$\left((A, B, C), \sum_{i,j,k} M(i, j, k) e_i \otimes e_j \otimes e_k \right) \mapsto \sum_{i,j,k} M(i, j, k) A e_i \otimes B e_j \otimes C e_k.$$

It can be shown that this action does not change the rank of a tensor. However, if it is extended to non-invertible matrices, this property does not hold: for example the zero matrix sends every tensor into the zero tensor.

6.2 GACE and Bit Commitment from Tensors

Given the group action defined above, we want to build a Group Action with Canonical Element. Since the computation of the rank is supposed to be hard, we set $T = \mathbb{N}$ and

$$f : \mathbf{V} \to \mathbb{N}, \ M \mapsto \mathrm{rk}(M).$$

In order to define the function $\langle \cdot \rangle$, we need to do some observations. From Eq. (1), we see that the rank of a tensor is at most n^3 and with a simple trick it can be shown that it is at most n^2. Actually, the maximal rank is strictly less that this value. As showed in [19], the maximal rank attainable by a tensor in $\mathbf{V}$ is between $\frac{1}{3}n^2$ and $\frac{3}{4}n^2$. Moreover, an open problem in this field is to exhibit the explicit construction of a high-rank tensor. Even if there are some results [2,6,36], we are not able to construct a tensor of any given rank. Luckily, there is a set of integers for which we can easily exhibit tensors of a given rank. Let $T' = \{1, \ldots, n\}$ and we can define the function

$$\langle \cdot \rangle : T' \to \mathbf{V},$$

$$r \mapsto \sum_{i=1}^r e_i \otimes e_i \otimes e_i.$$

We can see that $f(\langle r \rangle) = r$ for any r in $T' = \{1, \ldots, n\}$, hence the tuple $(G, \mathbf{V}, \star, f, \langle \cdot \rangle)$ is a GACE. In fact, computing the rank of a random tensor of promised rank between 1 and n is hard, while recognize the rank of $\langle r \rangle$ is easy.

The non-interactive bit commitment scheme we present is based on the general one in Fig. 4. During the parameter generation phase, we choose $n - 1$ and n as elements of T' encoding the bits 0 and 1, respectively.

Concretely, given a security parameter λ, a prime power q, an integer n and the tensor space $\mathbf{V} = \mathbb{F}_q^n \otimes \mathbb{F}_q^n \otimes \mathbb{F}_q^n$, the public parameters are

$$(G, \mathbf{V}, \star, f, \langle \cdot \rangle, n - 1, n).$$

Let us analyze the assumptions on this particular group action. The dGA-IP assumption for tensors is related to the Tensor Isomorphism problem [16,17], which is complete for a large class of problems and it is conjectured hard even for a quantum computer. The One-Way assumption on tensors is linked to the computational version of the dGA-IP problem: given two tensors in the same orbit, find the group element that links them. This problem is believed to be hard and it is directly used in various cryptosystem [10,20], while other constructions use polynomially equivalent problems [35]. When we consider just the orbits of rank n and $n - 1$, these assumptions seem to remain intractable.

Summarizing, to commit to a bit b, the sender picks a random g in G and obtains the commitment com equal to $g \star \langle n - 1 \rangle$ if $b = 0$ or $g \star \langle n \rangle$ if $b = 1$. The opening material is given by g. To open the commitment com, the sender communicates to the receiver b and g and the latter checks that $g^{-1} \star$ com is equal to $\langle n - 1 \rangle$ or $\langle n \rangle$. There is one additional check to take care during the opening phase: the receiver must verify the membership of g to G. In fact, if $g = (A, B, C)$ and A, B or C are non-invertible, then g can send a tensor of rank n to a tensor of rank $n - 1$, breaking the binding property.

Analogously, a linkable bit commitment can be designed on tensors with the constructions given in Subsection 5.1.

7   Conclusions

In this work, we have presented a framework based on group actions that makes use of invariant functions and canonical elements, namely a Group Action with Canonical Element (GACE). The considered invariant function must be hard to compute on a large class of elements, but at the same time its computation on the canonical elements must be feasible. Then, we showed how to design a bit commitment based on this framework that is proven secure in the standard model. More in detail, breaking the hiding assumption of our commitment scheme means breaking independently both 2GA-PR and dGA-IP. This leads to the first non-interactive bit commitment relying on group actions.

One of the most interesting aspects of our construction is that it requires the action to be non-transitive. This is somehow novel in the cryptographic group action literature, where previous schemes rely on transitive action or they restrict to a single orbit. Concretely, in our framework we need to exhibit two elements that belong to two different orbits.

Moreover, we introduce the notion of linkable commitment and we prove that our bit commitment can be easily extended to a linkable one. Finally, we show an instantiation of our framework and commitment using tensors on finite fields. In this case, the invariant function is the tensor rank, and the cryptographic assumption is linked to the computational version of the dGA-IP problem.

As a future work, a commitment based on more orbits or new cryptographic schemes starting from a GACE could be investigated. At the same time, it would be interesting to find other GACEs to concretely instantiate the framework.

Acknowledgements. The authors are members of GNSAGA of INdAM. The first and the third authors are members of CrypTO, the group of Cryptography and Number Theory of Politecnico di Torino. The first author acknowledges support from TIM S.p.A. through the PhD scholarship. The second author acknowledges support from Eustema S.p.A. through the PhD scholarship. The third author acknowledges support from Ripple's University Blockchain Research Initiative.

A   2GA-PR Reduces to Hiding(Π_{Com})

The reduction used to prove the hiding property under the 2GA-PR assumption is exactly the same given in the proof of Theorem 2, and the main difference between the proof of the hiding property under the dGA-IP assumption and the following is that the outcome of the adversaries of the Hiding(Π_{Com}) game $\mathcal{A}_1$ and $\mathcal{A}_2$ are not independent anymore, but are only conditionally independent once the input values (s and t) are fixed.

In fact, in the 2GA-PR game $\Pr[O(s) = O(t)] = \frac{3}{4}$ which means that the selection of the value of t, input to $\mathcal{A}_2$ depends on the selection of s, given in input to $\mathcal{A}_1$.

Theorem 5. *The bit commitment scheme in Fig. 4 instantiated with two orbits of similar size is computationally hiding under the 2GA-PR assumption.*

For simplicity, in the following proof we assume that the cardinality of the two orbits is the same, that is, the probability of picking an element at random inside any orbit is $\frac{1}{2}$. The proof can be easily generalized to the case where the probability of falling into one orbit is negligibly greater than the probability of falling into the other. In other words, the proof holds whenever there exists a negligible function $\nu(\lambda)$ such that, given the two orbits O_0 and O_1,

$$|\Pr[x \in O_0] - \Pr[x \in O_1]| = \nu(\lambda)$$

for a randomly chosen x in $O_0 \cup O_1$. This assumption seems admissible and not too strict for cryptographic purposes.

Proof. We must prove that the hiding property holds for Π_{Com}. We show that, given an adversary of the Hiding(Π_{Com}) game with non-negligible advantage, we can build an adversary of the 2GA-PR game with non-negligible advantage (recall that the advantage of $\mathcal{A}$ is defined as $\mathbf{Adv}(\mathcal{A}, 2\text{GA-PR}(\mathsf{pp})) = \Pr[\mathcal{A} \text{ wins } 2\text{GA-PR}(\mathsf{pp})] - \frac{1}{2}$).

1. *Reduction description.*
   To define $\mathcal{A}$, we use two independent instances of the same adversary $\mathcal{A}_1, \mathcal{A}_2$ of the hiding game as we did in the proof of Theorem 2; then, we perform the same reduction, as it is presented in Fig. 10.

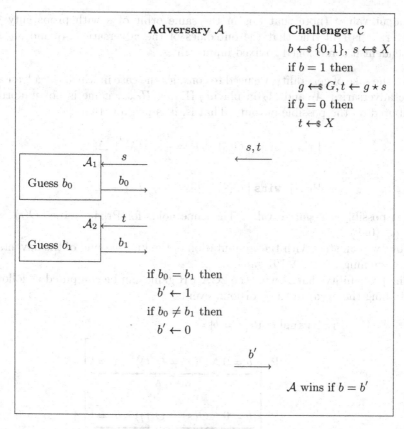

Fig. 10. Reduction from 2GA-PR to the hiding game for the bit commitment scheme.

2. $\mathcal{A}$ *correctly simulates the* Hiding(Π_{Com}) *challenger.*

   The adversary $\mathcal{A}$ correctly simulates the challenger of Hiding(Π_{Com}) with respect to the adversaries $\mathcal{A}_1$ and $\mathcal{A}_2$ separately, in fact both s and t are uniformly sampled from the set of commitment to 0 and 1. Therefore, $\mathcal{A}_1$ and $\mathcal{A}_2$ will output the right bit with advantage $\epsilon(\lambda)$.

3. *Measurement of $\mathcal{A}$'s advantage.*

   From now on, when we consider the orbits $O(s)$ and $O(t)$ of s and t respectively, they will assume binary values according to the relation used in the bit commitment scheme Π_{Com}: $O(s) = 1$ if s lives in the orbit of commitments to 1, and $O(s) = 0$ if s lives in the orbit of commitments to 0. The same holds for $O(t)$.

   Before computing the lower bound of the advantage of the adversary $\mathcal{A}$, we state the following remark.

Remark 2. The outcomes of the games performed by $\mathcal{A}_1$ and $\mathcal{A}_2$ in the reduction of Fig. 10 are not independent since the values given as inputs to them are dependent values (note that t is in the same orbit of s with probability $\frac{3}{4}$). However, it is still true that the outcomes of the adversaries $\mathcal{A}_1$ and $\mathcal{A}_2$ are independent if conditioned to fixed input values.

For the sake of generality, we need to consider the case in which the advantage of the adversaries $\mathcal{A}_1$ and $\mathcal{A}_2$ in playing Hiding(Π_{Com}) game is not uniformly distributed on the possible outputs. That is, it is possible that

$$\Pr[\mathcal{A}_1 \text{ wins} \mid O(s) = 1] = \frac{1}{2} + \epsilon(\lambda) + \Delta,$$

$$\Pr[\mathcal{A}_1 \text{ wins} \mid O(s) = 0] = \frac{1}{2} + \epsilon(\lambda) - \Delta,$$

with Δ possibly a negative value. The same holds for $\Pr[\mathcal{A}_2 \text{ wins} \mid O(t) = b]$, with $b \in \{0, 1\}$.

Now, we can start with the computation of the lower bound of the advantage of $\mathcal{A}$ in winning the 2GA-PR game.

The probability that $\mathcal{A}$ wins the 2GA-PR game can be computed as follows, partitioning the event in three disjoint events:

$$\Pr[\mathcal{A} \text{ wins}] = \Pr[b' = b] =$$

$$\Pr\left[\underbrace{(b = 0 \wedge O(s) \neq O(t)) \wedge b' = b}_{\text{Event A}}\right] +$$

$$\Pr\left[\underbrace{(b = 0 \wedge O(s) = O(t)) \wedge b' = b}_{\text{Event B}}\right] +$$

$$\Pr\left[\underbrace{b = 1 \wedge b' = b}_{\text{Event C}}\right].$$

We now separately quantify the three probabilities as follows. We recall that according to the event we are considering, the event $b = b'$ can be translated in terms of success of the adversaries $\mathcal{A}_1$ and $\mathcal{A}_2$

- **Event A**: when $b = 0$ and $O(s) \neq O(t)$, then $b = b'$ when both $\mathcal{A}_1$ and $\mathcal{A}_2$ win or when both of them lose. Therefore, it holds that

$$\begin{aligned}
\Pr[b = 0 \wedge O(s) \neq O(t) \wedge b' = b] = \\
\Pr[b = 0 \wedge O(s) \neq O(t) \wedge \mathcal{A}_1 \text{ wins} \wedge \mathcal{A}_2 \text{ wins}] + \quad (2) \\
\Pr[b = 0 \wedge O(s) \neq O(t) \wedge \mathcal{A}_1 \text{ loses} \wedge \mathcal{A}_2 \text{ loses}].
\end{aligned}$$

We can compute this probability by considering the general case $\Pr[b = 0 \wedge O(s) \neq O(t) \wedge \mathcal{A}_1 \text{ outcome} \wedge \mathcal{A}_2 \text{ outcome}]$ and then substituting outcome with wins or loses accordingly with the formula above.

It holds that

$$\Pr[b = 0 \wedge O(s) \neq O(t) \wedge \mathcal{A}_1 \text{ outcome} \wedge \mathcal{A}_2 \text{ outcome}] =$$

$$\sum_{c=0}^{1} \Pr[b = 0 \wedge O(s) = c \wedge O(t) = 1 - c \wedge \mathcal{A}_1 \text{ outcome} \wedge \mathcal{A}_2 \text{ outcome}] =$$

$$\sum_{c=0}^{1} \Big(\Pr[\mathcal{A}_1 \text{ outcome} \wedge \mathcal{A}_2 \text{ outcome} \mid b = 0 \wedge O(s) = c \wedge O(t) = 1 - c] \cdot$$

$$\cdot \Pr[b = 0 \wedge O(s) = c \wedge O(t) = 1 - c] \Big).$$

Since the outcomes of $\mathcal{A}_1$ and $\mathcal{A}_2$ are independent once their input values are fixed, we have that

$$\Pr[\mathcal{A}_1 \text{ outcome} \wedge \mathcal{A}_2 \text{ outcome} \mid b = 0 \wedge O(s) = c \wedge O(t) = 1 - c] =$$

$$\prod_{i=1}^{2} \Pr[\mathcal{A}_i \text{ outcome} \mid b = 0 \wedge O(s) = c \wedge O(t) = 1 - c],$$

with $c \in \{0, 1\}$.
Since the outcome of $\mathcal{A}_1$ only depends on the value of $O(s)$ and the outcome of $\mathcal{A}_2$ depends only on $O(t)$, then

$$\Pr[\mathcal{A}_1 \text{ outcome} \wedge \mathcal{A}_2 \text{ outcome} \mid b = 0 \wedge O(s) = c \wedge O(t) = 1 - c] =$$
$$\Pr[\mathcal{A}_1 \text{ outcome} \mid O(s) = c] \Pr[\mathcal{A}_2 \text{ outcome} \mid O(t) = 1 - c]$$

Therefore, since $\Pr\big[b = 0 \wedge O(s) = \bar{b} \wedge O(t) = 1 - \bar{b}\big] = \frac{1}{8}$ with $\bar{b} \in \{0, 1\}$ then

$$\Pr[b = 0 \wedge O(s) \neq O(t) \wedge \mathcal{A}_1 \text{ outcome} \wedge \mathcal{A}_2 \text{ outcome}] =$$

$$\frac{1}{8} \Big(\Pr[\mathcal{A}_1 \text{ outcome} \mid O(s) = 1] \cdot \Pr[\mathcal{A}_2 \text{ outcome} \mid O(t) = 0] +$$

$$\Pr[\mathcal{A}_1 \text{ outcome} \mid O(s) = 0] \cdot \Pr[\mathcal{A}_2 \text{ outcome} \mid O(t) = 1] \Big).$$

We can finally compute the initial probability given in Eq. (2), by substituting outcome with wins and loses and obtaining

$$\Pr[b = 0 \wedge O(s) \neq O(t) \wedge b' = b] = \frac{1}{8} + \frac{1}{2}\epsilon^2(\lambda) - \frac{1}{2}\Delta^2. \tag{3}$$

– **Event B**: when $b = 0$ and $O(s) = O(t)$, then $b = b'$ when either $\mathcal{A}_1$ wins and $\mathcal{A}_2$ loses or when $\mathcal{A}_1$ loses and $\mathcal{A}_2$ wins. Therefore, it holds that

$$\Pr[b = 0 \wedge O(s) = O(t) \wedge b' = b] =$$
$$\Pr[b = 0 \wedge O(s) = O(t) \wedge \mathcal{A}_1 \text{ wins} \wedge \mathcal{A}_2 \text{ loses}] + \tag{4}$$
$$\Pr[b = 0 \wedge O(s) = O(t) \wedge \mathcal{A}_1 \text{ loses} \wedge \mathcal{A}_2 \text{ wins}].$$

Since in this case the input of $\mathcal{A}_1$ and $\mathcal{A}_2$ are in the same orbit, then we can state

$$\Pr[b = 0 \wedge O(s) = O(t) \wedge b' = b] =$$
$$2\Pr[b = 0 \wedge O(s) = O(t) \wedge \mathcal{A}_1 \text{ wins} \wedge \mathcal{A}_2 \text{ loses}] =$$
$$2\sum_{c=0}^{1} \Pr[b = 0 \wedge O(s) = c \wedge O(t) = c \wedge \mathcal{A}_1 \text{ wins} \wedge \mathcal{A}_2 \text{ loses}].$$

Using arguments similar to the ones used for **Event A**, that is the conditional independence of the outcomes of the adversaries once the inputs are fixed, the fact that the output of $\mathcal{A}_1$ (resp. $\mathcal{A}_2$) depends only on $O(s)$ (resp. on $O(t)$) and finally that $\Pr[b = 0 \wedge O(s) = c \wedge O(t) = c] = \frac{1}{8}$, for $c \in \{0,1\}$, we can write the Eq. (4) as follows

$$\Pr[b = 0 \wedge O(s) = O(t) \wedge b' = b] = \frac{1}{8} - \frac{1}{2}\epsilon^2(\lambda) - \frac{1}{2}\Delta^2. \tag{5}$$

– **Event C**: when $b = 1$, $O(s) = O(t)$, then $b = b'$ when both $\mathcal{A}_1$ and $\mathcal{A}_2$ win or when both of them lose. Therefore, it holds that

$$\Pr[b = 1 \wedge b' = b] =$$
$$\Pr[b = 1 \wedge \mathcal{A}_1 \text{ wins} \wedge \mathcal{A}_2 \text{ wins}]+ \tag{6}$$
$$\Pr[b = 1 \wedge \mathcal{A}_1 \text{ loses} \wedge \mathcal{A}_2 \text{ loses}].$$

As in the computation of the probability of **Event A**, we must compute $\Pr[b = 1 \wedge \mathcal{A}_1 \text{ outcome} \wedge \mathcal{A}_2 \text{ outcome}]$. Using similar arguments as before, and noticing that $\Pr[b = 1 \wedge O(s) = c \wedge O(t) = c] = \frac{1}{4}$ with $c \in \{0,1\}$, it can be shown that

$$\Pr[b = 1 \wedge \mathcal{A}_1 \text{ outcome} \wedge \mathcal{A}_2 \text{ outcome}] =$$
$$\frac{1}{4}\sum_{c=0}^{1} \Pr[\mathcal{A}_1 \text{ outcome} \mid O(s) = c]\Pr[\mathcal{A}_2 \text{ outcome} \mid O(t) = c]$$

Therefore, substituting outcome with loses and wins, and using the probabilities of success of adversaries $\mathcal{A}_1$ and $\mathcal{A}_2$, from Eq. (6) we obtain

$$\Pr[b = 1 \wedge b' = b] = \frac{1}{4} + \epsilon^2(\lambda) + \Delta^2. \tag{7}$$

Combining the partial results derived analysing **Event A**, **Event B** and **Event C** from Equations (3),(5) and (7) respectively, we obtain the final result

$$\Pr[\mathcal{A} \text{ wins}] = \frac{1}{2} + \epsilon^2(\lambda),$$

which proves that we have built an adversary for the 2GA-PR game which wins with non-negligible advantage. Therefore, an adversary who wins the hiding game with non-negligible advantage does not exist due to the 2GA-PR assumption. This means that the binary commitment scheme we have described results to be perfectly binding and computationally hiding.

B Hiding(Π_{Com}) Reduces to dGA-IP

Theorem 6. *The* Hiding(Π_{Com}) *game reduces to dGA-IP game.*

Proof. We show how the existence of an adversary of dGA-IP problem with non-negligible advantage allows the creation of an adversary of the Hiding(Π_{Com}) game with non-negligible advantage.

1. *Reduction description.*

   The adversary $\mathcal{A}$ of the Hiding(Π_{Com}) game (see Fig. 11) receives from the challenger a commitment c to a randomly generated bit b. $\mathcal{A}$ generates a commitment c' to a random bit b' and sends c, c' to $\mathcal{A}'$, the adversary to the dGA-IP game with non-negligible advantage. $\mathcal{A}$ receives a response b_0 from $\mathcal{A}'$ and returns to the Hiding(Π_{Com}) challenger the bit b' if $b_0 = 1$ (i.e. $\mathcal{A}'$ has guessed that c and c' are in the same orbit), otherwise $\mathcal{A}$ returns $1 - b'$.

2. *$\mathcal{A}$ correctly simulates the dGA-IP challenger.*

   The adversary $\mathcal{A}$ receives a commitment to a random unknown bit b. Therefore, in order to simulate the dGA-IP challenger, it generates a random bit b' and a commitment to such bit. In this way, $\mathcal{A}$ generates couples of elements

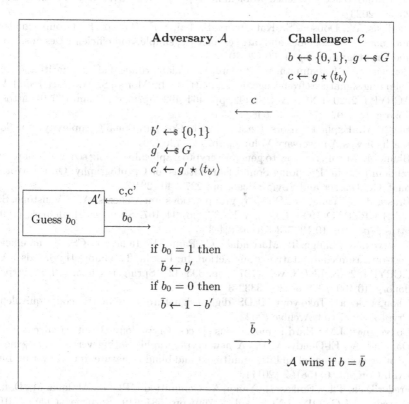

Fig. 11. Reduction from the hiding game for the bit commitment scheme to dGA-IP.

in X that live in the same orbit with probability $\frac{1}{2}$ as it does the dGA-IP challenger.

3. *Measurement of $\mathcal{A}$'s advantage.*
   The adversary $\mathcal{A}$ wins exactly with the same probability of $\mathcal{A}'$, since every time $\mathcal{A}'$ guesses the right answer to the dGA-IP game, $\mathcal{A}$ learns the orbit in which the element c lies since it knows the orbit of c'. Therefore, if $\mathcal{A}'$ wins the dGA-IP game with non-negligible advantage, also $\mathcal{A}$ wins the Hiding(Π_{Com}) game with non negligible advantage.

References

1. Alamati, N., De Feo, L., Montgomery, H., Patranabis, S.: Cryptographic group actions and applications. In: Moriai, S., Wang, H. (eds.) ASIACRYPT 2020. LNCS, vol. 12492, pp. 411–439. Springer, Cham (2020). https://doi.org/10.1007/978-3-030-64834-3_14

2. Alexeev, B., Forbes, M.A., Tsimerman, J.: Tensor rank: some lower and upper bounds. In: 2011 IEEE 26th Annual Conference on Computational Complexity, pp. 283–291. IEEE (2011)

3. Barenghi, A., Biasse, J.F., Persichetti, E., Santini, P.: On the computational hardness of the code equivalence problem in cryptography. Adv. Math. Commun. **17**(1), 23–55 (2023)

4. Beullens, W., Dobson, S., Katsumata, S., Lai, Y.F., Pintore, F.: Group signatures and more from isogenies and lattices: generic, simple, and efficient. Designs, Codes and Cryptography, pp. 1–60 (2023)

5. Beullens, W., Katsumata, S., Pintore, F.: Calamari and Falafl: logarithmic (linkable) ring signatures from isogenies and lattices. In: Moriai, S., Wang, H. (eds.) ASIACRYPT 2020. LNCS, vol. 12492, pp. 464–492. Springer, Cham (2020). https://doi.org/10.1007/978-3-030-64834-3_16

6. Bläser, M.: Explicit tensors. Perspectives in Computational Complexity: The Somenath Biswas Anniversary Volume, pp. 117–130 (2014)

7. Blum, M., Micali, S.: How to generate cryptographically strong sequences of pseudo random bits. In: Providing Sound Foundations for Cryptography: On the Work of Shafi Goldwasser and Silvio Micali, pp. 227–240 (2019)

8. Brassard, G., Yung, M.: One-way group actions. In: Menezes, A.J., Vanstone, S.A. (eds.) CRYPTO 1990. LNCS, vol. 537, pp. 94–107. Springer, Heidelberg (1991). https://doi.org/10.1007/3-540-38424-3_7

9. Castryck, W., Lange, T., Martindale, C., Panny, L., Renes, J.: CSIDH: an efficient post-quantum commutative group action. In: Peyrin, T., Galbraith, S. (eds.) ASIACRYPT 2018. LNCS, vol. 11274, pp. 395–427. Springer, Cham (2018). https://doi.org/10.1007/978-3-030-03332-3_15

10. Chou, T., et al.: Take your MEDS: digital signatures from matrix code equivalence. Cryptology ePrint Archive (2022)

11. Couveignes, J.M.: Hard homogeneous spaces. Cryptology ePrint Archive (2006)

12. Darwish, A., El-Gendy, M.M.: A new cryptographic voting verifiable scheme for e-voting system based on bit commitment and blind signature. Int. J. Swarm. Intel. Evol. Comput. **6**(158), 2 (2017)

13. Frederiksen, T.K., Pinkas, B., Yanai, A.: Committed MPC. In: Abdalla, M., Dahab, R. (eds.) PKC 2018. LNCS, vol. 10769, pp. 587–619. Springer, Cham (2018). https://doi.org/10.1007/978-3-319-76578-5_20

14. Goldreich, O., Micali, S., Wigderson, A.: Proofs that yield nothing but their validity or all languages in NP have zero-knowledge proof systems. J. ACM (JACM) **38**(3), 690–728 (1991)
15. Grigoriev, D., Shpilrain, V.: Authentication schemes from actions on graphs, groups, or rings. Ann. Pure Appl. Logic **162**(3), 194–200 (2010)
16. Grochow, J.A., Qiao, Y.: Isomorphism problems for tensors, groups, and cubic forms: completeness and reductions. arXiv preprint: arXiv:1907.00309 (2019)
17. Grochow, J.A., Qiao, Y.: On the complexity of isomorphism problems for tensors, groups, and polynomials I: tensor isomorphism-completeness. In: 12th Innovations in Theoretical Computer Science Conference (ITCS 2021). Schloss Dagstuhl-Leibniz-Zentrum für Informatik (2021)
18. Håstad, J.: Tensor rank is NP-complete. In: Ausiello, G., Dezani-Ciancaglini, M., Della Rocca, S.R. (eds.) ICALP 1989. LNCS, vol. 372, pp. 451–460. Springer, Heidelberg (1989). https://doi.org/10.1007/BFb0035776
19. Howell, T.D.: Global properties of tensor rank. Linear Algebra Appl. **22**, 9–23 (1978)
20. Ji, Z., Qiao, Y., Song, F., Yun, A.: General linear group action on tensors: a candidate for post-quantum cryptography. In: Hofheinz, D., Rosen, A. (eds.) TCC 2019. LNCS, vol. 11891, pp. 251–281. Springer, Cham (2019). https://doi.org/10.1007/978-3-030-36030-6_11
21. Juels, A., Luby, M., Ostrovsky, R.: Security of blind digital signatures. In: Kaliski, B.S. (ed.) Advances in Cryptology - CRYPTO '97. Lecture Notes in Computer Science, vol. 1294, pp. 150–164. Springer, Berlin (2006). https://doi.org/10.1007/bfb0052233
22. Leroux, A., Roméas, M.: Updatable encryption from group actions. Cryptology ePrint Archive (2022)
23. Lyubashevsky, V., Nguyen, N.K., Seiler, G.: Shorter lattice-based zero-knowledge proofs via one-time commitments. In: Garay, J.A. (ed.) PKC 2021. LNCS, vol. 12710, pp. 215–241. Springer, Cham (2021). https://doi.org/10.1007/978-3-030-75245-3_9
24. Naor, M.: Bit commitment using pseudorandomness. J. Cryptol. **4**, 151–158 (1991)
25. Ostrovsky, R., Persiano, G., Visconti, I.: Simulation-based concurrent non-malleable commitments and decommitments. In: Reingold, O. (ed.) TCC 2009. LNCS, vol. 5444, pp. 91–108. Springer, Heidelberg (2009). https://doi.org/10.1007/978-3-642-00457-5_7
26. Patarin, J.: Hidden fields equations (HFE) and isomorphisms of polynomials (IP): two new families of asymmetric algorithms. In: Maurer, U. (ed.) EUROCRYPT 1996. LNCS, vol. 1070, pp. 33–48. Springer, Heidelberg (1996). https://doi.org/10.1007/3-540-68339-9_4
27. Pedersen, T.P.: Non-interactive and information-theoretic secure verifiable secret sharing. In: Feigenbaum, J. (ed.) CRYPTO 1991. LNCS, vol. 576, pp. 129–140. Springer, Heidelberg (1992). https://doi.org/10.1007/3-540-46766-1_9
28. Petrank, E., Roth, R.M.: Is code equivalence easy to decide? IEEE Trans. Inf. Theory **43**(5), 1602–1604 (1997)
29. Poelstra, A., Back, A., Friedenbach, M., Maxwell, G., Wuille, P.: Confidential assets. In: Zohar, A., et al. (eds.) FC 2018. LNCS, vol. 10958, pp. 43–63. Springer, Heidelberg (2019). https://doi.org/10.1007/978-3-662-58820-8_4
30. Reijnders, K., Samardjiska, S., Trimoska, M.: Hardness estimates of the code equivalence problem in the rank metric. Cryptology ePrint Archive (2022)
31. Schaefer, M., Štefankovič, D.: The complexity of tensor rank. Theory Comput. Syst. **62**, 1161–1174 (2018)

32. Shitov, Y.: How hard is the tensor rank? arXiv preprint: arXiv:1611.01559 (2016)
33. Shor, P.W.: Algorithms for quantum computation: discrete logarithms and factoring. In: Proceedings 35th Annual Symposium on Foundations of Computer Science, pp. 124–134. IEEE (1994)
34. Stolbunov, A.: Cryptographic schemes based on isogenies (2012)
35. Tang, G., Duong, D.H., Joux, A., Plantard, T., Qiao, Y., Susilo, W.: Practical post-quantum signature schemes from isomorphism problems of trilinear forms. In: Dunkelman, O., Dziembowski, S. (eds.) Advances in Cryptology - EUROCRYPT 2022. Lecture Notes in Computer Science, vol. 13277, pp. 582–612. Springer, Cham (2022). https://doi.org/10.1007/978-3-031-07082-2_21
36. Weitz, B.: An improvement on ranks of explicit tensors. arXiv preprint: arXiv:1102.0580 (2011)

Pseudorandomness of Decoding, Revisited: Adapting OHCP to Code-Based Cryptography

Maxime Bombar[1,2](✉) , Alain Couvreur[1,2] ,
and Thomas Debris-Alazard[1,2]

[1] LIX, CNRS UMR 7161, École Polytechnique, Institut Polytechnique de Paris,
1 rue Honoré d'Estienne d'Orves, 91120 Palaiseau Cedex, France
[2] Inria, Paris, France
{maxime.bombar,alain.couvreur,thomas.debris}@inria.fr

Abstract. Recent code-based cryptosystems rely, among other things, on the hardness of the decisional decoding problem. If the search version is well understood, both from practical and theoretical standpoints, the decision version has been less studied in the literature, and little is known about its relationships with the search version, especially for structured variants. On the other hand, in the world of Euclidean lattices, the situation is rather different, and many reductions exist, both for unstructured and structured versions of the underlying problems. For the latter versions, a powerful tool called the OHCP framework (for Oracle with Hidden Center Problem), which appears to be very general, has been introduced by Peikert *et al.* (STOC 2017) and has proved to be very useful as a black box inside reductions.

In this work, we revisit this technique and extract the very essence of this framework, namely the Oracle Comparison Problem (OCP), to show how to recover the support of the error, solving an Oracle with Hidden Support Problem (OHSP), more suitable for code-based cryptography. This yields a new worst-case to average-case search-to-decision reduction for the Decoding Problem, as well as a new average-case to average-case reduction. We then turn to the structured versions and explain why this is not as straightforward as for Euclidean lattices. If we fail to give a search-to-decision reduction for structured codes, we believe that our work opens the way towards new reductions for structured codes, given that the OHCP framework proved to be so powerful in lattice-based cryptography. Furthermore, we also believe that this technique could be extended to codes endowed with other metrics, such as the rank metric, for which no reduction is known.

Keywords: Decoding Problem · OHCP · Search-to-Decision Reductions · Worst-Case to Average-Case

T. Debris-Alazard—This work was funded by the French Agence Nationale de la Recherche through ANR JCJC COLA (ANR-21-CE39-0011), ANR BARRACUDA (ANR-21-CE39-0009-BARRACUDA) and *Plan France 2030* ANR-22-PETQ-0008.

J. Guo and R. Steinfeld (Eds.): ASIACRYPT 2023, LNCS 14444, pp. 253–283, 2023.
https://doi.org/10.1007/978-981-99-8739-9_9

1   Introduction

Security Reductions in Post–quantum Cryptography. In the last two decades, there has been a longstanding trend to develop reductions between *generic* or even *worst-case* problems, in view to provide security guarantees of some encryption schemes and digital signatures. The most significant part of the known reductions concern lattice–based cryptography. In particular, the worst-case to average-case reductions between various lattice problems [28,29,32,33,35,37,39] provide a very convincing argument to assert that the security of cryptographic primitives rest only on the worst-case hardness of well-studied problems such as SVP or SIS. The recent conclusion of the third round of NIST standardisation process testifies from this trust: among the four selected schemes for standardisation, three of them are based on lattices.

In comparison, code–based cryptography appears to lag behind from the point of view of security reductions, despite being very promising in terms of simplicity of the designs, short length of ciphertexts, efficiency of encryption and decryption; and even short key sizes, for instance with BIKE [2] and HQC [4]. Indeed, in the last decades, a recurrent argument to claim the security of code–based cryptosystems was the NP–completeness of the so-called Decoding Problem [9]. This NP–completeness argument is only partially convincing since it is well–known that some NP–hard problems turn out to be easy for a large density of instances. In short, cryptographers are much more interested by problems which are hard *on average*, while NP–completeness only guarantees a worst-case hardness.

The Decoding Problem. A random $[n, k]$–code is the row–space of a uniformly random matrix $\mathbf{G} \in \mathbb{F}_2^{k \times n}$ (called a *generator matrix* of the code)[1]:

$$\mathcal{C} = \{\mathbf{mG} \mid \mathbf{m} \in \mathbb{F}_2^k\} \subset \mathbb{F}_2^n.$$

The (average-case) Decoding Problem can then be defined as follows:

Definition 1 ((Average-case) Search Decoding Problem). *Given a random code $\mathcal{C}$, a vector $\mathbf{y} \in \mathbb{F}_2^n$ and a target distance $t \in \mathbb{N}$, the goal is to find a codeword (if exists) $\mathbf{c} \in \mathcal{C}$ and an error vector $\mathbf{e} \in \mathbb{F}_2^n$ of Hamming weight $|\mathbf{e}| = t$ such that $\mathbf{y} = \mathbf{c} + \mathbf{e}$.*

Alternatively, this problem can be seen as solving a linear system with a non linear constraint given by the targetted Hamming weight. Indeed, a code $\mathcal{C}$ can also be defined by a *parity-check* matrix, that is to say a matrix $\mathbf{H} \in \mathbb{F}_2^{(n-k) \times n}$ such that

$$\mathcal{C} = \{\mathbf{x} \in \mathbb{F}_2^n \mid \mathbf{xH}^\top = \mathbf{0}\}.$$

The above decoding problem is then equivalent to finding a word $\mathbf{e} \in \mathbb{F}_2^n$ of Hamming weight t such that $\mathbf{eH}^\top = \mathbf{s}$ for a given *syndrome* $\mathbf{s} \overset{\text{def}}{=} \mathbf{yH}^\top \in \mathbb{F}_2^{n-k}$.

---

[1] Note that such a code has a dimension less than k when $\mathbf{G}$ has not full rank but this happens only with a negligible probability.

Note that for solving the Decoding Problem, it is enough to recover the positions i such that $\mathbf{e}_i \neq 0$, *i.e.* the support of the error. This is even true for larger fields $\mathbb{F}_q$, at the cost of solving an additional linear system to recover the exact coefficients. In other words, decoding is equivalent to recovering the *support* of the error.

This computational problem has been studied for over sixty years [8,13,18, 24,31,34,41], and is widely considered to be hard to solve, even with the help of a putative quantum computer. Moreover, it benefits from a search-to-decision reduction, due to Fischer and Stern [25], which asserts the hardness of the following *decisional* version:

Definition 2 ((Average-case) Decision Decoding Problem). *Given a random code $\mathcal{C}$ defined by a uniformly random generator matrix $\mathbf{G} \in \mathbb{F}_2^{k \times n}$, a target distance $t \in \mathbb{N}$ and a vector $\mathbf{y} \in \mathbb{F}_2^n$, decide whether $\mathbf{y}$ is uniformly distributed over $\mathbb{F}_2^n$, or of the form $\mathbf{mG} + \mathbf{e}$ for some $\mathbf{m} \in \mathbb{F}_2^k$ and $\mathbf{e} \in \mathbb{F}_2^n$ of Hamming weight $|\mathbf{e}| = t$.*

Such a reduction is very useful for cryptographic applications, since various cryptosystems, such as Alekhnovich cryptosystem [5], rely on the hardness of the decisional version. When the length n of the code is *a priori* unbounded, this problem is also known as LPN (Learning Parity with Noise) in the literature.

If the hypothesis that the Decoding Problem is hard on average is widely accepted by the community, we lack theoretical results to corroborate that, since the literature on security reductions for codes remains very limited. The first worst-case to average-case reduction for the Decoding Problem is due to Brakerski, Lyubashevsky, Vaikuntanathan and Wichs in the recent breakthrough work [16] (and subsequently Yu and Zhang [42]). This limited number of reductions is probably one of the reasons why NIST did not yet select any code–based submission. On the other hand, three of the four submissions selected to advance to the fourth round are based on binary error correcting codes. Moreover, with the recent attacks on SIDH [19,30,36], NIST announced its will to standardise at least one code-based candidate, which increases the importance of theoretical studies of the underlying assumptions.

Structured Variants. The plain Decoding Problem often leads to cryptosystems with large key sizes. In order to improve on that, it has been proposed to use codes with an additional structure, such as a large automorphism group $\text{Aut}(\mathcal{C})$. For example, quasi-cyclic codes, introduced in cryptography by Gaborit in [26], are very appealing since they offer a very good efficiency, while keeping the same security parameter as for truly random codes. Indeed, the best approach for solving the Decoding Problem of such structured codes remains the DOOM attack by Sendrier [38], which only allows a $\sqrt{\sharp\text{Aut}(\mathcal{C})}$ speed–up. Quasi–cyclic codes are in particular used in BIKE [1] and HQC [3] which are two of the three code–based proposals remaining in the fourth round of NIST competition. However, such structured codes are not restricted to encryption schemes. In particular, Bombar, Couteau, Couvreur and Ducros [10] have recently used the decision version of the Decoding Problem of random quasi-abelian codes, which generalise both random linear codes and quasi-cyclic codes, to build an efficient pseudorandom correlations generator for the OLE correlation (Oblivious Linear Evaluation) over any field $\mathbb{F}_q$ with $q > 2$. This allows to design the first efficient silent (*i.e.* which requires almost no communication in the preprocessing phase) N-party secure computation protocols for computing arbitrary arithmetic circuits over $\mathbb{F}_q$ for $q > 2$.

However, on the security reductions point of view, the situation is even worse than that of the plain Decoding Problem; there is even no complete search-to-decision reduction. The only known reduction for structured variants is the recent work of Bombar, Couvreur and Debris-Alazard [11], via the introduction of the new problem called *Function Field Decoding Problem* (FFDP), which yield a search-to-decision reduction for some quasi-cyclic codes. This reduction has been extended in [10] to slightly more general quasi-abelian codes, but the question remains fully open for the codes and parameter sets used in NIST submissions BIKE and HQC.

From Lattices to Codes. Motivated by this state-of-affairs, a recent trend of research in code–based cryptography has been to take inspiration from the literature on Euclidean lattices to provide new reductions for codes: [21] gives a quantum reduction from the Decoding Problem to the problem of finding a short codeword, in the way of [35,40]; the reduction of [11] is an average-case to average-case search-to-decision reduction for structured variants of the Decoding Problem, in the spirit of [29], replacing number fields used in the lattice setting by function fields (somehow the analogue in positive characteristics). However, their reduction only works when the irreducible modulus splits completely in the underlying ring of integers, which is not the case with the parameter choice of BIKE and HQC. In the latter situation, the problem remains fully open. Our motivation with this work was to advance towards a general search-to-decision reduction. In this context, one may wonder if all the tools used to design reductions for lattices have been translated in the context of error correcting codes.

The answer to this question is *negative*. Indeed, in the breakthrough paper [32], Peikert, Regev and Stephens-Davidowitz introduced a powerful tool for reductions called the OHCP framework (for Oracle with Hidden Center Problem). Until the aforementioned work, search-to-decision reductions for lattices had arithmetic and algebraic limitations in the choice of the modulus and the number field of the considered structured lattice problem: [29] required the modulus to split completely, and the chosen number field to be Galois. The arithmetic hypothesis on the modulus was removed in [28] with the use of the modulus switching technique. The work of [32] allows to completely get rid of such algebraic and arithmetic hypotheses, and Rosca, Stehlé and Wallet later used it in [37] to design a complete search-to-decision reduction. This OHCP technique proved itself extremely useful as a black box inside the latest reductions in the context of structured lattice problems such as ring-LWE [32,37], polynomial-LWE [37], module-LWE [14] or NTRU [33]. On the other hand, even if this technique is considered to be very general, it has never been used outside of the lattice world.

Contributions. In this article, we revisit the OHCP framework from [32] and adapt it to the coding theoretic setting (in Sect. 3). More precisely, we extract the very essence of this technique which appears to be the OCP technique (for Oracle Comparison Problem) ([32, Definition 4.1]) and was overlooked before as a mere technical step. Building on top of OCP, we show how given an algorithm solving the decisional Decoding Problem, it is possible to recover the support of the error, and hence to decode, solving the computational Decoding Problem. In other words, we show how to solve a problem which may be called OHSP for *Oracle with Hidden Support Problem*, and which is more suitable for code-based cryptography (see Fig. 1)[2]

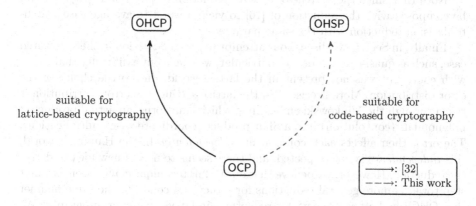

Fig. 1. Relationships between OCP, OHCP and OHSP.

Combining this framework with a recent result of Debris-Alazard and Resch [22] on smoothing bounds for codes which applies to any *radial* smoothing distribution (in particular, it applies to the Bernoulli noise, which was not captured before), we derive a new reduction from the worst-case search Decoding Problem to the average-case decision Decoding Problem, in the spirit of what has been done in the lattice-based setting.

In Sect. 4, we discuss instantiations and parameters for which our reduction holds for relevant parameters. It turns out that with this completely different approach, we recover the same parameters and noise ratio than the worst-case to average-case search-to-search reduction of Brakerski *et al.* [16]. In particular, we reduce a *worst-case* search decoding problem whose hardness is superpolynomial, to an average-case decisional problem, to get the following (informal) theorem.

---

[2] Note that it is possible to give a formal definitions of all the problems we mention, but instead, we choose to put forth the intuition (as well as rigorous proofs on how to solve them), in order to avoid superfluous technicalities which would only obfuscate the speech.

Theorem (Informal). *Let $n, k, t \in \mathbb{N}$, $D < 1/2$ be such that*

$$\frac{k}{n} = \frac{1}{n^D} \quad \text{and} \quad \frac{t}{n} = \frac{\log_2(n)^2}{n^{1-D}}.$$

Suppose that there exists an algorithm which distinguishes with polynomial advantage between $(\mathbf{A}, \mathbf{sA} + \mathbf{t})$ and $(\mathbf{A}, \mathbf{y})$ where $\mathbf{A}$ is a random binary $k \times n$ matrix, $\mathbf{y}$ is a random binary vector, and $\mathbf{t}$ is a random binary vector of Hamming weight $\frac{n}{2} \left(1 - 1/n^{D(1+o(1))}\right)$.

Then there exists an algorithm which solves the worst-case decoding problem for input codes of length n, dimension k and at decoding distance t^3.

Note that since the search-to-decision reduction of [25] is very tight, it can be composed with the reduction of [16] to yield a worst-to-average case search-to-decision reduction with the same parameters.

Finally, in Sect. 5, we discuss our attempt to give a reduction in the structured case, such as quasi-cyclic codes. In particular, we single out a difficulty that arises with codes but was not present in the lattice world, due to the choice of the error distribution. More precisely, in the lattice setting, the error distribution is taken through the Minkowski embedding, which transforms an actual product of polynomials (convolution) into a Shur product (coordinate-wise multiplication). The error then affects each component *independently*. In the Hamming world, this *independence* is not respected, and there seems to need a new idea to derive the reduction. However, we believe that our OHSP technique can be seen as a first step towards more general reductions for structured codes, in the same manner that OHCP had a huge impact for reductions in lattice–based cryptography. We also believe that this paves the way for reductions for other metrics used in cryptography, such as the rank metric, for which no search-to-decision reduction is known.

The diagram in Fig. 2 represents the relationships between problems in code–based cryptography. The black arrows represent previously known reductions.

Outline of the Article. The present article is organized as follows: In Sect. 2 we recall the notations and some elementary notions. Then we start Sect. 3 by giving formally our search-to-decision reduction in Theorem 1. It is followed by a high-level description of how this theorem is obtained. In Subsects. 3.1 and 3.2 we prove formally Theorem 1. In Sect. 4 we discuss instantiations of our search-to-decision reduction, first as an average-to-average reduction and ultimately as a worst-to-average reduction, in the context of the plain decoding problem. In Sect. 5 we describe our failed attempt to apply our reduction template to quasi-cyclic codes.

---

[3] Input codes are supposed to be *balanced* as in the reduction of [16].

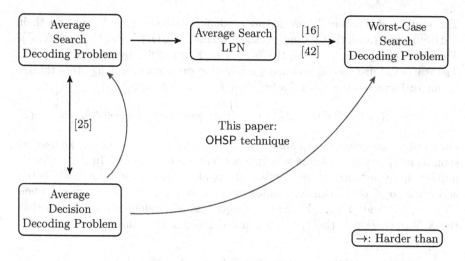

Fig. 2. Known reductions for the decoding problem used in code-based cryptography.

2 Preliminaries

Notation. When a and b are two integers, $[\![a, b]\!]$ denotes the set of integers $\{a, a+1, \ldots, b\}$, and we denote by $\mathsf{poly}(n)$ any quantity which is an $O(n^\alpha)$ for some constant α. Vectors are in *row notation* and they will be written with bold letters, such as $\mathbf{e}$. Uppercase bold letters are used to denote matrices (such as $\mathbf{G}$). The canonical inner product $\sum_{i=1}^{n} x_i y_i$ between two vectors $\mathbf{x}, \mathbf{y} \in \mathbb{F}_2^n$ is denoted by $\langle \mathbf{x}, \mathbf{y} \rangle$. The *support* $\mathsf{Supp}(\mathbf{x})$ of $\mathbf{x}$ is the positions of its non-zero coordinates

$$\mathsf{Supp}(\mathbf{x}) \stackrel{\text{def}}{=} \{i \in [\![1, n]\!] : x_i \neq 0\}$$

and its Hamming weight $|\mathbf{x}|$ is the cardinality of its support

$$|\mathbf{x}| \stackrel{\text{def}}{=} \sharp\mathsf{Supp}(\mathbf{x}).$$

The sphere in $\mathbb{F}_2^n$ centered at $\mathbf{0}$ and of radius t (for the Hamming metric $|\cdot|$) will be denoted by $\mathcal{S}_t^n$ (or simply $\mathcal{S}_t$ when the ambient space is clear).

In this article, we wish to emphasize on which probability space the probabilities or the expectations are taken. We will denote by a subscript the random variable specifying the associated probability space over which the probabilities or expectations are taken. For instance the probability $\mathbb{P}_X(E)$ of the event E is taken over the probability space Ω over which the random variable X is defined.

The *statistical distance* between two random variables X and Y taking their values in a same finite space $\mathcal{E}$ is defined as

$$\Delta(X, Y) \stackrel{\text{def}}{=} \frac{1}{2} \sum_{a \in \mathcal{E}} |\mathbb{P}(X = a) - \mathbb{P}(Y = a)|. \tag{1}$$

The statistical distance between two random variables depends only on their distributions. Recall that for any event E, we have $|\mathbb{P}_X(E) - \mathbb{P}_Y(E)| \leqslant \Delta(X, Y)$. Therefore, computing probabilities over X or Y will differ by at most $\Delta(X, Y)$. The statistical distance enjoys many interesting properties. Among other things, it cannot increase by applying a function f,

$$\Delta(f(X), f(Y)) \leqslant \Delta(X, Y) \quad (\textit{data processing inequality}). \tag{2}$$

For the data processing inequality to hold, the function f may be randomized as soon as its internal randomness is independent from X and Y. In particular, it implies that the "success" probability of any algorithm $\mathcal{A}$ for inputs distributed according to X or Y, can only differ by at most $\Delta(X, Y)$. Furthermore, when $(X_1, \ldots, X_r)$ and $(Y_1, \ldots, Y_r)$ are two sequences of random variables such that the X_i's (respectively the Y_i's) are pairwise independent, then

$$\Delta((X_1, \ldots, X_r), (Y_1, \ldots, Y_r)) \leqslant \sum_{i=1}^{r} \Delta(X_i, Y_i). \tag{3}$$

In the sequel, we denote by $X \leftarrow \mathcal{D}$ when X is a random variable following distribution $\mathcal{D}$. In addition when $\mathcal{E}$ is a finite set, we allow ourselves to denote $X \leftarrow \mathcal{E}$ when X is uniformly distributed over $\mathcal{E}$. A Bernoulli random variable $X \leftarrow \mathrm{Ber}(\omega)$ *of parameter* $\omega \in \mathbb{R}_+$ is any binary random variable $X \in \mathbb{F}_2$ such that

$$\mathbb{P}(X = 1) = \frac{1}{2}\left(1 - 2^{-\omega}\right).$$

Remark 1. This notation may seem surprising. It is however more comfortable to use in our setting. The rationale behind this choice is that in our reduction we strongly need to "focus" in the neighbourhood of $1/2$. This notation has also the following advantage: a simple calculation shows that given two independent random variables $X \leftarrow \mathrm{Ber}(\omega_1)$ and $Y \leftarrow \mathrm{Ber}(\omega_2)$, then $X + Y \leftarrow \mathrm{Ber}(\omega_1 + \omega_2)$. This will be comfortable in the sequel.

Finally, $X \leftarrow \mathrm{Ber}(\omega)^{\otimes N}$ means that $X \overset{\text{def}}{=} (X_1, \ldots, X_N)$ where the X_i's are independent and identically distributed Bernoulli random variables of parameter ω.

3 Search-to-Decision Reduction in the Oracle Comparison Problem (OCP) Framework

Let us assume that we have a probabilistic algorithm $\mathcal{A}$ running in time T that can distinguish noisy codewords at some Hamming distance and uniform random vectors over the ambient space. Its inputs are $\mathbf{A} \in \mathbb{F}_2^{k \times N}$ and $\mathbf{y} \in \mathbb{F}_2^N$. The aim of $\mathcal{A}$ is to output "1" if and only if $\mathbf{y} = \mathbf{s}\mathbf{A} + \mathbf{e}$ for some $\mathbf{s} \in \mathbb{F}_2^k$ and the bits of $\mathbf{e}$ are independent and identically distributed Bernoulli random variables of parameter ω. Namely, $\mathbf{y}$ is a noisy codeword $\mathbf{c} + \mathbf{e}$ where $\mathbf{c} \in \mathcal{C} \overset{\text{def}}{=} \{\mathbf{m}\mathbf{A} : \mathbf{m} \in \mathbb{F}_2^k\}$ and

$|\mathbf{e}| \approx \frac{N}{2}(1 - 2^{-\omega})$. Otherwise, $\mathcal{A}$ has to output "0". In addition, to be relevant in a cryptographic context, we suppose that $\mathcal{A}$ may give false answers. In that case we are interested in its *advantage* $\varepsilon(k, N, \omega)$ which is defined as follows

$$\varepsilon(k, N, \omega) \overset{\text{def}}{=} \frac{1}{2}\left(\mathbb{P}_{\mathbf{A},\mathbf{s},\mathbf{e}}\left(\mathcal{A}\left(\mathbf{A}, \mathbf{s}\mathbf{A} + \mathbf{e}\right) = 1\right) - \mathbb{P}_{\mathbf{A},\mathbf{y}}\left(\mathcal{A}\left(\mathbf{A}, \mathbf{y}\right) = 1\right)\right), \quad (4)$$

where the random variables satisfy

$$(i)\ \mathbf{A} \leftarrow \mathbb{F}_2^{k \times N}, \quad (ii)\ \mathbf{s} \leftarrow \mathbb{F}_2^k, \quad (iii)\ \mathbf{y} \leftarrow \mathbb{F}_2^N \quad \text{and} \quad (iv)\ \mathbf{e} \leftarrow \mathrm{Ber}(\omega)^{\otimes N}. \quad (5)$$

We say that $\mathcal{A}$ distinguishes between distributions $(\mathbf{A}, \mathbf{s}\mathbf{A} + \mathbf{e})$ and $(\mathbf{A}, \mathbf{y})$ with advantage $\varepsilon(k, N, \omega)$. It may happen that we omit the dependence in (k, N, w) and simply write ε (that will be clear from the context). The following general theorem shows that from any such putative "distinguishing" algorithm $\mathcal{A}$, we can build an algorithm solving a fixed decoding problem, namely recovering $\mathbf{t}$ from $(\mathbf{G}, \mathbf{m}\mathbf{G} + \mathbf{t})$.

Theorem 1. *Let* $N, n \in \mathbb{N}$ *and* $k \in [\![0, \min(N, n)]\!]$. *Let* $(\mathbf{G}, \mathbf{m}\mathbf{G} + \mathbf{t})$ *with* $\mathbf{G} \in \mathbb{F}_2^{k \times n}$, $\mathbf{m} \in \mathbb{F}_2^k$, *and* $|\mathbf{t}| = t \in [\![0, n]\!]$. *Suppose that there exists an algorithm* $\mathcal{A}$ *which distinguishes in time* T *distributions* $(\mathbf{A}, \mathbf{s}\mathbf{A}+\mathbf{e})$ *and* $(\mathbf{A}, \mathbf{y})$ *with advantage* $\varepsilon(k, N, \omega)$ *where* $\mathbf{A}, \mathbf{s}, \mathbf{e}, \mathbf{y}$ *satisfy* (5) *and* $\omega \in \mathbb{R}_+$ *verifying*

$$\omega = \Omega(1) \quad \text{and} \quad \omega = O(n). \quad (6)$$

Let $\omega_0, \alpha \in \mathbb{R}_+$ *be such that*

$$t\,\omega_0 = \omega \quad \text{and} \quad \alpha \overset{\text{def}}{=} \max\left(\frac{1}{\varepsilon(k, N, \omega)}, N, n\right). \quad (7)$$

Then, there exists an algorithm which takes as input $(\mathbf{G}, \mathbf{m}\mathbf{G} + \mathbf{t})$ *and which outputs* $\mathbf{t}$ *in time* $T\,\mathrm{poly}\,(\alpha)$ *with probability (over its internal randomness and* **not** *the choice of* $\mathbf{G}, \mathbf{m}$ *and* $\mathbf{t}$ *which are fixed) bigger than*

$$1 - 2^{-\Omega(n)} - N\,\mathrm{poly}(\alpha) \max_{x \geqslant 0} \Delta\left(\left(\mathbf{r}(x)\mathbf{G}^\top, \langle \mathbf{r}(x), \mathbf{t}\rangle\right), (\mathbf{a}, e(x))\right), \quad (8)$$

where $\mathbf{a} \leftarrow \mathbb{F}_2^k$, $\mathbf{r}(x) \leftarrow \mathrm{Ber}(2^x \omega_0)^{\otimes n}$ *and* $e(x) \leftarrow \mathrm{Ber}(2^x \omega_0 t)$ *with* $x \geqslant 0$.

This theorem will follow from a sequence of lemmas. Before providing a rigorous demonstration, let us give an informal sketch of the proof.

Remark 2. Similarly to [32], our algorithm rests on a distinguishing process between two distinct *oracles*. Informally, by *oracle* we mean a black box that we can query arbitrarily many times and whose outputs are independent random elements following a given distribution. Formally, an oracle $\mathcal{O}(x)$ can be modelised by a sequence $(X_i)_{i \in \mathbb{N}}$ of independent identically distributed random variables whose distribution may depend from some parameter x.

Step 1. (*From distinguishing* LPN *samples to distinguishing noisy codewords*). We start from an algorithm $\mathcal{A}$ that distinguishes, with advantage ε, between a noisy codeword $\mathbf{c}+\mathbf{e}$ (by outputting 1) and a uniform $\mathbf{y} \in \mathbb{F}_2^N$ (by outputting 0) with $\mathbf{c}$ drawn uniformly at random from some random binary $[N, k]$-code $\mathcal{C}$, and $\mathbf{e} \leftarrow \mathrm{Ber}(\omega)^{\otimes N}$. This algorithm can easily be turned into an algorithm $\mathcal{A}'$ distinguishing (with the same advantage ε) oracles

$$\mathcal{O}(\omega) : (\mathbf{a}, \langle \mathbf{a}, \mathbf{s} \rangle + e) \quad \text{and} \quad \mathcal{O}(\infty) : (\mathbf{a}, u) \tag{9}$$

where $\mathbf{s} \in \mathbb{F}_2^k$, $e \leftarrow \mathrm{Ber}(\omega)$, $\mathbf{a} \leftarrow \mathbb{F}_2^k$ and $u \leftarrow \mathbb{F}_2$[4]. Indeed, given one of the above oracles $\mathcal{O}$, in order to design $\mathcal{A}'$, it is enough to perform N queries $(\mathbf{a}_i, b_i)$ to $\mathcal{O}$ and gather them to generate the pair $(\mathbf{A}, \mathbf{b})$ where the columns of $\mathbf{A}$ are the $\mathbf{a}_i$'s and $\mathbf{b} = (b_1, \dots, b_N)$. Then, we feed $\mathcal{A}$ with the generated pair $(\mathbf{A}, \mathbf{b})$ to make our decision. Defining such an algorithm $\mathcal{A}'$ solving the above LPN-decisional problem with at most N queries may seem at first sight tautological, but for our reduction it is more convenient to emphasize this point.

This is why, for proving Theorem 1, we will suppose that we directly have an algorithm $\mathcal{A}'$ distinguishing LPN-oracles $\mathcal{O}(\omega)$ and $\mathcal{O}(\infty)$ with some advantage ε *and* querying at most N times the input oracle.

Step 2. (*From a noisy codeword to* LPN-*samples*). The starting point of the reduction consists in noticing that, from any input of a decoding problem, we can build some LPN-oracle. Given

$$\left(\mathbf{G}, \mathbf{y} \overset{\mathrm{def}}{=} \mathbf{m}\mathbf{G} + \mathbf{t} \right) \in \mathbb{F}_2^{k \times n} \times \mathbb{F}_2^n,$$

we can design the following oracle $\mathcal{O}_0$. Sample $\mathbf{r}$ according to $\mathrm{Ber}(\omega_0)^{\otimes n}$, then compute $\mathbf{r}\mathbf{G}^\top$ and

$$\langle \mathbf{y}, \mathbf{r} \rangle = \langle \mathbf{m}\mathbf{G} + \mathbf{t}, \mathbf{r} \rangle = \langle \mathbf{m}, \mathbf{r}\mathbf{G}^\top \rangle + \langle \mathbf{t}, \mathbf{r} \rangle. \tag{10}$$

The oracle $\mathcal{O}_0$ outputs LPN–like samples of the form:

$$\mathcal{O}_0 : (\mathbf{a}', \langle \mathbf{s}, \mathbf{a}' \rangle + e') \quad \text{where} \quad \begin{cases} \mathbf{s} \overset{\mathrm{def}}{=} \mathbf{m} \\ \mathbf{a}' \overset{\mathrm{def}}{=} \mathbf{r}\mathbf{G}^\top \\ e' \overset{\mathrm{def}}{=} \langle \mathbf{t}, \mathbf{r} \rangle. \end{cases} \tag{11}$$

The random variable e' follows a Bernoulli distribution of parameter $\omega_0 |\mathbf{t}| = \omega_0 t$ (see Lemma 1 further) which equals ω (under the notation of Theorem 1, Eq. (7)). However, one can notice that our above sample is not a valid LPN instance since $\mathbf{a}' = \mathbf{r}\mathbf{G}^\top$ is *a priori* not uniformly distributed and is correlated to e'. Nonetheless, thanks to the data processing inequality (see Eq. (2)), replacing the sample $(\mathbf{r}\mathbf{G}^\top, \langle \mathbf{m}, \mathbf{r}\mathbf{G}^\top \rangle + \langle \mathbf{t}, \mathbf{r} \rangle)$ by a genuine LPN sample $(\mathbf{a}, \langle \mathbf{a}, \mathbf{m} \rangle + e)$ changes the probabilities by at most the additive term

$$\Delta \left((\mathbf{r}\mathbf{G}^\top, \langle \mathbf{r}, \mathbf{t} \rangle), (\mathbf{a}, e) \right), \quad \text{where } e \leftarrow \mathrm{Ber}(\omega) \text{ and is independent from } \mathbf{a}.$$

---

[4] A sample from $\mathcal{O}(\cdot)$ is called an LPN sample.

Further, in Sect. 4, when we instantiate Theorem 1, parameters are chosen so that this statistical distance is negligible. This is obtained by carefully choosing ω_0. In particular, we use smoothing bounds as given in [16, 20, 22, 23].

Now, one may wonder how we can use $\mathcal{O}_0$ with our algorithm $\mathcal{A}'$ distinguishing between LPN-distributions to solve our underlying decoding problem. It is the aim of the next step.

Step 3. (*Applying the Oracle Comparison Problem* OCP *framework*). For a formal definition of OCP, the interested reader can refer to [32, Definition 4.1]. Intuitively, given access to two oracles $\mathcal{O}_1$ and $\mathcal{O}_2$ whose acceptance probability are just a "shift" of one another, the goal of OCP is to tell which one is in advance, and which one lags behind (see Fig. 3).

The first core idea of the reduction is to notice that in order to build the oracle $\mathcal{O}_0$ of (11), we have computed $\langle \mathbf{y}, \mathbf{r} \rangle$ (see (10)), leading to an LPN sample with parameter $\omega_0 |\mathbf{t}| = \omega$ (see Lemma 1 further). One could have done the same thing but this time by computing $\langle \mathbf{y}+\mathbf{z}, \mathbf{r} \rangle$ for some fixed $\mathbf{z} \in \mathbb{F}_2^n$ instead. This has the following consequence: our new oracle provides LPN-samples with Bernoulli noise of parameter $\omega_0 |\mathbf{t}+\mathbf{z}|$. Arguably this innocent looking fact is the key of our reduction, which follows the approach of [32, 37]. Let us define the oracle $\mathcal{O}^{\mathbf{v}_i}$ as $\mathcal{O}_0$, but instead of outputting $\langle \mathbf{y}, \mathbf{r} \rangle$ it outputs $\langle \mathbf{y}+\mathbf{v}_i, \mathbf{r} \rangle$ where $(\mathbf{v}_j)_{1 \leqslant j \leqslant n}$ is the canonical basis of $\mathbb{F}_2^n$. Then we feed $\mathcal{A}'$ with $\mathcal{O}^{\mathbf{v}_i}$. By assumption, $\mathcal{A}'$ distinguishes between an LPN oracle with noise $\mathrm{Ber}(\omega)$ and a uniform noise $\mathrm{Ber}(\infty)$ with advantage ε. Therefore, the probability that $\mathcal{A}'$ outputs 1 when fed with $\mathcal{O}_0$ is roughly $1/2 + \varepsilon$. On the other hand, $\mathcal{O}^{\mathbf{v}_i}$ defines an LPN oracle with Bernoulli parameter $\omega_0 |\mathbf{t}+\mathbf{v}_i|$, where $|\mathbf{t}| = t$ and $|\mathbf{v}_i| = 1$. Therefore, the noise is distributed either as $\mathrm{Ber}(\omega_0(t-1))$ or $\mathrm{Ber}(\omega_0(t+1))$ depending on whether $t_i = 1$ *or* not, that is to say on whether i belongs to the support of $\mathbf{t}$ *or* not. In other words, the behaviour of $\mathcal{O}^{\mathbf{v}_i}$ depends on the *hidden support* of $\mathbf{t}$. From then on, one may prematurely conclude that the acceptance probability of $\mathcal{A}'$ when fed with $\mathcal{O}^{\mathbf{v}_i}$ slightly differs from the one when fed with $\mathcal{O}_0$; a behaviour that could be detected. Unfortunately the success probability, $1/2 + \varepsilon$, may be the same in all these cases. This brings us to the second core idea of the reduction. Instead of defining $\mathcal{O}_0$ and $\mathcal{O}^{\mathbf{v}_i}$ by sampling $\mathbf{r}$ according to $\mathrm{Ber}(\omega_0)$, we choose $\mathbf{r} \leftarrow \mathrm{Ber}(2^x \omega_0)$ for $x \in \mathbb{R}_+$. The LPN-noise now follows the following distributions

$$\mathrm{Ber}(2^x \omega_0 t) \text{ in } \mathcal{O}_0 \quad \text{and} \quad \begin{cases} \mathrm{Ber}\left(2^x \omega_0 (t-1)\right) \text{ if } t_i = 1 \\ \\ \mathrm{Ber}\left(2^x \omega_0 (t+1)\right) \text{ if } t_i = 0 \end{cases} \text{ in } \mathcal{O}^{\mathbf{v}_i}. \quad (12)$$

We can notice that by letting $x \to \infty$, above distributions go to $\mathrm{Ber}(\infty)$. However, the fundamental remark is not here. By definition, our distinguishing algorithm $\mathcal{A}'$ does not behave "in the same way" when is given as input $\mathcal{O}(\omega_0 t)$ or $\mathcal{O}(\infty)$; fact which is quantified by its advantage ε.

Therefore, if one feeds $\mathcal{A}'$ with the oracle $\mathcal{O}_0$ (which outputs LPN samples with Bernoulli noise of parameter $\omega_0 t$ when $x = 0$), then playing on $x \geqslant 0$ one can detect a difference in its probability to output 1. Let us say that the change of behaviour happens at some x_0, namely for a noise $\mathrm{Ber}(2^{x_0}\omega_0 t)$. Let us suppose that now we feed $\mathcal{O}^{\mathbf{v}_i}$ to $\mathcal{A}'$. One can also choose different values x and look at the probability that $\mathcal{A}'$ outputs 1. But, we know that this change of behaviour will happen when the noise follows some Bernoulli distribution of parameter $2^{x_0}\omega_0 t$. Therefore, in that case, we will observe a difference at some $x_0' \geqslant 0$ when (according to Eq. (12); see also Fig. 3)

$$\begin{cases} 2^{x_0'}\omega_0(t-1) = 2^{x_0}\omega_0 t \iff x_0' = x_0 + \log\left(\frac{t}{t-1}\right) > x_0 \text{ if } t_i = 1, \\[2mm] 2^{x_0'}\omega_0(t+1) = 2^{x_0}\omega_0 t \iff x_0' = x_0 + \log\left(\frac{t}{t+1}\right) < x_0 \text{ if } t_i = 0. \end{cases}$$

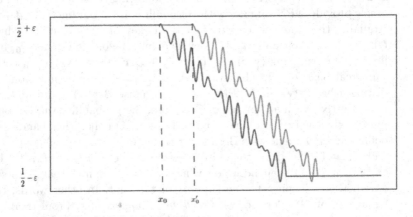

Fig. 3. Illustration of Step 3 (in the case $t_i = 1$).

It turns out that with classical statistical methods, we can now detect this difference in the acceptance probability of $\mathcal{A}'$. The idea is just to estimate when $\mathcal{A}'$ changes its behaviour given as input $\mathcal{O}_0$ and $\mathcal{O}^{\mathbf{v}_i}$. Depending whether $t_i = 1$ or not, this change of behaviour will happen for a smaller x with input $\mathcal{O}_0$, or a bigger x. This yields the claimed reduction: we are able to decide whether $t_i = 1$ or 0 for any $i \in [\![1, n]\!]$, *i.e.* we are able to recover the *hidden support* of the error, and hence to solve the decoding problem. In other words, we turned a "distinguishing decoding" algorithm into a "search decoding" algorithm.

From now on, $\mathcal{A}$ denotes an algorithm running in time T and taking as input an oracle $\mathcal{O}$ which can be queried at most N times and outputting vectors in $\mathbb{F}_2^k \times \mathbb{F}_2$. Furthermore, its advantage to distinguish between $\mathcal{O}(\omega)$ and $\mathcal{O}(\infty)$ (defined in (9)) is given by

$$\varepsilon = \frac{1}{2}\Big(\mathbb{P}\left(\mathcal{A}\left(\mathcal{O}(\omega)\right) = 1\right) - \mathbb{P}\left(\mathcal{A}\left(\mathcal{O}(\infty)\right) = 1\right)\Big) > 0. \tag{13}$$

Remark 3. After possibly replacing $\mathcal{A}(\mathcal{O})$ by $1 - \mathcal{A}(\mathcal{O})$, one can always suppose the advantage to be positive.

3.1 Building LPN-Oracles from a Decoding Instance: Step 2

Our aim in this step is to study oracles $\mathcal{O}^z(x)$ and $\mathcal{O}^z_{\text{ideal}}(x)$ which are given in Fig. 4, where $z \in \mathbb{F}_2^n$ is a parameter, $x \in \mathbb{R}$ an input and $y = mG + t$. Notice that (G, y) is known while (m, t) are unknown; preventing us from being able to run $\mathcal{O}^z_{\text{ideal}}(x)$. However, as we will explain below, $\mathcal{O}^z_{\text{ideal}}(x)$ is an ideal version of $\mathcal{O}^z(x)$ that we "only" use to analyse the success probability of the reduction.

Oracle $\mathcal{O}^z(x)$:
  Input: $x \in \mathbb{R}$
    Sample: $r \leftarrow \text{Ber}(2^x \omega_0)^{\otimes n}$
  Return: $\left(rG^\top, \langle y + z, r \rangle\right)$

Oracle $\mathcal{O}^z_{\text{ideal}}(x)$:
  Input: $x \in \mathbb{R}$
    Sample: $r \leftarrow \text{Ber}(2^x \omega_0)^{\otimes n}$
      and $a \leftarrow \mathbb{F}_2^k$
  Return: $(a, \langle a, m \rangle + \langle z + t, r \rangle)$

Fig. 4. Oracles $\mathcal{O}^z(x)$ and $\mathcal{O}^z_{\text{ideal}}(x)$

Oracle $\mathcal{O}^z_{\text{ideal}}(x)$ is an ideal version of $\mathcal{O}^z(x)$. It follows from the fact that $\mathcal{O}^z$ outputs LPN-like samples

$$\left(rG^\top, \langle m, rG^\top \rangle + \langle z + t, r \rangle\right).$$

Notice that, contrary to $\mathcal{O}^z_{\text{ideal}}$, oracle $\mathcal{O}^z$ does not provide genuine LPN samples (that is the reason why we said LPN *like*) since $rG^\top$ is not uniformly distributed and is correlated to $\langle z + t, r \rangle$. However, in both oracles the noise term is the same. In the following lemma (often called the piling-up lemma) we show how it behaves.

Lemma 1. *Let* $r \leftarrow \text{Ber}(\alpha)^{\otimes n}$, *then for any* $z \in \mathbb{F}_2^n$ *we have*

$$\langle z, r \rangle \leftarrow \text{Ber}(|z|\alpha).$$

Proof. Let $z \stackrel{\text{def}}{=} |\mathbf{z}|$ and $p \stackrel{\text{def}}{=} \frac{1}{2}(1 - 2^{-\alpha})$. By definition of $\mathbf{r} \leftarrow \text{Ber}(\alpha)^{\otimes n}$ we have the following computation

$$
\begin{aligned}
\mathbb{P}_{\mathbf{r}}\left(\langle \mathbf{z}, \mathbf{r}\rangle = 1\right) &= \sum_{j \text{ odd}} \binom{z}{j} p^j (1-p)^{z-j} \\
&= \frac{1}{2}\left(\sum_j \binom{z}{j} p^j (1-p)^{z-j} - \sum_j (-1)^j \binom{z}{j} p^j (1-p)^{z-j}\right) \\
&= \frac{1}{2}\left(1 - (1 - 2p)^z\right) \\
&= \frac{1}{2}\left(1 - 2^{-z\alpha}\right),
\end{aligned}
$$

which concludes the proof. $\qquad\square$

3.2   Oracle Comparison Problem Technique: Step 3

Let us introduce the following function

$$
p : x \in \mathbb{R} \longmapsto \mathbb{P}\left(\mathcal{A}(\mathcal{O}_{\text{ideal}}^{\mathbf{0}}(x)) = 1\right) \tag{14}
$$

where we feed to $\mathcal{A}$ the ideal oracle. Recall that $(\mathbf{v}_i)_{1 \leqslant i \leqslant n}$ denotes the canonical basis of $\mathbb{F}_2^n$; from Lemma 1, we notice that

$$
\begin{aligned}
p\left(x + \log \frac{|\mathbf{t} + \mathbf{v}_i|}{|\mathbf{t}|}\right) &= \mathbb{P}\left(\mathcal{A}\left(\mathcal{O}_{\text{ideal}}^{\mathbf{0}}\left(x + \log \frac{|\mathbf{t} + \mathbf{v}_i|}{|\mathbf{t}|}\right)\right) = 1\right) \\
&= \mathbb{P}\left(\mathcal{A}\left(\mathcal{O}_{\text{ideal}}^{\mathbf{v}_i}(x)\right) = 1\right) \tag{15}
\end{aligned}
$$

where the last equality follows from the fact that $\mathcal{O}_{\text{ideal}}^{\mathbf{0}}\left(x + \log \frac{|\mathbf{t}+\mathbf{v}_i|}{|\mathbf{t}|}\right)$ outputs proper LPN samples with Bernoulli noise of parameter

$$
2^{x + \log \frac{|\mathbf{t}+\mathbf{v}_i|}{|\mathbf{t}|}} \omega_0 |\mathbf{t}| = 2^x \omega_0 |\mathbf{t} + \mathbf{v}_i|.
$$

In other words, the probability that $\mathcal{A}$ outputs 1 when fed with $\mathcal{O}_{\text{ideal}}^{\mathbf{v}_i}(x)$ is the probability that $\mathcal{A}$ outputs 1 when fed with $\mathcal{O}_{\text{ideal}}^{\mathbf{0}}$ on x shifted by

$$
\log\left(\frac{|\mathbf{t} + \mathbf{v}_i|}{|\mathbf{t}|}\right) = \begin{cases} \log\left(1 - 1/t\right) \text{ if } t_i = 1 \\ \log\left(1 + 1/t\right) \text{ otherwise.} \end{cases}
$$

Let us stress that (15) would not hold if one had defined p in (14) by feeding $\mathcal{A}$ with $\mathcal{O}^{\mathbf{0}}$ instead of $\mathcal{O}_{\text{ideal}}^{\mathbf{0}}$. Indeed, notice that outputs $(\mathbf{a}, b)$ of $\mathcal{O}^{\mathbf{0}}(x)$ are such that *both* the distributions of b *and* $\mathbf{a}$ are functions of x. Hence, changing x in the non–ideal oracle $\mathcal{O}^{\mathbf{0}}(x)$ might change the distribution of the first component of the output and (15) would no longer hold. We crucially used that changing x in $\mathcal{O}_{\text{ideal}}^{\mathbf{0}}(x)$ only modifies the noise term.

As roughly described below Theorem 1, the core idea of the reduction is to feed to $\mathcal{A}$ oracles $\mathcal{O}^0_{\text{ideal}}(x)$ and $\mathcal{O}^{\mathbf{v}_i}_{\text{ideal}}(x)$ and then to draw the probability to output 1 when x ranges over $[0, +\infty[$. Practically, we compute statistical estimates of this probability when x ranges over a discretisation of $[0, X_{\max}]$, for some $X_{\max}$. In the choice of $X_{\max}$ and the discretisation step, a trade-off should be made. On the one hand, for the empirical estimates to be close enough to the actual probability function p of (14), the upper bound $X_{\max}$ should be large enough and the discretisation step should be small enough. On the other hand for the statistical estimator to run in polynomial time, $X_{\max}$ should not be too large and the discretisation step should not be too small.

Then, using that $\mathcal{A}$ discriminates oracles $\mathcal{O}(\omega_0 t) = \mathcal{O}^0_{\text{ideal}}(0)$ and $\mathcal{O}(\infty) = \mathcal{O}^0_{\text{ideal}}(\infty)$, we will be able for both oracles to determine the first input x that induces a change in the behaviour of $\mathcal{A}$. We will compare both values and depending on which one is the biggest, we will decide if $t_i = 1$, or not. The correction of this procedure relies on (15) showing that one distribution is the shift of the other one. However, one may note that we cannot run $\mathcal{A}\left(\mathcal{O}^0_{\text{ideal}}(x)\right)$ and $\mathcal{A}\left(\mathcal{O}^{\mathbf{v}_i}_{\text{ideal}}(x)\right)$ as $\mathbf{m}, \mathbf{t}$ are unknown. We have instead access to $\mathcal{A}\left(\mathcal{O}^0(x)\right)$ and $\mathcal{A}\left(\mathcal{O}^{\mathbf{v}_i}(x)\right)$ for which we do not know if their probabilities to output 1 are a shift of the other one. In order to be able to analyse our procedure, we will use the following remark: the probability of success when given the real oracles only differs by at most an additive term $\Delta\left(\left(\mathbf{r}\mathbf{G}^\top, \langle\mathbf{r}, \mathbf{t}\rangle\right), (\mathbf{a}, e)\right)$ (multiplied by the number of queries to the oracles) to the case where it is given the ideal oracles. Therefore, as soon as we can estimate the aforementioned statistical distance, it is enough to perform the analysis when given ideal oracles.

The following technical lemma (whose proof can be found in the extended version [12] but is essentially the same as the one of [32, Lemma 4.2]) shows how two oracles depending on a parameter x can be distinguished if the distribution of one is the shift of the other one. This statement was initially used to solve the Oracle Comparison Problem (OCP) problem introduced in [32, §4]. Think that we will instantiate this lemma using oracles $\mathcal{O}_{s_1}(x) = \mathcal{A}\left(\mathcal{O}^0_{\text{ideal}}(x)\right)$ with $s_1 = 0$ and $\mathcal{O}_{s_2}(x) = \mathcal{A}\left(\mathcal{O}^{\mathbf{v}_i}_{\text{ideal}}(x)\right)$ with $s_2 = \log\left(1 \pm \frac{1}{t}\right)$.

Lemma 2. *Let $s_1, s_2 \in \mathbb{R}$ and $p : \mathbb{R} \to [0,1]$. We suppose that there exists $\alpha > 0$ and $p_\infty \in [0,1]$ such that p verifies the following assumptions*

(i) $p(s_1) - p_\infty \geq \frac{1}{\alpha}$;
(ii) $\forall x \in \mathbb{R}_+, |p(x) - p_\infty| \leq \alpha 2^{-\frac{x}{\alpha}}$;
(iii) p is α-lipschitz.

Let $\mathcal{O}_{s_1}$ and $\mathcal{O}_{s_2}$ be two oracles that output 0 or 1 and such that

$$\forall x \in \mathbb{R}, \quad \mathbb{P}\left(\mathcal{O}_{s_1}(x) = 1\right) = p(s_1 + x) \quad \text{and} \quad \mathbb{P}\left(\mathcal{O}_{s_2}(x) = 1\right) = p(s_2 + x).$$

We suppose that a call to one of the above oracle costs a time T. Furthermore, s_1 and s_2 are such that

$$\text{either} \quad \text{(I)} \quad s_1 \leq s_2 \quad \text{or} \quad \text{(II)} \quad s_1 \geq s_2 + \frac{1}{\alpha}.$$

Then, there exists an algorithm, running in time T $\mathsf{poly}(\alpha)$, taking as inputs $(\mathcal{O}_{s_1}, \mathcal{O}_{s_2})$, querying them $\mathsf{poly}(\alpha)$ times and which can decide whether (I) or (II) holds, with a success probability $\geqslant 1 - e^{-\alpha}$ (over the outputs of the oracles $\mathcal{O}_{s_i}$'s).

Equipped with this statement, we are almost ready to prove Theorem 1. However, it still remains to verify that the function p given in (14) satisfies the assumption of the lemma for some parameters α and p_∞.

Lemma 3. *We use the notation of Theorem 1. Let p be the function defined in (14), and let*

$$p_\infty \stackrel{def}{=} \mathbb{P}\left(\mathcal{A}\left(\mathcal{O}^0_{\mathrm{ideal}}(\infty)\right) = 1\right) \quad (\mathcal{O}^0_{\mathrm{ideal}} \text{ is defined in Figure 4}). \tag{16}$$

Then, we have

(i) $p(0) - p_\infty \geqslant \frac{1}{\alpha}$;
(ii) $|p(x) - p_\infty| \leqslant \alpha 2^{-\frac{x}{\alpha}}$;
(iii) p is α-lipschitz;

for some α satisfying

$$\alpha = C \max\left(\frac{1}{\varepsilon}, N, n\right) \tag{17}$$

for some large enough constant C and where ε is the distinguishing advantage of $\mathcal{A}$ given in Eq. (13).

Proof. Let us first prove (i). Following the discussion in Step 1, let $\mathcal{O}(\omega) = \mathcal{O}^0_{\mathrm{ideal}}(0)$ and $\mathcal{O}(\infty) = \mathcal{O}^0_{\mathrm{ideal}}(\infty)$ (defined in (9)). By definition of p,

$$p(0) - p_\infty = \mathbb{P}\left(\mathcal{A}\left(\mathcal{O}(\omega)\right) = 1\right) - \mathbb{P}\left(\mathcal{A}\left(\mathcal{O}(\infty)\right) = 1\right)$$
$$= 2\varepsilon$$
$$\geqslant \frac{1}{\alpha},$$

where in the last line we used the assumption on α given in Eq. (17).

Let us prove (ii). Using the data processing inequality (2) together with (3), for $X \leftarrow \mathrm{Ber}(2^x \omega_0 t)$ and $Y \leftarrow \mathrm{Ber}(\infty)$, we have

$$|p(x) - p(\infty)| \leqslant N \, \Delta(X, Y)$$
$$= N \, 2^{-2^x \omega_0 t}.$$

Notice now that

$$N 2^{-2^x \omega_0 t} \leqslant \alpha 2^{-\frac{x}{\alpha}} \iff \log(N) - 2^x \omega_0 t \leqslant -\frac{x}{\alpha} + \log(\alpha),$$

and the last equality is verified for all $x \geqslant 0$ since, from (6), we know that $\omega_0 t = \omega = \Omega(1)$ and $\alpha \geqslant CN$ for some large enough constant C. It proves item (ii).

We are now ready to finish the proof by proving item (iii). In the same manner as before, for $X \leftarrow \mathrm{Ber}(2^x \omega_0 t)$ and $Y \leftarrow \mathrm{Ber}(2^y \omega_0 y)$ and for all $x, y \geqslant 0$, we have

$$
|p(x) - p(y)| \leqslant N \Delta(X, Y)
$$
$$
= N \left| 2^{-2^x \omega_0 t} - 2^{-2^y \omega_0 t} \right|
$$
$$
\leqslant N \omega_0 t \, |x - y|,
$$

where the last inequality follows from the mean value theorem. Notice now that $N \omega_0 t \leqslant \alpha$ as $N \omega_0 t = N \omega = O(Nn)$. It concludes the proof. $\quad\square$

We are now ready to prove Theorem 1.

Proof. The algorithm recovering $\mathbf{t}$ from $\mathbf{mG} + \mathbf{t}$ simply runs for any $i \in [\![1, n]\!]$ the procedure of Lemma 2 with oracles $\mathcal{A}(\mathcal{O}^0(x))$ and $\mathcal{A}(\mathcal{O}^{v_i}(x))$. However to see why it works, let us make the analyse of the success probability as if the following oracles were given

$$
\mathcal{O}_{s_1}(x) \stackrel{\text{def}}{=} \mathcal{A}\left(\mathcal{O}^0_{\text{ideal}}(x)\right) \quad \text{and} \quad \mathcal{O}_{s_2}(x) \stackrel{\text{def}}{=} \mathcal{A}\left(\mathcal{O}^{v_i}_{\text{ideal}}(x)\right).
$$

with $s_1 = 0$ and s_2 chosen later. Notice that according to the definition of p given in Eq. (14) we have

$$
\mathbb{P}\left(\mathcal{O}_{s_1}(x) = 1\right) = p(s_1 + x) \quad \text{and} \quad \mathbb{P}\left(\mathcal{O}_{s_2}(x) = 1\right) = p(s_2 + x)
$$

where s_2 is such that (see Eq. (15))

$$
s_2 = \begin{cases} \log\left(1 - \frac{1}{t}\right) & \text{if } t_i = 1 \\ \log\left(1 + \frac{1}{t}\right) & \text{otherwise.} \end{cases}
$$

Therefore, for $t \geqslant 1$, either

$$
s_2 > s_1 = 0 \quad \text{if} \quad t_i = 0
$$

or,

$$
s_2 + \frac{1}{t} = \log\left(1 - \frac{1}{t}\right) + \frac{1}{t} \leqslant 0 = s_1 \quad \text{if} \quad t_i = 1.
$$

Consequently, to apply Lemma 2 we need to have $\alpha \geqslant t$. But the function p has also to verify items (i), (ii) and (iii) of the lemma. According to Lemma 3, all these assumptions are met if we choose α as a $\Theta\left(\max\left(\frac{1}{\varepsilon}, N, n\right)\right)$ (recall that $t \leqslant n$). Notice that $\mathsf{poly}(\alpha) = \mathsf{poly}\left(\max\left(\frac{1}{\varepsilon}, N, n\right)\right)$.

Running the procedure of Lemma 2 for any $i \in [\![1, n]\!]$ will output the support of $\mathbf{t}$, namely $\{i \in [\![1, n]\!], t_i \neq 0\}$ with probability

$$
\geqslant \left(1 - e^{-\alpha}\right)^n = \left(1 - e^{-\Omega(n)}\right)^n = 1 - 2^{-\Omega(n)}.
$$

and in time $T\mathsf{poly}(\alpha)$. However, we will run this procedure with oracles $\mathcal{A}(\mathcal{O}^0(x))$ and $\mathcal{A}(\mathcal{O}^{\mathbf{v}_i}(x))$. But, according to Lemma 1, the statistical distance between outputs of $\mathcal{O}^0(x)$ and $\mathcal{O}^0_{\mathrm{ideal}}(x)$ is smaller than

$$\Delta\Big(\big(\mathbf{r}(x)\mathbf{G}^\top, \langle \mathbf{r}(x), \mathbf{t}\rangle\big), (\mathbf{a}, e(x))\Big)$$

where $\mathbf{a} \leftarrow \mathbb{F}_2^k$, $\mathbf{r}(x) \leftarrow \mathrm{Ber}(e^x\omega_0)^{\otimes n}$ and $e(x) \leftarrow \mathrm{Ber}(e^x\omega_0 t)$. Furthermore we have the same upper-bound between outputs of $\mathcal{O}^{\mathbf{v}_i}(x)$ and $\mathcal{O}^{\mathbf{v}_i}_{\mathrm{ideal}}(x)$ except that we have to replace $\mathbf{t}$ by $\mathbf{t} + \mathbf{v}_i$ and $e(x) \leftarrow \mathrm{Ber}(e^x\omega_0(t \pm 1))$ as $|\mathbf{v}_i| = 1$. But in both cases, the statistical distances are equal up to a factor $(1 + 2^{-\Omega(n)})$.

   Therefore, by using the data processing inequality and Eq. (3), the procedure will recover the support of $\mathbf{t}$ in the same time and with probability

$$\geqslant 1 - 2^{-\Omega(n)} - N' \max_{x \geqslant 0} \Delta\Big(\big(\mathbf{r}(x)\mathbf{G}^\top, \langle \mathbf{r}(x), \mathbf{t}\rangle\big), (\mathbf{a}, e(x))\Big)$$

where N' is the number of queries that our procedure makes to oracles $\mathcal{O}^0(x)$ and $\mathcal{O}^{\mathbf{v}_i}(x)$. According to Lemma 2, the procedure makes $\mathsf{poly}(\alpha)$ queries to its input oracle which is here $\mathcal{A}(\mathcal{O}^0(x))$ and $\mathcal{A}(\mathcal{O}^{\mathbf{v}_i}(x))$. But at the same time, $\mathcal{A}$ makes N queries to its input oracles. Therefore $N' = \mathsf{poly}(\alpha)N$ which concludes the proof. □

Remark 4. This algorithm bares similarities with the OHCP framework introduced in [32] to prove pseudorandomness of the ring-LWE distribution. However, contrary to the lattice-based setting, in the case of codes we do not need to introduce a random walk towards a center. Indeed, in the Hamming metric, the support gathers all the needed information to recover the error. The situation is even simpler in the case of the binary field $\mathbb{F}_2$, for there are only two situations: either the error is 1 or 0. For a bigger finite field $\mathbb{F}_q$, we would have to distinguish between a 0 value or a non-zero error, letting us with $q-1$ choices for the actual error value. However, the information "being in the support or not" is enough to recover the error, even if that means solving a linear system. Note that this remark also applies to the rank metric, which could be a good starting point to design search-to-decision reductions for codes endowed with this metric.

4   Instantiations

4.1   Plain Decoding

In order to instantiate the above reduction, we need to carefully understand how close our oracle $\mathcal{O}^z(x)$ is to output LPN-like samples, from genuine LPN samples which are produced by $\mathcal{O}^z_{\mathrm{ideal}}(x)$ (see Fig. 4). That is to say, we want to understand when the additive term

$$N\mathsf{poly}(\alpha)\,\Delta\Big(\big(\mathbf{r}(x)\mathbf{G}^\top, \langle \mathbf{r}(x), \mathbf{t}\rangle\big), (\mathbf{a}, e(x))\Big)$$

in Eq. (8) is negligible. Recall that $|\mathbf{t}| = t$, $\mathbf{r}(x) \leftarrow \mathrm{Ber}(e^x\omega_0)^{\otimes n}$ and $e \leftarrow \mathrm{Ber}(e^x\omega_0 t)^{\otimes n}$. In other words, we want to understand for which parameters ω_0, x

the distribution of $\mathbf{r}(x)$ *smoothes* the dual of the code generated by $\mathbf{G}$. We will consider two situations: *average-case to average-case* and *worst-case to average-case* reductions. It has to be noted that OCP-based reductions are fundamentally worst-case to average-case. In particular, the average-case to average-case reduction yields essentially the same parameters as the worst-case to average-case. The major difference is that the latter requires so-called *smoothing bounds*.

– **Average-case to Average-case reduction:** for cryptographic applications, we need to assess the hardness of our problem *on average*. In this situation, the matrix $\mathbf{G}$ is chosen uniformly at random in $\mathbb{F}_2^{k \times n}$. This yields another search to decision reduction for the plain decoding problem, completely different than that of [25]. Furthermore this gives a sense of the best sorts of trade-off between parameters that we can achieve with our reduction.

The main ingredient here will be the following lemma which is a variation of [23, Lemma 3, §C.1], itself a particular case of the famous leftover hash lemma (see [6]). A proof can be found in the extended version [12].

Lemma 4. *Let E, F be finite sets. Let $\mathcal{H} = (h_i)_{i \in I}$ be a finite family of applications from E to F and $T \subseteq E$. Let t be drawn uniformly at random in T and $r \in E$ be a random variable distributed according to some distribution $\mathcal{D}$. Let,*

$$p \stackrel{\mathrm{def}}{=} \mathbb{P}_{t,r}\left(\langle r, t \rangle = 1\right) \tag{18}$$

where $\langle \cdot, \cdot \rangle$ is a map from $E \times E \to \{0,1\}$. Let η be the "collision bias" defined by

$$\mathbb{P}_{h,t,r_0,r_1}\left(h(r_0) = h(r_1), \langle t, r_0 \rangle = \langle t, r_1 \rangle\right) \leqslant \frac{1}{\sharp F}(p^2 + (1-p)^2 + \eta) \tag{19}$$

where h, t are uniformly drawn in $\mathcal{H}$ and T respectively and r_0, r_1 be independent and distributed according to $\mathcal{D}$.

Let Y be the random variable (u, e) where u is uniform over F and $e \in \{0,1\}$ is a Bernoulli random variable of parameter p and u, e are independent. Let $Y(h, t)$ be the random variable $(h(r), \langle r, t \rangle)$ when r is distributed according to $\mathcal{D}$. We have,

$$\mathbb{E}_{h,t}\left(\Delta(Y(h, t), Y)\right) \leqslant \sqrt{\eta}.$$

In our case, the functions will be defined as $h(r) = \mathbf{r}\mathbf{G}^\top$ where $\mathbf{G}$ ranges over a family of matrices, typically double circulant matrices, or the full space of $k \times n$ matrices; and $\langle \cdot, \cdot \rangle$ will stand for the canonical inner product over $\mathbb{F}_2^n$.

– **Worst-case to Average-case reduction:** on a more theoretical perspective, one can wonder on the worst case hardness of the decision decoding problem. Such a result has been obtained for lattices, proving for instance that different flavors of LWE are at least as hard as *worst-case* problems on (different classes of) Euclidean lattices. The main ingredient here will be the *smoothing bounds* of [16,20,22,42]. This is the first time that such a reduction is derived from the OCP framework in the code–based setting.

Average-Case to Average-Case Reduction. In this paragraph, we consider the plain decoding problem. First, we prove the following lemma. It will yield the noise allowed in the decision problem of the reduction.

Lemma 5. *Let* $\beta, \eta \in (0,1)$, $k \leqslant n \in \mathbb{N}$, $t \in [\![1, n]\!]$ *and* $\omega_0 \in \mathbb{R}_+$ *be such that*

$$\omega_0 \geqslant -\log_2 \left(1 - 2\,\frac{1+\eta}{1-\beta}\,h^{-1}\left(\frac{k}{n}\right)\right) \tag{20}$$

with $h^{-1} : [0,1] \to [0, \frac{1}{2}]$ *being the inverse of the binary entropy function* h. *Then, for all* $x \geqslant 0$,

$$\mathbb{E}_{\mathbf{G},\mathbf{t}}\left(\Delta\Big((\mathbf{r}(x)\mathbf{G}^{\top}, \langle \mathbf{r}(x), \mathbf{t}\rangle), (\mathbf{a}, e(x))\Big)\right) = 2^{-\Omega(n)}$$

where $\mathbf{a} \leftarrow \mathbb{F}_2^k$, $\mathbf{r}(x) \leftarrow \mathrm{Ber}(e^x\omega_0)^{\otimes n}$, $e(x) \leftarrow \mathrm{Ber}(e^x\omega_0 t)$, $\mathbf{G} \leftarrow \mathbb{F}_2^{k\times n}$ *and* $\mathbf{t} \leftarrow \mathcal{S}_t^n$ *being the sphere of radius* t *around* $\mathbf{0}$ *in* $\mathbb{F}_2^n$.

It is a corollary of Lemma 4 and [22, Proposition 6.7] recalled below, which shows that the Bernoulli distribution inherits the smoothing properties of the uniform distribution over a Hamming sphere.

Proposition 1 ([22, **Proposition 6.7**]). *Let* $\mathbf{t} \in \mathbb{F}_2^n$, $\beta > 0$, $\rho \in \mathbb{R}_+$ *and* $p \stackrel{def}{=} \frac{1}{2}(1 - 2^{-\rho})$. *Let* $\mathbf{G} \in \mathbb{F}_2^{k\times n}$ *be the generator matrix of an* $[n,k]$-*code. Then,*

$$\Delta\Big((\mathbf{r}\mathbf{G}^{\top}, \langle \mathbf{r}, \mathbf{t}\rangle), (\mathbf{a}, e)\Big) \leqslant \sum_{r=(1-\beta)np}^{(1+\beta)np} \Delta\Big((\mathbf{r}_r\mathbf{G}^{\top}, \langle \mathbf{r}_r, \mathbf{t}\rangle), (\mathbf{a}, e_r)\Big) + 2^{-\Omega(n)}$$

where $\mathbf{r} \leftarrow \mathrm{Ber}(\rho)^{\otimes n}$, $\mathbf{a} \leftarrow \mathbb{F}_2^k$, $e \leftarrow \mathrm{Ber}(\rho|\mathbf{t}|)$, $\mathbf{r}_r \leftarrow \mathcal{S}_r$ *and the* e_r's *are distributed as the* $\langle \mathbf{r}_r, \mathbf{t}\rangle$'s.

Remark 5. Note that Equation (20) is equivalent to

$$\frac{1}{2}\left(1 - 2^{-\omega_0}\right)(1-\beta) \geqslant (1+\eta)h^{-1}\left(\frac{k}{n}\right). \tag{21}$$

That is to say, require the least index in the sum in Proposition 1 to be above the Gilbert-Varshamov bound. This is a necessary condition for the statistical distances to be negligible.

We are now ready to prove Lemma 5. We will proceed in two steps: first we show that it holds when $\mathbf{r}$ is instead uniformly distributed over the sphere of radius $\frac{n}{2}\left(1 - 2^{-e^x\omega_0}\right)(1-\beta)$; we then apply Proposition 1.

Proof. To ease the reading, let us drop the dependency in x (the maximum of the statistical distance is reached for $x = 0$; taking $x \geqslant 0$ can only decrease this statistical distance as it increases the noise). Let $r \stackrel{def}{=} \frac{n}{2}(1 - 2^{-\omega_0})(1-\beta)$

and $\mathbf{r} \leftarrow \mathcal{S}_r$. Our aim is to show that the result holds for this distribution. To conclude the proof it will just remain to apply Proposition 1. By Lemma 4, it suffices to compute the collision probability (where $\mathbf{r}_0, \mathbf{r}_1 \leftarrow \mathcal{S}_r$, $\mathbf{G} \leftarrow \mathbb{F}_2^{k \times n}$ and $\mathbf{t} \leftarrow \mathcal{S}_t$)

$$\mathbb{P}_{\mathbf{r}_0, \mathbf{r}_1, \mathbf{G}, \mathbf{t}} \left(\mathbf{r}_0 \mathbf{G}^\top = \mathbf{r}_1 \mathbf{G}^\top, \langle \mathbf{t}, \mathbf{r}_0 \rangle = \langle \mathbf{t}, \mathbf{r}_1 \rangle \right)$$

$$= \mathbb{P}_{\mathbf{r}_0, \mathbf{r}_1, \mathbf{G}, \mathbf{t}} \left((\mathbf{r}_0 - \mathbf{r}_1) \, \mathbf{G}^\top = 0, \langle \mathbf{t}, \mathbf{r}_0 - \mathbf{r}_1 \rangle = 0 \right)$$

$$= \sum_{\mathbf{r} \neq 0} \mathbb{P}_{\mathbf{G}} \left(\mathbf{r} \mathbf{G}^\top = 0 \right) \mathbb{P}_{\mathbf{t}} \left(\langle \mathbf{t}, \mathbf{r} \rangle = 0 \right) \mathbb{P}_{\mathbf{r}_0, \mathbf{r}_1} \left(\mathbf{r}_0 - \mathbf{r}_1 = \mathbf{r} \right) + \mathbb{P}_{\mathbf{r}_0, \mathbf{r}_1} \left(\mathbf{r}_0 = \mathbf{r}_1 \right)$$

$$= \frac{1}{2^k} \sum_{\mathbf{r} \neq 0} \mathbb{P}_{\mathbf{t}} \left(\langle \mathbf{t}, \mathbf{r} \rangle = 0 \right) \mathbb{P}_{\mathbf{r}_0, \mathbf{r}_1} \left(\mathbf{r}_0 - \mathbf{r}_1 = \mathbf{r} \right) + \mathbb{P}_{\mathbf{r}_0, \mathbf{r}_1} \left(\mathbf{r}_0 = \mathbf{r}_1 \right)$$

$$\leqslant \frac{1}{2^k} \left(\mathbb{P}_{\mathbf{t}, \mathbf{r}_0, \mathbf{r}_1} \left(\langle \mathbf{t}, \mathbf{r}_0 - \mathbf{r}_1 \rangle = 0 \right) + 2^k \mathbb{P}_{\mathbf{r}_0, \mathbf{r}_1} \left(\mathbf{r}_0 = \mathbf{r}_1 \right) \right)$$

$$= \frac{1}{2^k} \left(p^2 + (1-p)^2 + \frac{2^k}{\binom{n}{r}} \right)$$

where $p \stackrel{\text{def}}{=} \mathbb{P}_{\mathbf{r}, \mathbf{t}} \left(\langle \mathbf{t}, \mathbf{r} \rangle = 1 \right)$ and we used in the inequality the law of total probability. By Lemma 4,

$$\mathbb{E}_{\mathbf{G}, \mathbf{t}} \left(\Delta \left((\mathbf{r}_r \mathbf{G}^\top, \langle \mathbf{r}_r, \mathbf{t} \rangle), (\mathbf{a}, e_r) \right) \right) \leqslant \sqrt{\frac{2^k}{\binom{n}{r}}}.$$

Recall that $\binom{n}{r} = 2^{nh(r/n)(1+o(1))}$ where h denotes the binary entropy function. By Eq. (21), r verifies $(1 + \eta) h^{-1} \left(\frac{k}{n} \right) \leqslant \frac{r}{n} \leqslant 1/2$. Therefore, since h is a strictly increasing function, the above upper-bound is a $2^{-\Omega(n)}$. This yields the claimed result. $\square$

Recall that in Theorem 1, the considered (search) decoding problem is fixed once and for all. However, the above lemma tells us that on average, on the choice of $\mathbf{G}$ and $\mathbf{t}$, the considered statistical distance is negligible. We can actually prove that it holds for *almost all* choices.

Lemma 6. *Let $k \leqslant n \in \mathbb{N}, t \in [\![0, n]\!]$. For a matrix $\mathbf{G} \in \mathbb{F}_2^{k \times n}$ and a vector $\mathbf{t} \in \mathbb{F}_2^n$ of Hamming weight t, denote*

$$X(\mathbf{G}, \mathbf{t}) \stackrel{\text{def}}{=} \Delta \left((\mathbf{r}(x) \mathbf{G}^\top, \langle \mathbf{r}(x), \mathbf{t} \rangle), (\mathbf{a}, e(x)) \right).$$

Let,

$$\gamma \stackrel{\text{def}}{=} \mathbb{E}_{\mathbf{G}_u, \mathbf{t}_u} \left(X(\mathbf{G}_u, \mathbf{t}_u) \right)$$

where $\mathbf{G}_u \leftarrow \mathbb{F}_2^{k \times n}$ and $\mathbf{t}_u \leftarrow \mathcal{S}_t$. Then,

$$\frac{\#\{(\mathbf{G}, \mathbf{t}) \in \mathbb{F}_2^{k \times n} \times \mathcal{S}_t \mid X(\mathbf{G}, \mathbf{t}) \geqslant \sqrt{\gamma}\}}{2^{kn} \binom{n}{t}} \leqslant \sqrt{\gamma}.$$

Proof. Since $\mathbf{G}_u$ and $\mathbf{t}_u$ are independent and uniformly distributed over their respective domains, this proportion is nothing else than $\mathbb{P}_{\mathbf{G}_u, \mathbf{t}_u}(X(\mathbf{G}_u, \mathbf{t}_u) \geqslant \sqrt{\gamma})$. By Markov inequality, we have

$$\mathbb{P}_{\mathbf{G}_u, \mathbf{t}_u}(X(\mathbf{G}_u, \mathbf{t}_u) \geqslant \sqrt{\gamma}) \leqslant \frac{\mathbb{E}_{\mathbf{G}_u, \mathbf{t}_u}(X(\mathbf{G}_u, \mathbf{t}_u))}{\sqrt{\gamma}} \leqslant \sqrt{\gamma},$$

which concludes the proof. □

We are now ready to instantiate our search-to-decision average-to-average case reduction. However, in the same manner as discussed in [22, §6], parameters have to be carefully chosen to ensure that the decision problem is not *too hard* and its search counterpart into which we reduce is not *too easy*.

Notice that the noise of the decision decoding problem of the reduction is distributed as $\mathrm{Ber}(\omega_0 t)$ with ω_0 given in Eq. (20). If one chooses k, n such that $\frac{k}{n} = \Theta(1)$, one would obtain a noise distributed as $\mathrm{Ber}(\omega_0 t) = \mathrm{Ber}(\Theta(t))$. In that case, it seems that we need to choose t as a $O(\log_2(n))$ to reach a noise rate $1/2(1-2^{-\omega_0 t}) = 1/2 - 1/\mathsf{poly}(n)$ in the decision decoding problem. Otherwise, we would reduce the decoding problem into a decision decoding problem with a noise rate *exponentially or sub-exponentially* close to $1/2$; an extremely hard problem which is not very satisfactory. On the other hand, choosing $t = O(\log_2(n))$ is a real disaster for the reduction: decoding a code of length n at distance $O(\log_2(n))$ can be done in polynomial time (using for instance Prange algorithm [34]). That is, we would be reducing an *easy* worst-case search decoding problem to an average-case decision decoding problem; which says nothing about the hardness of the decision version. We therefore conclude that the only way to reach an error rate $1/2(1 - 2^{-\omega_0 t}) = 1/2 - 1/\mathsf{poly}(n)$ is to decrease as much as possible ω_0 given in Eq. (20). In particular, we are led to choose $k/n = o(1)$, since in that case $\omega_0 = -\log_2(1 - o(1)) = o(1)$. More precisely, for these parameters ω_0 verifies

$$\omega_0 = -\log_2\left(1 - \Theta\left(h^{-1}\left(\frac{k}{n}\right)\right)\right) \approx \frac{1}{\log_2\left(\frac{n}{k}\right)} \frac{k}{n}$$

where we used the expansion $h^{-1}(\varepsilon) \underset{\varepsilon \to 0}{\approx} \frac{\varepsilon}{\log_2(1/\varepsilon)}$. Therefore, to reach the noise rate $1/2 - 1/\mathsf{poly}(n)$ we need to choose parameters such that

$$\frac{k}{n} = o(1) \quad \text{and} \quad \omega_0 t = \frac{1}{\log_2\left(\frac{n}{k}\right)} \frac{k}{n} t = O(\log_2(n)). \tag{22}$$

Notice that necessarily in the above choice of parameters, we need t to be sublinear in n, since otherwise k would be too small, allowing an exhaustive search to decode in polynomial time. Fortunately, in that case the reduction is non-trivial. The cost of Prange's algorithm [34] (which is asymptotically the best known decoding algorithm when the decoding distance t is sublinear in the length of the input code) is given by

$$2^{\Theta\left(t \frac{k}{n}\right)} = 2^{\Theta(\log_2(n) \log_2(n/k))} = n^{\Theta(\log_2(n/k))}$$

(see [17]) which is super-polynomial.

In what follows we focus our attention to a noise rate $1/2 - 1/\mathrm{poly}(n)$ in the decision problem, that is to say we propose parameters where the rate k/n of the codes considered in the reduction verifies $k/n = o(1)$.

Theorem 2. *Let $\beta, \eta \in (0,1)$, $C > 0$ and $n, k, t \in \mathbb{N}$ be such that*

$$\frac{k}{n} = o(1) \quad and \quad \frac{2}{\ln(2)} \frac{1+\eta}{1-\beta} \frac{1}{\log_2\left(\frac{n}{k}\right)} \frac{k}{n} t = C \log_2(n). \tag{23}$$

Furthermore, let

$$\omega_0 = -\log_2\left(1 - 2\frac{1+\eta}{1-\beta} h^{-1}\left(\frac{k}{n}\right)\right) \tag{24}$$

$$i.e. \quad \frac{1-\beta}{2}\left(1 - 2^{-\omega_0}\right) = (1+\eta)h^{-1}\left(\frac{k}{n}\right).$$

Suppose that there exists an algorithm $\mathcal{A}$, with advantage $\varepsilon = \frac{1}{\mathrm{poly}(n)}$, which distinguishes in time T distributions $(\mathbf{A}, \mathbf{sA} + \mathbf{e})$ and $(\mathbf{A}, \mathbf{y})$ with

$$\mathbf{A} \leftarrow \mathbb{F}_2^{k \times n}, \ \mathbf{s} \leftarrow \mathbb{F}_2^k, \ \mathbf{y} \leftarrow \mathbb{F}_2^n \ and \ \mathbf{e} \leftarrow \mathrm{Ber}\left(\omega_0 t\right)^{\otimes n}.$$

Then, there exists an algorithm running in time $T\mathrm{poly}(n)$, which takes as inputs $\mathbf{G} \in \mathbb{F}_2^{k \times n}$, $\mathbf{mG} + \mathbf{t}$ where $\mathbf{m} \in \mathbb{F}_2^k$, $\mathbf{t} \in \mathcal{S}_t^n$, and outputs $\mathbf{t}$ (or equivalently $\mathbf{m}$) with probability at least $1 - 2^{-\Omega(n)}$ over a uniform choice of $\mathbf{G}$ and $\mathbf{t}$.

Remark 6. With the above parameter choice, we have

$$\omega_0 t = C \log_2(n)(1 + o(1))$$

i.e. the error rate in the *decision* problem is

$$\frac{1}{2}(1 - 2^{-\omega_0 t}) = \frac{1}{2} - \frac{1}{\mathrm{poly}(n)}.$$

Proof. We use the notations of Theorem 1 and Lemma 6. Let $\mathbf{G} \leftarrow \mathbb{F}_2^{k \times n}$ and $\mathbf{t} \leftarrow \mathcal{S}_t$. Notice that, since $k/n = o(1)$, the following computation holds

$$\omega_0 t = -\log_2\left(1 - 2\frac{1+\eta}{1-\beta} h^{-1}\left(\frac{k}{n}\right)\right) t$$

$$= \frac{2}{\ln(2)} \frac{1+\eta}{1-\beta} h^{-1}\left(\frac{k}{n}\right) t(1 + o(1))$$

$$= \frac{2}{\ln(2)} \frac{1+\eta}{1-\beta} \frac{1}{\log_2\left(\frac{n}{k}\right)} \frac{k}{n} t \, (1 + o(1)),$$

where we used the expansion $h^{-1}(x) = \frac{x}{\log_2(1/x)}(1 + o(1))$. Therefore, by Equation (23), we have

$$\omega_0 t = C \log_2(n)(1 + o(1)).$$

Let us consider now the algorithm $\mathcal{B}$ given by Theorem 1 which is obtained from an algorithm distinguishing distributions $(\mathbf{A}, \mathbf{sA} + \mathbf{e})$ and $(\mathbf{A}, \mathbf{y})$ with advantage $\varepsilon = \frac{1}{\text{poly}(n)}$. It will output some $\mathbf{t}'$ in time $T\text{poly}(\alpha)$ and with probability $1 - 2^{-\Omega(n)} - n\text{poly}(\alpha)X(\mathbf{G}, \mathbf{t})$. Notice that we do not have a max here because it is reached when $x = 0$: the higher is the noise, the closer our distribution is from the genuine LPN. Since $\alpha = \max\left(\frac{1}{\varepsilon}, n\right) = \text{poly}(n)$, then this probability is $1 - 2^{-\Omega(n)}$ when $X(\mathbf{G}, \mathbf{t}) = 2^{-\Omega(n)}$. But since ω_0 is chosen as in Eq. (24), we have $\mathbb{E}_{\mathbf{G}, \mathbf{t}}(X(\mathbf{G}, \mathbf{t})) = 2^{-\Omega(n)}$. Therefore, according to Lemma 6, the proportion of $(\mathbf{G}, \mathbf{t})$ for which it happens is $1 - 2^{-\Omega(n)}$ (since ω_0 was chosen such that $\gamma = \mathbb{E}_{\mathbf{G}, \mathbf{t}}(X(\mathbf{G}, \mathbf{t})) = 2^{-\Omega(n)}$). Moreover, the success probability of $\mathcal{B}$ is independent from $\mathbf{G}$ and $\mathbf{t}$. Therefore, the probability that $\mathcal{B}(\mathbf{G}, \mathbf{t})$ outputs 1 will be greater than $(1 - 2^{-\Omega(n)})(1 - 2^{-\Omega(n)}) = 1 - 2^{-\Omega(n)}$, which concludes the proof. $\qquad\square$

Remark 7. In Theorem 2, we instantiated Theorem 1 with $N = n$ to get a decisional version of the actual decoding problem. However, we are not really limited by the length N of the input code in the decision decoding problem; we have total liberty in the choice of N. Increasing N would only increase the running time of the reduction. In other words, this reduction would also apply in the context of LPN, where N is *a priori* unbounded.

Worst-Case to Average-Case Reduction. We will now deal with the worst-case to average-case reduction. Recall that in Theorem 1, we need to set the statistical distance between our produced samples and genuine LPN samples to be negligible. For a worst-case hardness we need it to be negligible for *any* code, *i.e.* for *any* matrix $\mathbf{G}$. To this end we will use smoothing bounds as given in [22, Proposition 7.6]. However, this bound is only stated when $\mathbf{G}$ is a generator matrix of an $[n, k]$-code which is balanced (in the same manner than in [16]).

Definition 3 (Balanced code). *An $[n, k]$-code is δ-balanced if its minimum distance is at least δn and all the codewords have Hamming weight at most $(1 - \delta)n$. That is, for all $\mathbf{x} \in \mathcal{C} \setminus \{\mathbf{0}\}$,*

$$\delta n \leqslant |\mathbf{x}| \leqslant (1 - \delta)n.$$

In the worst-case to average-case search-to-decision reduction we will restrict "worst" instances to δ-balanced codes. Therefore, we will first need to fix an $[n, k]$-code $\mathcal{C}$ which is δ-balanced. A natural choice for δ is given by the relative *Gilbert-Varshamov* bound $h^{-1}\left(1 - \frac{k}{n}\right)$ which appears ubiquitously in the coding-theoretic literature: amongst other contexts, it arises as the (expected) relative minimum distance of a random code of dimension k and length n (see for instance [7, §C]). However, for the same reasons as above with random codes, in order to reach a noise rate $1/2 - 1/\text{poly}(n)$ in the decision problem, we will choose parameters k, n so that $k/n = o(1)$. Many other interesting sets of parameters for the reduction can be proposed, for instance choosing $k/n = \Theta(1)$ and $t/n = o(n)$ leading to a noise rate in the decision decoding problem $1/2 - 2^{-o(n)}$.

To reach a negligible statistical distance we will use the following proposition.

Proposition 2 ([22, **Proposition 7.6**]). *Let* $G \in \mathbb{F}_2^{k \times n}$ *be the generator matrix of an* $[n, k]$-*code which is* δ-*balanced with* $1/2 \geqslant \delta \geqslant h^{-1}\left(1 - \frac{k}{n}\right) \geqslant C$ *for some constant* $C > 0$. *Let* $t \in \mathbb{F}_2^n$ *and suppose that* $\frac{|t|}{n} = o(1)$.
  Let $\beta, \eta > 0$ *and* $\rho \in \mathbb{R}_+$ *be such that*

$$(1 - \beta)\frac{1}{2}(1 - 2^{-\rho}) \geqslant (1 + \eta)h^{-1}\left(2\frac{k}{n} + D\frac{|t|}{n}\right)$$

for some large enough constant D. *Then,*

$$\Delta\Big(\big(rG^\top, \langle r, t \rangle\big), (a, e)\Big) = 2^{-\Omega(n)}$$

where $r \leftarrow \mathrm{Ber}(\rho)^{\otimes n}$, $a \leftarrow \mathbb{F}_2^k$ *and* $e \leftarrow \mathrm{Ber}(\rho|t|)$.

This proposition allows to instantiate our reduction in the worst-to-average case in the following theorem.

Theorem 3. *Let* $\beta, \eta \in (0, 1)$, $C > 0$ *and* $n, k, t \in \mathbb{N}$ *be such that*

$$\frac{k}{n} = o(1), \quad \frac{t}{n} = o\left(\frac{k}{n}\right) \quad and \quad \frac{4}{\ln(2)}\frac{1+\eta}{1-\beta}\frac{1}{\log_2\left(\frac{n}{k}\right)}\frac{k}{n}t = C\log_2(n). \quad (25)$$

Furthermore, let (for some large enough constant D)

$$\omega_0 = -\log_2\left(1 - 2\frac{1+\eta}{1-\beta}h^{-1}\left(2\frac{k}{n} + D\frac{t}{n}\right)\right) \quad (26)$$

i.e. $\quad \dfrac{1-\beta}{2}\left(1 - 2^{-\omega_0}\right) = 2(1+\eta)h^{-1}\left(2\dfrac{k}{n} + D\dfrac{t}{n}\right).$

Suppose that there exists an algorithm $\mathcal{A}$, *with advantage* $\varepsilon = \frac{1}{\mathrm{poly}(n)}$, *which distinguishes in time* T *distributions* $(A, sA + e)$ *and* (A, y) *with*

$$A \leftarrow \mathbb{F}_2^{k \times n}, \ s \leftarrow \mathbb{F}_2^k, \ y \leftarrow \mathbb{F}_2^n \quad and \quad e \leftarrow \mathrm{Ber}(\omega_0 t)^{\otimes n}$$

$$where \ \omega_0 t = C\log_2(n)(1 + o(1)).$$

Then, there exists an algorithm running in time $T\mathrm{poly}(n)$, *which takes as inputs* $G \in \mathbb{F}_2^{k \times n}$ *a (fixed) generator matrix of a* δ-*balanced* $[n, k]$ *code (with* $\delta \geqslant h^{-1}\left(1 - \frac{k}{n}\right) = \frac{1}{2} - \sqrt{\frac{k}{n}}(1 + o(1)))$, *a noisy codeword* $mG + t$ *with* t *of Hamming weight* t, *and outputs* t *(or equivalently* m) *with probability at least* $1 - 2^{-\Omega(n)}$ *(where the probability is not taken over the choice of* m, G *and* t).

Proof. We use the notations of Theorem 1 and Proposition 2. Notice that, since $k/n = o(1)$ and $t/n = o(k/n)$, we have the following computation

$$\omega_0 t = -\log_2\left(1 - 2\frac{1+\eta}{1-\beta}h^{-1}\left(2\frac{k}{n} + D\frac{t}{n}\right)\right)t$$

$$= \frac{4}{\ln(2)}\frac{1+\eta}{1-\beta}\frac{1}{\log_2\left(\frac{n}{k}\right)}\frac{k}{n}t(1 + o(1))$$

where we used the expansion $h^{-1}(x) = \frac{x}{\log_2(1/x)}(1 + o(1))$. Therefore, by Equation (25), we have

$$\omega_0 t = C \log_2(n)(1 + o(1)),$$

i.e.

$$\frac{1}{2}\left(1 - 2^{-\omega_0 t}\right) = \frac{1}{2}\left(1 - \frac{1}{n^{C(1+o(1))}}\right).$$

Let,

$$Y(\mathbf{G}, t) \overset{\text{def}}{=} \Delta\Big(\big(\mathbf{r}(x)\mathbf{G}^\top, \langle \mathbf{r}(x), t \rangle\big), (\mathbf{a}, e(x))\Big).$$

Let us consider now the algorithm $\mathcal{B}$ given by Theorem 1 which is obtained from an algorithm distinguishing distributions $(\mathbf{A}, \mathbf{sA} + \mathbf{e})$ and $(\mathbf{A}, \mathbf{y})$ with advantage $\varepsilon = \frac{1}{\mathsf{poly}(n)}$. It will output some t' in time $T\mathsf{poly}(\alpha)$ and with probability $1 - 2^{-\Omega(n)} - n\mathsf{poly}(\alpha)Y(\mathbf{G}, t)$. Notice that we do not have a max here because it is reached when $x = 0$: the higher is the noise, the closer our distribution is from the genuine LPN. Since $\alpha = \max\left(\frac{1}{\varepsilon}, n\right) = \mathsf{poly}(n)$, then this probability is $1 - 2^{-\Omega(n)}$ when $Y(\mathbf{G}, t) = 2^{-\Omega(n)}$. But since ω_0 is chosen as in Eq. (26) we have $Y(\mathbf{G}, t) = 2^{-\Omega(n)}$. Moreover, the success probability of $\mathcal{B}$ is independent from $\mathbf{G}$ which concludes the proof. $\square$

A Set of Parameters. One can apply Theorem 3 for instance with the following set of parameters

$$\frac{k}{n} = \frac{1}{n^D} \quad \text{and} \quad \frac{t}{n} = \frac{\log_2(n)^2}{n^{1-D}}$$

with $D < 1/2$. Theorem 3 shows that solving the decision-average decoding problem of codes with length n, dimension n^{1-D} at distance $1/2 - O\left(1/n^{D\ln(2)/4}\right)$ is at least as hard as decoding a fixed δ-balanced code (with $\delta \geqslant h^{-1}\left(1 - \frac{1}{n^D}\right)$) at distance $n^D \log_2(n)^2$. Note that, as noticed in [16, §1.1] or [42] and even [7] (though not under the same terminology), most of the codes are δ-balanced, and no generic decoding algorithm is known to take advantage of this property.

5 Failed Attempt: The Case of Structured Codes

In the manner of [32, 37], it would be very tempting to apply our reduction in the case of structured error correcting codes, such as quasi-cyclic codes. Such codes are used in NIST submissions BIKE and HQC because they offer a very good efficiency while keeping the same security parameter as truly random codes.

Quasi-cyclic codes are codes that have a generator matrix formed out by multiple circulant blocks, i.e. of the form

$$\begin{pmatrix} a_0 & a_{n-1} & \cdots & a_1 \\ a_1 & a_0 & \cdots & a_2 \\ a_2 & a_1 & \cdots & a_3 \\ \vdots & \vdots & \ddots & \vdots \\ a_{n-1} & a_{n-2} & \cdots & a_0 \end{pmatrix}.$$

In order to simplify the discourse, in the sequel we consider the situation of quasi-cyclic codes formed out by a *single* row of circulant blocks. This generalizes easily to multiple rows, which corresponds to what is sometimes called *module*-LPN in the literature (see for instance [15]).

Very conveniently, quasi-cyclic codes benefit from a so-called *polynomial* representation. Indeed, each vector of length n can be represented as an element of $\mathbb{F}_2[X]/(X^n - 1)$; such that the matrix-vector product is nothing but the usual product of polynomials.

Consider a quasi-cyclic code generated by a matrix $\mathbf{G}$ of rate R, *i.e.* with $1/R$ circulant blocks. A noisy codeword $\mathbf{y} = \mathbf{mG} + \mathbf{t}$ where $\mathbf{t}$ is a *regular* error of weight t (*i.e.* a concatenation of $1/R$ words of Hamming weight t, which is the usual noise considered with quasi-cyclic codes) yields $1/R$ noisy polynomials of the form $\mathbf{ma} + \mathbf{t}' \in \mathbb{F}_2[X]/(X^n - 1)$, using the polynomial representation.

Hence, we could change the inner product $\langle \cdot, \cdot \rangle$ in Theorem 1 by the following inner product (with value in $\mathbb{F}_2[X]/(X^n - 1)$): if $\mathbf{x} = (\mathbf{x}_1, \dots, \mathbf{x}_{1/R}) \in (\mathbb{F}_2[X]/(X^n - 1))^{1/R}$, define

$$\langle \mathbf{x}, \mathbf{y} \rangle \stackrel{\text{def}}{=} \sum_{i=1}^{1/R} \mathbf{x}_i \mathbf{y}_i.$$

With this inner product in hand, given $\mathbf{y} = (\mathbf{ma}_1 + \mathbf{t}'_1, \dots, \mathbf{ma}_{1/R} + \mathbf{t}'_{1/R}) \in (\mathbb{F}_2[X]/(X^n - 1))^{1/R}$, we can compute $\langle \mathbf{y}, \mathbf{r} \rangle$ where $\mathbf{r} = (\mathbf{r}_1, \dots, \mathbf{r}_{1/R})$ and each $\mathbf{r}_i$ are distributed according to $\mathrm{Ber}(\omega_0)$, meaning in this context that all the n coefficients of $\mathbf{r}_i$ are distributed according to $\mathrm{Ber}(\omega_0)$. Then,

$$\langle \mathbf{y}, \mathbf{r} \rangle = \mathbf{m} \left(\sum_{i=1}^{1/R} \mathbf{a}_i \mathbf{r}_i \right) + \underbrace{\sum_{i=1}^{1/R} \mathbf{t}'_i \mathbf{r}_j}_{\text{LPN noise}} \qquad (27)$$

We can then follow the same strategy than previously to prove a structured analogue of Theorem 1. However we have to show that sampling elements as in (27) is close to sample from the ring-LPN distribution instead of the plain LPN. Lemma 4 can be adapted to this case and collisions can be easily computed; therefore we are able to compute the noise from which the Bernoulli distribution smoothes the distribution, which would actually be roughly the same as in the unstructured case (this is actually a consequence of the fact that random quasi-cyclic codes of use in cryptography have on average a minimum distance reaching the Gilbert-Varshamov bound [27], so as genuine random codes). However there is a strong caveat when one wants to estimate the noise in a sample given in Eq. (27).

For the sake of simplicity, let us consider $R = 1$. Let $\mathbf{t} = \sum_{i=0}^{n-1} t_i X^i \in \mathbb{F}_2[X]/(X^n - 1)$ with Hamming weight t, namely with t non-zero coefficients. Now, sample $\mathbf{r} = \sum_{i=0}^{n-1} r_i X^i \in \mathbb{F}_2[X]/(X^n - 1)$ where $(r_0, \dots, r_{n-1}) \leftarrow \mathrm{Ber}(\omega_0)^{\otimes n}$. The noise in the built LPN-samples is given by the inner product between $\mathbf{t}$ and $\mathbf{r}$, namely

$$\mathbf{tr} = \sum_{k=0}^{n-1} \sum_{i+j \equiv k \bmod n} t_i r_j X^k. \tag{28}$$

Notice that each coefficient of $\mathbf{tr}$ is exactly the sum of t independent $\mathrm{Ber}(\omega_0)$ random variables, therefore is a Bernoulli random variable of parameter $t\omega_0$. It may seem at first glance that we obtain the same analysis than in the plain case, starting from a noisy codewords $\mathbf{y} = \mathbf{ma} + \mathbf{t}$ we build LPN like sample with Bernoulli noise given by $\mathrm{Ber}(\omega_0 t)$. There is a strong caveat here though: the coefficients of the product in Eq. (28) are *not* independent, even though this inner product would have the good Hamming weight on average. Therefore our new noise does not follow the right distribution.

It turns out that this distribution is very difficult to analyze, and this fact was already emphasized in the HQC submission to the NIST [4] when studying the Decoding Failure Rate (DFR) of the scheme. In particular, the authors replaced this weird distribution by an actual Bernoulli distribution and made experimental results to support their modelization. Such a modelization is not enough from a theoretical standpoint, and we cannot use it to build reductions. In other words, in order to apply our reduction, we lack a *random self reducibility* for structured codes, such as quasi-cyclic codes as the direct approach given in Eq. (27) does not seem to work directly.

In the world of Euclidean lattices, this caveat is avoided since the error distribution is taken through the Mikowski embedding. The noise would then affect each coordinate independently. The reduction from [37, Section 4] benefits from the fact that the Vandermonde matrix, which maps the so-called coefficient embedding onto the Mikowski embedding, does not distort the noise too much. In the case of codes, such a Fourier-based approach takes an exaggerated toll on the noise distribution.

6   Conclusion

We gave the first reduction from the worst-case search decoding problem to the average-case decision decoding problem by following the OCP framework introduced in [32]. This reduction paradigm applied to lattices also permitted to obtain many new reductions for structured variants. Therefore it is tantalizing to try to apply such an approach in order to get worst-case to average-case and search-to-decision reductions for structured codes such as quasi-cyclic codes which are used for instance in BIKE and HQC, two of the three code-based proposals remaining in the fourth round of NIST post-quantum competition. However, as mentioned in Sect. 5, such an extension to structured codes is far from being straightforward and represents a highly interesting challenge.

References

1. Aguilar Melchor, C., et al.: BIKE. Round 4 Submission to the NIST Post-Quantum Cryptography Call, v. 5.1, October 2022. https://bikesuite.org

2. Aguilar Melchor, C., et al.: BIKE. Round 3 Submission to the NIST Post-Quantum Cryptography Call, v. 4.2, September 2021. https://bikesuite.org

3. Aguilar Melchor, C., et al.: HQC. Round 4 Submission to the NIST Post-Quantum Cryptography Call, October 2022. https://pqc-hqc.org/

4. Aguilar Melchor, C., et al.: HQC. Round 3 Submission to the NIST Post-Quantum Cryptography Call, June 2021. https://pqc-hqc.org/doc/hqc-specification_2021-06-06.pdf

5. Alekhnovich, M.: More on average case vs approximation complexity. In: 44th Symposium on Foundations of Computer Science (FOCS 2003), 11–14 October 2003, Cambridge, MA, USA, Proceedings, pp. 298–307. IEEE Computer Society (2003). https://doi.org/10.1109/SFCS.2003.1238204

6. Barak, B., et al.: Leftover hash lemma, revisited. In: Rogaway, P. (ed.) CRYPTO 2011. LNCS, vol. 6841, pp. 1–20. Springer, Heidelberg (2011). https://doi.org/10.1007/978-3-642-22792-9_1

7. Barg, A., Forney., G.D.: Random codes: minimum distances and error exponents. IEEE Trans. Inf. Theory $48(9)$, 2568–2573 (2002). https://doi.org/10.1109/TIT.2002.800480

8. Becker, A., Joux, A., May, A., Meurer, A.: Decoding random binary linear codes in $2^{n/20}$: how $1 + 1 = 0$ improves information set decoding. In: Pointcheval, D., Johansson, T. (eds.) EUROCRYPT 2012. LNCS, vol. 7237, pp. 520–536. Springer, Heidelberg (2012). https://doi.org/10.1007/978-3-642-29011-4_31

9. Berlekamp, E., McEliece, R., van Tilborg, H.: On the inherent intractability of certain coding problems. IEEE Trans. Inform. Theory $24(3)$, 384–386 (1978)

10. Bombar, M., Couteau, G., Couvreur, A., Ducros, C.: Correlated pseudorandomness from the hardness of quasi-abelian decoding. In: Handschuh, H., Lysyanskaya, A. (eds.) CRYPTO 2023. LNCS, vol. 14084, pp. 567–601. Springer, Cham (2023). https://doi.org/10.1007/978-3-031-38551-3_18

11. Bombar, M., Couvreur, A., Debris-Alazard, T.: On codes and learning with errors over function fields. In: Dodis, Y., Shrimpton, T. (eds.) CRYPTO 2022. LNCS, vol. 13508, pp. 513–540. Springer, Cham (2022). https://doi.org/10.1007/978-3-031-15979-4_18, https://arxiv.org/pdf/2202.13990.pdf

12. Bombar, M., Couvreur, A., Debris-Alazard, T.: Pseudorandomness of decoding, revisited: adapting OHCP to code-based cryptography (2023). Extended version: https://eprint.iacr.org/2022/1751

13. Both, L., May, A.: Optimizing BJMM with nearest neighbors: full decoding in $2^{2/21n}$ and McEliece security. In: WCC Workshop on Coding and Cryptography, September 2017. http://wcc2017.suai.ru/Proceedings_WCC2017.zip

14. Boudgoust, K., Jeudy, C., Roux-Langlois, A., Wen, W.: Towards classical hardness of module-LWE: the linear rank case. In: Moriai, S., Wang, H. (eds.) ASIACRYPT 2020. LNCS, vol. 12492, pp. 289–317. Springer, Cham (2020). https://doi.org/10.1007/978-3-030-64834-3_10

15. Boyle, E., Couteau, G., Gilboa, N., Ishai, Y., Kohl, L., Scholl, P.: Efficient pseudorandom correlation generators from ring-LPN. In: Micciancio, D., Ristenpart, T. (eds.) CRYPTO 2020. LNCS, vol. 12171, pp. 387–416. Springer, Cham (2020). https://doi.org/10.1007/978-3-030-56880-1_14

16. Brakerski, Z., Lyubashevsky, V., Vaikuntanathan, V., Wichs, D.: Worst-case hardness for LPN and cryptographic hashing via code smoothing. In: Ishai, Y., Rijmen, V. (eds.) EUROCRYPT 2019. LNCS, vol. 11478, pp. 619–635. Springer, Cham (2019). https://doi.org/10.1007/978-3-030-17659-4_21

17. Canto Torres, R., Sendrier, N.: Analysis of information set decoding for a sub-linear error weight. In: Takagi, T. (ed.) PQCrypto 2016. LNCS, vol. 9606, pp. 144–161. Springer, Cham (2016). https://doi.org/10.1007/978-3-319-29360-8_10

18. Carrier, K., Debris-Alazard, T., Meyer-Hilfiger, C., Tillich, J.: Statistical decoding 2.0: reducing decoding to LPN. In: Agrawal, S., Lin, D. (eds.) ASIACRYPT 2022. LNCS, vol. 13794, pp. 477–507. Springer, Cham (2022). https://doi.org/10.1007/978-3-031-22972-5_17, https://eprint.iacr.org/2022/1000

19. Castryck, W., Decru, T.: An efficient key recovery attack on SIDH. In: Hazay, C., Stam, M. (eds.) EUROCRYPT 2023. LNCS, vol. 14008, pp. 423–447. Springer, Cham (2023). https://doi.org/10.1007/978-3-031-30589-4_15

20. Debris-Alazard, T., Ducas, L., Resch, N., Tillich, J.: Smoothing codes and lattices: systematic study and new bounds. CoRR abs/2205.10552 (2022). https://doi.org/10.48550/arXiv.2205.10552

21. Debris-Alazard, T., Remaud, M., Tillich, J.: Quantum reduction of finding short code vectors to the decoding problem. preprint, November 2021. https://arxiv.org/abs/2106.02747, arXiv:2106.02747

22. Debris-Alazard, T., Resch, N.: Worst and average case hardness of decoding via smoothing bounds. Preprint, December 2022, eprint

23. Debris-Alazard, T., Sendrier, N., Tillich, J.-P.: Wave: a new family of trapdoor one-way preimage sampleable functions based on codes. In: Galbraith, S.D., Moriai, S. (eds.) ASIACRYPT 2019, Part I. LNCS, vol. 11921, pp. 21–51. Springer, Cham (2019). https://doi.org/10.1007/978-3-030-34578-5_2

24. Dumer, I.: On minimum distance decoding of linear codes. In: Proceedings of 5th Joint Soviet-Swedish International Workshop Informatics and Theory, pp. 50–52. Moscow (1991)

25. Fischer, J.-B., Stern, J.: An efficient pseudo-random generator provably as secure as syndrome decoding. In: Maurer, U. (ed.) EUROCRYPT 1996. LNCS, vol. 1070, pp. 245–255. Springer, Heidelberg (1996). https://doi.org/10.1007/3-540-68339-9_22

26. Gaborit, P.: Shorter keys for code based cryptography. In: Proceedings of the 2005 International Workshop on Coding and Cryptography (WCC 2005), pp. 81–91. Bergen, Norway, March 2005

27. Gaborit, P., Zémor, G.: Asymptotic improvement of the Gilbert-Varshamov bound for linear codes. In: Proceedings of IEEE International Symposium Information and Theory - ISIT 2006, pp. 287–291. Seattle, USA (Jun 2006)

28. Langlois, A., Stehlé, D.: Worst-case to average-case reductions for module lattices. Des. Codes Cryptogr. 75, 565–599 (2015). https://hal.archives-ouvertes.fr/hal-01240452

29. Lyubashevsky, V., Peikert, C., Regev, O.: On ideal lattices and learning with errors over rings. In: Gilbert, H. (ed.) EUROCRYPT 2010. LNCS, vol. 6110, pp. 1–23. Springer, Heidelberg (2010). https://doi.org/10.1007/978-3-642-13190-5_1

30. Maino, L., Martindale, C., Panny, L., Pope, G., Wesolowski, B.: A direct key recovery attack on SIDH. In: Hazay, C., Stam, M. (eds.) EUROCRYPT 2023. LNCS, vol. 14008, pp. 423–447. Springer, Cham (2023). https://doi.org/10.1007/978-3-031-30589-4_16

31. May, A., Ozerov, I.: On computing nearest neighbors with applications to decoding of binary linear codes. In: Oswald, E., Fischlin, M. (eds.) EUROCRYPT 2015. LNCS, vol. 9056, pp. 203–228. Springer, Heidelberg (2015). https://doi.org/10.1007/978-3-662-46800-5_9

32. Peikert, C., Regev, O., Stephens-Davidowitz, N.: Pseudorandomness of ring-LWE for any ring and modulus. In: Proceedings of the 49th Annual ACM SIGACT Symposium on Theory of Computing, pp. 461–473 (2017)
33. Pellet-Mary, A., Stehlé, D.: On the hardness of the NTRU problem. In: ASIACRYPT 2021. LNCS, vol. 13090, pp. 3–35, Springer, Cham (2021). https://doi.org/10.1007/978-3-030-92062-3_1, https://hal.archives-ouvertes.fr/hal-03348022
34. Prange, E.: The use of information sets in decoding cyclic codes. IRE Trans. Inf. Theory 8(5), 5–9 (1962). https://doi.org/10.1109/TIT.1962.1057777
35. Regev, O.: On lattices, learning with errors, random linear codes, and cryptography. In: Proceedings of the 37th Annual ACM Symposium on Theory of Computing, Baltimore, MD, USA, 22–24 May 2005, pp. 84–93 (2005). https://doi.org/10.1145/1060590.1060603
36. Robert, D.: Breaking SIDH in polynomial time. In: Hazay, C., Stam, M. (eds.) EUROCRYPT 2023. LNCS, vol. 14008, pp. 423–447. Springer, Cham (2023). https://doi.org/10.1007/978-3-031-30589-4_17
37. Rosca, M., Stehlé, D., Wallet, A.: On the ring-LWE and polynomial-LWE problems. In: Nielsen, J.B., Rijmen, V. (eds.) EUROCRYPT 2018. LNCS, vol. 10820, pp. 146–173. Springer, Cham (2018). https://doi.org/10.1007/978-3-319-78381-9_6
38. Sendrier, N.: Decoding one out of many. In: Yang, B.-Y. (ed.) PQCrypto 2011. LNCS, vol. 7071, pp. 51–67. Springer, Heidelberg (2011). https://doi.org/10.1007/978-3-642-25405-5_4
39. Stehlé, D., Steinfeld, R.: Making NTRU as secure as worst-case problems over ideal lattices. In: Paterson, K.G. (ed.) EUROCRYPT 2011. LNCS, vol. 6632, pp. 27–47. Springer, Heidelberg (2011). https://doi.org/10.1007/978-3-642-20465-4_4
40. Stehlé, D., Steinfeld, R., Tanaka, K., Xagawa, K.: Efficient public key encryption based on ideal lattices. In: Matsui, M. (ed.) ASIACRYPT 2009. LNCS, vol. 5912, pp. 617–635. Springer, Heidelberg (2009). https://doi.org/10.1007/978-3-642-10366-7_36
41. Stern, J.: A method for finding codewords of small weight. In: Cohen, G., Wolfmann, J. (eds.) Coding Theory 1988. LNCS, vol. 388, pp. 106–113. Springer, Heidelberg (1989). https://doi.org/10.1007/BFb0019850
42. Yu, Yu., Zhang, J.: Smoothing out binary linear codes and worst-case subexponential hardness for LPN. In: Malkin, T., Peikert, C. (eds.) CRYPTO 2021. LNCS, vol. 12827, pp. 473–501. Springer, Cham (2021). https://doi.org/10.1007/978-3-030-84252-9_16

Blockwise Rank Decoding Problem and LRPC Codes: Cryptosystems with Smaller Sizes

Yongcheng Song[1], Jiang Zhang[1]($\boxtimes$), Xinyi Huang[2], and Wei Wu[3,4]

[1] State Key Laboratory of Cryptology, P. O. Box 5159, Beijing 100878, China
`jiangzhang09@gmail.com`

[2] Artificial Intelligence Thrust, Information Hub, The Hong Kong University of Science and Technology (Guangzhou), Guangzhou 511455, China
`xinyi@ust.hk`

[3] College of Education Sciences, The Hong Kong University of Science and Technology (Guangzhou), Guangzhou 511455, China
`serenaweiwu@hkust-gz.edu.cn`

[4] School of Mathematics and Statistics, Fujian Normal University, Fuzhou 350117, China

Abstract. In this paper, we initiate the study of the Rank Decoding (RD) problem and LRPC codes with blockwise structures in rank-based cryptosystems. First, we introduce the blockwise errors (ℓ-errors) where each error consists of ℓ blocks of coordinates with disjoint supports, and define the blockwise RD (ℓ-RD) problem as a natural generalization of the RD problem whose solutions are ℓ-errors (note that the standard RD problem is actually a special ℓ-RD problem with $\ell = 1$). We adapt the typical attacks on the RD problem to the ℓ-RD problem, and find that the blockwise structures do not ease the problem too much: the ℓ-RD problem is still exponentially hard for appropriate choices of $\ell > 1$. Second, we introduce blockwise LRPC (ℓ-LRPC) codes as generalizations of the standard LPRC codes whose parity-check matrices can be divided into ℓ sub-matrices with disjoint supports, i.e., the intersection of two subspaces generated by the entries of any two sub-matrices is a null space, and investigate the decoding algorithms for ℓ-errors. We find that the gain of using ℓ-errors in decoding capacity outweighs the complexity loss in solving the ℓ-RD problem, which makes it possible to design more efficient rank-based cryptosystems with flexible choices of parameters.

As an application, we show that the two rank-based cryptosystems submitted to the NIST PQC competition, namely, RQC and ROLLO, can be greatly improved by using the ideal variants of the ℓ-RD problem and ℓ-LRPC codes. Concretely, for 128-bit security, our RQC has total public key and ciphertext sizes of 2.5 KB, which is not only about 50% more compact than the original RQC, but also smaller than the NIST Round 4 code-based submissions HQC, BIKE, and Classic McEliece.

Keywords: Post-Quantum Cryptography · NIST PQC Candidates · Rank Metric Code-Based Cryptography · Rank Decoding Problem · LRPC Codes

© International Association for Cryptologic Research 2023
J. Guo and R. Steinfeld (Eds.): ASIACRYPT 2023, LNCS 14444, pp. 284–316, 2023.
https://doi.org/10.1007/978-981-99-8739-9_10

1 Introduction

Since traditional cryptographic schemes based on number theoretic assumptions are at risk from the possible attacks using quantum computers, the design of post-quantum cryptosystems, such as code-based cryptosystems, has become the consensus of industry and academia. Last year, three code-based cryptosystems using the Hamming metric codes, namely, BIKE, Classic McEliece, and HQC, had been selected to the fourth round of NIST post-quantum standardization process for future standardization [35]. As a nice alternative to Hamming metric code-based cryptography, code-based cryptography using the rank metric, namely, rank-based cryptography, is more efficient in computational efficiency and bandwidth, and deserves further research as encouraged by NIST [34].

$\mathbb{F}_{q^m}$-Linear Codes with Rank Metric and Rank Decoding Problem.
Codes used in rank-based cryptography are $\mathbb{F}_{q^m}$-linear codes with rank metric over a degree m extension field $\mathbb{F}_{q^m}$ of $\mathbb{F}_q$. Let $\boldsymbol{\alpha} = (\alpha_1, \alpha_2, \ldots, \alpha_m) \in \mathbb{F}_{q^m}^m$ be a basis of $\mathbb{F}_{q^m}$ viewed as an m-dimensional vector space over $\mathbb{F}_q$. Then, any $\boldsymbol{e} = (e_1, e_1, \ldots, e_n) \in \mathbb{F}_{q^m}^n$ has an associated matrix $\mathrm{Mat}(\boldsymbol{e}) \in \mathbb{F}_q^{m \times n}$ such that $\boldsymbol{e} = \boldsymbol{\alpha} \mathrm{Mat}(\boldsymbol{e})$. *The rank weight $\|\boldsymbol{e}\|_R$ of $\boldsymbol{e}$ is defined as the rank of $\mathrm{Mat}(\boldsymbol{e})$. The support $\mathrm{Supp}(\boldsymbol{e})$ of $\boldsymbol{e}$ is the $\mathbb{F}_q$-linear subspace of $\mathbb{F}_{q^m}$ spanned by the coordinates of $\boldsymbol{e}$.* It follows from definition that $\|\boldsymbol{e}\|_R$ equals to the dimension of $\mathrm{Supp}(\boldsymbol{e})$. The set of errors of length n and weight r is denoted by $\mathcal{S}_r^n$. An $\mathbb{F}_{q^m}$-linear code $([n,k]_{q^m})$ with rank metric of length n and dimension k is a dimension k subspace of $\mathbb{F}_{q^m}^n$, which can be represented by a generator matrix of size $k \times n$ or a parity-check matrix of size $(n-k) \times n$ over $\mathbb{F}_{q^m}$.

Let $\boldsymbol{G}$ be the generator matrix of a random $[n,k]_{q^m}$-linear code, $\boldsymbol{y} \in \mathbb{F}_{q^m}^n$, and $r \in \mathbb{N}$. The Rank Decoding (RD) problem is to find $\boldsymbol{x} \in \mathbb{F}_{q^m}^k$ and $\boldsymbol{e} \in \mathcal{S}_r^n$ such that $\boldsymbol{y} = \boldsymbol{x}\boldsymbol{G} + \boldsymbol{e}$. Although the RD problem is not shown to be NP-hard, it is very close to the Hamming metric decoding problem which is NP-hard [23], and can be seen as a structured version of the MinRank problem which is also NP-hard [17]. Moreover, after more than three decades of study, the best known algorithms for solving the RD problem are all exponential. This makes the RD problem a promising hard problem to construct secure cryptosystems.

Rank-Based Cryptography. The first rank-based cryptosystem, known as the GPT cryptosystem [19], was based on Gabidulin codes [18] which have analogous structures to Reed-Solomon codes. The GPT cryptosystem and its early variants were broken by Overbeck attack [38], in the much same way as McEliece schemes based on Reed-Solomon codes were attacked in [16,39]. The recent variant [28] was analyzed with some insecure parameters region being found in [15,24]. As these attacks [15,16,24,38,39] mainly expose the security flaws of the GPT cryptosystem by exploiting the strong algebraic structure of Gabidulin codes, it is still possible to construct secure and efficient rank-based cryptosystems.

A very significant step was using the Low Rank Parity Check (LRPC) codes [4,20] and the Gabidulin codes to build cryptosystems [2,20,22,29,30], which can be viewed as rank metric analogues of the MDPC cryptosystem [33], NTRU [25], or Alekhnovich [1]. Four cryptosystems of this kind, namely, RQC [30],

Lake, Locker [29], and Ouroboros-R [2], were submitted to the NIST PQC standardization process in 2017, with the latter three being merged into ROLLO in the second round. The combinatorial attacks [5,21,37] were once considered to be the most efficient attacks against the parameters region of RQC and ROLLO. However, it turned out later that the improved dedicated algebraic attacks [7,9] could greatly reduce the concrete security of RQC and ROLLO. This is the main reason that RQC and ROLLO were not selected to the third round of the NIST PQC standardization process. New parameter sets [2,29,30] for RQC and ROLLO were proposed to provide adequate security against algebraic attacks. As the new key and ciphertext sizes of RQC and ROLLO remain competitive, NIST encourages further research on rank-based cryptography [34].

1.1 Our Contribution

We initiate the study of the RD problem and LRPC codes with blockwise structures to design secure and efficient rank-based cryptosystems. First, we introduce the blockwise errors (ℓ-errors) where each error consists of ℓ blocks of coordinates with disjoint supports, and define the blockwise RD (ℓ-RD) problem as a natural generalization of the RD problem whose solutions are ℓ-errors. Notably, the standard RD problem can be seen as a special ℓ-RD problem with $\ell = 1$, or equivalently the ℓ-RD problem can be treated as a structured RD problem. Since the attacks may benefit from the blockwise structure, the ℓ-RD problem is inherently not harder than the standard one. Fortunately, this structure does not ease the problem too much: we only observe a reduction about ℓ times in the exponent to solve the ℓ-RD problem by carefully examining the typical attacks for the standard RD problem, implying that the ℓ-RD problem is still exponentially hard for appropriate choices of constant $\ell > 1$.

Second, we introduce the blockwise LRPC (ℓ-LRPC) codes as generalizations of the standard LPRC codes whose parity-check matrices can be divided into ℓ sub-matrices with disjoint supports, i.e., the intersection of two subspaces generated by the entries of any two sub-matrices is a null space, and investigate the decoding algorithms for ℓ-errors. We find that the decoding algorithm can also benefit from the blockwise structure: the decoding capacity can be significantly improved by a factor of ℓ. In particular, a suitably defined $[n, k]_{q^m}$ ℓ-LRPC code can actually decode an ℓ-error with weight up to $(n - k)/2$, which achieves the decoding capacity of rank codes of optimal distance. This makes it possible to design more efficient rank-based cryptosystems with flexible choices of parameters, by making a tradeoff between the hardness of the ℓ-RD problem and the decoding capacity of the ℓ-LPRC codes.

Finally, we show that the two rank-based cryptosystems submitted to the NIST PQC competition, namely, RQC and ROLLO, can be greatly improved by using the ideal variants of the ℓ-RD problem and ℓ-LRPC codes. Concretely, for 128-bit security, our RQC has total public key and ciphertext sizes of 2.5 KB, which is not only about 50% more compact than the original RQC, but also smaller than the NIST Round 4 code-based submissions HQC, BIKE, and Classic McEliece. A detailed comparison with related works is given in Subsect. 1.2.

1.2   Technical Overview

Recall that the set of errors of length n and weight r is denoted by $\mathcal{S}_r^n$. By definition, all n coordinates of an error $e \in \mathcal{S}_r^n$ belong to the same support of dimension r. In particular, let $\boldsymbol{\varepsilon} = (\varepsilon_1, \ldots, \varepsilon_r) \in \mathbb{F}_{q^m}^r$ be a basis of the support $\mathrm{Supp}(e)$, then there is an $r \times n$ coefficient matrix C such that $e = \boldsymbol{\varepsilon}C$.

The Blockwise Errors (ℓ-errors). Let $n = (n_1, \ldots, n_\ell)$ and $r = (r_1, \ldots, r_\ell)$ be vectors of positive integers. We say that an error $e \in \mathcal{S}_r^n$ with $n = \sum_{i=1}^{\ell} n_i$ and $r = \sum_{i=1}^{\ell} r_i$ is an ℓ-error with parameters n and r if it can be divided into ℓ sub-vectors $e = (e_1, e_2, \ldots, e_\ell)$ such that 1) the sub-vector $e_i \in \mathbb{F}_{q^m}^{n_i}$ has weight r_i for all $i \in \{1..\ell\}$; and 2) the supports of these sub-vectors are mutually disjoint, namely, $\mathrm{Supp}(e_i) \cap \mathrm{Supp}(e_j) = \{0\}$ for all $i \neq j$. Denote $\mathcal{S}_r^n$ as the set of blockwise errors with parameters n and r. By definition, the set $\mathcal{S}_r^n$ is exactly the set $\mathcal{S}_r^n$ of ℓ-errors with $\ell = 1$. For $\ell > 1$, $\mathcal{S}_r^n$ is a proper subset of $\mathcal{S}_r^n$. In particular, for any $e = (e_1, e_2, \ldots, e_\ell) \in \mathcal{S}_r^n$, if we let $\varepsilon_i = (\varepsilon_{i1}, \varepsilon_{i2}, \ldots, \varepsilon_{ir_i}) \in \mathbb{F}_{q^m}^{r_i}$ be a basis of $\mathrm{Supp}(e_i)$, then the coefficient matrix C of e w.r.t. the basis $\boldsymbol{\varepsilon} = (\varepsilon_1, \varepsilon_2, \ldots, \varepsilon_\ell)$, i.e., $e = \boldsymbol{\varepsilon}C$, has a special block-diagonal form:

$$C = \begin{pmatrix} C_1 & 0 & 0 & 0 \\ 0 & C_2 & 0 & 0 \\ \vdots & \vdots & \ddots & \vdots \\ 0 & 0 & 0 & C_\ell \end{pmatrix} \in \mathbb{F}_q^{r \times n} \tag{1}$$

where $e_i = \varepsilon_i C_i$. As we will show later, the attacks can benefit from the block-diagonal structure.

The Blockwise RD (ℓ-RD) Problem. We define the ℓ-RD problem as a natural generalization of the RD problem whose solutions are ℓ-errors. Recall that the RD problem asks an algorithm given as inputs a generator matrix G of random $[n, k]_{q^m}$-linear code $\mathcal{C}$, a vector $y \in \mathbb{F}_{q^m}^n$, and an integer $r \in \mathbb{N}$, outputs $x \in \mathbb{F}_{q^m}^k$ and $e \in \mathcal{S}_r^n$ such that $y = xG + e$. The RD problem can be solved by finding a codeword $e \in \mathcal{S}_r^n$ in the $[n, k+1]_{q^m}$ extended code $\mathcal{C}_y = \mathcal{C} + \langle y \rangle$ of $\mathcal{C}$. Let $H_y \in \mathbb{F}_{q^m}^{(n-k-1) \times n}$ be the parity-check matrix of $\mathcal{C}_y$. The problem can be further reduced to find an $e \in \mathcal{S}_r^n$ such that $eH_y^\top = \varepsilon C H_y^\top = 0$.

There are two main kinds of attacks for the RD problem, i.e., combinatorial attacks [5,14,21,37] and algebraic attacks [7–9,21]. The basic idea of the combinatorial attacks [5,14,21,37] is to guess some unknown variables about the equations $y = xG + e$ or $eH_y^\top = \varepsilon C H_y^\top = 0$ so that they can be directly solved by using Gaussian eliminations (note that number of equations are much less than that of the variables). The guess complexity is the main cost for the combinatorial attacks. In contrast, the algebraic attacks [7–9,21] resort to establish sufficiently more equations using different algebraic properties such as the annulator polynomial, so that the error e can be directly found by solving those equations. The complexity of the algebraic attacks is mainly determined by the number of the unknown variables of those equations. By carefully investigating the typical attacks, we find that both combinatorial and algebraic attacks can benefit from the blockwise structures, the basic reason is that the coefficient matrix C for an ℓ-error has a special block-diagonal form, which allows to greatly reduce the number of the unknown variables. The take-away message is that the best cost for solving the ℓ-RD problem is roughly equal to the ℓ-th square root of the cost for solving the standard RD problem (with the same parameters). This means that for appropriate choices of constant $\ell > 1$ such as $\ell = 2$ or 3 in our applications, the ℓ-RD problem is still exponentially hard.

The Blockwise LRPC (ℓ-LRPC) Codes. Let $H \in \mathbb{F}_{q^m}^{(n-k) \times n}$ be the parity-check matrix of an $[n, k]_{q^m}$ LRPC code. The entries of H generate an $\mathbb{F}_q$-linear subspace F of dimension d (for simplicity, we call H a matrix of weight d and support F). Let $e \in \mathcal{S}_r^n$ be an error of support E and let $s = He^\top$. Let EF be the product space of E and F, whose dimension is equal to rd with overwhelming probability when rd is sufficiently smaller than m. The decoding algorithm works by first recovering the product space EF using the support $\mathrm{Supp}(s)$ of s (which requires the weight $\|s\|_R$ is equal to the dimension of EF), then recovering the error support E from EF, and finally solving the linear equations $s = He^\top$ using E. The Decode Failure Rate (DFR) is about $q^{\|s\|_R-(n-k)} = q^{rd-(n-k)}$, implying that an LPRC code of weight d can decode errors of weight up to $\frac{n-k}{d}$.

We define the blockwise LRPC (ℓ-LRPC) codes as generalizations of the standard LPRC codes whose parity-check matrices can be divided by columns into ℓ sub-matrices with disjoint supports. Let $n = (n_1, \ldots, n_\ell)$ and $d = (d_1, \ldots, d_\ell)$ be vectors of positive integers and $k \in \mathbb{N}$. We say that an $[n, k]_{q^m}$ LRPC code is an ℓ-LRPC code with parameters $n = \sum_{i=1}^\ell n_i$ and $d = \sum_{i=1}^\ell d_i$ if its parity-check matrix $H \in \mathbb{F}_{q^m}^{(n-k) \times n}$ can be divided into ℓ sub-matrices $H = (H_1, H_2, \cdots, H_\ell)$ such that 1) the sub-matrix $H_i \in \mathbb{F}_{q^m}^{(n-k) \times n_i}$ has small weight d_i for all $i \in \{1..\ell\}$; and 2) the supports $\{F_i = \mathrm{Supp}(H_i)\}$ of these sub-matrices are mutually disjoint, namely, $F_i \cap F_j = \{0\}$ for all $i \neq j$.

The decoding algorithm for ℓ-LRPC codes works the same way as the one for standard LRPC codes. For traditional errors, an ℓ-LRPC code has the same decoding capacity as a standard LRPC code. However, it is more powerful when decoding ℓ-errors. This is because for an ℓ-error $e \in \mathcal{S}_r^n$ with supports $(E_1, E_2, \ldots, E_\ell)$ and $r = (r_1, \ldots, r_\ell)$, the product space in consideration becomes $\sum_{i=1}^\ell E_i F_i$, whose dimension is upper bounded by $\sum_{i=1}^\ell r_i d_i < rd$, where $r = \sum_{i=1}^\ell r_i$. This means that the ℓ-LRPC code can decode an ℓ-error with a much larger weight r. Formally, we have the following Theorem 1.1 (see the proofs in Sect. 4).

Theorem 1.1. *When $d_1 = d_2 = \cdots = d_\ell$, the ℓ-LRPC code allows to decode ℓ-errors of weight up to $r = \sum_{j=1}^\ell r_j = \frac{n-k}{d_1}$. By setting $d_1 = d_2 = \cdots = d_\ell = 2$, it can decode ℓ-errors of weight up to $\frac{n-k}{2}$.*

Theorem 1.1 implies that when dealing with ℓ-errors, the decoding capacity for the ℓ-LRPC codes is ℓ times larger than that of the standard LRPC codes. For example, fixing $d = 4$, $r = 8$, and the DFR of q^{32-n-k}, an $[n, k]_{q^m}$ LRPC code can decode errors of weight 8, but an $[n, k]_{q^m}$ 2-LRPC codes with parameter $\boldsymbol{d} = (d_1, d_2) = (2, 2)$ can decode ℓ-errors with parameter $\boldsymbol{r} = (r_1, r_2) = (8, 8)$ of weight up to $r = r_1 + r_2 = 16$.

Applications. By making a tradeoff between the hardness of the ℓ-RD problem and the decoding capacity of the ℓ-LRPC codes, it is possible to design more efficient and secure rank-based cryptosystems with flexible choices of parameters. In particular, the blockwise structures would lead to larger parameters to reserve the security, but the gain in decoding capacity still allows us to design more efficient cryptosystems. As an application, we show that both RQC and ROLLO cryptosystems can be greatly improved by using the ideal variants of the ℓ-RD problem and ℓ-LRPC codes. A brief comparison with related coded-based cryptosystems at the same 128-bit security is summarized in Table 1, which shows that our RQC is about 50% more compact than the original RQC, and has smaller sizes than the three code-based cryptosystems using the Hamming metric, namely, HQC, BIKE, and Classic McEliece.

Table 1. Comparisons of size and DFR for 128-bit security.

Schemes		pks (bytes)	cts (bytes)	total (bytes)	DFR
RQC	**Our**	860	1704	2564	–
	NIST [30]	1834	3652	5486	–
Lake (ROLLO-I)	**Our**	511	511	1022	2^{-31}
	NIST [29]	696	696	1392	2^{-28}
Locker (ROLLO-II)	**Our**	1814	1942	3756	2^{-131}
	NIST [29]	1941	2089	4030	2^{-134}
Ouroboros-R (ROLLO-III)	**Our**	623	1166	1789	2^{-33}
	TIT 2022 [2]	736	1431	2167	2^{-28}
HQC	NIST [31]	2249	4497	6746	–
BIKE	NIST [1]	1541	1573	3114	2^{-128}
Classic McEliece	NIST [10]	261120	96	261216	–
Ouroboros	TIT 2022 [2]	1566	3100	4666	2^{-128}

The public key size (pks), the ciphertext size (cts), total = pks+cts.

1.3   Other Related Works

The idea of using blockwise errors can be seen as an adaption of the LPN/LWE problem in rank metric [11]. Our blockwise codes are also related to the sum-rank metric codes [13], where the error is also divided into ℓ blocks and the sum-rank weight is defined as the sum of rank weight of each block. One main difference is that we explicitly require the ℓ blocks to have disjoint supports, which is very crucial for our results in this paper.

290 Y. Song et al.

1.4 Organization

After some notations given in Sect. 2, we define the ℓ-errors and analyze the complexity of solving the ℓ-RD problem in Sect. 3. Section 4 defines the ℓ-LRPC codes and analyzes decoding failure probability and error-correcting capability. In Sect. 5, we apply the ideal ℓ-RD problem and the ideal ℓ-LRPC codes to improve RQC and ROLLO. We conclude this paper in Sect. 6.

2 Notations

- We denote by $\mathbb{N}$ the set of positive integer numbers, q prime or prime power, and $\mathbb{F}_{q^m}$ an extension of degree m of the finite field $\mathbb{F}_q$.
- Let $\alpha \in \mathbb{F}_{q^m}$ be a primitive element and $\boldsymbol{\alpha} = (1, \alpha, \ldots, \alpha^{m-1})$ be a basis of $\mathbb{F}_{q^m}$ viewed as an $\mathbb{F}_q$ vector space.
- Vectors (resp. matrices) are represented by lower-case (resp. upper-case) bold letters. We say that an algorithm is a PPT algorithm if it is a probabilistic polynomial-time algorithm.
- If $\mathcal{X}$ is a finite set, $x \xleftarrow{\$} \mathcal{X}$ (resp. $x \xleftarrow{\text{seed}} \mathcal{X}$) denotes that x is chosen uniformly and randomly from the set $\mathcal{X}$ (resp. by a seed seed).
- For integers $a \leq b$, let $\{a..b\}$ denote all integers from a to b.
- The number of $\mathbb{F}_q$-subspaces of dimension r of $\mathbb{F}_{q^m}$ is given by the Gaussian coefficient $\begin{bmatrix} m \\ r \end{bmatrix}_q = \prod_{i=0}^{r-1} \frac{q^m - q^i}{q^r - q^i} \approx q^{r(m-r)}$.
- The submatrix of a matrix M formed from the rows in I and columns in J is denoted by $M_{I,J}$. When I (resp. J) consists of all the rows (resp. columns), we use the notation $M_{*,J}$ (resp. $M_{I,*}$).
- $|M|$, $|M|_{I,J}$, and $|M|_{*,J}$ are the determinant of the matrix M, the submatrix $M_{I,J}$, and the submatrix $M_{*,J}$, respectively.
- $\mathrm{GL}_\eta(\mathbb{F}_q)$ is a general linear group and represents the set of all invertible matrices of size η over $\mathbb{F}_q$. The matrix I_r is the identity matrix of size r.
- The maximal minor c_T of a matrix C of size $r \times n$ is the determinant of its submatrix $C_{*,T}$ whose column indexes $T \subset \{1..n\}$ and $\#T = r$.
- Cauchy-Binet formula that computes the determinant of the product of $A \in \mathbb{F}_{q^m}^{r \times n}$ and $B \in \mathbb{F}_{q^m}^{n \times r}$ is expressed as $|AB| = \sum_{T \subset \{1..n\}, \#T = r} |A|_{*,T} |B|_{T,*}$.
- The Gaussian elimination of a $\mu \times \nu$ matrix of rank ρ over an $\mathbb{F}_q$ has a complexity of $\mathcal{O}(\rho^{\omega-2} \mu \nu)$ operations in $\mathbb{F}_q$, where ω is the exponent of matrix multiplication with $2 \leq \omega \leq 3$ and a practical value is 2.81 when more than a few hundreds rows and columns.
- The complexities are estimated by operations in $\mathbb{F}_q$ if there is no ambiguity. All logarithms are of base 2.

3 The ℓ-RD Problem and Its Complexity

In this section, we first introduce the blockwise errors (ℓ-errors) and the blockwise RD (ℓ-RD) problem in Subsect. 3.1. Then, to analyze the complexity of the ℓ-RD problem, we refine a universal reduction from existing attacks on the RD problem and analyze the support and coefficient matrices of the ℓ-error in Subsect. 3.2. Finally, we adapt the typical combinatorial and algebraic attacks to the ℓ-RD problem in Subsects. 3.3, 3.4 and 3.5, and find that the ℓ-errors do not ease the problem too much: the ℓ-RD problem is still exponentially hard for appropriate choices of $\ell > 1$.

3.1   The ℓ-Errors and ℓ-RD Problem

Let $\ell, k \in \mathbb{N}$. Let $\boldsymbol{n} = (n_1, \ldots, n_\ell)$ and $\boldsymbol{r} = (r_1, \ldots, r_\ell)$ be vectors of positive integers. Let $n = \sum_{i=1}^{\ell} n_i$ and $r = \sum_{i=1}^{\ell} r_i$. We first define the disjointness of multiple subspaces. We say that ℓ $\mathbb{F}_q$-subspaces $\{V_i\}_{i \in \{1..\ell\}}$ of $\mathbb{F}_{q^m}$ are mutually *disjoint* if $\forall\, i, j \in \{1..\ell\}, i \neq j, V_i \cap V_j = \{0\}$.

Definition 3.1 (Blockwise Errors (ℓ-errors)). *Let $e_i \in \mathbb{F}_{q^m}^{n_i}$ be a vector of weight r_i for $i \in \{1..\ell\}$. An error $\boldsymbol{e} = (e_1, e_2, \ldots, e_\ell) \in \mathbb{F}_{q^m}^n$ is called an ℓ-error if the supports of ℓ vectors e_i's are mutually disjoint.*

Recall that $\boldsymbol{n} = (n_1, \ldots, n_\ell)$ and $\boldsymbol{r} = (r_1, \ldots, r_\ell)$ are two vectors of positive integers. We denote the set of such ℓ-errors by $\mathcal{S}_r^n$. Let E_i be the support of dimension r_i of e_i. Because all supports are mutually disjoint, the ℓ-error $\boldsymbol{e}$ can be viewed as the error of weight r and support $E = \sum_{i=1}^{\ell} E_i$.

We now define the ℓ-RD problem. This problem is the Rank Decoding (RD) problem finding the ℓ-errors.

Definition 3.2 (Blockwise RD (ℓ-RD) Problem). *Let $\boldsymbol{G}$ be the generator matrix of a random $[n, k]_{q^m}$-linear code $\mathcal{C}$ and $\boldsymbol{y} \in \mathbb{F}_{q^m}^n$. The problem is to find $\boldsymbol{x} \in \mathbb{F}_{q^m}^k$ and $\boldsymbol{e} \in \mathcal{S}_r^n$ such that $\boldsymbol{y} = \boldsymbol{xG} + \boldsymbol{e}$.*

Like the dual version of the RD problem using the generator matrix is the Rank Syndrome Decoding (RSD) problem [23] using the parity-check matrix, the dual version of the ℓ-RD problem is defined as the ℓ-RSD problem.

Definition 3.3 (Blockwise RSD (ℓ-RSD) Problem). *Let $\boldsymbol{H}$ be the parity-check matrix of a random $[n, k]_{q^m}$-linear code $\mathcal{C}$ and $\boldsymbol{s} \in \mathbb{F}_{q^m}^{n-k}$. The problem is to find $\boldsymbol{e} \in \mathcal{S}_r^n$ such that $\boldsymbol{s} = \boldsymbol{He}^\top$.*

Two variants are exactly the standard RD and RSD problems when $\ell = 1$. By the duality, the hardness of two variants is equivalent. Intuitively, two variants are also hard because they still find a small-weight error.

3.2   Reduction, Support and Coefficient Matrices

In this subsection, we first recall existing attacks on the RD problem, then adapt the reduction refined from typical attacks to the ℓ-RD problem, finally analyze support and coefficient matrices of the ℓ-error.

Attacks on the RD Problem. There currently exist the combinatorial and algebraic attacks [5,7–9,14,21,37] on the RD problem. Please see Appendix B of full version [40] for detailed overviews of these attacks. The first combinatorial attack [14] starts with the RSD problem and is significantly improved in [37] and further refined in [5,21]. The combinatorial attacks [5,14,21] consist of subtly guessing the support of error and solving a linear system. The attack [37] transforms a quadratic multivariate system obtained from the RD problem into a linear system by guessing the entries of support matrix and coefficient matrix. Another way is the algebraic attack [21], where one solves a multivariate system induced from the RD problem based on the annulator polynomial by linearization and Gröbner basis. A breakthrough paper [7] shows that the $\mathbb{F}_{q^m}$-linearity allows to devise a dedicated algebraic attack, i.e., the MaxMinors (MM) modeling. Then the MM modeling is refined and improved in [9] where the authors also introduced another algebraic modeling, the Support-Minors (SM) modeling. The SM modeling later is combined with the MM modeling (i.e., the SM-$\mathbb{F}_{q^m}^+$ modeling [8]). Both SM and MM modelings reduce the RD problem to solving a linear system. The analysis in [8] shows that the cost of the SM-$\mathbb{F}_{q^m}^+$ modeling is close to those of the combinatorial attack [5] and the MM modeling [9].

To measure the potential complexity loss and ensure the security of schemes, we adapt typical combinatorial attacks [5,37] and algebraic attacks [9,21] to the ℓ-RD problem in Subsects. 3.3, 3.4 and 3.5. The reduction technique in attacks [5,9,21,37] is still available to the ℓ-RD problem. We refine the reduction in Theorem 3.4.

Theorem 3.4. *Solving the ℓ-RD(q, m, n, k, r, ℓ) problem defined by $[n, k]_{q^m}$ linear code $\mathcal{C}$ (see Definition 3.2) can be reduced to finding a blockwise codeword (i.e., an ℓ-error) of weight r in the $[n, k+1]_{q^m}$ extended code of $\mathcal{C}$.*

Proof. Once obtaining word $\boldsymbol{y}$, one adds $\boldsymbol{y}$ to code $\mathcal{C}$ and obtains an $[n, k+1]_{q^m}$ extended code $\mathcal{C}_y = \mathcal{C} + \langle \boldsymbol{y} \rangle$ with a generator matrix $\begin{pmatrix} \boldsymbol{y} \\ \boldsymbol{G} \end{pmatrix}$ of size $(k+1) \times n$. In this way, $\boldsymbol{e} = \begin{pmatrix} 1 & -\boldsymbol{m} \end{pmatrix} \begin{pmatrix} \boldsymbol{y} \\ \boldsymbol{G} \end{pmatrix}$ is exactly a codeword of weight r of $\mathcal{C}_y$. Let $\boldsymbol{G}_y = (\boldsymbol{I}_{k+1} \; \boldsymbol{R}) \in \mathbb{F}_{q^m}^{(k+1)\times n}$ be a systematic generator matrix of $\mathcal{C}_y$ and $\boldsymbol{H}_y = \left(-\boldsymbol{R}^\top \; \boldsymbol{I}_{n-k-1} \right) \in \mathbb{F}_{q^m}^{(n-k-1)\times n}$ be a systematic parity-check matrix of $\mathcal{C}_y$, where $\boldsymbol{R} \in \mathbb{F}_{q^m}^{(k+1)\times(n-k-1)}$. Then solving the ℓ-RD problem consists in finding an $\boldsymbol{u} \in \mathbb{F}_{q^m}^{k+1}$ of weight $\leq r$ such that

$$\boldsymbol{u}\boldsymbol{G}_y = \boldsymbol{e}, \tag{2}$$

or finding an ℓ-error $\boldsymbol{e}$ of weight r such that

$$\boldsymbol{e}\boldsymbol{H}_y^\top = \boldsymbol{0}. \tag{3}$$

$\square$

The support and coefficient matrices of the ℓ-error are crucial tools to construct the specific attack modelings by exploiting the reduction in Theorem 3.4. The entries of two matrices determine the number of variables of algebraic equations in the attack modelings. We next analyze the forms of two matrices.

Support and Coefficient Matrices of the ℓ-error. Let $n = (n_1, \ldots, n_\ell)$ and $r = (r_1, \ldots, r_\ell)$ be vectors of positive integers. Let $e = (e_1, e_2, \ldots, e_\ell) \in \mathcal{S}_r^n$ be an ℓ-error. If let $\varepsilon_i = (\varepsilon_{i1}, \varepsilon_{i2}, \ldots, \varepsilon_{ir_i}) \in \mathbb{F}_{q^m}^{r_i}$ be a basis of support of dimension r_i, then there exists a matrix $C_i \in \mathbb{F}_q^{r_i \times n_i}$ of rank r_i such that $e_i = \varepsilon_i C_i$, If one expresses the basis ε_i as a matrix $S_i \in \mathbb{F}_q^{m \times r_i}$ of rank r_i under the basis α, then $e_i = \alpha S_i C_i$. We have $e = \varepsilon C = \alpha S C$, where $\varepsilon = (\varepsilon_1, \varepsilon_2, \ldots, \varepsilon_\ell) \in \mathbb{F}_{q^m}^r$,

$$S = \begin{pmatrix} S_1 & S_2 & \cdots & S_\ell \end{pmatrix} \in \mathbb{F}_q^{m \times r}, \qquad C = \begin{pmatrix} C_1 & 0 & 0 & 0 \\ 0 & C_2 & 0 & 0 \\ \vdots & \vdots & \ddots & \vdots \\ 0 & 0 & 0 & C_\ell \end{pmatrix} \in \mathbb{F}_q^{r \times n}. \qquad (4)$$

We call S and C respectively support matrix and coefficient matrix of e.

Remark 1. The main difference with the standard rank metric error is that the form of the coefficient matrix C of the ℓ-error is of block-diagonal form. For a standard rank metric error $e \in \mathcal{S}_r^n$, let $\varepsilon = (\varepsilon_1, \varepsilon_2, \ldots, \varepsilon_r) \in \mathbb{F}_{q^m}^r$ be a basis of Supp(e), the there is a coefficient matrix $C \in \mathbb{F}_q^{r \times n}$ of rank r such that $e = \varepsilon C$. Under the basis α, there is a support matrix $S \in \mathbb{F}_q^{m \times r}$ of rank r such that $\varepsilon = \alpha S$. Then $e = \alpha S C$.

Support and Coefficient Matrices with Less Entries. Because all multiples λe for $\lambda \in \mathbb{F}_{q^m}^*$ are solutions of Eq. (3) due to $\|\lambda e\|_R = r$, one can specify λ to be the inverse of the first coordinate of e. Without loss of generality, let the first coordinate of e be 1, then one can set the first column of C to $(1\, 0\, \cdots\, 0)^\top$ and the first column of S to $(1\, 0\, \cdots\, 0)^\top$. Then S and C can be further reduced to two forms with less entries.

- $S_{\{1..r\},*} = I_r$. By Gaussian elimination on column of S, there is a matrix $P \in \mathrm{GL}_r(q)$ such that $SP = \left(\begin{array}{c|c} I_r \\ \hline \mathbf{0}_{(m-r) \times 1} & S' \end{array} \right)$ and $P^{-1}C = \left(\begin{array}{c|c} 1 \\ \mathbf{0}_{(r-1) \times 1} & C' \end{array} \right)$ where $S' \in \mathbb{F}_q^{(m-r) \times (r-1)}$ and $C' \in \mathbb{F}_q^{r \times (n-1)}$. Then

$$e = \alpha S C = \alpha S P P^{-1} C = \alpha \left(\begin{array}{c|c} I_r \\ \hline \mathbf{0}_{(m-r) \times 1} & S' \end{array} \right) \left(\begin{array}{c|c} 1 \\ \mathbf{0}_{(r-1) \times 1} & C' \end{array} \right). \qquad (5)$$

Let $s := SP$ and $C := P^{-1}C$.
- C_i is of systematic form. By Gaussian elimination on row of C, there is a matrix $Q_i \in \mathrm{GL}_{r_i}(q)$ such that $Q_i C_i = (I_{r_i}\ C_i')$ and $SQ^{-1} = \left(\begin{array}{c|c} 1 \\ \mathbf{0}_{(m-1) \times 1} & S' \end{array} \right)$ where $C_i' \in \mathbb{F}_q^{r_i \times (n_i - r_i)}$, $S' \in \mathbb{F}_q^{m \times (r-1)}$, and $Q =$

$$\begin{pmatrix} Q_1 & 0 & 0 & 0 \\ 0 & Q_2 & 0 & 0 \\ \vdots & \vdots & \ddots & \vdots \\ 0 & 0 & 0 & Q_\ell \end{pmatrix} \in \mathrm{GL}_r(q). \text{ Then}$$

$$e = \alpha S C = \alpha S Q^{-1} Q C = \alpha \left(\begin{array}{c|c} 1 & \\ \hline 0_{(m-1)\times 1} & S' \end{array} \right) \begin{pmatrix} Q_1 C_1 & 0 & 0 & 0 \\ 0 & Q_2 C_2 & 0 & 0 \\ \vdots & \vdots & \ddots & \vdots \\ 0 & 0 & 0 & Q_\ell C_\ell \end{pmatrix}. \tag{6}$$

Let $S := SQ^{-1}$ and $C := QC$.

For solving the ℓ-RD problem, most attacks aim to recover S and C by solving the algebraic equations obtained from Eqs. (2)–(6). Equation (3) is used to build the AGHT attacks (Subsect. 3.3). Equations (2), (5) and (6) are used to build the OJ attack (Subsect. 3.3). Equations (3) and (6) are used to build the algebraic attack, the MM modeling (Subsect. 3.5). The details of constructing the algebraic equations can refer to the specific attacks in Subsects. 3.3, 3.4 and 3.5.

3.3   Combinatorial Attacks on the ℓ-RD Problem

In this subsection, we use the AGHT attack [5] and the OJ attack [37] to analyze the complexity of solving the ℓ-RD problem.

AGHT Attack [5]. The idea is that the solver tries to guess a subspace that contains the support of the ℓ-error, then checks if the choice is correct. The cost depends on how to successfully guess such a subspace.

- Guess randomly a t-dimensional subspace F that contains the support Supp(e) of dimension $r = \sum_{i=1}^{\ell} r_i$ of the ℓ-error e.
- Let $(f_1, f_2, \ldots, f_t) \in \mathbb{F}_{q^m}^t$ be a basis of F. One expresses e under this basis

$$e = (e_1, e_2, \ldots, e_n) = (f_1, f_2, \ldots, f_t) \begin{pmatrix} e_{11} & e_{12} & \cdots & e_{1n} \\ e_{21} & e_{22} & \cdots & e_{2n} \\ \vdots & \vdots & \cdots & \vdots \\ e_{t1} & e_{t2} & \cdots & e_{tn} \end{pmatrix} = (f_1, f_2, \ldots, f_t) \begin{pmatrix} \overline{e}_1 \\ \overline{e}_2 \\ \vdots \\ \overline{e}_t \end{pmatrix},$$

where $\overline{e}_i = (e_{i1}, e_{i2}, \ldots, e_{in}) \in \mathbb{F}_q^n$ for $i \in \{1..t\}$. By Eq. (3): $H_y e^\top = 0$, let h_j is the j-th row of H_y, we have

$$H_y e^\top = \begin{pmatrix} h_1 \\ h_2 \\ \vdots \\ h_{n-k-1} \end{pmatrix} (\overline{e}_1^\top, \overline{e}_2^\top, \ldots, \overline{e}_t^\top) \begin{pmatrix} f_1 \\ f_2 \\ \vdots \\ f_t \end{pmatrix}$$

$$= \begin{pmatrix} h_1 f_1 & h_1 f_2 & \cdots & h_1 f_t \\ h_2 f_1 & h_2 f_2 & \cdots & h_2 f_t \\ \vdots & \vdots & \cdots & \vdots \\ h_{n-k-1} f_1 & h_{n-k-1} f_2 & \cdots & h_{n-k-1} f_t \end{pmatrix} \begin{pmatrix} \overline{e}_1^\top \\ \overline{e}_2^\top \\ \vdots \\ \overline{e}_t^\top \end{pmatrix} = 0_{n-k-1}. \quad (7)$$

- Express Eq. (7) as a linear system over $\mathbb{F}_q$ and solve $\overline{e}_i$. By expressing $h_j f_i$ as a matrix $\mathrm{Mat}(h_j f_i) \in \mathbb{F}_q^{m \times n}$ under the basis α for $j \in \{1..n-k-1\}$ and $i \in \{1..t\}$, a linear system over $\mathbb{F}_q$ with nt unknowns and $m(n-k-1)$ equations is obtained. The linear system has only one solution with overwhelming probability if $nt \le m(n-k-1)$.

- The probability of $F \supset E$ is estimated as $\frac{\genfrac[]{0pt}{}{t}{r}_q}{\genfrac[]{0pt}{}{m}{r}_q} \approx q^{-r(m-t)}$. In this way, the complexity is $\mathcal{O}\left(((n-k-1)m)^\omega q^{r\lceil \frac{(k+1)m}{n} \rceil}\right)$.

- Use $\mathbb{F}_{q^m}$-linearity to decrease the cost. Since, for any $\lambda \in \mathbb{F}_{q^m}^*$, $\|\lambda e\|_R = r$ and all multiples λe are solutions of Eq. (3): $H_y e^\top = 0$, the complexity is divided by about q^m.

As a result, this attack has a complexity of $\mathcal{O}\left(((n-k-1)m)^\omega q^{r\lceil \frac{(k+1)m}{n} \rceil - m}\right)$.

In [12], the authors adapted the AGHT attack to the RD problem finding so-called non-homogeneous errors. Here, inspired by [12], the strategy guessing the subspace F is that the solver randomly guesses a subspace F_i of dimension t_i that contains the support $E_i = \mathrm{Supp}(e_i)$ of dimension r_i of e_i such that all F_i's are mutually disjoint, and sets $F = \sum_{i=1}^{\ell} F_i$. In this way, the dimension of F is of $\sum_{i=1}^{\ell} t_i$, and F must contain the support of the ℓ-error e.

If one knows F_i, then each entry of e_i can be expressed as an $\mathbb{F}_q$-linear combination of t_i elements in a basis of F_i. This means that one can write e_i using $n_i t_i$ unknowns in $\mathbb{F}_q$. Doing the same for all e_i's, one obtains $\sum_{i=1}^{\ell} n_i t_i$ unknowns. Then one solves the linear system with $\sum_{i=1}^{\ell} n_i t_i$ unknowns and $m(n-k-1)$ equations for single solution e as long as $\sum_{i=1}^{\ell} n_i t_i \le m(n-k-1)$. The most costly part of the attack consists in finding the F_i's containing E_i for $i \in \{1..\ell\}$. We estimate this probability in Lemma 3.5.

Lemma 3.5. Let $E_1, E_2, \ldots, E_\ell$ be fixed $\mathbb{F}_q$-subspaces of dimension respectively $r_1, r_2, \ldots, r_\ell$ of $\mathbb{F}_{q^m}$. The probability that one successfully guesses $\mathbb{F}_q$-subspaces $F_1, F_2, \ldots, F_\ell$ dimension respectively $t_1, t_2, \ldots, t_\ell$ of $\mathbb{F}_{q^m}$ such that all F_i's are mutually disjoint and $E_i \subset F_i$ is estimated as $\mathcal{O}\left(q^{-mr + \sum_{i=1}^{\ell-1} r_i^2 + \sum_{j=2}^{\ell} r_j \sum_{i=1}^{j-1} r_i + t_\ell r_\ell}\right)$.

We give the detailed proof for Lemma 3.5 in Appendix C.1 of full version [40]. Finally, one takes advantage of the $\mathbb{F}_{q^m}$-linearity to raise this probability: for any $\lambda \in \mathbb{F}_{q^m}^*$, $\|\lambda e\|_{\mathrm{R}} = r$ and all multiples λe are solutions of Eq. (3): $H_y e^{\top} = \mathbf{0}$, hence the complexity is divided by about q^m. The complexity of solving the ℓ-RD problem by the variant of AGHT attack is estimated as

$$\mathcal{O}\left((m(n-k-1))^{\omega} q^{mr - \sum_{i=1}^{\ell-1} r_i^2 - \sum_{j=2}^{\ell} r_j \sum_{i=1}^{j-1} r_i - t_{\ell} r_{\ell} - m}\right)$$

where t_i is chosen to maximize $t_{\ell} r_{\ell}$ under the constraints

$$\begin{cases} r_i \leq t_i, \quad \text{for } i \in \{1..\ell\}; \\ \sum_{i=1}^{\ell} t_i \leq m-1; \\ \sum_{i=1}^{\ell} n_i t_i \leq m(n-k-1). \end{cases}$$

OJ Attack. We now analyze the complexity of solving the ℓ-RD problem by the OJ attack [37]. Let $\bar{e}_1$ and $\bar{e}_2$ be the first $k+1$ and the last $n-k-1$ coordinates of e. Let A_1 and A_2 be the first $k+1$ columns and the last $n-k-1$ columns of C. Then $e = (\bar{e}_1, \bar{e}_2) = \varepsilon(A_1, A_2) = (\alpha S A_1, \alpha S A_2)$. Equation (2) means

$$u G_y = e \iff (u \ uR) = (\bar{e}_1, \bar{e}_2) \iff \bar{e}_1 R = \bar{e}_2 \iff \alpha S A_1 R = \alpha S A_2. \quad (8)$$

We first analyze the case of the 2-RD problem, then extend conclusions into general cases. By Equation (8), for $j \in \{1..n-k-1\}$, let r_j and a_j be the j-th column of R and A_2, respectively, then

$$\alpha S A_1 r_j = \alpha S a_j \iff \alpha S \left(A_1 \ a_j\right) \begin{pmatrix} r_j \\ -1 \end{pmatrix} = 0. \quad (9)$$

Let $\begin{pmatrix} r_j \\ -1 \end{pmatrix} = T_j \alpha^{\top}$ where $T_j \in \mathbb{F}_q^{(k+2) \times m}$ is the matrix expression of $\begin{pmatrix} r_j \\ -1 \end{pmatrix}$ under the basis α. Equation (9) can be written $\alpha S \left(A_1 \ a_j\right) T_j \alpha^{\top} = 0$. This means

$$S(A_1 \ a_j) T_j = \mathbf{0}_{m \times m}. \quad (10)$$

The entries of $S(A_1 \ a_j) T_j$ are quadratic polynomials. Then Eq. (10) gives a quadratic multivariate system over $\mathbb{F}_q$ with m^2 quadratic polynomials in the entries of S and C.

The OJ attack uses the basis enumeration and the coordinates enumeration to transform the quadratic multivariate system into a linear system. The former guesses all entries of S and solves the linear system about the entries of $(A_1 \ a_j)$ to determine C. The latter guesses the entries of C and solves the linear system about the entries of S to determine S.

When S and C are in the form of Eq. (5) and Eq. (6), the complexities are presented in Theorem 3.6 and Theorem 3.7. We give their detailed proofs in Appendix C.2 and Appendix C.3 of full version [40]. The ideas of proofs can be easily extended to the ℓ-RD problem.

Theorem 3.6. *If S and C are in the form of Eq. (5), the 2-RD problem can be solved with complexity $\mathcal{O}\left((kr+r)^\omega q^{(m-r)(r-1)}\right)$ by the basis enumeration.*

Theorem 3.7. *If $k = n_1$, S and C are in the form of Eq. (6), the 2-RD problem can be solved with complexity $\mathcal{O}\left((m(r-1)+(n_1-r_1))^\omega q^{(r_1-1)(n_1-r_1)+r_2}\right)$ by the coordinates enumeration.*

Theorem 3.8. *If $k = n_1$, the complexity of solving the ℓ-RD problem by the OJ attack is estimated as*

$$
\begin{cases}
\mathcal{O}\left((kr+r)^\omega q^{(m-r)(r-1)}\right), & \text{Basis Enumeration;} \\
\mathcal{O}\left((m(r-1)+(n_1-r_1))^\omega q^{(r_1-1)(n_1-r_1)+\gamma}\right), & \text{Coordinates Enumeration,}
\end{cases}
$$

where $\gamma = \max\left\{r_i : i \in \{2..\ell\}\right\}$ and $r = \sum_{i=1}^{\ell} r_i$.

3.4   Algebraic Attack by Annulator Polynomial

This algebraic attack [21] differs from attacks aiming to recover S and C with reductions described in Subsect. 3.2. It directly solves x from a multivariate system obtained from the ℓ-RD instance and the theory of q-polynomials [36], more specifically annulator polynomials (see Appendix A of full version [40]). The attack details are outlined in Appendix B.2 of full version [40].

For the ℓ-RD problem finding the ℓ-error $e = (e_1, e_2, \ldots, e_\ell) \in S_r^n$, the solver splits y as $(y_1, y_2, \ldots, y_\ell)$ and splits G as $(G_1, G_2, \ldots, G_\ell)$ by columns n. Then

$$(y_1, y_2, \ldots, y_\ell) = x(G_1, G_2, \ldots, G_\ell) + (e_1, e_2, \ldots, e_\ell).$$

In this way, the ℓ-RD problem is divided into ℓ subproblems, for $\nu \in \{1..\ell\}$, $y_\nu = xG_\nu + e_\nu$, then one solves x from *one* of ℓ subproblems.

Let $x = (x_1, x_2, \ldots, x_k)$. For $\nu \in \{1..\ell\}$, let $y_\nu = (y_1, y_2, \ldots, y_{n_\nu})$, $G_\nu = (g_{ij})_{\substack{i \in \{1..k\} \\ j \in \{1..n_\nu\}}}$, and $e_\nu = (e_1, e_2, \ldots, e_{n_\nu})$. Since the entries of e_ν lie in the support Supp(e_ν) of dimension r_ν, there exists a unique monic q-polynomials $P^{(\nu)}(u) = \sum_{\delta=0}^{r_\nu} p_\delta^{(\nu)} u^{q^\delta}$ of q-degree r_ν such that for $j \in \{1..n_\nu\}$

$$P^{(\nu)}\left(y_j - \sum_{i=1}^{k} x_i g_{ij}\right) = \sum_{\delta=0}^{r_\nu}\left(p_\delta^{(\nu)} y_j^{q^\delta} - \sum_{i=1}^{k} p_\delta^{(\nu)} x_i^{q^\delta} g_{ij}^{q^\delta}\right) = P^{(\nu)}(e_j) = 0. \quad (11)$$

Equation (11) gives a multivariate system with n_ν polynomials and $(r_\nu + k)$ variables $p_\delta^{(\nu)}$ and x_i. For solving the ℓ-RD problem, one solves x_i from this multivariate system.

The linearization and Gröbner basis techniques are applied to solve x_i. The complexities are given in Theorem 3.9 and the detailed proof is presented in Appendix C.4 of full version [40].

Theorem 3.9. *The complexity of solving the ℓ-RD problem by annulator polynomials is estimated as*

$$\begin{cases} \mathcal{O}\left(\min\left\{(r_\nu k)^\omega q^{r_\nu \left\lceil \frac{(k+1)(r_\nu+1)-(n_\nu+1)}{r_\nu}\right\rceil} : \nu \in \{1..\ell\}\right\}\right), & Linearization; \\ \mathcal{O}\left(\min\left\{n_\nu \binom{r_\nu+k+d_{reg}^{(\nu)}-1}{d_{reg}^{(\nu)}}^\omega : \nu \in \{1..\ell\}\right\}\right), & Gröbner\ Basis. \end{cases}$$

where $d_{reg}^{(\nu)}$ is the degree of regularity of the semi-regular system.

3.5   Algebraic Attacks by the MaxMinors Modeling

The MaxMinors (MM) modeling [9] is a powerful algebraic attack for cryptographic parameters and reduces the RD problem to solving a linear system. Equation $\varepsilon C H_y^\top = 0_{n-k-1}$ (obtained from Eq. (3) and $e = \varepsilon C$) implies that $C H_y^\top \in \mathbb{F}_{q^m}^{r \times (n-k-1)}$ is not of row full rank because a non-zero vector s belongs to its left kernel. Then all maximal minors $|C H_y^\top|_{*,J}$ of $C H_y^\top$ are equal to 0 for $J \subset \{1..n-k-1\}$ and $\#J = r$. By the Cauchy-Binet formula, each $|C H_y^\top|_{*,J}$ can be viewed a non-zero linear combination about all maximal minors $c_T = |C|_{*,T}$ for $T \subset \{1..n\}$ and $\#T = r$. One views non-zero c_T as unknowns and solves c_T from a linear system with $\binom{n}{r}$ unknowns and $\binom{n-k-1}{r}$ equations. Finally, one determines the entries of C from the c_T by using the fact that it is in systematic form. The MM modeling over $\mathbb{F}_{q^m}$ is built

$$\left\{P_J = |C H_y^\top|_{*,J} : J \subset \{1..n-k-1\}, \#J = r\right\}, \quad (\text{MM-}\mathbb{F}_{q^m}) \quad (12)$$

Unknowns: $\binom{n}{r}$ variables $c_T \in \mathbb{F}_q$ for $T \subset \{1..n\}$ and $\#T = r$,
Equations: $\binom{n-k-1}{r}$ linear equations $P_J = 0$ over $\mathbb{F}_{q^m}$ in c_T.

However, this system has many solutions due to $\binom{n-k-1}{r} < \binom{n}{r}$ whereas one wants more equations than unknowns for a unique solution. To obtain more equations than unknowns, one unfolds the coefficients of P_J over $\mathbb{F}_q$ and obtains the MM-$\mathbb{F}_q$ modeling

$$\left\{P_{i,J} = |C H_y^\top|_{*,J} : J \subset \{1..n-k-1\}, \#J = r, i \in \{1..m\}\right\}, \quad (\text{MM-}\mathbb{F}_q) \quad (13)$$

Unknowns: $\binom{n}{r}$ variables $c_T \in \mathbb{F}_q$ for $T \subset \{1..n\}$ and $\#T = r$,
Equations: $m\binom{n-k-1}{r}$ linear equations $P_{i,J} = 0$ over $\mathbb{F}_q$ in c_T.

We first analyze the case of the 2-RD problem, then extend conclusions to general cases. By Eq. (6), the matrix C is of form

$$C = \begin{pmatrix} I_{r_1} & C_1' & 0_{r_1 \times n_2} \\ 0_{r_2 \times n_1} & I_{r_2} & C_2' \end{pmatrix} \in \mathbb{F}_q^{r \times n}, \quad (14)$$

where $C = (c_{ij})_{\substack{i \in \{1..r\} \\ j \in \{1..n\}}} \in \mathbb{F}_q^{r \times n}$, $C_1' \in \mathbb{F}_q^{r_1 \times (n_1-r_1)}$, and $C_2' \in \mathbb{F}_q^{r_2 \times (n_2-r_2)}$. One can easily check

- $|C|_{*,(\{1..r_1\}\setminus\{i\}\cup\{j\})\cup\{n_1+1..n_1+r_2\}} = (-1)^{r_1-i}c_{ij}$ for $i \in \{1..r_1\}$ and $j \in \{r_1 + 1..n_1\}$,
- $|C|_{*,\{1..r_1\}\cup(\{n_1+1..n_1+r_2\}\setminus\{i\}\cup\{j\})} = (-1)^{n_1+r_2-i}c_{ij}$ for $i \in \{n_1 + 1..n_1 + r_2\}$ and $j \in \{n_1 + r_2 + 1..n\}$,
- $|C|_{*,\{1..r_1\}\cup\{n_1+1..n_1+r_2\}} = 1$.

Therefore, once all c_T's are solved, one can determine the entries of the matrix C. Lemma 3.10 bounds the number of equations and unknowns c_T.

Lemma 3.10. *Under block form of C in Eq. (14), the MM-$\mathbb{F}_q$ modeling obtained from the 2-RD problem contains $\binom{n_1}{r_1}\binom{n_2}{r_2}$ unknowns c_T and at most $m\binom{n-k-1}{r}$ equations.*

We give the detailed proof for Lemma 3.10 in Appendix C.5 of full version [40].

Remark 2. Our analysis follows the idea of updated RQC [30], where authors bounded the maximal number of equations. On the one hand, considering less equations could lead to a higher complexity because in this case one is more likely to solve an underdetermined system with more unknowns and would guess more entries of C to transform the system into an overdetermined case (see hybrid method in the proof of Theorem 3.11). This means that using the maximal number of equations would give a lower bound of complexity. Cryptographic parameters often lead to an underdetermined case. On the other hand, the number of zero and dependent equations is negligible to the maximal number $m\binom{n-k-1}{r}$ and their impact on complexity is very limited. A thorough analysis in [8,12] supported this point and we also experimentally verified this when $\ell = 2, 3$.

Remark 3. The number of non-zero variables c_T is easy to compute. When n and r are divisible by ℓ, by Stirling approximation, the loss of variables c_T is large due to $\binom{n/\ell}{r/\ell}^{\ell} \approx \ell^{\frac{\ell}{2}}\left(\frac{n}{2\pi r(n-r)}\right)^{\frac{\ell-1}{2}}\binom{n}{r}$ while comparing with the MM-$\mathbb{F}_q$ modeling obtained from the standard RD problem. See Lemma C.1 in Appendix C.6 of full version [40] for this proof.

Theorem 3.11. *The complexity of solving the 2-RD problem by the MM-$\mathbb{F}_q$ modeling is estimated as*

$$\begin{cases} \mathcal{O}\left(m\binom{n-p-k-1}{r}\left(\binom{n_1}{r_1}\binom{n_2-p}{r_2}\right)^{\omega-1}\right), & m\binom{n-k-1}{r} \geq \binom{n_1}{r_1}\binom{n_2}{r_2} - 1; \\ \mathcal{O}\left(q^{a_1r_1+a_2r_2}m\binom{n-k-1}{r}\left(\binom{n_1-a_1}{r_1}\binom{n_2-a_2}{r_2}\right)^{\omega-1}\right), & m\binom{n-k-1}{r} < \binom{n_1}{r_1}\binom{n_2}{r_2} - 1. \end{cases}$$

where $p = \max\left\{i \mid m\binom{n-i-k-1}{r} \geq \binom{n_1}{r_1}\binom{n_2-i}{r_2} - 1\right\}$ and (a_1, a_2) is an integer pair such that $m\binom{n-k-1}{r} \geq \binom{n_1-a_1}{r_1}\binom{n_2-a_2}{r_2} - 1$ exactly holds.

We give a proof with full details for Theorem 3.11 in Appendix C.7 of full version [40]. Theorem 3.11 can be extended to the case of the ℓ-RD problem.

Theorem 3.12. *The complexity of solving the ℓ-RD problem by the MM-$\mathbb{F}_q$ modeling is estimated as*

$$
\begin{cases}
\mathcal{O}\left(m\binom{n-p-k-1}{r}\left(\binom{n_\ell-p}{r_\ell}\prod_{i=1}^{\ell-1}\binom{n_i}{r_i}\right)^{\omega-1}\right), & m\binom{n-k-1}{r} \geq \prod_{i=1}^{\ell}\binom{n_i}{r_i} - 1; \\
\mathcal{O}\left(q^{\sum_{i=1}^{\ell}a_i r_i}m\binom{n-k-1}{r}\left(\prod_{i=1}^{\ell}\binom{n_i-a_i}{r_i}\right)^{\omega-1}\right), & m\binom{n-k-1}{r} < \prod_{i=1}^{\ell}\binom{n_i}{r_i} - 1.
\end{cases}
$$

where $p = \max\left\{i \mid m\binom{n-i-k-1}{r} \geq \binom{n_\ell-i}{r_\ell}\prod_{i=1}^{\ell-1}\binom{n_i}{r_i} - 1\right\}$ *and* $(a_1, a_2, \ldots, a_\ell)$ *is an integers sequence such that* $m\binom{n-k-1}{r} \geq \prod_{i=1}^{\ell}\binom{n_i-a_i}{r_i} - 1$ *exactly holds.*

3.6 Summary of Complexities for Solving the ℓ-RD Problem

At the end of this section, we summarize the complexity gain of solving the ℓ-RD problem compared with the standard RD problem in Table 2. For the first three attacks, we only compare the exponential terms.

Table 2. Complexity comparisons of solving the ℓ-RD and RD problems.

Attacks	RD(q, m, n, k, r)	ℓ-RD(q, m, n, k, r, ℓ)
AGHT	$q^{r\left\lceil\frac{(k+1)m}{n}\right\rceil - m}$	$q^{r\left\lceil\frac{(k+1)m}{n}\right\rceil - m}$
OJ	$q^{(m-r)(r-1)+2}{}_q{}^{(r-1)(k+1)}$	$q^{(m-r)(r-1)}{}_q{}^{(r_1-1)(k-r_1)+\gamma}$ $\gamma = \max\{r_i : i \in \{2..\ell\}\}$
Annulator Polynomial	$q^{r\left\lceil\frac{(k+1)(r+1)-(n+1)}{r}\right\rceil}$ $n^{\left(\frac{r+k+d_{reg}-1}{d_{reg}}\right)^\omega}$	$\min\left\{q^{r_\nu\left\lceil\frac{(k+1)(r_\nu+1)-(n_\nu+1)}{r_\nu}\right\rceil} : \nu \in \{1..\ell\}\right\}$ $\min\left\{n_\nu\left(\frac{r_\nu+k+d_{reg}^{(\nu)}-1}{d_{reg}^{(\nu)}}\right)^\omega : \nu \in \{1..\ell\}\right\}$
MM	$m\binom{n-p-k-1}{r}\left(\binom{n-p}{r}\right)^{\omega-1}$ $q^{ar}m\binom{n-k-1}{r}\left(\binom{n-a}{r}\right)^{\omega-1}$	$m\binom{n-p-k-1}{r}\left(\binom{n_\ell-p}{r_\ell}\prod_{i=1}^{\ell-1}\binom{n_i}{r_i}\right)^{\omega-1}$ $q^{\sum_{i=1}^{\ell}a_i r_i}m\binom{n-k-1}{r}\left(\prod_{i=1}^{\ell}\binom{n_i-a_i}{r_i}\right)^{\omega-1}$

Remark 4. The complexity analysis shows that the gain of most attacks on the ℓ-RD problem benefits from the blockwise structure of ℓ-errors. (1) the OJ and MM attacks benefits from the block-diagonal form of coefficient matrix C because the sparse C enables one to solve less variables (multivariable or linear) system; (2) the AGHT attack is limited because its cost depends on how to successfully guess a subspace that contains the support of the error; (3) the annulator polynomials attack benefits from the fact that the ℓ-errors allow to divide the ℓ-RD problem into ℓ subproblems with the smaller parameters.

For the powerful MM-$\mathbb{F}_q$ modeling, in the "underdetermined" case, an interesting result is that the complexity of solving the ℓ-RD problem allows to divide by a factor ℓ that of solving the standard RD problem.

Let $\ell|n$, $\ell|r$, $n' = n/\ell$, and $r' = r/\ell$. For both RD and ℓ-RD instances, when the parameters (m, n, k, r) satisfy respectively the "underdetermined" conditions: $m\binom{n-k-1}{r} < \binom{n}{r} - 1$ and $m\binom{n-k-1}{r} < \binom{n'}{r'}^\ell - 1$. The attacker chooses appropriate a and $(a_1, a_2, \ldots, a_\ell)$ such that

$$m\binom{n-k-1}{r} \geq \binom{n-a}{r} - 1 \quad \text{and} \quad m\binom{n-k-1}{r} \geq \prod_{i=1}^{\ell}\binom{n'-a_i}{r'} - 1$$

exactly hold. This means $\binom{n-a}{r} \approx \prod_{i=1}^{\ell}\binom{n'-a_i}{r'}$. From Lemma C.1 in Appendix C.6 of full version [40], an appropriate choice is $a_1 = a_2 = \cdots = a_\ell$ and $a_i = a/\ell$. At this point,

$$\frac{\log_q(T_{RD})}{\log_q(T_{\ell\text{-RD}})} \approx \frac{ar}{\sum_i^\ell a_i r_i} = \ell \implies T_{\ell\text{-RD}} \approx \sqrt[\ell]{T_{RD}},$$

where T_{RD} and $T_{\ell\text{-RD}}$ are the complexity of solving the RD and ℓ-RD problems, respectively. This further shows that the speedup really benefits from the block-diagonal form of C because having C sparse enables one to guess $\sum_{i=1}^{\ell} a_i r_i$ entries of C to convert the "underdetermined" system into an "overdetermined" system, instead of ar entries in the standard RD problem.

We simulate the complexity of MM-$\mathbb{F}_q$ for RD, 2-RD, and 3-RD in Fig. 1.

- (a) The RD instances are estimated with $(q, m, n, k) = (2, 200, 200, 100)$ and various even values $r = 2r'$ ($r' \in \{3..30\}$). The 2-RD instances are estimated with $(q, m, n, k, n_1, n_2) = (2, 200, 200, 100, 100, 100)$ and various values $r_1 = r_2 \in \{3..30\}$.
- (b) The RD instances are estimated with $(q, m, n, k) = (2, 100, 200, 100)$ and various even values $r \in \{6..40\}$. The 2-RD instances are estimated with $(q, m, n, k, n_1, n_2) = (2, 100, 200, 100, 100, 100)$ and various values $r_1 = r_2 \in \{3..20\}$.
- (c) The RD instances are estimated with $(q, m, n, k) = (2, 100, 300, 100)$ and various values $r = 3r'$ ($r' \in \{2..20\}$). The 3-RD instances are estimated with $(q, m, n, k, n_1, n_2, n_3) = (2, 100, 300, 100, 100, 100, 100)$ and various values $r_1 = r_2 = r_3 \in \{2..20\}$.

Our simulations become interesting as r increases. (a) and (b) in Fig. 1 show that, when r is divided equally into (r_1, r_2), the exponential complexity allows to divide by a factor 2 for $r \geq 10$, i.e., $T_{2\text{-RD}} \approx \sqrt{T_{RD}}$. (c) in Fig. 1 shows that, when r is divided equally into (r_1, r_2, r_3), the exponential complexity allows to divide by a factor 3 for $r \geq 12$, i.e., $T_{3\text{-RD}} \approx \sqrt[3]{T_{RD}}$. The parameters sizes in (b) and (c) are exactly the case of cryptography parameters in Sect. 5.

4 The ℓ-LRPC Codes and Decoding Algorithm

In this section, we define the blockwise LRPC (ℓ-LRPC) codes, give its decoding algorithm, and analyze the decoding failure probability and the error-correcting

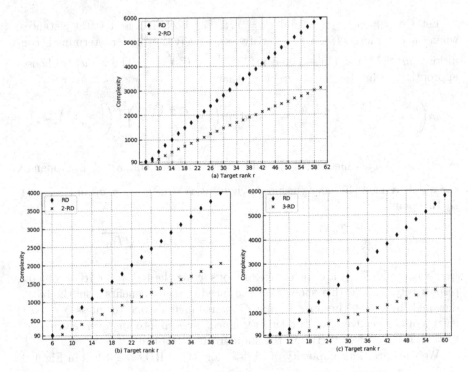

Fig. 1. Complexity trend of RD, 2-RD, and 3-RD by MM-$\mathbb{F}_q$.

capability. We find that the decoding algorithm can benefit from the blockwise structure: the decoding capacity can be significantly improved by a factor of ℓ. For cryptography applications in Sect. 5, we finally give the ℓ-Rank Support Recover (ℓ-RSR) algorithm which is used to recover the support of the ℓ-error.

4.1 The ℓ-LRPC Codes

An $[n, k]_{q^m}$ LRPC code [4, 20] is defined by a parity-check matrix $\boldsymbol{H} \in \mathbb{F}_{q^m}^{(n-k) \times n}$ with small weight. Our $[n, k]_{q^m}$ ℓ-LRPC code is defined by a parity-check matrix consisting of ℓ small-weight matrices of size $(n-k) \times n_i$.

Definition 4.1 (Blockwise LRPC (ℓ-LRPC) Codes). *Let $\ell, k \in \mathbb{N}$, $n_i, d_i \in \mathbb{N}$ for $i \in \{1..\ell\}$, and $n = \sum_{i=1}^{\ell} n_i$. Let $\boldsymbol{H}_i \in \mathbb{F}_{q^m}^{(n-k) \times n_i}$ be a matrix of weight d_i. Let the supports of ℓ matrices $\boldsymbol{H}_i$'s are mutually disjoint. An $[n, k]_{q^m}$ ℓ-LRPC code of length n and dimension k is defined by a parity-check matrix $\boldsymbol{H} = (\boldsymbol{H}_1 \ \boldsymbol{H}_2 \ \cdots \ \boldsymbol{H}_\ell) \in \mathbb{F}_{q^m}^{(n-k) \times n}$.*

Let $\boldsymbol{n} = (n_1, n_2, \ldots, n_\ell)$ and $\boldsymbol{d} = (d_1, d_2, \ldots, d_\ell)$ be vectors of positive integers. We denote the set of such parity-check matrices by $\mathcal{M}_{\boldsymbol{d}}^{\boldsymbol{n}}(k)$. Let F_i be the support of dimension d_i of $\boldsymbol{H}_i$. Because all supports are mutually disjoint, the matrix H can be viewed as the matrix of weight $d = \sum_{i=1}^{\ell} d_i$ and support $F = \sum_{i=1}^{\ell} F_i$.

We next consider decoding algorithms for two error distributions: the ℓ-errors and the standard rank metric errors. In this subsection, we analyze the case of decoding the ℓ-errors. The decoding algorithm is also applied to ROLLO in Sect. 5. The latter is presented in Appendix D of full version [40], where we show that for the standard errors, the ℓ-LRPC code has the same decoding capacity as the standard LRPC code.

4.2   Decoding ℓ-Errors

Let $r = (r_1, \ldots, r_\ell)$ be a vector of positive integers. Consider an $[n, k]_{q^m}$ ℓ-LRPC code $\mathcal{C}$ with generator matrix $G \in \mathbb{F}_{q^m}^{k \times n}$ and parity-check matrix $H = (H_1\ H_2\ \cdots\ H_\ell) \in \mathcal{M}_d^n(k)$ of support $(F_1, F_2, \ldots, F_\ell)$. Let $y = mG + e$ be a received word, where $m \in \mathbb{F}_{q^m}^k$ and $e = (e_1, e_2, \ldots, e_\ell) \in \mathcal{S}_r^n$ with the support $(E_1, E_2, \ldots, E_\ell)$. The syndrome $s = Hy^\top = He^\top = \sum_{j=1}^{\ell} H_j e_j^\top$.

The general idea of decoding ℓ-error e uses the fact that the subspace $S = \langle s_1, s_2, \ldots, s_{n-k} \rangle_{\mathbb{F}_q}$ generated by s enables one to recover the space $\sum_{i=1}^{\ell} E_i F_i$. Once obtaining $\sum_{j=1}^{\ell} E_j F_j$, one recovers $E_1, E_2, \ldots, E_\ell$ and computes the support $E = \sum_{j=1}^{\ell} E_j$ of the error e. Finally, the coordinates of e are computed by solving a linear system. The decoding algorithm is described in Algorithm 1.

4.3   Correctness of the Decoding Algorithm

The correctness of Algorithm 1 depends on the recovery of correct E_j, which requires $\dim S = \dim\left(\sum_{j=1}^{\ell} E_j F_j\right)$ and $\dim\left(\bigcap_{i=1}^{d_j} S_{ji}\right) = r_j$ for $j \in \{1..\ell\}$. We assume that these two conditions hold.

Step 1: the first step of the algorithm is obvious.

Step 2: we prove that $E_j = \bigcap_{i=1}^{d_j} S_{ji}$ for $j \in \{1..\ell\}$. Let $(\varepsilon_{j1}, \varepsilon_{j2}, \ldots, \varepsilon_{jr_j}) \in \mathbb{F}_{q^m}^{r_j}$ be the basis of E_j. Since $s = He^\top = \sum_{j=1}^{\ell} H_j e_j^\top$, $H \in \mathcal{M}_d^n(k)$ is a matrix of support $(F_1, F_2, \ldots, F_\ell)$, and $e \in \mathcal{S}_r^n$ is an ℓ-error of support $(E_1, E_2, \ldots, E_\ell)$, we have that the entries of $H_j e_j^\top$ respectively lie in $E_j F_j$. Thus, $S \subset \sum_{j=1}^{\ell} E_j F_j$. By assumption $\dim S = \dim\left(\sum_{j=1}^{\ell} E_j F_j\right)$, we have $S = \sum_{j=1}^{\ell} E_j F_j$. Further, for any $i \in \{1..d_j\}$, since $f_{ji}\varepsilon_{j\kappa} \in \sum_{j=1}^{\ell} E_j F_j$ for all $\kappa \in \{1..r_j\}$, we have $\varepsilon_{j\kappa} \subset S_{ji} = \{f_{ji}^{-1} x : x \in S\} \Rightarrow E_j \subset S_{ji}$. Then, $E_j \subset \bigcap_{i=1}^{d_j} S_{ji}$. By assumption $\dim\left(\bigcap_{i=1}^{d_j} S_{ji}\right) = r_j$, we have $E_j = \bigcap_{i=1}^{d_j} S_{ji}$.

Step 3: one expresses e under the basis ε of E:

$$e = (e_1, e_2, \ldots, e_n) = (\varepsilon_1, \varepsilon_2, \ldots, \varepsilon_r) \begin{pmatrix} e_{11} & e_{12} & \cdots & e_{1n} \\ e_{21} & e_{22} & \cdots & e_{2n} \\ \vdots & \vdots & \ddots & \vdots \\ e_{r1} & e_{r2} & \cdots & e_{rn} \end{pmatrix} = (\varepsilon_1, \varepsilon_2, \ldots, \varepsilon_r) \begin{pmatrix} \overline{e}_1 \\ \overline{e}_2 \\ \vdots \\ \overline{e}_r \end{pmatrix},$$

Algorithm 1. Decoding ℓ-errors for ℓ-LRPC codes

Input: the vector $\boldsymbol{y}$ and the parity-check matrix $\boldsymbol{H}$.

Output: the message $\boldsymbol{m}$

1: Computing syndrome space:
   - Compute the syndrome $\boldsymbol{H}\boldsymbol{y}^\top = \boldsymbol{H}\boldsymbol{e}^\top = \sum_{i=1}^{\ell} \boldsymbol{H}_i \boldsymbol{e}_i^\top = \boldsymbol{s} = (s_1, s_2, \ldots, s_{n-k})^\top$
     and the syndrome space $S = \langle s_1, s_2, \ldots, s_{n-k} \rangle_{\mathbb{F}_q}$.
2: Recovering the support E of the error $\boldsymbol{e}$:
   - Compute F_j from $\boldsymbol{H}$ for $j \in \{1..\ell\}$
   - Compute the basis $(f_{j1}, f_{j2}, \ldots, f_{jd_j}) \in \mathbb{F}_{q^m}^{d_j}$ of F_j for $j \in \{1..\ell\}$
   - Compute $S_{ji} = f_{ji}^{-1} S$, where all generators of S are multiplied by f_{ji}^{-1} for
     $j \in \{1..\ell\}$ and $i \in \{1..d_j\}$
   - Compute $E_j = \bigcap_{i=1}^{d_j} S_{ji}$ for $j \in \{1..\ell\}$
   - Compute $E = \sum_{j=1}^{\ell} E_j$
3: Recovering the error $\boldsymbol{e}$:
   - Compute the basis $\boldsymbol{\varepsilon} = (\varepsilon_1, \varepsilon_2, \ldots, \varepsilon_r) \in \mathbb{F}_{q^m}^r$ of E
   - Write each entry e_j of $\boldsymbol{e}$ as $e_j = \sum_{i=1}^{r} e_{ij} \varepsilon_i$ for $j \in \{1..n\}$ in the basis $\boldsymbol{\varepsilon}$
   - Solve e_{ij} from the linear system $\boldsymbol{H}\boldsymbol{e}^\top = \boldsymbol{s}$.
4: Recovering $\boldsymbol{m}$ from $\boldsymbol{m}\boldsymbol{G} = \boldsymbol{y} - \boldsymbol{e}$.

---

where $\overline{\boldsymbol{e}}_i = (e_{i1}, e_{i2}, \ldots, e_{in})$ for $i \in \{1..r\}$, and computes $\overline{\boldsymbol{e}}_i$ from Eq. (15):

$$
\boldsymbol{H}\boldsymbol{e}^\top = \begin{pmatrix} \boldsymbol{h}_1 \\ \boldsymbol{h}_2 \\ \vdots \\ \boldsymbol{h}_{n-k} \end{pmatrix} (\overline{\boldsymbol{e}}_1^\top, \overline{\boldsymbol{e}}_2^\top, \ldots, \overline{\boldsymbol{e}}_r^\top) \begin{pmatrix} \varepsilon_1 \\ \varepsilon_2 \\ \vdots \\ \varepsilon_r \end{pmatrix}
$$

$$
= \begin{pmatrix} \boldsymbol{h}_1\varepsilon_1 & \boldsymbol{h}_1\varepsilon_2 & \cdots & \boldsymbol{h}_1\varepsilon_r \\ \boldsymbol{h}_2\varepsilon_1 & \boldsymbol{h}_2\varepsilon_2 & \cdots & \boldsymbol{h}_2\varepsilon_r \\ \vdots & \vdots & \cdots & \vdots \\ \boldsymbol{h}_{n-k}\varepsilon_1 & \boldsymbol{h}_{n-k}\varepsilon_2 & \cdots & \boldsymbol{h}_{n-k}\varepsilon_r \end{pmatrix} \begin{pmatrix} \overline{\boldsymbol{e}}_1^\top \\ \overline{\boldsymbol{e}}_2^\top \\ \vdots \\ \overline{\boldsymbol{e}}_r^\top \end{pmatrix} = \begin{pmatrix} s_1 \\ s_2 \\ \vdots \\ s_{n-k} \end{pmatrix}, \quad (15)
$$

where $\boldsymbol{h}_j$ is the j-th row of $\boldsymbol{H}$.

There are two methods to solve Eq. (15):

1. **Solve-$\mathbb{F}_{q^m}$:** Obtaining a linear system with nr unknowns and $m(n-k)$ equations over $\mathbb{F}_q$ by expressing $\boldsymbol{h}_j\varepsilon_i$ and s_j as a matrix $\mathrm{Mat}(\boldsymbol{h}_j\varepsilon_i) \in \mathbb{F}_q^{m \times n}$ and column vector of length m, respectively, under the basis $\boldsymbol{\alpha}$. The system has one solution with overwhelming probability if $nr \leq m(n-k)$;

2. **Solve-EF:** As $\sum_{j=1}^{\ell} E_j F_j \subset EF$, where $F = \sum_{j=1}^{\ell} F_j$, the entries of $\boldsymbol{h}_j\varepsilon_i$ and s_j lie in EF. We then can express Equation (15) under the basis of EF by expressing $\boldsymbol{h}_j\varepsilon_i$ and s_j as a matrix of $rd \times n$ and column vector of length rd, respectively. Finally, we will obtain a linear system with nr unknowns and $rd(n-k)$ equations over $\mathbb{F}_q$. The system has one solution with overwhelming probability if $nr \leq rd(n-k)$, where $d = \sum_{j=1}^{\ell} d_j$ and $r = \sum_{j=1}^{\ell} r_j$.

Once all $\overline{e}_i$'s are obtained, one can recover e. We experimentally find that **Solve-**$\mathbb{F}_{q^m}$ is more efficient than **Solve-**EF on SageMath 9.0.

Step 4: the fourth step of the algorithm is obvious.

4.4 The Decoding Complexity

The most costly part is the intersection in Step 2 and solving linear systems in Step 3. The intersection $\bigcap_{i=1}^{d_j} S_{ji}$ of spaces S_{ji} of dimension $\mu = \sum_{j=1}^{\ell} r_j d_j$ costs $\mathcal{O}\left(4\mu^2 m \sum_{j=1}^{\ell} d_j\right)$ operations in $\mathbb{F}_q$ for $j \in \{1..\ell\}$. By **Solve-**EF, expressing $h_j \varepsilon_i$ as a matrix of $rd \times n$ in the basis of EF consists in solving n linear systems with rd unknowns and m equations. This costs $(n - k)nr^{\omega+1}d^{\omega}$ operations in $\mathbb{F}_q$. Expressing s_j as a column vector of length rd in the basis of EF consists in solving a linear system with rd unknowns and m equations. This costs $(n - k)(rd)^{\omega}$ operations in $\mathbb{F}_q$. Solving the linear system $He^{\top} = s$ with nr unknowns and $rd(n - k)$ equations costs about $\mathcal{O}((nr)^{\omega})$ operations in $\mathbb{F}_q$. Thus, the complexity of the decoding algorithm is bounded by $\mathcal{O}((nr)^{\omega})$.

4.5 Decoding Failure Probability

By the correctness assumption of Algorithm 1, two cases can make the algorithm fail: (i) $\dim S < \dim \left(\sum_{j=1}^{\ell} E_j F_j\right)$; (ii) $\dim \left(\bigcap_{i=1}^{d_j} S_{ji}\right) > r_j$ for $j \in \{1..\ell\}$. Propositions 4.2 and 4.3 estimate the probability of two cases.

Proposition 4.2. *The probability of* $\dim S < \dim \left(\sum_{j=1}^{\ell} E_j F_j\right)$ *is bounded by* $q^{-(n-k-\mu)}$ *where* $\mu = \sum_{j=1}^{\ell} r_j d_j$.

Proposition 4.3. *The probability that there is* $j \in \{1..\ell\}$ *such that* $\dim \left(\bigcap_{i=1}^{d_j} S_{ji}\right) > r_j$ *is bounded by* $\sum_{j=1}^{\ell} q^{\mu-r_j} \left(\frac{q^{\mu-r_j}-1}{q^{m-r_j}}\right)^{d_j-1}$ *where* $\mu = \sum_{j=1}^{\ell} r_j d_j$.

We give the detailed proofs for Propositions 4.2 and 4.3 in Appendices (C.8 and C.9) of full version [40]. Combining these two propositions, we deduce the decoding failure probability of Algorithm 1 in Theorem 4.4.

Theorem 4.4. *Under assumptions that S_{ji} behaves as independent and random subspaces containing E_j, the decoding failure probability of Algorithm 1 is bounded by* $q^{-(n-k-\mu)} + \sum_{j=1}^{\ell} q^{\mu-r_j} \left(\frac{q^{\mu-r_j}-1}{q^{m-r_j}}\right)^{d_j-1}$ *where* $\mu = \sum_{j=1}^{\ell} r_j d_j$.

The analysis shows that the failure probability can be made arbitrarily small.

4.6 Error Correction Capability

From the correctness of Algorithm 1, we have $nr \leq rd(n - k) \Rightarrow d \geq \frac{n}{n-k}$. Under this condition, the decoding capacity is constrained by $\sum_{j=1}^{\ell} r_j d_j \leq n - k$. The following Theorem 4.5 is obvious.

Theorem 4.5. *When $d_1 = d_2 = \cdots = d_\ell$, the ℓ-LRPC code allows to decode ℓ-errors of weight up to $r = \sum_{j=1}^{\ell} r_j = \frac{n-k}{d_1}$. By setting $d_1 = d_2 = \cdots = d_\ell = 2$, it can decode ℓ-errors of weight up to $\frac{n-k}{2}$.*

Theorem 4.5 implies that the decoding algorithm can benefit from the block-wise structure: the decoding capacity can be significantly improved by a factor of ℓ. An $[n,k]_{q^m}$ LRPC code defined by a parity-check matrix of weight d can decode the standard errors of weight up to $r = \frac{n-k}{d}$ with a DFR of about q^{rd-n-k}. Let $\ell | d$, $d_i = d/\ell$, $\boldsymbol{H} \in \mathcal{M}_{\boldsymbol{d}}^n(k)$ be a parity-check matrix of an $[n,k]_{q^m}$ ℓ-LRPC code. This ℓ-LRPC code can decode ℓ-errors in $\mathcal{S}_{\boldsymbol{r}}^n$ of weight up to ℓr with the same DFR, which comes from

$$\sum_{j=1}^{\ell} r_j d_j = \frac{d}{\ell} \sum_{j=1}^{\ell} r_j \le n - k \implies \sum_{j=1}^{\ell} r_j \le \frac{\ell(n-k)}{d} = \ell r.$$

For example, fixing $d = 4$, $r = 8$, and the DFR of q^{32-n-k}, an $[n,k]_{q^m}$ LRPC code can decode errors of weight 8, but an $[n,k]_{q^m}$ 2-LRPC codes with parameter $\boldsymbol{d} = (d_1, d_2) = (2,2)$ can decode ℓ-errors with parameter $\boldsymbol{r} = (r_1, r_2) = (8,8)$ of weight up to $r = r_1 + r_2 = 16$.

For the accurate failure probability of decoding errors of maximal weight, it is hard to estimate theoretical value and the value in Theorem 4.4 seems not practical for $q > 2$. We give a simulation of the decoding algorithm for 2-LRPC codes on SageMath 9.0. When $\ell = 2$ and $d_1 = d_2 = 2$, the 2-LRPC codes can decode 2-errors of weight up to $\frac{n-k}{2}$. The simulated result shows that the failure probability is about 0.73 for $q = 2$. Figure 2 shows the decreasing trend of the failure probability as q increases. For $q = 2$, the failure probability is bounded by $q^{-(n-k-\sum_{j=1}^{2} r_j d_j)} = 1$. For $q > 2$, the upper bound of failure probability seems to be $q^{-(n-k+1-\sum_{j=1}^{2} r_j d_j)}$. The code parameters are $(m, n, k, n_1, n_2, r_1, r_2, d_1, d_2) = (43, 44, 22, 22, 22, 6, 5, 2, 2)$ for $q = 2, 3, 5, 7, 11, 13, 17, 19$.

4.7   The ℓ-RSR Algorithm

For cryptography applications in Sect. 5, one just recovers the support of the error. In this subsection, we give the ℓ-Rank Support Recover (ℓ-RSR) algorithm (Algorithm 2), which is a shortened version of the decoding Algorithm 1 without the computation of the error. The correctness follows Algorithm 1. The failure probability follows Theorem 4.4. The cost is only the recovery of support and is given in Subsect. 4.4.

5   Applications to Cryptography

In this section, we apply the ideal variants of the ℓ-RD problem and the ℓ-LRPC codes to improve RQC [30] and ROLLO [29] kept in NIST PQC Round 2. Due to

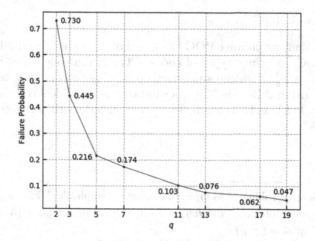

Fig. 2. Simulated failure probability of decoding 2-errors of weight $\frac{n-k}{2}$ for 2-LRPC codes.

Algorithm 2. ℓ-RSR Algorithm

Input: a parity-check matrix $H = (H_1 \ H_2 \ \cdots \ H_\ell) \in \mathcal{M}_d^n(k)$, a syndrome $s \in \mathbb{F}_{q^m}^{n-k}$, $r = (r_1, r_2, \ldots, r_\ell)$.
Output: ℓ spaces E_j of dimensions r_j.
  1: Compute the syndrome space $S = \langle s_1, s_2, \ldots, s_{n-k} \rangle_{\mathbb{F}_q}$.
  2: Recovering the support E_j for $j \in \{1..\ell\}$:
    – Compute F_j from H_j
    – Compute the basis $(f_{j1}, f_{j2}, \ldots, f_{jd_j})$ of F_j
    – Compute $S_{ji} = f_{ji}^{-1} S$, where all generators of S are multiplied by f_{ji}^{-1} for $i \in \{1..d_j\}$
    – Compute $E_j = \bigcap_{i=1}^{d_j} S_{ji}$

---

space limitations, we present the ideal variants in Appendix E of full version [40] and only list improved schemes and comparisons in this section.

RQC [30] and ROLLO [29] include Public Key Encryptions (PKE) and Key Encapsulation Mechanisms (KEM). RQC is an IND-CCA2 KEM built from its IND-CPA PKE construction based on the HHK transformation [26] and uses the Gabidulin codes. We only consider the PKE version of RQC for simplicity. ROLLO is the merge of the three cryptosystems Laker, Locker, and Ouroboros-R which all share the same decryption algorithm for the LRPC codes. Laker (ROLLO-I) and Ouroboros-R (ROLLO-III) are two IND-CPA KEM. Locker (ROLLO-II) is an IND-CCA2 PKE scheme built from its IND-CPA PKE construction based on the HHK transformation [26]. We only consider the IND-CPA PKE version of Locker for simplicity.

5.1 Improved RQC

In this subsection, we improve RQC [30] based on the 2-IRSD and 3-IRSD problems. Our RQC uses three types of codes: a Gabidulin code $\mathcal{C}$ [18] with generator matrix $G \in \mathbb{F}_{q^m}^{k \times n}$ which can correct up to $\lfloor \frac{n-k}{2} \rfloor$ errors by a deterministic decoding algorithm $\mathcal{C}$.Decode [6,27], a random $[2n, n]_{q^m}$-ideal code with parity-check matrix $(1 \ \ h)$, and a random $[3n, n]_{q^m}$-ideal code with parity-check matrix $\begin{pmatrix} 1 & 0 & h \\ 0 & 1 & s \end{pmatrix}$.

- RQC.KGen(λ): Taking 1^λ as input, it randomly samples $h \xleftarrow{\$} \mathbb{F}_{q^m}^n$ and $(x, y) \xleftarrow{\$} S_{(w_x, w_y)}^{(n,n)}$, computes $s = x + hy$, and sets the public key $pk = (h, s)$ and the private key $sk = (x, y)$.
- RQC.Enc(pk, m): Taking the public key $pk = (s, h)$ and a message $m \in \mathbb{F}_{q^m}^k$ as input, it randomly samples $(r_1, r_2, e) \xleftarrow{\$} S_{(w_{r_1}, w_{r_2}, w_e)}^{(n,n,n)}$, computes $u = r_1 + hr_2$ and $v = mG + sr_2 + e$, and returns the ciphertext $c = (u, v)$.
- RQC.Dec(sk, c): Taking a private key $sk = (x, y)$ and the ciphertext c as input, it computes $v - uy$ and returns $m \leftarrow \mathcal{C}$.Decode $(v - uy)$.

Fig. 3. Description of our RQC PKE scheme.

Correctness. We have $v - uy = mG + xr_2 + e - r_1 y$. The correctness of our encryption scheme is based on the decoding capability of the Gabidulin code $\mathcal{C}$, i.e., the error term $xr_2 + e - r_1 y$ must fulfill: $\|xr_2 + e - r_1 y\|_R = w_x w_{r_2} + w_y w_{r_1} + w_e \leq \lfloor \frac{n-k}{2} \rfloor$.

In the decryption step, one needs to decode an error of weight $w_x w_{r_2} + w_y w_{r_1} + w_e$. This weight increase is slow, which brings the gain of decoding capacity and saves code parameters. Although the ℓ-errors can also be used to speed up the attacks for decoding problems, the performance in Table 3 shows that the gain in the decoding method greatly outweighs the gain in the attacks, and eventually allows scheme with small parameters.

Theorem 5.1. *Under the decisional 2-IRSD and 3-IRSD problems, our RQC PKE in Fig. 3 is IND-CPA secure.*

Proof. The proof is similar to [30] with 2-IRSD and 3-IRSD instances. The two instances are defined by

$$s = (1 \ \ h) \begin{pmatrix} x \\ y \end{pmatrix}, \quad \begin{pmatrix} u \\ v - mG \end{pmatrix} = \begin{pmatrix} 1 & 0 & h \\ 0 & 1 & s \end{pmatrix} \begin{pmatrix} r_1 \\ r_2 \\ e \end{pmatrix}.$$

$\square$

5.2 Improved Lake (ROLLO-I)

In this subsection, we improve Lake based on the 2-IRSD problem and the 2-ILRPC codes indistinguishability problem. Our Laker has three building blocks: a random $[2n, n]_{q^m}$ 2-ILRPC code with parity-check matrix $(\boldsymbol{x} \ \boldsymbol{y})$, the algorithm 2-RSR (see Algorithm 2), and a random $[2n, n]_{q^m}$-ideal code with parity-check matrix $(\boldsymbol{1} \ \boldsymbol{h})$.

- Lake.KGen(λ): Taking 1^λ as input, it samples $(\boldsymbol{x}, \boldsymbol{y}) \overset{\$}{\leftarrow} \mathcal{S}_{(d_1,d_2)}^{(n,n)}$ and computes $\boldsymbol{h} = \boldsymbol{x}^{-1}\boldsymbol{y}$, then it sets the public key $pk = \boldsymbol{h}$ and the private key $sk = (\boldsymbol{x}, \boldsymbol{y})$.
- Lake.Encap(pk): Taking the public key $\boldsymbol{h}$ as input, it randomly chooses $(\boldsymbol{e}_1, \boldsymbol{e}_2) \overset{\$}{\leftarrow} \mathcal{S}_{(r_1,r_2)}^{(n,n)}$ and computes $\boldsymbol{c} = \boldsymbol{e}_1 + \boldsymbol{h}\boldsymbol{e}_2$, $E_1 = \mathrm{Supp}(\boldsymbol{e}_1)$, $E_2 = \mathrm{Supp}(\boldsymbol{e}_2)$, $E = E_1 + E_2$, and $K = \mathrm{Hash}(E)$, and returns $(\boldsymbol{c}, K)$.
- Lake.Decap($sk, \boldsymbol{c}$): Taking $(\boldsymbol{x}, \boldsymbol{y})$ and $\boldsymbol{c}$ as input, it computes $\boldsymbol{x}\boldsymbol{c} = \boldsymbol{x}\boldsymbol{e}_1 + \boldsymbol{y}\boldsymbol{e}_2$, executes $(E_1, E_2) \leftarrow$ 2-RSR$((\boldsymbol{x}, \boldsymbol{y}), \boldsymbol{x}\boldsymbol{c}, r_1, r_2)$, computes $E = E_1 + E_2$, and returns $K = \mathrm{Hash}(E)$.

Fig. 4. Description of our Lake KEM scheme.

5.3 Improved Locker (ROLLO-II)

Locker (ROLLO-II [29]) is a PKE scheme and is obtained from ROLLO-I. In this subsection, we improve ROLLO-II by the 2-IRSD problem. As our Lake, our Locker has three building blocks: a random $[2n, n]_{q^m}$ 2-ILRPC code with parity-check matrix $(\boldsymbol{x} \ \boldsymbol{y})$, the algorithm 2-RSR (see Algorithm 2), and a random $[2n, n]_{q^m}$-ideal code with parity-check matrix $(\boldsymbol{1} \ \boldsymbol{h})$.

- Locker.KGen(λ): Taking 1^λ as input, it samples $(\boldsymbol{x}, \boldsymbol{y}) \overset{\$}{\leftarrow} \mathcal{S}_{(d_1,d_2)}^{(n,n)}$ and computes $\boldsymbol{h} = \boldsymbol{x}^{-1}\boldsymbol{y}$, then it sets the public key $pk = \boldsymbol{h}$ and the private key $sk = (\boldsymbol{x}, \boldsymbol{y})$.
- Locker.Enc(pk, M): Taking the public key $\boldsymbol{h}$ and a message M as input, it randomly chooses $(\boldsymbol{e}_1, \boldsymbol{e}_2) \overset{\$}{\leftarrow} \mathcal{S}_{(r_1,r_2)}^{(n,n)}$, computes $\boldsymbol{c} = \boldsymbol{e}_1 + \boldsymbol{h}\boldsymbol{e}_2$, $E_1 = \mathrm{Supp}(\boldsymbol{e}_1)$, $E_2 = \mathrm{Supp}(\boldsymbol{e}_2)$, $E = E_1 + E_2$, and the ciphertext $C = (\boldsymbol{c}, M \oplus \mathrm{Hash}(E)) = (\boldsymbol{c}, \boldsymbol{c}')$, and returns C.
- Locker.Dec(sk, C): Taking the private key $(\boldsymbol{x}, \boldsymbol{y})$ and the ciphertext C as input, it computes $\boldsymbol{x}\boldsymbol{c} = \boldsymbol{x}\boldsymbol{e}_1 + \boldsymbol{y}\boldsymbol{e}_2$, executes $(E_1, E_2) \leftarrow$ 2-RSR$((\boldsymbol{x}, \boldsymbol{y}), \boldsymbol{x}\boldsymbol{c}, r_1, r_2)$, computes $E = E_1 + E_2$, and returns $M = \boldsymbol{c}' \oplus \mathrm{Hash}(E)$.

Fig. 5. Description of our Locker PKE scheme.

In Laker and Locker, the decapsulation and decryption steps obtain the support of $(\boldsymbol{e}_1, \boldsymbol{e}_2)$ from $\boldsymbol{x}\boldsymbol{e}_1 - \boldsymbol{y}\boldsymbol{e}_2$ of weight $r_1 d_1 + r_2 d_2$. This weight increase implies that the parameters (r_1, r_2) and (d_1, d_2) can be increased a lot. Although the 2-errors and the 2-LRPC codes can also be used to speed up the attacks for decoding problems, the performance in Tables 4, 5 and 7 shows that the gain in the decoding method outweighs the gain in the attacks, and eventually allows schemes with small parameters.

Theorem 5.2. *Under the 2-ILRPC codes indistinguishability, and 2-IRSR problems our Lake KEM in Fig. 4 and Locker PKE in Fig. 5 are IND-CPA secure in the random oracle model.*

Proof. The proofs are similar to [29] with the 2-ILRPC codes indistinguishability and 2-IRSR instances. The two instances are defined by

$$0 = \begin{pmatrix} 1 & h \end{pmatrix} \begin{pmatrix} y \\ -x \end{pmatrix}, \quad c = \begin{pmatrix} 1 & h \end{pmatrix} \begin{pmatrix} e_1 \\ e_2 \end{pmatrix}.$$

$\square$

5.4   Improved Ouroboros-R (ROLLO-III)

In this subsection, we improve ROLLO-III based on the 2-IRSD and 3-IRSD problems. Our Ouroboros-R has three building blocks: a 3-ILRPC code with parity-check matrix $\begin{pmatrix} h_0 & h_1 & 1 \end{pmatrix}$, the algorithm 3-RSR (see Algorithm 2), a $[2n, n]_{q^m}$-ideal code with parity-check matrix $\begin{pmatrix} 1 & f_1 \end{pmatrix}$, and a $[3n, n]_{q^m}$-ideal code with parity-check matrix $\begin{pmatrix} 1 & 0 & f_0 \\ 0 & 1 & f_1 \end{pmatrix}$.

- Ouroboros-R.KGen(λ): Taking 1^λ as input, it samples $f_1 \xleftarrow{\text{seed}} \mathbb{F}_{q^m}^n$, and $(h_0, h_1) \xleftarrow{\$} \mathcal{S}_{(d_1, d_2)}^{(n,n)}$, then it computes $f_0 = h_1 + f_1 h_0$ and sets the public key $pk = (f_0, \text{seed})$ and the private key $sk = (h_0, h_1)$.
- Ouroboros-R.Encap(pk): Taking the public key (f_0, seed) as input, it randomly chooses $(e_0, e_1, e) \xleftarrow{\$} \mathcal{S}_{(r_1, r_2, r_3)}^{(n,n,n)}$, computes $c_0 = f_0 e_1 + e$, $c_1 = f_1 e_1 + e_0$, $E_1 = \text{Supp}(e_1)$, $E_2 = \text{Supp}(e_2)$, $E = E_1 + E_2$, and $K = \text{Hash}(E)$, sets $c = (c_0, c_1)$, and returns (c, K).
- Ouroboros-R.Decap(sk, c): Taking (h_0, h_1) and c as input, it computes $s = c_0 - h_0 c_1 = -h_0 e_0 + h_1 e_1 + e$, executes $(E_1, E_2) \leftarrow \text{3-RSR}((h_0, h_1, 1), s, r_1, r_2, r_3)$, computes $E = E_1 + E_2$, and returns $K = \text{Hash}(E)$.

Fig. 6. Description of our Ouroboros-R KEM scheme.

In the decapsulation step, one obtains the support of (e_0, e_1) from $h_1 e_1 - h_0 e_0 + e$ of weight $r_1 d_1 + r_2 d_2 + r_3$. This weight increasing implies that the parameters (r_1, r_2, r_3) and (d_1, d_2) can be increased a lot. Although the blockwise errors and LRPC codes can also be used to speed up the attacks for decoding problems, the performance in Tables 6 and 7 shows that the gain in the decoding method outweighs the gain in the attacks, and eventually allows scheme with small parameters.

Theorem 5.3. *Under the decisional 2-IRSD and 3-IRSD problems, our Ouroboros-R KEM in Fig. 6 is IND-CPA secure in the random oracle model.*

Proof. The proof is similar to [2] with the (decisional) 2-IRSD and 3-IRSD instances. The two instances are defined by

$$f_0 = \begin{pmatrix} 1 & f_1 \end{pmatrix} \begin{pmatrix} h_1 \\ h_0 \end{pmatrix}, \quad \begin{pmatrix} c_0 \\ c_1 \end{pmatrix} = \begin{pmatrix} 1 & 0 & f_0 \\ 0 & 1 & f_1 \end{pmatrix} \begin{pmatrix} e \\ e_0 \\ e_1 \end{pmatrix}.$$

□

5.5 Performance and Comparison

In this subsection, we compare performance of our RQC and ROLLO with original versions.

In Tables 3, 4 and 5, parameters are chosen in two principles. First, the hardness of decoding problems (the 2-IRSD and 3-IRSD problems) is ensured to reach the target security level. The hardness is estimated by our complexity formulas. Secondly, the error-correcting capacity of rank metric codes is ensured to satisfy the decryption correctness condition. $[n,k]_{q^m}$ Gabidulin codes used in RQC require $k < n \leq m$ and correct errors of weight up to $\lfloor (n-k)/2 \rfloor$; in the decryption step, the weight of the decoded errors must $\leq \lfloor (n-k)/2 \rfloor$. The ℓ-LRPC codes used in ROLLO must satisfy a reasonable DFR in Theorem 4.4. In Tables 3 and 6, "2n" ("3n") represents the complexity of solving the 2-IRSD (3-IRSD) instances in RQC and Ouroboros-R. In Tables 4 and 5, the structural attack is estimated with parameters $(m, n, k, r_1, r_2) = (m, 2n - \lfloor \frac{n}{d} \rfloor, n - \lfloor \frac{n}{d} \rfloor, d_1.d_2)$; the message attack is estimated with parameters $(m, n, k, r_1, r_2) = (m, 2n, n, r_1, r_2)$.

From Tables (3, 4, 5 and 6), our parameters sizes are smaller than those of the original ones due to the blockwise stricture, which brings a low complexity redundancy, improved the public key/ciphertext sizes, and more efficient implementations. The improved performance benefits from that the gain of using ℓ-errors and ℓ-LRPC codes in decoding capacity outweighs the complexity loss in solving the ℓ-RD problem. As an example, we provide concrete timings of implementations for our ROLLO and original versions (Table 7). The benchmark is performed on Intel(R) Core(TM) i5-7440HQ CPU@ 3.40 GHz with SageMath 9.0. The tests are available online at https://github.com/YCSong232431/NH-ROLLO. Note that, we do not compare with most recent works [12,32], where the authors constructed a series of efficient PKE and KEM schemes without ideal structure by proposing augmented Gabidulin codes and LRPC codes with multiple syndromes. Our techniques are different from [12,32] and we only consider cryptosystems with ideal structure and one syndrome.

Table 3. Comparison of parameters and sizes for RQC.

Schemes	m	n	k	w_x	w_y	w_{r_1}	w_{r_2}	w_e	pks (bytes)	cts (bytes)	total (KB)	Attack $(2n, 3n)$	Security
Our RQC	83	79	7	4	4	4	4	4	860	1704	2.5	$(2^{130}, 2^{163})$	128
Our RQC	127	113	3	5	5	5	5	5	1834	3652	5.3	$(2^{258}, 2^{214})$	192
Our RQC	139	137	5	5	5	6	6	6	2421	4826	7.1	$(2^{271}, 2^{274})$	256

Schemes	m	n	k	w_x	w_y	w_{r_1}	w_{r_2}	w_e	pks (bytes)	cts (bytes)	total (KB)	Security
RQC (NIST [30])	127	113	3	7	7	7	7	13	1834	3652	5.3	128
RQC (NIST [30])	151	149	5	8	8	8	8	16	2853	5690	8.3	192
RQC (NIST [30])	181	179	3	9	9	9	9	16	4090	8164	12.0	256

pks: $\left(\left\lceil \frac{mn}{8} \right\rceil + 40\right)$ bytes; cts: $\left(2\left\lceil \frac{mn}{8} \right\rceil + 64\right)$ bytes; total = pks + cts.

Table 4. Comparison of parameters and sizes for Lake (ROLLO-I).

Schemes	m	n	r_1	r_2	d_1	d_2	DFR	pks/cts (bytes)	Structural attack $y - xh = 0$	Message attack $c = e_1 + he_2$	Security
Our Lake	61	67	4	4	5	4	2^{-31}	511	2^{160}	2^{144}	128
Our Lake	71	79	5	5	5	5	2^{-29}	702	2^{225}	2^{255}	192
Our Lake	79	89	5	5	6	5	2^{-34}	879	2^{281}	2^{266}	256

Schemes	m	n	r	d	DFR	pks/cts (bytes)	Security
Lake (NIST [29])	67	83	7	8	2^{-28}	696	128
Lake (NIST [29])	79	97	8	8	2^{-34}	958	192
Lake (NIST [29])	97	113	9	9	2^{-33}	1371	256

pks: $\left\lceil \frac{mn}{8} \right\rceil$ bytes. cts: $\left\lceil \frac{mn}{8} \right\rceil$ bytes.

Table 5. Comparison of parameters and sizes for Locker (ROLLO-II).

Schemes	m	n	r_1	r_2	d_1	d_2	DFR	pks (bytes)	cts (bytes)	Structural attack $y - xh = 0$	Message attack $c = e_1 + he_2$	Security
Our Locker	89	163	4	4	4	4	2^{-131}	1814	1942	2^{134}	2^{139}	128
Our Locker	97	179	4	5	5	5	2^{-134}	2171	2299	2^{254}	2^{231}	192
Our Locker	101	181	5	5	5	5	2^{-131}	2286	2414	2^{267}	2^{357}	256

Schemes	m	n	r	d	DFR	pks (bytes)	cts (bytes)	Security
Locker (NIST [29])	83	189	7	8	2^{-134}	1941	2089	128
Locker (NIST [29])	97	193	8	8	2^{-130}	2341	2469	192
Locker (NIST [29])	97	211	8	9	2^{-136}	2559	2687	256

pks: $\left\lceil \frac{mn}{8} \right\rceil$ bytes; cts: $\left\lceil \frac{mn}{8} \right\rceil + 64$ bytes. To obtain the IND-CCA2 security, another hash is added to the ciphertext such that cts = $\left\lceil \frac{mn}{8} \right\rceil + 2 * 64$ bytes.

Table 6. Comparison of parameters and sizes for Ouroboros-R (ROLLO-III).

Schemes	m	n	r_1	r_2	r_3	d_1	d_2	DFR	pks (bytes)	cts (bytes)	Attacks $(2n, 3n)$	Security
Our Ouroboros-R	53	79	4	4	5	4	4	2^{-33}	623	1166	$(2^{147}, 2^{175})$	128
Our Ouroboros-R	89	101	6	6	6	4	5	2^{-33}	1164	2248	$(2^{196}, 2^{266})$	192
Our Ouroboros-R	97	109	6	6	7	5	5	2^{-42}	1362	2644	$(2^{275}, 2^{308})$	256

Schemes	m	n	w	w_r	δ	DFR	pks (bytes)	cts (bytes)	Security
Ouroboros-R (TIT [2])	67	83	7	7	7	2^{-28}	736	1431	128
Ouroboros-R (TIT [2])	107	113	9	9	9	2^{-24}	1552	3023	192
Ouroboros-R (TIT [2])	149	151	11	11	11	2^{-20}	2853	5625	256

pks: $\left(\left\lceil \frac{mn}{8} \right\rceil + 40\right)$ bytes and cts: $\left\lceil \frac{2mn}{8} \right\rceil$ bytes. We update DFR of Ouroboros-R.

Table 7. Timings comparisons of our ROLLO and original ROLLO.

Schemes	KGen (ms)	Encap (ms)	Decap (ms)	Security
Our Lake	715	73	257	128
Our Lake	737	100	499	192
Our Lake	1020	118	553	256
Lake (NIST [29])	995	109	391	128
Lake (NIST [29])	1220	134	525	192
Lake (NIST [29])	1390	181	838	256

Schemes	KGen (ms)	Enc (ms)	Dec (ms)	Security
Our Locker	2300	232	388	128
Our Locker	2940	280	614	192
Our Locker	3210	301	644	256
Locker (NIST [29])	2760	258	446	128
Locker (NIST [29])	3410	314	583	192
Locker (NIST [29])	2780	333	715	256

Schemes	KGen (ms)	Encap (ms)	Decap (ms)	Security
Our Ouroboros-R	101	120	246	128
Our Ouroboros-R	206	247	633	192
Our Ouroboros-R	224	262	798	256
Ouroboros-R (TIT [2])	130	153	368	128
Ouroboros-R (TIT [2])	275	308	1040	192
Ouroboros-R (TIT [2])	504	614	2560	256

6 Conclusion and Future Work

In this paper, we studied blockwise structures in rank-based cryptosystems and introduced ℓ-errors, ℓ-RD problem, and ℓ-LRPC codes. They are natural generalizations of the standard errors, RD problem, and LRPC codes. We found that (1) the blockwise structure does not ease the problem too much: the ℓ-RD problem is still exponentially hard for appropriate choices of $\ell > 1$; (2) the decoding algorithm can benefit from the blockwise structure: the decoding capacity can be significantly improved by a factor of ℓ. Interestingly, the gain of the decoding capacity outweighs the complexity loss in solving the ℓ-RD problem, which allows to improve RQC and ROLLO. For 128-bit security, our RQC has total public key and ciphertext sizes of 2.5 KB, which is not only about 50% more compact than the original RQC, but also smaller than the NIST Round 4 code-based submissions HQC, BIKE, and Classic McEliece.

Recent works [3,12,32] proposed unstructured PKE and KEM without ideal structure for more reliable security. We would in next work analyze the complexity of blockwise rank support learning problem and apply the ℓ-LRPC codes with multiple syndromes to improve unstructured schemes.

Acknowledgement. We would like to thank the anonymous reviewers of ASIACRYPT 2023 for their helpful comments and suggestions on earlier versions of our paper. Jiang Zhang, the corresponding author, is supported by the National Key Research and Development Program of China (Grant No. 2022YFB2702000), and by the National Natural Science Foundation of China (Grant Nos. 62022018, 61932019). Xinyi Huang is supported by the National Natural Science Foundation of China (Grant No. 62032005). Wei Wu is supported by the National Natural Science Foundation of China (Grant No. 62372108). This research is also funded in part by the National Natural Science Foundation of China (Grant No. 62172096).

References

1. Alekhnovich, M.: More on average case vs approximation complexity. In: Proceedings of the 44th Symposium on Foundations of Computer Science (FOCS), pp. 298–307. IEEE Computer Society (2003)
2. Aragon, N., Blazy, O., Deneuville, J., Gaborit, P., Zémor, G.: Ouroboros: an efficient and provably secure KEM family. IEEE Trans. Inf. Theory **68**(9), 6233–6244 (2022)
3. Aragon, N., Dyseryn, V., Gaborit, P., Loidreau, P., Renner, J., Wachter-Zeh, A.: LowMS: a new rank metric code-based KEM without ideal structure. IACR Cryptology ePrint Archive, p. 1596 (2022). https://eprint.iacr.org/2022/1596
4. Aragon, N., Gaborit, P., Hauteville, A., Ruatta, O., Zémor, G.: Low rank parity check codes: new decoding algorithms and applications to cryptography. IEEE Trans. Inf. Theory **65**(12), 7697–7717 (2019)
5. Aragon, N., Gaborit, P., Hauteville, A., Tillich, J.: A new algorithm for solving the rank syndrome decoding problem. In: International Symposium on Information Theory (ISIT), pp. 2421–2425. IEEE (2018)
6. Augot, D., Loidreau, P., Robert, G.: Generalized Gabidulin codes over fields of any characteristic. Des. Codes Crypt. **86**(8), 1807–1848 (2018)
7. Bardet, M., et al.: An algebraic attack on rank metric code-based cryptosystems. In: Canteaut, A., Ishai, Y. (eds.) EUROCRYPT 2020. LNCS, vol. 12107, pp. 64–93. Springer, Cham (2020). https://doi.org/10.1007/978-3-030-45727-3_3
8. Bardet, M., Briaud, P., Bros, M., Gaborit, P., Tillich, J.: Revisiting algebraic attacks on MinRank and on the rank decoding problem. IACR Cryptology ePrint Archive, p. 1031 (2022). https://eprint.iacr.org/2022/1031

9. Bardet, M., et al.: Improvements of algebraic attacks for solving the rank decoding and MinRank problems. In: Moriai, S., Wang, H. (eds.) ASIACRYPT 2020. LNCS, vol. 12491, pp. 507–536. Springer, Cham (2020). https://doi.org/10.1007/978-3-030-64837-4_17

10. Bernstein, D.J., Chou, T., Cid, C., et al.: Classic McEliece. Fourth Round Submission to the NIST Post-quantum Cryptography Call (2022). https://classic.mceliece.org/

11. Bettaieb, S., Bidoux, L., Connan, Y., Gaborit, P., Hauteville, A.: The Learning with Rank Errors problem and an application to symmetric authentication. In: International Symposium on Information Theory, ISIT, pp. 2629–2633. IEEE (2018)

12. Bidoux, L., Briaud, P., Bros, M., Gaborit, P.: RQC revisited and more cryptanalysis for rank-based cryptography. CoRR (2022). https://doi.org/10.48550/arXiv.2207.01410

13. Byrne, E., Gluesing-Luerssen, H., Ravagnani, A.: Fundamental properties of sum-rank-metric codes. IEEE Trans. Inf. Theory $67(10)$, 6456–6475 (2021)

14. Chabaud, F., Stern, J.: The cryptographic security of the syndrome decoding problem for rank distance codes. In: Kim, K., Matsumoto, T. (eds.) ASIACRYPT 1996. LNCS, vol. 1163, pp. 368–381. Springer, Heidelberg (1996). https://doi.org/10.1007/BFb0034862

15. Coggia, D., Couvreur, A.: On the security of a Loidreau rank metric code based encryption scheme. Des. Codes Crypt. $88(9)$, 1941–1957 (2020)

16. Couvreur, A., Gaborit, P., Gauthier-Umaña, V., Otmani, A., Tillich, J.: Distinguisher-based attacks on public-key cryptosystems using Reed-Solomon codes. Des. Codes Crypt. $73(2)$, 641–666 (2014)

17. Faugère, J.-C., Levy-dit-Vehel, F., Perret, L.: Cryptanalysis of MinRank. In: Wagner, D. (ed.) CRYPTO 2008. LNCS, vol. 5157, pp. 280–296. Springer, Heidelberg (2008). https://doi.org/10.1007/978-3-540-85174-5_16

18. Gabidulin, E.M.: Theory of codes with maximum rank distance. Problemy Peredachi Informatsii $21(1)$, 3–16 (1985)

19. Gabidulin, E.M., Paramonov, A.V., Tretjakov, O.V.: Ideals over a non-commutative ring and their application in cryptology. In: Davies, D.W. (ed.) EUROCRYPT 1991. LNCS, vol. 547, pp. 482–489. Springer, Heidelberg (1991). https://doi.org/10.1007/3-540-46416-6_41

20. Gaborit, P., Murat, G., Ruatta, O., Zémor, G.: Low rank parity check codes and their application to cryptography. In: The Workshop on Coding and Cryptography (WCC) (2013). http://www.selmer.uib.no/WCC2013/pdfs/Gaborit.pdf

21. Gaborit, P., Ruatta, O., Schrek, J.: On the complexity of the rank syndrome decoding problem. IEEE Trans. Inf. Theory $62(2)$, 1006–1019 (2016)

22. Gaborit, P., Ruatta, O., Schrek, J., Zémor, G.: New results for rank-based cryptography. In: Pointcheval, D., Vergnaud, D. (eds.) AFRICACRYPT 2014. LNCS, vol. 8469, pp. 1–12. Springer, Cham (2014). https://doi.org/10.1007/978-3-319-06734-6_1

23. Gaborit, P., Zémor, G.: On the hardness of the decoding and the minimum distance problems for rank codes. IEEE Trans. Inf. Theory $62(12)$, 7245–7252 (2016)

24. Ghatak, A.: Extending Coggia-Couvreur attack on Loidreau's rank-metric cryptosystem. Des. Codes Crypt. $90(1)$, 215–238 (2022)

25. Hoffstein, J., Pipher, J., Silverman, J.H.: NTRU: a ring-based public key cryptosystem. In: Buhler, J.P. (ed.) ANTS 1998 (ANTS-III). LNCS, vol. 1423, pp. 267–288. Springer, Heidelberg (1998). https://doi.org/10.1007/BFb0054868

26. Hofheinz, D., Hövelmanns, K., Kiltz, E.: A modular analysis of the Fujisaki-Okamoto transformation. In: Kalai, Y., Reyzin, L. (eds.) TCC 2017. LNCS, vol. 10677, pp. 341–371. Springer, Cham (2017). https://doi.org/10.1007/978-3-319-70500-2_12

27. Loidreau, P.: A Welch–Berlekamp like algorithm for decoding Gabidulin codes. In: Ytrehus, Ø. (ed.) WCC 2005. LNCS, vol. 3969, pp. 36–45. Springer, Heidelberg (2006). https://doi.org/10.1007/11779360_4

28. Loidreau, P.: A new rank metric codes based encryption scheme. In: Lange, T., Takagi, T. (eds.) PQCrypto 2017. LNCS, vol. 10346, pp. 3–17. Springer, Cham (2017). https://doi.org/10.1007/978-3-319-59879-6_1

29. Melchor, C.A., Aragon, N., Bardet, M., et al.: ROLLO. Second Round Submission to the NIST Post-quantum Cryptography Call (2020). https://pqc-rollo.org/

30. Melchor, C.A., Aragon, N., Bettaieb, S., et al.: RQC. Second Round Submission to the NIST Post-quantum Cryptography Call (2020). http://pqc-rqc.org/

31. Melchor, C.A., Aragon, N., Bettaieb, S., et al.: HQC. Fourth Round Submission to the NIST Post-quantum Cryptography Call (2023). http://pqc-hqc.org

32. Melchor, C.A., Aragon, N., Dyseryn, V., Gaborit, P., Zémor, G.: LRPC codes with multiple syndromes: near ideal-size KEMs without ideals. In: Cheon, J.H., Johansson, T. (eds.) Post-Quantum Cryptography (PQCrypto), vol. 13512, pp. 45–68. Springer, Cham (2022). https://doi.org/10.1007/978-3-031-17234-2_3

33. Misoczki, R., Tillich, J., Sendrier, N., Barreto, P.S.L.M.: MDPC-McEliece: new McEliece variants from moderate density parity-check codes. In: IEEE International Symposium on Information Theory (ISIT), pp. 2069–2073. IEEE (2013)

34. NIST: Status report on the second round of the NIST post-quantum cryptography standardization process (2020). https://nvlpubs.nist.gov/nistpubs/ir/2020/NIST.IR.8309.pdf

35. NIST: Status report on the third round of the NIST post-quantum cryptography standardization process (2022). https://doi.org/10.6028/NIST.IR.8413-upd1

36. Ore, O.: On a special class of polynomials. Trans. Am. Math. Soc. **35**(3), 559–584 (1933)

37. Ourivski, A.V., Johansson, T.: New technique for decoding codes in the rank metric and its cryptography applications. Probl. Inf. Transm. **38**(3), 237–246 (2002)

38. Overbeck, R.: A new structural attack for GPT and variants. In: Dawson, E., Vaudenay, S. (eds.) Mycrypt 2005. LNCS, vol. 3715, pp. 50–63. Springer, Heidelberg (2005). https://doi.org/10.1007/11554868_5

39. Sidelnikov, V.M., Shestakov, S.O.: On insecurity of cryptosystems based on generalized Reed-Solomon codes. Discret. Appl. Math. **2**(4), 439–444 (1992)

40. Song, Y., Zhang, J., Huang, X., Wu, W.: Blockwise rank decoding problem and LRPC codes: cryptosystems with smaller sizes. Cryptology ePrint Archive, Paper 2023/1387 (2023). https://eprint.iacr.org/2023/1387

SDitH in the QROM

Carlos Aguilar-Melchor[1] , Andreas Hülsing[2]([⊠]) , David Joseph[1] ,
Christian Majenz[3] , Eyal Ronen[4] , and Dongze Yue[1]

[1] SandboxAQ, Palo Alto, USA
{Carlos.Aguilar-Melchor,David.Joseph,Dongze.Yue}@sandboxaq.com
[2] Eindhoven University of Technology, Eindhoven, The Netherlands
andreas@huelsing.net
[3] Technical University of Denmark, Kgs. Lyngby, Denmark
chmaj@dtu.dk
[4] Tel Aviv University, Tel Aviv, Israel
eyal.ronen@cs.tau.ac.il

Abstract. The MPC in the Head (MPCitH) paradigm has recently led
to significant improvements for signatures in the code-based setting. In
this paper we consider some modifications to a recent twist of MPCitH,
called Hypercube-MPCitH, that in the code-based setting provides the
currently best known signature sizes. By compressing the Hypercube-
MPCitH five-round code-based identification scheme into three-rounds
we obtain two main benefits. On the one hand, it allows us to further develop recent techniques to provide a tight security proof in the
quantum-accessible random oracle model (QROM), avoiding the catastrophic reduction losses incurred using generic QROM-results for Fiat-
Shamir. On the other hand, we can reduce the already low-cost online
part of the signature even further. In addition, we propose the use of
proof-of-work techniques that allow to reduce the signature size. On
the technical side, we develop generalizations of several QROM proof
techniques and introduce a variant of the recently proposed extractable
QROM.

Keywords: Post-quantum cryptography · code-based signatures ·
provable security · SDitH · MPCitH · QROM · QROM+ · Fiat-Shamir

1 Introduction

The advent of large scale quantum computers will render the security of virtually
all public-key cryptography that is deployed today obsolete [28]. While it is an
ongoing debate if and when such devices will be built (c.f., [18]) the potential
impact would be so catastrophic, that betting on this never happening is not an

Andreas Hülsing is supported by an NWO VIDI grant (Project No. VI.Vidi.193.066).
Christian Majenz is supported by a NWO VENI grant (Project No. VI.Veni.192.159).
Eyal Ronen is partially supported by Len Blavatnik and the Blavatnik Family founda-
tion, the Blavatnik ICRC, and Robert Bosch Technologies Israel Ltd.

J. Guo and R. Steinfeld (Eds.): ASIACRYPT 2023, LNCS 14444, pp. 317–350, 2023.
https://doi.org/10.1007/978-981-99-8739-9_11

option. For that reason, NIST initiated a competition to select future crypto-graphic standards for post-quantum secure signatures and key encapsulation, in 2016 [30]. In 2022, NIST selected one KEM (Kyber) and three digital signature systems (Dilithium, Falcon, SPHINCS+) as the end of the third round of the competition [29]. However, the competition is not over, yet. NIST is still about to select another KEM, and there are good candidates from coding-theory [1,4,5]. The situation is worse for signatures. Dilithium [26] and Falcon [31] are both based on lattice-assumptions, and SPHINCS+ [20] while solely relying on the security of a cryptographic hash function, has significantly worse performance. Just before the selection, the last remaining candidates from multivariate cryp-tography were fatally attacked [7]. Consequently, there is a lack of signature proposals that are not based on lattice-assumptions and have good overall per-formance. For that reason, NIST started an "on-ramp" process for new signature proposals.

A promising area for new signature proposals is code-based cryptography which dates back to the work of McEliece [27]. Code-based cryptography grounds the security of construction in the hardness of decoding problems, like the *general decoding problem* or the *syndrome decoding problem*. Traditionally, code-based cryptography is rather well-known for public key encryption schemes. Propos-als for signature schemes have also been known for a long time [32] but have never really been competitive. However, in recent years this area has received new interest with several new schemes proposed, like WAVE [11], and, most recently, Syndrome-Decoding in the Head (SDitH) [14]. SDitH is a new app-roach to code-based signatures that applies the MPCitH approach [22] to the Syndrome Decoding Problem to build an identification scheme (IDS). The lat-ter is then turned into a signature scheme using the Fiat-Shamir heuristic [15]. MPCitH is a well known approach in post-quantum cryptography (PQC). Pic-nic [33], one of the long-standing contenders in the NIST competition was built on this approach. The SDitH authors manage to show that applying the MPCitH concept to a coding theory problem enables one to achieve better performance for the overall protocol. This performance has further been improved by a recent work [2] that proposes what they call Hypercube-MPCitH, to amplify the sound-ness of MPCitH in an efficient way, and apply it to the SDitH signature. We will call the resulting scheme the *Hypercube-SDitH* scheme.

The works proposing SDitH and Hypercube-SDitH come with security proofs. However, these security arguments only consider classical adversaries. This does not give a formal post-quantum security guarantee, especially because they use the Random Oracle Model (ROM) which is insufficient in that setting. An oracle modeling a hash function, a public primitive, needs to permit quantum queries, as an attacker can implement a hash function on a quantum computer. Hence the Quantum-accessible Random Oracle Model (QROM) was introduced [8]. It is now common practice to provide a QROM proof for post-quantum security.

Our contribution. In this work, we present a security proof for (a minor modi-fication of) Hypercube-SDitH in the QROM. Our proof establishes the security of previously used parameters against quantum attacks at NIST security level 1 (the only parameter set considered for Hypercube-SDitH so far). For our proof we revist the Hypercube-SDitH and SDitH constructions. They build a 5-round IDS and turn this into a signature scheme. 5-round IDS are not that well understood and results about, e.g., the Fiat-Shamir transform are often only given for the canonical 3-round IDS. We notice that the IDS in both proposals can actually be viewed as 3-round IDS *in the (Q)ROM.*

On the one hand, this changed view increases the conceptual complexity of the scheme in two ways: i) The 3-round IDS needs to be constructed to readily include any parallel repetitions of the 5-round IDS. ii) While the 5-round IDS has statistical special soundness, the 3-round IDS only has *computational* special soundness, requiring additional work to prove security. On the other hand, the changed view has several benefits. First of all, it allows to use results for 3-round IDS. In particular, a recent result about the security of commit & open IDS in the QROM [12], which is only given for 3-round schemes, applies after a mild generalization. Second, for Hypercube-SDitH it was noticed that a huge part of the signing cost is caused by operations that do not depend on the message. This enables an online-offline trade-off in the sense of [13], where precomputation can be done during an offline phase to speed up signing during the online phase when messages to be signed become available. That way, it becomes easier to deal with traffic peaks. With our observation, the balance shifts even more further reducing the online phase. Finally, this enables a more modular proof than in previous approaches which hopefully makes the result more accessible.

Why is the reduction to three rounds possible? The previous proposals need two challenge rounds (and thereby five rounds total): one for a polynomial zero test that is used to probabilistically verify that the syndrome known by the prover / signer has low weight, and one for MPCitH. However, the first challenge is not necessary to achieve zero-knowledge. One indication for this is that the proofs in [2,14] allow to extract a syndrome from two valid transcripts that agree in the initial three messages but differ in the fourth (the second challenge). In our analysis we proceed in two Fiat-Shamir steps. First, we make the polynomial zero test non-interactive. This step is secure unless an adversary can solve a certain random oracle search problem that we characterize in the ROM as well as in the QROM. This step leads to the advertised 3-round IDS. More precisely we prove a reduction from a family of computational special soundness properties of the 3-round IDS to a family of QROM oracle search problems. The second step constructs a digital signature. We thus analyse (some form of special) soundness and honest-verifier zero knowledge (HVZK) of the three round IDS. Based on these properties, we prove UF-CMA-security of the Signature scheme.

As mentioned, the QROM proof we obtain is clean and modular. We analyze HVZK in the multi-transcript setting, necessary when considering computational in place of statistical HVZK as is the case in Hypercube-SDitH. We prove security of the now non-interactive polynomial test. For this, we apply recent QROM lower bound methods from [10] based on Zhandry's compressed oracle technique [34]. We then prove a computational version of special-soundness in the QROM. Next, we develop a generalization of the recent result of [12] to the case of computational special soundness, and apply them towards security for Fiat-Shamir transformed IDS under no-message attacks. For this last step we introduce the QROM+, a model similar to the extractable QROM as recently defined in [19] (which maybe of independent interest), and develop an extension of the techniques from [10] to the QROM+. The QROM+ serves as a proof tool: it allows us to generalize a common, modular proof strategy, where intermediate algorithms require to learn the preimages of certain queries to the QROM. To eventually obtain a security bound that does not refer to the QROM+, we prove an explicit bound for the adversarial advantage against computational special soundness in the QROM+. Finally, we extend the result to security under chosen message attacks using the adaptive reprogramming technique from [17].

Besides the change in point of view that allows for improved analysis including a QROM proof, we also make some actual modifications to the scheme. We note that we can optimize the computation cost without increasing the signature size. This is done in a counter-intuitive way: it turns out that by increasing the communication cost of the IDS sending certain data in the clear instead of just a commitment, we can reduce the signing cost. The considered data are the communication transcripts and final outputs of the MPC parties which will all be revealed eventually. We assume that this information was previously sent in committed form to optimize communication cost of the IDS. However, as the data is recomputable from the opening information provided in the last message, it does not have to be included in this first message. As a side effect, this simplifies the structure of the protocol and the security proof.

Finally, we present performance numbers of our proposed signature scheme. The total signature times are comparable to the original Hypercube-SDitH, but most of the computational cost is moved from online time to offline time. In addition, we also show that it is possible to make use of a proof-of-work (PoW) technique similar to the recently proposed SPHINCS+C in [24] to decrease signature sizes by minimally increasing signing and verification times.

Outline. We discuss the IDS in Sec. 2, including necessary background, and a summary of the ideas behind SDitH, and Hypercube-SDitH. We analyze the security of the IDS in Sec. 3. In Sec. 4, we discuss the signature scheme and its security. Finally, in Sec. 5 we provide performance results and the PoW trick.

2   SDitH as a 3-Round Identification Scheme

In this section we present SDitH and the hypercube variant thereof as a 3-round, public coin, commit & open identification scheme (IDS). We start with background on the used cryptographic tools. Afterwards, we give an intuition of the scheme, before we end with a detailed, modular description of the IDS.

2.1   Preliminaries

In the following we provide the definitions for a PRG, a TreePRG, commitments, and identification schemes. At the end of the section we introduce the syndrome decoding problem we use as hardness assumption.

PRG. A pseudorandom generator (PRG) is an efficiently computable function $\mathrm{PRG} : \{0,1\}^n \rightarrow \{0,1\}^{en}$ where e is the expansion factor. Security of a PRG is defined in terms of a real-or-random game. The advantage of a possibly quantum adversary A is defined as

$$\mathrm{Adv}_{\mathsf{PRG}}^{\mathrm{ror}}(\mathsf{A}) := \left| \Pr[x \leftarrow \{0,1\}^{en} : 1 \leftarrow \mathsf{A}(x)] - \Pr[x \leftarrow \{0,1\}^n : 1 \leftarrow \mathsf{A}(\mathrm{PRG}(x))] \right|.$$

TreePRG. In this work we make use of a specific PRG called TreePRG, initially proposed by Goldreich, Goldwasser, and Micali [16]. TreePRG makes use of a standard PRG with expansion factor $e = 2$ and reaches $e = 2^\lambda$ building a binary tree of height λ. The root of the tree is the input and the leaves are the outputs. To build the tree, every inner node is fed to PRG to generate its two child nodes. Let Out_i denote the ith leaf / output block of TreePRG. We define as TP.extract the function that given a seed x and an index i returns the sibling path for Out_i, i.e., the minimal set of inner nodes that allows to compute all Out values except Out_i. For our construction we require that Out_i is pseudorandom even when given the output of $\mathsf{TP.extract}(x, i)$. We define an even stronger notion as it is easily achievable: For a possibly quantum adversary A we define the advantage against TreePRG as

$$\mathrm{Adv}_{\mathsf{TreePRG}}^{\mathrm{ror}}(\mathsf{A}) := \left| \Pr[\{x_j\}_{j=0}^\lambda \leftarrow (\{0,1\}^n)^\lambda : 1 \leftarrow \mathsf{A}(\{x_j\}_{j=0}^\lambda)] \right.$$
$$\left. - \Pr[x, y \leftarrow \{0,1\}^n : 1 \leftarrow \mathsf{A}(\mathsf{TP.extract}(x,i), \mathsf{Out}_i))] \right|.$$

A standard hybrid argument can be used to show that $\mathrm{Adv}_{\mathsf{TreePRG}}^{\mathrm{ror}}(\mathsf{A}) \leq (\lambda - 1)\mathrm{Adv}_{\mathsf{PRG}}^{\mathrm{ror}}(\mathsf{B})$ where $\mathsf{TIME}(\mathsf{B}) \leq \mathsf{TIME}(\mathsf{A}) + (\lambda - 1)\mathsf{TIME}(\mathrm{PRG})$: One replaces the outputs on the path to leaf i by random values, one by one. The beginning is the real case (right probability above). Once all outputs on the pathare replaced, we get the random case (left probability above). The computational distance between any two consecutive hybrids is bounded by $\mathrm{Adv}_{\mathsf{PRG}}^{\mathrm{ror}}(\mathsf{B})$ where B replaces the outputs where the two hybrids differ by its input and then runs A.

Com. In this work we consider only hash-based commitments. Hence, we define commitment scheme as an algorithm Com that given an input x and randomness $\rho \in \{0,1\}^r$ produces a commitment $\mathsf{com} = \mathsf{Com}(x; \rho) \in \{0,1\}^c$. We make the randomness explicit as given (com, x, ρ) everybody can check that indeed $\mathsf{com} = \mathsf{Com}(x; \rho)$. We require two properties: binding and hiding.

We define the advantage of a possibly quantum adversary A against the computational binding property of Com as

$$\mathrm{Adv}_{\mathsf{Com}}^{\mathrm{bind}}(\mathsf{A}) := \Pr[((x_1, \rho_1), (x_2, \rho_2)) \leftarrow \mathsf{A} : \mathsf{Com}(x_1; \rho_1) = \mathsf{Com}(x_2; \rho_2)].$$

We define the advantage of a possibly quantum adversary A against the computational hiding property of Com as

$$\mathrm{Adv}_{\mathsf{Com}}^{\mathrm{hide}}(\mathsf{A}) := \left| \Pr[((x_1, x_2) \leftarrow \mathsf{A}; \rho \leftarrow \{0,1\}^k : 1 \leftarrow \mathsf{A}(\mathsf{Com}(x_1; \rho))] \right.$$
$$\left. - \Pr[((x_1, x_2) \leftarrow \mathsf{A}; \rho \leftarrow \{0,1\}^k : 1 \leftarrow \mathsf{A}(\mathsf{Com}(x_2; \rho))] \right|.$$

2.1.1   Identification Schemes. In this work we are concerned with 3-round, public coin, commit and open identification schemes which we will denote by IDS. An IDS is an interactive protocol between a prover P and a verifier V. It is defined by a tuple of algorithms (Keygen, Commit, Resp, Vrf) and a challenge space $\mathcal{C}$. Prior to any interaction, Keygen is run and outputs a key pair (pk, sk). A protocol run starts with P running (st, w) ← Commit(sk). The commitment message w is sent to V which samples a challenge c from the uniform distribution over $\mathcal{C}$ and sends it to P. Upon receiving c, the prover P runs z ← Resp(st, c) and sends z to V. The verifier accepts if Vrf(pk, w, c, z) = 1 and rejects otherwise.

The *transcript* of a run of the IDS is the tuple (w, c, z) of messages exchanged. We are only interested in IDS that are *correct*, i.e., for any key pair output by Keygen, we want that the execution of IDS between honest P and V always accepts. A property that can be handy when turning IDS into signatures is that of *commitment-recoverable* IDS. An IDS is commitment recoverable if there exists an algorithm Rcvr, such that for any valid transcript (w, c, z), we have Rcvr(c, z) = w.

We expect IDS to provide two security propertes which are defined below.

HVZK. The most commonly used version of honest-verifier zero-knowledge (HVZK) is the statistical version. This version has the advantage that it trivially also gives a bound for multiple transcripts. However, in our setting where we use hash-based commitments the amount of commitment randomness required to achieve statistical HVZK in place of computational HVZK is greater by a factor 2.5 as shown in [25]. This has a huge impact on signature size and so we aim only at computational HVZK. As pointed out in [17], deriving a bound for HVZK of multiple transcripts is not straight-forward when in the computational setting. Hence, we directly prove multiple transcript, computational HVZK below. To define this property, we first have to define an honest transcript generator Trans and an HVZK simulator Sim. In our definitions we closely follow [17] as we later use the HVZK property in a result of that work.

Definition 1 (HVZK simulator and honest transcript generator). *An HVZK simulator for IDS is an algorithm Sim that takes as input the public key pk and outputs a transcript (w, c, z). An honest transcript generator for IDS is an algorithm Trans that takes as input the secret key sk and outputs a transcript (w, c, z) by means of an honest execution of IDS.*

Based on this definition we can define computational t-HVZK of an IDS as follows:

Definition 2 (Computational t-HVZK). *We define the advantage of a possibly quantum adversary A against the computational t-HVZK of IDS with simulator Sim, making no more than t queries to its (transcript-)oracle as*

$$\mathrm{Adv}_{\mathsf{IDS,Sim}}^{t-\mathsf{HVZK}}(A) := \Big| \Pr[(\mathsf{pk,sk}) \leftarrow \mathsf{Keygen}() : 1 \leftarrow A^{\mathsf{Sim(pk)}}(\mathsf{pk})]$$
$$- \Pr[(\mathsf{pk,sk}) \leftarrow \mathsf{Keygen}() : 1 \leftarrow A^{\mathsf{Trans(sk)}}(\mathsf{pk})] \Big|.$$

Special Soundness. Also for special soundness (spS) we slightly deviate from the common definition. The reason is again that statistical special soundness would be too expensive in terms of signature size (requiring length preserving commitments). Moreover, as we turn the five- into a three-round protocol it becomes inherently impossible to achieve statistical special soundness: the polynomial test can now be cheated by solving a search problem for the hash function. Bounding the hardness of this search problem will be a large part of the spS-proof.

It turns out that we need an even more fine-grained notion of special soundness as we are considering a τ-fold parallel-composition of some basic IDS'. Looking ahead, in the case we are interested in, IDS is the parallel repetition of the five-round identification scheme considered in [2], with the Fiat-Shamir transform for proof systems applied to the first three rounds. As an abstraction of this parallel composition, we say IDS has a *splittable challenge* if a challenge c of IDS has form $c = (c_1, \ldots, c_\tau)$, where c_i are challenges of IDS'. We let the distance between two IDS challenges $\text{Dist}(c_1, c_2)$ as the number of IDS' challenges on which they disagree, i.e., the number of indices $1 \leq i \leq \tau$ for which $(c_1)_i \neq (c_2)_i$.

Definition 3 ((Query-bounded) distance-d special soundness for IDSwith splittable challenge). *We define the advantage of a possibly quantum adversary A against the query bounded special soundness of a composed IDS with respect to extractor Ext in the (quantum-accessible) random oracle model as follows*

$$\text{Adv}_{\text{IDS,Ext}}^{d-\text{spS}}(A) := \Pr[(\text{sk}, \text{pk}) \leftarrow \text{Keygen}(); ((w_1, c_1, z_1), (w_2, c_2, z_2)) \leftarrow A^{\text{RO}}(\text{pk});$$

$$\text{sk}' \leftarrow \text{Ext}^{\text{RO}}((w_1, c_1, z_1), (w_2, c_2, z_2)) : \text{Vrf}(\text{pk}, w_i, c_i, z_i) = 1$$

$$, i \in \{1, 2\} \wedge (w_1 = w_2) \wedge d = \text{Dist}(c_1, c_2) \wedge (\text{sk}', \text{pk}) \notin \text{Keygen}()],$$

where q is the maximum number of queries that A makes to RO and we consider it understood that in this case all IDS algorithms may depend on RO.

Syndrome Decoding. The hardness assumption that we use in this work is that of the Coset Weights variant of the Syndrome Decoding (SD) problem, shown to be NP-complete [6].

Definition 4 (Coset Weights Syndrome Decoding problem). *Sample a uniformly random parity check matrix $H \in \mathbb{F}_{SD}^{(m-k) \times m}$, and binary vector $x \in \mathbb{F}_{SD}^m$ with $wt(x) = \omega$. Let syndrome $y = Hx$. Then given only H, y, it is difficult to find $x' \in \mathbb{F}_{SD}^m$ such that $Hx' = y$ with $wt(x') \leq \omega$.*

Furthermore, for cryptographically relevant parameters, with overwhelming likelihood there exists only one short preimage of weight $\leq \omega$, and that is the x sampled initially.

2.2 SDitH and the Hypercube Approach

In the following we summarize the previous works that we build on. We first briefly sketch the MPC in the Head (MPCitH) paradigm [22]. Then we discuss the work syndrome decoding in the head [14], and finally a recent extension to that work called the hypercube approach [2].

MPCitH. The MPCitH approach is a technique to build a zero-knowledge proof (ZKP) by simulating an MPC computation *in the head* and building on the security properties of the MPC protocol. More precisely, MPCitH can be used to prove knowledge of some x such that $F(x) = \texttt{ACCEPT}$ for a function F that outputs either $\texttt{ACCEPT}$ or $\texttt{REJECT}$ in zero-knowledge. Roughly, the protocol works as follows. The input x is secret shared among all parties (we limit ourselves here to additive secret sharing over a finite field) and the MPC protocol is used to evaluate F on this shared x. For this the MPC protocol would exchange messages between parties to implement multiplications of secret shared data while linear operations can be done locally by every party on their shares. Finally, all parties output their secret share of the result which can be summed up to get the result.

To turn this into a ZKP, in MPCitH the prover P first does the secret sharing and then executes the MPC protocol for all parties to compute the communication transcript of in- and outgoing messages for each party, as well as the secret share of the result. Then, P commits to the view of all parties which contains the initial secret share, their random tape, and communication transcripts. The commitments together with all secret shares of the result are sent to the verifier V. In response, V sends a random number i between 1 and t. As last message, P then sends the openings for the views of all parties but the ith. (We limit ourselves to the case where all but one state are opened. In general, less than $t-1$ parties might be opened.) For verification, V checks the views of all opened parties, making sure that the communications agree with the initial state and both together lead to the secret share of the result for this party.

Intuitively, zero-knowledge is obtained due to the privacy of the MPC protocol and one party not being opened. Soundness is obtained by the correctness of the MPC protocol, and the observation that a P that does not know x can at most compute $t-1$ consistent views. Consequently, the view of one party has to be inconsistent which is observed by V with probability $1 - t^{-1}$.

SDitH. In [14], an application of MPCitH to the syndrome decoding problem is proposed. Intuitively, it is clear that we can use MPCitH to prove knowledge of an $\mathbf{x}$ such that $\mathbf{Hx} = \mathbf{y}$ setting $F(\mathbf{x}) := \mathbf{Hx} - \mathbf{y}$ and defining 0 to indicate $\texttt{ACCEPT}$ and any other value to indicate $\texttt{REJECT}$. The problem is that this does not guarantee that $wt(\mathbf{x}) \le \omega$.

The crucial novelty in [14] is to overcome this problem by proposing a weight check routine which we describe in detail later. Roughly, this routine computes a polynomial S from $\mathbf{x}$ as well as some other polynomials Q, P, and F such that $S \cdot Q - P \cdot F = 0$ iff $wt(\mathbf{x}) \le \omega$. This equation is then probabilistically checked on a set of random points, chosen by the verifier (which makes their protocol five-round). To avoid running two MPCitH instances, the authors link the two as follows. They consider only $\mathbf{H} = (\mathbf{H}'|\mathbf{I})$ given in standard form. This means, one can split $\mathbf{x} = (\mathbf{x}_A|\mathbf{x}_B)$ such that $\mathbf{y} = \mathbf{H}'\mathbf{x}_A + \mathbf{x}_B$. Exploiting this, they store only $\mathbf{x}_A$ as secret and start the weight check routine by recomputing $\mathbf{x}_B = \mathbf{y} - \mathbf{H}'\mathbf{x}_A$, and then deriving S from the recombined $\mathbf{x} = (\mathbf{x}_A|\mathbf{x}_B)$. Thereby, this extended weight check also verifies that $\mathbf{Hx} = \mathbf{y}$.

The final protocol is then obtained applying MPCitH to F being the extended weight check function that starts with $\mathbf{x}_A$. The protocol deviates from the basic MPCitH recipe as it obtains the random evaluation points from V. For this, P generates the initial secret shares of $\mathbf{x}_A$, Q, and P (F is public and the secret share of S is derived from the secret share of $\mathbf{x}_A$). It commits to all this and sends it to V that responds with the random evaluation points (and some values necessary for multiplication of shares). Then P can simulate the MPC computation of F and the protocol from there on follows the standard MPCitH receipt.

A standard optimization. One way to reduce the size of the opening information above is based on the properties of additive secret sharing. Namely, the initial state of all parties consists of a secret sharing of the secret x and in case of SDitH also of some secret sharings of further values (the polynomials Q, and P, as well as values needed to do multiplication of shares). Generation of the secret shares in additive secret sharing can be done by picking the first $t-1$ shares at random and then computing the final share as the difference of the shared value and the sum of the $t-1$ shares. The first $t-1$ shares can hence be replaced by short random seeds which are expanded to the full shares using a PRG. These seeds can be bitstrings of the length of the security parameter while the secret shares in the above protocols are significantly longer. Given that we commonly send the shares together with the commitment randomness as opening information, this massively reduces communication cost as we now only have to send the seeds to open parties 1 to $t-1$. Only for party t we are unable to compress the opening information. We call this the auxiliary state aux.

A further way of optimizing communication cost can be achieved using TreePRG. Instead of sampling $t-1$ random seeds for the initial secret sharing, these seeds are generated using TreePRG. This allows to open all seeds with $\log_2(t-1)$ values and if $i \neq t$ (using TP.extract) and with just a single value in case $i = t$ (in the former case we still have to send along the full auxiliary state aux to open that one). This reduces the biggest part of the communication cost from linear in the number of parties to logarithmic.

Hypercubes. In a recent work [2], an improvement to the SDitH protocol is proposed that allows to boost soundness in a size efficient way. The protocols above have soundness error $1/t$. To achieve a negligible soundness error, we require amplification. There are two common ways to get a soundness error of $t^{-\tau}$: First, we can increase the number of parties to t^τ causing an exponential increase in runtime and communication cost but the number of aux states remains the same. Second, we can run τ iterations of the protocol in parallel at the cost of a τ fold increase in communication, especially, we get τ aux states, but also only a τ fold increase in runtime (compared to the exponential increase).

The improvement proposed in [2] is the hypercube approach. The idea is to generate an N^D secret sharing of the initial state values, i.e., all the values that are secret shared for the initial states of parties. This means we get a single auxiliary state. Then, these shares are used to create D instances of the MPC protocol with N parties each. For each of these D instances, they partition the

N^D shares into N subsets of D shares each and recombine the secret shares in each subset by summing them up. This recombination results in N secret shares of the shared values, i.e., the initial states of N parties necessary for the MPC protocol. This is related to a hypercube as the partitioning is done by arranging the original N^D shares in a hypercube and for each of the D partitions we recombine by projection onto one of the D dimensions. The protocol essentially then runs the SDitH protocol for D instances with a few little differences. First, P commits to all the N^D initial shares independently instead of committing to the shares of the parties in the actual MPC protocol. This is intuitively fine as P thereby still commits to all the information. Second, V still only picks one index i now between 1 and N^D. Then P opens all secret shares of the original N^D shares except share i (which is possible because of the independent commitments). Due to the properties of the partitioning and the secret sharing scheme, this means that in each protocol instance, there is one party for which the initial state remains unopened as one share is lacking for the partial recombination.

All in all, this approach allows us to achieve the best of both worlds: We get the soundness error N^{-D} at computational and communication cost of parallel composition (D parallel repetitions of the N party protocol), while we get just one auxiliary state as if we had increased the number of protocol parties to N^D (as pointed out in [2], there are more computational improvements possible when looking at the details, like balancing the party preparation phase and the MPC phase; for those we refer to [2]).

2.3 Polynomial Zero Test

In the identification schemes presented here, the prover P gives a zero knowledge proof (ZKP) that he knows a solution $\mathbf{x} \in \mathbb{F}_{SD}^m$ to the syndrome decoding problem, i.e., such that $\mathbf{Hx} = \mathbf{y}$ with $wt(\mathbf{x}) \leq \omega$. In order to do this, P constructs four polynomials S, Q, P, F in $\mathbb{F}_{poly}[X]$ which should satisfy the relation $S \cdot Q = P \cdot F$, and the ZKP proceeds by checking the relation is true at various points in a space $\mathbb{F}_{points} \supseteq \mathbb{F}_{poly}$.

Let $\phi \colon \mathbb{F}_{SD} \to \mathbb{F}_{poly}$ be the canonical embedding. Then S is computed by interpolating over the coordinates of $\mathbf{x}$. That is, $S(f_i) = \phi(x_i)$ where f_i runs over the first m elements of $\mathbb{F}_{poly}$, so $deg(S) \leq m - 1$ as S is the interpolation over the m coordinates of $\mathbf{x}$. Next, Q is $\prod_{f_i \in E}(X - f_i)$, where E is a set of order ω which contains the nonzero coordinates of S. Thus, the nonzero points of S are all roots of $Q[X]$ which has degree ω. Polynomial F is public, and is $F[X] = \prod_{[m]}(X - f_i)$, meaning it has roots everywhere in the first m coordinates of $\mathbb{F}_{poly}$. And finally, P is defined as $S \cdot Q / F$, in order to ensure that both sides of the relation have the same degree, which is $\leq m + \omega - 1$.

Checking the polynomial is not done by directly checking the polynomials, but implicitly by checking that the polynomial relation is true at several points $r \in \mathbb{F}_{points}$. This is because if two polynomials are equal, then they will be equal at every point at which they are evaluated, however if they are not equal, then it becomes increasingly unlikely that they will be equal if we check them at an increasing number t of randomly selected points, by the Schwarz-Zippel lemma

[14]. When selecting points at which to evaluate the polynomials, we draw from a larger domain $\mathbb{F}_{\text{points}} \supseteq \mathbb{F}_{\text{poly}}$, in order to make it harder to find points at random where non-equivalent polynomials coincide.

In summary, when evaluated on the first m coordinates of $\mathbb{F}_{\text{poly}}$, S has zeros everywhere except the ω nonzero coordinates of $\mathbf{x}$; Q has zeroes everywhere that S does not by construction, F has zeroes everywhere, and P serves to make left and right hand sides equal. Any party that knows a valid solution to the Coset Weights SD problem can therefore build polynomials S, Q, P that satisfy this relation. Note that a party who can solve the SD problem and finds $\mathbf{x}'$ such that $wt(\mathbf{x}') < \omega$ would also be able to construct a valid but different set of S, Q, P.

2.4   Protocol Formulation

SDitH and Hypercube-SDitH are presented as five round IDS. Here we give a description as three-round IDS. The advantage of observing that they can be turned into three-round IDS, is threefold. First, it reduces the number of interactions between parties. Second, when turning it into a signature scheme using the Fiat-Shamir transform, we can apply the tight QROM proof recently introduced in [12] which only applies to three round IDS. Third, more of the computation done during signature generation is independent of the message, thus can be precomputed. Indeed, the required online computation consists merely of computing a hash and assembling a message from the local state.

In the following we describe the protocol in terms of the different steps it encompasses. For a full picture of the protocol see Algs. 1 and 2. We give our description for $\tau = 1$ and explain a detailed change to the standard parallel compoisition for $\tau > 1$ afterwards.

Parameters. Hypercube-SDitH has the following building blocks and parameters. The seed length for the used PRG is n. We assume that PRG can produce an arbitrary number of n byte output blocks and we truncate to the required amount. Commitments take r bits of randomness and produce commitments of length c. It uses a hypercube of dimension D and N parties per MPC computation. We use parallel composition of τ instances to reduce the soundness error. Finally, the parameters of the syndrome decoding problem are m, k, and ω.

Key Generation. Prover P samples $\mathbf{H}' \xleftarrow{\$} \mathbb{F}_{\text{SD}}^{(m-k) \times k}$ and $\mathbf{x} \xleftarrow{\$} \mathbb{F}_{\text{SD},\omega}^{m}$ where $\mathbb{F}_{\text{SD},\omega}^{m}$ is the set of all elements $\mathbf{a} \in \mathbb{F}_{\text{SD}}^{m}$ with $wt(\mathbf{a}) = \omega$. It splits $\mathbf{x} = (\mathbf{x}_A | \mathbf{x}_B)$ with $\mathbf{x}_A \in \mathbb{F}_{\text{SD},\omega}^{m-k}$ and sets $\mathsf{sk} = \mathbf{x}_A$. Then it computes $\mathbf{y} = (\mathbf{H}' | \mathbf{I}_{m-k})\mathbf{x}$ and sets $\mathsf{pk} = (\mathbf{H}', \mathbf{y})$.

Generating leaf parties. The prover P first generates the polynomials S, Q, P as explained above. Then it creates a secret sharing for each of them as follows. P first picks a fresh random seed and generates shares for all N^D leaf parties using TreePRG to generate $(state_i, \rho_i)$ which are the leaf's seed, and its commitment randomness. From $state_i$, the prover then derives the ith share of each of the

Algorithm 1. 3-round Hypercube-SDitH – Part 1: P.Commit

Algorithm P.Commit:

Input: Secret key $\mathsf{sk} = \mathbf{x}_A \in \mathbb{F}_{\mathrm{SD}}^{m-k}$.

Output: Commitment message w (For simplicity we keep st implicit).

Set-up:
1: Choose $E \subset [m]$ such that $|E| = w$ and the non-zero coordinates of x are in E.
2: Compute $Q(X) = \prod_{i \in E}(X - \gamma_i) \in \mathbb{F}_{\mathrm{poly}}(X)$.
3: Compute $S(X) \in \mathbb{F}_{\mathrm{poly}}(X)$ by interpolation over the coordinates of $\mathbf{x}$.
4: Compute $P(X) = S(X) \cdot Q(X)/F(X)$ with $F(X) \in \mathbb{F}_{\mathrm{poly}}(X)$ s.t. $F(X) = \prod_{i=1}^{m}(X - \gamma_i)$.
5: Sample a root seed: $\mathsf{seed} \leftarrow \{0,1\}^{\lambda}$.
6: Expand root seed seed recursively using TreePRG to obtain N^D leafs seed'_i which are further expanded to $(\mathsf{seed}_i, \rho_i) \leftarrow \mathsf{PRG}(\mathsf{seed}'_i), 0 \le i < N^D$.
7: The index of a main party is $(k,j) \in \{0,\ldots,D-1\} \times \{0,\ldots,N-1\}$ and contains all leaf parties i whose k-th coordinate is j when i is represented as radix N integer.
8: **for** each party $(k,j) \in \{0,\ldots,D-1\} \times \{0,\ldots,N-1\}$ **do**
9:     Set $[\mathbf{x}_A]_{(k,j)}, [Q]_{(k,j)}, [P]_{(k,j)}, [a]_{(k,j)}, [b]_{(k,j)}$, and $[c]_{(k,j)}$ to zero.

Expand leaf party seeds and commit:
10: **for** each leaf $i \in \{0,\ldots,N^D-1\}$ **do**
11:     **if** $i \ne N^D - 1$ **then**
12:         $([a]_i, [b]_i, [c]_i, [\mathbf{x}_A]_i, [Q]_i, [P]_i) \leftarrow \mathsf{PRG}(\mathsf{seed}_i)$
13:         $\mathsf{state}_i = \mathsf{seed}_i$
14:     **else**
15:         $[a]_{N^D-1}, [b]_{N^D-1} \leftarrow \mathsf{PRG}(\mathsf{seed}_{N^D-1})$, $[c]_{N^D-1} = \langle a, b \rangle - \sum_{i \ne N^D-1}[c]_i$
16:         $[\mathbf{x}_A]_{N^D-1} = \mathbf{x}_A - \sum_{i \ne N^D-1}[\mathbf{x}_A]_i$
17:         $[Q]_{N^D-1} = Q - \sum_{i \ne N^D-1}[Q]_i$, $[P]_{N^D-1} = P - \sum_{i \ne N^D-1}[P]_i$,
18:         $aux = ([\mathbf{x}_A]_{N^D-1}, [Q]_{N^D-1}, [P]_{N^D-1}, [c]_{N^D-1})$, and $\mathsf{state}_{N^D-1} = \mathsf{seed}_{N^D-1} \| aux$
19:     Leaf parties commit to their state $\mathsf{com}_i = \mathsf{Com}(\mathsf{state}_i, \rho_i)$.
20: Compute $\mathsf{w}_1 = \mathsf{Hash}(\mathsf{com}_0, \ldots, \mathsf{com}_{N^D-1})$.

Derive evaluation points and masks:
21: P derives t challenge points $r \in \mathbb{F}_{\mathrm{points}}$ and masks $\epsilon \in \mathbb{F}_{\mathrm{points}}$ from commitment hash: $\{r, \varepsilon\}_0^{t-1} = \mathsf{PRG}(\mathsf{w}_1)$.

Build main parties:
22: **for** Dimension $k \in \{0,\ldots,D-1\}$ **do**
23:     **for** Main party $j \in \{0,\ldots,N-1\}$ **do**
24:         Let $(i_1,\ldots,i_D)$ be the radix N representation of i.
25:         Let S be the set of leaf parties with $i_k = j$.
26:         $[\mathbf{x}_A]_{(k,j)} = \sum_{i \in S}[\mathbf{x}_A]_i$, $[Q]_{(k,j)} = \sum_{i \in S}[Q]_i$, $[P]_{(k,j)} = \sum_{i \in S}[P]_i$
27:         $[a]_{(k,j)} = \sum_{i \in S}[a]_i$, $[b]_{(k,j)} = \sum_{i \in S}[b]_i$, $[c]_{(k,j)} = \sum_{i \in S}[c]_i$

Execute MPC protocol:
28: **for** Dimension $k \in \{0,\ldots,D-1\}$ **do**
29:     Execute MPC protocol between the main parties $(k,1),\ldots,(k,N)$ to compute communication and result shares $\{[\alpha]_{(k,j)}, [\beta]_{(k,j)}, [v]_{(k,j)}\}_{j=0}^{N-1}$.
30: Set $\mathsf{w}_2 = \left\{\left\{[\alpha]_{(k,j)}, [\beta]_{(k,j)}, [v]_{(k,j)}\right\}_{j=0}^{N-1}\right\}_{k=0}^{D-1}$, and send $\mathsf{w} = (\mathsf{w}_1, \mathsf{w}_2)$ to V.

Algorithm 2. 3-round Hypercube-SDitH – Part 2: V.Challenge, P.Resp, V.Vrf

Algorithm V.Challenge:
Input: Commitment message w.
Output: Challenge c.
1: V samples $c \xleftarrow{\$} \{0, \ldots, N^D - 1\}$ and sends it to P.

Algorithm P.Resp:
Input: Commitment message w, challenge c (and internal state st that we left implicit).
Output: Response z.
2: Run the local computations of the MPC protocol using the shares of leaf party c to obtain its contribution to the overall communication ($[\![\alpha]\!]_c, [\![\beta]\!]_c$).
3: P sets $z = (\mathsf{TP.extract}(\mathsf{seed}, c), \mathsf{com}_c, ([\![\alpha]\!]_c, [\![\beta]\!]_c)$, adds aux if $c \neq N^D - 1$ and sends it to V.

Algorithm V.Vrf:
Input: Public key $\mathsf{pk} = (\mathbf{H}', \mathbf{y}) \in \mathbb{F}_{\mathrm{SD}}^{(m-k) \times k} \times \mathbb{F}_{\mathrm{SD}}^{(m-k)}$, commitment message w, challenge c and response z.
Output: Decision (ACCEPT/REJECT).
4: **for** $i \in (\{0, \ldots, N^D - 1\} \setminus c)$ **do**
5:     Compute $(state_i, \rho_i)$ from z using TreePRG.
6:     Compute $\mathsf{com}'_i = \mathsf{Com}(state_i, \rho_i)$.
7:     Compute $\mathsf{w}'_1 = \mathsf{Hash}(\mathsf{com}'_0, \ldots, \mathsf{com}_c, \ldots \mathsf{com}'_{N^D - 1})$.
8: **for** $(k \in \{0, \ldots, D - 1\})$ **do**
9:     Run verification of main parties [3] on inputs derived from $\{state_i\}_{i \neq c, i=0}^{N^D - 1}$,
        $([\![\alpha]\!]_c, [\![\beta]\!]_c)$, and $\{r, \varepsilon\}_0^{t-1} = \mathsf{PRG}(\mathsf{w}_1)$ to get $\left\{[\alpha']_{(k,j)}, [\beta']_{(k,j)}, [v']_{(k,j)}\right\}_{j=0}^{N-1}$.
10: **if** $(\mathsf{w}'_1, \mathsf{w}'_2) \neq \mathsf{w}$ where $\mathsf{w}'_2 = \left\{\left\{[\alpha']_{(k,j)}, [\beta']_{(k,j)}, [v']_{(k,j)}\right\}_{j=0}^{N-1}\right\}_{k=0}^{D-1}$ **then return**
    REJECT.
11: **return** ACCEPT.

---

polynomials $[\![S]\!]_i, [\![P]\!]_i, [\![Q]\!]_i$, as well as its share of the Beaver triple $[\![a]\!]_i, [\![b]\!]_i, [\![c]\!]_i$ using PRG to expand $state_i$. For the auxiliary party $(i = N^D - 1)$, the secret share is then computed such that the shares sum up to the right values. This share is then appended to the auxiliary party's $state_i$. Then P commits to each state: $\mathsf{com}_i = \mathsf{Com}(state_i, \rho_i)$.

Building main parties. Next the prover builds the main parties for the MPC computations. The prover runs D MPC computations. For this, [2] aggregates the secret shares of the N^D leaf parties into an N party protocol in D different ways. This is done using D different partitions of the N^D leaf parties.

The partitions are computed as follows. First the index i of a leave party is turned into a vector of D values, the *hypercube representation*, taking its radix N representation $i = (i_0, \ldots, i_{D-1})$. The leaf parties that are summed up to form the share of the j-th main party of the k-th MPC instance are those parties for which $i_k = j$. For $K = 1$, i.e., considering the first hypercube index, one obtains an N party MPCitH protocol, where the first party is the aggregation of all leave parties of the form $(0, i_1, \ldots, i_{D-1})$, the second contains leaves of the form $(1, i_1, \ldots, i_{D-1})$, and so on. This process is repeated for each of the D dimensions of the hypercube, giving D independent N-party MPCitH protocols.

Evaluation points. The next step is generating the points for validating the polynomial relation $S \cdot Q = P \cdot F$, the objective of which is for the prover to demonstrate that the preimage $\mathbf{x}$ they know for the syndrome decoding problem $\mathbf{y} = \mathbf{Hx}$ has *low weight*, i.e. $wt(\mathbf{x}) \leq \omega$. To that end, points $r_j \in \mathbb{F}_{points}$ and masks ϵ_j for $j = 0, \ldots, t-1$ are sampled. Then for each j, $S(r_j), Q(r_j)$, $P(r_j), F(r_j)$ are computed via MPC and the identity $S(r_j) \cdot Q(r_j) = (P \cdot F)(r_j)$ is checked probabilistically via an MPC protocol using the mask ϵ_j.

In the five-round IDS of [2] and [14], the evaluation points and masks are selected at random by the verifier as the first challenge. However in the three round scheme we present here, the evaluation points are derived from the transcript of the previous steps that have occurred up to that point, i.e. they are generated by expanding the hash of the commitments w_1 using PRG.

MPC operations. At this stage P has all the information required to perform the MPC operations - the inputs being the shared main party polynomials evaluated at the challenge points to give $[s], [q], [pf]$. Beaver multiplication is then performed to verify the triple s, q, pf by sacrificing the Beaver triple a, b, c. This creates the communication shares $[\alpha], [\beta], [v]$. In each of the D dimensions $k \in D$ the prover runs Γ on each set of main party inputs, resulting in communication and output shares $\{[\alpha]_{(k,j)}, [\beta]_{(k,j)}, [v]_{(k,j)}\}_{j=0}^{N-1}$. This is repeated for each of the D dimensions of the hypercube, and all communications. Note that for honest P, $v_k = 0$ for all $k \in \{0, \ldots, D-1\}$. For more details on the MPC computation see the full version [3].

Challenge. P sends the commitment hash w_1 together with all the communication and main party sharings $w_2 = \left\{ \left\{ [\alpha]_{(k,j)}, [\beta]_{(k,j)}, [v]_{(k,j)} \right\}_{j=0}^{N-1} \right\}_{k=0}^{D-1}$ to V. The MPCitH challenge is then randomly sampled by the verifier and returned to the prover. This challenge is interpreted as an index c of one of the N^D leaf parties that does not need to be opened.

Response. P opens the views of all leaf parties except for c, by sending $(state_i, \rho_i)$. This is done more efficiently using TP.extract(seed, c) to extract the sibling path path for leaf c from TreePRG and sending this instead. The prover also sends the initial commitment com_c and communications $([\alpha]_c, [\beta]_c)$ for the hidden (leaf) party, and aux in case that c $\neq N^D - 1$. Note that the communication shares would not have to be sent for the IDS as they are already part of w. However, we send them as we want Hypercube-SDitH to be commitment-recoverable.

Verification. The verifier first recomputes the commitment hash w_1 by computing commitments $\{com_i'\}_{i \neq c}$ for each of the states of the $N^D - 1$ leaf parties that have been revealed, and then combining with com_c to compute w_1'. Next the verifier expands the commitment hash to get the evaluation points and masks, and compiles the polynomial shares for each of the main parties from the given state information. Once this is done, they execute the MPCitH protocol on main parties as in the original SDitH proposal [14] for each of the D dimensions k using $[\![\alpha]\!]_c, [\![\beta]\!]_c$. Here we exploit that by linearity of the calculations of $[\alpha]$ and $[\beta]$ the communications of the main party k, i'_k that contains the unopened leaf party c can be computed by assembling the respective leaf party shares, and that $v = 0$ when determine $[v]_{k,c_k}$. The final main party communications and output shares $\{[\alpha]_{k,j}, [\beta]_{k,j}, [v]_{k,j}\}_{j=0}^{N-1}$ for each dimension $k \in \{0, \ldots, D-1\}$ are then assembled to obtain w'_2. This part also represents the commitment recovery algorithm Rcvr for Hypercube-SDitH. The final output is the result of the comparison $(\mathsf{w}'_1, \mathsf{w}'_2) \overset{?}{=} \mathsf{w}$.

Parallel composition (Π). In the above, we did describe the routines performed in the atomic three round IDS ($\tau = 1$), which takes soundness error $\simeq 1/N^D$. In order to reach negligible soundness error of 2^{-n} one can repeat the IDS many times independently in parallel such that $(1/N^D)^\tau \leq 2^{-n}$.

However, we note here that since the evaluation points are generated offline by the prover, it is possible to make the polynomial test harder to cheat by deriving the challenge points from a hash of the commitments com from all τ parallel repetitions. Denote the τ-fold parallel IDS as Π. Then to generate the challenge points/masking point pairs $\left\{ \{r_i^j, \varepsilon_i^j\}_{i=0}^{t-1} \right\}_{j=0}^{\tau-1}$ we take $\mathsf{w}_1 = \mathsf{PRG} \circ \mathsf{Hash}(\mathsf{com}_1, \ldots, \mathsf{com}_{\tau N^D - 1})$, therefore the evaluation points for all τ repetitions depend on the state commitments of all leaves in the entire τ-fold protocol Π.

3 Security of the 3-Round IDS

In this section we discuss the security of our IDS. We prove that the IDS is multi-transcript honest-verifier zero-knowledge (HVZK) and has special-soundness. We begin with HVZK proving the following theorem:

Theorem 1 (Honest-Verifier Zero Knowledge (HVZK)). *The algorithm* Sim_Π *shown in Alg. 3 is an HVZK simulator for* Π *such that for any quantum algorithm* A *in distinguishing* Trans_Π *from* Sim_Π *making at most* q_{zk} *queries to its oracle there exist algorithms* B– *distinguishing the outputs of* TreePRG *from random – and* C– *breaking the hiding property of* Com– *which fulfill*

$$\mathsf{Adv}_{\Pi,\mathsf{Sim}}^{\mathsf{hvzk}}(\mathsf{A}) := \left| \Pr[1 \leftarrow \mathsf{A}^{\mathsf{Sim}_\Pi}] - \Pr[1 \leftarrow \mathsf{A}^{\mathsf{Trans}_\Pi}] \right|$$
$$\leq q_{zk}\tau(\mathsf{Adv}_{\mathsf{Com}}^{\mathsf{hide}}(\mathsf{C}) + \mathsf{Adv}_{\mathsf{TreePRG}}^{\mathsf{ror}}(\mathsf{B})),$$

where B *and* C *run in time* $\mathsf{TIME}(\mathsf{B}) = \mathsf{TIME}(\mathsf{C}) = \mathsf{TIME}(\mathsf{A}) + \mathsf{TIME}(\mathsf{Trans})$ *respectively.*

On a high level, our proof follows a sequence of game hops, where we slowly change the oracle given to the adversary. We start with Trans, i.e., the honest execution of the protocol, in GAME_0. First, we switch the order of operations

---

Algorithm 3. HVZK simulator Sim_Π (Simplified version $[\tau = 1]$)

Step 1: Sample challenge.

1: $c \leftarrow \{0, \ldots, N^D - 1\}$.

Step 2: generate N^D leaf party states and witness shares.

2: Sample sibling path $\mathsf{path} \leftarrow\!\!\$\ \{0,1\}^{n \times \log_2 N^D}$ for leaf c and $\{(\mathsf{seed}_c, \rho_c)\} \leftarrow\!\!\$\ \{0,1\}^n$.

3: **for** $i' \neq c$ **do**

4:     Generate $\{(\mathsf{seed}_i, \rho_i)\}$ via $\mathsf{TreePRG}(\mathsf{path})$ and PRG.

5:     **if** $i' \neq N^D - 1$ **then**

6:         Set $\mathsf{state}_i = \mathsf{seed}_i$.

7:         Expand seed_i into witness shares.

8:     **else**

9:         To generate aux for the last leaf party, $i' = N^D - 1$, randomly draw
             $[\![x_A]\!]_{N^D - 1}$, $[\![Q]\!]_{N^D - 1}$, $[\![P]\!]_{N^D - 1}$, and $[\![c]\!]_{N^D - 1}$.

10:        Set $\mathsf{state}_{N^D - 1} = (\mathsf{seed}_{N^D - 1} \| aux)$.

Step 3: generate leaf party commitments

11: **for** $i' \neq c$ **do** Compute $\mathsf{com}_{i'} = \mathsf{Hash}(\mathsf{state}_{i'}, \rho_{i'})$

12: Draw com_c at random.

13: Compute commitment hash $\mathsf{w}_1 = \mathsf{Hash}(\mathsf{com}_0, \ldots, \mathsf{com}_{i*}, \ldots, \mathsf{com}_{N^D - 1})$.

Step 4: compute evaluation points

14: $\{r_l, \epsilon_l\}_{l=1}^t \leftarrow \mathsf{PRG}(\mathsf{w}_1)$

Step 5: generate party communications

15: Draw $[\![\alpha]\!]_c$ and $[\![\beta]\!]_c$ uniformly at random from their respective domains.

16: **for** $k \in \{0, \ldots, D-1\}$ **do**

17:     Let the main party to which c belongs be (k, j^*)

18:     **for** $(k, j) \neq (k, j^*)$ **do**

19:         Compute communications $[\alpha]_{k,j^*}, [\beta]_{k,j^*}, [v]_{k,j^*}$ following Alg. 1

20:     **for** (k, j^*) **do**

21:         Compute party communication shares $[\alpha]_{k,j^*}, [\beta]_{k,j^*}, [v]_{k,j^*}$ by running Π
            on the sum of the witnesses of the $N^{D-1} - 1$ *revealed* leaf parties in main party
            (k, j^*), as described in Algorithm 1, then add on $[\![\alpha]\!]_c$ and $[\![\beta]\!]_c$.

22:         Set $v_c = -\sum_{i' \neq c} [\![v]\!]$.

Step 6: Output transcript $((\mathsf{w}_1, \mathsf{w}_2), c, z)$:

23: $\mathsf{w}_2 = \{\{[\alpha]_{(k,j)}, [\beta]_{(k,j)}, [v]_{(k,j)}\}_{k=0}^{D-1}\}_{j=0}^{N-1}$, $c = c$

24: $z = \mathsf{com}_c, \{(\mathsf{state}_c, \rho_c) \forall i \neq c\}$.

---

and sample the challenges first. This defines GAME_1. In GAME_2, we replace the seed seed_c and the commitment pseudorandomness ρ_c for the commitments that remain unopened by truly random bits. To be consistent with $\mathsf{TreePRG}$, we also sample a random sibling path path which we use to derive the values for the opened commitments. This whole change is only detectable up to a τ-fold distinguishing advantage against $\mathsf{TreePRG}$ per oracle query. Next, we replace the state of the unopened parties by truly random bits in GAME_3. This is undetectable up to a τ-fold advantage against the hiding property of the commitment scheme per oracle query. Now, the distribution of the auxiliary state (of party $N^D - 1$) is independent of the sum of the other shares. Hence, in GAME_4 we sample that state uniformly at random. To preserve consistency of the communications, we compute the communications of all opened parties using the original algorithm. Then we compute the communication of the unopened parties to agree with these. Now we don't need the secret key anymore and observe that the oracle in GAME$_4$ corresponds to Sim. The full proof can be found in the full version [3].

We now move on to prove soundness of Π. Maybe not surprisingly, this is based on the binding property of the used commitment and the soundness of the non-interactive polynomial test which we prove first.

Soundness of the Non-interactive Polynomial Test. Here, we prove a query lower bound on the oracle search problem of finding inputs x, P and Q that "cheat" on the polynomial test implemented as MPC computation in Commit of Π (c.f., Algorithm 1). More generally, we will show concrete query lower bounds for the *family* of search problems where the goal is to cheat ℓ out of τ parallel repetitions of the polynomial test, where the challenge points for all repetitions are generated by hashing all commitments together.

We begin by finding a more abstract formulation that is a common generalization of all the mentioned problems of cheating (some of) the polynomial zero tests. To that end, let $\mathcal{P}(P_1, ..., P_{n_p})$ be a predicate on polynomials $P_i \in \mathfrak{P}_i \subset \mathbb{F}_{\text{poly}}[X], i = 1, ..., n_p$. The domains $\mathfrak{P}_i$ can be different for every polynomial and can, e.g., reflect degree limitations (e.g. for polynomials P and Q in Π) or that a polynomial has been obtained via interpolation (e.g. for polynomial S in Π). Let $\mathbf{T} = (T_1, ..., T_{n_t})$ be a list of test polynomials $T_i \in R[X_1, ..., X_{n_p}], i = 1, ..., n_t$ for $R = \mathbb{F}_{\text{poly}}[X]$ such that $\mathcal{P}(\mathbf{P}) = 0 \implies T_i(\mathbf{P}) = 0$ for all i, where $\mathbf{P} = (P_1, ..., P_{n_p}) \in \mathfrak{P} = \mathfrak{P}_1 \times \mathfrak{P}_2 \times ... \times \mathfrak{P}_{n_p}$.[1] In addition, let $\mathcal{M}$ be a randomized algorithm that takes as input a testing polynomial T, a tuple of polynomials $\mathbf{P}$, an evaluation point r and a random masking point $\epsilon \in \mathfrak{E}$, with the purpose that if $T(\mathbf{P})(r) \neq 0$ then the probability that $\mathcal{M}$ outputs 0 is small. We define the false-positive probability

$$p_{\mathbf{T},\ell}^{\text{fp}} = \max_{\mathbf{P}:\mathcal{P}(\mathbf{P})=1} \left(\Pr_{\substack{r \leftarrow \mathbb{F}_{\text{points}}^{n_t} \\ \epsilon \leftarrow \mathfrak{E}^{n_t}}} \left[|\{i \in [n_t] | \mathcal{M}(T_i, \mathbf{P}, r; \epsilon_i) = 0\}| \geq \ell \right] \right), \quad (1)$$

where the maximum is over $\mathbf{P} = (P_1, ..., P_{n_p})$ such that $P_i \in \mathfrak{P}_i$. In words, this is the maximum probability for any set of polynomials that doesn't fulfil the predicate to pass a test where each testing polynomials T_i is evaluated at a random point using $\mathcal{M}$, and at least ℓ of the results are 0.

In Round 1 of Π, $\mathbf{P}$ is secret shared. The secret shares of $\mathbf{P}$ are generated using a two stage PRG structure, first using TreePRG to generate seeds $seed_i$ from a single root seed $seed$ followed by PRG to expand the $seed_i$ into secret shares, commitment randomness, and other objects irrelevant here). The evaluation points and masks for the polynomial test are then derived from the individual commitments to all $seed_i$ by hashing all these commitments together. This complicates the analysis because this three-step process is not exactly indistinguishable from a random oracle. We will not need the pseudorandomness properties to give a query bound for our search problems. For

---

[1] In our application, we only need T_i with coefficients in $\mathbb{F}_{\text{poly}} \subset \mathbb{F}_{\text{poly}}[X]$.

Algorithm 4. Abstract non-interactive polynomial zero test for secret-shared polynomials $\mathcal{T}$

Input: Secret-shared polynomials $(state_i, \rho_i)_{i=1}^{n_c}$, threshold ℓ
Output: Boolean value $b \in \{0, 1\}$.

$state = (state_i)_{i=1}^{n_c}$
$\mathbf{P} = \mathcal{R}(state)$
$com_i = \text{Com}(state_i, \rho_i)$ for all $i = 1, \ldots, n_c$
$\left((r_{i,j})_{(i,j) \in [n_t] \times [t]}, (\epsilon_{i,j})_{(i,j) \in [n_t] \times [t]}\right) = G((com_i)_{i=1}^{n_c})$

Perform zero checks:
count$= 0$
for $i \in [n_t]$ **do**
    for $j \in [t]$ **do**
        if $\mathcal{M}(T_i, \mathbf{P}, r_{i,j}; \epsilon_{i,j}) = 0$ **then**
            count$=$count$+1$
$b = 1$
if count$\geq \ell$ **then** $b = 0$
return b

---

this section it is sufficient to define two black box algorithms $\mathcal{S}$, and $\mathcal{R}$ which abstract away the generation of the secret shared values and their recombination as follows: $\mathcal{S}(\mathbf{P}; seed) = (state_i, \rho_i)_{i=1}^{n_c}$ and $\mathcal{R}(state) = \mathbf{P}$, where we set $state = (state_i)_{i=1}^{n_c}$. Let $\mathfrak{S}$ be such that $(state_i, \rho_i) \in \mathfrak{S}$ for all i, $\mathbf{T}$ a tuple of testing polynomials for a predicate $\mathcal{P}$, t a non-negative integer and $\text{Com} : \mathfrak{S} \to \mathfrak{C}$ and $G : \mathfrak{C}^{n_c} \to \mathbb{F}_{\text{points}}^{2t \cdot n_t}$ two hash functions modeling the commitment scheme and the use of PRG for computing the challenge points and masks. We define the abstract non-interactive polynomial zero test algorithm $\mathcal{T}$ in Algorithm 4.

We now model the hash functions Com and G as random oracles. The most natural oracle search problem associated with the task of cheating the polynomial test in Algorithm 4 would be to find inputs $\mathbf{P}$ and $seed$ such that $\mathcal{P}(\mathbf{P}) = 1$, i.e., the predicate is not satisfied, yet $\mathbf{P}$ evaluates to zero at the challenge points, i.e. running algorithm $\mathcal{S}$ followed by $\mathcal{T}$ (Algorithm 4) returns 0. Unfortunately, a special soundness extractor for Π cannot solve this problem, as the root seed is never revealed. A search problem that can be solved using a special soundness extractor for the protocol in Algs. 1 and 2 is to find $(state_i, \rho_i)_{i=1}^{n_c}$ such that for $\mathcal{R}(state) = \mathbf{P}$ we have $\mathcal{P}(\mathbf{P}) = 1$ but executing Algorithm 4 directly results in output $b = 0$. We are now ready to define our search problem.

Definition 5 (Non-interactive polynomial zero test cheating problem).
Let $\mathcal{P}, \mathbf{T}, t$ be as above. An oracle algorithm $\mathsf{A}^{\text{Com}, G}$ with access to random oracles Com *and G as above solves the non-interactive polynomial zero test cheating problem* $\text{Cheat}_{\mathcal{P}, \mathbf{T}, t, \ell}$ *if it outputs* $o = (state_i, \rho_i)_{i=1}^{n_c}$ *such that $\mathcal{P}(\mathcal{R}(o)) = 1$ but* $\mathcal{T}_{\mathbf{T}, t}(o, \ell) = 0$.

We first give a query bound for the case where A has classical oracle access only. In the following, for $O \in \{\text{Com}, G\}$, let D_O be the list of pairs $(x, O(x))$ for queries x made by A to its oracle O. We overload the list symbols by writing

$$D_O(x) = \begin{cases} y & (x,y) \in D_O \\ \perp & \text{else.} \end{cases}$$

Remark 1. We can now regard Com and G as domain-separated parts of the same random oracle F. We assume that F has a sufficiently large output space $\mathfrak{F}$ and introduce truncation functions trunc_O such that $\text{Com} = \text{trunc}_{\text{Com}} \circ F|_{\mathfrak{S}}$ and $G = \text{trunc}_G \circ F|_{\mathfrak{C}^{n_c}}$. We let D be the query list for F. The lists D_O for $O \in \{\text{Com}, G\}$ are obtained as sublists of D with trunc_O applied to all outputs. In the following, we try to keep the notation lean by omitting the truncation functions.

Following [10] we call a predicate on query lists a *database property*. For database properties P and Q, the classical transition capacity is defined as

$$[P \to Q] = \max_{\substack{L:P(D) \\ s \in \mathfrak{S} \cup \mathfrak{C}^{n_c}}} \Pr_{u \leftarrow \mathfrak{F}}[Q(D \cup (s,u))].$$

Here, $D \cup (s,u)$ denotes the query list D with the pair (s,u) added if D did not contain a pair (s,y) yet. The proof strategy for the following theorems bears some similarity to the proof of Lemma 4.1 in [12].

Theorem 2. *Let* $\mathsf{A}^{\text{Com},G}$ *be an algorithm that makes* q_{Com}, *and* q_G *classical queries to its oracles* Com, *and* G, *respectively and let* $q = q_{\text{Com}} + q_G$. *Then*

$$\Pr_{o \leftarrow \mathsf{A}^{\text{Com},G}}[(\mathcal{P}(\mathcal{R}(o)) = 1) \wedge (\mathcal{T}(o,\ell) = 0)] \leq (q + n_c + 1) \max\left(p_{\mathbf{T},\ell}^{\text{fp}}, n_c \frac{q_G}{|\mathfrak{C}|} \right).$$

Proof. We denote by $\mathcal{T}_D$ the variant of the zero test $\mathcal{T}$ where for $O \in \{\text{Com}, G\}$, any call to the oracle O is replaced by a call to D_O. If any such call outputs $\perp$, $\mathcal{T}_D$ outputs $\perp$. Let $\mathsf{A}^{\text{Com},G}$ be an algorithm as in the theorem statement. We define $\mathsf{A}'^{\text{Com},G}$ as follows. $\mathsf{A}'^{\text{Com},G}$ computes $o \leftarrow \mathsf{A}^{\text{Com},G}$, makes queries $\text{com}_i = \text{Com}(o_i)$ and $\mathbf{r} = G(\text{com}_1, \ldots, \text{com}_{n_c})$, and outputs o. Now we have

$$\Pr_{o \leftarrow \mathsf{A}^{\text{Com},G}}[(\mathcal{P}(\mathcal{R}(o)) = 1) \wedge (\mathcal{T}(o,\ell) = 0)] = \Pr_{o \leftarrow \mathsf{A}'^{\text{Com},G}}[(\mathcal{P}(\mathcal{R}(o)) = 1) \wedge (\mathcal{T}_D(o,\ell) = 0)]$$

$$\leq \Pr_{o \leftarrow \mathsf{A}'^{\text{Com},G}}[\exists o' : (\mathcal{P}(\mathcal{R}(o')) = 1) \wedge (\mathcal{T}_D(o',\ell) = 0)]. \tag{2}$$

On an intuitive level the above inequality reflect the fact that the adversary A′ is guaranteed to perform the test $\mathcal{T}$ on its own output, so if the test checks out, a combination of input-output pairs which certifies the existence of a successful output can be found in the query list. The event in the last probability expression defines the database property

$$\text{Found}(D) = (\exists o' : \mathcal{P}(\mathcal{R}(o')) = 1 \wedge \mathcal{T}_D(o') = 0).$$

Now let D_i be the list of queries after A' has been run until its ith query (of any kind). Clearly, Found(D_i) $\implies$ Found(D). We thus get

$$\Pr[\text{Found}(D)] = \Pr[\text{Found}(D_{\tilde{q}})] = \sum_{k=1}^{\tilde{q}} \Pr[\text{Found}(D_k) \wedge \neg\text{Found}(D_{k-1})]$$

$$\leq \sum_{k=1}^{\tilde{q}} [\neg\text{Found} \wedge (|D| \leq k-1) \to \text{Found}], \tag{3}$$

where the right hand side represents the sum of transition probabilities, and

$$\tilde{q} = q + n_c + 1. \tag{4}$$

It remains to bound the transition capacities in the sum. For this we now make a case distinction. Setting $P = \neg\text{Found} \wedge (|D| \leq k-1)$, we have

$$[P \to \text{Found}] = \max_{\substack{D:P(D) \\ s \in \mathfrak{S} \cup \mathfrak{C}^{n_c}}} \Pr_{u \leftarrow \mathfrak{F}}[\text{Found}(D \cup (s, u))]$$

$$= \max \left(\max_{\substack{D:P(D) \\ s \in \mathfrak{S}}} \Pr_{u \leftarrow \mathfrak{F}}[\text{Found}(D \cup (s, u))], \max_{\substack{D:P(D) \\ s \in \mathfrak{C}^{n_c}}} \Pr_{u \leftarrow \mathfrak{F}}[\text{Found}(D \cup (s, u))] \right)$$

If $\neg\text{Found}(D)$ and $\text{Found}(D \cup (s, u))$ for some $s \in \mathfrak{S}$, then there exist $i \in n_c$ and $(o_{i'}, \text{com}_{i'}) \in D_{\text{Com}}$ for $i' \neq i$ such that $(\text{com}_1, \ldots, \text{com}_{i-1}, u, \text{com}_{i+1}, \ldots, \text{com}_{n_c}) \in D_G$. Upper-bounding the first event by 1, we obtain the bound

$$\max_{\substack{D:P(D) \\ s \in \mathfrak{S}}} \Pr_{u \leftarrow \mathfrak{F}}[\text{Found}(D \cup (s, u))] \leq n_c |D_G||\mathfrak{C}|^{-1} \leq n_c q_G |\mathfrak{C}|^{-1}, \tag{5}$$

as for each entry of D_G there are n_c targets for the output of Com to match. If $\neg\text{Found}(D)$ and $\text{Found}(D \cup (s, u))$ for some $s \in \mathfrak{C}^{n_c}$, then $(o_i, \text{com}_i) \in D_{\text{Com}}$ for $i \in [n_c]$ such that $s = (\text{com}_1, \ldots, \text{com}_{n_c})$, and $\mathbf{T}(\mathcal{R}(o_1, \ldots, o_{n_c}))(G(x)) = 0$. Based on only the last condition, we get

$$\max_{\substack{D:P(D) \\ s \in \mathfrak{C}^{n_c}}} \Pr_{u \leftarrow \mathfrak{F}}[\text{Found}(D \cup (s, u))] \leq p_{\mathbf{T},\ell}^{\text{fp}} \tag{6}$$

Combining the last three equations we get

$$\Pr[\text{Found}(L)] = \tilde{q} \max \left(p_{\mathbf{T},\ell}^{\text{fp}}, n_c q_G |\mathfrak{C}|^{-1} \right). \tag{7}$$

Combining Equations (2), (3) and (7) yields the desired bound. $\qquad\square$

We now move on to bound the success probability of an algorithm trying to solve $\text{Cheat}_{P,\mathbf{T},t}$ given quantum access to the random oracle(s). This is necessary to later prove the security of our digital signature scheme in the quantum-accessible random oracle model (QROM).

In [10], a generic method for proving such bounds is introduced that essentially generalizes (a very general version of) the technique used in the proof of Theorem 2 to the QROM. Their technique uses Zhandry's compressed oracle method [34], but their results are sufficiently versatile to allow us to prove our desired bound without introducing compressed oracles.

In fact, we need to prove a bound in a slightly stronger model. As we will use the technique of [12] to construct a special soundness adversary from an adversary against the signature scheme, that special soundness adversary can only work in a model where the quantum-accessible random oracle is instantiated with the efficient oracle simulation via Zhandry's compressed oracle, and any adversary can proceed by i) making a number of queries to the oracle, ii) obtain the measurement outcome of measuring the internal state of the oracle simulation, and iii) computing the output. The measured internal state of the oracle essentially contains a query transcript of the adversarial algorithm. A classical adversary can just compile such a query transcript themselves, without relying on augmented access to the random oracle. In the quantum setting, the no-cloning principle prevents the adversary from recording a query transcript. This can be an issue if the adversary has a black-box subroutine that makes queries and relies knowledge of these queries. For solving an oracle search problem, however, the additional power of obtaining the measured query transcript does not help. It is important to notice that we use this model as a proof tool and don't have to ascribe it any predictive power for real-world hash functions. We call this model QROM+. In the full version [3], we prove the following lemma, specializing and slightly improving a combination of results from [10].

Lemma 1 (A compressed oracle query bound lemma). *Let $F : \mathcal{X} \to \mathcal{Y}$ be a random oracle and let $\mathcal{P}^F$ be a predicate on some set $\mathcal{Z}$ that can be computed using at most $q_\mathcal{P}$ classical queries to F. Let further A^F be a QROM+ algorithm making at most q quantum queries to F and outputing $z \in \mathcal{Z}$. Then*

$$\sqrt{\Pr_{z \leftarrow A^F}[P(z)]} \leq \sum_{k=1}^{q+q_\mathcal{P}} \max_{\substack{x,D: \\ |D| \leq k \\ \neg\mathsf{Found}(D)}} \sqrt{10 \Pr_{u \leftarrow \mathcal{Y}}[\mathsf{Found}_\mathcal{P}(D[x \mapsto u])]} \qquad (8)$$

where $\mathsf{Found}_\mathcal{P}$ is the database property

$$\mathsf{Found}_\mathcal{P} = (\exists z \in \mathcal{Z} : \mathcal{P}^D(z)) \qquad (9)$$

and $\mathcal{P}^D$ is the algorithm that computes $\mathcal{P}$ but makes queries to D instead of F, and if any query returns $\bot$, $\mathcal{P}^D$ ouputs 'false'.

We use this lemma to prove a quantum query complexity bound for $\mathsf{Cheat}_{\mathcal{P},\mathbf{T},t,\ell}$.

Theorem 3. *Let $A^{\mathsf{Com},G}$ be a QROM+ algorithm that makes q_{Com} and q_G quantum queries to its oracles Com and G, respectively, and let $\tilde{q} = q_{\mathsf{Com}} + q_G + n_c + 1$. Then*

$$\Pr_{o \leftarrow A^{\mathsf{Com},G}}[\mathcal{P}(\mathcal{R}(o)) = 1 \wedge \mathcal{T}(o, \ell) = 0] \leq 10 \cdot \begin{cases} \tilde{q}^2 p_{\mathbf{T},\ell}^{\mathsf{fp}} & \text{if } n_c \tilde{q} \leq p_{\mathbf{T},\ell}^{\mathsf{fp}} |\mathcal{C}| \\ n_c \frac{\tilde{q}^3}{|\mathcal{C}|} & \text{else.} \end{cases}$$

Proof. We again view the two random oracles as being constructed from a single one using domain separation and truncation, see Remark 1. Using the same reasoning as for Equations (5) and (6), but without taking a maximal size of the sub-database corresponding to G into account, we get for $|D| \leq k$ that

$$\Pr_{u \leftarrow \mathfrak{F}}[\mathsf{Found}_{\mathcal{P}}(D[x \mapsto u])] \leq \max\left(p_{\mathbf{T},\ell}^{\mathrm{fp}}, n_c k |\mathfrak{C}|^{-1}\right).$$

Suppose now first that $n_c \tilde{q} \leq p_{\mathbf{T},\ell}^{\mathrm{fp}} |\mathfrak{C}|$. Then we have $n_c k |\mathfrak{C}|^{-1} \leq n_c \tilde{q} |\mathfrak{C}|^{-1} \leq p_{\mathbf{T},\ell}^{\mathrm{fp}}$ and thus $\max(p_{\mathbf{T},\ell}^{\mathrm{fp}}, n_c k |\mathfrak{C}|^{-1}) = p_{\mathbf{T},\ell}^{\mathrm{fp}}$. If on the other hand $n_c \tilde{q} > p_{\mathbf{T},\ell}^{\mathrm{fp}} |\mathfrak{C}|$, we have $\max(p_{\mathbf{T},\ell}^{\mathrm{fp}}, n_c k |\mathfrak{C}|^{-1}) \leq \max\left(p_{\mathbf{T},\ell}^{\mathrm{fp}}, n_c \tilde{q} |\mathfrak{C}|^{-1}\right) = n_c \tilde{q} |\mathfrak{C}|^{-1}$. Note that the predicate checking whether A has solved $\mathsf{Cheat}_{\mathcal{P},\mathbf{T},t}$ makes $n_c + 1$ queries. Setting

$$\eta = \begin{cases} p_{\mathbf{T},\ell}^{\mathrm{fp}} & \text{if } n_c \tilde{q} \leq p_{\mathbf{T},\ell}^{\mathrm{fp}} |\mathfrak{C}| \\ n_c \frac{\tilde{q}}{|\mathfrak{C}|} & \text{else,} \end{cases}$$

we apply Lemma 1 to obtain

$$\sqrt{\Pr_{o \leftarrow \mathsf{A}^{\mathrm{Com},G}}[\mathcal{P}(\mathcal{R}(o)) = 1 \wedge \mathcal{T}(o,\ell) = 0]} \leq \sum_{k=1}^{\tilde{q}} \max_{\substack{x,D: \\ |D| \leq k \\ \neg \mathsf{Found}(D)}} \sqrt{10 \Pr_{u \leftarrow y}[\mathsf{Found}_{\mathcal{P}}(D[x \mapsto u])]}$$

$$\leq \sum_{k=1}^{\tilde{q}} \sqrt{10\eta} = \tilde{q}\sqrt{10\eta}.$$

Squaring both sides of the inequality yields the desired bound.   □

We proceed to apply the above theorems to the particular polynomial zero test that appears in Hypercube-SDitH. In this test, there are τ parallel repetitions of the atomic test described in Section 2.3, and the evaluation points for all of them are generated by hashing all commitments together. Each test involves 3 polynomials in addition to the public polynomial F, , i.e. we have $n_p = 3\tau + 1$. Denoting the polynomials involved in the ith test by $S^{(i)}, P^{(i)}, Q^{(i)}$ and F, we set $P_i = S^{(i)}$, $P_{\tau+i} = P^{(i)}$ and $P_{2\tau+i} = Q^{(i)}$ for $i = 1, \ldots, \tau$, and $P_{3\tau+1} = F$. We define the corresponding domains. For $i = 1, \ldots, \tau$ we set

$$\mathfrak{P}_i = \{S \in \mathbb{F}_{\mathrm{poly}}[X] | \deg(S) \leq m\}, \qquad \mathfrak{P}_{\tau+i} = \mathbb{F}_{\mathrm{poly}}[X]$$
$$\mathfrak{P}_{2\tau+i} = \{Q \in \mathbb{F}_{\mathrm{poly}}[X] | Q(x) = x^{\omega} + Q'(x) \text{ with } \deg(Q') \leq \omega - 1\}, \text{ and}$$
$$\mathfrak{P}_{3\tau+1} = \{F\}.$$

The predicate $\mathcal{P}$ is defined by

$$\mathcal{P}(\mathbf{P}) = \neg(\exists i \in [\tau] : P_i P_{2\tau+i} = P_{\tau+i} P_{3\tau+1}) \tag{10}$$

and $T_i = P_i P_{2\tau+i} - P_{\tau+i} P_{3\tau+1}$. The intuition behind this predicate is, that any one out of the τ sets of four polynomials can be used to extract the secret key if it fulfils the polynomial identity. Define

$$p = \max_{\mathbf{P}:T_i(\mathbf{P}) \neq 0} \Pr_{(r,\epsilon) \leftarrow \mathbb{F}_{\mathrm{points}}^2}[\mathcal{M}(T_i, \mathbf{P}, r; \epsilon) = 0]. \tag{11}$$

A bound for this probability can be obtained as follows. The polynomial $SQ - FP$ is non-zero and has degree at most $m + w - 1$. Setting $|\mathbb{F}_{\text{points}}| = \Delta$, we get

$$\Pr_{r \leftarrow \mathbb{F}_{\text{points}}} [(SQ - FP)(r) = 0] \leq \frac{m + \omega - 1}{\Delta}.$$

If $(SQ - FP)(r) \neq 0$, the product verification fails with probability $\frac{1}{\Delta}$. We get

$$p \leq \frac{m + \omega - 1}{\Delta} + \left(1 - \frac{m + \omega - 1}{\Delta}\right)\frac{1}{\Delta} = \frac{m + \omega}{\Delta} - \frac{m + \omega - 1}{\Delta^2}. \tag{12}$$

The t evaluation points and t masks are sampled independently, so the false positive probability for a single test with t points is just p^t. The probability that the t tests with random masks and evaluation points all fail for T_i, for all $i \in J \subset [\tau]$ with $|J| = \ell$ is just $p^{t\ell}$. Via a union bound, we obtain

$$p_{\mathbf{T},\ell}^{\text{fp}} \leq \binom{\tau}{\ell} p^{t\ell}.$$

Combining the discussion above, we get the following

Corollary 1. *Let* $\mathsf{A}^{\mathsf{Com},G}$ *be an adversary that makes* q_{Com}, *and* q_G *queries to its oracles* Com, *and* G, *respectively, and let* $\tilde{q} = q_{\mathsf{Com}} + q_G + n_c + 1$, *where* $n_c = \tau \cdot N^D$ *is the number of commitments. The probability that its output wins* $\mathsf{Cheat}_{\mathcal{P},\mathbf{T},t,\ell}$ *in this case is bounded by*

$$\Pr_{o \leftarrow \mathsf{A}^{\mathsf{Com},G}}[\mathcal{P}(\mathcal{R}(o)) = 1 \wedge \mathcal{T}(o, \ell) = 0] \leq \tilde{q} \max\left(\binom{\tau}{\ell} p^{t\ell}, \tau \cdot N^D \frac{q_G}{2^c}\right) \quad (ROM)$$

$$\Pr_{o \leftarrow \mathsf{A}^{\mathsf{Com},G}}[\mathcal{P}(\mathcal{R}(o)) = 1 \wedge \mathcal{T}(o, \ell) = 0] \leq 10 \cdot \begin{cases} \tilde{q}^2\binom{\tau}{\ell} p^{t\ell} & \text{if } \tilde{q} \leq \binom{\tau}{\ell} p^{t\ell} 2^c \\ \tau \cdot N^D \frac{\tilde{q}^3}{2^c} & \text{else} \end{cases} \quad (QROM+)$$

Distance-d Special Soundness in the QROM+. We now use Cor. 1 to prove that the identification scheme in Algs. 1 and 2 has query-bounded distance-d special soundness. The special soundness extractor $\mathsf{Ext}_d^{\mathsf{Com},G}$ is straightforward: Given two valid transcripts with the same w and challenges of distance d, for all repetitions i where the challenges differ do the following: If the openings are not consistent, abort. Here consistency means that all openings of the same commitments agree. Otherwise, reconstruct x from the secret shares and check if $Hx = y$ and $wt(x) \leq \omega$. If not, move on to the next i, if yes, output x.

Theorem 4. *Our identification scheme* Π *has query-bounded distance-d special soundness. More precisely, let* $\mathsf{A}^{\mathsf{Com},G}$ *be a distance-d special soundness adversary making at most* q_{Com} *and* q_G *queries to its oracles* Com *and* G, *respectively, and set* $q = q_{\mathsf{Com}} + q_G$ *and* $\tilde{q} = q + \tau \cdot N^D + 1$. *Then the bounds*

$$\mathsf{Adv}_{\mathsf{IDS},\mathsf{Ext}}^{d-\mathsf{spS}}(\mathsf{A}) \leq \begin{cases} (\tau N^D + 1)\frac{\tilde{q}^2}{2^c} + \tilde{q}\binom{\tau}{d} p^{t \cdot d} & \text{in the ROM} \\ (10\tau N^D + 47)\frac{\tilde{q}^3}{2^c} + 10\tilde{q}^2\binom{\tau}{d} p^{t \cdot d} & \text{in the QROM+} \end{cases}$$

hold, where c is the output length of Com.

Proof. Given adversary A and extractor Ext_d, we construct adversaries B against the binding property of the commitment scheme and C against $\mathsf{Cheat}_{\mathcal{P},\mathbf{T},t,d}$ as follows. Let E be the event that the side-conditions for spS are fulfilled,

$$E = (\mathsf{Vrf}(\mathsf{pk},\mathsf{w}_i,\mathsf{c}_i,\mathsf{z}_i) = 1, i \in \{1,2\} \wedge (\mathsf{w}_1 = \mathsf{w}_2) \wedge d = \mathsf{Dist}(\mathsf{c}_1,\mathsf{c}_2)).$$

The adversary B runs $((\mathsf{w}_1,\mathsf{c}_1,\mathsf{z}_1),(\mathsf{w}_2,\mathsf{c}_2,\mathsf{z}_2)) \leftarrow \mathsf{A}^{\mathsf{Com},G}(\mathsf{pk})$. If z_1 and z_2 are consistent, B outputs $\perp$. Otherwise, B uses the inconsistency to break the binding property: Let com_i and $(state_i, \rho_i) \neq (\widetilde{state}_i, \tilde{\rho}_i)$ be a commitment and two distinct openings for it that are present in $((\mathsf{w}_1,\mathsf{c}_1,\mathsf{z}_1),(\mathsf{w}_2,\mathsf{c}_2,\mathsf{z}_2))$ causing the inconsistency of z_1 and z_2. The two transcripts are valid, so the openings must be as well. B outputs $(state_i, \rho_i),(\widetilde{state}_i, \tilde{\rho}_i)$.

The adversary C runs $((\mathsf{w}_1,\mathsf{c}_1,\mathsf{z}_1),(\mathsf{w}_2,\mathsf{c}_2,\mathsf{z}_2)) \leftarrow \mathsf{A}^{\mathsf{Com},G}(\mathsf{pk})$. If A aborts, C aborts. Otherwise, C outputs the set $(state_i, \rho_i)_{i=1}^{\tau \cdot N^D} = \mathsf{z}_1 \cup \mathsf{z}_2$.

Moreover, we observe that Ext_d successfully extracts a matching secret key for pk whenever A outputs transcripts such that E holds, B fails (i.e., z_1 and z_2 are consistent), and C fails (implying that the polynomial test was cheated for at most $d - 1$ challenges). The reason is that if B fails, we know that E will be able to extract $\mathbf{x}$ such that $\mathbf{Hx} = \mathbf{y}$ and the result of the polynomial zero test is 0, according to the correctness of the MPC protocol. If C fails, we additionally have that the polynomial test cannot have been cheated for all d challenges and therefore we can extract at least one $\mathbf{x}$ such that $\mathbf{Hx} = \mathbf{y}$ *and* $wt(\mathbf{x}) \leq w$.

Putting things together, we now bound the success probability of A. Consider the experiment where Ext_d, B and C use the same runs of A. The probabilities are taken over $(\mathsf{sk},\mathsf{pk}) \leftarrow \mathsf{Keygen}(); ((\mathsf{w}_1,\mathsf{c}_1,\mathsf{z}_1),(\mathsf{w}_2,\mathsf{c}_2,\mathsf{z}_2)) \leftarrow \mathsf{A}^{\mathsf{Com},G}(\mathsf{pk}); \mathsf{sk}' \leftarrow \mathsf{Ext}^{\mathsf{Com},G}((\mathsf{w}_1,\mathsf{c}_1,\mathsf{z}_1),(\mathsf{w}_2,\mathsf{c}_2,\mathsf{z}_2))$ and abusing notation we define the event that B or C succeed by B and C, respectively. We bound

$$\mathsf{Adv}_{\mathsf{IDS},\mathsf{Ext}}^{d-\mathsf{spS}}(\mathsf{A}) = \Pr[E \wedge (\mathsf{sk}',\mathsf{pk}) \notin \mathsf{Keygen}()]$$
$$\leq \Pr[E \wedge (A \vee B)] \leq \Pr[A] + \Pr[B],$$

where the inequality results from dropping the condition E and a union bound. Considering that we implement Com using a random oracle and applying a standard bound for collision finding in the ROM, we obtain

$$\Pr[B] \leq q^2 2^{-c} \quad , \text{ in the ROM}.$$

The bound in Theorem 5.29 in [10], for $k = 1$, which generalizes to the QROM+ by Lemma 2 in the full version [3], yields

$$\Pr[B] \leq 47(q+1)^3 2^{-c} \quad , \text{ in the QROM+}$$

after simplifying the constants. The adversary C plays the $\mathsf{Cheat}_{\mathcal{P},\mathbf{T},t,d}$ game. According to Corollary 1, we thus have

$$\Pr[C] \leq \begin{cases} \tilde{q}\left(\binom{\tau}{d} p^{t \cdot d} + \tau N^D \frac{q_G}{2^c}\right) & \text{in the ROM} \\ 10\tilde{q}^2 \binom{\tau}{d} p^{t \cdot d} + 10\tau N^D \frac{\tilde{q}^3}{2^c} & \text{in the QROM+} \end{cases}$$

Combining the inequalities with $q_G \leq q + 1 \leq \tilde{q}$ yields the claimed bound. $\square$

Sign(sk, m)	Vrfy(pk, m, $\sigma = (\mathsf{w}, \mathsf{z})$)
$(\mathsf{w}, \mathsf{st}) \leftarrow$ Commit(sk)	$\mathsf{c} = \mathsf{RO}(\mathsf{w}, m)$
$\mathsf{c} := \mathsf{RO}(\mathsf{w}, m)$	return Vrf(pk, w, c, z)
$\mathsf{z} \leftarrow$ Resp(sk, w, c, st)	
return $\sigma := (\mathsf{w}, \mathsf{z})$	

Fig. 1. Signing and verification algorithms of DSS = FS[IDS, RO].

4   The Signature Scheme

The main target of this paper is not the security of Π but that of the resulting signature scheme that we obtain by applying the Fiat-Shamir transform to it. This is what we focus on now. We first introduce the Fiat-Shamir transform and recall previous results, then we present our results for the security of the signature scheme. The definitions for signatures are available in the full version [3].

The Fiat-Shamir transform. Here we describe the standard Fiat-Shamir transform. To an identification scheme IDS = (Keygen, Commit, Resp, Vrf) with commitment space $\mathcal{COM}$, and random oracle RO : $\mathcal{COM} \times \mathcal{M} \to \mathcal{C}$ for some message space $\mathcal{M}$, we associate FS[IDS, RO] := DSS := (Keygen, Sign, Vrfy) , where algorithms Sign and Vrfy of DSS are defined in Fig. 1.

In [17] the following result was stated that relates the UF-NMA and UF-CMA security of a Fiat-Shamir transformed IDS in the QROM, and the HVZK property of the IDS. The bound makes use of what they call commitment entropy: $\gamma_{\mathsf{w}} :=$ $\mathbb{E} \max_{\mathsf{w}} \Pr[\mathsf{w}]$, where the expectation is taken over (pk, sk) $\leftarrow$ Keygen, and the probability is taken over $(\mathsf{w}, \mathsf{st}) \leftarrow$ Commit(sk).

Theorem 5. *[17, Theorem 3] For any (quantum) UF-CMA adversary A issuing at most q_S (classical) queries to the signing oracle* sign *and at most q_H quantum queries to* RO, *there exists a UF-NMA adversary B and a q_S-HVZK adversary C such that*

$$\mathrm{Succ}_{\mathsf{FS[IDS,RO]}}^{\mathsf{UF\text{-}CMA}} (A) \leq \mathrm{Succ}_{\mathsf{FS[IDS,RO]}}^{\mathsf{UF\text{-}NMA}} (B) + \mathrm{Adv}_{\mathsf{IDS}}^{q_S\text{-}\mathsf{HVZK}} (C)$$
$$+ \frac{3q_S}{2} \sqrt{(q_H + q_S + 1) \cdot \gamma_{\mathsf{w}}} \ , \tag{13}$$

and the running time of B and C is about that of A, where γ_{w} is the maximum over the probability that w *takes any given value. The bound given in Eq. (13) also holds for the modified Fiat-Shamir transform that defines challenges by letting* $\mathsf{c} := \mathsf{RO}(\mathsf{w}, m, \mathsf{pk})$ *instead of letting* $\mathsf{c} := \mathsf{RO}(\mathsf{w}, m)$.

In our actual construction, for efficiency reasons, we use a variant called Fiat-Shamir for *commitment-recoverable* IDS (see e.g., [23]), where the challenge c is sent instead of the first message w (sometimes referred to as the *commitment*). As defined in Sec. 2.1.1 a commitment-recoverable scheme like Π provides a function

Rcvr that allows to recover the first message from the other two Rcvr(c, z) = w. In Fiat-Shamir for commitment-recoverable IDS the verifier first *recovers* w using Rcvr and then checks that indeed c = RO(w, m). From a security perspective the two are equivalent as Rcvr allows to compute the values of a standard Fiat-Shamir signature from one resulting from a commitment recoverable scheme. The other direction, i.e., get c from w– RSP is not needed – is as simple as c = RO(w, m).

In our implementation, we use a nonce per signature, which we call *salt*. The nonce is included as a prefix in calls to all commitments, PRG operations, and Hash functions, in order to domain separate between distinct signature queries. This allows to minimize the impact of multi-target attacks. For the sake of readability, we do not consider the nonce in our formal security arguments (and therefore gain a loss in tightness) but we discuss the impact on practical security when selecting parameters.

4.1 Signature Scheme Security

The security of the signature scheme FS[Π, RO] obtained by applying the Fiat-Shamir transform to our three round IDS, can be argued in two steps as is commonly done. First, we show that we can turn any UF-NMA adversary against the scheme into an adversary against the special soundness of Π. This step follows the recipe of [12]. Afterwards, we apply Thm. 5 to argue full UF-CMA security. In [12], a tight online-extractability result is proven for the Fiat-Shamir transform of sigma-protocols with commit-and-open structure, both for simple random-oracle-based commitments and for tree commitments. The following is a specialized variant of the tree commitment variant of the result for query-bounded distance-d special soundness. We give a description of how the proof of Theorem 5.2 in [12] implies the below variant in the full version [3].

Theorem 6 (Variant of Theorem 5.2 from [12]). *Let $\Pi^{\mathsf{Com},G}$ be a distance-d special-sound commit-and-open identification scheme with ϕ-ary tree commitment with n_c leaves using a random oracle Com with output length c, splittable challenge, challenge space $\mathcal{C}^\tau$ and an additional random oracle G. Let further A be a UF-NMA-adversary against FS[Π, RO] making q_{RO}, q_{Com} and q_G queries to RO, Com and G respectively. Then there exists a (q_{Com}, q_G)-query QROM+ adversary B against the query-bounded distance-d special soundness of $\Pi^{\mathsf{Com},G}$ with respect to the special soundness extractor Ext_d of Π such that*

$$\mathsf{Adv}^{\mathsf{UF\text{-}NMA}}_{\mathsf{FS[IDS,RO]}}(\mathsf{A}) \leq \Pr[\mathsf{sk}' \leftarrow \mathsf{Ext}_d \circ \mathsf{B} : (\mathsf{sk}', \mathsf{pk}) \in \mathsf{Keygen}()]$$

$$+ \mathsf{Adv}^{d\text{-}\mathsf{spS}}_{\mathsf{IDS,Ext}}(\mathsf{B}) + (22n_c \log_\phi n_c + 60)q^3 2^{-c} + 20q^2 \frac{1}{|\mathcal{C}|^{\tau-d}},$$

where $q = q_{\mathsf{Com}} + q_{\mathsf{RO}}$. The runtime of B is bounded as $\mathsf{TIME}(\mathsf{B}) \leq \mathsf{TIME}(\mathsf{A}) + \gamma(q + q_G)^2))$, where γ is polynomial in the input and output lengths of the random oracles.

As a corollary, we get a UF-NMA-security result for our signature scheme in the QROM. We note that this corollary does not need to refer to the QROM+ anymore, as it combines a reduction to an adversary agains the query-bounded distance-d special soundness in the QROM+ with an explicit bound on the success probability of such an adversary.

Corollary 2. *Let A be a UF-NMA-adversary against FS[Π, RO] that makes $q_{RO} \geq \tau \cdot N^D + 1$, q_{Com} and q_G quantum queries to RO, Com and G respectively. Then for all $d = 0, 1, \ldots, \tau$ we get*

$$\mathrm{Adv}_{FS[IDS,RO]}^{UF\text{-}NMA} (A) \leq \epsilon_{SD} + (32\tau N^D + 107)\frac{q^3}{2^c} + 10 \cdot q^2 \binom{\tau}{d} p^{t \cdot d} + 20q^2 \frac{1}{N^{D \cdot (\tau - d)}}.$$

Here, ϵ_{SD} is the maximal success probability that an adversary with runtime $\mathrm{TIME}(A) + \mathrm{TIME}(\mathrm{CompOr}(q)) + \mathrm{TIME}(\mathrm{Ext}_d)$, *where* $\mathrm{TIME}(\mathrm{CompOr}(q))$ *is the runtime of a compressed oracle simulation for q queries, can solve syndrome decoding. Also $q = q_{Com} + q_{RO} + q_G$ is the total number of random oracle queries of A, c is the output length of Com, and the atomic polynomial zero test false-positive probability p is defined and bounded in Equation (11) and Equation (12).*

Note that the restriction on q_{RO} is almost without loss of generality ($\tau \cdot N^D + 1$, q_{Com} queries to RO can be made in time similar to, e.g., the signing time) and is only needed to allow for a less cluttered bound expression.

Proof. Π uses a commitment that works by hashing each state with some randomness, and then hashing all theses hashes together to produce a single collective commitment. This is a $\tau \cdot N^D$-ary tree commitment with $\tau \cdot N^D$ leaves, so we can apply Theorem 6 for these parameters. Plugging in the number of possible split-challenges N^D, we get

$$\mathrm{Adv}_{FS[IDS,RO]}^{UF\text{-}NMA} (A) \leq \Pr[\mathrm{sk}' \leftarrow \mathrm{Ext}_d \circ B : (\mathrm{sk}', \mathrm{pk}) \in \mathrm{Keygen}()]$$
$$+ \mathrm{Adv}_{IDS,Ext}^{d\text{-}spS} (B) + (22n_c + 60)q^3 2^{-c} + 20q^2 N^{-D \cdot (\tau - d)},$$

where c is the length of the commitments. $\Pr[\mathrm{sk}' \leftarrow \mathrm{Ext}_d \circ B : (\mathrm{sk}', \mathrm{pk}) \in \mathrm{Keygen}()]$ is the success probability of $\mathrm{Ext}_d \circ B$ as a syndrome decoding algorithm and thus

$$\Pr[\mathrm{sk}' \leftarrow \mathrm{Ext}_d \circ B : (\mathrm{sk}', \mathrm{pk}) \in \mathrm{Keygen}()] \leq \epsilon_{SD}.$$

Setting $\tilde{q} = q_{Com} + q_G + N^D + 1$, by Theorem 4, we have the bound

$$\mathrm{Adv}_{IDS,Ext}^{d\text{-}spS} (B) \leq (10\tau N^D + 47)\frac{\tilde{q}^3}{|\mathcal{C}|} + 10\tilde{q}^2 \binom{\tau}{d} p^{t \cdot d} \leq (10\tau N^D + 47)\frac{q^3}{|\mathcal{C}|} + 10q^2 \binom{\tau}{d} p^{t \cdot d}$$

where the second inequality holds because $\tilde{q} \leq q$ by assumption on q_{RO}. Combining the inequalities yields the desired bound. □

Finally we obtain a bound for the UF-CMA security as follows:

Corollary 3. *Let* A *be a* UF-CMA-*adversary against* FS[Π, RO] *that makes* $q_{RO} \geq \tau \cdot N^D + 1$, q_{PRG}, q_{Com} *and* q_G *quantum queries to* RO, PRG, Com *and* G *respectively, and* q_S *(classical) signing queries. Then for all* $d = 0, 1, \ldots, \tau$,

$$\mathsf{Adv}^{\mathsf{UF\text{-}CMA}}_{\mathsf{FS[IDS,RO]}}(\mathsf{A}) \leq \epsilon_{SD} + (32\tau N^D + 107)q^3 2^{-c} + 10 \cdot q^2 \binom{\tau}{d} p^{t \cdot d} + 20q^2 \frac{1}{N^{D \cdot (\tau - d)}}$$

$$+ q_S \tau \left(16 q_{Com} 2^{-r/2} + \log(N^D - 1) \frac{(q_{PRG} + q_S \tau)^2}{2^n} \right) + \frac{3 q_S}{2} \sqrt{\frac{q_{RO} + q_S + 1}{2^n}}, \quad (14)$$

Here ϵ_{SD} *is the maximal success probability that an adversary that runs in time* $\mathsf{TIME}(\mathsf{A}) + \mathsf{TIME}(\mathsf{CompOr}(q)) + \mathsf{TIME}(\mathsf{Ext}_d)$, *where* $\mathsf{TIME}(\mathsf{CompOr}(q))$ *is the runtime of a compressed oracle simulation for* q *queries, can solve syndrome decoding. Moreover,* $q = q_{Com} + q_{RO} + q_G$ *is the total number of random oracle queries of* A, c *is the output length of* Com, *and the atomic polynomial zero test false-positive probability* p *is defined in Equation* (11) *and bounded in Equation* (12), n *is the seed length of* TreePRG, r *is the length of commitment randomness.*

Proof. This follows by applying Thm. 5 to Cor. 2. Moreover, we plug in the HVZK bound from Thm. 1 and observe that γ_w, the entropy of the commitment messages, in Π is n bits. Further we note that the reduction in the HVZK proof makes up to τq_S additional calls to TreePRG, and use the bound for the security of TreePRG given in Sec. 2.1. We finally apply the QROM bound for hiding of Com from [25] and note that for the security of PRG when modeled as QRO, a standard search bound applies. The reason is that without seeing an input that maps to a challenge, the adversary can do no better than guessing. □

Discussion. Cor. 3 provides a tight bound for UF-CMA security in terms of the hardness of syndrome decoding. The additive terms are all benign. The first additive term is matched by a collision finding attack on the hash function used for commitment [9], up to the constant preceding $q^3 2^{-c}$. The second and third additive terms are similar to the ones appearing in the bounds in [2,14], and are matched by a "divide-and-conquer" attack: An adversary can first search for polynomials allowing them to cheat d out of τ polynomial zero tests, and then search for a message to be signed that allows cheating the MPCitH proof of the remaining $\tau - d$ repetitions. When $p \simeq (1/N^D)$ the divide and conquer attack is most powerful, with $d = \frac{\tau}{2}$. But when $p \ll (1/N^D)$ the attack complexity tends towards $(1/N^D)^\tau$, and parameters in section 5 are selected accordingly. The $16 q_{Com} 2^{r/2}$ term in the second line stems from the computational hiding property of the commitments and is matched by a Grover search for the used commitment randomness. The term in the last line is negligible compared to the last term in the second line, which is matched by a Grover search attack on PRG.

Comparing the bound in Cor. 3 to the ROM bound proven in [2], we observe that each term in Cor. 3 either has been neglected in [2] (e.g. the term corresponding to the hiding security of RO-based committments), or leaves at most the possibility for a quadratic speed-up due to Grover search, up to small mutiplicative constants (e.g. the terms characterizing the security of the polynomial identity test and MPCitH proof).

Algorithm 5. PoW - Proof-of-Work for challenge derivation

Input: Commitment-message hash $h_{\mathsf{w}} \leftarrow H(\mathsf{w}, m)$, number of iterations $2^{k_{iter}}$.

1: $dgst \leftarrow h_{\mathsf{w}}$
2: **for** $ctr \in \{0, \dots, 2^{k_{iter}} - 1\}$ **do** $dgst \leftarrow H(dgst \| h_{\mathsf{w}})$
3: **return** $dgst$

---

5   Performance

The tweaks introduced to the original Hypercube-SDitH scheme not only make possible a security proof in the QROM setting, they also have a positive impact on the performance of the scheme. They allow to slightly reduce signature size and to significantly reduce the online signing time.

Fast online signing. The original Hypercube-SDitH signature is based on a 5-round IDS with two verifier challenges, the first challenge being between the evaluation points. When applying the Fiat-Shamir transform, the message is required to compute the first challenge, so the online phase of the original Hypercube-SDitH signature scheme (the part that requires presence of the message) includes both the MPC computation and the MPC party opening. In the 3-round version, the online phase of the signature corresponds just to one random oracle call and the MPC party opening. In practice this can be as fast as one hash call, plus arithmetic to compute $[\![\alpha]\!]_\mathsf{c}$, $[\![\beta]\!]_\mathsf{c}$, plus building sibling paths required for the openings. Reducing the online cost of a signature is amazing. However, some applications may prefer smaller signatures at the cost of a slower online phase. For this we introduce an online-time - signature-size trade-off which *stretches* the challenge generation time in order to reduce the signature size.

Proof-of-Work. Our trade-off is inspired by the Proof-of-Work (PoW) technique used in SPHINCS+C [24]. In our scheme, we exchange the counter based PoW, with $2^{k_{iter}}$ times iterative hashing. To generate the challenge c, we first generate the hash $h_{\mathsf{w}} \leftarrow H(\mathsf{w}, m)$. We then apply the PoW routine (Alg. 5) to increase the cost of the hash computation, such that the final challenge is $\mathsf{c} \leftarrow PoW(h_{\mathsf{w}})$.

The proof-of-work technique (PoW) does not change the applicability of the security proof as it only replaces one hash function by a more costly one. However, the choice of parameters according to the PoW cannot be supported by our security proof. Because of this, we only introduce the proof-of-work trick here as an optimization. To be covered by the security proof, we would need our bound to distinguish between queries made to the different functions that are modeled as random oracles. This is not possible with our current proof as we are using the technique from [12] in a black box manner where possible and [12] does not distinguish between queries to different functions.

We note, that unlike the PoW counter-based solution of [24], there is no variability in the runtime of our PoW algorithm. The downside, is that unlike the counter-based solution, our iterative solution adds the same running time to the verifier. However, at the same time it reduces the running time as we are able to reduce the number of parallel repetitions τ of Π (c.f.,Table 1).

For concrete parameters, we increase the cost of the message-hash query by $2^{k_{iter}}$, but can in turn reduce the requirement on D and τ to $\approx (1/N^D)^\tau \le 2^{-\lambda} \cdot 2^{k_{iter}} = 2^{-\lambda+k_{iter}}$. As discussed below, we use $N = 2$. Choosing $k_{iter} = D$ increases the attack complexity by a factor 2^D, and each additional parallel repetition increases the attack complexity by a factor $\approx N^D = 2^D$. Thus selecting $k_{iter} = D$ allows us to use $\tau' = \tau - 1$ at the same security level. This means that we need one less repetition of the protocol and can thereby reduce the overall size of the signature. However, this is clearly not the only possible choice for k_{iter}. Reasonable values would be any multiple of D, as $k_{iter} = kD$ means that we can run the protocol with $\tau' = \tau - k$ parallel repetitions. Moreover, as D and τ are integers, we might find cases where $(1/N^D)^\tau$ is slightly larger than $2^{-\lambda}$, forcing us to increase the parameters and signature size, also this could be compensated for using the PoW. Thereby, we can increase our degree of freedom in choosing parameters, possibly resulting in better-optimized variants.

Parameters. For our implementation we stick with the parameters from [14] also used in [2]. Our security bound is (except for some small constants) the same as in [2] up to the generic Grover search and quantum collision finding bounds. These were already (heuristically) considered in the parameter selection by the previous works. For security we target NIST security level I which refers to 128bit security against conventional attacks and 64 bit security against quantum attacks. We use the Variant 3 parameters of the original SDitH scheme (also used in the Hypercube scheme). These parameters use the syndrome decoding problem in $\mathbb{F}_{SD} = \mathbb{F}_{2^8}$ with $m = 256, k = 128$, and $w = 80$. When looking at the original Hypercube proposal, they fix $N = 2$ and define further parameters applying different trade-offs between signature-size and speed (chosen to match the equally named parameter sets proposed in [14]). We focus on the "Short" $(D = 8, \tau = 17)$ and "Shorter" $(D = 12, \tau = 12)$ configurations from Hypercube-SDitH since they offer the most interesting trade-offs in our opinion. We use these parameters as baseline to demonstrate the impact of our results.

It remains to fix the values for the seed length n, the commitment randomness length r, and the commitment length c. For these values we use $n = r = 128$ bit and $c = 256$ bit. Taking a close look at the terms of the sum on the RHS of Equation (14) shows that our choice for the values of n and r are ignoring the $q_S\tau \log(N^D - 1)$ and $q_S\tau$ factors respectively. Examining the proof shows that these factors are caused by the hybrid arguments which reflect multi-target attacks. When modeling the PRG and the commitment as random oracles, these attacks can be mitigated using domain separation (as for example demonstrated in [21]). Hence, as mentioned previously, our implementation makes use of an additional random 128 bit nonce, called *salt*, which is freshly chosen for each signature. This nonce is used as a prefix to the inputs to the PRG, the commitment, and the hash function. Thereby, it domain-separates these calls over different signature calls, effectively removing the need of the factor q_S in the bound. This leaves as worst case the $\tau \log(N^D - 1)$ factor to be considered for the seed length. For our parameters, this accounts to a less then 8 bit loss in security. Given that we count hash function calls as a single operation while this takes more than 256 bit operations, we consider this compensated for. We note that we did not consider this domain separation in our proof as it would significantly hurt readability of the arguments at rather limited novelty given that this kind of solution was discussed already in previous works.

Implementation Results. We base our implementation of the tweaked scheme on top of the previous Hypercube-SDitH implementation from [2], using the XKCP library (SHAKE) for all symmetric primitives (hashes, commitments, and PRGs). Before making modifications, we thoroughly examined the Hypercube-SDitH implementation regarding constant execution time and identified and hardened several key routines that rely on signer-private information and could leak information if done naively.

Next, we benchmarked the original 5-round Hypercube-SDitH scheme with the updated implementation to obtain reference values. Then, we benchmarked the 3-round version of this scheme (Ours - Vanilla), and the same scheme but applying the PoW algorithm above (Ours - PoW) with parameter $k_{iter} = D$. For the benchmarks we used an optimized implementation that leverages AVX2 instructions to parallelize SHAKE and SHA3 calls. The experiments ran on an Intel Xeon E-2378 with frequency fixed at 2.6 GHz and Turbo Boost disabled. We prepared a test routine that runs keygen, sign, and verify on a fixed text input. Finally, we run the test routine for 100 times sequentially on a single CPU core and average the timing measurement results. The implementation is available at https://github.com/sandbox-quantum/sdith-impl-release.

Table 1. Implementation benchmarks of Hypercube-SDitH vs our tweaked scheme for NIST security level I. For the PoW, the parameter $k_{iter} = D$ is used.

Scheme	Aim	Signature Size (bytes)	Parameters				Sign Time (in ms)			Verify Time (in ms) Total
			$\|\mathbb{F}_{points}\|$	t	D	τ	Offline	Online	Total	
Hypercube-SDitH [2]	Short	8464	2^{24}	5	8	17	3.83	0.68	4.51	4.16
	Shorter	6760	2^{24}	5	12	12	44.44	0.60	45.04	42.02
Ours Vanilla	Short	8464	2^{24}	5	8	17	4.45	0.049	4.50	4.17
	Shorter	6760	2^{24}	5	12	12	44.98	0.080	45.06	42.02
Ours PoW	Short	7968	2^{24}	5	8	16	4.20	0.14	4.34	4.00
	Shorter	6204	2^{24}	5	12	11	41.06	1.49	42.55	39.75

References

1. C. Aguilar Melchor, N. Aragon, S. Bettaieb, L. Bidoux, O. Blazy, J.-C. Deneuville, P. Gaborit, E. Persichetti, G. Zémor, J. Bos, A. Dion, J. Lacan, J.-M. Robert, and P. Veron. *HQC.* Tech. rep. available at https://csrc.nist.gov/Projects/post-quantum-cryptography/round-4-submissions. National Institute of Standards and Technology, 2022

2. C. Aguilar Melchor, N. Gama, J. Howe, A. Hülsing, D. Joseph, and D. Yue. "The Return of the SDitH". In: *EUROCRYPT 2023, Part V.* Ed. by C. Hazay and M. Stam. Vol. 14008. LNCS. Springer, Heidelberg, Apr. 2023, pp. 564–596. https://doi.org/10.1007/978-3-031-30589-4_20

3. C. Aguilar-Melchor, A. Hülsing, D. Joseph, C. Majenz, E. Ronen, and D. Yue. *SDitH in the QROM.* Cryptology ePrint Archive, Report 2023/756. https://eprint.iacr.org/2023/756. 2023

4. M. R. Albrecht, D. J. Bernstein, T. Chou, C. Cid, J. Gilcher, T. Lange, V. Maram, I. von Maurich, R. Misoczki, R. Niederhagen, K. G. Paterson, E. Persichetti, C. Peters, P. Schwabe, N. Sendrier, J. Szefer, C. J. Tjhai, M. Tomlinson, and W. Wang. *Classic McEliece.* Tech. rep. available at https://csrc.nist.gov/projects/post-quantum-cryptography/round-4-submissions. National Institute of Standards and Technology, 2022

5. N. Aragon, P. Barreto, S. Bettaieb, L. Bidoux, O. Blazy, J.-C. Deneuville, P. Gaborit, S. Gueron, T. Guneysu, C. Aguilar Melchor, R. Misoczki, E. Persichetti, N. Sendrier, J.-P. Tillich, G. Zémor, V. Vasseur, S. Ghosh, and J. Richter-Brokmann. *BIKE.* Tech. rep. available at https://csrc.nist.gov/Projects/post-quantum-cryptography/round-4-submissions. National Institute of Standards and Technology, 2022

6. E. Berlekamp, R. McEliece, and H. Van Tilborg. "On the inherent intractability of certain coding problems (corresp.)" In: *IEEE Transactions on Information Theory* 24.3 (1978), pp. 384–386

7. W. Beullens. "Breaking Rainbow Takes a Weekend on a Laptop". In: *CRYPTO 2022, Part II.* Ed. by Y. Dodis and T. Shrimpton. Vol. 13508. LNCS. Springer, Heidelberg, Aug. 2022, pp. 464–479. https://doi.org/10.1007/978-3-031-15979-4_16

8. D. Boneh, Ö. Dagdelen, M. Fischlin, A. Lehmann, C. Schaffner, and M. Zhandry. "Random Oracles in a Quantum World". In: *ASIACRYPT 2011.* Ed. by D. H. Lee and X. Wang. Vol. 7073. LNCS. Springer, Heidelberg, Dec. 2011, pp. 41–69. https://doi.org/10.1007/978-3-642-25385-0_3

9. G. Brassard, P. Høyer, and A. Tapp. "Quantum Cryptanalysis of Hash and Claw-Free Functions". In: *LATIN '98.* Ed. by C. L. Lucchesi and A. V. Moura. Vol. 1380. Lecture Notes in Computer Science. Springer, 1998, pp. 163–169. https://doi.org/10.1007/BFb0054319

10. K.-M. Chung, S. Fehr, Y.-H. Huang, and T.-N. Liao. "On the Compressed- Oracle Technique, and Post-Quantum Security of Proofs of Sequential Work". In: *EUROCRYPT 2021, Part II.* Ed. by A. Canteaut and F.-X. Standaert. Vol. 12697. LNCS. Springer, Heidelberg, Oct. 2021, pp. 598–629. https://doi.org/10.1007/978-3-030-77886-6_21

11. T. Debris-Alazard, N. Sendrier, and J.-P. Tillich. "Wave: A New Family of Trapdoor One-Way Preimage Sampleable Functions Based on Codes". In: *ASIACRYPT 2019, Part I.* Ed. by S. D. Galbraith and S. Moriai. Vol. 11921. LNCS. Springer, Heidelberg, Dec. 2019, pp. 21–51. https://doi.org/10.1007/978-3-030-34578-5_2

12. J. Don, S. Fehr, C. Majenz, and C. Schaffner. "Efficient NIZKs and Signatures from Commit-and-Open Protocols in the QROM". In: *CRYPTO 2022, Part II.* Ed. by Y. Dodis and T. Shrimpton. Vol. 13508. LNCS. Springer, Heidelberg, Aug. 2022, pp. 729–757. https://doi.org/10.1007/978-3-031-15979-4_25

13. S. Even, O. Goldreich, and S. Micali. "On-Line/Off-Line Digital Schemes". In: *CRYPTO'89.* Ed. by G. Brassard. Vol. 435. LNCS. Springer, Heidelberg, Aug. 1990, pp. 263–275. https://doi.org/10.1007/0-387-34805-0_24

14. T. Feneuil, A. Joux, and M. Rivain. "Syndrome Decoding in the Head: Shorter Signatures from Zero-Knowledge Proofs". In: *CRYPTO 2022, Part II*. Ed. by Y. Dodis and T. Shrimpton. Vol. 13508. LNCS. Springer, Heidelberg, Aug. 2022, pp. 541–572. https://doi.org/10.1007/978-3-031-15979-4_19

15. A. Fiat and A. Shamir. "How to Prove Yourself: Practical Solutions to Identification and Signature Problems". In: *CRYPTO'86*. Ed. by A. M. Odlyzko. Vol. 263. LNCS. Springer, Heidelberg, Aug. 1987, pp. 186–194. https://doi.org/10.1007/3-540-47721-7_12

16. O. Goldreich, S. Goldwasser, and S. Micali. "How to Construct Random Functions (Extended Abstract)". In: *25th FOCS*. IEEE Computer Society Press, Oct. 1984, pp. 464–479. https://doi.org/10.1109/SFCS.1984.715949

17. A. B. Grilo, K. Hövelmanns, A. Hülsing, and C. Majenz. "Tight Adaptive Reprogramming in the QROM". In: *ASIACRYPT 2021, Part I*. Ed. by M. Tibouchi and H. Wang. Vol. 13090. LNCS. Springer, Heidelberg, Dec. 2021, pp. 637–667. https://doi.org/10.1007/978-3-030-92062-3_22

18. E. Grumbling and M. Horowitz. *Quantum Computing: Progress and Prospects*. 1st. National Academies of Sciences, Engineering, and Medicine. The National Academies Press, Apr. 2019. isbn: 9780309479691. DOI: https://doi.org/10.17226/25196

19. K. Hövelmanns, A. Hülsing, and C. Majenz. "Failing Gracefully: Decryption Failures and the Fujisaki-Okamoto Transform". In: *ASIACRYPT 2022, Part IV*. LNCS. Springer, Heidelberg, Dec. 2022, pp. 414–443. https://doi.org/10.1007/978-3-031-22972-5_15

20. A. Hülsing, D. J. Bernstein, C. Dobraunig, M. Eichlseder, S. Fluhrer, S.-L. Gazdag, P. Kampanakis, S. Kolbl, T. Lange, M. M. Lauridsen, F. Mendel, R. Niederhagen, C. Rechberger, J. Rijneveld, P. Schwabe, J.-P. Aumasson, B. Westerbaan, and W. Beullens. *SPHINCS+*. Tech. rep. available at https://csrc.nist.gov/Projects/post-quantum-cryptography/selectedalgorithms-2022. National Institute of Standards and Technology, 2022

21. A. Hülsing, J. Rijneveld, and F. Song. "Mitigating Multi-target Attacks in Hash-Based Signatures". In: *PKC 2016, Part I*. Ed. by C.-M. Cheng, K.-M. Chung, G. Persiano, and B.-Y. Yang. Vol. 9614. LNCS. Springer, Heidelberg, Mar. 2016, pp. 387–416. https://doi.org/10.1007/978-3-662-49384-7_15

22. Y. Ishai, E. Kushilevitz, R. Ostrovsky, and A. Sahai. "Zero-knowledge from secure multiparty computation". In: *39th ACM STOC*. Ed. by D. S. Johnson and U. Feige. ACM Press, June 2007, pp. 21–30. https://doi.org/10.1145/1250790.1250794

23. E. Kiltz, V. Lyubashevsky, and C. Schaffner. "A Concrete Treatment of Fiat-Shamir Signatures in the Quantum Random-Oracle Model". In: *EUROCRYPT 2018, Part III*. Ed. by J. B. Nielsen and V. Rijmen. Vol. 10822. LNCS. Springer, Heidelberg, 2018, pp. 552–586. https://doi.org/10.1007/978-3-319-78372-7_18

24. M. A. Kudinov, A. Hülsing, E. Ronen, and E. Yogev. "SPHINCS+C: Compressing SPHINCS+ With (Almost) No Cost". In: *IACR Cryptol. ePrint Arch.* (2022), p. 778. URL: https://eprint.iacr.org/2022/778

25. D. Leichtle. *Post-quantum signatures from identification schemes*. Master's thesis, Technische Universiteit Eindhoven. https://pure.tue.nl/ws/portalfiles/portal/125545339/Dominik_Leichtle_thesis_final_IAM_307.pdf. 2018

26. V. Lyubashevsky, L. Ducas, E. Kiltz, T. Lepoint, P. Schwabe, G. Seiler, D. Stehlé, and S. Bai. *CRYSTALS-DILITHIUM*. Tech. rep. available at https://csrc.nist.gov/Projects/post-quantum-cryptography/selectedalgorithms-2022. National Institute of Standards and Technology, 2022

27. R. J. McEliece. *A public-key cryptosystem based on algebraic coding theory.* The Deep Space Network Progress Report 42–44. https://ipnpr.jpl.nasa.gov/progress_report2/42-44/44N.PDF. Jet Propulsion Laboratory, California Institute of Technology, 1978, pp. 114–116

28. Mosca, M.: Cybersecurity in an Era with Quantum Computers: Will We Be Ready? IEEE Security & Privacy **16**, 38–41 (2018). https://doi.org/10.1109/MSP.2018.3761723

29. NIST. *National Institute for Standards and Technology. PQC Standardization Process: Announcing Four Candidates to be Standardized, Plus Fourth Round Candidates.* https://csrc.nist.gov/News/2022/pqccandidates-to-be-standardized-and-round-4. Mar. 2022

30. NIST. *Submission Requirements and Evaluation Criteria for the Post- Quantum Cryptography Standardization Process.* https://csrc.nist.gov/CSRC/media/Projects/Post-Quantum-Cryptography/documents/callfor-proposals-final-dec-2016.pdf. 2016

31. T. Prest, P.-A. Fouque, J. Hoffstein, P. Kirchner, V. Lyubashevsky, T. Pornin, T. Ricosset, G. Seiler, W. Whyte, and Z. Zhang. *FALCON.* Tech. rep. available at https://csrc.nist.gov/Projects/post-quantumcryptography/selected-algorithms-2022. National Institute of Standards and Technology, 2022

32. J. Stern. "Designing Identification Schemes with Keys of Short Size". In: *CRYPTO'94.* Ed. by Y. Desmedt. Vol. 839. LNCS. Springer, Heidelberg, Aug. 1994, pp. 164–173. https://doi.org/10.1007/3-540-48658-5_18

33. G. Zaverucha, M. Chase, D. Derler, S. Goldfeder, C. Orlandi, S. Ramacher, C. Rechberger, D. Slamanig, J. Katz, X. Wang, V. Kolesnikov, and Đ. Kales. *Picnic.* Tech. rep. available at https://csrc.nist.gov/projects/post-quantum-cryptography/post-quantum-cryptography-standardization/round-3-submissions. National Institute of Standards and Technology, 2020

34. M. Zhandry. "How to Record Quantum Queries, and Applications to Quantum Indifferentiability". In: *CRYPTO 2019*, Part II. Ed. by A. Boldyreva and D. Micciancio. Vol. 11693. LNCS. Springer, Heidelberg, Aug. 2019, pp. 239–268. https://doi.org/10.1007/978-3-030-26951-7_9

A New Formulation of the Linear Equivalence Problem and Shorter LESS Signatures

Edoardo Persichetti[1,2]([✉]) and Paolo Santini[3]

[1] Florida Atlantic University, Boca Raton, USA
epersichetti@fau.edu
[2] Sapienza University of Rome, Rome, Italy
[3] Marche Polytechnic University, Ancona, Italy

Abstract. The Linear Equivalence Problem (LEP) asks to find a linear isometry between a given pair of linear codes; in the Hamming weight this is known as a *monomial map*. LEP has been used in cryptography to design the family of LESS signatures, which includes also some advanced schemes, such as ring and identity-based signatures. All of these schemes are obtained applying the Fiat-Shamir transformation to a Sigma protocol, in which the prover's responses contain a description of how the monomial map acts on all code coordinates; such a description constitutes the vast majority of the signature size. In this paper, we propose a new formulation of LEP, which we refer to as Information-Set (IS)-LEP. Exploiting IS-LEP, it is enough for the prover to provide the description of the monomial action only on an information set, instead of all the coordinates. Thanks to this new formulation, we are able to drastically reduce signature sizes for all LESS signature schemes, without any relevant computational overhead. We prove that IS-LEP and LEP are completely equivalent (indeed, the same problem), which means that improvement comes with no additional security assumption, either.

1 Introduction

The Code Equivalence Problem (CEP) is a traditional problem of coding theory, which asks to determine whether two given linear codes are equivalent to each other. For the canonical (and most studied) case of isometries in the Hamming metric, the notion of equivalence is linked to the existence of a generalized permutation (i.e. with non-unitary scaling factors), also known as *monomial* transformation. In such a setting, the problem is normally referred to as the Linear Equivalence Problem (LEP).

The computational version of LEP, which is of interest in cryptography, may appear to be somewhat less secure than other problems from coding theory such as the well-known Syndrome Decoding Problem (SDP); unlike SDP, in fact, LEP is probably not NP-hard, since this would imply the collapse of the polynomial hierarchy [PR97]. Nevertheless, perhaps surprisingly, the best known algorithms for LEP (at least, for the regime of interest) utilize an SDP solver as a subroutine.

J. Guo and R. Steinfeld (Eds.): ASIACRYPT 2023, LNCS 14444, pp. 351–378, 2023.
https://doi.org/10.1007/978-981-99-8739-9_12

Moreover, the application of an isometry to a linear code can be described as a (non-commutative) group action with certain nice properties, which is exactly the key for its use in cryptographic applications.

1.1 Related Works

The first cryptosystem built on LEP was presented in 2020 as LESS, acronym for Linear Equivalence Signature Scheme [BMPS20]. The paper describes a simple 3-pass Zero-Knowledge Identification (ZK-ID) protocol, following in the footsteps of [GMW19], and then shows how this can be transformed into a full-fledged signature scheme via Fiat-Shamir. It is worth noting that LESS is part of a collection of schemes leveraging this framework, relying on tools from a wide variety of setting, including polynomials [Pat96], isogenies [FG19], lattices [DvW22], matrix codes [CNP+23], trilinear forms [TDJ+22, DG22] etc.

In a follow-up work [BBPS21], the authors refine the scheme using some familiar protocol-level techniques such as the use of multiple keys (to amplify soundness) and fixed-weight challenge strings (to reduce signature length), as seen for instance in [BKV19]; the work also features new parameters, adjusted to withstand a novel LEP solver introduced by Beullens [Beu21]. In fact, a comprehensive study of solvers for LEP was subsequently put together in [BBPS23], with the aim of presenting a clear picture of the best attack techniques, and a tool for selecting secure parameters. The group action structure connected to LEP proved to be appealing as a potential building block in many constructions, developed in ensuing works: some successfully, such as the ring and identity-based signatures proposed in [BBN+22], some unsuccessfully (e.g. [ZZ21, PRS22]).

The essential structure of the LESS protocol is as follows. Starting from a public code $\mathscr{C}$, the prover generates their public key as $\mathscr{C}' = \mu(\mathscr{C})$ where μ is a linear isometry. Then, the protocol goes as in Fig. 1.

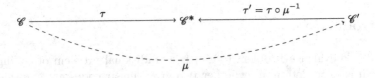

Fig. 1. Representation of the proof of knowledge structure in LESS

In each execution of the protocol, the prover samples an ephemeral map τ and commits to $\mathscr{C}^* = \tau(\mathscr{C})$. The verifier then asks to disclose one of the following two maps: the one *on the left* between $\mathscr{C}$ and $\mathscr{C}^*$, or the one *on the right* between $\mathscr{C}^*$ and $\mathscr{C}'$. The honest prover is always able to provide both maps, i.e., can always construct a graph like the one in Fig. 1. A cheating prover, instead, can only craft one of the two maps at a given time and try to guess which one is going to be asked; he cannot, however, reproduce the full graph, without knowing the secret key (which requires to solve a LEP instance). This informal argument of witness extractability intuitively leads to a soundness error of 1/2; to achieve λ bits of security, it is then necessary to utilize standard error amplification techniques such as parallel repetitions.

Linear codes are customarily represented through their generator matrices, whereas isometries consist of column transformations together with a change of basis. This means that, in practice, $\mathscr{C}'$ is represented as $\mathbf{S}\mu(\mathbf{G})$, where $\mathbf{G} \in \mathbb{F}_q^{k\times n}$ is a generator matrix for $\mathscr{C}$ and $\mathbf{S}$ is non-singular of size k. To check that two codes are equal, one can compute a special generator matrix, say, the one in systematic form, which can be naturally obtained with one Gaussian elimination. This allows to greatly reduce the communication cost, because the prover can commit to the hash of the systematic generator of $\mathscr{C}^*$: the verifier will recompute such a matrix, hash it, and check consistence with the commitment. Without this consideration, the LESS scheme would not be practical, since the size of commitments would be gigantic.

Two meaningful improvements appeared in [BBPS21]. The first one consists in allowing for more than two equivalent codes in the public key, which allows to enrich the graph in Fig. 1 with some additional maps on the right. The corresponding graph is reported in Fig. 2; in the figure, we are denoting $\tau_i' = \tau \circ \mu_i^{-1}$ and are using s for the number of codes.

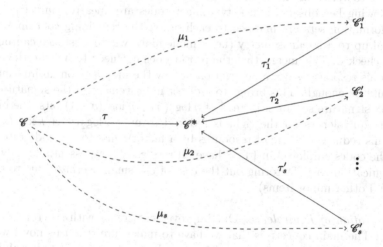

Fig. 2. The LESS-FM proof of knowledge with multiple keys

With this variant, the verifier will choose either the map on the left or one of the $s-1$ maps on the right. It is easy to see that an adversary can reply correctly only by guessing, in advance, which instance will be selected by the prover. This leads to an amplified soundness error of $\frac{1}{s}$ and, consequently, only $\frac{\lambda}{\log_2(s)}$ repetitions are required. With respect to the LESS scheme, this leads to an improvement for what concerns both the signature size and the computational overhead on the verifier's side, since the number of parallel repetitions is reduced by a factor $\log_2(s)$. Obviously, the price to pay is a steep increase in public key size.

The second optimization introduced in LESS-FM consists of using challenges with a non-uniform distribution, so that the map on the left is the one queried most frequently. This is because such a map, being entirely random, can be represented compactly by the seed used to generate it. To preserve the soundness error, which now behaves like a binomial coefficient, one needs to increase the number of overall repetitions; however, the number of maps on the right which are verified (which cannot be compressed with seeds) is much smaller. This yields a significant reduction in signature size, which is further improved by utilizing a seed tree [BKP20] to efficiently transmit the seeds.

1.2 Our Contributions

In this work, we describe a new technique which greatly improves the performance of the scheme. Unlike the ones described in LESS-FM, which are somewhat standard techniques applicable to any Sigma protocol with the same structure, our improvement is specific to the LEP setting.

A New Method for Verification. In a nutshell, our technique consists of a compact way to verify the maps of the graph in Fig. 2. The main idea is based on the following key observation: if two linear codes are linearly equivalent, once two information sets are mapped to each other, the remaining coordinates are identical up to a linear isometry (i.e. a monomial), whose existence can be efficiently checked. This means that the prover does not need to include the entire map in his response, since a description of how the map acts on an information set would be enough. This brings to a direct improvement in the signature size of LESS signature schemes: instead of $n \log_2(n) + n \log_2(q - 1)$ bits, the binary size for equivalences on the right is reduced to only $k \log_2(n) + k \log_2(q - 1)$ bits. This reduces the size of responses by a factor equal to the code rate k/n: since the codes employed in LESS have all rate $\approx 1/2$, we essentially halve the communication cost (factoring out the cost of the small overhead due to seeds, salts and other minor items).

A New Notion of Equivalence. Our improvement comes with several technical caveats. The main concern is that we have to make sure that this novel way to verify that two codes are indeed equivalent, does not introduce vulnerabilities. To do this, we introduce a new notion of equivalence, which we call Information Set (IS) - linear equivalence, to emphasize that the focus is on how the linear map acts on an information set. We then show that the associated decisional problem, which we call IS-LEP, is literally the same as LEP: any solver for IS-LEP can in fact be used to solve LEP, and viceversa. Formally, what we prove is something stronger, namely that any "YES" (resp. "NO") instance for LEP is also a "YES" (resp. "NO") instance for IS-LEP: this implies that IS-LEP and LEP are actually the same problem. The definition of IS-LEP is the focus of Sect. 4.

Application to Proofs of Knowledge. In Sect. 5 we deal with the practical problem of embedding the verification of IS-LEP into proof-of-knowledge protocols as in Figs. 1 and 2. Indeed, unlike the existing schemes, in this case the prover cannot commit anymore to the systematic form of $\mathscr{C}^*$. The issue is that now the prover provides only a *truncated* representation for the maps on the right: the verifier computes a code which is identical to $\mathscr{C}^*$ only in k out of n coordinates, so its systematic form will be different from the one of $\mathscr{C}^*$. To circumvent this issue, we modify the verification procedure and require that, after the computation of the systematic form, both the verifier and the prover execute an ad-hoc function which is an invariant under truncated monomial maps. We show that these extra steps have a cost which is much smaller than that of Gaussian elimination so that, in practice, the overall computational cost is only slightly affected. We also address the problem of communicating the information set which is used for verification: with a proper way to represent the truncated map, this cost can be entirely removed.

Practical Outlook. Finally, in Sect. 6 we present some new instances of LESS signatures. These include new instances also for the ring signatures described in [BBN+22]. These are formulated with additional constraints and guidelines in mind, oriented at providing the best performance for the intended use case, and desired security level. Indeed, after recalling the state-of-the-art attacks on LEP, we propose a simple procedure to design secure LEP instances. This leads to parameters that are slightly larger than those employed in [BBPS21,BBN+22] but are more conservative. To be sure, this new procedure not only rules out the best attacks, i.e. the ones based on finding low-weight codewords (which is computationally equivalent to SDP), but also possible improvements to such attacks. This provides a very high level of confidence on the new parameters: new attacks, in order to significantly lower the security level, would need to be radically different from those based on low-weight codeword finding.

As mentioned before, the sizes resulting from this process are nearly half of those that would be obtained without our improvement. To be precise, we are able to produce signature sizes that range between 5 and 8.5 KiB, for NIST's security category 1. We also propose parameters for categories 3 and 5, ranging respectively between 14 and 18.5 KiB for the former, and 26 and 32.5 KiB for the latter. In all cases except one, the sum of our public keys and signatures is below 100KiB. To complete the picture, we include also some implementation figures, that we obtain by a reference implementation in ANSI C. While these numbers are far from optimized, they are still useful to show that the scheme is practical: indeed, the number of cycles is comparable with that obtained measuring the reference code of e.g. SPHINCS+.

2   Notation and Background

In this section we establish the notation that we will use throughout the paper, as well as recall basic concepts about linear codes.

2.1 Notation

As usual, we use $\mathbb{F}_q$ to indicate the finite field with q elements and $\mathbb{F}_q^*$ to indicate its multiplicative group. Given a matrix $\mathbf{A}$ over $\mathbb{F}_q$, we write $\mathbf{a}_i$ to indicate its i-th column. The general linear group formed by the non singular $k \times k$ matrices over $\mathbb{F}_q$ is indicated as GL_k. For an ordered set J, we write $\mathbf{A}_J$ to indicate the matrix formed by the columns of $\mathbf{A}$ that are indexed by the elements in J; equivalent notation is adopted for vectors. The identity with size k is indicated as $\mathbf{I}_k$, while $\mathbf{0}$ denotes the null-matrix (its dimensions will always be clear from the context). The standard matrix product between $\mathbf{A}$ and $\mathbf{B}$ is indicated as $\mathbf{AB}$, i.e., without any operator. In some cases, to avoid confusion with other operations, we will make it explicit and write the product as $\mathbf{A} \cdot \mathbf{B}$.

We denote by S_n the symmetric group on n elements, and consider its elements as permutations of n objects. We represent permutations in one-line notation, as n-tuples of the form $\pi := (i_1, i_2, \cdots, i_n)$, so that $\pi(j) = i_j$, i.e., π moves the j-th element to position i_j. For a vector $\mathbf{a} = (a_1, \cdots, a_n)$, it holds that

$$\pi(\mathbf{a}) = \left(a_{\pi^{-1}(1)}, \cdots, a_{\pi^{-1}(n)}\right).$$

We denote by M_n the set of monomial transformations, that is, transformations of the form $\mu := (\pi, \mathbf{v})$ with $\pi \in S_n$ and $\mathbf{v} \in \mathbb{F}_q^{*n}$, acting as follows

$$\mu(\mathbf{a}) = \pi(\mathbf{a}) \begin{pmatrix} v_1 & & & \\ & v_2 & & \\ & & \ddots & \\ & & & v_n \end{pmatrix} = \left(v_1 a_{\pi^{-1}(1)}, \cdots, v_n a_{\pi^{-1}(n)}\right).$$

We naturally extend the action of monomials on matrices $\mathbf{A}$, i.e., $\mu(\mathbf{A})$ indicates the matrix resulting from the action of μ on the columns of $\mathbf{A}$. For two monomials $\mu, \mu' \in M_n$, we write $\mu \circ \mu'$ to denote the monomial resulting from their combination.

2.2 Linear Codes

A linear code $\mathscr{C} \subseteq \mathbb{F}_q^n$ is a k-dimensional subspace of $\mathbb{F}_q^n$. The quantity $R = k/n$ is called *code rate*, and any vector $\mathbf{c} \in \mathscr{C}$ is called *codeword*. A canonical representation for a code is through a *generator matrix*, that is, a full-rank matrix $\mathbf{G} \in \mathbb{F}_q^{k \times n}$ such that $\mathscr{C} = \{\mathbf{uG} \mid \mathbf{u} \in \mathbb{F}_q^k\}$. Codes admit multiple generator matrices: for any $\mathbf{S} \in \mathrm{GL}_k$, which can be seen as a change of basis, it holds that $\mathbf{SG}$ and $\mathbf{G}$ generate the same code. The dual code $\mathscr{C}^\perp$ is the set of all vectors that are orthogonal to codewords in $\mathscr{C}$, that is, $\mathscr{C}^\perp = \{\mathbf{v} \in \mathbb{F}_q^n \mid \mathbf{cv}^\top = 0, \forall \mathbf{c} \in \mathscr{C}\}$. It is easy to see that $\mathscr{C}^\perp$ is a linear subspace of $\mathbb{F}_q^n$ with dimension $r = n - k$ (which is normally called *redundancy*). The dual code is generated by a full-rank matrix $\mathbf{H} \in \mathbb{F}_q^{r \times n}$, which is called *parity-check matrix* and is such that $\mathbf{GH}^\top = \mathbf{0}$. Obviously, for any $\mathbf{S} \in \mathrm{GL}_r$, $\mathbf{H}$ and $\mathbf{SH}$ are parity-check matrices for the same code.

For $J \subseteq \{1, \cdots, n\}$, we write $\mathscr{C}_J := \{\mathbf{c}_J \mid \mathbf{c} \in \mathscr{C}\}$. We say that a set J with size k is an *information set* for a code $\mathscr{C}$ if, for any two distinct $\mathbf{c}, \mathbf{c}' \in \mathscr{C}$, it holds that $\mathbf{c}_J \neq \mathbf{c}'_J$, which implies that $\mathscr{C}_J$ contains q^k elements. Equivalently, J is an information set if, for $\mathbf{G}$ being a generator matrix for $\mathscr{C}$, it holds that $\mathbf{G}_J$ is non singular. Normally, we say that a generator matrix $\mathbf{G}$ is in *systematic form* if $\mathbf{G} = (\mathbf{I}_k, \mathbf{V})$, where $\mathbf{I}_k$ is the identity matrix of size k and $\mathbf{V} \in \mathbb{F}_q^{k \times (n-k)}$. This matrix exists whenever $J = \{1, \cdots, k\}$ is an information set: starting from any generator matrix $\mathbf{G}$, we obtain the one in systematic form as $\mathbf{G}_J^{-1}\mathbf{G}$. Also, the systematic matrix is an invariant under changes of basis: if $\mathbf{G}' = \mathbf{S}\mathbf{G}$, then its systematic form is $\mathbf{G}_J'^{-1}\mathbf{G}' = \mathbf{G}_J^{-1}\mathbf{S}^{-1}\mathbf{S}\mathbf{G} = \mathbf{G}_J^{-1}\mathbf{G}$.

In principle, there is no guarantee that $\{1, \cdots, k\}$ is an information set. Thus, sometimes one considers a slightly more general definition: given a matrix $\mathbf{G}$, its systematic form is $\mathbf{G}_J^{-1}\mathbf{G}$, where J is the first (according to some lexicographic ordering) subset of $\{1, \cdots, n\}$ of size k and such that $\mathbf{G}_J$ is non-singular. We refer to this operation as Row Reduced Echelon Form (RREF) with respect to J. To encompass the canonical definition of systematic matrix, we impose that the lexicographically first set is $\{1, \cdots, k\}$. It is easy to see that also this generalized definition is invariant under changes of basis: to emphasize this property, we will write $\mathsf{SF}(\mathscr{C})$ to denote the function that, on input a linear code, returns its systematic form.

Finally, we summarize here the traditional notion of equivalence between two codes, in the Hamming metric. To do this, we first clarify that we indicate with $\mu(\mathscr{C})$ the linear code obtained by applying the monomial transformation μ to all the codewords $\mathbf{c} \in \mathscr{C}$.

Definition 1 (Linear Equivalence). *We say that two codes $\mathscr{C}, \mathscr{C}' \subseteq \mathbb{F}_q^n$ are linearly equivalent, and write $\mathscr{C} \sim \mathscr{C}'$, if there exists a monomial transformation $\mu \in M_n$ such that $\mathscr{C}' = \mu(\mathscr{C})$. That is, given generator matrices $\mathbf{G}, \mathbf{G}' \in \mathbb{F}_q^{k \times n}$ for $\mathscr{C}$ and $\mathscr{C}'$, respectively, the two codes are linearly equivalent if $\mathbf{G}' = \mathbf{S}\mu(\mathbf{G})$ for some non-singular matrix $\mathbf{S} \in \mathrm{GL}_k$, or analogously, if $\mathsf{SF}(\mathscr{C}') = \mathsf{SF}(\mu(\mathscr{C}))$.*

The above definition encompasses the weaker notion of *permutation equivalence*, which is the particular case where the monomial μ is a permutation.

3   The Code Equivalence Problem

The code equivalence problem generically asks, on input two codes $\mathscr{C}$ and $\mathscr{C}'$, to find a linear isometry mapping one code into the other. The problem is sometimes distinguished into two versions, depending on the type of isometry that one desires to identify. We present here only the more general one.

Problem 1 (Linear Equivalence Problem (LEP)). *Given $\mathscr{C}, \mathscr{C}' \subseteq \mathbb{F}_q^n$ with dimension k, decide if $\mathscr{C} \sim \mathscr{C}'$, i.e., if there exists $\mu \in M_n$ such that $\mathscr{C}' = \mu(\mathscr{C})$. Equivalently, given $\mathbf{G}, \mathbf{G}' \in \mathbb{F}_q^{k \times n}$ (generators for $\mathscr{C}$ and $\mathscr{C}'$, respectively), decide whether there exist $\mu \in M_n$ and $\mathbf{S} \in \mathrm{GL}_k$ such that $\mathbf{G}' = \mathbf{S}\mu(\mathbf{G})$.*

The *Permutation Equivalence Problem (PEP)* is just a special case of LEP, since any permutation is a monomial with scalar factors equal to 1.

Avoiding Weak Instances. Given its importance in coding theory, LEP has been studied for decades. As we have already mentioned, a well-known result states that the NP-completeness of LEP would imply a collapse of the polynomial hierarchy [PR97]. For PEP, there exist certain algorithms that can have a polynomial running time [Sen00,BOS19]. Namely, these attacks take times in $O\left(n^3 + q^{\tilde{k}}\right)$ and $O\left(n^{2.3+\tilde{k}}\right)$, respectively, where $\tilde{k}$ is the dimension of the hull, that is, the linear code $\mathscr{C} \cap \mathscr{C}^\perp$. For random codes, the size of the hull tends to a small constant [Sen97], so that the above attacks become essentially polynomial in the code length. To counter these attacks, it suffices to use codes with large enough hull, or even *self-orthogonal codes*, that is, codes such that $\mathscr{C} \subseteq \mathscr{C}^\perp$. In this extreme case, in fact, the hull is equal to the code itself, so that $\tilde{k} = k = Rn$, and the attacks in [Sen00,BOS19] take exponential time.

For LEP, however, it is still safe to use random codes, provided that the underlying finite field is sufficiently large. Indeed, there exists a polynomial time map that takes any LEP instance into a PEP instance, so that any solver for PEP can be used to solve LEP. However, when $q \geqslant 5$, this reduction always ends in a self-dual code [SS13]. This guarantees that the algorithms in [Sen00,BOS19] have maximum, exponential running time.

Attacks Based on Low-Weight Codeword Finding. The other class of attacks against PEP and LEP is characterized by the search for codewords with low Hamming weight (or subcodes with small support) [Leo82,Beu21,BBPS23]. The description of these attacks requires several technicalities which, due to lack of space, we cannot report here. Yet, they all share the common principle of looking at a small set of codewords (or subcodes) from which the action of μ can be recovered. For instance, Leon's algorithm [Leo82] requires to find, for each code, all codewords with weight $\leqslant w$, that is,

$$A = \{\mathbf{c} \in \mathscr{C} \mid \mathrm{wt}(\mathbf{c}) \leqslant w\}, \quad A' = \{\mathbf{c}' \in \mathscr{C}' \mid \mathrm{wt}(\mathbf{c}') \leqslant w\}.$$

This guarantees that $\mu(A) = A'$ and, when $w \ll n$, we have $|A| \ll |\mathscr{C}| = q^k$: roughly, since A and A' contain a few codewords, reconstructing μ gets easy. Modern algorithms relax the requirements of Leon and, instead, aim to find a sufficiently large number of *collisions*. This idea has been first proposed in [Beu21] and then refined in [BBPS23]. Here, by collision, we refer to a pair of codewords $\mathbf{c} \in \mathscr{C}$, $\mathbf{c}' \in \mathscr{C}'$ such that $\mu(\mathbf{c}) = \mathbf{c}'$. When the Hamming weights of $\mathbf{c}$ and $\mathbf{c}'$ are sufficiently small, collisions can be determined efficiently. The gain with respect to Leon's algorithm depends on several technicalities but, as a rule of thumb, it is enough to consider that this attack outperforms Leon's only if q is sufficiently large.

Note that the attack in [Beu21] actually uses two-dimensional subcodes instead of codewords. However, as observed in [BBPS23], this attack can be improved by first finding low-weight codewords and then using them to build subcodes. This allows to improve upon the attack in [Beu21] since the component codewords have a much smaller support size than the resulting subcode, hence finding them is much easier.

Conservative Design Criteria. In practice, once weak instances are excluded, the best attacks against LEP are those based on low-weight codeword finding. Fortunately, this is one of the oldest and most studied problems in coding theory and we have a pretty consolidated picture about the cost of the best solvers, which are Information-Set Decoding (ISD) algorithms. In particular, for non-binary fields, the state-of-the-art is Peters' ISD [Pet10]. In the following, we will denote by $C_{\mathrm{ISD}}(q, n, k, w)$ the cost of finding a single codeword with weight w, in a code defined over $\mathbb{F}_q$, with length n and dimension k.

Looking at the attacks summarized above, we see that they all follow a general model, where an attacker always pursues the following strategy: i) produce two lists L_1 and L_2 with short codewords, ii) find collisions, i.e., pairs of elements in L_1 and L_2 that are presumably mapped by μ, and iii) use collisions to reconstruct the secret monomial. To obtain a conservative point of view on these attacks, we make the following choices:

- we assume that the technique employed to find collisions has no cost;
- we assume that the attacker never finds *fake collisions*, i.e., never considers $(\mathbf{c}, \mathbf{c}')$ as a collision even if $\mathbf{c} \neq \mu(\mathbf{c}')$. Note that fake collisions may make the monomial reconstruction unfeasible or, at the very least, much more complicated. In fact, the possibility of fake collisions is exactly the reason why the attacks in [Beu21,BBPS23] focus only on short codewords and, most importantly, work only when the finite field is large enough;
- we assume that knowing one collision is enough to retrieve significant and useful information about the secret monomial. Notice that all attacks, instead, require to find a sufficiently large number of collisions. For instance, Leon's algorithm requires to determine all codewords with some bounded weight. Analogously, the attacks in [Beu21,BBPS23] reconstruct exactly the secret monomial only if a sufficiently large number of (not fake) collisions is available. Yet, there may be ways to improve the monomial reconstruction phase (i.e., efficient techniques that require a smaller number of collisions), or to make use of some partial information. To show why this a concrete possibility, consider the case in which $\mathscr{C}$ contains only one minimum weight codeword $\mathbf{c}$. This gets mapped into $\mathbf{c}' = \mu(\mathbf{c}) \in \mathscr{C}'$. The pair $(\mathbf{c}, \mathbf{c}')$ already provides some information about μ: for instance, if $c_i = 0$ and $c'_j \neq 0$, we learn that μ does not move i in position j.

Taking into account the above three conservative assumptions, we use the following criterion to select secure LEP instances.

Criterion 1. *Let q, n, k denote, respectively, the finite field size, code length and dimension. We consider only $q \geqslant 5$ and random codes. We select n, k, q so that, for any $w \in \{1, \cdots, n\}$, finding lists $L_1 \subseteq \mathscr{C}$ and $L_2 \subseteq \mathscr{C}'$ with weight-w codewords and such that $L_2 \cap \mu(L_1)$ is non empty (where $\{\mu(\mathbf{c}) \mid \mathbf{c} \in L_1\}$), takes time greater than 2^λ.*

This translates into a very simple way to select parameters. Indeed, let L_1 and L_2 have the same size ℓ. Then, the cost to produce these lists is

$$f(\ell, N(w)) \cdot \frac{C_{\text{ISD}}(n, k, q, w)}{N(w)},$$

where $f(\ell, N(w))$ counts the number of ISD calls to find ℓ distinct codewords. The term $N(w)$ accounts for the number of codewords with weight w: since codes are random, this is well estimated as

$$N(w) = \binom{n}{w}(q-1)^w q^{-(n-k)}.$$

The cost of each ISD call is divided by $N(w)$ to take into account existence of multiple solutions.

We now observe that, on average, we have

$$|L_2 \cap \mu(L_1)| = \frac{|L_1| \cdot |L_2|}{N(w)} = \frac{\ell^2}{N(w)}.$$

Indeed, for each codeword in L_2, there is only one good collision among the $N(w)$ codewords in $\mathscr{C}$. Since we populate L_1 with ℓ random codewords, the probability that such a codeword is indeed in L_1 is $\frac{\ell}{N(w)}$. It follows that, in order to have at least one collision in the expectation, it must hold that $\ell^2 \geqslant N(w)$, which implies $\ell \geqslant \sqrt{N(w)}$. So, $\ell \ll N(w)$ and ℓ calls to ISD return, with high probability, ℓ distinct codewords [Beu21]. Consequently, we have

$$f(\ell, N(w)) \approx \ell = \sqrt{N(w)}.$$

Consequently, Criterion 1 translates into the following criterion.

Criterion 2. *We consider random codes defined over $\mathbb{F}_q$ with $q \geqslant 5$, and choose q, n, k so that, for any w, it holds that*

$$\frac{1}{\sqrt{N(w)}} \cdot C_{\text{ISD}}(n, k, q, w) > 2^\lambda.$$

The above criterion emphasizes the fact that, when weak instances are avoided and in light of existing attacks, solving LEP reduces to finding low-weight codewords.

At the end of the day, as we will see in Sect. 6, the parameters we consider in this paper are only slightly bigger than those previously proposed in [BBPS21].

4   A New Formulation

In this section we show that LEP can be reformulated using a more convenient notion of equivalence, which allows for a much more compact representation for the solution to the equivalence problem. We introduce a new definition of equivalence between codes, which we call *Information Set (IS) - Linear Equivalence*, and then define the associated decisional problem, which we call IS-LEP. The main difference between LEP and IS-LEP is in that, for the latter, one is interested only in how the linear map acts on an information set (i.e., on k positions instead of n). We then show that IS-LEP is effectively the same as LEP, namely, that any "YES" (resp., "NO") instance of IS-LEP is also a "YES" (resp., "NO") instance for LEP.

4.1   Splitting Monomials with Respect to Information Sets

To begin, we introduce some additional notation, which will help improve the readability of the next topics.

Definition 2. *Let* $\mathbf{G} = (\mathbf{g}_1, \cdots, \mathbf{g}_n) \in \mathbb{F}_q^{k \times n}$, $\mu = (\pi, \mathbf{v}) \in M_n$ *and* $\mathbf{G}' = \mu(\mathbf{G})$. *For any* $J' = \{j'_1, \cdots, j'_k\} \subseteq \{1, \cdots, n\}$, *we define* $J = \pi^{-1}(J') = \{\pi^{-1}(j') \mid j' \in J'\}$. *We define* $\mu^{(J \mapsto J')} \in M_k$ *as the monomial transformation such that* $\mu^{(J \mapsto J')}(\mathbf{G}_J) = \mathbf{G}'_{J'}$. *Equivalently, we define* $\mu^{(\backslash J \mapsto \backslash J')} \in M_{n-k}$ *as the monomial transformation such that* $\mu^{(\backslash J \mapsto \backslash J')}(\mathbf{G}_{\{1, \cdots, n\} \backslash J}) = \mathbf{G}'_{\{1, \cdots, n\} \backslash J'}$.

Determining $\mu^{(J \mapsto J')}$ from the knowledge of $\mu = (\pi, \mathbf{v})$ and J' is easy. Indeed, let us express $\mu^{(J \mapsto J')} = \left(\pi^{(J \mapsto J')}, \mathbf{v}^{(J \mapsto J')} \right)$. Then, it is enough to apply the following rule: if the i-th column of $\mathbf{G}'_{J'}$ corresponds to the j-th column of $\mathbf{G}_J$, multiplied by α, then we set $\pi^{(J \mapsto J')}(j) = i$ and $v_i^{(J \mapsto J')} = \alpha$. With analogous reasoning, one can compute $\mu^{(\backslash J \mapsto \backslash J')}$.

Splitting the action of a monomial with respect to a set J' is useful to understand how the map acts inside and outside an information set. Indeed, it is easy to verify that the following relation holds

$$\mathbf{G}' = \mathbf{S} \cdot \mu(\mathbf{G}) \implies \begin{cases} \mathbf{G}'_{J'} = \mathbf{S} \cdot \mu^{(J \mapsto J')}(\mathbf{G}_J), \\ \mathbf{G}'_{\{1, \cdots, n\} \backslash J'} = \mathbf{S} \cdot \mu^{(\backslash J \mapsto \backslash J')}(\mathbf{G}_{\{1, \cdots, n\} \backslash J}). \end{cases} \tag{1}$$

We will frequently make use of the above relations to describe how monomial transformations act on specific sets of coordinates.

Example 1. Let us consider the example of $n = 8$ and $\mu = (\pi, \mathbf{v})$, with $\pi = (6, 5, 1, 3, 4, 7, 8, 2)$ and $\mathbf{v} = (2, 3, 1, 5, 3, 4, 6, 1)$ over $\mathbb{F}_7$. We describe how μ can be split, considering the set $J' = \{2, 3, 6, 7\}$. We observe that the permutation acts as follows (we are denoting $\mathbf{a}' = \pi(\mathbf{a})$):

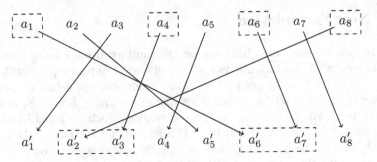

We have $J = \{1, 4, 6, 8\}$, $\pi^{(J \mapsto J')} = (3, 2, 4, 1)$ and $\pi^{(\backslash J \mapsto \backslash J')} = (3, 1, 2, 4)$. Considering also the action of $\mathbf{v}$, we have that $\mu(\mathbf{a})$ is:

$$2a_3 \quad \boxed{3a_8 \quad 1a_4} \quad 5a_5 \quad 3a_2 \quad \boxed{4a_1 \quad 6a_6} \quad 1a_7$$

Hence, $\mathbf{v}^{(J \mapsto J')} = (3, 1, 4, 6)$ and $\mathbf{v}^{(\backslash J \mapsto \backslash J')} = (2, 5, 3, 1)$.

4.2   LEP with Information Sets

We are now ready to introduce the new notion of equivalence between codes which, at a first glance, may seem rather different from the traditional notion used to define LEP. Perhaps surprisingly, we are able to prove that the two notions are exactly the same.

Definition 3 (Information Set (IS) - Linear Equivalence). *We say that two codes* $\mathscr{C}, \mathscr{C}' \subseteq \mathbb{F}_q^n$ *are Information Set (IS) linearly equivalent, and write* $\mathscr{C} \overset{*}{\sim} \mathscr{C}'$, *if there exist monomial transformations* $\widetilde{\mu} \in M_n$, $\zeta \in M_{n-k}$ *and an information set* J' *for both* $\mathscr{C}'$ *and* $\widetilde{\mathscr{C}} = \widetilde{\mu}(\mathscr{C})$ *such that, for any codeword* $\widetilde{\mathbf{c}} \in \widetilde{\mathscr{C}}$, *there exists a codeword in* $\mathbf{c}' \in \mathscr{C}'$ *with*

i) $\widetilde{\mathbf{c}}_{J'} = \mathbf{c}'_{J'}$;
ii) $\widetilde{\mathbf{c}}_{\{1,\cdots,n\} \backslash J'} = \zeta(\mathbf{c}'_{\{1,\cdots,n\} \backslash J'})$.

Equivalently, given generator matrices $\widetilde{\mathbf{G}}, \mathbf{G}' \in \mathbb{F}_q^{k \times n}$ *for* $\widetilde{\mathscr{C}}$ *and* $\mathscr{C}'$, *it must be*

$$\widetilde{\mathbf{G}}_{J'}^{-1} \widetilde{\mathbf{G}}_{\{1,\cdots,n\} \backslash J'} = \zeta(\mathbf{G}'^{-1}_{J'} \mathbf{G}'_{\{1,\cdots,n\} \backslash J'}).$$

In other words, the two systematic generator matrices (computed with respect to the set J'*) have the non-systematic parts which are identical, up to a monomial transformation.*

We associate this new notion of equivalence with the following decisional problem.

Problem 2 (Information Set-Linear Equivalence (IS-LEP)). *Given two linear codes* $\mathscr{C}, \mathscr{C}'$, *determine whether* $\mathscr{C} \overset{*}{\sim} \mathscr{C}'$.

In the next theorem we prove the core result of this section: LEP is equivalent to IS-LEP. Technically, we show that two codes are linearly equivalent if and only if they are also IS-linearly equivalent: this implies that any "YES" (resp. "NO") instance $(\mathscr{C}, \mathscr{C}')$ for LEP is a "YES" (resp. "NO") instance for IS-LEP, and viceversa. Hence, IS-linear equivalence is merely a different formulation of the traditional notion of linear equivalence.

Before showing the full proof, as a warm up, we provide a small example which captures the essence of the relation between LEP and IS-LEP. Let $\mathscr{C}$ and $\mathscr{C}'$ be two equivalent codes and assume that $J' = \{1, \cdots, k\}$ is an information set for $\mathscr{C}'$. First, note that any solution μ for LEP is also a solution for IS-LEP: this corresponds to the special case of ζ in Definition 3 being the identity. Now, let $\widetilde{\mu}$ be a solution for IS-LEP and $\widetilde{\mathscr{C}} = \widetilde{\mu}(\mathscr{C})$: since we are considering RREF to the first k columns, we get

$$\mathsf{SF}(\mathscr{C}') = (\mathbf{I}_k, \mathbf{A}), \quad \mathsf{SF}(\widetilde{\mathscr{C}}) = (\mathbf{I}_k, \zeta(\mathbf{A})).$$

Then, $\widetilde{\mathscr{C}} \sim \mathscr{C}'$ are equivalent. But since $\widetilde{\mathscr{C}} \sim \mathscr{C}$, by transitive property we get that $\mathscr{C} \sim \mathscr{C}'$. The proof of the following theorem makes use of the above ideas, but does not restrict to a particular choice for J'; also, the proof is constructive, i.e., it shows explicit relations between solutions for LEP and IS-LEP.

Theorem 1 (Equivalence between IS-LEP and LEP). *For any pair of linear codes $\mathscr{C}, \mathscr{C}' \subseteq \mathbb{F}_q^n$, it holds $\mathscr{C} \sim \mathscr{C}' \iff \mathscr{C} \overset{*}{\sim} \mathscr{C}'$.*

Proof. We first prove that $\mathscr{C} \sim \mathscr{C}'$ implies $\mathscr{C} \overset{*}{\sim} \mathscr{C}'$. Let us consider two generator matrices $\mathbf{G}, \mathbf{G}' \in \mathbb{F}_q^{k \times n}$ for two equivalent codes $\mathscr{C}$ and $\mathscr{C}'$. Consequently, it holds $\mathbf{G}' = \mathbf{S}\mu(\mathbf{G})$ for some non-singular $\mathbf{S} \in \mathbb{F}_q^{k \times k}$ and $\mu = (\pi, \mathbf{v}) \in M_n$. We now show that $\mathscr{C}$ and $\mathscr{C}'$ are also IS-linearly equivalent. Let J' be an information set for $\mathscr{C}'$, and $J = \pi^{-1}(J')$ (recall Definition 2). Because of (1), we have

$$\mathbf{G}'_{J'} = \mathbf{S}\mu^{(J \mapsto J')}(\mathbf{G}_J), \qquad \mathbf{G}'_{\{1, \cdots, n\} \backslash J'} = \mathbf{S}\mu^{(\backslash J \mapsto \backslash J')}(\mathbf{G}_{\{1, \cdots, n\} \backslash J}).$$

Representing the action of monomials through matrices, we rewrite the above relations as

$$\mathbf{G}'_{J'} = \mathbf{S}\mathbf{G}_J\mathbf{M}', \qquad \mathbf{G}'_{\{1, \cdots, n\} \backslash J'} = \mathbf{S}\mathbf{G}_{\{1, \cdots, n\} \backslash J}\mathbf{M}'',$$

with $\mathbf{M}' \in \mathbb{F}_q^{k \times k}$ and $\mathbf{M}'' \in \mathbb{F}_q^{(n-k) \times (n-k)}$. Reducing $\mathbf{G}'$ with respect to J', and considering only the non-systematic part, we obtain the matrix

$$\begin{aligned}
\mathbf{A} &= \mathbf{G}'^{-1}_{J'}\mathbf{G}'_{\{1, \cdots, n\} \backslash J'} \\
&= (\mathbf{S}\mathbf{G}_J\mathbf{M}')^{-1}\mathbf{S}\mathbf{G}_{\{1, \cdots, n\} \backslash J}\mathbf{M}'' \\
&= \mathbf{M}'^{-1}\mathbf{G}_J^{-1}\mathbf{G}_{\{1, \cdots, n\} \backslash J}\mathbf{M}''.
\end{aligned}$$

Let $\widetilde{\mu} \in M_n$ be an arbitrary monomial such that $\widetilde{\mu}^{(J \mapsto J')} = \mu^{(J \mapsto J')}$ and, generically, $\widetilde{\mu}^{(\backslash J \mapsto \backslash J')} = \mu^{(\backslash J \mapsto \backslash J')} \circ \zeta$, where $\zeta \in M_{n-k}$ can be any monomial transformation. Using again matrices to represent monomials, we associate

$\tilde{\mu}^{(J \mapsto J')} = \mu^{(J \mapsto J')}$ with $\mathbf{M}'$ and $\tilde{\mu}^{(\backslash J \mapsto \backslash J')}$ with $\widetilde{\mathbf{M}}''$ which, in general, is different from $\mathbf{M}''$. Let $\tilde{\mathbf{G}} = \tilde{\mu}(\mathbf{G})$, and consider the non-systematic part of the matrix we obtain by row reducing with respect to J'. Taking again (1) into account, we have

$$\tilde{\mathbf{G}}_{J'}^{-1}\tilde{\mathbf{G}}_{\{1,\cdots,n\}\backslash J'} = (\mathbf{G}_J\mathbf{M}')^{-1}\mathbf{G}_{\{1,\cdots,n\}\backslash J}\widetilde{\mathbf{M}}''$$
$$= \underbrace{\mathbf{M}'^{-1}\mathbf{G}_J^{-1}\mathbf{G}_{\{1,\cdots,n\}\backslash J}}_{\mathbf{A}\mathbf{M}''^{-1}}\widetilde{\mathbf{M}}''$$
$$= \mathbf{A}\mathbf{M}''^{-1}\widetilde{\mathbf{M}}'' = \zeta(\mathbf{A})$$

with $\zeta \in M_{n-k}$ being the monomial associated to $\mathbf{M}''^{-1}\widetilde{\mathbf{M}}''$. This proves that $\mathscr{C}$ and $\mathscr{C}'$ are indeed IS-linearly equivalent.

We now show the other way around, i.e., that two codes that are IS-linearly equivalent are also linearly equivalent. We consider again two generator matrices $\mathbf{G}$ and $\mathbf{G}'$ and assume we know an information set J' and monomials $\tilde{\mu} \in M_n$, $\zeta \in M_{n-k}$ that satisfy the requirements for IS-linear equivalence. Let $\tilde{\mathbf{G}} = \tilde{\mu}(\mathbf{G})$. The non-systematic parts of $\mathbf{G}'$ and $\tilde{\mathbf{G}}$, when reducing with respect to J', are

$$\mathbf{A}' = \mathbf{G}_{J'}'^{-1}\mathbf{G}_{\{1,\cdots,n\}\backslash J'}', \qquad \tilde{\mathbf{A}} = \tilde{\mathbf{G}}_{J'}^{-1}\tilde{\mathbf{G}}_{\{1,\cdots,n\}\backslash J'}.$$

By definition of IS-linear equivalence, we have that $\mathbf{A}'$ and $\tilde{\mathbf{A}}$ are linearly equivalent, i.e.,

$$\tilde{\mathbf{A}} = \zeta(\mathbf{A}') = \mathbf{A}'\mathbf{Z} = \mathbf{G}_{J'}'^{-1}\mathbf{G}_{\{1,\cdots,n\}\backslash J'}'\mathbf{Z},$$

for some monomial $\zeta \in M_{n-k}$ associated with the matrix $\mathbf{Z} \in \mathbb{F}_q^{(n-k)\times(n-k)}$. Let us again split the action of $\tilde{\mu}$, using the information set J'. We write $\tilde{\mu} = (\tilde{\pi}, \tilde{\mathbf{v}})$, set $J = \tilde{\pi}^{-1}(J')$ and represent $\tilde{\mu}^{(J\mapsto J')}$ and $\tilde{\mu}^{(\backslash J\mapsto\backslash J')}$ through the monomial matrices $\widetilde{\mathbf{M}}' \in \mathbb{F}_q^{k\times k}$ and $\widetilde{\mathbf{M}}'' \in \mathbb{F}_q^{(n-k)\times(n-k)}$. We then have

$$\tilde{\mathbf{G}}_{J'} = \tilde{\mu}^{(J\mapsto J')}(\mathbf{G}_J) = \mathbf{G}_J\widetilde{\mathbf{M}}',$$

$$\tilde{\mathbf{G}}_{\{1,\cdots,n\}\backslash J'} = \tilde{\mu}^{(\backslash J\mapsto\backslash J')}(\mathbf{G}_{\{1,\cdots,n\}\backslash J}) = \mathbf{G}_{\{1,\cdots,n\}\backslash J}\widetilde{\mathbf{M}}''.$$

Thus

$$\tilde{\mathbf{A}} = \tilde{\mathbf{G}}_{J'}^{-1}\tilde{\mathbf{G}}_{\{1,\cdots,n\}\backslash J'}$$
$$= (\mathbf{G}_J\widetilde{\mathbf{M}}')^{-1}(\mathbf{G}_{\{1,\cdots,n\}\backslash J}\widetilde{\mathbf{M}}'').$$

Recalling that $\tilde{\mathbf{A}} = \mathbf{A}'\mathbf{Z} \implies \tilde{\mathbf{A}}\mathbf{Z}^{-1} = \mathbf{A}'$, we get

$$\underbrace{(\mathbf{G}_J\widetilde{\mathbf{M}}')^{-1}\mathbf{G}_{\{1,\cdots,n\}\backslash J}}_{\tilde{\mathbf{A}}}\widetilde{\mathbf{M}}''\mathbf{Z}^{-1} = \underbrace{\mathbf{G}_{J'}'^{-1}\mathbf{G}_{\{1,\cdots,n\}\backslash J'}'}_{\mathbf{A}'},$$

from which

$$\mathbf{G}_{\{1,\cdots,n\}\backslash J}\widetilde{\mathbf{M}}''\mathbf{Z}^{-1} = \mathbf{G}_J\widetilde{\mathbf{M}}'\mathbf{G}_{J'}'^{-1}\mathbf{G}_{\{1,\cdots,n\}\backslash J'}'. \tag{2}$$

We are now finally ready to determine the $\mathbf{S} \in GL_k$ and $\mu \in M_n$ that would solve LEP on $\mathbf{G}$ and $\mathbf{G}'$. Indeed, let μ such that $\mu^{(J \mapsto J')}$ corresponds to $\widetilde{\mathbf{M}}'$ and $\mu^{(\backslash J \mapsto \backslash J')}$ corresponds to $\widetilde{\mathbf{M}}''\mathbf{Z}^{-1}$, and $\mathbf{S} = \mathbf{G}'_{J'}\widetilde{\mathbf{M}}'^{-1}\mathbf{G}_J^{-1}$. In the positions of $\mathbf{S}\mu(\mathbf{G})$ which are indexed by J', we have

$$\mathbf{S}\mu^{(J \mapsto J')}(\mathbf{G}_J) = \mathbf{S}\mathbf{G}_J\widetilde{\mathbf{M}}'$$
$$= \mathbf{G}'_{J'}\widetilde{\mathbf{M}}'^{-1}\mathbf{G}_J^{-1}\mathbf{G}_J\widetilde{\mathbf{M}}' = \mathbf{G}'_{J'},$$

while in the positions which are not indexed by J',

$$\mathbf{S}\mu^{(\backslash J \mapsto \backslash J')}(\mathbf{G}) = \mathbf{S}\mathbf{G}_{\{1,\cdots,n\}\backslash J}\widetilde{\mathbf{M}}''\mathbf{Z}^{-1}$$
$$= \underbrace{\mathbf{G}'_{J'}\widetilde{\mathbf{M}}'^{-1}\mathbf{G}_J^{-1}}_{\mathbf{S}}\underbrace{\mathbf{G}_J\widetilde{\mathbf{M}}'\mathbf{G}_{J'}^{-1}\mathbf{G}'_{\{1,\cdots,n\}\backslash J'}}_{\mathbf{G}_{\{1,\cdots,n\}\backslash J}\widetilde{\mathbf{M}}''\mathbf{Z}^{-1}} \quad \text{(Using (2))}$$
$$= \mathbf{G}'_{\{1,\cdots,n\}\backslash J'}.$$

□

We conclude this section by showing how, from the knowledge of a solution for LEP, one can derive a solution to IS-LEP, which is more convenient in terms of communication cost. This depends on how the action of a monomial can be represented. To this end, we introduce the following functions, which we will use to represent the action of $\widetilde{\mu}$.

Definition 4. *Let* $\mu = (\pi, \mathbf{v}) \in M_n$. *For* $J' = \{j'_1, \cdots, j'_k\} \subseteq \{1, \cdots, n\}$ *with size* k, *we define*

$$\mathsf{Trunc}(\mu, J') = (\pi^*, \mathbf{v}^*)$$
$$= \left((\pi^{-1}(j'_1), \pi^{-1}(j'_2), \cdots, \pi^{-1}(j'_k)) \ , \ (v_{j'_1}, v_{j'_2}, \cdots, v_{j'_k}) \right).$$

Notice that π^* *is an ordered subset of* $\{1, \cdots, n\}$ *with size* k, *that is,* $\pi^* = (j^*_1, \cdots, j^*_k)$. *Also,* $\mathbf{v}^* = (v^*_1, \cdots, v^*_k) = \mathbf{v}_{J'}$ *is represented as a length-k vector over* $\mathbb{F}_q^*$.

Definition 5. *We define* $\mathsf{Apply}((\pi^*, \mathbf{v}^*), \mathbf{G})$ *as the function that outputs the matrix* $\mathbf{U} \in \mathbb{F}_q^{k \times k}$ *such that, if the i-th entry of* π^* *is* $j \in \{1, \cdots, n\}$, *has i-th column* $\mathbf{u}_i = v^*_i \mathbf{g}_j$, *where* $\mathbf{g}_j$ *denotes the j-column of* $\mathbf{G}$.

Remark 1. The elements of π^* and $J = \pi^{-1}(J')$ are the same, but have a different order. While J represents an information set (and, coherently with the notation we are using, is a non-ordered set), π^* is meant to describe how π acts on the coordinates which are moved to J'. Consequently, it is important that π^* is seen as an ordered set. Notice that π^* describes the action of π only on k coordinates (hence, the function is called Trunc, which stand for truncated).

Remark 2. If J' is the information set that has been used to compute $(\pi^*, \mathbf{v}^*)$ using the monomial μ and $J = \pi^{-1}(J')$, then $\mathbf{U} = \mu^{(J \mapsto J')}(\mathbf{G})$.

We first observe that representing π^* requires $k \log_2(n)$ bits while $\mathbf{v}^*$ takes $k \log_2(q-1)$ bits. The implication on signatures based on LEP is easy to see. In fact, all existing schemes communicate monomial transformations using $n \log_2(n) + n \log_2(q-1)$ bits, i.e., the action of the monomial is fully represented. We are aiming at reducing this size thanks to the convenient representation we have defined above. However, this requires some additional technical steps (e.g. modifications in how commitments are computed). Thus, we postpone this discussion to the next section, and we conclude the current one by showing that communicating $\mathsf{Trunc}(\mu, J')$ is enough to verify a solution to IS-LEP, in a time which is essentially not modified with respect to LEP.

Proposition 1. *Let $\mathscr{C}$ and $\mathscr{C}'$ be two linearly equivalent codes, i.e., there exists $\mu = (\pi, \mathbf{v}) \in M_n$ such that $\mathscr{C}' = \mu(\mathscr{C})$. Let $\mathbf{G}, \mathbf{G}' \in \mathbb{F}_q^{k \times n}$ be generator matrices for such codes. To show that $\mathscr{C}$ and $\mathscr{C}'$ are IS-linearly equivalent, it is enough to provide J' and $\mathsf{Trunc}(\mu, J')$. Verifying the solution for IS-LEP takes a time which is polynomial in n and, in practice, is the same as computing two RREFs.*

Proof. Since the codes are linearly equivalent, there exists $\mathbf{S} \in GL_k$ such that $\mathbf{G}' = \mathbf{S}\mu(\mathbf{G})$. Let us indicate $J = \pi^{-1}(J')$; notice that J is known because of π^* (see Remark 1). Thanks to (1), we can write

$$\mathbf{G}'_{J'} = \mathbf{S}\mu^{(J \mapsto J')}(\mathbf{G}_J),$$

$$\mathbf{G}'_{\{1,\cdots,n\}\backslash J'} = \mathbf{S}\mu^{(\backslash J \mapsto \backslash J')}(\mathbf{G}_{\{1,\cdots,n\}\backslash J}).$$

Let $\mathbf{U} = \mathsf{Apply}\big((\pi^*, \mathbf{v}^*), \mathbf{G}\big)$, and notice that

$$\mathbf{U} = \mathbf{G}_{\{1,\cdots,n\}\backslash\pi^*} = \mathbf{G}_{\{1,\cdots,n\}\backslash J}.$$

Indeed, we consider that π^* is identical to J, up to a reordering of the elements, hence $\{1, \cdots, n\} \backslash \{j_1^*, \cdots, j_k^*\} = \{1, \cdots, n\} \backslash J$. Let $\widetilde{\mu} \in M_n$ be any monomial such that $\mathsf{Trunc}(\mu, J') = \mathsf{Trunc}(\widetilde{\mu}, J')$ and $\widetilde{\mathbf{G}} = \widetilde{\mu}(\mathbf{G})$. We now compute the RREFs of both $\mathbf{G}'$ and $\widetilde{\mathbf{G}}$ with respect to J'. The non-systematic parts of the two matrices are, respectively,

$$\begin{aligned}
\mathbf{A}' &= \mathbf{G}'^{-1}_{J'}\mathbf{G}'_{\{1,\cdots,n\}\backslash J'} \\
&= \big(\mathbf{S} \cdot \mu^{(J \mapsto J')}(\mathbf{G}_J)\big)^{-1} \cdot \mathbf{S} \cdot \mu^{(\backslash J \mapsto \backslash J')}(\mathbf{G}_{\{1,\cdots,n\}\backslash J}) \\
&= \big(\mu^{(J \mapsto J')}(\mathbf{G}_J)\big)^{-1} \cdot \mu^{(\backslash J \mapsto \backslash J')}(\mathbf{G}_{\{1,\cdots,n\}\backslash J}) \\
&= \big(\mu^{(J \mapsto J')}(\mathbf{G}_J)\big)^{-1} \cdot \mathbf{G}_{\{1,\cdots,n\}\backslash J}\mathbf{Z},
\end{aligned}$$

and

$$\begin{aligned}
\widetilde{\mathbf{A}} &= \widetilde{\mathbf{G}}_{J'}^{-1}\widetilde{\mathbf{G}}_{\{1,\cdots,n\}\backslash J'} \\
&= \big(\mu^{(J \mapsto J')}(\mathbf{G}_J)\big)^{-1} \cdot \mathbf{G}_{\{1,\cdots,n\}\backslash J} \\
&= \mathbf{A}' \cdot \mathbf{Z}^{-1},
\end{aligned}$$

where $\mathbf{Z}$ is the matrix associated to $\mu^{(\backslash J \mapsto \backslash J')}$. To conclude verification, one should acknowledge that indeed $\mathbf{A}'$ and $\widetilde{\mathbf{A}}$ are identical, up to a monomial transformation. This can be easily verified. For instance, it is enough to consider scalar multiples of the columns in $\mathbf{A}'$ and search whether $\widetilde{\mathbf{A}}$ contains an identical column. Namely, we start with $i = 1$ (i.e., consider the first column $\mathbf{a}'_i = \mathbf{a}'_1$): if, in $\widetilde{\mathbf{A}}$, we find a column in position $j \in \{1, \cdots, n - k\}$ and such that $z\mathbf{a}'_1 = \widetilde{\mathbf{a}}'_j$, then we know that ζ moves the first coordinate in position j, and scales it by z. We then repeat the reasoning, considering $i = 2$ and searching for the matching column in the positions $\{1, \cdots, n - k\} \setminus \{j\}$. Iterating this procedure, we have that we successfully end the search (i.e., we find a match for all columns of $\mathbf{A}'$) if and only if there indeed exists such a monomial $\mathbf{Z}$. The cost of this procedure is $O(n^2)$, which is smaller than that of computing the RREFs, which is in $O(n^3)$.
□

In the next section, we show how IS-LEP can be employed to build ZK proofs. We anticipate that, in such applications, we will not need to transmit J'; furthermore, we will use a different approach to determine if the non systematic parts of two matrices are equal up to a monomial transformation (based on the computation of an ad-hoc invariant).

Remark 3. Even though we stated LEP and IS-LEP as decisional problems, they can be reformulated as search problems. The proofs of Theorem 1 and Proposition 1 show, constructively, reductions in both ways, even for the search versions.

Example 2. Let $q = 11$, $n = 5$ and $k = 2$. Let $\mathscr{C}$ be the code generated by

$$\mathbf{G} = \begin{pmatrix} 9 & 3 & 1 & 1 & 4 \\ 2 & 5 & 5 & 10 & 1 \end{pmatrix}.$$

Let $\mu = (\pi, \mathbf{v})$ with $\pi = (2, 1, 5, 3, 4)$ and $\mathbf{v} = (5, 6, 8, 9, 3)$ and $\mathscr{C}' = \mu(\mathscr{C})$. To represent the code, we use the generator matrix $\mathbf{G}' = \mathbf{S}\mu(\mathbf{G})$ with $\mathbf{S} = \begin{pmatrix} 0 & 4 \\ 4 & 10 \end{pmatrix}$, so that

$$\mathbf{G}' = \begin{pmatrix} 1 & 4 & 1 & 3 & 5 \\ 2 & 6 & 7 & 3 & 8 \end{pmatrix}.$$

Let $J' = \{1, 4\}$, which is an information set for $\mathscr{C}'$ since $\mathbf{G}'_{J'} = \begin{pmatrix} 1 & 3 \\ 2 & 3 \end{pmatrix}$ is non-singular (its determinant is 8). We have $\mathsf{Trunc}(\mu, J') = (\pi^*, \mathbf{v}^*)$ where $\pi^* = \{\pi^{-1}(1), \pi^{-1}(4)\} = \{j_1^*, j_2^*\} = \{2, 5\}$ and $\mathbf{v}^* = \mathbf{v}_{J'} = (v_1^*, v_2^*) = (5, 9)$. We now consider $\mathbf{U} = \mathsf{Apply}((\pi^*, \mathbf{v}^*), \mathbf{G})$ and have

$$\mathbf{U} = (v_1^* \mathbf{g}_{j_1^*}, v_2^* \mathbf{g}_{j_2^*}) = (5\mathbf{g}_2, 9\mathbf{g}_5) = \left(5 \cdot \begin{pmatrix} 3 \\ 5 \end{pmatrix}, 9 \cdot \begin{pmatrix} 4 \\ 1 \end{pmatrix}\right) = \begin{pmatrix} 4 & 3 \\ 3 & 9 \end{pmatrix}.$$

Since $\{1, \cdots, n\} \setminus \{j_1^*, j_2^*\} = \{1, 3, 4\}$, we have

$$\mathbf{G}_{\{1, \cdots, n\} \setminus \pi^*} = (\mathbf{g}_1, \mathbf{g}_3, \mathbf{g}_4) = \begin{pmatrix} 9 & 1 & 1 \\ 2 & 5 & 10 \end{pmatrix}.$$

We now compute the non-systematic part of $\mathbf{G}'$, after RREF with respect to J', and obtain

$$\mathbf{A}' = \mathbf{G}'^{-1}_{J'}\mathbf{G}'_{\{1,\cdots,n\}\setminus J'} = (\mathbf{g}'_1, \mathbf{g}'_4)^{-1}(\mathbf{g}'_2, \mathbf{g}'_3, \mathbf{g}'_5)$$

$$= \begin{pmatrix} 1 & 3 \\ 2 & 3 \end{pmatrix}^{-1} \begin{pmatrix} 4 & 1 & 5 \\ 6 & 7 & 8 \end{pmatrix} = \begin{pmatrix} 2 & 6 & 3 \\ 8 & 2 & 8 \end{pmatrix}.$$

Finally, we have

$$\widetilde{\mathbf{A}} = \mathbf{U}^{-1}\mathbf{G}_{\{1,\cdots,n\}\setminus \pi^*} = \begin{pmatrix} 4 & 3 \\ 3 & 9 \end{pmatrix}^{-1} \begin{pmatrix} 9 & 1 & 1 \\ 2 & 5 & 10 \end{pmatrix} = \begin{pmatrix} 4 & 1 & 9 \\ 5 & 10 & 3 \end{pmatrix}.$$

Now, we observe that

$$\mathbf{a}'_1 = 6 \cdot \widetilde{\mathbf{a}}_1, \qquad \mathbf{a}'_2 = 8 \cdot \widetilde{\mathbf{a}}_3, \qquad \widetilde{\mathbf{a}}_3 = 8 \cdot \mathbf{a}'_2.$$

This confirms that $\mathbf{A}'$ and $\widetilde{\mathbf{A}}$ are equal, up to a monomial transformation.

5   Compact Proofs of Equivalence from IS-LEP

Recall that, in a proof-of-knowledge constructed from LEP, the protocol goes as follows (see Fig. 1):

- there are two equivalent (public) codes $\mathcal{C}$ and $\mathcal{C}'$, with $\mathcal{C}' = \sigma(\mathcal{C})$ for some (secret) map μ;
- the prover samples a random transformation $\tau \in M_n$ and commits to $\mathcal{C}^* = \tau(\mathcal{C})$; this is done by applying a function $\mathsf{Commit}(\mathcal{C}^*)$ whose output is $h \in \{0;1\}^{2\lambda}$;
- the verifier either asks for the random map (i.e., a proof that $\mathcal{C} \sim \mathcal{C}^*$) and receives τ, or for the one involving the public code (i.e., a proof that $\mathcal{C}^* \sim \mathcal{C}'$) and receives $\tau' = \tau \circ \mu^{-1}$;
- the verifier either checks that $h = \mathsf{Commit}(\tau(\mathcal{C}))$, or that $h = \mathsf{Commit}(\tau'(\mathcal{C}'))$.

Note that we must necessarily assume that the commitment is obtained via a hash function, since otherwise one would need to publish $\mathcal{C}^*$, which requires at least $k(n-k)\log_2(q)$ bits (assuming a generator matrix in systematic form is employed). Currently, the commitment function is implemented as

$$\mathsf{Commit} = \mathsf{Hash}(\mathsf{SF}(\mathcal{C})) : \mathcal{C} \mapsto \{0,1\}^{2\lambda}.$$

This works well since it satisfies two fundamental properties:

i) the systematic generator matrix is an invariant of the code;
ii) the commitment function is relatively easy to compute.

The second property is obviously necessary to have a practical scheme, while the first one is crucial to guarantee verification, when the verifier asks for the equivalence on the right. Indeed, in this case he computes $\tau'(\mathbf{G}')$, which generates the same code as $\tau(\mathbf{G})$. However, the two generator matrices are not the same: generically, it holds that $\tau(\mathbf{G}') = \mathbf{S} \cdot \tau'(\mathbf{G})$ for some non-singular $\mathbf{S} \in GL_k$. Thanks to use of the systematic form, we get rid of this discrepancy.

To put it differently, the systematic form is used as an easy-to-compute representative for a code[1]. As we have seen in the previous section, with the IS-LEP formulation we can reduce significantly the communication cost. However, the commitment function which is currently employed will not work anymore, since the prover provides only a portion of τ'. In this section we describe an efficient solution to circumvent this issue. This requires to modify the commitment function and use a new invariant which, fortunately, can be computed with a cost which is comparable with that of a RREF. This leads to a direct improvement in all schemes based on LEP, for what concerns all relevant aspects: we reduce the communication cost (in practice $k \approx 0.5n$ so we almost halve it) and essentially keep the computational cost unchanged. Also, we do not introduce a new security assumption since, as we showed in the previous section, IS-LEP and LEP are two different formulations of the very same problem.

5.1   A New Invariant for Codes

Let us recall the concept of *lexicographic ordering* for vectors and matrices over a finite field.

Definition 6 (Lexicographic Ordering). *We define a lexicographic ordering over* $\mathbb{F}_q = \{x_1, x_2, \cdots, x_q\}$ *as*

$$x_1 \overset{\text{Lex}}{<} x_2 \overset{\text{Lex}}{<} \cdots \overset{\text{Lex}}{<} x_q.$$

For two vectors $\mathbf{a}, \mathbf{b}$, *we write* $\mathbf{a} \overset{\text{Lex}}{<} \mathbf{b}$ *if there exists an* i *such that* $a_j = b_j$ *for all* $j < i$, *and* $a_i \overset{\text{Lex}}{<} b_i$. *Analogously, for two matrices* $\mathbf{A}$ *and* $\mathbf{B}$, *we write* $\mathbf{A} \overset{\text{Lex}}{<} \mathbf{B}$ *if there exists an* i *such that* $\mathbf{a}_j = \mathbf{b}_j$ *for all* $j < i$ *and* $\mathbf{a}_i \overset{\text{Lex}}{<} \mathbf{b}_i$, *where* $\mathbf{a}_i$ *and* $\mathbf{b}_i$ *denote the* i-th *columns of* $\mathbf{A}$ *and* $\mathbf{B}$, *respectively. We write* $\mathbf{A} \overset{\text{Lex}}{\leqslant} \mathbf{B}$ *if either* $\mathbf{A} = \mathbf{B}$ *or* $\mathbf{A} \overset{\text{Lex}}{<} \mathbf{B}$.

Using the notion of lexicographic ordering defined above, we can define a representative for the orbit of a matrix, under the action of monomial transformations[2].

---

[1] There exist other invariants, but their computation is much harder. For instance, the prover may commit to the hash of the weight enumerator function. However, its computation requires $O(q^k)$ operations and is obviously unfeasible.

[2] In the context of code linear equivalence, these concepts have been first used by Beullens [Beu21].

Definition 7 (First Lexicographic Matrix). *Given* $\mathbf{A} \in \mathbb{F}_q^{m \times u}$, *we denote its orbit under the action of* M_u *as* $M_u(\mathbf{A}) = \{\tau(\mathbf{A}) \,|\, \tau \in M_u\}$. *Then, we define* MinLex($\mathbf{A}$) *as the function that returns the first lexicographic matrix in the orbit, that is*

$$\mathsf{MinLex}(\mathbf{A}) = \mathbf{A}^* \iff \mathbf{A}^* \overset{\mathsf{Lex}}{\leqslant} \widehat{\mathbf{A}}, \ \forall \widehat{\mathbf{A}} \in M_u(\mathbf{A}).$$

Note that the above definitions hold for any arbitrary choice of lexicographic ordering. However, since we are mostly interested in prime finite fields, from now on we focus on the simplest and most natural ordering, that is $0 \overset{\mathsf{Lex}}{<} 1 \overset{\mathsf{Lex}}{<} 2 \overset{\mathsf{Lex}}{<} \cdots \overset{\mathsf{Lex}}{<} q-1$. If $\mathbf{A}$ has m rows and u columns, computing MinLex takes in the worst case $O(um)$ operations over $\mathbb{F}_q$: indeed, it is enough to first scale each column so that the first non null element is 1 and then sort the columns so that they are in ascending lexicographic ordering. An example is given in Fig. 3.

$$\begin{pmatrix} 5 & 0 & 3 & 8 \\ 10 & 5 & 7 & 0 \end{pmatrix} \xrightarrow{\text{Scale columns}} \begin{pmatrix} 1 & 0 & 1 & 1 \\ 2 & 1 & 6 & 0 \end{pmatrix} \xrightarrow{\text{Reorder columns}} \begin{pmatrix} 0 & 1 & 1 & 1 \\ 1 & 0 & 2 & 6 \end{pmatrix}$$

Fig. 3. Example of computation of MinLex, for a matrix with $m = 2$ rows, $u = 4$ columns, with values over $\mathbb{F}_{11}$.

We finally have all the necessary tools to define our proposed invariant function, which we call SF*. Details about how the function operates are given in Algorithm 1. Basically, it computes the systematic form and then computes MinLex on the non systematic part. Since computing MinLex is much easier than a RREF, computing SF* comes with a cost which is slightly larger than that of SF. We observe that, in the wide majority of cases, the employed information set is $J^* = \{1, \cdots, k\}$ (i.e., the one that is tested first). Indeed, the probability that this set is valid can be estimated by considering the probability that a random $k \times k$ matrix over $\mathbb{F}_q$ is non-singular, that is

$$\prod_{i=1}^{k-1} 1 - q^{-i} \approx 1 - \frac{1}{q}.$$

For instance, for $q = 127$, this is approximately 0.992.

To conclude this section, we show that the function SF* possesses exactly the invariance properties we need.

Proposition 2. *Let* $\mathbf{G}, \mathbf{G}' \in \mathbb{F}_q^{k \times n}$ *be the generator matrices of two linearly equivalent codes, i.e.,* $\mathbf{G}' = \mathbf{S}\mu(\mathbf{G})$ *for some* $\mathbf{S} \in \mathrm{GL}_k$ *and* $\mu \in M_n$. *Let* $J^*, \mathbf{A}^* = \mathsf{SF}^*(\mathbf{G}')$. *Let* $(\pi^*, \mathbf{v}^*) = \mathsf{Trunc}(\mu, J^*)$ *and* $\mathbf{U} = \mathsf{Apply}\big((\pi^*, \mathbf{v}^*), \mathbf{G}\big)$. *Then, for any* μ *and any* $\mathbf{S}$, *it holds that*

$$\mathbf{A}^* = \mathsf{MinLex}(\mathbf{U}^{-1}\mathbf{G}_{\{1,\cdots,n\}\setminus\pi^*}).$$

Proof. Let J be the set of columns that get moved to J^*. Because of RREF, the effect of $\mathbf{S}$ gets canceled. So, RREF with respect to J^* yields

$$\mathbf{A}' = \mathbf{U}^{-1}\mathbf{G}'_{\{1,\cdots,n\}\backslash J^*} = \mathbf{U}^{-1}\mu^{(J\mapsto J^*)}(\mathbf{G}_{\{1,\cdots,n\}\backslash J}),$$

which is identical (up to a monomial transformation) to

$$\mathbf{A}'' = \mathbf{U}^{-1}\mathbf{G}_{\{1,\cdots,n\}\backslash\pi^*} = \mathbf{U}^{-1}\mathbf{G}_{\{1,\cdots,n\}\backslash J}.$$

This means that they are in the same orbit, i.e., $\mathbf{A}' \in M_{n-k}(\mathbf{A}'')$: computation of MinLex returns the same matrix. □

Algorithm 1: Function SF*

Input: matrix $\mathbf{G} \in \mathbb{F}_q^{k\times n}$
Output: set $J^* \subseteq \{1,\cdots,n\}$, matrix $\mathbf{A}^* \in \mathbb{F}_q^{k\times(n-k)}$

1 Find the first $J^* \subseteq \{1,\cdots,n\}$ of size k and such that $\text{Rank}(\mathbf{G}_{J^*}) = k$;
2 Set $\mathbf{A} = \mathbf{G}_{J^*}^{-1}\mathbf{G}_{\{1,\cdots,n\}\backslash J^*}$;// Non systematic part after RREF
3 Compute $\mathbf{A}^* = \text{MinLex}(\mathbf{A})$;// Compute first lexicographic matrix
4 Return $J^*, \mathbf{A}^*$.

5.2 Proof-of-Knowledge with IS-LEP

We now describe how the proof-of-knowledge protocol used in the family of LESS schemes [BMPS20, BBPS21, BBN+22] can be reformulated to take into account IS-LEP. In Fig. 4 we have reported the description of one round of the LESS-FM protocol, taking into account verification based on IS-LEP.

The protocol possesses all the properties that are required by a ZK proof of knowledge. Completeness holds because of Proposition 2, while Zero-Knowledge is guaranteed by the fact that $(\pi^*, \mathbf{v}^*)$ is a truncated representation of τ', which is uniformly distributed over M_n. The only property which is not obvious is special soundness; for this reason, we present a detailed analysis next.

Proposition 3. *The protocol of Fig. 4 is 2-special sound.*

Proof. Let us consider two accepting transcripts, associated with the same commitment h and two different challenges b and $\tilde{b}$. We assume that both b and $\tilde{b}$ are different from 0 (the case where one of the challenges is 0 trivially follows and is therefore omitted). We denote by $(\pi^*, \mathbf{v}^*)$ the response for challenge b, and by $(\tilde{\pi}^*, \tilde{\mathbf{v}}^*)$ the one for challenge $\tilde{b}$. We now show that, from the knowledge of these two accepting transcripts, either a hash collision has been found, or a monomial map from $\mathscr{C}_b$ to $\mathscr{C}_{\tilde{b}}$ can be computed in polynomial time.

| Private Key | $\mu_1, \cdots, \mu_s \in M_n$ |
| Public Key | Matrices $\{\mathbf{G}'_i = \mathsf{SF}(\mu_i(\mathbf{G}))\}_{1 \leqslant i \leqslant s}$ |

PROVER   **VERIFIER**

Sample $\tau \xleftarrow{\$} M_n$
Compute $\mathbf{G}^* = \tau(\mathbf{G})$
Compute $J^*, \mathbf{A}^* = \mathsf{SF}^*(\mathbf{G}^*)$
Compute $h = \mathsf{Hash}(\mathbf{A}^*)$

$$\xrightarrow{\quad h \quad}$$

Sample $b \xleftarrow{\$} \{0, \cdots, s\}$

$$\xleftarrow{\quad b \quad}$$

If $b = 0$:
  Set $f := \tau$
Else:
  Set $\tau' = \tau \circ \mu_b^{-1}$
  Set $(\pi^*, \mathbf{v}^*) = \mathsf{Trunc}(\tau', J^*)$
  Set $f = (\pi^*, \mathbf{v}^*)$

$$\xrightarrow{\quad f \quad}$$

          If $b = 0$:
            Compute $\mathbf{G}^* = \tau(\mathbf{G})$
            Compute $J^*, \mathbf{A}^* = \mathsf{SF}^*(\mathbf{G}^*)$
            Verify $h = \mathsf{Hash}(\mathbf{A}^*)$
          Else:
            Compute $\mathbf{U} = \mathsf{Apply}((\pi^*, \mathbf{v}^*), \mathbf{G}'_b)$
            Verify $h = \mathsf{Hash}\left(\mathsf{MinLex}(\mathbf{U}^{-1}(\mathbf{G}'_b)_{\{1, \cdots, n\} \setminus \pi^*})\right)$

Fig. 4. One round of LESS-FM using IS-LEP

Let $\mathbf{U} = \mathsf{Apply}((\pi^*, \mathbf{v}^*,)\mathbf{G}_b)$ and $\widetilde{\mathbf{U}} = \mathsf{Apply}((\widetilde{\pi}^*, \widetilde{\mathbf{v}}^*), \mathbf{G}_{\widetilde{b}})$. Since both are accepting transcripts, it follows that either a hash collision has been found, or

$$\mathsf{MinLex}\big(\underbrace{\mathbf{U}^{-1}(\mathbf{G}'_b)_{\{1, \cdots, n\} \setminus \pi^*}}_{\mathbf{A}}\big) = \mathsf{MinLex}\big(\underbrace{\widetilde{\mathbf{U}}^{-1}(\mathbf{G}'_{\widetilde{b}})_{\{1, \cdots, n\} \setminus \widetilde{\pi}^*}}_{\widetilde{\mathbf{A}}}\big).$$

This means that one knows two monomial transformations $\zeta, \widetilde{\zeta} \in M_{n-k}$ such that $\zeta(\mathbf{A}) = \widetilde{\zeta}(\widetilde{\mathbf{A}}) = \mathbf{A}^*$.

Remember that what Apply does is applying a monomial transformation that modifies only the k coordinates which are included in π^*. In other words, starting from $\mathbf{G}_b$, one possesses the generator matrix for an equivalent code, in the form $(\mathbf{U}, \mathbf{G}'_{b\{1, \cdots, n\} \setminus \pi^*})$. Let us denote by $\sigma \in M_n$ the monomial such that $\sigma(\mathbf{G}'_b) = (\mathbf{U}, \mathbf{G}'_{b\{1, \cdots, n\} \setminus \pi^*})$. Doing RREF with respect to the first k positions, we find a generator matrix for the same code, in the form $(\mathbf{I}_k, \mathbf{A})$. If we now apply another monomial transformation $\sigma' \in M_n$, acting as the identity in the first k positions and as ζ in the last $n - k$ positions, we end up with $(\mathbf{I}_k, \zeta(\mathbf{A})) = (\mathbf{I}_k, \mathbf{A}^*)$. This means that $\mathscr{C}_b$, the code generated by $\mathbf{G}_b$, is equivalent to the one $\mathscr{C}^*$ generated by $(\mathbf{I}_k, \mathbf{A}^*)$: the equivalence between the two codes is given by $\sigma' \circ \sigma$.

The same chain of transformations can be applied to $\mathbf{G}'_{\widetilde{b}}$, and would bring us to the code generated by $(\mathbf{I}_k, \widetilde{\zeta}(\widetilde{\mathbf{A}})) = (\mathbf{I}_k, \mathbf{A}^*)$. To summarize all the transformations we used, see Fig. 5.

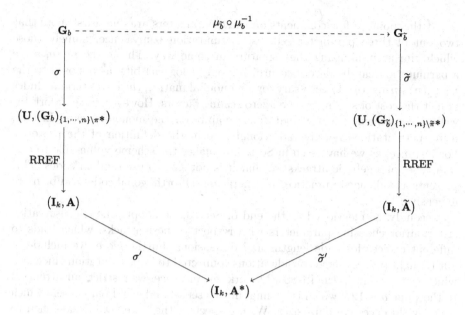

Fig. 5. Transformations from $\mathscr{C}_b$ and $\mathscr{C}_{\tilde{b}}$ to a common code $\mathscr{C}^*$

In the end, we found a code $\mathscr{C}^*$ which is equivalent to both $\mathscr{C}_b$ and $\mathscr{C}_{\tilde{b}}$, and we also know the transformations that map $\mathscr{C}_b$ into $\mathscr{C}^*$ and $\mathscr{C}_{\tilde{b}}$ into $\mathscr{C}^*$. Combining such transformations, we are able to find a map between $\mathscr{C}_b$ and $\mathscr{C}_{\tilde{b}}$.   □

For what concerns computational complexity, as in LESS-FM, the most time consuming operation remains the systematic form computation.

6   New Instances for LESS Signatures

In this section, we report on the practical impact of our new techniques, in the context of LESS, as well as schemes derived from it. To begin with, we recall the parameters that were proposed in LESS-FM. Table 1, below, is an excerpt from [BBPS21].

Table 1. Parameter sets for LESS-FM, for $\lambda = 128$ classical bits of security.

Optimization Criterion	Type	Code Params			Prot. Params			pk (KiB)	sig (KiB)
		n	k	q	t	ω	s		
Min. pk size	Mono	198	94	251	283	28	2	9.77	15.2
Min. sig size	Perm	235	108	251	66	19	16	205.74	5.25
Min. pk + sig size	Perm	230	115	127	233	31	2	11.57	10.39

At this point, a few comments on these parameters are due. First, note that two out of three parameter sets use permutation equivalence, namely those which aim at minimizing the signature in some way. This make sense, since a permutation can be described utilizing only $n \log_2(n)$ bits, as opposed to the $n \log_2(n) + n \log_2(q-1)$ necessary for a monomial matrix; the latter term includes in fact the cost of storing the non-zero scaling factors. However, in this work (as well as subsequent ones) we will focus mainly on the monomial case. In fact, using permutations requires additional care in the definition of the protocol. For instance, as we have seen in Sect. 3, it makes the scheme vulnerable to certain types of algebraic attacks, so that it is not safe to use random codes. This presents a challenge in practice, as generating self-orthogonal codes can be quite expensive.

Secondly, as mentioned at the end of Sect. 3, we adopt a new, conservative criterion for choosing parameters with respect to best attacks, which leads to different choices for code lengths and dimensions. Furthermore, we include in our thought process some considerations connected to implementation efficiency, which were absent in the LESS-FM work: for instance, we restrict our attention to the value $q = 127$, which is optimal in this sense, and avoid parameters which would yield excessive data sizes. With respect to the latter, we decide then to remain within the psychological threshold of 100 kB.

Finally, as we transition from a mostly theoretical design, to one with a practical outlook, we provide parameters for higher security levels. For this, we follow NIST's guidance and align with their proposed definitions for categories 1, 3 and 5. We report the new data in Table 2, with a slightly different layout. Indeed, we no longer need to specify the type of equivalence considered, since this is always monomial. Also, the optimization criterion is no longer purely aimed at "minimizing" quantities. Instead, we use the nomenclature LESS-$\alpha\beta$ which recalls simultaneously the security level achieved (via the number $\alpha \in \{1, 3, 5\}$), and the characteristics of the resulting choice (via the letter β). To be precise, we use "b" for "balanced", i.e. a set which yields similar sizes for public key and signature; "s" for "short", i.e. a set which sacrifices public-key size in favor of signature; and "i", only for category 1, for an "intermediate" set.

To illustrate the advantage of our technique, in Table 2 we have reported signature sizes for both the scheme with, and without the new technique; to do so, we have use the format $x(y)$ where x is the optimized signature size, and y the unoptimized one.

Next, we report some timings. We start with those obtained for an unoptimized reference implementation in ANSI C, which are to be considered purely in the spirit of exemplification. The values are collected on an Intel Core i7-12700K, on a P-core, clocked at 4.9 GHz. Clock cycle values collected via `rtdscp`, as averages of 100 primitive runs. The computer is endowed with 64 GiB of PC5-19200 DDR5 and is running Debian 11. The source was compiled with `gcc` 10.2.1-20210110 (version packaged with the distribution), with `-O3 -march=native` compilation options (Table 3).

Table 2. New parameter sets for LESS, for different security categories.

NIST Cat.	Parameter Set	Code Params			Prot. Params			pk (KiB)	sig (KiB)
		n	k	q	t	ω	s		
1	LESS-1b	252	126	127	247	30	2	13.6	8.4 (15.3)
	LESS-1i				244	20	4	40.8	5.8 (10.7)
	LESS-1s				198	17	8	95.2	5.0 (9.2)
3	LESS-3b	400	200	127	759	33	2	34.2	16.8 (30.5)
	LESS-3s				895	26	3	68.5	13.4 (24.2)
5	LESS-5b	548	274	127	1352	40	2	64.2	29.8 (53.8)
	LESS-5s				907	37	3	128.5	26.6 (48.8)

Table 3. Timings for the reference implementation of LESS.

NIST Cat.	Parameter Set	KeyGen (Mcycles)	Sign (Mcycles)	Verify (Mcycles)
1	LESS-1b	3.4	878.7	890.8
	LESS-1i	9.8	876.6	883.6
	LESS-1s	23.0	703.6	714.7
3	LESS-3b	9.3	7224.1	7315.8
	LESS-3s	18.3	8527.4	8608.6
5	LESS-5b	24.4	33787.7	34014.0
	LESS-5s	48.0	22621.5	22703.3

To provide a hint at the improved performance that we can obtain by leveraging more advanced tools, we report below the results of an additional implementation. Since, as explained above, the RREF computation is by far the most expensive operation, this implementation is realized by amending the ANSI C reference code with Gaussian Elimination code implemented using AVX2 C intrinsics. The test system was a Dell OptiPlex XE4, a mid-range 2022 desktop system with Intel Core i7-12700 CPU running at 2.1 GHz. The test programs were executed on a single CPU thread with frequency scaling disabled. The system has 64GB of physical RAM and was running Ubuntu 22.04.2 LTS Linux operating system, and the C test code was compiled with gcc 11.3.0 packaged in that operating system. Compilation and optimization flags were \verb|-Wall -Wextra -Ofast -march=native|.

To complete our showcase, we report below the data obtained while applying our technique to the LESS-based ring signature scheme (Table 4).

Table 5 is an excerpt from [BBN+22], with some caveats. First, note that the parameter s is missing, as the optimization involving multiple codes was not used; instead, we have a new parameter r corresponding to the size of the ring of users. Secondly, all the instances presented in [BBN+22] were based on permutation equivalence (and thus the "Type" column is omitted). In this case,

Table 4. Timings for the additional implementation of LESS.

NIST Cat.	Parameter Set	KeyGen (Mcycles)	Sign (Mcycles)	Verify (Mcycles)
1	LESS-1b	0.9	263.6	271.4
	LESS-1i	2.3	254.3	263.4
	LESS-1s	5.1	206.6	213.4
3	LESS-3b	2.8	2446.9	2521.4
	LESS-3s	5.2	2984.3	3075.1
5	LESS-5b	6.4	10212.6	10458.8
	LESS-5s	11.7	6763.2	7016.5

Table 5. Parameter sets for ring signatures based on LESS, for $\lambda = 128$ classical bits of security.

Parameter Set	Code Params			Prot. Params			pk (kB)	sig (kB)
	n	k	q	t	ω	r		
I	230	115	127	233	31	2^3	11.6	8.6 (10.8)
II						2^6		11.6 (13.8)
III						2^{12}		17.5 (19.7)
IV						2^{21}		26.5 (28.7)

rather than presenting entirely new parameters based on (IS-)LEP, we simply calculate the sizes that we would obtain applying our technique to PEP, i.e. replacing $n \log_2(n)$ bits with $k \log_2(n)$ bits whenever a permutation needs to be transmitted. We use the same $x(y)$ format as above, where now the unoptimized value y corresponds to the sizes appearing in [BBN+22].

Note that, compared to the reduction obtained for LESS, in the case of ring signature the improvement is considerably less relevant. This is mainly because a large part of the signature size, in such a scheme, is comprised of the cost of transmitting a Merkle proof, which is proportional to the (logarithm) of the number of users in the ring. It is worth considering, however, that this is exactly the feature that makes the scheme appealing in the first place, and so we are satisfied with our improvement being less impactful in this case.

Acknowledgements. The work of the first author is generously sponsored by NSF grant 1906360 and NSA grant H98230-22-1-0328.

References

[BBN+22] Barenghi, A., Biasse, J.-F., Ngo, T., Persichetti, E., Santini, P.: Advanced signature functionalities from the code equivalence problem. Int. J. Comput. Math. Comput. Syst. Theory **7**(2), 112–128 (2022)

[BBPS21] Barenghi, A., Biasse, J.-F., Persichetti, E., Santini, P.: LESS-FM: fine-tuning signatures from the code equivalence problem. In: Cheon, J.H., Tillich, J.-P. (eds.) PQCrypto 2021 2021. LNCS, vol. 12841, pp. 23–43. Springer, Cham (2021). https://doi.org/10.1007/978-3-030-81293-5_2

[BBPS23] Barenghi, A., Biasse, J.-F., Persichetti, E., Santini, P.: On the computational hardness of the code equivalence problem in cryptography. Adv. Math. Commun. **17**(1), 23–55 (2023)

[Beu21] Beullens, W.: Not enough LESS: an improved algorithm for solving code equivalence problems over $\mathbb{F}_q$. In: Dunkelman, O., Jacobson, Jr., M.J., O'Flynn, C. (eds.) SAC 2020. LNCS, vol. 12804, pp. 387–403. Springer, Cham (2021). https://doi.org/10.1007/978-3-030-81652-0_15

[BKP20] Beullens, W., Katsumata, S., Pintore, F.: Calamari and Falafl: logarithmic (linkable) ring signatures from isogenies and lattices. In: Moriai, S., Wang, H. (eds.) ASIACRYPT 2020, Part II. LNCS, vol. 12492, pp. 464–492. Springer, Cham (2020). https://doi.org/10.1007/978-3-030-64834-3_16

[BKV19] Beullens, W., Kleinjung, T., Vercauteren, F.: CSI-FiSh: efficient isogeny based signatures through class group computations. In: Galbraith, S.D., Moriai, S. (eds.) ASIACRYPT 2019. LNCS, vol. 11921, pp. 227–247. Springer, Cham (2019). https://doi.org/10.1007/978-3-030-34578-5_9

[BMPS20] Biasse, J.-F., Micheli, G., Persichetti, E., Santini, P.: LESS is more: code-based signatures without syndromes. In: Nitaj, A., Youssef, A. (eds.) AFRICACRYPT 2020. LNCS, vol. 12174, pp. 45–65. Springer, Cham (2020). https://doi.org/10.1007/978-3-030-51938-4_3

[BOS19] Bardet, M., Otmani, A., Saeed-Taha, M.: Permutation code equivalence is not harder than graph isomorphism when hulls are trivial. In: IEEE ISIT 2019, pp. 2464–2468 (2019)

[CNP+23] Chou, T., et al.: Take your MEDS: digital signatures from matrix code equivalence. In: El Mrabet, N., De Feo, L., Duquesne, S. (eds.) AFRICACRYPT 2023. LNCS, vol. 14064, pp. 28–52. Springer, Cham (2023). https://doi.org/10.1007/978-3-031-37679-5_2

[DG22] D'Alconzo, G., Gangemi, A.: Trifors: Linkable trilinear forms ring signature. Cryptology ePrint Archive (2022)

[DvW22] Ducas, L., van Woerden, W.: On the lattice isomorphism problem, quadratic forms, remarkable lattices, and cryptography. In: Dunkelman, O., Dziembowski, S. (eds.) EUROCRYPT 2022, Part III. LNCS, vol. 13277, pp. 643–673. Springer, Cham (2022). https://doi.org/10.1007/978-3-031-07082-2_23

[FG19] De Feo, L., Galbraith, S.D.: SeaSign: compact isogeny signatures from class group actions. In: Ishai, Y., Rijmen, V. (eds.) EUROCRYPT 2019. LNCS, vol. 11478, pp. 759–789. Springer, Cham (2019). https://doi.org/10.1007/978-3-030-17659-4_26

[GMW19] Goldreich, O., Micali, S., Wigderson, A.: Proofs that yield nothing but their validity and a methodology of cryptographic protocol design. In: Providing Sound Foundations for Cryptography: On the Work of Shafi Goldwasser and Silvio Micali, pp. 285–306 (2019)

[Leo82] Leon, J.: Computing automorphism groups of error-correcting codes. IEEE Trans. Inf. Theory **28**(3), 496–511 (1982)

[Pat96] Patarin, J.: Hidden Fields Equations (HFE) and Isomorphisms of Polynomials (IP): two new families of asymmetric algorithms. In: Maurer, U. (ed.) EUROCRYPT 1996. LNCS, vol. 1070, pp. 33–48. Springer, Heidelberg (1996). https://doi.org/10.1007/3-540-68339-9_4

[Pet10] Peters, C.: Information-set decoding for linear codes over $\mathbf{F}_q$. In: Sendrier, N. (ed.) PQCrypto 2010. LNCS, vol. 6061, pp. 81–94. Springer, Heidelberg (2010). https://doi.org/10.1007/978-3-642-12929-2_7

[PR97] Petrank, E., Roth, R.M.: Is code equivalence easy to decide? IEEE Trans. Inf. Theory **43**(5), 1602–1604 (1997)

[PRS22] Persichetti, E., Randrianarisoa, T.H., Santini, P.: An attack on a non-interactive key exchange from code equivalence. Tatra Mt. Math. Publ. **82**(2), 53–64 (2022)

[Sen97] Sendrier, N.: On the dimension of the hull. SIAM J. Discret. Math. **10**(2), 282–293 (1997)

[Sen00] Sendrier, N.: The support splitting algorithm. IEEE Trans. Inf. Theory **46**, 1193–1203 (2000)

[SS13] Sendrier, N., Simos, D.E.: The hardness of code equivalence over $\mathbb{F}_q$ and its application to code-based cryptography. In: Gaborit, P. (ed.) PQCrypto 2013. LNCS, vol. 7932, pp. 203–216. Springer, Heidelberg (2013). https://doi.org/10.1007/978-3-642-38616-9_14

[TDJ+22] Gang, G., Duong, D.H., Joux, A., Plantard, T., Qiao, Y., Susilo, W.: Practical post-quantum signature schemes from isomorphism problems of trilinear forms. In: Dunkelman, O., Dziembowski, S. (eds.) EUROCRYPT 2022, Part III. LNCS, vol. 13277, pp. 582–612. Springer, Cham (2022). https://doi.org/10.1007/978-3-031-07082-2_21

[ZZ21] Zhang, Z., Zhang, F.: Code-based non-interactive key exchange can be made. Cryptology ePrint Archive, Report 2021/1619 (2021)

Correction to: Cryptographic Smooth Neighbors

Giacomo Bruno, Maria Corte-Real Santos, Craig Costello, Jonathan Komada Eriksen,
Michael Meyer, Michael Naehrig, and Bruno Sterner

Correction to:
Chapter 7 in: J. Guo and R. Steinfeld (Eds.): *Advances*
in Cryptology – ASIACRYPT 2023, **LNCS 14444,**
https://doi.org/10.1007/978-981-99-8739-9_7

In the originally published version of chapter 7, the name of the author Maria Corte-Real
Santos had been tagged incorrectly with regard to first name and last name. This has
been corrected.

The updated version of this chapter can be found at
https://doi.org/10.1007/978-981-99-8739-9_7

Author Index

© International Association for Cryptologic Research 2023, corrected publication 2024
J. Guo and R. Steinfeld (Eds.): ASIACRYPT 2023, LNCS 14444, p. 379, 2023.
https://doi.org/10.1007/978-981-99-8739-9

Printed in the United States
by Baker & Taylor Publisher Services